Cisco IOS Solutions for Network Protocols, Volume I: IP

Cisco Systems, Inc

Macmillan Technical Publishing
201 West 103rd Street
Indianapolis, IN 46290 USA

Cisco Systems, Inc.

Copyright © 1998 Cisco Systems, Inc

Cisco Press logo is a trademark of Cisco Systems, Inc.

Published by:

Macmillan Technical Publishing

201 West 103rd Street

Indianapolis, IN 46290 USA

Printed in the United States of America   2 3 4 5 6 7 8 9 0

Library of Congress Cataloging-in-Publication Number 98-84216

ISBN: 1-57870-049-3

Warning and Disclaimer

This book is designed to provide information about **Cisco IOS Solutions for Network Protocols Volume I: IP.** Every effort has been made to make this book as complete and as accurate as possible, but no warranty or fitness is implied.

The information is provided on an "as is" basis. The author, Macmillan Technical Publishing, and Cisco Systems, Inc. shall have neither liability nor responsibility to any person or entity with respect to any loss or damages arising from the information contained in this book or from the use of the discs or programs that may accompany it.

The opinions expressed in this book belong to the author and are not necessarily those of Cisco Systems, Inc.

Associate Publisher	Jim LeValley
Executive Editor	Julie Fairweather
Cisco Systems Program Manager	H. Kim Lew
Managing Editor	Caroline Roop
Acquisitions Editor	Tracy Hughes
Copy Editors	Brad Miser Michael Hughes
Team Coordinator	Amy Lewis
Book Designer	Trina Wurst
Cover Designer	Karen Ruggles
Production Team	Deb Kincaid, Lisa Stumpf
Indexer	Tim Wright

Trademark Acknowledgments

All terms mentioned in this book that are known to be trademarks or service marks have been appropriately capitalized. Macmillan Technical Publishing or Cisco Systems, Inc. cannot attest to the accuracy of this information. Use of a term in this book should not be regarded as affecting the validity of any trademark or service mark.

Acknowledgments

The Cisco IOS Reference Library is a result of collaborative efforts of many Cisco technical writers and editors over the years. This bookset represents the continuing development and integration of user documentation for the ever-increasing set of Cisco IOS networking features and functionality.

The current team of Cisco IOS technical writers and editors includes Katherine Anderson, Jennifer Bridges, Joelle Chapman, Christy Choate, Meredith Fisher, Tina Fox, Marie Godfrey, Dianna Johansen, Sheryl Kelly, Yvonne Kucher, Doug MacBeth, Lavanya Mandavilli, Mary Mangone, Spank McCoy, Greg McMillan, Madhu Mitra, Oralee Murillo, Vicki Payne, Jane Phillips, George Powers, Teresa Oliver Schuetz, Wink Schuetz, Karen Shell, Grace Tai, and Bethann Watson.

This writing team wants to acknowledge the many engineering, customer support, and marketing subject-matter experts for their participation in reviewing draft documents and, in many cases, providing source material from which this bookset is developed.

v

Contents at a Glance

TINH NGUYEN

Table of Contents

About the Cisco IOS Reference Library

The Cisco IOS Reference Library books are Cisco documentation that describe the tasks and commands necessary to configure and maintain your Cisco IOS network.

The Cisco IOS software bookset is intended primarily for users who configure and maintain access servers and routers, but are not necessarily familiar with the tasks, the relationship between tasks, or the commands necessary to perform particular tasks.

CISCO IOS REFERENCE LIBRARY ORGANIZATION

The Cisco IOS Reference library consists of eight books. Each book contains technology-specific configuration chapters with corresponding command reference chapters. Each configuration chapter describes Cisco's implementation of protocols and technologies, related configuration tasks, and contains comprehensive configuration examples. Each command reference chapter complements the organization of its corresponding configuration chapter and provides complete command syntax information.

OTHER BOOKS AVAILABLE IN THE CISCO IOS REFERENCE LIBRARY

- *Cisco IOS Configuration Fundamentals.* 1-57870-044-2; December 1997

    This comprehensive guide details Cisco IOS software configuration basics. *Cisco IOS Configuration Fundamentals* offers thorough coverage of router and access server configuration and maintenance techniques. In addition to hands-on implementation and task instruction, this book also presents the complete syntax for router and access server commands and individual examples for each command. Learn to configure interfaces in addition to system management, file loading, AutoInstall, and set up functions.

1

- *Cisco IOS Dial Solutions.* 1-57870-055-8; March 1998

  This book provides readers with real-world solutions and how to implement them on a network. Customers interested in implementing dial solutions across their network environment include remote sites dialing in to a central office, Internet Service Providers (ISPs), ISP customers at home offices, and enterprise WAN system administrators implementing dial-on-demand routing (DDR).

- *Cisco IOS Wide Area Networking Solutions.* 1-57870-054-x; March 1998

  This book offers thorough, comprehensive coverage of internetworking technologies, particularly ATM, Frame Relay, SMDS, LAPB, and X.25, teaching the reader how to configure the technologies in a LAN/WAN environment.

- *Cisco IOS Switching Services.* 1-57870-053-1; March 1998

  This book is a comprehensive guide detailing available Cisco IOS switching alternatives. Cisco's switching services range from fast switching and Netflow switching to LAN Emulation.

- *Cisco IOS Solutions for Network Protocols, Volume II: IPX, AppleTalk, and More.* 1-57870-050-7; April 1998

  This book is a comprehensive guide detailing available network protocol alternatives. It describes how to implement various protocols in your network. This book includes documentation of the latest functionality for the IPX and AppleTalk desktop protocols as well as the following network protocols: Apollo Domain, Banyan VINES, DECNet, ISO CLNS, and XNS.

- *Cisco IOS Bridging and IBM Network Solutions.* 1-57870-051-5; May 1998

  This book describes Cisco's support for networks in IBM and bridging environments. Support includes: transparent and source-route transparent bridging, source-route bridging (SRB), remote source-route bridging (RSRB), data link switching plus (DLS+), serial tunnel and block serial tunnel, SDLC and LLC2 parameter, IBM network media translation, downstream physical unit and SNA service point, SNA Frame Relay access support, Advanced Peer-to-Peer Networking, and native client interface architecture (NCIA).

- *Cisco IOS Network Security.* 1-57870-057-4; May 1998

  This book documents security configuration from a remote site and for a central enterprise or service provider network. It describes AAA, Radius, TACACS+, and Kerberos network security features. It also explains how to encrypt data across enterprise networks. The book includes many illustrations that show configurations and functionality, along with a discussion of network security policy choices and some decision-making guidelines.

BOOK CONVENTIONS

Software and hardware documentation uses the following conventions:

- The caret character (^) represents the Control key.

    For example, the key combinations ^D and Ctrl-D are equivalent: Both mean hold down the Control key while you press the D key. Keys are indicated in capital letters, but are not case-sensitive.

- A string is defined as a nonquoted set of characters.

    For example, when setting an SNMP community string to *public*, do not use quotation marks around the string; otherwise, the string will include the quotation marks.

Command descriptions use these conventions:

- Vertical bars (|) separate alternative, mutually exclusive, elements.
- Square brackets ([ ]) indicate optional elements.
- Braces ({ }) indicate a required choice.
- Braces within square brackets ([{ }]) indicate a required choice within an optional element.
- **Boldface** indicates commands and keywords that are entered literally as shown.
- *Italics* indicate arguments for which you supply values; in contexts that do not allow italics, arguments are enclosed in angle brackets (< >).

Examples use these conventions:

- Examples that contain system prompts denote interactive sessions, indicating that the user enters commands at the prompt. The system prompt indicates the current command mode. For example, the prompt Router(config)# indicates global configuration mode.
- Terminal sessions and information the system displays are in screen font.
- Information you enter is in **boldface screen** font.
- Nonprinting characters, such as passwords, are in angle brackets (< >).
- Default responses to system prompts are in square brackets ([ ]).
- Exclamation points (!) at the beginning of a line indicate a comment line. They are also displayed by the Cisco IOS software for certain processes.

CAUTION ──

Means *reader be careful*. In this situation, you might do something that could result in equipment damage or loss of data.

NOTES ──

Means *reader take note*. Notes contain helpful suggestions or references to materials not contained in this manual.

TIMESAVER ──

Means *the described action saves time.* You can save time by performing the action described in the paragraph.

Within the Cisco IOS Reference Library, the term *router* is used to refer to both access servers and routers. When a feature is supported on the access server only, the term *access server* is used. When a feature is supported on one or more specific router platforms (such as the Cisco 4500), but not on other platforms (such as the Cisco 2500), the text specifies the supported platforms.

Within examples, routers and access servers are alternately shown. These products are used only for example purposes—an example that shows one product does not indicate that the other product is not supported.

PART 1

IP

CHAPTER 1

IP Overview

The Cisco IOS software supports a variety of routing protocols. In this book, the following network protocols are discussed:

- Internet Protocol
- IP Routing Protocols

For each type of protocol, a chapter showing you how to configure that protocol is followed by a command reference chapter.

This introductory chapter provides an overview of IP.

INTERNET PROTOCOL

The Internet Protocol (IP) is a packet-based protocol that is used to exchange data over computer networks. IP handles addressing, fragmentation, reassembly, and protocol demultiplexing. It is the foundation on which all other IP protocols (collectively referred to as the IP Protocol suite) are built. A network-layer protocol, IP contains addressing and control information that allows data packets to be routed.

The Transmission Control Protocol (TCP) is built upon the IP layer. TCP is a connection-oriented protocol that specifies the format of data and acknowledgments used in the transfer of data. TCP also specifies the procedures that computers use to ensure that the data arrives correctly. TCP allows multiple applications on a system to communicate concurrently because it handles all demultiplexing of the incoming traffic among the application programs.

IP addressing features such as Address Resolution Protocol, Next Hop Resolution Protocol, and Network Address Translation are described in Chapter 2, "Configuring IP Addressing." IP services such as ICMP, Hot Standby Router Protocol, IP accounting, and performance parameters are described in Chapter 4, "Configuring IP Services."

Cisco's implementation of IP provides most of the major services contained in the various protocol specifications. Cisco IOS software also provides the TCP and User Datagram Protocol (UDP) services called Echo and Discard, which are described in RFCs 862 and 863, respectively.

Cisco supports both TCP and UDP at the transport layer, for maximum flexibility in services. Cisco also supports all standards for IP broadcasts.

Resource Reservation Protocol (RSVP)

RSVP is a signalling protocol that a host uses to request Quality of Service (QoS) guarantees from the network. The need for network resource reservations for data traffic differs from real-time traffic. Data applications (with little need for resource guarantees) frequently demand relatively lower bandwidth than real-time traffic. The almost constant high bit-rate demands of a video conference application and the bursty, low bit-rate demands of an interactive data application share available network resources.

IP ROUTING PROTOCOLS

Cisco's implementation of each IP routing protocol is discussed at the beginning of the individual protocol chapters in this book.

With any of the IP routing protocols, you must create the routing process, associate networks with the routing process, and customize the routing protocol for your particular network. You will need to perform some combination of the tasks in the respective chapters to configure one or more IP routing protocols.

Determining a Routing Process

Choosing a routing protocol is a complex task. When choosing a routing protocol, consider at least the following:

- Internetwork size and complexity
- Support for variable-length subnet masks (VLSM). Enhanced IGRP, IS-IS, static routes, and OSPF support VLSM
- Internetwork traffic levels
- Security needs
- Reliability needs
- Internetwork delay characteristics
- Organizational policies
- Organizational acceptance of change

The chapters in this book describe the configuration tasks associated with each supported routing protocol or service. This chapter presents the routing protocols that best suit your needs.

Interior and Exterior Gateway Protocols

IP routing protocols are divided into two classes: Interior Gateway Protocols (IGPs) and Exterior Gateway Protocols (EGPs). The IGPs and EGPs that Cisco supports are listed in the following sections.

— **NOTES** ——————————————————————————————

Many routing protocol specifications refer to routers as *gateways*, so the word *gateway* often appears as part of routing protocol names. However, a router usually is defined as a Layer 3 internetworking device, whereas a protocol translation gateway usually is defined as a Layer 7 internetworking device. You should understand that regardless of whether a routing protocol name contains the word "gateway," routing protocol activities occur at Layer 3 of the OSI reference model.

Interior Gateway Protocols

Interior protocols are used for routing networks that are under a common network administration. All IP interior gateway protocols must be specified with a list of associated networks before routing activities can begin. A routing process listens to updates from other routers on these networks and broadcasts its own routing information on those same networks. Cisco IOS software supports the following interior routing protocols:

- On-Demand Routing (ODR)
- Routing Information Protocol (RIP)
- Internet Gateway Routing Protocol (IGRP)
- Open Shortest Path First (OSPF)
- Enhanced Internet Gateway Routing Protocol (Enhanced IGRP)
- Integrated Intermediate System-to-Intermediate System (Integrated IS-IS)

Exterior Gateway Protocol

Exterior protocols are used to exchange routing information between networks that do not share a common administration. IP exterior gateway protocols require the following three sets of information before routing can begin:

- A list of neighbor (or peer) routers with which to exchange routing information
- A list of networks to advertise as directly reachable
- The autonomous system number of the local router

The supported exterior gateway protocol is Border Gateway Protocol (BGP).

Configuring Multiple Routing Protocols

You can configure multiple routing protocols in a single router to connect networks that use different routing protocols. You can, for example, run RIP on one subnetted network, IGRP on another subnetted network, and exchange routing information between them in a controlled fashion. The available routing protocols were not designed to interoperate, so each protocol collects different types of information and reacts to topology changes in its own way.

For example, RIP uses a hop-count metric and IGRP uses a five-element vector of metric information. If routing information is being exchanged between different networks that use different routing protocols, you can use many configuration options to filter the exchange of routing information.

The Cisco IOS software can handle simultaneous operation of up to 30 dynamic IP routing processes. The combination of routing processes on a router consists of the following protocols (with the limits noted):

- Up to 30 IGRP routing processes
- Up to 30 OSPF routing processes
- One RIP routing process
- One IS-IS process
- One BGP routing process

IP Multicast Routing

IP multicast routing provides an alternative to unicast and broadcast transmission. It allows a host to send packets to a subset of all hosts, known as *group transmission*. IP multicast runs on top of the other IP routing protocols.

CHAPTER 2

Configuring IP Addressing

This chapter describes how to configure IP addressing. For a complete description of the commands in this chapter, see Chapter 3, "IP Addressing Commands."

THE IP ADDRESSING TASK LIST

A basic and required task for configuring IP is to assign IP addresses to network interfaces. Doing so enables the interfaces and allows communication with hosts on those interfaces using IP. Associated with this task are decisions about subnetting and masking the IP addresses.

To configure various IP addressing features, complete the tasks in the following list. The first task is required; the remaining tasks are optional.

- Assigning IP Addresses to Network Interfaces
- Configuring Address Resolution Methods
- Enabling IP Routing
- Enabling IP Bridging
- Enabling Integrated Routing and Bridging
- Configuring a Routing Process
- Configuring Broadcast Packet Handling
- Configuring Network Address Translation (NAT)
- Monitoring and Maintaining IP Addressing

At the end of this chapter, there are examples that illustrate how you might establish IP addressing in your network.

ASSIGNING IP ADDRESSES TO NETWORK INTERFACES

An IP address identifies a location to which IP datagrams can be sent. Some IP addresses are reserved for special uses and cannot be used for host, subnet, or network addresses. Table 2–1 lists ranges of IP addresses, and shows which addresses are reserved and which are available for use.

Table 2–1   *Reserved and Available IP Addresses*

Class	Address or Range	Status
A	0.0.0.0 1.0.0.0 to 126.0.0.0 127.0.0.0	Reserved Available Reserved
B	128.0.0.0 to 191.254.0.0 191.255.0.0	Available Reserved
C	192.0.0.0 192.0.1.0 to 223.255.254 223.255.255.0	Reserved Available Reserved
D	224.0.0.0 to 239.255.255.255	Multicast group addresses
E	240.0.0.0 to 255.255.255.254 255.255.255.255	Reserved Broadcast

The official description of IP addresses is found in RFC 1166, "Internet Numbers."

To receive an assigned network number, contact your Internet service provider.

An interface can have one primary IP address. To assign a primary IP address and a network mask to a network interface, perform the following task in interface configuration mode:

Task	Command
Set a primary IP address for an interface.	**ip address** *ip-address mask*

A mask identifies the bits that denote the network number in an IP address. When you use the mask to subnet a network, the mask is then referred to as a *subnet mask*.

NOTES

Cisco software only supports network masks that use contiguous bits that are flush left against the network field.

The tasks required to enable additional, optional IP addressing features are shown in the following list:

- Assigning Multiple IP Addresses to Network Interfaces
- Enabling Use of Subnet Zero
- Enabling Classless Routing Behavior
- Enabling IP Processing on a Serial Interface

Assigning Multiple IP Addresses to Network Interfaces

The software supports multiple IP addresses per interface. You can specify an unlimited number of secondary addresses. Secondary IP addresses can be used in a variety of situations. The following are the most common applications:

- There might not be enough host addresses for a particular network segment. For example, suppose your subnetting allows up to 254 hosts per logical subnet, but on one physical subnet you must have 300 host addresses. Using secondary IP addresses on the routers or access servers allows you to have two logical subnets using one physical subnet.

- Many older networks were built using Level 2 bridges and were not subnetted. The judicious use of secondary addresses can aid in the transition to a subnetted, router-based network. Routers on an older, bridged segment can easily be made aware that many subnets are on that segment.

- Two subnets of a single network might otherwise be separated by another network. You can create a single network from subnets that are physically separated by another network by using a secondary address. In these instances, the first network is *extended*, or layered on top of the second network. Note that a subnet cannot appear on more than one active interface of the router at a time.

NOTES
_____

If any router on a network segment uses a secondary address, all other routers on that same segment must also use a secondary address from the same network or subnet.

To assign multiple IP addresses to network interfaces, perform the following task in interface configuration mode:

Task	Command
Assign multiple IP addresses to network interfaces.	**ip address** *ip-address mask* **secondary**

NOTES

IP routing protocols sometimes treat secondary addresses differently when sending routing updates. See the description of IP split horizon in Chapter 10, "Configuring RIP," Chapter 12, "Configuring IGRP," and Chapter 16, "Configuring IP Enhanced IGRP."

See the "Creating a Network from Separated Subnets Example" section at the end of this chapter for an example of creating a network from separated subnets.

Enabling Use of Subnet Zero

Subnetting with a subnet address of zero is illegal and strongly discouraged (as stated in RFC 791) because of the confusion that can arise between a network and a subnet that have the same addresses. For example, if network 131.108.0.0 is subnetted as 255.255.255.0, subnet zero would be written as 131.108.0.0—which is identical to the network address.

You can use the all zeros and all ones subnet (131.108.255.0), even though it is discouraged. Configuring interfaces for the all ones subnet is explicitly allowed. However, if you need the entire subnet space for your IP address, perform the following task in global configuration mode to enable subnet zero:

Task	Command
Enable the use of subnet zero for interface addresses and routing updates.	ip subnet-zero

Enabling Classless Routing Behavior

At times, a router might receive packets destined for a subnet of a network that has no network default route. Figure 2–1 shows a router in network 128.20.0.0 connected to subnets 128.20.1.0, 128.20.2.0, and 128.20.3.0. Suppose that the host sends a packet to 120.20.4.1. By default, if the router receives a packet destined for a subnet it does not recognize, and there is no network default route, the router discards the packet.

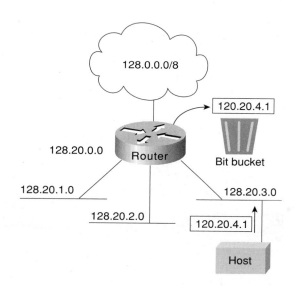

Figure 2–1
An example of a network with
no IP classless routing.

In Figure 2–2, classless routing is enabled in the router. Therefore, when the host sends a packet to 120.20.4.1, instead of discarding the packet, the router forwards the packet to the best supernet route.

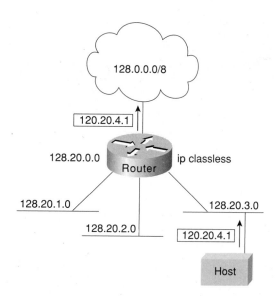

Figure 2–2
An example network with IP
classless routing.

To have the Cisco IOS software forward packets destined for unrecognized subnets to the best supernet route possible, perform the following task in global configuration mode:

Task	Command
Enable classless routing behavior.	ip classless

Enabling IP Processing on a Serial Interface

You might want to enable IP processing on a serial or tunnel interface without assigning an explicit IP address to the interface. Whenever the unnumbered interface generates a packet (for example, for a routing update), it uses the address of the interface you specified as the source address of the IP packet. It also uses the specified interface address in determining which routing processes are sending updates over the unnumbered interface. Restrictions are as follows:

- Serial interfaces using HDLC, PPP, LAPB, and Frame Relay encapsulations, as well as SLIP and tunnel interfaces, can be unnumbered. Serial interfaces using Frame Relay encapsulation can also be unnumbered, but the interface must be a point-to-point subinterface. It is not possible to use the unnumbered interface feature with X.25 or SMDS encapsulations.

- You cannot use the **ping** EXEC command to determine whether the interface is up, because the interface has no IP address. The Simple Network Management Protocol (SNMP) can be used to monitor interface status remotely.

- You cannot netboot a runnable image over an unnumbered serial interface.

- You cannot support IP security options on an unnumbered interface.

If you are configuring Intermediate System-to-Intermediate System (IS-IS) across a serial line, you should configure the serial interfaces as unnumbered. This allows you to conform with RFC 1195, which states that IP addresses are not required on each interface.

NOTES

Using an unnumbered serial line between different major networks requires special care. If, at each end of the link, there are different major networks assigned to the interfaces you specified as unnumbered, any routing protocols running across the serial line should be configured not to advertise subnet information.

To enable IP processing on an unnumbered serial interface, perform the following task in interface configuration mode:

Task	Command
Enable IP processing on a serial or tunnel interface without assigning an explicit IP address to the interface.	**ip unnumbered** *type number*

The interface you specify must be the name of another interface in the router that has an IP address, not another unnumbered interface. The interface you specify also must be enabled (listed as "up" in the **show interfaces** command display).

See the "Serial Interfaces Configuration Example" section at the end of this chapter for an example of how to configure serial interfaces.

CONFIGURING ADDRESS RESOLUTION METHODS

Cisco's IP implementation allows you to control interface-specific handling of IP addresses by facilitating address resolution, name services, and other functions. The next sections describe how to configure the following address resolution methods:

- Establishing Address Resolution
- Mapping Host Names to IP Addresses
- Configuring HP Probe Proxy Name Requests
- Configuring the Next Hop Resolution Protocol

Establishing Address Resolution

A device in the IP can have both a local address (which uniquely identifies the device on its local segment or LAN) and a network address (which identifies the network to which the device belongs). The local address is more properly known as a *data link* address, because it is contained in the data link layer (Layer 2 of the OSI model) part of the packet header and is read by data link devices (bridges and all device interfaces, for example). The more technically inclined will refer to local addresses as *MAC addresses*, because the Media Access Control (MAC) sublayer within the data link layer processes addresses for the layer.

To communicate with a device on Ethernet, for example, the Cisco IOS software first must determine the 48-bit MAC or local data link address of that device. The process of determining the local data link address from an IP address is called *address resolution*. The process of determining the IP address from a local data link address is called *reverse address resolution*.

The software uses three forms of address resolution: Address Resolution Protocol (ARP), proxy ARP, and Probe (similar to ARP). The software also uses the Reverse Address Resolution Protocol (RARP). ARP, proxy ARP, and RARP as defined in RFCs 826, 1027, and 903, respectively. Probe is a protocol developed by the Hewlett-Packard Company (HP) for use on IEEE-802.3 networks.

ARP is used to associate IP addresses with media or MAC addresses. Taking an IP address as input, ARP determines the associated media address. Once a media or MAC address is determined, the IP address/media address association is stored in an ARP cache for rapid retrieval. Then the IP datagram is encapsulated in a link-layer frame and sent over the network. Encapsulation of IP datagrams and ARP requests and replies on IEEE 802 networks other than Ethernet is specified by the Subnetwork Access Protocol (SNAP).

RARP works the same way as ARP, except that the RARP Request packet requests an IP address instead of a local data link address. Use of RARP requires a RARP server on the same network segment as the router interface. RARP often is used by diskless nodes that do not know their IP addresses when they boot. The Cisco IOS software attempts to use RARP if it does not know the IP address of an interface at startup. Also, Cisco routers are able to act as RARP servers by responding to RARP requests that they are able to answer.

Perform the following tasks to set address resolution:

- Defining a Static ARP Cache
- Setting ARP Encapsulations
- Enabling Proxy ARP
- Configuring Local-Area Mobility

The procedures for performing these tasks are described in the following sections.

Defining a Static ARP Cache

ARP and other address resolution protocols provide a dynamic mapping between IP addresses and media addresses. Because most hosts support dynamic address resolution, you generally do not need to specify static ARP cache entries. If you must define them, you can do so globally. Doing this task installs a permanent entry in the ARP cache. The Cisco IOS software uses this entry to translate 32-bit IP addresses into 48-bit hardware addresses.

Optionally, you can specify that the software respond to ARP requests as if it was the owner of the specified IP address. In case you do not want the ARP entries to be permanent, you have the option of specifying an ARP entry timeout period when you define ARP entries.

The following two tables list the tasks required to provide static mapping between IP addresses and media address.

Perform either of the following tasks in global configuration mode:

Task	Command
Globally associate an IP address with a media (hardware) address in the ARP cache.	**arp** *ip-address hardware-address type*
Specify that the software respond to ARP requests as if it were the owner of the specified IP address.	**arp** *ip-address hardware-address type* **alias**

Perform the following task in interface configuration mode:

Task	Command
Set the length of time an ARP cache entry will stay in the cache.	**arp timeout** *seconds*

To display the type of ARP being used on a particular interface and also display the ARP timeout value, use the **show interfaces** EXEC command. Use the **show arp** EXEC command to examine the contents of the ARP cache. Use the **show ip arp** EXEC command to show IP entries. To remove all nonstatic entries from the ARP cache, use the privileged EXEC command **clear arp-cache**.

Setting ARP Encapsulations

By default, standard Ethernet-style ARP encapsulation (represented by the **arpa** keyword) is enabled on the IP interface. You can change this encapsulation method to SNAP or HP Probe, as required by your network, to control the interface-specific handling of IP address resolution into 48-bit Ethernet hardware addresses.

When you set HP Probe encapsulation, the Cisco IOS software uses the Probe protocol whenever it attempts to resolve an IEEE-802.3 or Ethernet local data link address. The subset of Probe that performs address resolution is called Virtual Address Request and Reply. Using Probe, the router can communicate transparently with Hewlett-Packard IEEE-802.3 hosts that use this type of data encapsulation. You must explicitly configure all interfaces for Probe that will use it.

To specify the ARP encapsulation type, perform the following task in interface configuration mode:

Task	Command
Specify one of three ARP encapsulation methods for a specified interface.	arp {arpa	probe	snap}

Enabling Proxy ARP

The Cisco IOS software uses proxy ARP (as defined in RFC 1027) to help hosts with no knowledge of routing determine the media addresses of hosts on other networks or subnets. For example, if the router receives an ARP request for a host that is not on the same interface as the ARP request sender, and if the router has all of its routes to that host through other interfaces, then it generates a proxy ARP reply packet giving its own local data link address. The host that sent the ARP request then sends its packets to the router, which forwards them to the intended host. Proxy ARP is enabled by default.

To enable proxy ARP if it has been disabled, perform the following task in interface configuration mode (as necessary) for your network:

Task	Command
Enable proxy ARP on the interface.	ip proxy-arp

Configuring Local-Area Mobility

Local-area mobility provides the capability to relocate IP hosts within a limited area without reassigning host IP addresses and without changes to the host software. Local-area mobility is supported only on Ethernet, Token Ring, and FDDI interfaces.

To create a mobility area with only one router, perform the following tasks:

	Task	Command
Step 1	Enable bridging.	bridge *group* protocol {dec	ieee}
Step 2	Enter interface configuration mode.	interface *type number*
Step 3	Enable local-area mobility.	ip mobile arp [timers *keepalive hold-time*] [access-group *access-list-number*	*name*]
Step 4	Configure bridging on the interface.	bridge-group *group*

To create larger mobility areas, you must first redistribute the mobile routes into your IGP. The IGP must support host routes. You can use Enhanced IGRP, OSPF, or IS-IS; you can also use RIP in some cases, but this is not recommended. To redistribute the mobile routes into your existing IGP configuration, perform the following tasks:

Task	Command
Step 1 Enter router configuration mode.	**router** {**eigrp** *autonomous-system* | **isis** [*tag*] | **ospf** *process-id*}
Step 2 Set default metric values.	**default-metric** *number* or **default-metric** *bandwidth delay reliability loading mtu*
Step 3 Redistribute the mobile routes.	**redistribute mobile**

If your IGP supports summarization, you should also restrict the mobile area so that it falls completely inside an IGP summarization area. This lets hosts roam within the mobile area without affecting routing outside the area.

The mobile area must consist of a contiguous set of subnets.

Hosts that roam within a mobile area should rely on a configured default router for their routing.

Mapping Host Names to IP Addresses

Each unique IP address can have a host name associated with it. The Cisco IOS software maintains a cache of host name-to-address mappings for use by the EXEC **connect, telnet, ping,** and related Telnet support operations. This cache speeds the process of converting names to addresses.

IP defines a naming scheme that allows a device to be identified by its location in the IP. This is a hierarchical naming scheme that provides for *domains*. Domain names are pieced together with periods (.) as the delimiting characters. For example, Cisco Systems is a commercial organization that the IP identifies by a *com* domain name, so its domain name is *cisco.com*. A specific device in this domain, the File Transfer Protocol (FTP) system for example, is identified as *ftp.cisco.com*.

To keep track of domain names, IP has defined the concept of a *name server*, whose job is to hold a cache (or database) of names mapped to IP addresses. To map domain names to IP addresses, you must first identify the host names, then specify a name server, and enable the Domain Naming System (DNS), the Internet's global naming scheme that uniquely identifies network devices. These tasks are described in the following sections:

- Mapping IP Addresses to Host Names
- Specifying the Domain Name
- Specifying a Name Server
- Enabling the DNS
- Using the DNS to Discover ISO CLNS Addresses

Mapping IP Addresses to Host Names

The Cisco IOS software maintains a table of host names and their corresponding addresses, also called a *host name-to-address mapping*. Higher-layer protocols such as Telnet use host names to identify network devices (hosts). The router and other network devices must be able to associate host names with IP addresses to communicate with other IP devices. Host names and IP addresses can be associated with one another through static or dynamic means.

Manually assigning host names to addresses is useful when dynamic mapping is not available.

To assign host names to addresses, perform the following task in global configuration mode:

Task	Command
Statically associate host names with IP addresses.	**ip host** *name* [*tcp-port-number*] *address1* [*address2...address8*]

Specifying the Domain Name

You can specify a default domain name that the Cisco IOS software will use to complete domain name requests. You can specify either a single domain name or a list of domain names. Any IP host name that does not contain a domain name will have the domain name you specify appended to it before being added to the host table.

To specify a domain name or names, perform either of the following tasks in global configuration mode:

Task	Command
Define a default domain name that the Cisco IOS software will use to complete unqualified host names.	**ip domain-name** *name*
Define a list of default domain names to complete unqualified host names.	**ip domain-list** *name*

See the "IP Domains Example" section at the end of this chapter for an example of establishing IP domains.

Specifying a Name Server

To specify one or more hosts (up to six) that can function as a name server to supply name information for the DNS, perform the following task in global configuration mode:

Task	Command
Specify one or more hosts that supply name information.	ip name-server *server-address1* [[*server-address2*]...*server-address6*]

Enabling the DNS

If your network devices require connectivity with devices in networks for which you do not control name assignment, you can assign device names that uniquely identify your devices within the entire internetwork. The Internet's global naming scheme, the DNS, accomplishes this task. This service is enabled by default.

If the DNS has been disabled, you may re-enable it by performing the following task in global configuration mode:

Task	Command
Enable DNS-based host name-to-address translation.	ip domain-lookup

See the "Dynamic Lookup Example" section at the end of this chapter for an example of enabling the DNS.

Using the DNS to Discover ISO CLNS Addresses

If your router has both IP and International Organization for Standardization Connectionless Network Service (ISO CLNS) enabled and you want to use ISO CLNS Network Service Access Point (NSAP) addresses, you can use the DNS to query these addresses, as documented in RFC 1348. This feature is enabled by default.

To disable DNS queries for ISO CLNS addresses, perform the following task in global configuration mode:

Task	Command
Disable DNS queries for ISO CLNS addresses.	no ip domain-lookup nsap

Configuring HP Probe Proxy Name Requests

HP Probe Proxy support allows the Cisco IOS software to respond to HP Probe Proxy name requests. These requests are typically used at sites that have Hewlett-Packard equipment and are already using HP Probe Proxy. Tasks associated with HP Probe Proxy are shown in the following two tables.

To configure HP Probe Proxy, perform the following task in interface configuration mode:

Task	Command
Allow the Cisco IOS software to respond to HP Probe Proxy name requests.	**ip probe proxy**

Perform the following task in global configuration mode:

Task	Command
Enter the host name of an HP host (for which the router is acting as a proxy) into the host table.	**ip hp-host** *hostname ip-address*

See the "HP Hosts on a Network Segment Example" section at the end of this chapter for an example of configuring HP hosts on a network segment.

Configuring the Next Hop Resolution Protocol

Routers, access servers, and hosts can use Next Hop Resolution Protocol (NHRP) to discover the addresses of other routers and hosts connected to a nonbroadcast, multiaccess (NBMA) network. Partially meshed NBMA networks are typically configured with multiple logical networks to provide full network layer connectivity. In such configurations, packets might make several hops over the NBMA network before arriving at the exit router (the router nearest the destination network). In addition, such NBMA networks (whether partially or fully meshed) typically require tedious static configurations. These static configurations provide the mapping between network layer addresses (such as IP) and NBMA addresses (such as E.164 addresses for Switched Multimegabit Data Service, or SMDS).

NHRP provides an ARP-like solution that alleviates these NBMA network problems. With NHRP, systems attached to an NBMA network dynamically learn the NBMA address of the other systems that are part of that network, allowing these systems to communicate directly without requiring traffic to use an intermediate hop.

The NBMA network is considered nonbroadcast either, because it technically does not support broadcasting (for example, an X.25 network) or because broadcasting is too expensive (for example, an SMDS broadcast group that would otherwise be too large).

Understanding Cisco's Implementation of NHRP

Cisco's implementation of NHRP supports IP Version 4, Internet Packet Exchange (IPX) network layers, and, at the link layer, ATM, Ethernet, SMDS, and multipoint tunnel networks. Although NHRP is available on Ethernet, it is not necessary to implement NHRP over Ethernet media because Ethernet is capable of broadcasting. Ethernet support is unnecessary (and not provided) for IPX.

Figure 2–3 illustrates four routers connected to an NBMA network. Within the network are ATM or SMDS switches necessary for the routers to communicate with each other. Assume that the switches have virtual circuit connections represented by hops 1, 2, and 3 of the figure. When Router A attempts to forward an IP packet from the source host to the destination host, NHRP is triggered. On behalf of the source host, Router A sends an NHRP request packet encapsulated in an IP packet, which takes three hops across the network to reach Router D, connected to the destination host. After receiving a positive NHRP reply, Router D is determined to be the "NBMA next hop," and Router A sends subsequent IP packets for the destination to Router D in one hop.

Figure 2–3

Four routers connected to an NBMA network using Next Hop Resolution Protocol (NHRP).

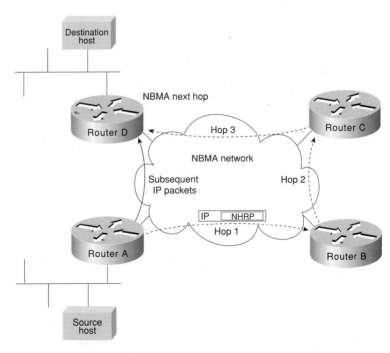

With NHRP, once the NBMA next hop is determined, the source either starts sending data packets to the destination (in a connectionless NBMA network such as SMDS) or establishes a virtual circuit connection to the destination with the desired bandwidth and QoS characteristics (in a connection-oriented NBMA network such as ATM).

Other address resolution methods can be used while NHRP is deployed. IP hosts that rely upon the LIS (Logical IP Subnet) model might require ARP servers and services over NBMA networks, and deployed hosts might not implement NHRP, but might continue to support ARP variations. NHRP is designed to eliminate the suboptimal routing that results from the LIS model, and can be deployed with existing ARP services without interfering with them.

NHRP is used to facilitate building a virtual private network. In this context, a virtual private network consists of a virtual Layer 3 network that is built on top of an actual Layer 3 network. The topology you use over the virtual private network is largely independent of the underlying network, and the protocols you run over it are completely independent of it.

Connected to the NBMA network are one or more stations that implement NHRP, and are known as *Next Hop Servers*. All routers running Release 10.3 or later are capable of implementing NHRP and, thus, can act as Next Hop Servers.

Each Next Hop Server serves a set of destination hosts, which might or might not be directly connected to the NBMA network. Next Hop Servers cooperatively resolve the NBMA next hop addresses within their NBMA network. In addition to NHRP, Next Hop Servers typically participate in protocols used to disseminate routing information across (and beyond the boundaries of) the NBMA network, and might also support ARP service.

A Next Hop Server maintains a "next-hop resolution" cache, which is a table of network layer address to NBMA address mappings. The table is created from information gleaned from NHRP register packets, extracted from NHRP request or reply packets that traverse the Next Hop Server as they are forwarded, or through other means such as ARP and preconfigured tables.

Understanding Protocol Operation

NHRP requests traverse one or more hops within an NBMA subnetwork before reaching the station that is expected to generate a response. Each station (including the source station) chooses a neighboring Next Hop Server to forward the request to. The Next Hop Server selection procedure typically involves performing a routing decision based upon the network layer destination address of the NHRP request. Ignoring error situations, the NHRP request eventually arrives at a station that generates an NHRP reply. This responding station either serves the destination, is the destination itself, or is a client that specified it should receive NHRP requests when it registered with its server. The responding station generates a reply using the source address from within the NHRP packet to determine where the reply should be sent.

NHRP Configuration Task List

To configure NHRP, perform the tasks shown in the following list. The first task is required, the remainder are optional.

- Enabling NHRP on an Interface
- Configuring a Station's Static IP-to-NBMA Address Mapping
- Statically Configuring a Next Hop Server
- Configuring NHRP Authentication
- Controlling NHRP Rate
- Suppressing Forward and Reverse Record Options
- Specifying the NHRP Responder Address
- Changing the Time Period NBMA Addresses Are Advertised as Valid
- Configuring a GRE Tunnel for Multipoint Operation

Enabling NHRP on an Interface

To enable NHRP for an interface on a router, perform the following task in interface configuration mode. In general, all NHRP stations within a logical NBMA network must be configured with the same network identifier.

Task	Command
Enable NHRP on an interface.	**ip nhrp network-id** *number*

See the "Logical NBMA Example" section and the "NHRP over ATM Example" section at the end of this chapter for examples of enabling NHRP.

Configuring a Station's Static IP-to-NBMA Address Mapping

To participate in NHRP, a station connected to an NBMA network should be configured with the IP and NBMA addresses of its Next Hop Server(s). The format of the NBMA address depends on the medium you are using. For example, ATM uses an NSAP address, Ethernet uses a MAC address, and SMDS uses an E.164 address.

These Next Hop Servers may also be the stations's default or peer routers, so their addresses can be obtained from the station's network layer forwarding table.

If the station is attached to several link layer networks (including logical NBMA networks), the station should also be configured to receive routing information from its Next Hop Server(s) and peer routers so that it can determine which IP networks are reachable through which link layer networks.

To configure static IP-to-NBMA address mapping on a station (host or router), perform the following task in interface configuration mode:

Task	Command
Configure static IP-to-NBMA address mapping.	**ip nhrp map** *ip-address nbma-address*

Statically Configuring a Next Hop Server

A Next Hop Server normally uses the network layer forwarding table to determine where to forward NHRP packets, and to find the egress point from an NBMA network. A Next Hop Server may alternately be statically configured with a set of IP address prefixes that correspond to the IP addresses of the stations it serves and their logical NBMA network identifiers.

To statically configure a Next Hop Server, perform the following task in interface configuration mode:

Task	Command
Statically configure a Next Hop Server.	**ip nhrp nhs** *nhs-address* [*net-address* [*netmask*]]

To configure multiple networks that the Next Hop Server serves, repeat the **ip nhrp nhs** command with the same Next Hop Server address, but different IP network addresses. To configure additional Next Hop Servers, repeat the **ip nhrp nhs** command.

Configuring NHRP Authentication

Configuring an authentication string ensures that only routers configured with the same string can communicate with each other using NHRP. Therefore, if the authentication scheme is to be used, the same string must be configured in all devices configured for NHRP on a fabric. To specify the authentication string for NHRP on an interface, perform the following task in interface configuration mode:

Task	Command
Specify an authentication string.	**ip nhrp authentication** *string*

Controlling NHRP Rate

There are three ways to control NHRP:

- Triggering NHRP by IP Packets

- Triggering NHRP on a Per-Destination Basis
- Controlling the NHRP Packet Rate

These methods are described in this section.

Triggering NHRP by IP Packets

You can specify an IP access list that is used to decide which IP packets can trigger the sending of NHRP requests. By default, all non-NHRP packets trigger NHRP requests. To limit which IP packets trigger NHRP requests, define an access list and then apply it to the interface.

To define an access list, perform one of the following tasks in global configuration mode:

Task	Command
Define a standard IP access list.	**access-list** *access-list-number* {**deny** | **permit**} *source* [*source-wildcard*]
Define an extended IP access list.	**access-list** *access-list-number* {**deny** | **permit**} *protocol source source-wildcard destination destination-wildcard* [**precedence** *precedence*] [**tos** *tos*] [**established**] [**log**]

Then apply the IP access list to the interface by performing the following task in interface configuration mode:

Task	Command
Specify an IP access list that controls NHRP requests.	**ip nhrp interest** *access-list-number*

Triggering NHRP on a Per-Destination Basis

By default, when the software attempts to transmit a data packet to a destination for which it has determined that NHRP can be used, it transmits an NHRP request for that destination. You can configure the system to wait until a specified number of data packets have been sent to a particular destination before NHRP is attempted. To do so, perform the following task in interface configuration mode:

Task	Command
Specify how many data packets are sent to a destination before NHRP is attempted.	**ip nhrp use** *usage-count*

Controlling the NHRP Packet Rate

By default, the maximum rate at which the software sends NHRP packets is 5 packets per 10 seconds. The software maintains a per interface quota of NHRP packets (whether generated locally or forwarded) that can be transmitted. To change this maximum rate, perform the following task in interface configuration mode:

Task	Command
Change the NHRP packet rate per interface.	**ip nhrp max-send** *pkt-count* **every** *interval*

Suppressing Forward and Reverse Record Options

To dynamically detect link-layer filtering in NBMA networks (for example, SMDS address screens) and to provide loop detection and diagnostic capabilities, NHRP incorporates a Route Record in requests and replies. The Route Record options contain the network (and link layer) addresses of all intermediate Next Hop Servers between source and destination (in the forward direction) and between destination and source (in the reverse direction).

By default, forward record options and reverse record options are included in NHRP request and reply packets. To suppress the use of these options, perform the following task in interface configuration mode:

Task	Command
Suppress forward and reverse record options.	**no ip nhrp record**

Specifying the NHRP Responder Address

If an NHRP requestor wants to know which Next Hop Server generates an NHRP reply packet, it can request that information by including the responder address option in its NHRP request packet. The Next Hop Server that generates the NHRP reply packet then complies by inserting its own IP address in the NHRP reply. The Next Hop Server uses the primary IP address of the specified interface.

To specify which interface that the Next Hop Server uses for the NHRP responder IP address, perform the following task in interface configuration mode:

Task	Command
Specify which interface the Next Hop Server uses to determine the NHRP responder address.	**ip nhrp responder** *type number*

If an NHRP reply packet being forwarded by a Next Hop Server contains that Next Hop Server's own IP address, the Next Hop Server generates an Error Indication of type "NHRP Loop Detected" and discards the reply.

Changing the Time Period NBMA Addresses Are Advertised as Valid

You can change the length of time that NBMA addresses are advertised as valid in positive and negative NHRP responses. In this context, *advertised* means how long the Cisco IOS software tells other routers to keep the addresses it is providing in NHRP responses. The default length of time for each response is 7,200 seconds (2 hours). To change the length of time, perform the following task in interface configuration mode:

Task	Command
Specify the number of seconds that NBMA addresses are advertised as valid in positive or negative NHRP responses.	**ip nhrp holdtime** *seconds-positive* [*seconds-negative*]

Configuring a GRE Tunnel for Multipoint Operation

You can enable a generic routing encapsulation (GRE) tunnel to operate in multipoint fashion. A tunnel network of multipoint tunnel interfaces can be thought of as an NBMA network. To configure the tunnel, perform the following tasks in interface configuration mode:

Task	Command
Step 1 Enable a GRE tunnel to be used in multipoint fashion.	**tunnel mode gre multipoint**
Step 2 Configure a tunnel identification key.	**tunnel key** *key-number*

The tunnel key should correspond to the NHRP network identifier specified in the **ip nhrp network-id** command. See the "NHRP on a Multipoint Tunnel Example" section at the end of this chapter for an example of NHRP configured on a multipoint tunnel.

ENABLING IP ROUTING

IP routing is automatically enabled in the Cisco IOS software. If you choose to set up the router to bridge rather than route IP datagrams, you must disable IP routing. To re-enable IP routing if it has been disabled, perform the following task in global configuration mode:

Task	Command
Enable IP routing.	**ip routing**

When IP routing is disabled, the router will act as an IP end host for IP packets destined for or sourced by it, whether or not bridging is enabled for those IP packets not destined for the device. To reenable IP routing, use the **ip routing** command.

Routing Assistance When IP Routing Is Disabled

The Cisco IOS software provides three methods by which the router can learn about routes to other networks when IP routing is disabled and the device is acting as an IP host. These methods are the following:

- Proxy ARP
- Default Gateway (also known as *default router*)
- ICMP Router Discovery Protocol (IRDP)

When IP routing is disabled, the default gateway feature and the router discovery client are enabled, and proxy ARP is disabled. When IP routing is enabled, the default gateway feature is disabled and you can configure proxy ARP and the router discovery servers.

Proxy ARP

The most common method of learning about other routes is by using proxy ARP. Proxy ARP, defined in RFC 1027, enables an Ethernet host with no knowledge of routing to communicate with hosts on other networks or subnets. Such a host assumes that all hosts are on the same local Ethernet, and that it can use ARP to determine their hardware addresses.

Under proxy ARP, if a device receives an ARP Request for a host that is not on the same network as the ARP Request sender, the Cisco IOS software evaluates whether it has the best route to that host. If it does, the device sends an ARP Reply packet giving its own Ethernet hardware address. The host that sent the ARP Request then sends its packets to the device, which forwards them to the intended host. The software treats all networks as if they are local and performs ARP requests for every IP address. This feature is enabled by default. If it has been disabled, see the section "Enabling Proxy ARP" earlier in this chapter.

Proxy ARP works as long as other routers support it. Many other routers, especially those loaded with host-based routing software, do not.

Default Gateway

Another method for locating routes is to define a default router (or gateway). The Cisco IOS software sends all nonlocal packets to this router, which either routes them appropriately or sends an IP Control Message Protocol (ICMP) redirect message back, telling it of a better route. The ICMP redirect message indicates which local router the host should use. The software caches the redirect messages and routes each packet thereafter as efficiently as possible. The limitations of this method are that there is no means of detecting when the default router has gone down or is unavailable, and there is no method of picking another device if one of these events should occur.

To set up a default gateway for a host, perform the following task in global configuration mode:

Task	Command
Set up a default gateway (router).	**ip default-gateway** *ip-address*

To display the address of the default gateway, use the **show ip redirects** EXEC command.

ICMP Router Discovery Protocol (IRDP)

The Cisco IOS software provides a third method, called *router discovery*, by which the router dynamically learns about routes to other networks using the ICMP Router Discovery Protocol (IRDP). IRDP allows hosts to locate routers. When operating as a client, router discovery packets are generated. When operating as a host, router discovery packets are received. Cisco's IRDP implementation fully conforms to the router discovery protocol outlined in RFC 1256.

The software is also capable of wire-tapping Routing Information Protocol (RIP) and Interior Gateway Routing Protocol (IGRP) routing updates and inferring the location of routers from those updates. The server/client implementation of router discovery does not actually examine or store the full routing tables sent by routing devices; it merely keeps track of which systems are sending such data.

You can configure the four protocols in any combination. When possible, Cisco recommends that you use IRDP because it allows each router to specify *both* a priority and the time after which a device should be assumed down if no further packets are received. Devices discovered using IGRP are assigned an arbitrary priority of 60. Devices discovered through RIP are assigned a priority of 50. For IGRP and RIP, the software attempts to measure the time between updates, and assumes that the device is down if no updates are received for 2.5 times that interval.

Each device discovered becomes a candidate for the default router. The list of candidates is scanned and a new highest-priority router is selected when any of the following events occur:

- When a higher-priority router is discovered (the list of routers is polled at 5-minute intervals).
- When the current default router is declared down.

- When a TCP connection is about to time out because of excessive retransmissions. In this case, the server flushes the ARP cache and the ICMP redirect cache, and picks a new default router in an attempt to find a successful route to the destination.

Enabling IRDP Processing

The only required task for configuring IRDP routing on a specified interface is to enable IRDP processing on an interface. To do so, perform the following task in interface configuration mode:

Task	Command
Enable IRDP processing on an interface.	**ip irdp**

Changing IRDP Parameters

When you enable IRDP processing, the default parameters will apply. Optionally, you can change any of these IRDP parameters. To change these parameters, perform the following tasks in interface configuration mode:

Task		Command
Step 1	Send IRDP advertisements to the all-systems multicast address (224.0.0.1) on a specified interface.	**ip irdp multicast**
Step 2	Set the IRDP period for which advertisements are valid.	**ip irdp holdtime** *seconds*
Step 3	Set the IRDP maximum interval between advertisements.	**ip irdp maxadvertinterval** *seconds*
Step 4	Set the IRDP minimum interval between advertisements.	**ip irdp minadvertinterval** *seconds*
Step 5	Set a device's IRDP preference level.	**ip irdp preference** *number*
Step 6	Specify an IRDP address and preference to proxy-advertise.	**ip irdp address** *address* [*number*]

The Cisco IOS software can proxy-advertise other machines that use IRDP; however, this is not rec-ommended because it is possible to advertise nonexistent machines or machines that are down.

ENABLING IP BRIDGING

To transparently bridge IP on an interface, perform the following tasks beginning in global config-uration mode:

Task		Command
Step 1	Disable IP routing.	**no ip routing**
Step 2	Specify an interface.	**interface** *type number*
Step 3	Add the interface to a bridge group.	**bridge-group** *group*

ENABLING INTEGRATED ROUTING AND BRIDGING

With integrated routing and bridging (IRB), you can route IP traffic between routed interfaces and bridge groups, or route IP traffic between bridge groups. Specifically, local or unroutable traffic is bridged among the bridged interfaces in the same bridge group, while routable traffic is routed to other routed interfaces or bridge groups. Using IRB, you can do the following:

- Switch packets from a bridged interface to a routed interface
- Switch packets from a routed interface to a bridged interface
- Switch packets within the same bridge group

CONFIGURING A ROUTING PROCESS

At this point in the configuration process, you can choose to configure one or more of the many routing protocols that are available based on your individual network needs. Routing protocols provide topology information of an internetwork. Refer to subsequent chapters in this book for the tasks involved in configuring IP routing protocols such as BGP, On-Demand Routing (ODR), RIP, IGRP, OSPF, IP Enhanced IGRP, Integrated IS-IS, and IP multicast routing. The following sections of this chapter describe what to do if you want to continue performing IP addressing tasks.

CONFIGURING BROADCAST PACKET HANDLING

A *broadcast* is a data packet destined for all hosts on a particular physical network. Network hosts recognize broadcasts by special addresses. Broadcasts are heavily used by some protocols, including several important Internet protocols. Control of broadcast messages is an essential part of the IP network administrator's job.

The Cisco IOS software supports two kinds of broadcasting: *directed broadcasting* and *flooding*. A directed broadcast is a packet sent to a specific network or series of networks, while a flooded broadcast packet is sent to every network. A directed broadcast address includes the network or subnet fields.

Several early IP implementations do not use the current broadcast address standard. Instead, they use the old standard, which calls for all zeros instead of all ones to indicate broadcast addresses. Many of these implementations do not recognize an all-ones broadcast address and fail to respond to the broadcast correctly. Others forward all-ones broadcasts, which causes a serious network overload known as a *broadcast storm*. Implementations that exhibit these problems include systems based on versions of BSD UNIX prior to Version 4.3.

Routers provide some protection from broadcast storms by limiting their extent to the local cable. Bridges (including intelligent bridges), because they are Layer 2 devices, forward broadcasts to all network segments, thus propagating all broadcast storms.

The best solution to the broadcast storm problem is to use a single broadcast address scheme on a network. Most modern IP implementations allow the network manager to set the address to be used as the broadcast address. Many implementations, including the one in the Cisco IOS software, accept and interpret all possible forms of broadcast addresses.

For detailed discussions of broadcast issues in general, see RFC 919, "Broadcasting Internet Datagrams," and RFC 922, "Broadcasting IP Datagrams in the Presence of Subnets." The support for Internet broadcasts generally complies with RFC 919 and RFC 922; it does not support multisubnet broadcasts as defined in RFC 922.

The current broadcast address standard provides specific addressing schemes for forwarding broadcasts. Perform the tasks in the following list to enable these schemes:

- Enabling Directed Broadcast-to-Physical Broadcast Translation
- Forwarding UDP Broadcast Packets and Protocols
- Establishing an IP Broadcast Address
- Flooding IP Broadcasts

See the "Broadcasting Examples" section at the end of this chapter for broadcasting configuration examples.

Enabling Directed Broadcast-to-Physical Broadcast Translation

To enable forwarding of directed broadcasts on an interface where the broadcast becomes a physical broadcast, perform one of the tasks that follow. By default, this feature is enabled only for those protocols configured using the **ip forward-protocol** global configuration command. You can specify an access list to control which broadcasts are forwarded. When an access list is specified, only those IP packets permitted by the access list are eligible to be translated from directed broadcasts to physical broadcasts.

Perform either of the following tasks in interface configuration mode as required for your network:

Task	Command
Enable directed broadcast-to-physical broadcast translation on an interface.	**ip directed-broadcast** [*access-list-number*]
Disable directed broadcast-to-physical broadcast translation on an interface.	**no ip directed-broadcast** [*access-list-number*]

Forwarding UDP Broadcast Packets and Protocols

Network hosts occasionally use UDP broadcasts to determine address, configuration, and name information. If such a host is on a network segment that does not include a server, UDP broadcasts are normally not forwarded. You can remedy this situation by configuring the interface of your router to forward certain classes of broadcasts to a helper address. You can use more than one helper address per interface.

You can specify a UDP destination port to control which UDP services are forwarded; you can specify multiple UDP protocols. You can also specify the Network Disk (ND) protocol, which is used by older diskless Sun workstations, and you can specify the network security protocol SDNS. By default, both UDP and ND forwarding are enabled if a helper address has been defined for an interface. The description for the **ip forward-protocol** command in Chapter 3 lists the ports that are forwarded by default if you do not specify any UDP ports.

If you do not specify any UDP ports when you configure the forwarding of UDP broadcasts, you are configuring the router to act as a BOOTP forwarding agent. BOOTP packets carry Dynamic Host Configuration Protocol (DHCP) information. (DHCP is defined in RFC 1531.) This means that the Cisco IOS software is now compatible with DHCP clients.

To enable forwarding and to specify the destination address, perform the following task in interface configuration mode:

Task	Command
Enable forwarding and specify the destination address for forwarding UDP broadcast packets, including BOOTP.	**ip helper-address** *address*

To specify which protocols will be forwarded, perform the following task in global configuration mode:

Task	Command
Specify which protocols will be forwarded over which ports.	**ip forward-protocol** {**udp** [*port*]	**nd**	**sdns**}

See the "Helper Addresses Example" section at the end of this chapter for an example of how to configure helper addresses.

Establishing an IP Broadcast Address

The Cisco IOS software supports IP broadcasts on both LANs and WANs. There are several ways to indicate an IP broadcast address. Currently, the most popular way, and the default, is an address consisting of all ones (255.255.255.255), although the software can be configured to generate any form of IP broadcast address. Cisco software also receives and understands any form of IP broadcast.

To set the IP broadcast address, perform the following task in interface configuration mode:

Task	Command
Establish a different broadcast address (other than 255.255.255.255).	**ip broadcast-address** [*ip-address*]

If the router does not have nonvolatile memory, and you need to specify the broadcast address to use before the software is configured, you must change the IP broadcast address by setting jumpers in the processor configuration register. Setting bit 10 causes the device to use all zeros. Bit 10 interacts with bit 14, which controls the network and subnet portions of the broadcast address. Setting bit 14 causes the device to include the network and subnet portions of its address in the broadcast address. Table 2–2 shows the combined effect of setting bits 10 and 14.

Table 2–2 *Configuration Register Settings for Broadcast Address Destination*

Bit 14	Bit 10	Address (<net><host>)
Out	Out	<ones><ones>
Out	In	<zeros><zeros>
In	In	<net><zeros>
In	Out	<net><ones>

Some router platforms allow the configuration register to be set through the software. For other router platforms, the configuration register must be changed through hardware; see the appropriate hardware installation and maintenance manual for your system.

Flooding IP Broadcasts

You can allow IP broadcasts to be flooded throughout your internetwork in a controlled fashion using the database created by the bridging spanning-tree protocol. Turning on this feature also prevents loops. In order to support this capability, the routing software must include the transparent bridging, and bridging must be configured on each interface that is to participate in the flooding. If bridging is not configured on an interface, it still will be able to receive broadcasts. However, the interface will never forward broadcasts it receives, and the router will never use that interface to send broadcasts received on a different interface.

Packets that are forwarded to a single network address using the IP helper address mechanism can be flooded. Only one copy of the packet is sent on each network segment.

In order to be considered for flooding, packets must meet the following criteria (note that these are the same conditions used to consider packets forwarding via IP helper addresses):

- The packet must be a MAC-level broadcast.
- The packet must be an IP-level broadcast.
- The packet must be a TFTP, DNS, Time, NetBIOS, ND, or BOOTP packet, or a UDP protocol specified by the **ip forward-protocol udp** global configuration command.
- The packet's Time-To-Live (TTL) value must be at least two.

A flooded UDP datagram is given the destination address you specified with the **ip broadcast-address** command on the output interface. The destination address can be set to any desired address. Thus, the destination address may change as the datagram propagates through the network. The source address is never changed. The TTL value is decremented.

After a decision has been made to send the datagram out on an interface (and the destination address possibly changed), the datagram is handed to the normal IP output routines and is, therefore, subject to access lists, if they are present on the output interface.

To use the bridging spanning-tree database to flood UDP datagrams, perform the following task in global configuration mode:

Task	Command
Use the bridging spanning-tree database to flood UDP datagrams.	**ip forward-protocol spanning-tree**

If no actual bridging is desired, you can configure a type-code bridging filter that will deny all packet types from being bridged. The spanning-tree database is still available to the IP forwarding code to use for the flooding.

Speeding Up Flooding of UDP Datagrams

You can speed up flooding of UDP datagrams using the spanning-tree algorithm. Used in conjunction with the **ip forward-protocol spanning-tree** command, this feature boosts the performance of spanning tree-based UDP flooding by a factor of about four to five times. The feature, called *turbo flooding*, is supported over Ethernet interfaces configured for ARPA encapsulated, Fiber Distributed Data Interface (FDDI), and HDLC-encapsulated serial interfaces. However, it is not supported on Token Ring interfaces. As long as the Token Rings and the non-HDLC serial interfaces are not part of the bridge group being used for UDP flooding, turbo flooding will behave normally.

To enable turbo flooding, perform the following task in global configuration mode:

Task	Command
Use the bridging spanning-tree database to speed up flooding of UDP datagrams.	**ip forward-protocol turbo-flood**

CONFIGURING NETWORK ADDRESS TRANSLATION (NAT)

Two of the key problems facing the Internet are depletion of IP address space and scaling in routing. Network Address Translation (NAT) is a feature that allows an organization's IP network to appear from the outside to use different IP address space than what it is actually using. Thus, NAT allows an organization with nonglobally routable addresses to connect to the Internet by translating those addresses into globally routable address space. NAT also allows a more graceful renumbering strategy for organizations that are changing service providers or voluntarily renumbering into CIDR blocks. NAT is also described in RFC 1631.

NAT Applications

NAT has several applications. Use it for the following purposes:

- You want to connect to the Internet, but not all your hosts have globally unique IP addresses. NAT enables private IP internetworks that use nonregistered IP addresses to connect to the Internet. NAT is configured on the router at the border of a stub domain (referred to as the *inside network*) and a public network such as the Internet (referred to as the *outside network*). NAT translates the internal local addresses to globally unique IP addresses before sending packets to the outside network.

- You must change your internal addresses. Instead of changing them, which can be a considerable amount of work, you can translate them by using NAT.

- You want to do basic load sharing of TCP traffic. You can map a single global IP address to many local IP addresses by using the TCP load distribution feature.

As a solution to the connectivity problem, NAT is practical only when relatively few hosts in a stub domain communicate outside of the domain at the same time. When this is the case, only a small subset of the IP addresses in the domain must be translated into globally unique IP addresses when outside communication is necessary, and these addresses can be reused when no longer in use.

Benefits of NAT

A significant advantage of NAT is that it can be configured without requiring changes to hosts or routers other than those few routers on which NAT will be configured. As discussed previously, NAT may not be practical if large numbers of hosts in the stub domain communicate outside of the domain. Furthermore, some applications use embedded IP addresses in such a way that it is impractical for a NAT device to translate. These applications may not work transparently or at all through a NAT device. NAT also hides the identity of hosts, which may be an advantage or a disadvantage.

A router configured with NAT will have at least one interface to the inside and one to the outside. In a typical environment, NAT is configured at the exit router between a stub domain and backbone. When a packet is leaving the domain, NAT translates the locally significant source address into a globally unique address. When a packet is entering the domain, NAT translates the globally unique destination address into a local address. If more than one exit point exists, each NAT must have the same translation table. If the software cannot allocate an address because it has run out of addresses, it drops the packet and sends an ICMP Host Unreachable packet.

A router configured with NAT must not advertise the local networks to the outside. However, routing information that NAT receives from the outside can be advertised in the stub domain as usual.

NAT Terminology

As mentioned previously, the term *inside* refers to those networks that are owned by an organization and that must be translated. Inside this domain, hosts will have address in the one address space, while on the outside, they will appear to have addresses in another address space when NAT is configured. The first address space is referred to as the *local* address space while the second is referred to as the *global* address space.

Similarly, *outside* refers to those networks to which the stub network connects, and which are generally not under the organization's control. As will be described later, hosts in outside networks can be subject to translation also, and thus, can have local and global addresses.

In summary, NAT uses the following definitions:

- **Inside local address**—The IP address that is assigned to a host on the inside network. The address is probably not a legitimate IP address assigned by the Network Information Center (NIC) or service provider.
- **Inside global address**—A legitimate IP address (assigned by the NIC or service provider) that represents one or more inside local IP addresses to the outside world.

- **Outside local address**—The IP address of an outside host as it appears to the inside network. Not necessarily a legitimate address, it was allocated from address space routable on the inside.

- **Outside global address**—The IP address assigned to a host on the outside network by the host's owner. The address was allocated from globally routable address or network space.

NAT Configuration Task List

Before configuring any NAT translation, you must know your inside local addresses and inside global addresses. The next sections show you how to use NAT to perform the following optional tasks:

- Translating Inside Source Addresses
- Overloading an Inside Global Address
- Translating Overlapping Addresses
- Providing TCP Load Distribution
- Changing Translation Timeouts
- Monitoring and Maintaining NAT

Translating Inside Source Addresses

Use this feature to translate your own IP addresses into globally unique IP addresses when communicating outside of your network. You can configure static or dynamic inside source translation as follows:

- *Static translation* establishes a one-to-one mapping between your inside local address and an inside global address. Static translation is useful when a host on the inside must be accessible by a fixed address from the outside.

- *Dynamic translation* establishes a mapping between an inside local address and a pool of global addresses.

Figure 2–4 illustrates a router that is translating a source address inside a network to a source address outside the network.

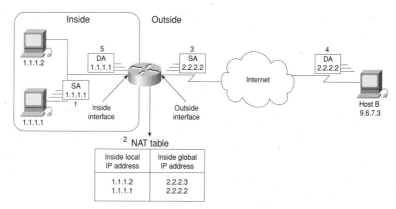

Figure 2–4
A router using a NAT translation for an inside source.

The following steps describe inside source address translation, as shown in Figure 2–4:

1. The user at Host 1.1.1.1 opens a connection to Host B.

2. The first packet that the router receives from Host 1.1.1.1 causes the router to check its NAT table.

   - If a static translation entry was configured, the router goes to Step 3.

   - If no translation entry exists, the router determines that the Source Address (SA) 1.1.1.1 must be translated dynamically, then selects a legal, global address from the dynamic address pool, and finally creates a translation entry. This type of entry is called a *simple entry*.

3. The router replaces the inside local source address of Host 1.1.1.1 with the translation entry's global address, and forwards the packet.

4. Host B receives the packet and responds to Host 1.1.1.1 by using the inside global IP Destination Address (DA) 2.2.2.2.

5. When the router receives the packet with the inside global IP address, it performs a NAT table lookup by using the inside global address as a key. It then translates the address to the inside local address of Host 1.1.1.1 and forwards the packet to Host 1.1.1.1.

6. Host 1.1.1.1 receives the packet and continues the conversation. The router performs Steps 2 through 5 for each packet.

Configuring Static Translation

To configure static inside source address translation, perform the following tasks beginning in global configuration mode:

Task	Command
Step 1 Establish static translation between an inside local address and an inside global address.	**ip nat inside source static** *local-ip global-ip*
Step 2 Specify the inside interface.	**interface** *type number*
Step 3 Mark the interface as connected to the inside.	**ip nat inside**
Step 4 Specify the outside interface.	**interface** *type number*
Step 5 Mark the interface as connected to the outside.	**ip nat outside**

The previous steps are the minimum you must configure. You can configure multiple inside and outside interfaces.

Configuring Dynamic Translation

To configure dynamic inside source address translation, perform the following tasks beginning in global configuration mode:

Task	Command
Step 1 Define a pool of global addresses to be allocated as needed.	**ip nat pool** *name start-ip end-ip* {**netmask** *netmask* | **prefix-length** *prefix-length*}
Step 2 Define a standard access list permitting those addresses that are to be translated.	**access-list** *access-list-number* **permit** *source* [*source-wildcard*]
Step 3 Establish dynamic source translation, specifying the access list defined in the prior step.	**ip nat inside source list** *access-list-number* **pool** *name*
Step 4 Specify the inside interface.	**interface** *type number*

Task		Command
Step 5	Mark the interface as connected to the inside.	ip nat inside
Step 6	Specify the outside interface.	interface *type number*
Step 7	Mark the interface as connected to the outside.	ip nat outside

NOTES

The access list must permit only those addresses that are to be translated. (Remember that there is an implicit "deny all" at the end of each access list.) An access list that is too permissive can lead to unpredictable results.

See the "Dynamic Inside Source Translation Example" section at the end of this chapter for an example of dynamic inside source translation.

Overloading an Inside Global Address

You can conserve addresses in the inside global address pool by allowing the router to use one global address for many local addresses. When this overloading is configured, the router maintains enough information from higher-level protocols (for example, TCP or UDP port numbers) to translate the global address back to the correct local address. When multiple local addresses map to one global address, the TCP or UDP port numbers of each inside host distinguish between the local addresses.

Figure 2–5 illustrates NAT operation when one inside global address represents multiple inside local addresses. The TCP port numbers act as differentiators.

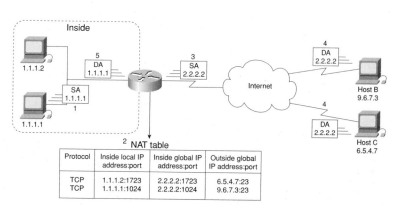

Figure 2–5
NAT operation while overloading inside global addresses.

Protocol	Inside local IP address:port	Inside global IP address:port	Outside global IP address:port
TCP	1.1.1.2:1723	2.2.2.2:1723	6.5.4.7:23
TCP	1.1.1.1:1024	2.2.2.2:1024	9.6.7.3:23

The router performs the following process in overloading inside global addresses, as shown in Figure 2–5. Both Host B and Host C think they are talking to a single host at address 2.2.2.2. They are actually talking to different hosts; the port number is the differentiator. In fact, many inside hosts could share the inside global IP address by using many port numbers.

1. The user at Host 1.1.1.1 opens a connection to Host B.

2. The first packet that the router receives from Host 1.1.1.1 causes the router to check its NAT table.

   If no translation entry exists, the router determines that address 1.1.1.1 must be translated, and sets up a translation of inside local address 1.1.1.1 to a legal global address. If overloading is enabled, and another translation is active, the router reuses the global address from that translation and saves enough information to be able to translate back. This type of entry is called an *extended entry*.

3. The router replaces the inside local source address 1.1.1.1 with the selected global address and forwards the packet.

4. Host B receives the packet and responds to Host 1.1.1.1 by using the inside global IP address 2.2.2.2.

5. When the router receives the packet with the inside global IP address, it performs a NAT table lookup using the protocol, inside global address and port, and outside address and port as a key. It then translates the address to inside local address 1.1.1.1 and forwards the packet to Host 1.1.1.1.

6. Host 1.1.1.1 receives the packet and continues the conversation. The router performs Steps 2 through 5 for each packet.

To configure overloading of inside global addresses, perform the following tasks beginning in global configuration mode:

Task	Command
Step 1 Define a pool of global addresses to be allocated as needed.	**ip nat pool** *name start-ip end-ip* {**netmask** *netmask* | **prefix-length** *prefix-length*}
Step 2 Define a standard access list.	**access-list** *access-list-number* **permit** *source* [*source-wildcard*]
Step 3 Establish dynamic source translation, identifying the access list defined in the prior step.	**ip nat inside source list** *access-list-number* **pool** *name* **overload**
Step 4 Specify the inside interface.	**interface** *type number*

Task	Command
Step 5 Mark the interface as connected to the inside.	**ip nat inside**
Step 6 Specify the outside interface.	**interface** *type number*
Step 7 Mark the interface as connected to the outside.	**ip nat outside**

NOTES

The access list must permit only those addresses that are to be translated. (Remember that there is an implicit "deny all" at the end of each access list.) An access list that is too permissive can lead to unpredictable results.

See the "Overloading Inside Global Addresses Example" section at the end of this chapter for an example of overloading inside global addresses.

Translating Overlapping Addresses

The NAT overlap translates IP addresses in certain situations, for example, when your IP addresses are not legal, officially assigned IP addresses. Perhaps you chose IP addresses that officially belong to another network. The case of an address used both illegally and legally is called *overlapping*. You can use NAT to translate inside addresses that overlap with outside addresses. Use this feature if your IP addresses in the stub network are legitimate IP addresses belonging to another network, and you want to communicate with those hosts or routers.

Figure 2–6 shows how NAT translates overlapping networks.

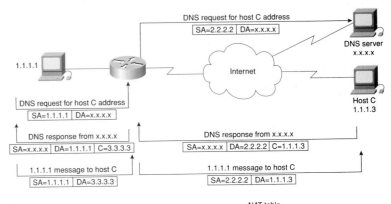

Figure 2–6

NAT translation of overlapping addresses.

The router performs the following steps when translating overlapping addresses:

1. The user at Host 1.1.1.1 opens a connection to Host C by name, requesting a name-to-address lookup from a DNS server.

2. The router intercepts the DNS reply and translates the returned address if there is an overlap (that is, the resulting legal address resides illegally in the inside network). To translate the return address, the router creates a simple translation entry mapping the overlapping address 1.1.1.3 to an address from a separately configured, outside local address pool.

   The router examines every DNS reply from everywhere, ensuring that the IP address is not in the stub network. If it is, the router translates the address.

3. Host 1.1.1.1 opens a connection to 3.3.3.3.

4. The router sets up translations, mapping inside local and global addresses to each other and outside global and local addresses to each other.

5. The router replaces the source address with the inside global address and replaces the destination address with the outside global address.

6. Host C receives the packet and continues the conversation.

7. The router does a lookup, replaces the destination address with the inside local address, and replaces the source address with the outside local address.

8. Host 1.1.1.1 receives the packet and the conversation continues, using this translation process.

Configuring Static Translation

To configure static outside source address translation, perform the following tasks beginning in global configuration mode:

Task	Command
Step 1 Establish static translation between an outside local address and an outside global address.	**ip nat outside source static** *global-ip local-ip*
Step 2 Specify the inside interface.	**interface** *type number*
Step 3 Mark the interface as connected to the inside.	**ip nat inside**
Step 4 Specify the outside interface.	**interface** *type number*
Step 5 Mark the interface as connected to the outside.	**ip nat outside**

Configuring Dynamic Translation

To configure dynamic outside source address translation, perform the following tasks beginning in global configuration mode:

Task	Command
Step 1 Define a pool of local addresses to be allocated as needed.	**ip nat pool** *name start-ip end-ip* {**netmask** *netmask* | **prefix-length** *prefix-length*}
Step 2 Define a standard access list.	**access-list** *access-list-number* **permit** *source* [*source-wildcard*]
Step 3 Establish dynamic outside source translation, specifying the access list defined in the prior step.	**ip nat outside source list** *access-list-number* **pool** *name*

Task		Command
Step 4	Specify the inside interface.	interface *type number*
Step 5	Mark the interface as connected to the inside.	**ip nat inside**
Step 6	Specify the outside interface.	interface *type number*
Step 7	Mark the interface as connected to the outside.	**ip nat outside**

NOTES

The access list must permit only those addresses that are to be translated. (Remember that there is an implicit "deny all" at the end of each access list.) An access list that is too permissive can lead to unpredictable results.

See the "Translating Overlapping Address Example" section at the end of this chapter for an example of translating an overlapping address.

Providing TCP Load Distribution

Another use of NAT is unrelated to Internet addresses. Your organization may have multiple hosts that must communicate with a heavily used host. Using NAT, you can establish a virtual host on the inside network that coordinates load sharing among real hosts. Destination addresses that match an access list are replaced with addresses from a rotary pool. Allocation is done in a round-robin basis, and only when a new connection is opened from the outside to the inside. Non-TCP traffic is passed untranslated (unless other translations are in effect). Figure 2–7 illustrates this feature.

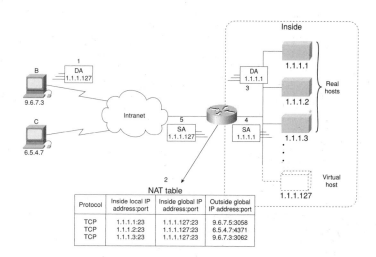

Figure 2–7
NAT TCP load distribution
feature.

The router performs the following steps when translating rotary addresses:

1. The user on Host B (9.6.7.3) opens a connection to virtual host at 1.1.1.127.

2. The router receives the connection request and creates a new translation, allocating the next real host (1.1.1.1) for the inside local IP address.

3. The router replaces the destination address with the selected real host address and forwards the packet.

4. Host 1.1.1.1 receives the packet and responds.

5. The router receives the packet and performs a NAT table lookup using the inside local address and port number and the outside address and port number as the key. The router then translates the source address to the address of the virtual host and forwards the packet.

The next connection request will cause the router to allocate 1.1.1.2 for the inside local address.

To configure destination address rotary translation, perform the following tasks beginning in global configuration mode. These tasks allow you to map one virtual host to many real hosts. Each new TCP session opened with the virtual host will be translated into a session with a different real host.

Task	Command
Step 1 Define a pool of addresses containing the addresses of the real hosts.	**ip nat pool** *name start-ip end-ip* {**netmask** *netmask* ǀ **prefix-length** *prefix-length*} **type rotary**
Step 2 Define an access list permitting the address of the virtual host.	**access-list** *access-list-number* **permit** *source* [*source-wildcard*]

Task	Command
Step 3 Establish dynamic inside destination translation, identifying the access list defined in the prior step.	**ip nat inside destination list** *access-list-number* **pool** *name*
Step 4 Specify the inside interface.	**interface** *type number*
Step 5 Mark the interface as connected to the inside.	**ip nat inside**
Step 6 Specify the outside interface.	**interface** *type number*
Step 7 Mark the interface as connected to the outside.	**ip nat outside**

NOTES

The access list must permit only those addresses that are to be translated. (Remember that there is an implicit "deny all" at the end of each access list.) An access list that is too permissive can lead to unpredictable results.

See the "TCP Load Distribution Example" section at the end of this chapter for an example of rotary translation.

Changing Translation Timeouts

By default, dynamic address translations time out after some period of non-use. You can change the default values on timeouts if necessary. When overloading is not configured, simple translation entries time out after 24 hours. To change this value, perform the following task in global configuration mode:

Task	Command
Change the timeout value for dynamic address translations that do not use overloading.	**ip nat translation timeout** *seconds*

If you have configured overloading, you have finer control over translation entry timeout because each entry contains more context about the traffic that is using it. To change timeouts on extended entries, perform one or more of the following tasks in global configuration mode:

Task	Command
Change the UDP timeout value from 5 minutes.	**ip nat translation udp-timeout** *seconds*
Change the DNS timeout value from 1 minute.	**ip nat translation dns-timeout** *seconds*
Change the TCP timeout value from 24 hours.	**ip nat translation tcp-timeout** *seconds*
Change the Finish and Reset timeout value from 1 minute.	**ip nat translation finrst-timeout** *seconds*

Monitoring and Maintaining NAT

By default, dynamic address translations will time out from the NAT translation table at some point. You can clear the entries before the timeout by performing one of the following tasks in EXEC mode:

Task	Command
Clear all dynamic address translation entries from the NAT translation table.	**clear ip nat translation ***
Clear a simple dynamic translation entry containing an inside translation, or both inside and outside translations.	**clear ip nat translation inside** *global-ip local-ip* [**outside** *local-ip global-ip*]
Clear a simple dynamic translation entry containing an outside translation.	**clear ip nat translation outside** *local-ip global-ip*
Clear an extended dynamic translation entry.	**clear ip nat translation** *protocol* **inside** *global-ip global-port local-ip local-port* [**outside** *local-ip local-port global-ip global-port*]

You can display translation information by performing one of the following tasks in EXEC mode:

Task	Command
Display active translations.	**show ip nat translations** [verbose]
Display translation statistics.	**show ip nat statistics**

MONITORING AND MAINTAINING IP ADDRESSING

To monitor and maintain your network, perform the tasks in the following list:

- Clearing Caches, Tables, and Databases
- Specifying the Format of Network Masks
- Displaying System and Network Statistics
- Monitoring and Maintaining NHRP

Clearing Caches, Tables, and Databases

You can remove all contents of a particular cache, table, or database. Clearing a cache, table, or database can become necessary when the contents of the particular structure have become or are suspected to be invalid.

The following table lists the tasks associated with clearing caches, tables, and databases. Perform the following tasks in EXEC mode as needed:

Task		Command
Step 1	Clear the IP ARP cache and the fast-switching cache.	**clear arp-cache**
Step 2	Remove one or all entries from the host name and address cache.	**clear host** {*name* | ***}
Step 3	Remove one or more routes from the IP routing table.	**clear ip route** {*network* [*mask*] | ***}

Specifying the Format of Network Masks

IP uses a 32-bit mask that indicates which address bits belong to the network and subnetwork fields, and which bits belong to the host field. This is called a *netmask*. By default, **show** commands display an IP address and then its netmask in dotted decimal notation. For example, a subnet would be displayed as 131.108.11.55 255.255.255.0.

You might find it more convenient to display the network mask in hexadecimal or bitcount format instead. The hexadecimal format is commonly used on UNIX systems. The previous example would be displayed as 131.108.11.55 0XFFFFFF00.

The bitcount format for displaying network masks is to append a slash (/) and the total number of bits in the netmask to the address itself. In this format, the previous example would be displayed as 131.108.11.55/24.

To specify the format in which netmasks appear for the current session, perform the following task in EXEC mode:

Task	Command
Specify the format of network masks for the current session.	**term ip netmask-format** {bitcount	decimal	hexadecimal}

To configure the format in which netmasks appear for an individual line, perform the following task in line configuration mode:

Task	Command
Configure the format of network masks for a line.	**ip netmask-format** {bitcount	decimal	hexadecimal}

Displaying System and Network Statistics

You can display specific statistics such as the contents of IP routing tables, caches, and databases. The resulting information can be used to determine resource utilization and to solve network problems. You also can display information about node reachability and discover the routing path that your device's packets are taking through the network.

These tasks are summarized in the table that follows. See Chapter 3 for details about the commands listed in these tasks. Perform any of the following tasks in privileged EXEC mode:

Task	Command
Display the entries in the ARP table.	**show arp**

Task	Command
Display the default domain name, style of lookup service, the name server hosts, and the cached list of host names and addresses.	**show hosts**
Display IP addresses mapped to TCP ports (aliases).	**show ip aliases**
Display the IP ARP cache.	**show ip arp**
Display the usability status of interfaces.	**show ip interface** [*type number*]
Display IRDP values.	**show ip irdp**
Display the masks used for network addresses and the number of subnets using each mask.	**show ip masks** *address*
Display the address of a default gateway.	**show ip redirects**
Display the current state of the routing table.	**show ip route** [*address* [*mask*]]	[*protocol*]
Display the current state of the routing table in summary form.	**show ip route summary**
Test network node reachability (privileged).	**ping** [*protocol*] {*host*	*address*}
Test network node reachability using a simple ping facility (user).	**ping** [*protocol*] {*host*	*address*}
Trace packet routes through the network (privileged).	**trace** [*destination*]
Trace packet routes through the network (user).	**trace ip** *destination*

See the "Ping Command Example" section at the end of this chapter for an example of pinging.

Monitoring and Maintaining NHRP

To monitor the NHRP cache or traffic, perform either of the following tasks in EXEC mode:

Task	Command
Display the IP NHRP cache, optionally limited to dynamic or static cache entries for a specific interface.	**show ip nhrp [dynamic | static]** [*type number*]
Display NHRP traffic statistics.	**show ip nhrp traffic**

The NHRP cache can contain static entries caused by statically configured addresses and dynamic entries caused by the Cisco IOS software learning addresses from NHRP packets. To clear static entries, use the **no ip nhrp map** command. To clear the NHRP cache of dynamic entries, perform the following task in EXEC mode:

Task	Command
Clear the IP NHRP cache of dynamic entries.	clear ip nhrp

IP ADDRESSING EXAMPLES

The following sections provide IP configuration examples:

- Creating a Network from Separated Subnets Example
- Serial Interfaces Configuration Example
- IP Domains Example
- Dynamic Lookup Example
- HP Hosts on a Network Segment Example
- Logical NBMA Example
- NHRP over ATM Example
- NHRP on a Multipoint Tunnel Example
- Broadcasting Examples

- Helper Addresses Example
- NAT Configuration Examples
- Ping Command Example

Creating a Network from Separated Subnets Example

In the following example, subnets 1 and 2 of network 131.108.0.0 are separated by a backbone, as shown in Figure 2–8. The two networks are brought into the same logical network through the use of secondary addresses.

Figure 2–8
Creating a network from separated subnets.

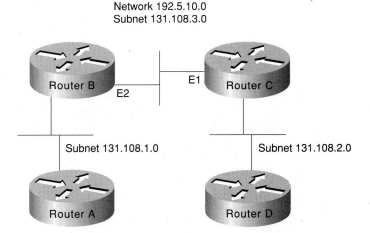

The following examples show the configurations for Routers B and C:

Configuration for Router B

```
interface ethernet 2
  ip address 192.5.10.1 255.255.255.0
  ip address 131.108.3.1 255.255.255.0 secondary
```

Configuration for Router C

```
interface ethernet 1
  ip address 192.5.10.2 255.255.255.0
  ip address 131.108.3.2 255.255.255.0 secondary
```

Serial Interfaces Configuration Example

In the following example, the second serial interface (serial 1) is given Ethernet 0's address. The serial interface is unnumbered.

```
interface ethernet 0
 ip address 145.22.4.67 255.255.255.0
interface serial 1
 ip unnumbered ethernet 0
```

IP Domains Example

The example that follows establishes a domain list with several alternate domain names:

```
ip domain-list csi.com
ip domain-list telecomprog.edu
ip domain-list merit.edu
```

Dynamic Lookup Example

A cache of host name-to-address mappings is used by **connect, telnet, ping, trace, write net,** and **configure net** EXEC commands to speed the process of converting names to addresses. The commands used in this example specify the form of dynamic name lookup to be used. Static name lookup also can be configured.

The following example configures the host name-to-address mapping process. IP DNS-based translation is specified, the addresses of the name servers are specified, and the default domain name is given.

```
! IP Domain Name System (DNS)-based host name-to-address translation is enabled
ip domain-lookup
! Specifies host 131.108.1.111 as the primary name server and host 131.108.1.2
! as the secondary server
ip name-server 131.108.1.111 131.108.1.2
! Defines cisco.com as the default domain name the router uses to complete
! unqualified host names
ip domain-name cisco.com
```

HP Hosts on a Network Segment Example

The following example has a network segment with Hewlett-Packard devices on it. The commands in this example customize the first Ethernet port to respond to Probe name requests for bl4zip and to use Probe as well as ARP.

```
ip hp-host bl4zip 131.24.6.27
interface ethernet 0
 arp probe
 ip probe proxy
```

Logical NBMA Example

A logical NBMA network is considered to be the group of interfaces and hosts participating in NHRP and having the same network identifier. Figure 2–9 illustrates two logical NBMA networks (shown as circles) configured over a single physical NBMA network. Router A can communicate with Routers B and C because they share the same network identifier (2). Router C can also communicate with Routers D and E, as they share network identifier 7. After address resolution is complete, Router A can send IP packets to Router C in one hop, and Router C can send them to Router E in one hop, as shown by the dotted lines.

Figure 2–9

Two logical NBMA networks over one physical NBMA network.

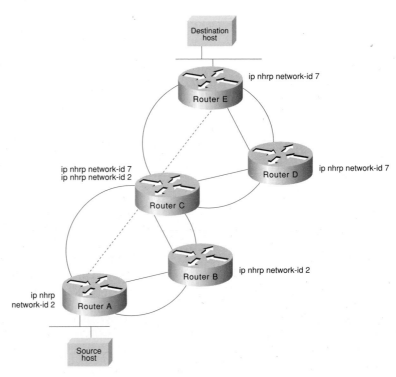

The physical configuration of the five routers in Figure 2–9 might actually be that shown in Figure 2–10. The source host is connected to Router A and the destination host is connected to Router E. The same switch serves all five routers, making one physical NBMA network.

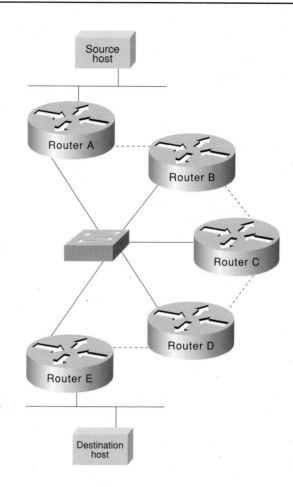

Figure 2–10
Physical configuration of a sample NBMA network.

Take another look at Figure 2–9. Initially, before NHRP has resolved any NBMA addresses, IP packets from the source host to the destination host travel through all five routers connected to the switch before reaching the destination. When Router A first forwards the IP packet toward the destination host, Router A also generates an NHRP request for the destination host's IP address. The request is forwarded to Router C, whereupon a reply is generated. Router C replies, because it is the egress router between the two logical NBMA networks.

Similarly, Router C generates an NHRP request of its own, to which Router E replies. In this example, subsequent IP traffic between the source and the destination still requires two hops to traverse the NBMA network because the IP traffic must be forwarded between the two logical NBMA networks. Only one hop would be required if the NBMA network were not logically divided.

NHRP over ATM Example

The following example shows a configuration of three routers using NHRP over ATM. Additionally, subinterfaces and dynamic routing are used. Router A obtains an OSPF route that it can use to reach the LIS where Router B resides. Router A can then initially reach Router B through Router C. Router A and Router B are able to communicate directly without Router C once NHRP has resolved Router A's and Router C's respective NSAP addresses.

The significant portions of the configurations for Routers A, B, and C follow:

Router A

```
interface ATM0/0
 ip address 10.1.0.1 255.255.0.0
 ip nhrp network-id 1
 map-group a
 atm nsap-address 11.1111.11.111111.1111.1111.1111.1111.1111.1111.11
 atm rate-queue 1 10
 atm pvc 1 0 5 qsaal

router ospf 1
 network 10.0.0.0 0.255.255.255 area 0

map-list a
 ip 10.1.0.3 atm-nsap 33.3333.33.333333.3333.3333.3333.3333.3333.3333.33
```

Router B

```
interface ATM0/0
 ip address 10.2.0.2 255.255.0.0
 ip nhrp network-id 1
 map-group a
 atm nsap-address 22.2222.22.222222.2222.2222.2222.2222.2222.2222.22
 atm rate-queue 1 10
 atm pvc 2 0 5 qsaal

router ospf 1
 network 10.0.0.0 0.255.255.255 area 0

map-list a
 ip 10.2.0.3 atm-nsap 33.3333.33.333333.3333.3333.3333.3333.3333.3333.33
```

Router C

```
interface ATM0/0
 no ip address
 atm rate-queue 1 10
 atm pvc 2 0 5 qsaal

interface ATM0/0.1 multipoint
 ip address 10.1.0.3 255.255.0.0
 ip nhrp network-id 1
```

```
map-group a
atm nsap-address 33.3333.33.333333.3333.3333.3333.3333.3333.3333.33
atm rate-queue 1 10

interface ATM0/0.2 multipoint
 ip address 10.2.0.3 255.255.0.0
 ip nhrp network-id 1
 map-group b
 atm nsap-address 33.3333.33.333333.3333.3333.3333.3333.3333.3333.33
 atm rate-queue 1 10

router ospf 1
 network 10.0.0.0 0.255.255.255 area 0
 neighbor 10.1.0.1 priority 1
 neighbor 10.2.0.2 priority 1

map-list a
 ip 10.1.0.1 atm-nsap 11.1111.11.111111.1111.1111.1111.1111.1111.1111.11

map-list b
 ip 10.2.0.2 atm-nsap 22.2222.22.222222.2222.2222.2222.2222.2222.2222.22
```

NHRP on a Multipoint Tunnel Example

With multipoint tunnels, a single tunnel interface may be connected to multiple neighboring routers. Unlike point-to-point tunnels, a tunnel destination need not be configured. In fact, if configured, the tunnel destination must correspond to an IP multicast address. Broadcast or multicast packets to be sent over the tunnel interface can then be transmitted by sending the GRE packet to the multicast address configured as the tunnel destination.

Multipoint tunnels require that you configure a tunnel key. Otherwise, unexpected GRE traffic could easily be received by the tunnel interface. For simplicity, it is recommended that the tunnel key correspond to the NHRP network identifier.

In the following example, Routers A, B, C, and D all share a common Ethernet segment. Minimal connectivity over the multipoint tunnel network is configured, thus creating a network that can be treated as a partially meshed NBMA network. Due to the static NHRP map entries, Router A knows how to reach Router B, Router B knows how to reach Router C, Router C knows how to reach Router D, and Router D knows how to reach Router A.

When Router A initially attempts to send an IP packet to Router D, the packet is forwarded through Routers B and C. Through NHRP, the routers quickly learn each other's NBMA addresses (in this case, IP addresses assigned to the underlying Ethernet network). The partially meshed tunnel network readily becomes fully meshed, at which point any of the routers can directly communicate over the tunnel network without their IP traffic requiring an intermediate hop.

The significant portions of the configurations for Routers A, B, C, and D follow:

Router A

```
interface tunnel 0
 no ip redirects
 ip address 11.0.0.1 255.0.0.0
 ip nhrp map 11.0.0.2 10.0.0.2
 ip nhrp network-id 1
 ip nhrp nhs 11.0.0.2
 tunnel source ethernet 0
 tunnel mode gre multipoint
 tunnel key 1

interface ethernet 0
 ip address 10.0.0.1 255.0.0.0
```

Router B

```
interface tunnel 0
 no ip redirects
 ip address 11.0.0.2 255.0.0.0
 ip nhrp map 11.0.0.3 10.0.0.3
 ip nhrp network-id 1
 ip nhrp nhs 11.0.0.3
 tunnel source ethernet 0
 tunnel mode gre multipoint
 tunnel key 1

interface ethernet 0
 ip address 10.0.0.2 255.0.0.0
```

Router C

```
interface tunnel 0
 no ip redirects
 ip address 11.0.0.3 255.0.0.0
 ip nhrp map 11.0.0.4 10.0.0.4
 ip nhrp network-id 1
 ip nhrp nhs 11.0.0.4
 tunnel source ethernet 0
 tunnel mode gre multipoint
 tunnel key 1

interface ethernet 0
 ip address 10.0.0.3 255.0.0.0
```

Router D

```
interface tunnel 0
 no ip redirects
 ip address 11.0.0.4 255.0.0.0
```

```
ip nhrp map 11.0.0.1 10.0.0.1
ip nhrp network-id 1
ip nhrp nhs 11.0.0.1
tunnel source ethernet 0
tunnel mode gre multipoint
tunnel key 1

interface ethernet 0
ip address 10.0.0.4 255.0.0.0
```

Broadcasting Examples

The Cisco IOS software supports two types of broadcasting: directed broadcasting and flooding. A directed broadcast is a packet sent to a specific network or series of networks, while a flooded broadcast packet is sent to every network. The following examples describe configurations for both types of broadcasting.

Flooded Broadcast Example

Figure 2–11 shows a flooded broadcast packet being sent to every network. The packet that is incoming from interface E0 is flooded to interfaces E1, E2, and S0.

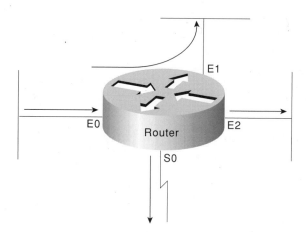

Figure 2–11
IP flooded broadcast.

A directed broadcast address includes the network or subnet fields. For example, if the network address is 128.1.0.0, the address 128.1.255.255 indicates all hosts on network 128.1.0.0. This would be a directed broadcast. If network 128.1.0.0 has a subnet mask of 255.255.255.0 (the third octet is the subnet field), the address 128.1.5.255 specifies all hosts on subnet 5 of network 128.1.0.0—another directed broadcast.

Flooding of IP Broadcasts Example

In the following example, flooding of IP broadcasts is enabled on all interfaces (two Ethernet and two serial). No bridging is permitted. The access list denies all protocols. No specific UDP protocols are listed by a separate **ip forward-protocol udp** interface configuration command, so the default protocols (TFTP, DNS, Time, NetBIOS, and BOOTP) will be flooded.

```
ip forward-protocol spanning-tree
 bridge 1 protocol dec
access-list 201 deny 0x0000 0xFFFF
 interface ethernet 0
 bridge-group 1
 bridge-group 1 input-type-list 201
interface ethernet 1
 bridge-group 1
 bridge-group 1 input-type-list 201
interface serial 0
 bridge-group 1
 bridge-group 1 input-type-list 201
interface serial 1
 bridge-group 1
 bridge-group 1 input-type-list 201
```

Helper Addresses Example

In the following example, one router is on network 191.24.1.0 and the other is on network 110.44.0.0, and you want to permit IP broadcasts from hosts on either network segment to reach both servers. Figure 2–12 illustrates how to configure the router that connects network 110 to network 191.24.1.

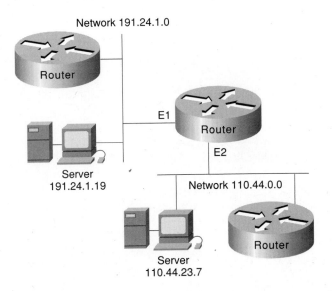

Figure 2–12

IP helper addresses.

Network 191.24.1.0

Router

E1

Router

E2

Server
191.24.1.19

Network 110.44.0.0

Router

Server
110.44.23.7

The following example shows the configuration of this router:

```
ip forward-protocol udp
!
interface ethernet 1
 ip helper-address 110.44.23.7
interface ethernet 2
 ip helper-address 191.24.1.19
```

NAT Configuration Examples

The following are NAT configuration examples.

Dynamic Inside Source Translation Example

The following example translates all source addresses passing access list 1 (having a source address from 192.168.1.0/24) to an address from the pool named net-208. The pool contains addresses from 171.69.233.208 to 171.69.233.233.

```
ip nat pool net-208 171.69.233.208 171.69.233.233 netmask 255.255.255.240
ip nat inside source list 1 pool net-208
!
interface serial 0
 ip address 171.69.232.182 255.255.255.240
 ip nat outside
!
interface ethernet 0
 ip address 192.168.1.94 255.255.255.0
 ip nat inside
!
access-list 1 permit 192.168.1.0 0.0.0.255
```

Overloading Inside Global Addresses Example

The following example creates a pool of addresses named net-208. The pool contains addresses from 171.69.233.208 to 171.69.233.233. Access list 1 allows packets having the source address from 192.168.1.0 to 192.168.1.255. If no translation exists, packets matching access list 1 are translated to an address from the pool. The router allows multiple local addresses (192.168.1.0 to 192.168.1.255) to use the same global address. The router retains port numbers to differentiate the connections.

```
ip nat pool net-208 171.69.233.208 171.69.233.233 netmask 255.255.255.240
ip nat inside source list 1 pool net-208 overload
!
interface serial0
 ip address 171.69.232.182 255.255.255.240
 ip nat outside
!
interface ethernet0
 ip address 192.168.1.94 255.255.255.0
 ip nat inside
!
access-list 1 permit 192.168.1.0 0.0.0.255
```

Translating Overlapping Address Example

In the following example, the addresses in the local network are being used legitimately by someone else on the Internet. An extra translation is required to access that external network. Pool net-10 is a pool of outside local IP addresses. The statement **ip nat outside source list 1 pool net-10** translates the addresses of hosts from the outside overlapping network to addresses in that pool.

```
ip nat pool net-208 171.69.233.208 171.69.233.223 prefix-length 28
ip nat pool net-10 10.0.1.0 10.0.1.255 prefix-length 24
ip nat inside source list 1 pool net-208
ip nat outside source list 1 pool net-10
!
interface serial 0
 ip address 171.69.232.192 255.255.255.240
 ip nat outside
!
interface ethernet0
 ip address 192.168.1.94 255.255.255.0
 ip nat inside
!
access-list 1 permit 192.168.1.0 0.0.0.255
```

TCP Load Distribution Example

In the following example, the goal is to define a virtual address, connections to which are distributed among a set of real hosts. The pool defines the addresses of the real hosts. The access list defines the virtual address. If a translation does not already exist, TCP packets from serial 0 (the outside interface) whose destination matches the access list are translated to an address from the pool.

```
ip nat pool real-hosts 192.168.15.2 192.168.15.15 prefix-length 28 type rotary
ip nat inside destination list 2 pool real-hosts
!
interface serial 0
 ip address 192.168.15.129 255.255.255.240
 ip nat outside
!
interface ethernet 0
 ip address 192.168.15.17 255.255.255.240
 ip nat inside
!
access-list 2 permit 192.168.15.1
```

Ping Command Example

You can specify the address to use as the source address for ping packets. In the following example, it is 131.108.105.62:

```
Sandbox# ping
Protocol [ip]:
Target IP address: 131.108.1.111
Repeat count [5]:
```

```
Datagram size [100]:
Timeout in seconds [2]:
Extended commands [n]: yes
Source address: 131.108.105.62
Type of service [0]:
Set DF bit in IP header? [no]:
Data pattern [0xABCD]:
Loose, Strict, Record, Timestamp, Verbose[none]:
Sweep range of sizes [n]:
Type escape sequence to abort.
Sending 5, 100-byte ICMP Echos to 131.108.1.111, timeout is 2 seconds:
!!!!!
Success rate is 100 percent, round-trip min/avg/max = 4/4/4 ms
```

CHAPTER 3

IP Addressing Commands

The Internet Protocol (IP) is a packet-based protocol used to exchange data over computer networks. IP handles addressing, fragmentation, reassembly, and protocol demultiplexing. It is the foundation on which all other Internet protocols, collectively referred to as the *Internet Protocol suite*, are built. IP is a network-layer protocol that contains addressing information and some control information that allows data packets to be routed.

The Transmission Control Protocol (TCP) is built upon the IP layer. TCP is a connection-oriented protocol that specifies the format of data and acknowledgments used in the transfer of data. TCP also specifies the procedures that computers use to ensure that data arrives correctly. TCP allows multiple applications on a system to communicate concurrently because it handles all demultiplexing of the incoming traffic among the application programs.

Use the commands in this chapter to configure and monitor the addressing of IP networks. For IP addressing configuration information and examples, see Chapter 2, "Configuring IP Addressing."

ARP (GLOBAL)

To add a permanent entry in the Address Resolution Protocol (ARP) cache, use the **arp** global configuration command. To remove an entry from the ARP cache, use the **no** form of this command.

> **arp** *ip-address hardware-address type* [**alias**]
> **no arp** *ip-address hardware-address type* [**alias**]

Syntax	Description
ip-address	IP address in four-part dotted-decimal format corresponding to the local data link address.
hardware-address	Local data link address (a 48-bit address).

Syntax	Description
type	Encapsulation description. For Ethernet interfaces, this is typically the **arpa** keyword. For Fiber Distributed Data Interface (FDDI) and Token Ring interfaces, this is always **snap**.
alias	(Optional.) Indicates that the Cisco IOS software should respond to ARP requests as if it were the owner of the specified address.

Default

No entries are permanently installed in the ARP cache.

Command Mode

Global configuration

Usage Guidelines

This command first appeared in Cisco IOS Release 10.0.

The Cisco IOS software uses ARP cache entries to translate 32-bit IP addresses into 48-bit hardware addresses. Because most hosts support dynamic resolution, you generally do not need to specify static ARP cache entries.

To remove all nonstatic entries from the ARP cache, use the **clear arp-cache** privileged EXEC command.

Example

The following is an example of a static ARP entry for a typical Ethernet host:

```
arp 192.31.7.19 0800.0900.1834 arpa
```

Related Commands

clear arp-cache

ARP (INTERFACE)

To control the interface-specific handling of IP address resolution into 48-bit Ethernet, FDDI, and Token Ring hardware addresses, use the **arp** interface configuration command. To disable an encapsulation type, use the **no** form of this command.

> arp {arpa | probe | snap}
> no arp {arpa | probe | snap}

Syntax	Description
arpa	Standard Ethernet-style ARP (RFC 826).

Syntax   *Description*

probe   HP Probe protocol for IEEE-802.3 networks.

snap   ARP packets conforming to RFC 1042.

Default

Standard Ethernet-style ARP

Command Mode

Interface configuration

Usage Guidelines

This command first appeared in Cisco IOS Release 10.0.

Unlike most commands that can have multiple arguments, arguments to the **arp** command are not mutually exclusive. Each command enables or disables a specific type of ARP. For example, if you enter the **arp arpa** command followed by the **arp probe** command, the Cisco IOS software would send three packets (two for **probe** and one for **arpa**) each time it needed to discover a Media Access Control (MAC) address.

The **arp probe** command allows the software to use the Probe protocol (in addition to ARP) whenever it attempts to resolve an IEEE-802.3 or Ethernet local data link address. The subset of Probe that performs address resolution is called Virtual Address Request and Reply. Using Probe, the software can communicate transparently with Hewlett-Packard IEEE-802.3 hosts that use this type of data encapsulation.

NOTES

Cisco's support for HP Probe proxy support changed as of Software Release 8.3(2) and subsequent releases. The **no arp probe** command is now the default. All interfaces that will use Probe must now be explicitly configured for **arp probe**.

The **show interfaces** EXEC command displays the type of ARP being used on a particular interface. To remove all nonstatic entries from the ARP cache, use the **clear arp-cache** privileged EXEC command.

Example

The following example enables probe services:

```
interface ethernet 0
 arp probe
```

Related Commands

clear arp-cache
show interfaces

ARP TIMEOUT

To configure how long an entry remains in the ARP cache, use the **arp timeout** interface configuration command. To restore the default value, use the **no** form of this command.

> **arp timeout** *seconds*
> **no arp timeout** *seconds*

Syntax	Description
seconds	Time (in seconds) that an entry remains in the ARP cache. A value of zero means that entries are never cleared from the cache.

Default

14400 seconds (4 hours)

Command Mode

Interface configuration

Usage Guidelines

This command first appeared in Cisco IOS Release 10.0.

This command is ignored when issued on interfaces that do not use ARP. The **show interfaces** EXEC command displays the ARP timeout value. The value follows the "Entry Timeout:" heading, as seen in this sample **show interfaces** display:

```
ARP type: ARPA, PROBE, Entry Timeout: 14400 sec
```

Example

The following example sets the ARP timeout to 12000 seconds to allow entries to time out more quickly than the default:

```
interface ethernet 0
 arp timeout 12000
```

Related Commands
show interfaces

CLEAR ARP-CACHE

To delete all dynamic entries from the ARP cache, to clear the fast-switching cache, and to clear the IP route cache, use the **clear arp-cache** EXEC command.

    clear arp-cache

Syntax   *Description*

This command has no arguments or keywords.

Command Mode

EXEC

Usage Guidelines

This command first appeared in IOS Release 10.0.

Example

The following example removes all dynamic entries from the ARP cache and clears the fast-switching cache:

```
clear arp-cache
```

Related Commands

arp (global)
arp (interface)

CLEAR HOST

To delete entries from the hostname-and-address cache, use the **clear host** EXEC command.

    clear host {*name* | ***}

Syntax	*Description*
name	Particular host entry to remove.
*	Removes all entries.

Command Mode

EXEC

Usage Guidelines

This command first appeared in IOS Release 10.0.

The host name entries will not be removed from Nonvolatile Random Access Memory (NVRAM), but will be cleared from running memory.

Example

The following example clears all entries from the host name-and-address cache:

```
clear host *
```

Related Commands

ip host
show hosts

CLEAR IP NAT TRANSLATION

To clear dynamic Network Address Translation (NAT) translations from the translation table, use the **clear ip nat translation** EXEC command.

> **clear ip nat translation** {* | [**inside** *global-ip local-ip*] [**outside** *local-ip global-ip*]}
> **clear ip nat translation** *protocol* **inside** *global-ip global-port local-ip local-port*
> [**outside** *local-ip global-ip*]

Syntax	Description
*	Clears all dynamic translations.
inside	Clears the inside translations containing the specified *global-ip* and *local-ip* addresses.
global-ip	When used without the arguments *protocol*, *global-port*, and *local-port*, clears a simple translation that also contains the specified *local-ip* address. When used with the arguments *protocol*, *global-port*, and *local-port*, clears an extended translation.
local-ip	(Optional.) Clears an entry that contains this local IP address and the specified *global-ip* address.
outside	Clears the outside translations containing the specified *global-ip* and *local-ip* addresses.
protocol	(Optional.) Clears an entry that contains this protocol and the specified *global-ip* address, *local-ip* address, *global-port*, and *local-port*.
global-port	(Optional.) Clears an entry that contains this *global-port* and the specified *protocol*, *global-ip* address, *local-ip* address, and *local-port*.
local-port	(Optional.) Clears an entry that contains this *local-port* and the specified *protocol*, *global-ip* address, *local-ip* address, and *global-port*.

Command Mode

EXEC

Usage Guidelines

This command first appeared in Cisco IOS Release 11.2.

Use this command to clear entries from the translation table before they time out.

Example

The following example shows the NAT entries before and after the UDP entry being cleared:

```
Router# show ip nat translation
Pro Inside global      Inside local       Outside local     Outside global
udp 171.69.233.209:1220 192.168.1.95:1220 171.69.2.132:53   171.69.2.132:53
tcp 171.69.233.209:11012 192.168.1.89:11012 171.69.1.220:23  171.69.1.220:23
tcp 171.69.233.209:1067 192.168.1.95:1067 171.69.1.161:23   171.69.1.161:23

Router# clear ip nat translation udp inside 171.69.233.209 1220 192.168.1.95 1220
171.69.2.132 53 171.69.2.132 53

Router# show ip nat translation
Pro Inside global      Inside local       Outside local     Outside global
tcp 171.69.233.209:11012 192.168.1.89:11012 171.69.1.220:23  171.69.1.220:23
tcp 171.69.233.209:1067 192.168.1.95:1067 171.69.1.161:23   171.69.1.161:23
```

Related Commands

ip nat
ip nat inside destination
ip nat inside source
ip nat outside source
ip nat pool
ip nat translation
show ip nat statistics
show ip nat translations

CLEAR IP NHRP

To clear all dynamic entries from the Next Hop Resolution Protocol (NHRP) cache, use the
clear ip nhrp EXEC command.

clear ip nhrp

Syntax   Description

This command has no arguments or keywords.

Command Mode

EXEC

Usage Guidelines

This command first appeared in Cisco IOS Release 11.0.

This command does not clear any static (configured) IP-to-Nonbroadcast Multiaccess (NBMA) address mappings from the NHRP cache.

Example

The following example clears all dynamic entries from the NHRP cache for the interface:

```
clear ip nhrp
```

Related Commands

show ip nhrp

CLEAR IP ROUTE

To delete routes from the IP routing table, use the **clear ip route** EXEC command.

    clear ip route {*network* [*mask*] | ***}

Syntax	Description
network	Network or subnet address to remove.
mask	(Optional.) Subnet address to remove.
*	Removes all routing table entries.

Default

All entries are removed.

Command Mode

EXEC

Usage Guidelines

This command first appeared in Cisco IOS Release 10.0.

Example

The following example removes a route to network 132.5.0.0 from the IP routing table:

```
clear ip route 132.5.0.0
```

IP ADDRESS

To set a primary or secondary IP address for an interface, use the **ip address** interface configuration command. To remove an IP address or disable IP processing, use the **no** form of this command.

ip address *ip-address mask* [**secondary**]
no ip address *ip-address mask* [**secondary**]

Syntax	Description
ip-address	IP address.
mask	Mask for the associated IP subnet.
secondary	(Optional.) Specifies that the configured address is a secondary IP address. If this keyword is omitted, the configured address is the primary IP address.

Default

No IP address is defined for the interface.

Command Mode

Interface configuration

Usage Guidelines

This command first appeared in Cisco IOS Release 10.0.

An interface can have one primary IP address and multiple secondary IP addresses. Packets generated by the Cisco IOS software always use the primary IP address. Therefore, all routers and access servers on a segment should share the same primary network number.

Hosts can determine subnet masks using the Internet Control Message Protocol (ICMP) Mask Request message. Routers respond to this request with an ICMP Mask Reply message.

You can disable IP processing on a particular interface by removing its IP address with the **no ip address** command. If the software detects another host using one of its IP addresses, it will print an error message on the console.

The optional keyword **secondary** allows you to specify an unlimited number of secondary addresses. Secondary addresses are treated like primary addresses, except that the system never generates datagrams other than routing updates with secondary source addresses. IP broadcasts and ARP requests are handled properly, as are interface routes in the IP routing table.

Secondary IP addresses can be used in a variety of situations. The following are the most common applications:

- There may not be enough host addresses for a particular network segment. For example, your subnetting allows up to 254 hosts per logical subnet, but on one physical subnet you need to have 300 host addresses. Using secondary IP addresses on the routers or access servers allows you to have two logical subnets using one physical subnet.

- Many older networks were built using Level 2 bridges. The judicious use of secondary addresses can aid in the transition to a subnetted, router-based network. Routers on an older, bridged segment can easily be made aware that there are many subnets on that segment.

- Two subnets of a single network might otherwise be separated by another network. This situation is not permitted when subnets are in use. In these instances, the first network is *extended*, or layered, on top of the second network using secondary addresses.

— NOTES ——

If any router on a network segment uses a secondary address, all other devices on that same segment must also use a secondary address from the same network or subnet. Inconsistent use of secondary addresses on a network segment can very quickly cause routing loops.

— NOTES ——

When you are routing Open Shortest Path First (OSPF), ensure that all secondary addresses of an interface fall into the same OSPF area as the primary addresses.

To transparently bridge IP on an interface, you must do two things:

- Disable IP routing (specify **no ip routing**).

- Add the interface to a bridge group. (See the **bridge-group** command.)

To concurrently route and transparently bridge IP on an interface, see the **bridge crb** command.

Example

In the following example, 131.108.1.27 is the primary address while 192.31.7.17 and 192.31.8.17 are secondary addresses for Ethernet interface 0:

```
interface ethernet 0
 ip address 131.108.1.27 255.255.255.0
 ip address 192.31.7.17 255.255.255.0 secondary
 ip address 192.31.8.17 255.255.255.0 secondary
```

Related Commands

bridge crb
bridge-group

IP BROADCAST-ADDRESS

To define a broadcast address for an interface, use the **ip broadcast-address** interface configuration command. To restore the default IP broadcast address, use the **no** form of this command.

 ip broadcast-address [*ip-address*]
 no ip broadcast-address [*ip-address*]

Syntax   *Description*

ip-address   (Optional.) IP broadcast address for a network.

Default

Default address: 255.255.255.255 (all ones)

Command Mode

Interface configuration

Usage Guidelines

This command first appeared in Cisco IOS Release 10.0.

Example

The following example specifies an IP broadcast address of 0.0.0.0:

```
ip broadcast-address 0.0.0.0
```

IP CLASSLESS

At times, the router might receive packets destined for a subnet of a network that has no network
default route. To have the Cisco IOS software forward such packets to the best supernet route possible, use the **ip classless** global configuration command. To disable this feature, use the **no** form of
this command.

> **ip classless**
> **no ip classless**

Syntax   *Description*

This command has no arguments or keywords.

Default

Disabled

Command Mode

Global configuration

Usage Guidelines

This command first appeared in Cisco IOS Release 10.0.

This command allows the software to forward packets that are destined for unrecognized subnets
of directly connected networks. By default, the software discards the packets when a router receives
packets for a subnet that numerically falls within its subnetwork addressing scheme, if there is no

such subnet number in the routing table and there is no network default route. However, when the **ip classless** command is enabled, the software instead forwards those packets to the best supernet route.

Example

The following example configures the software to forward packets destined for an unrecognized subnet to the best supernet possible:

```
ip classless
```

IP DEFAULT-GATEWAY

To define a default gateway (router) when IP routing is disabled, use the **ip default-gateway** global configuration command. To disable this function, use the **no** form of this command.

> **ip default-gateway** *ip-address*
> **no ip default-gateway** *ip-address*

Syntax	Description
ip-address	IP address of the router.

Default

Disabled

Command Mode

Global configuration

Usage Guidelines

This command first appeared in Cisco IOS Release 10.0.

The Cisco IOS software sends any packets that need the assistance of a gateway to the address you specify. If another gateway has a better route to the requested host, the default gateway sends an ICMP redirect message back. The ICMP redirect message indicates which local router the Cisco IOS software should use.

Example

The following example defines the router on IP address 192.31.7.18 as the default router:

```
ip default-gateway 192.31.7.18
```

Related Commands

show ip redirects

IP DIRECTED-BROADCAST

To enable the translation of directed broadcast to physical broadcasts, use the **ip directed-broadcast** interface configuration command. To disable this function, use the **no** form of this command.

> **ip directed-broadcast** [*access-list-number*]
> **no ip directed-broadcast** [*access-list-number*]

Syntax	Description
access-list-number	(Optional.) Number of the access list. If specified, a broadcast must pass the access list to be forwarded. If not specified, all broadcasts are forwarded.

Default

Enabled, with no list specified

Command Mode

Interface configuration

Usage Guidelines

This command first appeared in Cisco IOS Release 10.0.

This feature is enabled only for those protocols configured using the **ip forward-protocol** global configuration command. An access list may be specified to control which broadcasts are forwarded. When an access list is specified, only those IP packets permitted by the access list are eligible to be translated from directed broadcasts to physical broadcasts.

Example

The following example enables forwarding of IP directed broadcasts on Ethernet interface 0:

```
interface ethernet 0
 ip directed-broadcast
```

Related Commands

ip forward-protocol

IP DOMAIN-LIST

To define a list of default domain names to complete unqualified host names, use the **ip domain-list** global configuration command. To delete a name from a list, use the **no** form of this command.

> **ip domain-list** *name*
> **no ip domain-list** *name*

Syntax   *Description*

name   Domain name. Do not include the initial period that separates an unqualified
                  name from the domain name.

Default

No domain names are defined.

Command Mode

Global configuration

Usage Guidelines

This command first appeared in Cisco IOS Release 10.0.

If there is no domain list, the domain name that you specified with the **ip domain-name** global configuration command is used. If there is a domain list, the default domain name is not used. The **ip domain-list** command is similar to the **ip domain-name** command, except that with **ip domain-list** you can define a list of domains, each to be tried in turn.

Examples

The following example adds several domain names to a list:

```
ip domain-list martinez.com
ip domain-list stanford.edu
```

The following example adds a name to, and then deletes a name from, the list:

```
ip domain-list sunya.edu
no ip domain-list stanford.edu
```

Related Commands

ip domain-name

IP DOMAIN-LOOKUP

To enable the IP Domain Naming System (DNS)-based host name-to-address translation, use the **ip domain-lookup** global configuration command. To disable the DNS, use the **no** form of this command.

> ip domain-lookup
> no ip domain-lookup

Syntax   *Description*

This command has no arguments or keywords.

Default

Enabled

Command Mode

Global configuration

Usage Guidelines

This command first appeared in Cisco IOS Release 10.0.

Example

The following example enables the IP Domain Naming System-based host name-to-address translation:

```
ip domain-lookup
```

Related Commands

ip domain-lookup nsap
ip domain-name
ip name-server

IP DOMAIN-LOOKUP NSAP

To allow DNS queries for Connectionless Network System (CLNS) addresses, use the **ip domain-lookup nsap** global configuration command. To disable this feature, use the **no** form of this command.

> **ip domain-lookup nsap**
> **no ip domain-lookup nsap**

Syntax   Description

This command has no arguments or keywords.

Default

Enabled

Command Mode

Global configuration

Usage Guidelines

This command first appeared in Cisco IOS Release 10.0.

With both IP and International Organization for Standardization (ISO) CLNS enabled, this feature allows the Cisco IOS software to dynamically determine a CLNS address given a host name. This feature is useful for the ISO CLNS **ping** EXEC command and when making CLNS Telnet connections.

Example

The following example disables DNS queries of CLNS addresses:

```
no ip domain-lookup nsap
```

Related Commands

ip domain-lookup
ping (for ISO CLNS)

IP DOMAIN-NAME

To define a default domain name that the Cisco IOS software will use to complete unqualified host names (names without a dotted-decimal domain name), use the **ip domain-name** global configuration command. To disable use of the DNS, use the **no** form of this command.

> **ip domain-name** *name*
> **no ip domain-name**

Syntax	*Description*
name	Default domain name used to complete unqualified host names. Do not include the initial period that separates an unqualified name from the domain name.

Default

Enabled

Command Mode

Global configuration

Usage Guidelines

This command first appeared in Cisco IOS Release 10.0.

Any IP host name that does not contain a domain name (that is, any name without a dot), will have the dot and cisco.com appended to it before being added to the host table.

Example

The following example defines cisco.com as the default domain name:

```
ip domain-name cisco.com
```

Related Commands

ip domain-list
ip domain-lookup
ip name-server

IP FORWARD-PROTOCOL

To specify which protocols and ports the router forwards when forwarding broadcast packets, use the **ip forward-protocol** global configuration command. To remove a protocol or port, use the **no** form of this command.

> ip forward-protocol {udp [*port*] | nd | sdns}
> no ip forward-protocol {udp [*port*] | nd | sdns}

Syntax	*Description*
udp	Forward User Datagram Protocol (UDP) datagrams. See the "Default" section below for a list of port numbers forwarded by default.
port	(Optional.) Destination port that controls which UDP services are forwarded.
nd	Forward Network Disk (ND) datagrams. This protocol is used by older diskless Sun workstations.
sdns	Secure Data Network Service.

Default

If an IP helper address is defined, UDP forwarding is enabled on default ports. If UDP flooding is configured, UDP flooding is enabled on the default ports.

If a helper address is specified and UDP forwarding is enabled, broadcast packets destined to the following port numbers are forwarded by default:

- Trivial File Transfer Protocol (TFTP, port 69)
- Domain Naming System (port 53)
- Time service (port 37)
- NetBIOS Name Server (port 137)
- NetBIOS Datagram Server (port 138)
- Boot Protocol (BOOTP) client and server datagrams (ports 67 and 68)
- TACACS service (port 49)

NOTES

Using the **ip directed-broadcast** interface configuration command with the optional *access-list-number* argument overrides the behavior of the **ip forward-protocol** command.

Command Mode

Global configuration

Usage Guidelines

This command first appeared in Cisco IOS Release 10.0.

Enabling a helper address or UDP flooding on an interface causes the Cisco IOS software to forward particular broadcast packets. You can use the **ip forward-protocol** command to specify exactly which types of broadcast packets you would like to have forwarded. A number of commonly forwarded applications are enabled by default.

CAUTION

Enabling forwarding for some ports (for example, RIP) may be hazardous to your network.

If you use the **ip forward-protocol** command, specifying just UDP, without the port, enables forwarding and flooding on the default ports.

One common application that requires helper addresses is Dynamic Host Configuration Protocol (DHCP). DHCP is defined in RFC 1531. DHCP protocol information is carried inside BOOTP packets. To enable BOOTP broadcast forwarding for a set of clients, configure a helper address on the router interface closest to the client. The helper address should specify the address of the DHCP server. If you have multiple servers, you can configure one helper address for each server. Because BOOTP packets are forwarded by default, DHCP information can now be forwarded by the software. The DHCP server now receives broadcasts from the DHCP clients.

Example

The following example uses the **ip forward-protocol** command to specify forwarding of UDP port 3001 in addition to the default ports, and then defines a helper address:

```
ip forward-protocol udp 3001
!
interface ethernet 1
 ip helper-address 131.120.1.0
```

Related Commands

ip directed-broadcast
ip forward-protocol spanning-tree
ip forward-protocol turbo-flood
ip helper-address

IP FORWARD-PROTOCOL ANY-LOCAL-BROADCAST

To forward any broadcasts, including local subnet broadcasts, use the **ip forward-protocol any-local-broadcast** global configuration command. To disable this type of forwarding, use the **no** form of this command.

> **ip forward-protocol any-local-broadcast**
> **no ip forward-protocol any-local-broadcast**

Syntax   Description

This command has no arguments or keywords.

Default

Disabled

Command Mode

Global configuration

Usage Guidelines

This command first appeared in Cisco IOS Release 10.3.

The **ip forward-protocol any-local-broadcast** command forwards packets similarly to how the **ip forward-protocol spanning-tree** command does. That is, it forwards packets whose contents are all ones (255.255.255.255), all zeros (0.0.0.0), and, if subnetting is enabled, all networks (131.108.255.255 as an example in the network number 131.108.0.0). This mechanism also forwards packets whose contents are the zeros version of the all-networks broadcast when subnetting is enabled (for example, 131.108.0.0). In addition, it forwards any local subnet broadcast packets.

Use the **ip forward-protocol any-local-broadcast** command in conjunction with the **ip forward-protocol spanning-tree** command, not as a replacement for it.

Example

Assume a router is directly connected to subnet 1 of network 131.108.0.0 and that the netmask is 255.255.255.0. The following command enables the forwarding of IP broadcasts destined to 131.108.1.255 and 131.108.1.0 in addition to the broadcast addresses mentioned in the "Usage Guidelines" section:

```
ip forward-protocol any-local-broadcast
```

Related Commands

ip forward-protocol spanning-tree

IP FORWARD-PROTOCOL SPANNING-TREE

To permit IP broadcasts to be flooded throughout the internetwork in a controlled fashion, use the **ip forward-protocol spanning-tree** global configuration command. To disable the flooding of IP broadcasts, use the **no** form of this command.

> **ip forward-protocol spanning-tree**
> **no ip forward-protocol spanning-tree**

Syntax　　Description

This command has no arguments or keywords.

Default

Disabled

Command Mode

Global configuration

Usage Guidelines

This command first appeared in Cisco IOS Release 10.0.

Packets must meet the following criteria to be considered for flooding:

- The packet must be a MAC-level broadcast.
- The packet must be an IP-level broadcast; that is, an all-network broadcast (255.255.255.255) or major network broadcast (131.108.255.255, for example).
- The packet must be a TFTP, DNS, Time, NetBIOS, ND, or BOOTP packet, or a UDP protocol specified by the **ip forward-protocol udp** global configuration command.
- The packet's Time-to-Live (TTL) value must be at least 2.

A flooded UDP datagram is given the destination address specified by the **ip broadcast-address** interface configuration command on the output interface. The destination address can be set to any desired address. Thus, the destination address may change as the datagram propagates through the network. The source address is never changed. The TTL value is decremented.

After a decision has been made to send the datagram out on an interface (and the destination address possibly changed), the datagram is handed to the normal IP output routines and is therefore subject to access lists, if they are present on the output interface.

The **ip forward-protocol spanning-tree** command uses the database created by the bridging spanning-tree protocol. Therefore, the transparent bridging option must be in the routing software, and bridging must be configured on each interface that is to participate in the flooding in order to support this capability.

If an interface does not have bridging configured, it still will be able to receive broadcasts, but it will never forward broadcasts received on that interface. Also, it will never use that interface to send broadcasts received on a different interface.

If no bridging is desired, you can configure a type-code bridging filter that will deny all packet types from being bridged. The spanning-tree database is still available to the IP forwarding code to use for the flooding.

The spanning-tree-based flooding mechanism forwards packets whose contents are all ones (255.255.255.255), all zeros (0.0.0.0), and, if subnetting is enabled, all networks (131.108.255.255 as an example in the network number 131.108.0.0). This mechanism also forwards packets whose contents are the zeros version of the all-networks broadcast when subnetting is enabled (for example, 131.108.0.0).

This command is an extension of the **ip helper-address** interface configuration command, in that the same packets that may be subject to the helper address and forwarded to a single network can now be flooded. Only one copy of the packet will be put on each network segment.

Example

The following example permits IP broadcasts to be flooded through the internetwork in a controlled fashion:

```
ip forward-protocol spanning-tree
```

Related Commands

ip broadcast-address
ip forward-protocol
ip forward-protocol turbo-flood
ip helper-address

IP FORWARD-PROTOCOL TURBO-FLOOD

To speed up flooding of User Datagram Protocol (UDP) datagrams using the spanning-tree algorithm, use the **ip forward-protocol turbo-flood** global configuration command. To disable this feature, use the **no** form of this command.

> **ip forward-protocol turbo-flood**
> **no ip forward-protocol turbo-flood**

Syntax   Description

This command has no arguments or keywords.

Default

Disabled

Command Mode

Global configuration

Usage Guidelines

This command first appeared in Cisco IOS Release 10.0.

Used in conjunction with the **ip forward-protocol spanning-tree** global configuration command, this feature is supported over Advanced Research Projects Agency (ARPA)-encapsulated Ethernets, FDDI, and HDLC-encapsulated serials, but is not supported on Token Rings. As long as the Token Rings and the non-HDLC serials are not part of the bridge group being used for UDP flooding, turbo flooding will behave normally.

Example

The following is an example of a two-port router using this feature:

```
ip forward-protocol turbo-flood
ip forward-protocol spanning-tree
!
interface ethernet 0
 ip address 128.9.1.1
 bridge-group 1
!
interface ethernet 1
 ip address 128.9.1.2
 bridge-group 1
!
 bridge 1 protocol dec
```

Related Commands

ip forward-protocol
ip forward-protocol spanning-tree

IP HELPER-ADDRESS

To have the Cisco IOS software forward UDP broadcasts, including BOOTP, received on an interface, use the **ip helper-address** interface configuration command. To disable the forwarding of broadcast packets to specific addresses, use the **no** form of this command.

> **ip helper-address** *address*
> **no ip helper-address** *address*

Syntax	Description
address	Destination broadcast or host address to be used when forwarding UDP broadcasts. There can be more than one helper address per interface.

Default

Disabled

Command Mode

Interface configuration

Usage Guidelines

This command first appeared in Cisco IOS Release 10.0.

Combined with the **ip forward-protocol** global configuration command, the **ip helper-address** command allows you to control which broadcast packets and which protocols are forwarded.

One common application that requires helper addresses is Dynamic Host Configuration Protocol (DHCP), which is defined in RFC 1531. DHCP protocol information is carried inside BOOTP packets. To enable BOOTP broadcast forwarding for a set of clients, configure a helper address on the router interface closest to the client. The helper address should specify the address of the DHCP server. If you have multiple servers, you can configure one helper address for each server. Since BOOTP packets are forwarded by default, DHCP information can now be forwarded by the router. The DHCP server then receives broadcasts from the DHCP clients.

NOTES

The **ip helper-address** command does not work on an X.25 interface on a destination router because the router cannot tell if the packet was intended as a physical broadcast.

Example

The following example defines an address that acts as a helper address:

```
interface ethernet 1
  ip helper-address 121.24.43.2
```

Related Commands

ip forward-protocol

IP HOST

To define a static host name-to-address mapping in the host cache, use the **ip host** global configuration command. To remove the name-to-address mapping, use the **no** form of this command.

ip host *name* [*tcp-port-number*] *address1* [*address2...address8*]
no ip host *name address1*

Syntax	Description
name	Name of the host. The first character can be either a letter or a number. If you use a number, the operations you can perform are limited.
tcp-port-number	(Optional.) TCP port number to connect to when using the defined host name in conjunction with an EXEC connect or Telnet command. The default is Telnet (port 23).
address1	Associated IP address.
address2...address8	(Optional.) Additional associated IP addresses. You can bind up to eight addresses to a host name.

Default

Disabled

Command Mode

Global configuration

Usage Guidelines

This command first appeared in Cisco IOS Release 10.0.

The first character can be either a letter or a number. If you use a number, the operations you can perform (such as **ping**) are limited.

Example

The following example defines two static mappings:

```
ip host croff 192.31.7.18
ip host bisso-gw 10.2.0.2 192.31.7.33
```

IP HP-HOST

To enter the host name of an HP host to be used for HP Probe Proxy service into the host table, use the **ip hp-host** global configuration command. To remove a host name, use the **no** form of this command.

> **ip hp-host** *hostname ip-address*
> **no ip hp-host** *hostname ip-address*

Syntax	Description
hostname	Name of the host.
ip-address	IP address of the host.

Default

No host names are defined.

Command Mode

Global configuration

Usage Guidelines

This command first appeared in Cisco IOS Release 10.0.

To use the HP Proxy service, you must first enter the host name of the HP host into the host table using this command.

Example

The following example specifies an HP host's name and address, and then enables Probe Proxy:

```
ip hp-host BCWjo 131.108.1.27
interface ethernet 0
  ip probe proxy
```

Related Commands

ip probe proxy

IP IRDP

To enable ICMP Router Discovery Protocol (IRDP) processing on an interface, use the **ip irdp** interface configuration command. To disable IRDP routing, use the **no** form of this command.

ip irdp [**multicast** | **holdtime** *seconds* | **maxadvertinterval** *seconds* | **minadvertinterval**
seconds | **preference** *number* | **address** *address* [*number*]]
no ip irdp

Syntax	Description
multicast	(Optional.) Use the multicast address (224.0.0.1) instead of IP broadcasts.
holdtime *seconds*	(Optional.) Length of time, in seconds, advertisements are held valid. The default is three times the **maxadvertinterval** value. This must be greater than **maxadvertinterval**, but cannot be greater than 9000 seconds.
maxadvertinterval *seconds*	(Optional.) The maximum interval, in seconds, between advertisements. The default is 600 seconds.

Syntax	Description
minadvertinterval *seconds*	(Optional.) Minimum interval, in seconds, between advertisements. The default is 0.75 times the **maxadvertinterval**. If you change the **maxadvertinterval** value, this value defaults to three-fourths of the new value.
preference *number*	(Optional.) Preference value. The allowed range is -2^{31} to 2^{31}. The default is 0. A higher value increases the router's preference level. You can modify a particular router so that it will be the preferred router to which others home.
address *address* [*number*]	(Optional.) IP address (*address*) to proxy-advertise, and optionally, its preference value (*number*).

Default

Disabled

When enabled, IRDP uses these defaults:

- Broadcast IRDP advertisements
- Maximum interval between advertisements: 600 seconds
- Minimum interval between advertisements: 0.75 times **maxadvertinterval**
- Preference: 0

Command Mode

Interface configuration

Usage Guidelines

This command first appeared in Cisco IOS Release 10.0.

If you change **maxadvertinterval**, the other two values also change, so it is important to change **maxadvertinterval** before changing either **holdtime** or **minadvertinterval**.

The **ip irdp multicast** command allows for compatibility with Sun Microsystems Solaris, which requires IRDP packets to be sent out as multicasts. Many implementations cannot receive these multicasts; ensure end-host ability before using this command.

Example

The following example sets the various IRDP processes:

```
! enable irdp on interface Ethernet 0
interface ethernet 0
 ip irdp
! send IRDP advertisements to the multicast address
 ip irdp multicast
! increase router preference from 100 to 50
 ip irdp preference 50
```

```
! set maximum time between advertisements to 400 secs
 ip irdp maxadvertinterval 400
! set minimum time between advertisements to 100 secs
 ip irdp minadvertinterval 100
! advertisements are good for 6000 seconds
 ip irdp holdtime 6000
! proxy-advertise 131.108.14.5 with default router preference
 ip irdp address 131.108.14.5
! proxy-advertise 131.108.14.6 with preference of 50
 ip irdp address 131.108.14.6 50
```

Related Commands

show ip irdp

IP MOBILE ARP

To enable local-area mobility, use the **ip mobile arp** interface configuration command. To disable local-area mobility, use the **no** form of this command.

ip mobile arp [**timers** *keepalive hold-time*] [**access-group** *access-list-number* | *name*]
no ip mobile arp [**timers** *keepalive hold-time*] [**access-group** *access-list-number* | *name*]

Syntax	Description
timers	(Optional.) Indicates that you are setting local-area mobility timers.
keepalive	(Optional.) Frequency, in seconds, at which the Cisco IOS software sends unicast ARP messages to a relocated host to verify that the host is present and has not moved. The default keepalive time is 300 seconds (5 minutes).
hold-time	(Optional.) Hold time, in seconds. This is the length of time the software considers that a relocated host is present without receiving some type of ARP broadcast or unicast from the host. Normally, the hold time should be at least three times greater than the keepalive time. The default hold time is 900 seconds (15 minutes).
access-group	(Optional.) Indicates that you are applying an access list. This access list applies only to local-area mobility.
access-list-number	(Optional.) Number of a standard IP access list. It is a decimal number from 1 to 99. Only hosts with addresses permitted by this access list are accepted for local-area mobility.
name	(Optional.) Name of an IP access list. The name cannot contain a space or quotation mark, and must begin with an alphabetic character to avoid ambiguity with numbered access lists.

Defaults

Local-area mobility is disabled.

If you enable local-area mobility:

- *keepalive*: 300 seconds (5 minutes)
- *hold-time*: 900 seconds (15 minutes)

Command Mode

Interface configuration

Usage Guidelines

This command first appeared in Cisco IOS Release 11.0.

Local-area mobility is supported on Ethernet, Token Ring, and FDDI interfaces only.

To create larger mobility areas, you must first redistribute the mobile routes into your Interior Gateway Protocol (IGP). The IGP must support host routes. You can use Enhanced IGRP, OSPF, or Intermediate System-to-Intermediate System (IS-IS); you can also use RIP, but this is not recommended. The mobile area must consist of a contiguous set of subnets.

Using an access list to control the list of possible mobile nodes is strongly encouraged. Without an access list, misconfigured hosts can be taken for mobile nodes and disrupt normal operations.

Example

The following example configures local-area mobility on Ethernet interface 0:

```
    bridge 1 protocol ieee
    access-list 10 permit 198.92.37.114
    interface ethernet 0
     ip mobile arp access-group 10
     bridge-group 1
```

Related Commands

access-list (standard)
bridge-group
bridge protocol
default-metric (BGP, EGP, OSPF, and RIP)
network (BGP)
network (EGP)
network (IGRP)
network (RIP)
redistribute
router eigrp
router isis
router ospf

IP NAME-SERVER

To specify the address of one or more name servers for name and address resolution, use the **ip name-server** global configuration command. To remove the addresses specified, use the **no** form of this command.

> **ip name-server** *server-address1* [[*server-address2*]...*server-address6*]
> **no ip name-server** *server-address1* [[*server-address2*]...*server-address6*]

Syntax	Description
server-address1	IP addresses of name server.
server-address2...server-address6	(Optional.) IP addresses of additional name servers (a maximum of six name servers).

Default

No name server addresses are specified.

Command Mode

Global configuration

Usage Guidelines

This command first appeared in Cisco IOS Release 10.0.

Example

The following example specifies host 131.108.1.111 as the primary name server and host 131.108.1.2 as the secondary server:

```
ip name-server 131.108.1.111 131.108.1.2
```

This command will be reflected in the configuration file as follows:

```
ip name-server 131.108.1.111
ip name-server 131.108.1.2
```

Related Commands

ip domain-lookup
ip domain-name

IP NAT

To designate that traffic originating from or destined for the interface is subject to Network Address Translation (NAT), use the **ip nat** interface configuration command. To prevent the interface from being able to translate, use the **no** form of this command.

> **ip nat** {inside | outside}
> **no ip nat** {inside | outside}

Syntax	Description
inside	Indicates that the interface is connected to the inside network (the network is subject to NAT translation).
outside	Indicates the interface is connected to the outside network.

Default

Traffic leaving or arriving at this interface is not subject to network address translation.

Command Mode

Interface configuration

Usage Guidelines

This command first appeared in Cisco IOS Release 11.2.

Only packets moving between "inside" and "outside" interfaces can be translated. You must specify at least one inside interface and outside interface for each border router where you intend to use NAT.

Example

The following example translates between inside hosts addressed from either the 192.168.1.0 or 192.168.2.0 networks to the globally unique 171.69.233.208/28 network:

```
ip nat pool net-208 171.69.233.208 171.69.233.223 prefix-length 28
ip nat inside source list 1 pool net-208
!
interface ethernet 0
 ip address 171.69.232.182 255.255.255.240
 ip nat outside
!
interface ethernet 1
 ip address 192.168.1.94 255.255.255.0
 ip nat inside
!
access-list 1 permit 192.168.1.0 0.0.0.255
access-list 1 permit 192.168.2.0 0.0.0.255
```

Related Commands

clear ip nat translation
ip nat inside destination
ip nat inside source
ip nat outside source
ip nat pool
ip nat translation
show ip nat statistics
show ip nat translations

IP NAT INSIDE DESTINATION

To enable NAT of the inside destination address, use the **ip nat inside destination** global configuration command. To remove the dynamic association to a pool, use the **no** form of this command.

ip nat inside destination list {*access-list-number* | *name*} **pool** *name*
no ip nat inside destination list {*access-list-number* | *name*}

Syntax	Description
list *access-list-number*	Standard IP access list number. Packets with destination addresses that pass the access list are translated using global addresses from the named pool.
list *name*	Name of a standard IP access list. Packets with destination addresses that pass the access list are translated using global addresses from the named pool.
pool *name*	Name of the pool from which global IP addresses are allocated during dynamic translation.

Default

No inside destination addresses are translated.

Command Mode

Global configuration

Usage Guidelines

This command first appeared in Cisco IOS Release 11.2.

This command has two forms: dynamic and static address translation. The form with an access list establishes dynamic translation. Packets from addresses that match the standard access list are translated using global addresses allocated from the pool named with the **ip nat pool** command.

Example

The following example translates between inside hosts addressed to either the 192.168.1.0 or 192.168.2.0 networks and to the globally unique 171.69.233.208/28 network:

```
ip nat pool net-208 171.69.233.208 171.69.233.223 prefix-length 28
ip nat inside destination list 1 pool net-208
!
interface ethernet 0
 ip address 171.69.232.182 255.255.255.240
 ip nat outside
!
interface ethernet 1
 ip address 192.168.1.94 255.255.255.0
 ip nat inside
```

```
!
access-list 1 permit 192.168.1.0 0.0.0.255
access-list 1 permit 192.168.2.0 0.0.0.255
```

Related Commands

clear ip nat translation
ip nat
ip nat inside source
ip nat outside source
ip nat pool
ip nat translation
show ip nat statistics
show ip nat translations

IP NAT INSIDE SOURCE

To enable NAT of the inside source address, use the **ip nat inside source** global configuration command. To remove the static translation or remove the dynamic association to a pool, use the **no** form of this command.

> **ip nat inside source** {**list** {*access-list-number* | *name*} **pool** *name* [**overload**] | **static** *local-ip global-ip*}
>
> **no ip nat inside source** {**list** {*access-list-number* | *name*} **pool** *name* [**overload**] | **static** *local-ip global-ip*}

Syntax	Description
list *access-list-number*	Standard IP access list number. Packets with source addresses that pass the access list are dynamically translated using global addresses from the named pool.
list *name*	Name of a standard IP access list. Packets with source addresses that pass the access list are dynamically translated using global addresses from the named pool.
pool *name*	Name of the pool from which global IP addresses are allocated dynamically.
overload	(Optional.) Enables the router to use one global address for many local addresses. When overloading is configured, each inside host's TCP or UDP port number distinguishes between the multiple conversations using the same local IP address.

Syntax	Description
static *local-ip*	Sets up a single static translation; this argument establishes the local IP address assigned to a host on the inside network. The address could be randomly chosen, allocated from RFC 1918, or be obsolete.
global-ip	Sets up a single static translation; this argument establishes the globally unique IP address of an inside host as it appears to the outside world.

Default

No NAT translation of inside source addresses occurs.

Command Mode

Global configuration

Usage Guidelines

This command first appeared in Cisco IOS Release 11.2.

This command has two forms: dynamic and static address translation. The form with an access list establishes dynamic translation. Packets from addresses that match the standard access list are translated using global addresses allocated from the pool named with the **ip nat pool** command.

Alternatively, the syntax form with the keyword **static** establishes a single static translation.

Example

The following example translates between inside hosts addressed from either the 192.168.1.0 or 192.168.2.0 networks to the globally unique 171.69.233.208/28 network:

```
ip nat pool net-208 171.69.233.208 171.69.233.223 prefix-length 28
ip nat inside source list 1 pool net-208
!
interface ethernet 0
 ip address 171.69.232.182 255.255.255.240
 ip nat outside
!
interface ethernet 1
 ip address 192.168.1.94 255.255.255.0
 ip nat inside
!
access-list 1 permit 192.168.1.0 0.0.0.255
access-list 1 permit 192.168.2.0 0.0.0.255
```

Related Commands

clear ip nat translation
ip nat

ip nat inside destination
ip nat outside source
ip nat pool
ip nat translation
show ip nat statistics
show ip nat translations

IP NAT OUTSIDE SOURCE

To enable NAT of the outside source address, use the **ip nat outside source** global configuration command. To remove the static entry or the dynamic association, use the **no** form of this command.

> **ip nat outside source** {**list** {*access-list-number* | *name*} **pool** *name* | **static** *global-ip*
> *local-ip*}
> **no ip nat outside source** {**list** {*access-list-number* | *name*} **pool** *name* | **static** *global-ip*
> *local-ip*}

Syntax	Description
list *access-list-number*	Standard IP access list number. Packets with source addresses that pass the access list are translated using global addresses from the named pool.
list *name*	Name of a standard IP access list. Packets with source addresses that pass the access list are translated using global addresses from the named pool.
pool *name*	Name of the pool from which global IP addresses are allocated.
static *global-ip*	Sets up a single static translation. This argument establishes the globally unique IP address assigned to a host on the outside network by its owner. It is allocated from globally routable network space.
local-ip	Sets up a single static translation. This argument establishes the local IP address of an outside host as it appears to the inside world. The address is allocated from address space routable on the inside (RFC 1918, perhaps).

Default

No translation of source addresses coming from the outside to the inside network occurs.

Command Mode

Global configuration

Usage Guidelines

This command first appeared in Cisco IOS Release 11.2.

You might have IP addresses that are not legal, officially assigned IP addresses. Perhaps you chose IP addresses that officially belong to another network. The case of an address used illegally and legally is called *overlapping*. You can use NAT to translate inside addresses that overlap with outside addresses. Use this feature if your IP addresses in the stub network happen to be legitimate IP addresses belonging to another network, and you need to communicate with those hosts or routers.

This command has two forms: dynamic and static address translation. The form with an access list establishes dynamic translation. Packets from addresses that match the standard access list are translated using global addresses allocated from the pool named with the **ip nat pool** command.

Alternatively, the syntax form with the keyword **static** establishes a single static translation.

Example

The following example translates between inside hosts addressed from the 9.114.11.0 network to the globally unique 171.69.233.208/28 network. Further packets from outside hosts addressed from the 9.114.11.0 network (the true 9.114.11.0 network) are translated to appear to be from the network 10.0.1.0/24.

```
ip nat pool net-208 171.69.233.208 171.69.233.223 prefix-length 28
ip nat pool net-10 10.0.1.0 10.0.1.255 prefix-length 24
ip nat inside source list 1 pool net-208
ip nat outside source list 1 pool net-10
!
interface ethernet 0
 ip address 171.69.232.182 255.255.255.240
 ip nat outside
!
interface ethernet 1
 ip address 9.114.11.39 255.255.255.0
 ip nat inside
!
access-list 1 permit 9.114.11.0 0.0.0.255
```

Related Commands

clear ip nat translation
ip nat
ip nat inside destination
ip nat inside source
ip nat pool
ip nat translation
show ip nat statistics
show ip nat translations

IP NAT POOL

To define a pool of IP addresses for NAT, use the **ip nat pool** global configuration command. To remove one or more addresses from the pool, use the **no** form of this command.

> **ip nat pool** *name start-ip end-ip* {**netmask** *netmask* | **prefix-length** *prefix-length*}
>   [**type rotary**]
> **no ip nat pool** *name start-ip end-ip* {**netmask** *netmask* | **prefix-length** *prefix-length*}
>   [**type rotary**]

Syntax	Description
name	Name of the pool.
start-ip	Starting IP address that defines the range of addresses in the address pool.
end-ip	Ending IP address that defines the range of addresses in the address pool.
netmask *netmask*	Network mask that indicates which address bits belong to the network and subnetwork fields and which bits belong to the host field. Specifies the netmask of the network to which the pool addresses belong.
prefix-length *prefix-length*	Number that indicates how many bits of the netmask are ones (how many bits of the address indicate network). Specifies the netmask of the network to which the pool addresses belong.
type rotary	(Optional.) Indicates that the range of address in the address pool identify real, inside hosts among which TCP load distribution will occur.

Default

No pool of addresses is defined.

Command Mode

Global configuration

Usage Guidelines

This command first appeared in Cisco IOS Release 11.2.

This command defines a pool of addresses using start address, end address, and either netmask or prefix length. The pool can define either an inside global pool, an outside local pool, or a rotary pool.

Example

The following example translates between inside hosts addressed from either the 192.168.1.0 or 192.168.2.0 networks to the globally unique 171.69.233.208/28 network:

```
ip nat pool net-208 171.69.233.208 171.69.233.223 prefix-length 28
ip nat inside source list 1 pool net-208
```

```
!
interface ethernet 0
 ip address 171.69.232.182 255.255.255.240
 ip nat outside
!
interface ethernet 1
 ip address 192.168.1.94 255.255.255.0
 ip nat inside
!
access-list 1 permit 192.168.1.0 0.0.0.255
access-list 1 permit 192.168.2.0 0.0.0.255
```

Related Commands

clear ip nat translation
ip nat
ip nat inside destination
ip nat inside source
ip nat outside source
ip nat translation
show ip nat statistics
show ip nat translations

IP NAT TRANSLATION

To change the amount of time after which NAT translations time out, use the **ip nat translation** global configuration command. To disable the timeout, use the **no** form of this command.

> **ip nat translation** {**timeout** | **udp-timeout** | **dns-timeout** | **tcp-timeout** | **finrst-timeout**}
> *seconds*
> **no ip nat translation** {**timeout** | **udp-timeout** | **dns-timeout** | **tcp-timeout** | **finrst-timeout**}

Syntax	Description
timeout	Specifies that the timeout value applies to dynamic translations except for overload translations. The default is 86400 seconds (24 hours).
udp-timeout	Specifies that the timeout value applies to the UDP port. The default is 300 seconds (5 minutes).
dns-timeout	Specifies that the timeout value applies to connections to the Domain Naming System (DNS). The default is 60 seconds.
tcp-timeout	Specifies that the timeout value applies to the TCP port. The default is 86400 seconds (24 hours).
finrst-timeout	Specifies that the timeout value applies to Finish and Reset TCP packets, which terminate a connection. The default is 60 seconds.
seconds	Number of seconds after which the specified port translation times out. The default values are listed in the "Defaults" section.

Defaults

The default values are:

- **timeout:** 86400 seconds (24 hours)
- **udp-timeout:** 300 seconds (5 minutes)
- **dns-timeout:** 60 seconds (1 minute)
- **tcp-timeout:** 86400 seconds (24 hours)
- **finrst-timeout:** 60 seconds (1 minute)

Command Mode

Global configuration

Usage Guidelines

This command first appeared in Cisco IOS Release 11.2.

When port translation is configured, there is finer control over translation entry timeouts because each entry contains more context about the traffic that is using it. Non-Domain Naming System UDP translations time out after 5 minutes, while DNS times out in 1 minute. TCP translations timeout in 24 hours, unless a RST or FIN is seen on the stream, in which case they will time out in 1 minute.

Example

The following example causes UDP port translation entries to timeout after 10 minutes:

```
ip nat translation udp-timeout 600
```

Related Commands

clear ip nat translation
ip nat
ip nat inside destination
ip nat inside source
ip nat outside source
ip nat pool
show ip nat statistics
show ip nat translations

IP NETMASK-FORMAT

To specify the format in which netmasks are displayed in **show** command output, use the **ip netmask-format** line configuration command. To restore the default display format, use the **no** form of this command.

ip netmask-format {bitcount | decimal | hexadecimal}
no ip netmask-format [bitcount | decimal | hexadecimal]

Syntax	Description
bitcount	Addresses are followed by a slash and the total number of bits in the netmask. For example, 131.108.11.0/24 indicates that the netmask is 24 bits.
decimal	Network masks are displayed in dotted decimal notation (for example, 255.255.255.0).
hexadecimal	Network masks are displayed in hexadecimal format, as indicated by the leading 0X (for example, 0XFFFFFF00).

Default

Netmasks are displayed in dotted decimal format.

Command Mode

Line configuration

Usage Guidelines

This command first appeared in Cisco IOS Release 10.3.

IP uses a 32-bit mask that indicates which address bits belong to the network and subnetwork fields, and which bits belong to the host field. This is called a *netmask*. By default, **show** commands display an IP address and then its netmask in dotted decimal notation. For example, a subnet would be displayed as 131.108.11.0 255.255.255.0.

However, you can specify that the display of the network mask appear in hexadecimal format or bit count format instead. The hexadecimal format is commonly used on UNIX systems. The previous example would be displayed as 131.108.11.0 0XFFFFFF00.

The bitcount format for displaying network masks is to append a slash (/) and the total number of bits in the netmask to the address itself. The previous example would be displayed as 131.108.11.0/24.

Example

The following example configures network masks for the specified line to be displayed in bitcount notation in the output of **show** commands:

```
line vty 0 4
  ip netmask-format bitcount
```

IP NHRP AUTHENTICATION

To configure the authentication string for an interface using Next Hop Resolution Protocol (NHRP), use the **ip nhrp authentication** interface configuration command. To remove the authentication string, use the **no** form of this command.

ip nhrp authentication *string*
no ip nhrp authentication [*string*]

Syntax	Description
string	Authentication string configured for the source and destination stations that controls whether NHRP stations allow intercommunication. The string can be up to eight characters long.

Default

No authentication string is configured; the Cisco IOS software adds no authentication option to NHRP packets it generates.

Command Mode

Interface configuration

Usage Guidelines

This command first appeared in Cisco IOS Release 10.3.

All routers configured with NHRP within one logical NBMA network must share the same authentication string.

Example

In the following example, the authentication string named *specialxx* must be configured in all devices using NHRP on the interface before NHRP communication occurs:

```
ip nhrp authentication specialxx
```

IP NHRP HOLDTIME

To change the number of seconds that NHRP nonbroadcast, multiaccess (NBMA) addresses are advertised as valid in authoritative NHRP responses, use the **ip nhrp holdtime** interface configuration command. To restore the default value, use the **no** form of this command.

> **ip nhrp holdtime** *seconds-positive* [*seconds-negative*]
> **no ip nhrp holdtime** [*seconds-positive* [*seconds-negative*]]

Syntax	Description
seconds-positive	Time, in seconds, that NBMA addresses are advertised as valid in positive authoritative NHRP responses.
seconds-negative	(Optional.) Time, in seconds, that NBMA addresses are advertised as valid in negative authoritative NHRP responses.

Default

7200 seconds (2 hours) for both arguments

Command Mode

Interface configuration

Usage Guidelines

This command first appeared in Cisco IOS Release 10.3.

The **ip nhrp holdtime** command affects authoritative responses only. The advertised holding time is the length of time that the Cisco IOS software tells other routers to keep information that it is providing in authoritative NHRP responses. The cached IP-to-NBMA address mapping entries are discarded after the holding time expires.

The NHRP cache can contain static and dynamic entries. The static entries never expire. Dynamic entries expire regardless of whether they are authoritative or nonauthoritative.

If you want to change the valid time period for negative NHRP responses, you must also include a value for positive NHRP responses, as the arguments are position dependent.

Examples

In the following example, NHRP NBMA addresses are advertised as valid in positive authoritative NHRP responses for one hour:

```
ip nhrp holdtime 3600
```

In the following example, NHRP NBMA addresses are advertised as valid in negative authoritative NHRP responses for one hour and in positive authoritative NHRP responses for two hours:

```
ip nhrp holdtime 7200 3600
```

IP NHRP INTEREST

To control which IP packets can trigger sending a Next Hop Resolution Protocol (NHRP) Request, use the **ip nhrp interest** interface configuration command. To restore the default value, use the **no** form of this command.

> **ip nhrp interest** *access-list-number*
> **no ip nhrp interest** [*access-list-number*]

Syntax	Description
access-list-number	Standard or extended IP access list number in the range 1 to 199.

Default

All non-NHRP packets can trigger NHRP requests.

Command Mode

Interface configuration

Usage Guidelines

This command first appeared in Cisco IOS Release 10.3.

Use this command with the **access-list** command to control which IP packets trigger NHRP Requests.

The **ip nhrp interest** command controls *which* packets cause NHRP address resolution to take place; the **ip nhrp use** command controls *how readily* the system attempts such address resolution.

Example

In the following example, any TCP traffic can cause NHRP Requests to be sent, but no other IP packets will cause NHRP Requests:

```
ip nhrp interest 101
access-list 101 permit tcp any any
```

Related Commands

access-list (extended)
access-list (standard)
ip nhrp use

IP NHRP MAP

To statically configure the IP-to-NBMA address mapping of IP destinations connected to an NBMA network, use the **ip nhrp map** interface configuration command. To remove the static entry from NHRP cache, use the **no** form of this command.

> **ip nhrp map** *ip-address nbma-address*
> **no ip nhrp map** *ip-address nbma-address*

Syntax	Description
ip-address	IP address of the destinations reachable through the NBMA network. This address is mapped to the NBMA address.
nbma-address	NBMA address that is directly reachable through the NBMA network. The address format varies depending on the medium that you are using. For example, ATM has an NSAP address, Ethernet has a MAC address, and SMDS has an E.164 address. This address is mapped to the IP address.

Default

No static IP-to-NBMA cache entries exist.

Command Mode

Interface configuration

Usage Guidelines

This command first appeared in Cisco IOS Release 10.3.

You will probably have to configure at least one static mapping in order to reach the Next Hop Server. Repeat this command to statically configure multiple IP-to-NBMA address mappings.

Example

In the following example, this station in a multipoint tunnel network is statically configured to be served by two Next Hop Servers 100.0.0.1 and 100.0.1.3. The NBMA address for 100.0.0.1 is statically configured to be 11.0.0.1 and the NBMA address for 100.0.1.3 is 12.2.7.8.

```
interface tunnel 0
 ip nhrp nhs 100.0.0.1
 ip nhrp nhs 100.0.1.3
 ip nhrp map 100.0.0.1 11.0.0.1
 ip nhrp map 100.0.1.3 12.2.7.8
```

Related Commands

clear ip nhrp

IP NHRP MAP MULTICAST

To configure NBMA addresses used as destinations for broadcast or multicast packets to be sent over a tunnel network, use the **ip nhrp map multicast** interface configuration command. To remove the destinations, use the **no** form of this command.

ip nhrp map multicast *nbma-address*
no ip nhrp map multicast *nbma-address*

Syntax	Description
nbma-address	NBMA address which is directly reachable through the NBMA network. The address format varies depending on the medium you are using.

Default

No NBMA addresses are configured as destinations for broadcast or multicast packets.

Command Mode

Interface configuration

Usage Guidelines

This command first appeared in Cisco IOS Release 10.3, and applies only to tunnel interfaces.

The command is useful for supporting broadcasts over a tunnel network when the underlying network does not support IP multicast. If the underlying network does support IP multicast, you should use the **tunnel destination** command to configure a multicast destination for transmission of tunnel broadcasts or multicasts.

When multiple NBMA addresses are configured, the system replicates the broadcast packet for each address.

Example

In the following example, if a packet is sent to 10.255.255.255, it is replicated to destinations 11.0.0.1 and 11.0.0.2. Addresses 11.0.0.1 and 11.0.0.2 are the IP addresses of two other routers that are part of the tunnel network, but those addresses are their addresses in the underlying network, not the tunnel network. They would have tunnel addresses that are in network 10.0.0.0.

```
interface tunnel 0
  ip address 10.0.0.3 255.0.0.0
  ip nhrp map multicast 11.0.0.1
  ip nhrp map multicast 11.0.0.2
```

IP NHRP MAX-SEND

To change the maximum frequency at which NHRP packets can be sent, use the **ip nhrp max-send** interface configuration command. To restore this frequency to the default value, use the **no** form of this command.

> **ip nhrp max-send** *pkt-count* **every** *interval*
> **no ip nhrp max-send**

Syntax	Description
pkt-count	Number of packets which can be transmitted in the range from 1 to 65535. The default is 5 packets.
every *interval*	Time, in seconds, in the range from 10 to 65535. The default is 10 seconds.

Defaults

The defaults are

- *pkt-count*: 5 packets
- *interval*: 10 seconds

Command Mode

Interface configuration

Usage Guidelines

This command first appeared in Cisco IOS Release 11.1.

The software maintains a per-interface quota of NHRP packets that can be transmitted. NHRP traffic, whether locally generated or forwarded, cannot be sent at a rate that exceeds this quota. The quota is replenished at the rate specified by *interval*.

Example

In the following example, only one NHRP packet can be sent from serial interface 0 each minute:

```
interface serial 0
  ip nhrp max-send 1 every 60
```

Related Commands

ip nhrp interest
ip nhrp use

IP NHRP NETWORK-ID

To enable the NHRP on an interface, use the **ip nhrp network-id** interface configuration command. To disable NHRP on the interface, use the **no** form of this command.

    ip nhrp network-id *number*
    no ip nhrp network-id [*number*]

Syntax	*Description*
number	Globally unique, 32-bit network identifier for an NBMA network. The range is 1 to 4294967295.

Default

NHRP is disabled on the interface.

Command Mode

Interface configuration

Usage Guidelines

This command first appeared in Cisco IOS Release 10.3.

In general, all NHRP stations within one logical NBMA network must be configured with the same network identifier.

Example

The following example enables NHRP on the interface:

```
ip nhrp network-id 1
```

IP NHRP NHS

To specify the address of one or more NHRP Next Hop Servers, use the **ip nhrp nhs** interface configuration command. To remove the address, use the **no** form of this command.

    ip nhrp nhs *nhs-address* [*net-address* [*netmask*]]
    no ip nhrp nhs *nhs-address* [*net-address* [*netmask*]]

Syntax	Description
nhs-address	Address of the Next Hop Server being specified.
net-address	(Optional.) IP address of a network served by the Next Hop Server.
netmask	(Optional.) IP network mask to be associated with the *net* IP address. The *net* IP address is logically ANDed with the mask.

Default

No Next Hop Servers are explicitly configured, so normal network layer routing decisions are used to forward NHRP traffic.

Command Mode

Interface configuration

Usage Guidelines

This command first appeared in Cisco IOS Release 10.3.

Use this command to specify the address of a Next Hop Server and the networks it serves. Normally, NHRP consults the network layer forwarding table to determine how to forward NHRP packets. When Next Hop Servers are configured, these next hop addresses override the forwarding path that would otherwise be used for NHRP traffic.

For any Next Hop Server that is configured, you can specify multiple networks that it serves by repeating this command with the same *nhs-address*, but with different *net-address* IP network addresses.

Example

In the following example, the Next Hop Server with address 131.108.10.11 serves IP network 10.0.0.0. The mask is 255.0.0.0.

```
ip nhrp nhs 131.108.10.11 10.0.0.0 255.0.0.0
```

IP NHRP RECORD

To re-enable the use of forward record and reverse record options in NHRP Request and Reply packets, use the **ip nhrp record** interface configuration command. To suppress the use of such options, use the **no** form of this command.

ip nhrp record
no ip nhrp record

Syntax   Description

This command has no arguments or keywords.

Default

Forward record and reverse record options are used in NHRP Request and Reply packets.

Command Mode

Interface configuration

Usage Guidelines

This command first appeared in Cisco IOS Release 10.3.

Forward record and reverse record options provide loop detection and are enabled by default. Using the **no** form of this command disables this method of loop detection. For another method of loop detection, see the **ip nhrp responder** command.

Example

The following example suppresses forward record and reverse record options:

```
no ip nhrp record
```

Related Commands

ip nhrp responder

IP NHRP RESPONDER

To designate which interface's primary IP address the Next Hop Server will use in NHRP Reply packets when the NHRP requestor uses the Responder Address option, use the **ip nhrp responder** interface configuration command. To remove the designation, use the **no** form of this command.

ip nhrp responder *type number*
no ip nhrp responder [*type*] [*number*]

Syntax	Description
type	Interface type whose primary IP address is used when a Next Hop Server complies with a Responder Address option (for example, **serial, tunnel**).
number	Interface number whose primary IP address is used when a Next Hop Server complies with a Responder Address option.

Default

The Next Hop Server uses the IP address of the interface where the NHRP Request was received.

Command Mode

Interface configuration

Usage Guidelines

This command first appeared in Cisco IOS Release 10.3.

If an NHRP requestor wants to know which Next Hop Server generates an NHRP Reply packet, it can request that information through the Responder Address option. The Next Hop Server that generates the NHRP Reply packet then complies by inserting its own IP address in the Responder Address option of the NHRP Reply. The Next Hop Server uses the primary IP address of the specified interface.

If an NHRP Reply packet being forwarded by a Next Hop Server contains that Next Hop Server's own IP address, the Next Hop Server generates an Error Indication of type "NHRP Loop Detected" and discards the Reply.

Example

In the following example, any NHRP requests for the Responder Address will cause this router acting as a Next Hop Server to supply the primary IP address of serial interface 0 in the NHRP Reply packet:

```
ip nhrp responder serial 0
```

IP NHRP USE

To configure the software so that NHRP is deferred until the system has attempted to send data traffic to a particular destination multiple times, use the **ip nhrp use** interface configuration command. To restore the default value, use the **no** form of this command.

> **ip nhrp use** *usage-count*
> **no ip nhrp use** *usage-count*

Syntax	Description
usage-count	Packet count in the range from 1 to 65535. The default is 1.

Default

The default is *usage-count* = 1. The first time a data packet is sent to a destination for which the system determines NHRP can be used, an NHRP request is sent.

Command Mode

Interface configuration

Usage Guidelines

This command first appeared in Cisco IOS Release 11.1.

When the software attempts to transmit a data packet to a destination for which it has determined that NHRP address resolution can be used, an NHRP request for that destination is normally transmitted immediately. Configuring the *usage-count* causes the system to wait until that many data packets have been sent to a particular destination before it attempts NHRP. The *usage-count* for a particular destination is measured over 1-minute intervals (the NHRP cache expiration interval).

The usage-count applies *per destination*. So if *usage-count* is configured to be 3, and 4 data packets are sent toward 10.0.0.1 and 1 packet toward 10.0.0.2, then an NHRP request is generated for 10.0.0.1 only.

If the system continues to need to forward data packets to a particular destination, but no NHRP response has been received, retransmission of NHRP requests is performed. This retransmission occurs only if data traffic continues to be sent to a destination.

The **ip nhrp interest** command controls *which* packets cause NHRP address resolution to take place; the **ip nhrp use** command controls *how readily* the system attempts such address resolution.

Example

In the following example, if in the first minute four packets are sent to one destination and five packets are sent to a second destination, then a single NHRP request is generated for the second destination.

If in the second minute the same traffic is generated and no NHRP responses have been received, then the system retransmits its request for the second destination.

```
ip nhrp use 5
```

Related Commands

ip nhrp interest
ip nhrp max-send

IP PROBE PROXY

To enable the HP Probe Proxy support, which allows the Cisco IOS software to respond to HP Probe Proxy Name requests, use the **ip probe proxy** interface configuration command. To disable HP Probe Proxy, use the **no** form of this command.

ip probe proxy
no ip probe proxy

Syntax   Description

This command has no arguments or keywords.

Default

Disabled

Command Mode

Interface configuration

Usage Guidelines

This command first appeared in Cisco IOS Release 10.0.

HP Probe Proxy Name requests are typically used at sites that have HP equipment and are already using HP Probe.

To use the HP Proxy service, you must first enter the host name of the HP host into the host table using the **ip hp-host** global configuration command.

Example

The following example specifies an HP host's name and address, and then enables Probe Proxy:

```
ip hp-host BCWjo 131.108.1.27
interface ethernet 0
 ip probe proxy
```

Related Commands

ip hp-host

IP PROXY-ARP

To enable proxy ARP on an interface, use the **ip proxy-arp** interface configuration command. To disable proxy ARP on the interface, use the **no** form of this command.

> **ip proxy-arp**
> **no ip proxy-arp**

Syntax   Description

This command has no arguments or keywords.

Default

Enabled

Command Mode

Interface configuration

Usage Guidelines

This command first appeared in Cisco IOS Release 10.0.

Example

The following example enables proxy ARP on Ethernet interface 0:

```
interface ethernet 0
  ip proxy-arp
```

IP REDIRECTS

To enable the sending of redirect messages if the Cisco IOS software is forced to resend a packet through the same interface on which it was received, use the **ip redirects** interface configuration command. To disable the sending of redirect messages, use the **no** form of this command.

    ip redirects
    no ip redirects

Syntax   Description

This command has no arguments or keywords.

Default

Enabled, unless Hot Standby Router Protocol is configured.

Command Mode

Interface configuration

Usage Guidelines

This command first appeared in Cisco IOS Release 10.0.

If the Hot Standby Router Protocol is configured on an interface, ICMP Redirect messages are disabled by default for the interface.

Example

The following example enables the sending of IP redirects on Ethernet interface 0:

```
interface ethernet 0
  ip redirects
```

Related Commands

show ip redirects

IP ROUTING

To enable IP routing, use the **ip routing** global configuration command. To disable IP routing, use the **no** form of this command.

    ip routing
    no ip routing

Syntax   Description

This command has no arguments or keywords.

Default

Enabled

Command Mode

Global configuration

Usage Guidelines

This command first appeared in Cisco IOS Release 10.0.

To bridge IP, the **no ip routing** command must be configured to disable IP routing. However, you need not specify **no ip routing** in conjunction with concurrent routing and bridging to bridge IP.

Example

The following example enables IP routing:

```
ip routing
```

IP SUBNET-ZERO

To enable the use of subnet zero for interface addresses and routing updates, use the **ip subnet-zero** global configuration command. To restore the default, use the **no** form of this command.

> **ip subnet-zero**
> **no ip subnet-zero**

Syntax   Description

This command has no arguments or keywords.

Default

Disabled

Command Mode

Global configuration

Usage Guidelines

This command first appeared in Cisco IOS Release 10.0.

The **ip subnet-zero** command provides the ability to configure and route to subnet-zero subnets.

Subnetting with a subnet address of zero is discouraged because of the confusion inherent in having a network and a subnet with indistinguishable addresses.

Example

In the following example, subnet-zero is enabled:

```
ip subnet-zero
```

IP UNNUMBERED

To enable IP processing on a serial interface without assigning an explicit IP address to the interface, use the **ip unnumbered** interface configuration command. To disable the IP processing on the interface, use the **no** form of this command.

    ip unnumbered *type number*
    no ip unnumbered *type number*

Syntax	Description
type number	Type and number of another interface on which the router has an assigned IP address. It cannot be another unnumbered interface.

Default

Disabled

Command Mode

Interface configuration

Usage Guidelines

This command first appeared in Cisco IOS Release 10.0.

Whenever the unnumbered interface generates a packet (for example, for a routing update), it uses the address of the specified interface as the source address of the IP packet. It also uses the address of the specified interface in determining which routing processes are sending updates over the unnumbered interface. Restrictions include the following:

- Serial interfaces using HDLC, PPP, Link Access Procedure, Balanced (LAPB), and Frame Relay encapsulations, as well as Serial Line Internet Protocol (SLIP) and tunnel interfaces, can be unnumbered. It is not possible to use this interface configuration command with X.25 or Switched Multimegabit Data Service (SMDS) interfaces.

- You cannot use the **ping** EXEC command to determine whether the interface is up, because the interface has no address. Simple Network Management Protocol (SNMP) can be used to remotely monitor interface status.

- You cannot netboot a runnable image over an unnumbered serial interface.

- You cannot support IP security options on an unnumbered interface.

The interface you specify by the *type* and *number* arguments must be enabled (listed as "up" in the **show interfaces** command display).

If you are configuring IS-IS across a serial line, you should configure the serial interfaces as unnumbered. This allows you to conform with RFC 1195, which states that IP addresses are not required on each interface.

NOTES

Using an unnumbered serial line between different major networks (or *majornets*) requires special care. If at each end of the link there are different majornets assigned to the interfaces you specified as unnumbered, then any routing protocol running across the serial line must not advertise subnet information.

Example

In the following example, the first serial interface is given Ethernet 0's address:

```
interface ethernet 0
 ip address 131.108.6.6 255.255.255.0
 !
interface serial 0
 ip unnumbered ethernet 0
```

PING (PRIVILEGED)

To check host reachability and network connectivity, use the **ping** (IP packet internet groper function) privileged EXEC command.

   ping [*protocol*] {*host* | *address*}

Syntax	Description
protocol	(Optional.) Protocol keyword. The default is IP.
host	Host name of system to ping.
address	IP address of system to ping.

Command Mode

Privileged EXEC

Usage Guidelines

This command first appeared in Cisco IOS Release 10.0.

The **ping** command sends ICMP Echo messages. If the Cisco IOS software receives an ICMP Echo message, it sends an ICMP Echo Reply message to the source of the ICMP Echo message.

You can use the IP **ping** command to diagnose serial line problems. By placing the local or remote CSU/DSU into loopback mode and pinging your own interface, you can isolate the problem to the router, or to a leased line.

Multicast and broadcast pings are fully supported. When you ping the broadcast address of 255.255.255.255, the system will send out pings and print a list of all stations responding. You can also ping a local network to get a list of all systems that respond, as in the following example, where 128.111.3 is a local network:

```
ping 128.111.3.255
```

As a side effect, you also can get a list of all multicast-capable hosts that are connected directly to the router from which you are pinging, as in the following example:

```
ping 224.0.0.1
```

To abort a ping session, type the escape sequence (by default, Ctrl-^ X, which is done by simultaneously pressing the Ctrl, Shift, and 6 keys, letting go, then pressing the X key).

Table 3–1 describes the test characters that the ping facility sends.

Table 3–1 *Ping Test Characters*

Char	Description
!	Each exclamation point indicates receipt of a reply.
.	Each period indicates the network server timed out while waiting for a reply.
U	Destination unreachable.
N	Network unreachable.
P	Protocol unreachable.
Q	Source quench.
M	Could not fragment.
?	Unknown packet type.

You can use the extended command mode of the **ping** command to specify the supported Internet header options, as shown in the following sample display.

Sample Display Showing Extended Command Sequence

To enter **ping** extended command mode, enter **yes** at the extended commands prompt of the **ping** command. The following display shows a sample **ping** extended command sequence:

```
Router# ping

Protocol [ip]:
Target IP address: 192.31.7.27
Repeat count [5]:
Datagram size [100]:
Timeout in seconds [2]:
Extended commands [n]: y
Source address: 131.108.1.1
Type of service [0]:
Set DF bit in IP header? [no]:
Data pattern [0xABCD]:
Loose, Strict, Record, Timestamp, Verbose[none]:
Sweep range of sizes [n]:
Type escape sequence to abort.
Sending 5, 100-byte ICMP Echos to 192.31.7.27, timeout is 2 seconds:
!!!!!
Success rate is 100 percent, round-trip min/avg/max = 1/3/4 ms
```

Table 3–2 describes the significant fields shown in the display.

Table 3–2 *IP Ping Internet Header Options Field Descriptions*

Field	Description
Protocol [ip]:	Default is IP.
Target IP address:	Prompts for the IP address or host name of the destination node you plan to ping.
Repeat count [5]:	Number of ping packets that will be sent to the destination address. The default is 5.
Datagram size [100]:	Size of the ping packet (in bytes). The default is 100 bytes.
Timeout in seconds [2]:	Timeout interval. The default is 2 (seconds).
Extended commands [n]:	Specifies whether a series of additional commands appears. Many of the following displays and tables show and describe these commands. The default is no.
Source address:	IP address that appears in the ping packet as the source address.
Type of service [0]:	Internet service quality selection. See RFC 791 for more information. The default is 0.
Set DF bit in IP header?	Don't Fragment. Specifies that if the packet encounters a node in its path that is configured for a smaller MTU than the packet's MTU, then the packet is to be dropped and an error message is to be sent to the router at the packet's source address. If performance problems are encountered on the network, a node configured for a small MTU could be a contributing factor. This feature can be used to determine the smallest MTU in the path. The default is no.
Data pattern [0xABCD]:	Sets 16-bit hexadecimal data pattern. The default is 0xABCD. Varying the data pattern in this field (to all ones or all zeros, for example) can be useful when debugging data sensitivity problems on CSU/DSUs, or detecting cable-related problems such as cross talk.

Table 3-2 *IP Ping Internet Header Options Field Descriptions, Continued*

Field	Description
Loose, Strict, Record, Timestamp, Verbose [none]:	Supported Internet header options. The Cisco IOS software examines the header options for every packet that passes through it. If it finds a packet with an invalid option, the software sends an ICMP Parameter Problem message to the source of the packet and discards the packet. The Internet header options are as follows: • Loose • Strict • Record (see the following section for more information on this helpful option) • Timestamp • Verbose The default is none. For more information on these header options, see RFC 791.
Sweep range of sizes [n]:	Allows you to vary the sizes of the echo packets being sent. This capability is useful for determining the minimum sizes of the MTUs configured on the nodes along the path to the destination address. Packet fragmentation contributing to performance problems can then be reduced.
!!!!!	Each exclamation point (!) indicates receipt of a reply. A period (.) indicates the network server timed out while waiting for a reply. Other characters may appear in the **ping** output display, depending on the protocol type.
Success rate is 100 percent	Percentage of packets successfully echoed back to the router. Anything less than 80 percent usually indicates a problem.
round-trip min/avg/max = 1/3/4 ms	Round-trip travel time intervals for the protocol echo packets, including minimum/average/maximum (in milliseconds).

Use the Record Route Option

Use the Record Route option to trace a path to a particular destination address. Be aware, however, that the **trace** EXEC command performs a similar function, but the latter does not have the nine-hop limitation.

Sample Display Showing the Record Route Option

The following display shows sample extended **ping** output when this option is specified:

```
Router# ping

Protocol [ip]:
Target IP address: fred
Repeat count [5]:
Datagram size [100]:
Timeout in seconds [2]:
Extended commands [n]: y
Source address:
Type of service [0]:
Set DF bit in IP header? [no]:
Data pattern [0xABCD]:
Loose, Strict, Record, Timestamp, Verbose[none]: r
Number of hops [ 9 ]:
Loose, Strict, Record, Timestamp, Verbose[RV]:
Sweep range of sizes [n]:
Type escape sequence to abort.
Sending 5, 100-byte ICMP Echos to 131.108.1.115, timeout is 2 seconds:
Packet has IP options: Total option bytes= 39, padded length=40
 Record route: <*> 0.0.0.0 0.0.0.0 0.0.0.0 0.0.0.0
            0.0.0.0 0.0.0.0 0.0.0.0 0.0.0.0 0.0.0.0
```

The following display is a detail of the Echo packet section:

```
0 in 4 ms.  Received packet has options
 Total option bytes= 40, padded length=40
 Record route: 160.89.80.31 131.108.6.10 131.108.1.7 131.108.1.115
        131.108.1.115 131.108.6.7 160.89.80.240 160.89.80.31 <*> 0.0.0.0
 End of list

1 in 8 ms.  Received packet has options
 Total option bytes= 4 padded length=40
 Record route: 160.89.80.31 131.108.6.10 131.108.1.6 131.108.1.115
        131.108.1.115 131.108.6.7 160.89.80.240 160.89.80.31 <*> 0.0.0.0
 End of list

2 in 4 ms.  Received packet has options
 Total option bytes= 40, padded length=40
 Record route: 160.89.80.31 131.108.6.10 131.108.1.7 131.108.1.115
131.108.1.115 131.108.6.7 160.89.80.240 160.89.80.31 <*> 0.0.0.0
 End of list

3 in 8 ms.  Received packet has options
 Total option bytes= 40, padded length=40
 Record route: 160.89.80.31 131.108.6.10 131.108.1.6 131.108.1.115
        131.108.1.115 131.108.6.7 160.89.80.240 160.89.80.31 <*> 0.0.0.0
 End of list

4 in 4 ms.  Received packet has options
 Total option bytes= 40, padded length=40
 Record route: 160.89.80.31 131.108.6.10 131.108.1.7 131.108.1.115
        131.108.1.115 131.108.6.7 160.89.80.240 160.89.80.31 <*> 0.0.0.0
 End of list
```

```
Success rate is 100 percent, round-trip min/avg/max = 4/5/8 ms
Router#
```

In this display, five ping echo packets are sent to the destination address 131.108.1.115. The echo packet detail section includes specific information about each of these echo packets.

The lines of **ping** output that are unique when the Record Route option is specified are described as follows.

The following line of output allows you to specify the number of hops that will be recorded in the route. The range is 1 to 9. The default is 9.

```
Number of hops [ 9 ]:
```

The following line of output indicates that IP header options have been enabled on the outgoing echo packets, and it shows the number of option bytes and padded bytes in the headers of these packets:

```
Packet has IP options:  Total option bytes= 39, padded length=40
```

The following lines of output indicate that the fields that will contain the IP addresses of the nodes in the routes have been zeroed out in the outgoing packets:

```
Record route: <*> 0.0.0.0 0.0.0.0 0.0.0.0 0.0.0.0
              0.0.0.0 0.0.0.0 0.0.0.0 0.0.0.0 0.0.0.0
```

The following lines of output display statistics for the first of the five echo packets sent, where 0 is the number assigned to this packet to indicate that it is the first in the series, and 4 ms indicates the round-trip travel time for the packet:

```
0 in 4 ms.  Received packet has options
 Total option bytes= 40, padded length=40
 Record route: 160.89.80.31 131.108.6.10 131.108.1.7 131.108.1.115
        131.108.1.115 131.108.6.7 160.89.80.240 160.89.80.31 <*> 0.0.0.0
```

The following line of output indicates that four nodes were included in the packet's route, including the router at source address 160.89.80.31, two intermediate nodes at addresses 131.108.6.10 and 131.108.1.7, and the destination node at address 131.108.1.115. The underlined address shows where the original route differs from the return route.

```
Record route: 160.89.80.31 131.108.6.10 131.108.1.7 131.108.1.115
```

The following line of output includes the addresses of the four nodes in the return path of the echo packet. The underlined address shows where the return route differs from the original route shown in the previous line of output.

```
131.108.1.115 131.108.6.7 160.89.80.240 160.89.80.31 <*> 0.0.0.0
```

Related Commands

ping (user)

PING (USER)

To check host reachability and network connectivity, use the **ping** (IP packet internet groper function) user EXEC command.

> **ping** [*protocol*] {*host* | *address*}

Syntax	*Description*
protocol	(Optional.) Protocol keyword. The default is IP.
host	Host name of system to ping.
address	IP address of system to ping.

Command Mode

User EXEC

Usage Guidelines

This command first appeared in Cisco IOS Release 10.0.

The **ping** command sends ICMP Echo messages. If the Cisco IOS software receives an ICMP Echo message, it sends an ICMP Echo Reply message to the source of the ICMP Echo message.

The user ping feature provides a basic ping facility for IP users who do not have system privileges. This feature allows the software to perform the simple default ping functionality for the IP protocol. Only the nonverbose form of the **ping** command is supported for user pings.

If the system cannot map an address for a host name, it will return an "%Unrecognized host or address" error message.

To abort a ping session, type the escape sequence (by default, Ctrl-^ X, which is done by simultaneously pressing the Ctrl, Shift, and 6 keys, letting go, then pressing the X key).

In the **ping** (**privileged**) section, Table 3–1 describes the test characters that the ping facility sends.

Sample Display Using an IP Host Name

The following display shows sample ping output when you ping a host named fred:

```
Router> ping fred

Type escape sequence to abort.
Sending 5, 100-byte ICMP Echos to 192.31.7.27, timeout is 2 seconds:
!!!!!
Success rate is 100 percent, round-trip min/avg/max = 1/3/4 ms
```

Sample Display Using the Broadcast Address

The following display shows sample ping output when you ping the broadcast address of 255.255.255.255:

```
Router> ping 255.255.255.255

Type escape sequence to abort.
Sending 5, 100-byte ICMP Echos to 255.255.255.255, timeout is 2 seconds:

Reply to request 0 from 160.89.48.15 (4 ms)
Reply to request 0 from 160.89.48.10 (4 ms)
```

```
Reply to request 0 from 160.89.48.19 (4 ms)
Reply to request 0 from 160.89.49.15 (4 ms)
Reply to request 1 from 160.89.48.15 (4 ms)
Reply to request 1 from 160.89.48.10 (4 ms)
Reply to request 1 from 160.89.48.19 (4 ms)
Reply to request 1 from 160.89.49.15 (4 ms)
Reply to request 2 from 160.89.48.15 (4 ms)
Reply to request 2 from 160.89.48.10 (4 ms)
Reply to request 2 from 160.89.48.19 (4 ms)
Reply to request 2 from 160.89.49.15 (4 ms)
Reply to request 3 from 160.89.48.15 (4 ms)
Reply to request 3 from 160.89.48.10 (4 ms)
Reply to request 3 from 160.89.48.19 (4 ms)
Reply to request 3 from 160.89.49.15 (4 ms)
Reply to request 4 from 160.89.48.15 (4 ms)
Reply to request 4 from 160.89.48.10 (4 ms)
Reply to request 4 from 160.89.48.19 (4 ms)
Reply to request 4 from 160.89.49.15 (4 ms)
```

Related Commands

ping (privileged)

SHOW ARP

To display the entries in the ARP table, use the **show arp** privileged EXEC command.

show arp

Syntax   Description

This command has no arguments or keywords.

Command Mode

Privileged EXEC

Usage Guidelines

This command first appeared in Cisco IOS Release 10.0.

Sample Display

The following is sample output from the **show arp** command:

```
Router# show arp

Protocol   Address        Age (min)   Hardware Addr   Type   Interface

Internet   131.108.42.112  120        0000.a710.4baf  ARPA   Ethernet3
AppleTalk  4028.5          29         0000.0c01.0e56  SNAP   Ethernet2
Internet   131.108.42.114  105        0000.a710.859b  ARPA   Ethernet3
AppleTalk  4028.9          -          0000.0c02.a03c  SNAP   Ethernet2
```

```
Internet    131.108.42.121   42        0000.a710.68cd   ARPA   Ethernet3
Internet    131.108.36.9     -         0000.3080.6fd4   SNAP   TokenRing0
AppleTalk   4036.9           -         0000.3080.6fd4   SNAP   TokenRing0
Internet    131.108.33.9     -         0000.0c01.7bbd   SNAP   Fddi0
```

Table 3–3 describes significant fields shown in the first line of output in the display.

Table 3–3   *Show Hosts Field Descriptions*

Field	Description
Protocol	Indicates the type of network address that this entry includes.
Address	Network address that is mapped to the MAC address in this entry.
Age (min)	Indicates the interval, in minutes, since this entry was entered in the table, rather than the interval since the entry was last used. (The timeout value is 4 hours.)
Hardware Addr	In this entry, MAC address mapped to the network address.
Type	Indicates the encapsulation type that the Cisco IOS software is using for the network address. Possible values include: • ARPA • SNAP • ETLK (EtherTalk) • SMDS
Interface	Indicates the interface associated with this network address.

SHOW HOSTS

To display the default domain name, the style of name lookup service, a list of name server hosts, and the cached list of host names and addresses, use the **show hosts** EXEC command.

show hosts

Syntax   *Description*

This command has no arguments or keywords.

Command Mode

EXEC

Usage Guidelines

This command first appeared in Cisco IOS Release 10.0.

Sample Display

The following is sample output from the **show hosts** command:

```
Router# show hosts

Default domain is CISCO.COM
Name/address lookup uses domain service
Name servers are 255.255.255.255
Host            Flag       Age  Type   Address(es)
SLAG.CISCO.COM  (temp, OK) 1    IP     131.108.4.10
CHAR.CISCO.COM  (temp, OK) 8    IP     192.31.7.50
CHAOS.CISCO.COM (temp, OK) 8    IP     131.108.1.115
DIRT.CISCO.COM  (temp, EX) 8    IP     131.108.1.111
DUSTBIN.CISCO.COM (temp, EX) 0  IP     131.108.1.27
DREGS.CISCO.COM (temp, EX) 24   IP     131.108.1.30
```

Table 3–4 describes the significant fields shown in the display.

Table 3–4 *Show Hosts Field Descriptions*

Field	Description
Flag	A temporary entry is entered by a name server; the Cisco IOS software removes the entry after 72 hours of inactivity. A permanent entry is entered by a configuration command and is not timed out. Entries marked OK are believed to be valid. Entries marked ?? are considered suspect and subject to revalidation. Entries marked EX are expired.
Age	Indicates the number of hours since the software last referred to the cache entry.
Type	Identifies the type of address, for example, IP, CLNS, or X.121. If you have used the **ip hp-host** global configuration command, the **show hosts** command will display these host names as type HP-IP.
Address(es)	Shows the address of the host. One host may have up to eight addresses.

Related Commands

clear host

SHOW IP ALIASES

To display the IP addresses mapped to TCP ports (aliases) and SLIP addresses, which are treated similarly to aliases, use the **show ip aliases** EXEC command.

> **show ip aliases**

Syntax   Description

This command has no arguments or keywords.

Command Mode
EXEC

Usage Guidelines
This command first appeared in Cisco IOS Release 10.0.

To distinguish a SLIP address from a normal alias address, the command output uses the form SLIP TTY1 for the "port" number, where 1 is the auxiliary port.

Sample Display
The following is sample output from the **show ip aliases** command:

```
Router# show ip aliases

   IP Address    Port
131.108.29.245  SLIP TTY1
```

The display lists the IP address and corresponding port number.

Related Commands
show line

SHOW IP ARP

To display the Address Resolution Protocol (ARP) cache, where SLIP addresses appear as permanent ARP table entries, use the **show ip arp** EXEC command.

> **show ip arp** [*ip-address*] [*hostname*] [*mac-address*] [*type number*]

Syntax	Description
ip-address	(Optional.) ARP entries matching this IP address are displayed.
hostname	(Optional.) Host name.
mac-address	(Optional.) 48-bit MAC address.
type number	(Optional.) ARP entries learned via this interface type and number are displayed.

Command Mode
EXEC

Usage Guidelines
ARP establishes correspondences between network addresses (an IP address, for example) and LAN hardware addresses (Ethernet addresses). A record of each correspondence is kept in a cache for a predetermined amount of time and then discarded.

Sample Display

The following is sample output from the **show ip arp** command:

```
Router# show ip arp

Protocol    Address         Age(min)   Hardware Addr    Type    Interface
Internet    171.69.233.22      9        0000.0c59.f892   ARPA    Ethernet0/0
Internet    171.69.233.21      8        0000.0c07.ac00   ARPA    Ethernet0/0
Internet    171.69.233.19      -        0000.0c63.1300   ARPA    Ethernet0/0
Internet    171.69.233.30      9        0000.0c36.6965   ARPA    Ethernet0/0
Internet    172.19.168.11      -        0000.0c63.1300   ARPA    Ethernet0/0
Internet    172.19.168.254     9        0000.0c36.6965   ARPA    Ethernet0/0
```

Table 3–5 describes significant fields shown in the display.

Table 3–5 *Show IP ARP Field Descriptions*

Field	Description
Protocol	Protocol for network address in the Address field.
Address	The network address that corresponds to Hardware Addr.
Age (min)	Age, in minutes, of the cache entry.
Hardware Addr	LAN hardware address or a MAC address that corresponds to the network address.
Type	Type of encapsulation: • ARPA—Ethernet • SNAP—RFC 1042 • SAP—IEEE 802.3
Interface	Interface to which this address mapping has been assigned.

SHOW IP INTERFACE

To display the usability status of interfaces configured for IP, use the **show ip interface** EXEC command.

    show ip interface [*type number*]

Syntax	*Description*
type	(Optional.) Interface type.
number	(Optional.) Interface number.

Command Mode

EXEC

Usage Guidelines

This command first appeared in Cisco IOS Release 10.0.

The Cisco IOS software automatically enters a directly connected route in the routing table if the interface is usable. A usable interface is one through which the software can send and receive packets. If the software determines that an interface is not usable, it removes the directly connected routing entry from the routing table. Removing the entry allows the software to use dynamic routing protocols to determine backup routes (if any) to the network.

If the interface can provide two-way communication, the line protocol is marked "up." If the interface hardware is usable, the interface is marked "up."

If you specify an optional interface type, you will see only information on that specific interface.

If you specify no optional arguments, you will see information on all the interfaces.

When an asynchronous interface is encapsulated with PPP or SLIP, IP fast switching is enabled. A **show ip interface** command on an asynchronous interface encapsulated with PPP or SLIP displays a message indicating that IP fast switching is enabled.

Sample Display

The following is sample output from the **show ip interface** command:

```
Router# show ip interface

Ethernet0 is up, line protocol is up
  Internet address is 192.195.78.24, subnet mask is 255.255.255.240
  Broadcast address is 255.255.255.255
  Address determined by non-volatile memory
  MTU is 1500 bytes
  Helper address is not set
  Secondary address 131.192.115.2, subnet mask 255.255.255.0
  Directed broadcast forwarding is enabled
  Multicast groups joined: 224.0.0.1 224.0.0.2
  Outgoing access list is not set
  Inbound  access list is not set
  Proxy ARP is enabled
  Security level is default
  Split horizon is enabled
  ICMP redirects are always sent
  ICMP unreachables are always sent
  ICMP mask replies are never sent
  IP fast switching is enabled
  IP fast switching on the same interface is disabled
  IP SSE switching is disabled
  Router Discovery is disabled
  IP output packet accounting is disabled
  IP access violation accounting is disabled
  TCP/IP header compression is disabled
  Probe proxy name replies are disabled
```

Table 3–6 describes the fields shown in the display.

Table 3–6 *Show IP Interface Field Descriptions*

Field	Description
Ethernet0 is up	If the interface hardware is usable, the interface is marked "up." For an interface to be usable, both the interface hardware and line protocol must be up.
Line protocol is up	If the interface can provide two-way communication, the line protocol is marked "up." For an interface to be usable, both the interface hardware and line protocol must be up.
Internet address and subnet mask	IP Internet address and subnet mask of the interface.
Broadcast address	Shows the broadcast address.
Address determined by ...	Indicates how the IP address of the interface was determined.
MTU	Shows the MTU value set on the interface.
Helper address	Shows a helper address, if one has been set.
Secondary address	Shows a secondary address, if one has been set.
Directed broadcast forwarding	Indicates whether directed broadcast forwarding is enabled.
Multicast groups joined	Indicates the multicast groups of which this interface is a member.
Outgoing access list	Indicates whether the interface has an outgoing access list set.
Inbound access list	Indicates whether the interface has an incoming access list set.
Proxy ARP	Indicates whether Proxy ARP is enabled for the interface.
Security level	Specifies the IPSO security level set for this interface.
Split horizon	Indicates that split horizon is enabled.
ICMP redirects	Specifies whether redirects will be sent on this interface.
ICMP unreachables	Specifies whether unreachable messages will be sent on this interface.
ICMP mask replies	Specifies whether mask replies will be sent on this interface.
IP fast switching	Specifies whether fast switching has been enabled for this interface. It is generally enabled on serial interfaces, such as this one.

Table 3–6 *Show IP Interface Field Descriptions, Continued*

Field	Description
IP SSE switching	Specifies whether IP SSE switching is enabled.
Router Discovery	Specifies whether the discovery process has been enabled for this interface. It is generally disabled on serial interfaces.
IP output packet accounting	Specifies whether IP accounting is enabled for this interface and what the threshold (maximum number of entries) is.
TCP/IP header compression	Indicates whether compression is enabled or disabled.
Probe proxy name	Indicates whether HP Probe proxy name replies are generated.

SHOW IP IRDP

To display IRDP values, use the **show ip irdp** EXEC command.

> **show ip irdp**

Syntax   Description

This command has no arguments or keywords.

Command Mode

EXEC

Usage Guidelines

This command first appeared in Cisco IOS Release 10.0.

Sample Display

The following is sample output from the **show ip irdp** command:

```
Router# show ip irdp

Ethernet 0 has router discovery enabled

Advertisements will occur between every 450 and 600 seconds.
Advertisements are valid for 1800 seconds.
Default preference will be 100.
  --More--
Serial 0 has router discovery disabled
  --More--
Ethernet 1 has router discovery disabled
```

As the display shows, **show ip irdp** output indicates whether router discovery has been configured for each router interface, and it lists the values of router discovery configurables for those interfaces on which router discovery has been enabled. Explanations for the less obvious lines of output in the display are as follows:

```
Advertisements will occur between every 450 and 600 seconds.
```

This indicates the configured minimum and maximum advertising interval for the interface.

```
Advertisements are valid for 1800 seconds.
```

This indicates the configured holdtime values for the interface.

```
Default preference will be 100.
```

This indicates the configured (or in this case default) preference value for the interface.

Related Commands

ip irdp

SHOW IP MASKS

To display the masks used for network addresses and the number of subnets using each mask, use the **show ip masks** EXEC command.

show ip masks *address*

Syntax	Description
address	Network address for which a mask is required.

Command Mode

EXEC

Usage Guidelines

This command first appeared in Cisco IOS Release 10.0.

The **show ip masks** command is useful for debugging when a Variable-Length Subnet Mask (VLSM) is used. It shows the number of masks associated with the network and the number of routes for each mask.

Sample Display

The following is sample output from the **show ip masks** command:

```
Router# show ip masks 131.108.0.0

Mask             Reference count
255.255.255.255 2
255.255.255.0    3
255.255.0.0      1
```

SHOW IP NAT STATISTICS

To display NAT statistics, use the **show ip nat statistics** EXEC command.

> **show ip nat statistics**

Syntax   Description

This command has no arguments or keywords.

Command Mode

EXEC

Usage Guidelines

This command first appeared in Cisco IOS Release 11.2.

Sample Display

The following is sample output from the **show ip nat statistics** command:

```
Router# show ip nat statistics
Total translations: 2 (0 static, 2 dynamic; 0 extended)
Outside interfaces: Serial0
Inside interfaces: Ethernet1
Hits: 135  Misses: 5
Expired translations: 2
Dynamic mappings:
-- Inside Source
access-list 1 pool net-208 refcount 2
 pool net-208: netmask 255.255.255.240
        start 171.69.233.208 end 171.69.233.221
        type generic, total addresses 14, allocated 2 (14%), misses 0
```

Table 3–7 describes the significant fields in the display.

Table 3–7   *Show IP NAT Statistics Field Descriptions*

Field	Description
Total translations	Number of translations active in the system. This number is incremented each time a translation is created and is decremented each time a translation is cleared or times out.
Outside interfaces	List of interfaces marked as outside with the **ip nat outside** command.
Inside interfaces	List of interfaces marked as inside with the **ip nat inside** command.
Hits	Number of times the software does a translations table lookup and finds an entry.
Misses	Number of times the software does a translations table lookup, fails to find an entry, and must try to create one.

Table 3-7 *Show IP NAT Statistics Field Descriptions, Continued*

Field	Description
Expired translations	Cumulative count of translations that have expired since the router was booted.
Dynamic mappings	Indicates that the information that follows is about dynamic mappings.
Inside Source	The information that follows is about an inside source translation.
access-list	Access list number being used for the translation.
pool	Name of the pool (in this case, net-208).
refcount	Number of translations that are using this pool.
netmask	IP network mask being used in the pool.
start	Starting IP address in the pool range.
end	Ending IP address in the pool range.
type	Type of pool. Possible types are generic or rotary.
total addresses	Number of addresses in the pool that are available for translation.
allocated	Number of addresses being used.
misses	Number of failed allocations from the pool.

Related Commands

clear ip nat translation
ip nat
ip nat inside destination
ip nat inside source
ip nat outside source
ip nat pool
ip nat translation
show ip nat statistics
show ip nat translations

SHOW IP NAT TRANSLATIONS

To display active NAT translations, use the **show ip nat translations** EXEC command.

show ip nat translations [verbose]

Syntax	*Description*
verbose	(Optional.) Displays additional information for each translation table entry, including how long ago the entry was created and used.

Command Mode

EXEC

Usage Guidelines

This command first appeared in Cisco IOS Release 11.2.

Sample Displays

The following is sample output from the **show ip nat translations** command. Without overloading, two inside hosts are exchanging packets with some outside hosts.

```
Router# show ip nat translations
Pro Inside global      Inside local    Outside local    Outside global
--- 171.69.233.209     192.168.1.95    ---              ---
--- 171.69.233.210     192.168.1.89    ---              --
```

With overloading, a translation for a DNS transaction is still active, and translations for two Telnet sessions (from two different hosts) are also active. Note that two different inside hosts appear on the outside with a single IP address.

```
Router# show ip nat translations
Pro Inside global        Inside local      Outside local     Outside global
udp 171.69.233.209:1220  192.168.1.95:1220 171.69.2.132:53   171.69.2.132:53
tcp 171.69.233.209:11012 192.168.1.89:11012 171.69.1.220:23  171.69.1.220:23
tcp 171.69.233.209:1067  192.168.1.95:1067 171.69.1.161:23   171.69.1.161:23
```

The following is sample output that includes the **verbose** keyword.

```
Router# show ip nat translations verbose
Pro Inside global        Inside local      Outside local     Outside global
udp 171.69.233.209:1220  192.168.1.95:1220 171.69.2.132:53   171.69.2.132:53
        create 00:00:02, use 00:00:00, flags: extended
tcp 171.69.233.209:11012 192.168.1.89:11012 171.69.1.220:23  171.69.1.220:23
        create 00:01:13, use 00:00:50, flags: extended
tcp 171.69.233.209:1067  192.168.1.95:1067 171.69.1.161:23   171.69.1.161:23
        create 00:00:02, use 00:00:00, flags: extended
```

Table 3–8 describes the significant fields in the display.

Table 3–8   *Show IP NAT Translations Field Descriptions*

Field	Description
Pro	Protocol of the port identifying the address.
Inside global	The legitimate IP address (assigned by the NIC or service provider) that represents one or more inside local IP addresses to the outside world.

Table 3–8 *Show IP NAT Translations Field Descriptions, Continued*

Field	Description
Inside local	The IP address assigned to a host on the inside network; probably not a legitimate address assigned by the NIC or service provider.
Outside local	IP address of an outside host as it appears to the inside network; probably not a legitimate address assigned by the NIC or service provider.
Outside global	The IP address assigned to a host on the outside network by its owner.
create	How long ago the entry was created (in hours:minutes:seconds).
use	How long ago the entry was last used (in hours:minutes:seconds).
flags	Indication of the type of translation. Possible flags are the following: • extended—Extended translation • static—Static translation • destination—Rotary translation • outside—Outside translation • timing out—Translation will no longer be used, due to a TCP FIN or RST

Related Commands

clear ip nat translation
ip nat
ip nat inside destination
ip nat inside source
ip nat outside source
ip nat pool
ip nat translation
show ip nat statistics

SHOW IP NHRP

To display the NHRP cache, use the **show ip nhrp** EXEC command.

> **show ip nhrp** [**dynamic** | **static**] [*type number*]

Syntax	Description
dynamic	(Optional.) Displays only the dynamic (learned) IP-to-NBMA address cache entries.
static	(Optional.) Displays only the static IP-to-NBMA address entries in the cache (configured through the **ip nhrp map** command).
type	(Optional.) Interface type about which to display the NHRP cache (for example, **atm**, **tunnel**).
number	(Optional.) Interface number about which to display the NHRP cache.

Command Mode

EXEC

Usage Guidelines

This command first appeared in Cisco IOS Release 10.3.

Sample Display

The following is sample output from the **show ip nhrp** command:

```
Router# show ip nhrp

10.0.0.2 255.255.255.255, ATM0/0 created 0:00:43 expire 1:59:16
   Type: dynamic Flags: authoritative
   NBMA address: 11.1111.1111.1111.1111.1111.1111.1111.1111.1111.11
10.0.0.1 255.255.255.255, Tunnel0 created 0:10:03 expire 1:49:56
   Type: static Flags: authoritative
   NBMA address: 11.1.1.2
```

Table 3–9 describes the fields in the display.

Table 3–9   *Show IP NHRP Field Descriptions*

Field	Description
100.0.0.2 255.255.255.255	IP address and its network mask in the IP-to-NBMA address cache. The mask is currently always 255.255.255.255 because Cisco does not support aggregation of NBMA information through NHRP.
ATM0/0 created 0:00:43	Interface type and number (in this case, ATM slot and port numbers) and how long ago it was created (hours:minutes:seconds).
expire 1:59:16	Time in which the positive and negative authoritative NBMA address will expire (hours:minutes:seconds). This value is based on the **ip nhrp holdtime** command.

Table 3–9 *Show IP NHRP Field Descriptions, Continued*

Field	Description
Type	This value can be one of the following: • dynamic—NBMA address was obtained from NHRP Request packet. • static—NBMA address was statically configured.
Flags	This value can be one of the following: • authoritative—Indicates that the NHRP information was obtained from the Next Hop Server or router that maintains the NBMA-to-IP address mapping for a particular destination. • implicit—Indicates that the information was learned not from an NHRP request generated from the local router, but from an NHRP packet being forwarded or from an NHRP request being received by the local router. • negative—For negative caching; indicates that the requested NBMA mapping could not be obtained.
NBMA address	Nonbroadcast, multiaccess address. The address format is appropriate for the type of network being used (for example, ATM, Ethernet, SMDS, multipoint tunnel).

Related Commands

ip nhrp map

SHOW IP NHRP TRAFFIC

To display NHRP traffic statistics, use the **show ip nhrp traffic** EXEC command.

   show ip nhrp traffic

Syntax   Description

This command has no arguments or keywords.

Command Mode

EXEC

Usage Guidelines

This command first appeared in Cisco IOS Release 10.3.

Sample Display

The following is sample output from the **show ip nhrp traffic** command:

```
Router# show ip nhrp traffic
Tunnel0
  request packets sent: 2
  request packets received: 4
  reply packets sent: 4
  reply packets received: 2
  register packets sent: 0
  register packets received: 0
  error packets sent: 0
  error packets received: 0
Router#
```

Table 3–10 describes the fields in the display.

Table 3–10   *Show IP NHRP Traffic Field Descriptions*

Field	Description
Tunnel 0	Interface type and number.
request packets sent	Number of NHRP Request packets originated from this station.
request packets received	Number of NHRP Request packets received by this station.
reply packets sent	Number of NHRP Reply packets originated from this station.
reply packets received	Number of NHRP Reply packets received by this station.
register packets sent	Number of NHRP Register packets originated from this station. Currently, Cisco routers and access servers do not send Register packets, so this value is 0.
register packets received	Number of NHRP Register packets received by this station. Currently, Cisco routers or access servers do not send Register packets, so this value is 0.
error packets sent	Number of NHRP Error packets originated by this station.
error packets received	Number of NHRP Error packets received by this station.

SHOW IP REDIRECTS

To display the address of a default gateway (router) and the address of hosts for which a redirect has been received, use the **show ip redirects** EXEC command.

show ip redirects

Syntax   Description

This command has no arguments or keywords.

Command Mode

EXEC

Usage Guidelines

This command first appeared in Cisco IOS Release 10.0.

Sample Display

The following is sample output from the **show ip redirects** command:

```
Router# show ip redirects

Default gateway is 160.89.80.29

Host               Gateway          Last Use   Total Uses  Interface
131.108.1.111      160.89.80.240      0:00             9   Ethernet0
128.95.1.4         160.89.80.240      0:00             4   Ethernet0
Router#
```

Related Commands

ip redirects

TERM IP NETMASK-FORMAT

To specify the format in which netmasks are displayed in **show** command output, use the **term ip netmask-format** EXEC command. To restore the default display format, use the **no** form of this command.

> **term ip netmask-format** {bitcount | decimal | hexadecimal}
> **term no ip netmask-format** [bitcount | decimal | hexadecimal]

Syntax	*Description*
bitcount	Addresses are followed by a slash and the total number of bits in the netmask. For example, 131.108.11.55/24 indicates that the netmask is 24 bits.
decimal	Netmasks are displayed in dotted decimal notation (for example, 255.255.255.0).
hexadecimal	Netmasks are displayed in hexadecimal format, as indicated by the leading 0X (for example, 0XFFFFFF00).

Default

Netmasks are displayed in dotted decimal format.

Command Mode

EXEC

Usage Guidelines

This command first appeared in Cisco IOS Release 10.3.

IP uses a 32-bit mask that indicates which address bits belong to the network and subnetwork fields, and which bits belong to the host field. This is called a *netmask*. By default, **show** commands display an IP address and then its netmask in dotted decimal notation. For example, a subnet would be displayed as 131.108.11.55 255.255.255.0.

However, you can specify that the display of the network mask appears in hexadecimal format or bit count format instead. The hexadecimal format is commonly used on UNIX systems. The previous example would be displayed as 131.108.11.55 0XFFFFFF00.

The bitcount format for displaying network masks is to append a slash (/) and the total number of bits in the netmask to the address itself. The previous example would be displayed as 131.108.11.55/24.

Example

The following example specifies that network masks for the session be displayed in bitcount notation in the output of **show** commands:

```
term ip netmask-format bitcount
```

TRACE (PRIVILEGED)

To discover the routes that the packets follow when traveling to their destination from the router, use the **trace** privileged EXEC command.

      trace [*destination*]

Syntax	Description
destination	(Optional.) Destination address or host name on the command line. The default parameters for the appropriate protocol are assumed and the tracing action begins.

Command Mode

Privileged EXEC

Usage Guidelines

This command first appeared in Cisco IOS Release 10.0.

The **trace** command works by taking advantage of the error messages generated by the Cisco IOS software when a datagram exceeds its TTL value.

The **trace** command starts by sending probe datagrams with a TTL value of one. This causes the first router to discard the probe datagram and send back an error message. The **trace** command sends several probes at each TTL level and displays the round-trip time for each.

The **trace** command sends out one probe at a time. Each outgoing packet may result in one or two error messages. A *time exceeded* error message indicates that an intermediate router has seen and discarded the probe. A *destination unreachable* error message indicates that the destination node has received the probe and discarded it because it could not deliver the packet. If the timer goes off before a response comes in, **trace** prints an asterisk (*).

The **trace** command terminates when the destination responds, when the maximum TTL is exceeded, or when the user interrupts the trace with the escape sequence. By default, to invoke the escape sequence, press Ctrl-^ X, which is done by simultaneously pressing the Ctrl, Shift, and 6 keys, letting go, then pressing the X key.

To use parameters other than the default parameters and invoke an extended **trace** test, enter the command without a destination argument. You will be stepped through a dialog to select the desired parameters.

Common Trace Problems

Due to bugs in the IP implementation of various hosts and routers, the IP **trace** command may behave in odd ways.

Not all destinations will respond correctly to a *probe* message by sending back an *ICMP port unreachable* message. A long sequence of TTL levels with only asterisks, terminating only when the maximum TTL has been reached, may indicate this problem.

There is a known problem with the way some hosts handle an *ICMP TTL exceeded* message. Some hosts generate an *ICMP* message but they reuse the TTL of the incoming packet. Since this is zero, the ICMP packets do not make it back. When you trace the path to such a host, you may see a set of TTL values with asterisks (*). Eventually the TTL gets high enough that the *ICMP* message can get back. For example, if the host is six hops away, **trace** will time out on responses 6 through 11.

Sample Display Showing Trace IP Routes

The following display shows sample IP **trace** output when a destination host name has been specified:

```
Router# trace ABA.NYC.mil

Type escape sequence to abort.
Tracing the route to ABA.NYC.mil (26.0.0.73)
  1 DEBRIS.CISCO.COM (131.108.1.6) 1000 msec 8 msec 4 msec
  2 BARRNET-GW.CISCO.COM (131.108.16.2) 8 msec 8 msec 8 msec
  3 EXTERNAL-A-GATEWAY.STANFORD.EDU (192.42.110.225) 8 msec 4 msec 4 msec
  4 BB2.SU.BARRNET.NET (131.119.254.6) 8 msec 8 msec 8 msec
  5 SU.ARC.BARRNET.NET (131.119.3.8) 12 msec 12 msec 8 msec
  6 MOFFETT-FLD-MB.in.MIL (192.52.195.1) 216 msec 120 msec 132 msec
  7 ABA.NYC.mil (26.0.0.73) 412 msec 628 msec 664 msec
```

Table 3–11 describes the fields shown in the display.

Table 3–11   *Trace Field Descriptions for IP Routes*

Field	Description
1	Indicates the sequence number of the router in the path to the host.
DEBRIS.CISCO.COM	Host name of this router.
131.108.1.61	Internet address of this router.
1000 msec 8 msec 4 msec	Round-trip time for each of the three probes that are sent.

Sample Display Showing Extended IP Trace Dialog

The following display shows a sample **trace** session involving the extended dialog of the **trace** command:

```
Router# trace

Protocol [ip]:
Target IP address: mit.edu
Source address:
Numeric display [n]:
Timeout in seconds [3]:
Probe count [3]:
Minimum Time to Live [1]:
Maximum Time to Live [30]:
Port Number [33434]:
Loose, Strict, Record, Timestamp, Verbose[none]:
Type escape sequence to abort.
Tracing the route to MIT.EDU (18.72.2.1)
  1 ICM-DC-2-V1.ICP.NET (192.108.209.17) 72 msec 72 msec 88 msec
  2 ICM-FIX-E-H0-T3.ICP.NET (192.157.65.122) 80 msec 128 msec 80 msec
  3 192.203.229.246 540 msec 88 msec 84 msec
  4 T3-2.WASHINGTON-DC-CNSS58.T3.ANS.NET (140.222.58.3) 84 msec 116 msec 88 msec
  5 T3-3.WASHINGTON-DC-CNSS56.T3.ANS.NET (140.222.56.4) 80 msec 132 msec 88 msec
  6 T3-0.NEW-YORK-CNSS32.T3.ANS.NET (140.222.32.1) 92 msec 132 msec 88 msec
  7 T3-0.HARTFORD-CNSS48.T3.ANS.NET (140.222.48.1) 88 msec 88 msec 88 msec
  8 T3-0.HARTFORD-CNSS49.T3.ANS.NET (140.222.49.1) 96 msec 104 msec 96 msec
  9 T3-0.ENSS134.T3.ANS.NET (140.222.134.1) 92 msec 128 msec 92 msec
 10 W91-CISCO-EXTERNAL-FDDI.MIT.EDU (192.233.33.1) 92 msec 92 msec 112 msec
 11 E40-RTR-FDDI.MIT.EDU (18.168.0.2) 92 msec 120 msec 96 msec
 12 MIT.EDU (18.72.2.1) 96 msec 92 msec 96 msec
```

Table 3–12 describes the fields that are unique to the extended trace sequence, as shown in the display.

Table 3–12 *Trace Field Descriptions*

Field	Description
Target IP address	You must enter a host name or an IP address. There is no default.
Source address	One of the interface addresses of the router to use as a source address for the probes. The Cisco IOS software will normally pick the best source address to use.
Numeric display	The default is to have both a symbolic and numeric display; however, you can suppress the symbolic display.
Timeout in seconds	The number of seconds to wait for a response to a probe packet. The default is 3 seconds.
Probe count	The number of probes to be sent at each TTL level. The default count is 3.
Minimum Time to Live [1]	The TTL value for the first probes. The default is 1, but it can be set to a higher value to suppress the display of known hops.
Maximum Time to Live [30]	The largest TTL value that can be used. The default is 30. The **trace** command terminates when the destination is reached or when this value is reached.
Port Number	The destination port used by the UDP probe messages. The default is 33434.
Loose, Strict, Record, Timestamp, Verbose	IP header options. You may specify any combination. The **trace** command issues prompts for the required fields. Note that **trace** will place the requested options in each probe; however, there is no guarantee that all routers (or end nodes) will process the options.
Loose Source Routing	Allows you to specify a list of nodes that must be traversed when going to the destination.
Strict Source Routing	Allows you to specify a list of nodes that must be the only nodes traversed when going to the destination.
Record	Allows you to specify the number of hops to leave room for.
Timestamp	Allows you to specify the number of time stamps to leave room for.
Verbose	If you select any option, the verbose mode is automatically selected and **trace** prints the contents of the option field in any incoming packets. You can prevent verbose mode by selecting it again, thus toggling its current setting.

Table 3–13 describes the characters that can appear in **trace** output.

Table 3–13 *IP Trace Text Characters*

Character	Description
nn msec	For each node, the round-trip time (in milliseconds) for the specified number of probes.
*	The probe timed out.
?	Unknown packet type.
A	Administratively unreachable (possibly due to an access list).
Q	Source quench.
P	Protocol unreachable.
N	Network unreachable.
U	Port unreachable.
H	Host unreachable.

Related Commands

trace (user)

TRACE (USER)

To discover the routes that the router packets follow when traveling to their destination, use the **trace** user EXEC command.

> **trace ip** *destination*

Syntax	Description
destination	Destination address or host name on the command line. The default parameters for the appropriate protocol are assumed and the tracing action begins.

Command Mode

User EXEC

Usage Guidelines

This command first appeared in Cisco IOS Release 10.0.

The **trace** command works by taking advantage of the error messages generated by the Cisco IOS software when a datagram exceeds its TTL value.

The **trace** command starts by sending probe datagrams with a TTL value of one. This causes the first router to discard the probe datagram and send back an error message. The **trace** command sends several probes at each TTL level and displays the round-trip time for each.

The **trace** command sends out one probe at a time. Each outgoing packet may result in one or two error messages. A *time exceeded* error message indicates that an intermediate router has seen and discarded the probe. A *destination unreachable* error message indicates that the destination node has received the probe and discarded it because it could not deliver the packet. If the timer goes off before a response comes in, **trace** prints an asterisk (*).

The **trace** command terminates when the destination responds, when the maximum TTL is exceeded, or when the user interrupts the trace with the escape sequence. By default, to invoke the escape sequence, press Ctrl-^ X, which is done by simultaneously pressing the Ctrl, Shift, and 6 keys, letting go, then pressing the X key.

Common Trace Problems

Due to bugs in the IP implementation of various hosts and routers, the IP **trace** command may behave in odd ways.

Not all destinations will respond correctly to a *probe* message by sending back an *ICMP port unreachable* message. A long sequence of TTL levels with only asterisks, terminating only when the maximum TTL has been reached, may indicate this problem.

There is a known problem with the way some hosts handle an *ICMP TTL exceeded* message. Some hosts generate an *ICMP* message but they reuse the TTL of the incoming packet. Because this is zero, the ICMP packets do not make it back. When you trace the path to such a host, you may see a set of TTL values with asterisks (*). Eventually the TTL gets high enough that the *ICMP* message can get back. For example, if the host is six hops away, **trace** will time out on responses 6 through 11.

Sample Display

The following display shows sample IP **trace** output when a destination host name has been specified:

```
Router# trace ip ABA.NYC.mil

Type escape sequence to abort.
Tracing the route to ABA.NYC.mil (26.0.0.73)
  1 DEBRIS.CISCO.COM (131.108.1.6) 1000 msec 8 msec 4 msec
  2 BARRNET-GW.CISCO.COM (131.108.16.2) 8 msec 8 msec 8 msec
  3 EXTERNAL-A-GATEWAY.STANFORD.EDU (192.42.110.225) 8 msec 4 msec 4 msec
  4 BB2.SU.BARRNET.NET (131.119.254.6) 8 msec 8 msec 8 msec
  5 SU.ARC.BARRNET.NET (131.119.3.8) 12 msec 12 msec 8 msec
  6 MOFFETT-FLD-MB.in.MIL (192.52.195.1) 216 msec 120 msec 132 msec
  7 ABA.NYC.mil (26.0.0.73) 412 msec 628 msec 664 msec
```

In the **trace** (**privileged**) command section, Table 3–11 describes the fields shown in the display. Table 3–13 describes the characters that can appear in **trace** output.

Related Commands

trace (privileged)

TUNNEL MODE

To set the encapsulation mode for the tunnel interface, use the **tunnel mode** interface configuration command. To set to the default, use the **no** form of this command.

> **tunnel mode {aurp | cayman | dvmrp | eon | gre ip [multipoint] | nos}**
> **no tunnel mode**

Syntax	Description
aurp	AppleTalk Update-Based Routing Protocol (AURP).
cayman	Cayman TunnelTalk AppleTalk encapsulation.
dvmrp	Distance Vector Multicast Routing Protocol.
eon	EON compatible CLNS tunnel.
gre ip	Generic Routing Encapsulation (GRE) protocol over IP.
multipoint	(Optional.) Enables a GRE tunnel to be used in a multipoint fashion. Can be used with the **gre ip** keyword only, and requires the use of the **tunnel key** command.
nos	KA9Q/NOS compatible IP over IP.

Default

GRE tunneling

Command Mode

Interface configuration

Usage Guidelines

This command first appeared in Cisco IOS Release 10.0.

You cannot have two tunnels using the same encapsulation mode with exactly the same source and destination address. The workaround is to create a loopback interface and source packets off of the loopback interface.

Cayman tunneling implements tunneling as designed by Cayman Systems. This enables Cisco routers and access servers to interoperate with Cayman GatorBoxes. With Cayman tunneling, you can establish tunnels between two routers or between our device and a GatorBox. When using Cayman tunneling, you must not configure the tunnel with an AppleTalk network address. This means that there is no way to ping the other end of the tunnel.

Use Distance Vector Multicast Routing Protocol (DVMRP) when a router connects to an mrouted router to run DVMRP over a tunnel. It is required to configure Protocol-Independent Multicast (PIM) and an IP address on a DVMRP tunnel.

Generic Routing Encapsulation (GRE) tunneling can be done between our routers and access servers only. When using GRE tunneling for AppleTalk, you configure the tunnel with an AppleTalk network address. This means that you can ping the other end of the tunnel.

For multipoint GRE tunnels, a tunnel key must be configured. Unlike other tunnels, the tunnel destination is optional. However, if the tunnel destination is supplied, it must map to an IP multicast address.

Examples

The following example enables Cayman tunneling:

```
interface tunnel 0
 tunnel source ethernet 0
 tunnel destination 131.108.164.19
 tunnel mode cayman
```

The following example enables GRE tunneling:

```
interface tunnel 0
 appletalk cable-range 4160-4160 4160.19
 appletalk zone Engineering
 tunnel source ethernet0
 tunnel destination 131.108.164.19
 tunnel mode gre ip
```

Related Commands

appletalk cable-range
appletalk zone
tunnel destination
tunnel source

CHAPTER 4

Configuring IP Services

This chapter describes how to configure optional IP services. For a complete description of the commands in this chapter, see Chapter 5, "IP Services Commands."

IP SERVICES TASK LIST

To configure optional IP services, complete any of the tasks in the following list:

- Managing IP Connections
- Filtering IP Packets
- Configuring the Hot Standby Router Protocol
- Configuring IP Accounting
- Configuring Performance Parameters
- Configuring IP over WANs
- Monitoring and Maintaining the IP Network

Remember that not all the tasks in this list are required. The tasks you must perform will depend on your network and your needs.

At the end of this chapter, the examples in the "IP Services Configuration Examples" section illustrate how you might configure your network using IP.

MANAGING IP CONNECTIONS

The IP suite offers a number of services that control and manage IP connections. Internet Control Message Protocol (ICMP) provides many of these services. When a problem is discovered with the Internet header, ICMP messages are sent by routers or access servers to hosts or other routers. For detailed information on ICMP, see RFC 792.

To manage various aspects of IP connections, perform the appropriate tasks in the following list:

- Enabling ICMP Protocol Unreachable Messages
- Enabling ICMP Redirect Messages
- Enabling ICMP Mask Reply Messages
- Understanding Path MTU Discovery
- Setting the MTU Packet Size
- Enabling IP Source Routing
- Configuring Simplex Ethernet Interfaces
- Configuring a DRP Server Agent

See the "ICMP Services Example" section at the end of this chapter for examples of ICMP services.

Enabling ICMP Protocol Unreachable Messages

If the Cisco IOS software receives a nonbroadcast packet destined for itself that uses an unknown protocol, it sends an ICMP Protocol Unreachable message back to the source. Similarly, if the software receives a packet that it is unable to deliver to the ultimate destination because it knows of no route to the destination address, it sends an ICMP Host Unreachable message to the source. This feature is enabled by default.

You can enable this service if it has been disabled by performing the following task in interface configuration mode:

Task	Command
Enable the sending of ICMP Protocol Unreachable and Host Unreachable messages.	**ip unreachables**

Enabling ICMP Redirect Messages

Routes are sometimes less than optimal. For example, it is possible for the router to be forced to resend a packet through the same interface on which it was received. If this happens, the Cisco IOS software sends an ICMP Redirect message to the packet's originator telling it that it is on a subnet directly connected to the receiving device, and that it must forward the packet to another system on the same subnet. The software does this because the originating host presumably could have sent that packet to the next hop without involving this device at all. The Redirect message instructs the sender to remove the receiving device from the route and substitute a specified device representing a more direct path. This feature is enabled by default. However, when Hot Standby Router Protocol is configured on an interface, ICMP Redirect messages are disabled by default for the interface.

You can enable the sending of ICMP Redirect messages if this feature was disabled by performing the following task in interface configuration mode:

Task	Command
Enable the sending of ICMP Redirect messages to learn routes.	ip redirects

Enabling ICMP Mask Reply Messages

Occasionally, network devices must know the subnet mask for a particular subnetwork in the internetwork. To determine this information, such devices can send ICMP Mask Request messages. These messages are responded to by ICMP Mask Reply messages from devices that have the requested information. The Cisco IOS software can respond to ICMP Mask Request messages if this function is enabled.

To enable the sending of ICMP Mask Reply messages, perform the following task in interface configuration mode:

Task	Command
Enable the sending of ICMP Mask Reply messages.	ip mask-reply

Understanding Path MTU Discovery

The Cisco IOS software supports the IP Path MTU Discovery mechanism, as defined in RFC 1191. IP Path MTU Discovery allows a host to dynamically discover and cope with differences in the maximum allowable Maximum Transmission Unit (MTU) size of the various links along the path. Sometimes a router is unable to forward a datagram because it requires fragmentation (the packet is larger than the MTU you set for the interface with the **ip mtu** command), but the "don't fragment" (DF) bit is set. The Cisco IOS software sends a message to the sending host, alerting it to the problem. The host will have to fragment packets for the destination so that they fit the smallest packet size of all the links along the path. This technique is shown in Figure 4–1.

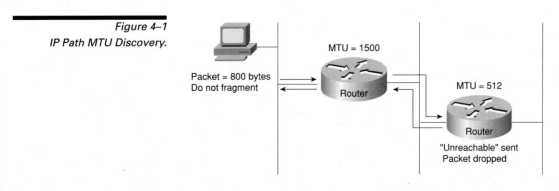

Figure 4–1
IP Path MTU Discovery.

IP Path MTU Discovery is useful when a link in a network goes down, forcing the use of another, different MTU-sized link (and different routers). As shown in Figure 4–1, suppose a router is sending IP packets over a network where the MTU in the first router is set to 1,500 bytes, but the second router is set to 512 bytes. If the datagram's "don't fragment" bit is set, the datagram would be dropped because the 512-byte router is unable to forward it. In this case, all packets larger than 512 bytes are dropped. The second router returns an ICMP Destination Unreachable message to the source of the datagram with its Code field indicating, "Fragmentation needed and DF set." To support IP Path MTU Discovery, it would also include the MTU of the next-hop network link in the low-order bits of an unused header field.

IP Path MTU Discovery is also useful when a connection is first being established and the sender has no information about the intervening links. It is always advisable to use the largest MTU that the links will bear; the larger the MTU, the fewer packets the host must send.

NOTES ──

IP Path MTU Discovery is a process initiated by end hosts. If an end host does not support IP Path MTU Discovery, the receiving device will have no mechanism available to avoid fragmenting datagrams generated by the end host.

The Cisco 7000 and Cisco 4000 routers support fast switching of IP packets between Ethernet and Fiber Distributed Data Interface (FDDI) interfaces. When packets are being sent from FDDI to Ethernet interfaces and you are not using IP Path MTU Discovery, FDDI packets with data lengths larger than 1,500 bytes will be fragmented into multiple Ethernet packets. This slows performance. If the majority of your traffic travels off the FDDI ring, you might want to either lower the MTU size on your host FDDI interfaces to 1,500 bytes or run IP Path MTU Discovery on your hosts.

Because the CTR card does not support the switching of frames larger than 4,472 bytes, some interoperability problems may occur if CTR cards are intermixed with other Token Ring cards on the same network. You can minimize this by setting lower (and the same) IP maximum packet sizes for all devices on the network with the **ip mtu** interface command.

To enable Path MTU Discovery for connections initiated by the router (when the router is acting as a host), see the section "Enabling TCP Path MTU Discovery" later in this chapter.

Setting the MTU Packet Size

All interfaces have a default MTU packet size. You can adjust the IP MTU size so that if an IP packet exceeds the MTU set for an interface, the Cisco IOS software will fragment it.

Changing the MTU value (with the **mtu** interface configuration command) can affect the IP MTU value. If the current IP MTU value is the same as the MTU value, and you change the MTU value, the IP MTU value will be modified automatically to match the new MTU. However, the reverse is not true; changing the IP MTU value has no effect on the value for the **mtu** interface configuration command.

Also, all devices on a physical medium must have the same protocol MTU in order to operate.

To set the MTU packet size for a specified interface, perform the following task in interface configuration mode:

Task	Command
Set the IP MTU packet size for an interface.	**ip mtu** *bytes*

Enabling IP Source Routing

The Cisco IOS software examines IP header options on every packet. It supports the IP header options *Strict Source Route*, *Loose Source Route*, *Record Route*, and *Time Stamp*, which are defined in RFC 791. If the software finds a packet with one of these options enabled, it performs the appropriate action. If it finds a packet with an invalid option, it sends an ICMP Parameter Problem message to the source of the packet and discards the packet.

IP provides a provision that allows the source IP host to specify a route through the IP network. This provision is known as *source routing*. Source routing is specified as an option in the IP header. If source routing is specified, the software forwards the packet according to the specified source route. This feature is employed when you want to force a packet to take a certain route through the network. The default is to perform source routing.

You can enable IP source-route header options if they have been disabled by performing the following task in global configuration mode:

Task	Command
Enable IP source routing.	**ip source-route**

Configuring Simplex Ethernet Interfaces

You can configure simplex Ethernet interfaces. This feature is useful for setting up dynamic IP routing over a simplex circuit (a circuit that receives only or transmits only). When a route is learned on a receive-only interface, the interface designated as the source of the route is converted to the interface you specify. When packets are routed out this specified interface, they are sent to the IP address of the source of the routing update. To reach this IP address on a transmit-only Ethernet link, a static ARP entry mapping this IP address to the hardware address of the other end of the link is required.

To assign a transmit interface to a receive-only interface, perform the following task in interface configuration mode:

Task	Command
Assign a transmit interface to a receive-only interface.	**transmit-interface** *type number*

See the "Simplex Ethernet Interfaces Example" section at the end of this chapter for an example of configuring a simplex Ethernet interface.

Configuring a DRP Server Agent

The Director Response Protocol (DRP) is a simple User Datagram Protocol (UDP)-based application developed by Cisco Systems. It enables Cisco's DistributedDirector product to query routers (DRP Server Agents) in the field for Border Gateway Protocol (BGP) and Interior Gateway Protocol (IGP) routing table metrics between distributed servers and clients. DistributedDirector, a separate, standalone product, uses DRP to transparently redirect end-user service requests to the topologically closest responsive server. DRP enables DistributedDirector to provide dynamic, scalable, and "network intelligent" Internet traffic load distribution between multiple geographically dispersed servers.

DRP Server Agents are border routers (or peers-to-border routers) that support the geographically distributed servers for which DistributedDirector service distribution is desired. Note that, because DistributedDirector makes decisions based on BGP and IGP information, all DRP Server Agents must have access to full BGP and IGP routing tables.

Perform the tasks in the following list to configure and maintain the DRP Server Agent. The first task is required; the remaining tasks are optional:

- Enabling the DRP Server Agent
- Limiting the Source of DRP Queries
- Configuring Authentication of DRP Queries and Responses

To monitor and maintain the DRP Server Agent, see the section "Monitoring and Maintaining the DRP Server Agent" later in this chapter.

For an example of configuring a DRP Server Agent, see the section "DRP Server Agent Example" at the end of this chapter.

Enabling the DRP Server Agent

The DRP Server Agent is disabled by default. To enable it, perform the following task in global configuration mode:

Task	Command
Enable the DRP Server Agent.	ip drp server

Limiting the Source of DRP Queries

As a security measure, you can limit the source of valid DRP queries. If a standard IP access list is applied to the interface, the Server Agent will respond only to DRP queries originating from an IP address in the list. If no access list is configured, the server agent will answer all queries.

If both an access group and a key chain (described in the next section) have been configured, both security mechanisms must allow access before a request is processed.

To limit the source of valid DRP queries, perform the following task in global configuration mode:

Task	Command
Control the sources of valid DRP queries by applying a standard IP access list.	ip drp access-group *access-list-number*

Configuring Authentication of DRP Queries and Responses

Another available security measure is to configure the DRP Server Agent to authenticate DRP queries and responses. You define a key chain, identify the keys that belong to the key chain, and specify how long each key is valid. To do so, perform the following tasks beginning in global configuration mode:

	Task	Command
Step 1	Identify which key chain to use to authenticate all DRP requests and responses.	ip drp authentication key-chain *name-of-chain*
Step 2	Identify a key chain (match the name configured in Step 1).	key chain *name-of-chain*
Step 3	In key chain configuration mode, identify the key number.	key *number*
Step 4	In key chain key configuration mode, identify the key string.	key-string *text*

Task	Command
Step 5 Optionally specify the time period during which the key can be received.	**accept-lifetime** *start-time* {**infinite** | *end-time* | **duration** *seconds*}
Step 6 Optionally specify the time period during which the key can be sent.	**send-lifetime** *start-time* {**infinite** | *end-time* | **duration** *seconds*}

When configuring your key chains and keys, keep the following points in mind:

- The key chain configured for the DRP Server Agent in Step 1 must match the key chain in Step 2.
- The key configured in the primary agent in the remote router must match the key configured in the DRP Server Agent in order for responses to be processed.
- You can configure multiple keys with lifetimes, and the software will rotate through them. Note that the router needs to know the time.
- If authentication is enabled and multiple keys on the key chain happen to be active based on the **send-lifetime** values, the software uses only the first key it encounters for authentication.
- Use the **show key chain** command to display key chain information.

FILTERING IP PACKETS

Packet filtering helps control packet movement through the network. Such control can help limit network traffic and restrict network use by certain users or devices. To permit or deny packets from crossing specified interfaces, Cisco provides *access lists*.

You can use access lists in the following ways:

- To control the transmission of packets on an interface
- To control virtual terminal line access
- To restrict contents of routing updates

This section summarizes how to create IP access lists and how to apply them.

See the "IP Services Configuration Examples" section at the end of this chapter for examples of configuring IP access lists.

An access list is a sequential collection of permit and deny conditions that apply to IP addresses. The Cisco IOS software tests addresses against the conditions in an access list one by one. The first match determines whether the software accepts or rejects the address. Because the software stops testing conditions after the first match, the order of the conditions is critical. If no conditions match, the software rejects the address.

The two steps involved in using access lists are the following:

Step 1   Create an access list by specifying an access list number or name and access conditions.

Step 2   Apply the access list to interfaces or terminal lines.

These steps are described in the next sections.

Creating Standard and Extended Access Lists Using Numbers

— **CAUTION** ———————————————————————————————

Release 11.1 and later introduced substantial changes to IP access lists. These extensions are backward compatible; migrating from a release earlier than Release 11.1 to the current image will convert your access lists automatically. However, previous releases are not upwardly compatible with these changes. Thus, if you save an access list with the current image and then use older software, the resulting access list will not be interpreted correctly. **This could cause you severe security problems.** Save your old configuration file before booting Release 11.1-or-later images.

———

The software supports the following styles of access lists for IP:

- Standard IP access lists that use source addresses for matching operations.

- Extended IP access lists that use source and destination addresses for matching operations and optional protocol type information for finer granularity of control.

- Dynamic extended IP access lists that grant access per user to a specific source or destination host basis through a user authentication process. In essence, you can allow user access through a firewall dynamically, without compromising security restrictions.

To create a standard access list, perform one of the following tasks in global configuration mode:

Task	Command
Define a standard IP access list using a source address and wildcard.	**access-list** *access-list-number* {**deny** | **permit**} *source* [*source-wildcard*]
Define a standard IP access list using an abbreviation for the source and source mask of 0.0.0.0 255.255.255.255.	**access-list** *access-list-number* {**deny** | **permit**} **any**

To create an extended access list, perform one of the following tasks in global configuration mode:

Task	Command
Define an extended IP access list number and the access conditions. Use the **log** keyword to get access list logging messages, including violations.	**access-list** *access-list-number* {**deny** I **permit**} *protocol source source-wildcard destination destination-wildcard* [**precedence** *precedence*] [**tos** *tos*] [**established**] [**log**]
Define an extended IP access list using an abbreviation for a source and source wildcard of 0.0.0.0 255.255.255.255, and an abbreviation for a destination and destination wildcard of 0.0.0.0 255.255.255.255.	**access-list** *access-list-number* {**deny** I **permit**} *protocol* **any any**
Define an extended IP access list using an abbreviation for a source and source wildcard of *source* 0.0.0.0, and an abbreviation for a destination and destination wildcard of *destination* 0.0.0.0.	**access-list** *access-list-number* {**deny** I **permit**} *protocol* **host** *source* **host** *destination*
Define a dynamic access list.	**access-list** *access-list-number* [**dynamic** *dynamic-name* [**timeout** *minutes*]] {**deny** I **permit**} *protocol source source-wildcard destination destination-wildcard* [**precedence** *precedence*] [**tos** *tos*] [**established**] [**log**]

After an access list is created initially, any subsequent additions (possibly entered from the terminal) are placed at the end of the list. In other words, you cannot selectively add or remove access list command lines from a specific access list.

NOTES

When creating an access list, remember that by default the end of the access list contains an implicit deny statement for everything if it did not find a match before reaching the end. Further, with standard access lists, if you omit the mask from an associated IP host address access list specification, 0.0.0.0 is assumed to be the mask.

NOTES

Autonomous switching is not used when you have extended access lists.

After creating an access list, you must apply it to a line or interface, as shown in the section "Applying the Access List to an Interface or Terminal Line" later in this chapter.

See the "Implicit Masks in Access Lists Examples" section at the end of this chapter for examples of implicit masks.

Creating Standard and Extended Access Lists Using Names

CAUTION

Named access lists will not be recognized by any software release prior to Cisco IOS Release 11.2.

You can identify IP access lists with an alphanumeric string (a name) rather than a number (1 to 199). This feature allows you to configure more than 99 standard IP and 100 extended IP access lists in a router. If you identify your access list with a name rather than a number, the mode and command syntax are slightly different. Currently, only packet and route filters can use a named list.

Before configuring named access lists, consider the following points:

- Access lists specified by name are not compatible with older releases.
- Not all access lists that accept a number will accept a name. Access lists for packet filters and route filters on interfaces can use a name.
- A standard access list and an extended access list cannot have the same name.
- Numbered access lists are also available, as described in the earlier section, "Creating Standard and Extended Access Lists Using Numbers."

To create a standard access list, perform the following tasks beginning in global configuration mode:

Task	Command
Step 1 Define a standard IP access list using a name.	**ip access-list standard** *name*
Step 2 In access-list configuration mode, specify one or more conditions allowed or denied. This determines whether the packet is passed or dropped.	**deny** {*source* [*source-wildcard*] | **any**} or **permit** {*source* [*source-wildcard*] | **any**}
Step 3 Exit access-list configuration mode.	exit

To create an extended access list, perform the following tasks beginning in global configuration mode:

Task		Command
Step 1	Define an extended IP access list using a name.	**ip access-list extended** *name*
Step 2	In access-list configuration mode, specify the conditions allowed or denied. Use the **log** keyword to get access list logging messages, including violations.	{**deny** | **permit**} *protocol source source-wildcard destination destination-wildcard* [**precedence** *precedence*] [**tos** *tos*] [**established**] [**log**]
	or	
	Define an extended IP access list using an abbreviation for a source and source wildcard of 0.0.0.0 255.255.255.255, and an abbreviation for a destination and destination wildcard of 0.0.0.0 255.255.255.255.	{**deny** | **permit**} *protocol* **any any**
	or	
	Define an extended IP access list using an abbreviation for a source and source wildcard of *source* 0.0.0.0, and an abbreviation for a destination and destination wildcard of *destination* 0.0.0.0.	{**deny** | **permit**} *protocol* **host** *source* **host** *destination*
	or	
	Define a dynamic access list.	**dynamic** *dynamic-name* [**timeout** *minutes*] {**deny** | **permit**} *protocol source source-wildcard destination destination-wildcard* [**precedence** *precedence*] [**tos** *tos*] [**established**] [**log**]

NOTES

Autonomous switching is not used when you have extended access lists.

After you initially create an access list, you place any subsequent additions (possibly entered from the terminal) at the end of the list. In other words, you cannot selectively add access list command lines to a specific access list. However, you can use **no permit** and **no deny** commands to remove entries from a named access list.

NOTES

When making the standard and extended access list, remember that by default the end of the access list contains an implicit deny statement for everything if it did not find a match before reaching the end. Further, with standard access lists, if you omit the mask from an associated IP host address access list specification, 0.0.0.0 is assumed to be the mask.

After creating an access list, you must apply it to a line or interface, as shown in the following section, "Applying the Access List to an Interface or Terminal Line."

See the "Named Access List Example" section at the end of this chapter for an example of a named access list.

Applying the Access List to an Interface or Terminal Line

After you create an access list, you can apply it to one or more interfaces. Access lists can be applied on *either* outbound or inbound interfaces. The following two tables show how to accomplish this task for both terminal lines and network interfaces. Remember the following guidelines:

- When controlling access to a line, you must use a number.
- When controlling access to an interface, you can use a name or number.

Perform the following task in line configuration mode. Only numbered access lists can be applied to lines. Set identical restrictions on all the virtual terminal lines, because a user can attempt to connect to any of them.

Task	Command
Restrict incoming and outgoing connections between a particular virtual terminal line (into a device) and the addresses in an access list.	**access-class** *access-list-number* {**in** | **out**}

Perform the following task in interface configuration mode:

Task	Command
Control access to an interface.	ip access-group {*access-list-number*	*name*} {in	out}

For inbound access lists, after receiving a packet, the Cisco IOS software checks the source address of the packet against the access list. If the access list permits the address, the software continues to process the packet. If the access list rejects the address, the software discards the packet and returns an ICMP Host Unreachable message.

For outbound access lists, after receiving and routing a packet to a controlled interface, the software checks the source address of the packet against the access list. If the access list permits the address, the software transmits the packet. If the access list rejects the address, the software discards the packet and returns an ICMP Host Unreachable message.

When you apply an access list that has not yet been defined to an interface, the software will act as if the access list has not been applied to the interface and will accept all packets. Remember this behavior if you use undefined access lists as a means of security in your network.

CONFIGURING THE HOT STANDBY ROUTER PROTOCOL

The Hot Standby Router Protocol provides high network availability because it routes IP traffic from hosts on Ethernet, FDDI, or Token Ring networks without relying on the availability of any single router.

This feature is useful for hosts that do not support a router discovery protocol (such as IRDP) and do not have the functionality to switch to a new router when their selected router reloads or loses power. Because existing TCP sessions can survive the *failover*, this protocol also provides a more transparent means of recovery for hosts that dynamically select a next hop for routing IP traffic.

When the Hot Standby Router Protocol is configured on a network segment, it provides a virtual MAC address and an IP address that is shared among routers in a group of routers that is running the Hot Standby Router Protocol. One of these devices is selected by the protocol to be the active router. The active router receives and routes packets destined for the group's MAC address. For n routers running the Hot Standby Router Protocol, there are $n + 1$ IP and MAC addresses assigned.

The Hot Standby Router Protocol detects when the designated active router fails, at which point a selected standby router assumes control of the Hot Standby group's MAC and IP addresses. A new standby router is also selected at that time.

Devices that are running the Hot Standby Router Protocol send and receive multicast UDP-based hello packets to detect router failure and to designate active and standby routers.

When the Hot Standby Router Protocol is configured on an interface, ICMP Redirect messages are disabled by default for the interface.

You can configure multiple Hot Standby groups on an interface, thereby making fuller use of the redundant routers. To do so, specify a group number for each Hot Standby command you configure for the interface.

— **NOTES** ——

Token Ring interfaces allow up to three Hot Standby groups each.

— **NOTES** ——

The Cisco 1000 series, Cisco 2500 series, Cisco 3000 series, and Cisco 4000 series that use Lance Ethernet hardware do not support multiple Hot Standby groups on a single Ethernet interface.

The Hot Standby Router Protocol is supported over Inter-Switch Link (ISL) encapsulation.

To enable the Hot Standby Router Protocol on an interface, perform the following task in interface configuration mode:

Task	Command
Enable the Hot Standby Router Protocol.	**standby** [*group-number*] **ip** [*ip-address* [**secondary**]]

To configure other Hot Standby group attributes that affect how the local router participates in the Hot Standby Router Protocol, perform one or more of the following tasks in interface configuration mode:

Task	Command
Configure the time between hello packets and the hold time before other routers declare the active router to be down.	**standby** [*group-number*] **timers** *hellotime holdtime*
Set the Hot Standby priority used in choosing the active router. Specify that, if the local router has priority over the current active router, the local router should attempt to take its place as the active router. Configure a preemption delay, after which the Hot Standby router preempts and becomes the active router.	**standby** [*group-number*] **priority** *priority* [**preempt** [**delay** *delay*]] or **standby** [*group-number*] [**priority** *priority*] **preempt** [**delay** *delay*]

Task	Command
Configure the interface to track other interfaces, so that if one of the other interfaces goes down, the device's Hot Standby priority is lowered.	**standby** [*group-number*] **track** *type number* [*interface-priority*]
Select an authentication string to be carried in all Hot Standby Router Protocol messages.	**standby** [*group-number*] **authentication** *string*
Configure the Hot Standby Router Protocol to use the interface's burned-in address as its virtual MAC address instead of the preassigned MAC address (on Ethernet and FDDI) or the functional address (on Token Ring).	**standby use-bia**

CONFIGURING IP ACCOUNTING

Cisco's IP accounting support provides basic IP accounting functions. By enabling IP accounting, users can see the number of bytes and packets switched through the Cisco IOS software on a source and destination IP address basis. Only transit IP traffic is measured and only on an outbound basis; traffic generated by the software or terminating in the software is not included in the accounting statistics. To maintain accurate accounting totals, the software maintains two accounting databases: an active database and a checkpointed database.

Cisco's IP accounting support also provides information identifying IP traffic that fails IP access lists. Identifying IP source addresses that violate IP access lists alerts you to possible attempts to breach security. This data also indicates that you should verify IP access list configurations. To make this feature available to users, you must enable IP accounting of access list violations using the **ip accounting access-violations** command. Users can then display the number of bytes and packets from a single source that attempted to breach security against the access list for the source destination pair. By default, IP accounting displays the number of packets that have passed the access lists and were routed.

To enable IP accounting, perform one of the following tasks for each interface in interface configuration mode:

Task	Command
Enable basic IP accounting.	**ip accounting**
Enable IP accounting with the ability to identify IP traffic that fails IP access lists.	**ip accounting access-violations**

To configure other IP accounting functions, perform one or more of the following tasks in global configuration mode:

Task	Command
Set the maximum number of accounting entries to be created.	**ip accounting-threshold** *threshold*
Filter accounting information for hosts.	**ip accounting-list** *ip-address wildcard*
Control the number of transit records that will be stored in the IP accounting database.	**ip accounting-transits** *count*

To display IP access violations for a specific IP accounting database, perform the following task in EXEC mode:

Task	Command
Display IP access-violation information.	**show ip accounting** [checkpoint] **access-violations**

To display IP access violations, you must give the **access-violations** keyword on the command. If you do not specify the keyword, the command defaults to displaying the number of packets that have passed access lists and were routed. The access violations output displays the number of the access list failed by the last packet for the source and destination pair. The number of packets reveals how aggressive the attack is upon a specific destination.

Use the EXEC command **show ip accounting** to display the active accounting database. To display the checkpointed database, use the **show ip accounting checkpoint** EXEC command. The **clear ip accounting** EXEC command clears the active database and creates the checkpointed database.

CONFIGURING PERFORMANCE PARAMETERS

To tune IP performance, complete any of the tasks in the following list:

- Compressing TCP Packet Headers
- Setting the TCP Connection Attempt Time
- Enabling TCP Path MTU Discovery
- Enabling TCP Selective Acknowledgment
- Enabling TCP Timestamp
- Setting the TCP Maximum Read Size

- Setting the TCP Window Size
- Setting the TCP Outgoing Queue Size

Compressing TCP Packet Headers

You can compress the headers of your TCP/IP packets in order to reduce their size, thereby increasing performance. Header compression is particularly useful on networks with a large percentage of small packets (such as those supporting many Telnet connections). This feature only compresses the TCP header, so it has no effect on UDP packets or other protocol headers. The TCP header compression technique, described fully in RFC 1144, is supported on serial lines using HDLC or PPP encapsulation. You must enable compression on both ends of a serial connection.

Optionally, you can specify outgoing packets to be compressed only if TCP incoming packets on the same interface are compressed. If you do not specify this option, the Cisco IOS software will compress all traffic. The default is no compression.

You also can specify the total number of header compression connections that can exist on an interface. You should configure one connection for each TCP connection through the specified interface.

To enable compression, perform either of the following optional tasks in interface configuration mode:

Task	Command
Enable TCP header compression.	**ip tcp header-compression** [passive]
Specify the total number of header compression connections that can exist on an interface.	**ip tcp compression-connections** *number*

NOTES

When compression is enabled, fast switching is disabled. Fast processors can handle several fast interfaces, such as T1s, that are running header compression. However, you should think carefully about your network's traffic characteristics before compressing TCP headers. You might want to use the monitoring commands to help compare network utilization before and after enabling header compression.

Setting the TCP Connection Attempt Time

You can set the amount of time the Cisco IOS software will wait to attempt to establish a TCP connection. In previous versions of software, the system would wait a fixed 30 seconds when attempting to establish a connection. This amount of time is not sufficient in networks that have dial-up asynchronous connections (such as a network consisting of dial-on-demand links that are implemented over modems) because it will affect your ability to Telnet over the link (from the router) if the link must be brought up.

Because the connection attempt time is a host parameter, it does not pertain to traffic going through the device, just to traffic originated at the device.

To set the TCP connection attempt time, perform the following task in global configuration mode:

Task	Command
Set the amount of time the Cisco IOS software will wait to attempt to establish a TCP connection.	**ip tcp synwait-time** *seconds*

Enabling TCP Path MTU Discovery

Path MTU Discovery is a method for maximizing the use of available bandwidth in the network between the end points of a TCP connection, and is described in RFC 1191. By default, this feature is disabled. Existing connections are not affected when this feature is turned on or off. To enable Path MTU Discovery, perform the following task in interface configuration mode:

Task	Command
Enable Path MTU Discovery.	**ip tcp path-mtu-discovery** [**age-timer** {*minutes*	**infinite**}]

Customers using TCP connections to move bulk data between systems on distinct subnets will benefit most by enabling this feature. This might include customers using RSRB with TCP encapsulation, STUN, X.25 Remote Switching (also known as XOT or X.25 over TCP), and some protocol translation configurations.

The **ip tcp path-mtu-discovery** command is to enable Path MTU Discovery for connections initiated by the router when it is acting as a host. For a discussion of how the Cisco IOS software supports Path MTU Discovery when the device is acting as a router, see the section "Understanding Path MTU Discovery" earlier in this chapter.

The age-timer is a time interval for how often TCP should re-estimate the Path MTU with a larger maximum segment size (MSS). The default path MTU Discovery age-timer is 10 minutes; its maximum is 30 minutes. You can turn off the age-timer by setting it to infinite.

Enabling TCP Selective Acknowledgment

The TCP selective acknowledgment feature improves performance in the event that multiple packets are lost from one TCP window of data.

Prior to this feature, with the limited information available from cumulative acknowledgments, a TCP sender could learn about only one lost packet per round trip time. An aggressive sender could choose to retransmit packets early, but such retransmitted segments might have already been successfully received.

The TCP selective acknowledgment mechanism helps improve performance. The receiving TCP host returns selective acknowledgment packets to the sender, informing the sender of data that has been received. In other words, the receiver can acknowledge packets received out of order. The sender can then retransmit only the missing data segments (instead of everything since the first missing packet).

Prior to selective acknowledgment, if TCP lost packets 4 and 7 out of an 8-packet window, TCP would receive acknowledgment of only packets 1, 2, and 3. Packets 4 through 8 would have to be resent. With selective acknowledgment, TCP receives acknowledgment of packets 1, 2, 3, 5, 6, and 8. Only packets 4 and 7 have to be resent.

Refer to RFC 2018 for more detailed information on TCP selective acknowledgment.

The feature is used only when multiple packets are dropped within one TCP window. There is no performance impact when the feature is enabled but not used. To enable TCP selective acknowledgment, perform the following task in global configuration mode:

Task	Command
Enable TCP selective acknowledgment.	ip tcp selective-ack

Enabling TCP Timestamp

The TCP timestamp option provides better TCP round-trip time measurements. Because the timestamps are always sent and echoed in both directions and the timestamp value in the header is always changing, TCP header compression will not compress the outgoing packet. To allow TCP header compression over a serial link, the TCP timestamp option is disabled.

Refer to RFC 1323 for more detailed information on TCP timestamp.

To enable TCP timestamp, perform the following task in global configuration mode:

Task	Command
Enable TCP timestamp.	ip tcp timestamp

If you want to use TCP header compression over a serial line, TCP timestamp and TCP selective acknowledgment must be disabled; both features are disabled by default. To disable TCP selective acknowledgment once it is enabled, see the "Enabling TCP Selective Acknowledgment" section earlier in this chapter.

Setting the TCP Maximum Read Size

By default, for Telnet and rlogin, the maximum number of characters that TCP reads from the input queue at once is a very large number (the largest possible 32-bit positive number). Cisco does not recommend that you change this value. However, you can change this value by performing the following task in global configuration mode:

Task	Command
Set the TCP maximum read size for Telnet or rlogin.	**ip tcp chunk-size** *characters*

Setting the TCP Window Size

The default TCP window size is 2144 bytes. Cisco recommends you keep the default value, unless you know your router is sending large packets (greater than 536 bytes). To change the default window size, perform the following task in global configuration mode:

Task	Command
Set the TCP window size.	**ip tcp window-size** *bytes*

Setting the TCP Outgoing Queue Size

The default TCP outgoing queue size per connection is 5 segments if the connection has a TTY associated with it (such as a Telnet connection). If there is no TTY connection associated with it, the default queue size is 20 segments. To change the 5-segment default value, perform the following task in global configuration mode:

Task	Command
Set the TCP outgoing queue size.	**ip tcp queuemax** *packets*

CONFIGURING IP OVER WANS

You can configure IP over X.25, SMDS, Frame Relay, and DDR networks. To do this, configure the address mappings.

MONITORING AND MAINTAINING THE IP NETWORK

To monitor and maintain your network, perform the tasks in the following list:

- Clearing Caches, Tables, and Databases
- Monitoring and Maintaining the DRP Server Agent
- Clearing the Access List Counters
- Displaying System and Network Statistics

Clearing Caches, Tables, and Databases

You can remove all contents of a particular cache, table, or database. Clearing a cache, table, or database can become necessary when the contents of the particular structure have become, or are suspected to be, invalid.

The following table lists the tasks associated with clearing caches, tables, and databases. Perform the following tasks, as needed, in EXEC mode:

Task	Command
Clear the active IP accounting or checkpointed database when IP accounting is enabled.	**clear ip accounting** [checkpoint]
Clear TCP statistics.	**clear tcp statistics**

Monitoring and Maintaining the DRP Server Agent

To monitor and maintain the DRP Server Agent, perform the following tasks in EXEC mode:

Task	Command
Clear statistics being collected on DRP requests and responses.	**clear ip drp**
Display information about the DRP Server Agent.	**show ip drp**

Clearing the Access List Counters

The system counts how many packets pass each line of an access list; the counters are displayed by the **show access-lists** command. You can clear the counters of an access list by performing the following task in EXEC mode:

Task	Command
Clear the access list counters.	**clear access-list counters** *access-list-number* | *name*

Displaying System and Network Statistics

You can display specific statistics such as the contents of IP routing tables, caches, and databases. The resulting information can be used to determine resource utilization and to solve network problems.

These tasks are summarized in the table that follows; perform any of the following tasks in privileged EXEC mode:

Task	Command
Display the contents of one or all current access lists.	**show access-lists** [*access-list-number* | *name*]
Display the contents of current IP access lists.	**show ip access-list** [*access-list-number* | *name*]
Display the active IP accounting or checkpointed database.	**show ip accounting** [**checkpoint**]
Show statistics on TCP header compression.	**show ip tcp header-compression**
Display IP protocol statistics.	**show ip traffic**
Display the status of the standby router.	**show standby** [*interface* [*group*]] [**brief**]
Display TCP statistics.	**show tcp statistics**

IP SERVICES CONFIGURATION EXAMPLES

The following sections provide IP configuration examples:

- ICMP Services Example
- Simplex Ethernet Interfaces Example

- DRP Server Agent Example
- Numbered Access List Examples
- Named Access List Example

ICMP Services Example

The example that follows changes some of the ICMP defaults for the first Ethernet interface 0. Disabling the sending of redirects could mean that you do not think your devices on this segment will ever have to send a redirect. Disabling the Unreachables messages will have a secondary effect—it also will disable IP Path MTU Discovery, because path discovery works by having the Cisco IOS software send Unreachables messages. If you have a network segment with a small number of devices and an absolutely reliable traffic pattern—which could easily happen on a segment with a small number of little-used user devices—you would be disabling options that your device would be unlikely to use anyway.

```
interface ethernet 0
 no ip unreachables
 no ip redirects
```

Simplex Ethernet Interfaces Example

The following is an example of configuring a simplex Ethernet interface. Figure 4–2 illustrates how to configure IP on two routers sharing transmit-only and receive-only Ethernet connections.

Figure 4–2
Simplex Ethernet
connections on two routers.

Configuration for Router 1

```
interface ethernet 0
 ip address 128.9.1.1
 !
interface ethernet 1
 ip address 128.9.1.2
 transmit-interface ethernet 0
 !
 !use show interfaces command to find router2-MAC-address-E0
 arp 128.9.1.4 router2-MAC-address-E0 arpa
```

Configuration for Router 2

```
interface ethernet 0
 ip address 128.9.1.3
 transmit-interface ethernet 1
```

```
!
interface ethernet 1
 ip address 128.9.1.4
!
!use show interfaces command to find router1-MAC-address-E1
arp 128.9.1.1 router1-MAC-address-E1 arpa
```

DRP Server Agent Example

The following example enables the DRP Server Agent. Sources of DRP queries are limited by access list 1, which permits only queries from the host at 33.45.12.4. Authentication is also configured for the DRP queries and responses.

```
ip drp server
access-list 1 permit 33.45.12.4
ip drp access-group 1
ip drp authentication key-chain mktg
key chain mktg
 key 1
   key-string internal
exit
exit
```

Numbered Access List Examples

In the following example, network 36.0.0.0 is a Class A network whose second octet specifies a subnet; that is, its subnet mask is 255.255.0.0. The third and fourth octets of a network 36.0.0.0 address specify a particular host. Using access list 2, the Cisco IOS software would accept one address on subnet 48 and reject all others on that subnet. The last line of the list shows that the software would accept addresses on all other network 36.0.0.0 subnets.

```
access-list 2 permit 36.48.0.3
access-list 2 deny 36.48.0.0  0.0.255.255
access-list 2 permit 36.0.0.0  0.255.255.255
interface ethernet 0
 ip access-group 2 in
```

Implicit Masks in Access Lists Examples

IP access lists contain *implicit* masks. For instance, if you omit the mask from an associated IP host address access list specification, 0.0.0.0 is assumed to be the mask. Consider the following example configuration:

```
access-list 1 permit 0.0.0.0
access-list 1 permit 131.108.0.0
access-list 1 deny 0.0.0.0 255.255.255.255
```

For this example, the following masks are implied in the first two lines:

```
access-list 1 permit 0.0.0.0 0.0.0.0
access-list 1 permit 131.108.0.0 0.0.0.0
```

The last line in the configuration (using the **deny** keyword) can be left off, because IP access lists implicitly *deny* all other access. This is equivalent to finishing the access list with the following command statement:

```
access-list 1 deny 0.0.0.0 255.255.255.255
```

The following access list only allows access for those hosts on the three specified networks. It assumes that subnetting is not used; the masks apply to the host portions of the network addresses. Any hosts with a source address that does not match the access list statements will be rejected.

```
access-list 1 permit 192.5.34.0  0.0.0.255
access-list 1 permit 128.88.0.0  0.0.255.255
access-list 1 permit 36.0.0.0  0.255.255.255
! (Note: all other access implicitly denied)
```

To specify a large number of individual addresses more easily, you can omit the address mask that is all zeros from the **access-list** global configuration command. Thus, the following two configuration commands are identical in effect:

```
access-list 2 permit 36.48.0.3
access-list 2 permit 36.48.0.3  0.0.0.0
```

Extended Access List Examples

In the following example, the first line permits any incoming TCP connections with destination ports greater than 1023. The second line permits incoming TCP connections to the SMTP port of host 128.88.1.2. The last line permits incoming ICMP messages for error feedback.

```
access-list 102 permit tcp 0.0.0.0 255.255.255.255 128.88.0.0 0.0.255.255 gt 1023
access-list 102 permit tcp 0.0.0.0 255.255.255.255 128.88.1.2 0.0.0.0 eq 25
access-list 102 permit icmp 0.0.0.0 255.255.255.255 128.88.0.0 255.255.255.255
interface ethernet 0
 ip access-group 102 in
```

For another example of using an extended access list, suppose that you have a network connected to the Internet, and you want any host on an Ethernet to be able to form TCP connections to any host on the Internet. However, you do not want IP hosts to be able to form TCP connections to hosts on the Ethernet except to the mail (SMTP) port of a dedicated mail host.

SMTP uses TCP port 25 on one end of the connection and a random port number on the other end. The same two port numbers are used throughout the life of the connection. Mail packets coming in from the Internet will have a destination port of 25. Outbound packets will have the port numbers reversed. The fact that the secure system behind the router always will be accepting mail connections on port 25 is what makes it possible to separately control incoming and outgoing services. The access list can be configured on either the outbound or inbound interface.

In the following example, the Ethernet network is a Class B network with the address 128.88.0.0, and the mail host's address is 128.88.1.2. The keyword **established** is used only for the TCP protocol to indicate an established connection. A match occurs if the TCP datagram has the ACK or RST bits set, which indicate that the packet belongs to an existing connection.

```
access-list 102 permit tcp 0.0.0.0 255.255.255.255 128.88.0.0 0.0.255.255 established
access-list 102 permit tcp 0.0.0.0 255.255.255.255 128.88.1.2 0.0.0.0 eq 25
interface ethernet 0
 ip access-group 102 in
```

Named Access List Example

The following configuration creates a standard access list named Internet_filter and an extended access list named marketing_group:

```
interface Ethernet0/5
 ip address 2.0.5.1 255.255.255.0
 ip access-group Internet_filter out
 ip access-group marketing_group in
...
ip access-list standard Internet_filter
 permit 1.2.3.4
 deny any
ip access-list extended marketing_group
 permit tcp any 171.69.0.0 0.0.255.255 eq telnet
 deny tcp any any
 permit icmp any any
 deny udp any 171.69.0.0 0.0.255.255 lt 1024
 deny ip any any log
```

CHAPTER 5

IP Services Commands

Use the commands in this chapter to configure various IP services. For configuration information and examples on IP services, see Chapter 4, "Configuring IP Services."

ACCESS-CLASS

To restrict incoming and outgoing connections between a particular virtual terminal line (into a Cisco device) and the addresses in an access list, use the **access-class** line configuration command. To remove access restrictions, use the **no** form of this command.

> **access-class** *access-list-number* {**in** | **out**}
> **no access-class** *access-list-number* {**in** | **out**}

Syntax	Description
access-list-number	Number of an access list. This is a decimal number from 1 to 199.
in	Restricts incoming connections between a particular Cisco device and the addresses in the access list.
out	Restricts outgoing connections between a particular Cisco device and the addresses in the access list.

Default
No access lists are defined.

Command Mode
Line configuration

Usage Guidelines

This command first appeared in Cisco IOS Release 10.0.

Remember to set *identical restrictions* on all the virtual terminal lines because a user can connect to any of them. To display the access lists for a particular terminal line, use the **show line** EXEC command and specify the line number.

Examples

The following example defines an access list that permits only hosts on network 192.89.55.0 to connect to the virtual terminal ports on the router:

```
access-list 12 permit 192.89.55.0  0.0.0.255
  line 1 5
  access-class 12 in
```

The following example defines an access list that denies connections to networks other than network 36.0.0.0 on terminal lines 1 through 5:

```
access-list 10 permit 36.0.0.0 0.255.255.255
  line 1 5
  access-class 10 out
```

Related Commands

show line

ACCESS-LIST (EXTENDED)

To define an extended IP access list, use the extended version of the **access-list** global configuration command. To remove the access lists, use the **no** form of this command.

> **access-list** *access-list-number* [**dynamic** *dynamic-name* [**timeout** *minutes*]] {**deny** | **permit**}
> *protocol source source-wildcard destination destination-wildcard* [**precedence** *precedence*]
> [**tos** *tos*] [**log**]
> **no access-list** *access-list-number*

For Internet Control Message Protocol (ICMP), you can also use the following syntax:

> **access-list** *access-list-number* [**dynamic** *dynamic-name* [**timeout** *minutes*]] {**deny** | **permit**}
> **icmp** *source source-wildcard destination destination-wildcard* [*icmp-type* [*icmp-code*] |
> *icmp-message*] [**precedence** *precedence*] [**tos** *tos*] [**log**]

For Internet Group Management Protocol (IGMP), you can also use the following syntax:

> **access-list** *access-list-number* [**dynamic** *dynamic-name* [**timeout** *minutes*]] {**deny** | **permit**}
> **igmp** *source source-wildcard destination destination-wildcard* [*igmp-type*]
> [**precedence** *precedence*] [**tos** *tos*] [**log**]

For TCP, you can also use the following syntax:

> **access-list** *access-list-number* [**dynamic** *dynamic-name* [**timeout** *minutes*]] {**deny** | **permit**}
> **tcp** *source source-wildcard* [*operator port* [*port*]] *destination destination-wildcard*
> [*operator port* [*port*]] [**established**] [**precedence** *precedence*] [**tos** *tos*] [**log**]

For User Datagram Protocol (UDP), you can also use the following syntax:

> **access-list** *access-list-number* [**dynamic** *dynamic-name* [**timeout** *minutes*]] {**deny** | **permit**}
> **udp** *source source-wildcard* [*operator port* [*port*]] *destination destination-wildcard*
> [*operator port* [*port*]] [**precedence** *precedence*] [**tos** *tos*] [**log**]

CAUTION

Enhancements to this command are backward compatible; migrating from releases prior to Release 11.1 will convert your access lists automatically. However, releases prior to Release 11.1 are not upwardly compatible with these enhancements. Therefore, if you save an access list with these images and then use software prior to Release 11.1, the resulting access list will not be interpreted correctly. **This could cause you severe security problems.** Save your old configuration file before booting these images.

Syntax	*Description*
access-list-number	Number of an access list. This is a decimal number from 100 to 199.
dynamic *dynamic-name*	(Optional.) Identifies this access list as a dynamic access list.
timeout *minutes*	(Optional.) Specifies the absolute length of time (in minutes) that a temporary access list entry can remain in a dynamic access list. The default is an infinite length of time and allows an entry to remain permanently.
deny	Denies access if the conditions are matched.
permit	Permits access if the conditions are matched.
protocol	Name or number of an IP protocol. It can be one of the keywords **eigrp**, **gre**, **icmp**, **igmp**, **igrp**, **ip**, **ipinip**, **nos**, **ospf**, **tcp**, or **udp**, or an integer in the range 0 to 255 representing an IP protocol number. To match any Internet protocol (including ICMP, TCP, and UDP) use the keyword **ip**. Some protocols allow further qualifiers explained in the following descriptions.
source	Number of the network or host from which the packet is being sent. There are three ways to specify the source:
	Use a 32-bit quantity in four-part, dotted-decimal format.
	Use the keyword **any** as an abbreviation for a *source* and *source-wildcard* of 0.0.0.0 255.255.255.255.
	Use **host** *source* as an abbreviation for a *source* and *source-wildcard* of *source* 0.0.0.0.

Syntax	Description
source-wildcard	Wildcard bits to be applied to source. There are three ways to specify the source wildcard:
	• Use a 32-bit quantity in four-part, dotted-decimal format. Place ones in the bit positions you want to ignore.
	• Use the keyword **any** as an abbreviation for a *source* and *source-wildcard* of 0.0.0.0 255.255.255.255.
	• Use **host** *source* as an abbreviation for a *source* and *source-wildcard* of *source* 0.0.0.0.
destination	Number of the network or host to which the packet is being sent. There are three ways to specify the destination:
	• Use a 32-bit quantity in four-part, dotted-decimal format.
	• Use the keyword **any** as an abbreviation for the *destination* and *destination-wildcard* of 0.0.0.0 255.255.255.255.
	• Use **host** *destination* as an abbreviation for a *destination* and *destination-wildcard* of *destination* 0.0.0.0.
destination-wildcard	Wildcard bits to be applied to the destination. There are three ways to specify the destination wildcard:
	• Use a 32-bit quantity in four-part, dotted-decimal format. Place ones in the bit positions you want to ignore.
	• Use the keyword **any** as an abbreviation for a *destination* and *destination-wildcard* of 0.0.0.0 255.255.255.255.
	• Use **host** *destination* as an abbreviation for a *destination* and *destination-wildcard* of *destination* 0.0.0.0.
precedence *precedence*	(Optional.) Packets can be filtered by precedence level, as specified by a number from 0 to 7 or by name as listed in the section "Usage Guidelines."
tos *tos*	(Optional.) Packets can be filtered by type of service level, as specified by a number from 0 to 15 or by name as listed in the section "Usage Guidelines."
icmp-type	(Optional.) ICMP packets can be filtered by ICMP message type. The type is a number from 0 to 255.
icmp-code	(Optional.) ICMP packets that are filtered by ICMP message type can also be filtered by the ICMP message code. The code is a number from 0 to 255.

Syntax	Description
icmp-message	(Optional.) ICMP packets can be filtered by an ICMP message type name or ICMP message type and code name. The possible names are found in the section "Usage Guidelines."
igmp-type	(Optional.) IGMP packets can be filtered by IGMP message type or message name. A message type is a number from 0 to 15. IGMP message names are listed in the section "Usage Guidelines."
operator	(Optional.) Compares source or destination ports. Possible operands include **lt** (less than), **gt** (greater than), **eq** (equal), **neq** (not equal), and **range** (inclusive range).
	If the operator is positioned after the *source* and *source-wildcard*, it must match the source port.
	If the operator is positioned after the *destination* and *destination-wildcard*, it must match the destination port.
	The **range** operator requires two port numbers. All other operators require one port number.
port	(Optional.) The decimal number or name of a TCP or UDP port. A port number is a number from 0 to 65535. TCP port names are listed in the section "Usage Guidelines." TCP port names can only be used when filtering TCP. UDP port names are listed in the section "Usage Guidelines."
	TCP port names can only be used when filtering TCP. UDP port names can only be used when filtering UDP.
established	(Optional.) For the TCP protocol only; indicates an established connection. A match occurs if the TCP datagram has the ACK or RST bits set. The nonmatching case is that of the initial TCP datagram to form a connection.
log	(Optional.) Causes an informational logging message about the packet that matches the entry to be sent to the console. (The level of messages logged to the console is controlled by the **logging console** command.)
	The message includes the access list number, whether the packet was permitted or denied; the protocol, whether it was TCP, UDP, ICMP, or a number; and, if appropriate, the source and destination addresses and source and destination port numbers. The message is generated for the first packet that matches, and then at five-minute intervals, including the number of packets permitted or denied in the prior five-minute interval.

Default

An extended access list defaults to a list that denies everything. An extended access list is terminated by an implicit deny statement.

Command Mode

Global configuration

Usage Guidelines

The UDP form of this command first appeared in Cisco IOS Release 10.0. All other forms of the command, as well as the following arguments and keywords, first appeared in Cisco IOS Release 10.3:

> *source*
> *source-wildcard*
> *destination*
> *destination-wildcard*
> **precedence** *precedence*
> *icmp-type*
> *icm-code*
> *icmp-message*
> *igmp-type*
> *operator*
> *port*
> **established**

The following keywords and arguments first appeared in Cisco IOS Release 11.1:

> **dynamic** *dynamic-name*
> **timeout** *minutes*

You can use access lists to control the transmission of packets on an interface, control virtual terminal line access, and restrict contents of routing updates. The Cisco IOS software stops checking the extended access list after a match occurs.

Fragmented IP packets, other than the initial fragment, are immediately accepted by any extended IP access list. Extended access lists used to control virtual terminal line access or restrict contents of routing updates must not match against the TCP source port, the type of service value, or the packet's precedence.

> **NOTES**
>
> After an access list is created initially, any subsequent additions (possibly entered from the terminal) are placed at the end of the list. In other words, you cannot selectively add or remove access list command lines from a specific access list.

The following list contains precedence names:

- critical
- flash
- flash-override
- immediate
- internet
- network
- priority
- routine

The following list shows Type of Service (ToS) names:

- max-reliability
- max-throughput
- min-delay
- min-monetary-cost
- normal

ICMP message type names and ICMP message type and code names are the following:

- administratively-prohibited
- alternate-address
- conversion-error
- dod-host-prohibited
- dod-net-prohibited
- echo
- echo-reply
- general-parameter-problem
- host-isolated
- host-precedence-unreachable
- host-redirect
- host-tos-redirect

- host-tos-unreachable
- host-unknown
- host-unreachable
- information-reply
- information-request
- mask-reply
- mask-request
- mobile-redirect
- net-redirect
- net-tos-redirect
- net-tos-unreachable
- net-unreachable
- network-unknown
- no-room-for-option
- option-missing
- packet-too-big
- parameter-problem
- port-unreachable
- precedence-unreachable
- protocol-unreachable
- reassembly-timeout
- redirect
- router-advertisement
- router-solicitation
- source-quench
- source-route-failed
- time-exceeded
- timestamp-reply
- timestamp-request
- traceroute
- ttl-exceeded
- unreachable

The following list contains IGMP message names:

- dvmrp
- host-query
- host-report
- pim
- trace

The following list shows TCP port names that can be used instead of port numbers. Refer to the current Assigned Numbers RFC to find a reference to these protocols. Port numbers corresponding to these protocols can also be found by typing a ? in the place of a port number.

- bgp
- chargen
- daytime
- discard
- domain
- echo
- finger
- ftp
- ftp-data
- gopher
- hostname
- irc
- klogin
- kshell
- lpd
- nntp
- pop2
- pop3
- smtp
- sunrpc
- syslog
- tacacs-ds
- talk
- telnet

- time
- uucp
- whois
- www

UDP port names that can be used instead of port numbers are shown in the following list. Refer to the current Assigned Numbers RFC to find a reference to these protocols. Port numbers corresponding to these protocols can also be found by typing a ? in the place of a port number.

- biff
- bootpc
- bootps
- discard
- dns
- dnsix
- echo
- mobile-ip
- nameserver
- netbios-dgm
- netbios-ns
- ntp
- rip
- snmp
- snmptrap
- sunrpc
- syslog
- tacacs-ds
- talk
- tftp
- time
- who
- xdmcp

Examples

In the following example, serial interface 0 is part of a Class B network with the address 128.88.0.0, and the mail host's address is 128.88.1.2. The keyword **established** is used only for the TCP protocol to indicate an established connection. A match occurs if the TCP datagram has the ACK or RST bits set, which indicate that the packet belongs to an existing connection.

```
access-list 102 permit tcp 0.0.0.0 255.255.255.255 128.88.0.0 0.0.255.255 established
access-list 102 permit tcp 0.0.0.0 255.255.255.255 128.88.1.2 0.0.0.0 eq 25
interface serial 0
 ip access-group 102 in
```

The following example also permits Domain Naming System (DNS) packets and ICMP echo and echo reply packets:

```
access-list 102 permit tcp any 128.88.0.0 0.0.255.255 established
access-list 102 permit tcp any host 128.88.1.2 eq smtp
access-list 102 permit tcp any any eq domain
access-list 102 permit udp any any eq domain
access-list 102 permit icmp any any echo
access-list 102 permit icmp any any echo-reply
```

The following examples show how wildcard bits are used to indicate the bits of the prefix or mask that are relevant. They are similar to the bitmasks that are used with normal access lists. Prefix/mask bits corresponding to wildcard bits set to 1 are ignored during comparisons and prefix/mask bits corresponding to wildcard bits set to 0 are used in comparison.

The following code permits 192.108.0.0 255.255.0.0 but denies any more specific routes of 192.108.0.0 (including 192.108.0.0 255.255.255.0):

```
access-list 101 permit ip 192.108.0.0 0.0.0.0    255.255.0.0 0.0.0.0
access-list 101 deny ip 192.108.0.0 0.0.255.255  255.255.0.0 0.0.255.255
```

In the following example, 131.108.0/24 is permitted, but 131.108/16 and all other subnets of 131.108.0.0 are denied:

```
access-list 101 permit ip 131.108.0.0 0.0.0.0    255.255.255.0 0.0.0.0
access-list 101 deny ip 131.108.0.0 0.0.255.255 255.255.0.0   0.0.255.255
```

Related Commands

access-class
access-list (standard)
clear access-temp
distribute-list in
distribute-list out
ip access-group
ip access-list
logging console
priority-list
queue-list
show access-lists
show ip access-list

ACCESS-LIST (STANDARD)

To define a standard IP access list, use the standard version of the **access-list** global configuration command. To remove standard access lists, use the **no** form of this command.

> **access-list** *access-list-number* {**deny** | **permit**} *source* [*source-wildcard*]
> **no access-list** *access-list-number*

CAUTION

Enhancements to this command are backward compatible; migrating from releases prior to Release 10.3 will convert your access lists automatically. However, releases prior to Release 10.3 are not upwardly compatible with these enhancements. Therefore, if you save an access list with these images and then use software prior to Release 10.3, the resulting access list will not be interpreted correctly. This could cause you severe security problems! Save your old configuration file before booting these images.

Syntax	Description
access-list-number	Number of an access list. This is a decimal number from 1 to 99.
deny	Denies access if the conditions are matched.
permit	Permits access if the conditions are matched.
source	Number of the network or host from which the packet is being sent. There are two ways to specify the source:
	Use a 32-bit quantity in four-part, dotted-decimal format.
	Use the keyword **any** as an abbreviation for a *source* and *source-wildcard* of 0.0.0.0 255.255.255.255.
source-wildcard	(Optional.) Wildcard bits to be applied to the source. There are two ways to specify the source wildcard:
	Use a 32-bit quantity in four-part, dotted-decimal format. Place ones in the bit positions you want to ignore.
	Use the keyword **any** as an abbreviation for a *source* and *source-wildcard* of 0.0.0.0 255.255.255.255.

Default

The access list defaults to an implicit deny statement for everything. The access list is always terminated by an implicit deny statement for everything.

Command Mode

Global configuration

Usage Guidelines

This command first appeared in Cisco IOS Release 10.3.

Plan your access conditions carefully and be aware of the implicit deny statement at the end of the access list.

You can use access lists to control the transmission of packets on an interface, control virtual terminal line access, and restrict the contents of routing updates.

Use the **show access-lists** EXEC command to display the contents of all access lists.

Use the **show ip access-list** EXEC command to display the contents of one access list.

Examples

The following example of a standard access list allows access for only those hosts on the three specified networks. The wildcard bits apply to the host portions of the network addresses. Any host with a source address that does not match the access list statements will be rejected.

```
access-list 1 permit 192.5.34.0  0.0.0.255
access-list 1 permit 128.88.0.0  0.0.255.255
access-list 1 permit 36.0.0.0  0.255.255.255
! (Note: all other access implicitly denied)
```

To specify a large number of individual addresses more easily, you can omit the wildcard if it is all zeros. Thus, the following two configuration commands are identical in effect:

```
access-list 2 permit 36.48.0.3
access-list 2 permit 36.48.0.3  0.0.0.0
```

Related Commands

access-class
access-list (extended)
distribute-list in
distribute-list out
ip access-group
priority-list
queue-list
show access-lists
show ip access-list

CLEAR ACCESS-LIST COUNTERS

To clear the counters of an access list, use the **clear access-list counters** EXEC command.

    clear access-list counters {*access-list-number* | *name*}

Syntax	Description
access-list-number	Access list number from 0 to 1199 for which to clear the counters.
name	Name of an IP access list. The name cannot contain a space or quotation mark, and must begin with an alphabetic character to avoid ambiguity with numbered access lists.

Command Mode
EXEC

Usage Guidelines
This command first appeared in Cisco IOS Release 11.0.

Some access lists keep counters that count the number of packets that pass each line of an access list. The **show access-lists** command displays the counters as a number of matches. Use the **clear access-list counters** command to restart the counters for a particular access list to 0.

Example
The following example clears the counters for access list 101:

```
clear access-list counters 101
```

Related Commands
show access-lists

CLEAR IP ACCOUNTING

To clear the active or checkpointed database when IP accounting is enabled, use the **clear ip accounting** EXEC command.

> **clear ip accounting** [**checkpoint**]

Syntax	Description
checkpoint	(Optional.) Clears the checkpointed database.

Command Mode
EXEC

Usage Guidelines
This command first appeared in Cisco IOS Release 10.0.

You can also clear the checkpointed database by issuing the **clear ip accounting** command twice in succession.

Example

The following example clears the active database when IP accounting is enabled:

```
clear ip accounting
```

Related Commands

ip accounting
ip accounting-list
ip accounting-threshold
ip accounting-transits
show ip accounting

CLEAR IP DRP

To clear all statistics being collected on Director Response Protocol (DRP) requests and replies, use the **clear ip drp** EXEC command.

clear ip drp

Syntax   Description

This command has no arguments or keywords.

Command Mode

EXEC

Usage Guidelines

This command first appeared in Cisco IOS Release 11.2 F.

Example

The following example clears all DRP statistics:

```
clear ip drp
```

Related Commands

ip drp access-group
ip drp authentication key-chain

CLEAR TCP STATISTICS

To clear TCP statistics, use the **clear tcp statistics** EXEC command.

clear tcp statistics

Syntax   Description

This command has no arguments or keywords.

Command Mode

Privileged EXEC

Usage Guidelines

This command first appeared in Cisco IOS Release 11.3.

Example

The following example clears all TCP statistics:

```
clear tcp statistics
```

Related Commands

show tcp statistics

DENY

To set conditions for a named IP access list, use the **deny** access-list configuration command. To remove a deny condition from an access list, use the **no** form of this command.

> **deny** *source* [*source-wildcard*]
> **no deny** *source* [*source-wildcard*]

> **deny** *protocol source source-wildcard destination destination-wildcard* [**precedence**
>   *precedence*] [**tos** *tos*] [**log**]
> **no deny** *protocol source source-wildcard destination destination-wildcard*

For ICMP, you can also use the following syntax:

> **deny icmp** *source source-wildcard destination destination-wildcard* [*icmp-type* [*icmp-code*] |
>   *icmp-message*] [**precedence** *precedence*] [**tos** *tos*] [**log**]

For IGMP, you can also use the following syntax:

> **deny igmp** *source source-wildcard destination destination-wildcard* [*igmp-type*]
>   [**precedence** *precedence*] [**tos** *tos*] [**log**]

For TCP, you can also use the following syntax:

> **deny tcp** *source source-wildcard* [*operator port* [*port*]] *destination destination-wildcard*
>   [*operator port* [*port*]] [**established**] [**precedence** *precedence*] [**tos** *tos*] [**log**]

For UDP, you can also use the following syntax:

> **deny udp** *source source-wildcard* [*operator port* [*port*]] *destination destination-wildcard*
>   [*operator port* [*port*]] [**precedence** *precedence*] [**tos** *tos*] [**log**]

Syntax	Description
source	Number of the network or host from which the packet is being sent. There are two ways to specify the source:
	• Use a 32-bit quantity in four-part, dotted-decimal format.
	• Use the keyword **any** as an abbreviation for a *source* and *source-wildcard* of 0.0.0.0 255.255.255.255.
source-wildcard	(Optional.) Wildcard bits to be applied to the *source*. There are two ways to specify the source wildcard:
	• Use a 32-bit quantity in four-part, dotted-decimal format. Place ones in the bit positions you want to ignore.
	• Use the keyword **any** as an abbreviation for a *source* and *source-wildcard* of 0.0.0.0 255.255.255.255.
protocol	Name or number of an IP protocol. It can be one of the keywords **eigrp, gre, icmp, igmp, igrp, ip, ipinip, nos, ospf, tcp,** or **udp,** or an integer in the range 0 to 255 representing an IP protocol number. To match any Internet protocol (including ICMP, TCP, and UDP), use the keyword **ip.** Some protocols allow further qualifiers, which are described later.
source	Number of the network or host from which the packet is being sent. There are three ways to specify the source:
	• Use a 32-bit quantity in four-part, dotted-decimal format.
	• Use the keyword **any** as an abbreviation for a *source* and *source-wildcard* of 0.0.0.0 255.255.255.255.
	• Use **host** *source* as an abbreviation for a *source* and *source-wildcard* of *source* 0.0.0.0.
source-wildcard	Wildcard bits to be applied to source. There are three ways to specify the source wildcard:
	• Use a 32-bit quantity in four-part, dotted-decimal format. Place ones in the bit positions you want to ignore.
	• Use the keyword **any** as an abbreviation for a *source* and *source-wildcard* of 0.0.0.0 255.255.255.255.
	• Use **host** *source* as an abbreviation for a *source* and *source-wildcard* of *source* 0.0.0.0.

Syntax	Description
destination	Number of the network or host to which the packet is being sent. There are three ways to specify the destination: • Use a 32-bit quantity in four-part, dotted-decimal format. • Use the keyword **any** as an abbreviation for the *destination* and *destination-wildcard* of 0.0.0.0 255.255.255.255. • Use **host** *destination* as an abbreviation for a *destination* and *destination-wildcard* of *destination* 0.0.0.0.
destination-wildcard	Wildcard bits to be applied to the destination. There are three ways to specify the destination wildcard: • Use a 32-bit quantity in four-part, dotted-decimal format. Place ones in the bit positions you want to ignore. • Use the keyword **any** as an abbreviation for a *destination* and *destination-wildcard* of 0.0.0.0 255.255.255.255. • Use **host** *destination* as an abbreviation for a *destination* and *destination-wildcard* of destination 0.0.0.0.
precedence *precedence*	(Optional.) Packets can be filtered by precedence level, as specified by a number from 0 to 7 or by name as listed in the section "Usage Guidelines."
tos *tos*	(Optional.) Packets can be filtered by type of service level, as specified by a number from 0 to 15 or by name as listed in the "Usage Guidelines" section of the **access-list** (**extended**) command.
icmp-type	(Optional.) ICMP packets can be filtered by ICMP message type. The type is a number from 0 to 255.
icmp-code	(Optional.) ICMP packets which are filtered by ICMP message type can also be filtered by the ICMP message code. The code is a number from 0 to 255.
icmp-message	(Optional.) ICMP packets can be filtered by an ICMP message type name or ICMP message type and code name. The possible names are found in the "Usage Guidelines" section of the **access-list** (**extended**) command.
igmp-type	(Optional.) IGMP packets can be filtered by IGMP message type or message name. A message type is a number from 0 to 15. IGMP message names are listed in the "Usage Guidelines" section of the **access-list** (**extended**) command.

Syntax	Description
operator	(Optional.) Compares source or destination ports. Possible operands include **lt** (less than), **gt** (greater than), **eq** (equal), **neq** (not equal), and **range** (inclusive range).
	If the operator is positioned after the *source* and *source-wildcard*, it must match the source port.
	If the operator is positioned after the *destination* and *destination-wildcard*, it must match the destination port.
	The **range** operator requires two port numbers. All other operators require one port number.
port	(Optional.) The decimal number or name of a TCP or UDP port. A port number is a number from 0 to 65535. TCP and UDP port names are listed in the "Usage Guidelines" section of the **access-list (extended)** command. TCP port names can only be used when filtering TCP. UDP port names can only be used when filtering UDP.
established	(Optional.) For the TCP protocol only; indicates an established connection. A match occurs if the TCP datagram has the ACK or RST bits set. The nonmatching case is that of the initial TCP datagram to form a connection.
log	(Optional.) Causes an informational logging message about the packet that matches the entry to be sent to the console. (The level of messages logged to the console is controlled by the **logging console** command.)
	The message includes the access list number, whether the packet was permitted or denied; the protocol, whether it was TCP, UDP, ICMP, or a number; and, if appropriate, the source and destination addresses and source and destination port numbers. The message is generated for the first packet that matches, and then at 5-minute intervals, including the number of packets permitted or denied in the prior 5-minute interval.

Default

There is no specific condition under which a packet is denied passing the named access list.

Command Mode

Access-list configuration

Usage Guidelines

This command first appeared in Cisco IOS Release 11.2.

Use this command following the **ip access-list** command to specify conditions under which a packet cannot pass the named access list.

Example

The following example sets a deny condition for a standard access list named Internetfilter:

```
ip access-list standard Internetfilter
 deny 192.5.34.0  0.0.0.255
 permit 128.88.0.0  0.0.255.255
 permit 36.0.0.0  0.255.255.255
 ! (Note: all other access implicitly denied)
```

Related Commands

ip access-group
ip access-list
permit
show ip access-list

DYNAMIC

To define a named, dynamic-IP access list, use the **dynamic** access-list configuration command. To remove the access lists, use the **no** form of this command.

> **dynamic** *dynamic-name* [**timeout** *minutes*] {**deny** | **permit**} *protocol source source-wildcard destination destination-wildcard* [**precedence** *precedence*] [**tos** *tos*] [**log**]
> **no dynamic** *dynamic-name*

For ICMP, you can also use the following syntax:

> **dynamic** *dynamic-name* [**timeout** *minutes*] {**deny** | **permit**} **icmp** *source source-wildcard destination destination-wildcard* [*icmp-type* [*icmp-code*] | *icmp-message*] [**precedence** *precedence*] [**tos** *tos*] [**log**]

For IGMP, you can also use the following syntax:

> **dynamic** *dynamic-name* [**timeout** *minutes*] {**deny** | **permit**} **igmp** *source source-wildcard destination destination-wildcard* [*igmp-type*] [**precedence** *precedence*] [**tos** *tos*] [**log**]

For TCP, you can also use the following syntax:

> **dynamic** *dynamic-name* [**timeout** *minutes*] {**deny** | **permit**} **tcp** *source source-wildcard* [*operator port* [*port*]] *destination destination-wildcard* [*operator port* [*port*]] [**established**] [**precedence** *precedence*] [**tos** *tos*] [**log**]

For UDP, you can also use the following syntax:

> **dynamic** *dynamic-name* [**timeout** *minutes*] {**deny** | **permit**} **udp** *source source-wildcard* [*operator port* [*port*]] *destination destination-wildcard* [*operator port* [*port*]] [**precedence** *precedence*] [**tos** *tos*] [**log**]

─── CAUTION ───

Named IP access lists will not be recognized by any software release prior to Cisco IOS Release 11.2.

───

Syntax	*Description*
dynamic-name	Identifies this access list as a dynamic access list.
timeout *minutes*	(Optional.) Specifies the absolute length of time, in minutes, that a temporary access list entry can remain in a dynamic access list. The default is an infinite length of time and allows an entry to remain permanently.
deny	Denies access if the conditions are matched.
permit	Permits access if the conditions are matched.
protocol	Name or number of an IP protocol. It can be one of the keywords **eigrp, gre, icmp, igmp, igrp, ip, ipinip, nos, ospf, tcp,** or **udp,** or an integer in the range 0 to 255 representing an IP protocol number. To match any Internet protocol (including ICMP, TCP, and UDP), use the keyword **ip.** Some protocols allow further qualifiers which are described later.
source	Number of the network or host from which the packet is being sent. There are three ways to specify the source:
	Use a 32-bit quantity in four-part, dotted-decimal format.
	Use the keyword **any** as an abbreviation for a *source* and *source-wildcard* of 0.0.0.0 255.255.255.255.
	Use **host** *source* as an abbreviation for a *source* and *source-wildcard* of *source* 0.0.0.0.
source-wildcard	Wildcard bits to be applied to source. There are three ways to specify the source wildcard:
	• Use a 32-bit quantity in four-part, dotted-decimal format. Place ones in the bit positions you want to ignore.
	• Use the keyword **any** as an abbreviation for a *source* and *source-wildcard* of 0.0.0.0 255.255.255.255.
	• Use **host** *source* as an abbreviation for a *source* and *source-wildcard* of *source* 0.0.0.0.

Syntax	Description
destination	Number of the network or host to which the packet is being sent. There are three ways to specify the destination: • Use a 32-bit quantity in four-part, dotted-decimal format. • Use the keyword **any** as an abbreviation for the *destination* and *destination-wildcard* of 0.0.0.0 255.255.255.255. • Use **host** *destination* as an abbreviation for a *destination* and *destination-wildcard* of *destination* 0.0.0.0.
destination-wildcard	Wildcard bits to be applied to the destination. There are three ways to specify the destination wildcard: • Use a 32-bit quantity in four-part, dotted-decimal format. Place ones in the bit positions you want to ignore. • Use the keyword **any** as an abbreviation for a *destination* and *destination-wildcard* of 0.0.0.0 255.255.255.255. • Use **host** *destination* as an abbreviation for a *destination* and *destination-wildcard* of *destination* 0.0.0.0.
precedence *precedence*	(Optional.) Packets can be filtered by precedence level, as specified by a number from 0 to 7 or by name as listed in the section "Usage Guidelines."
tos *tos*	(Optional.) Packets can be filtered by type of service level, as specified by a number from 0 to 15 or by name as listed in the section "Usage Guidelines."
icmp-type	(Optional.) ICMP packets can be filtered by ICMP message type. The type is a number from 0 to 255.
icmp-code	(Optional.) ICMP packets which are filtered by ICMP message type can also be filtered by the ICMP message code. The code is a number from 0 to 255.
icmp-message	(Optional.) ICMP packets can be filtered by an ICMP message type name or ICMP message type and code name. The possible names are found in the section "Usage Guidelines."
igmp-type	(Optional.) IGMP packets can be filtered by IGMP message type or message name. A message type is a number from 0 to 15. IGMP message names are listed in the section "Usage Guidelines."

Syntax	Description
operator	(Optional.) Compares source or destination ports. Possible operands include **lt** (less than), **gt** (greater than), **eq** (equal), **neq** (not equal), and **range** (inclusive range).
	If the operator is positioned after the *source* and *source-wildcard*, it must match the source port.
	If the operator is positioned after the *destination* and *destination-wildcard*, it must match the destination port.
	The **range** operator requires two port numbers. All other operators require one port number.
port	(Optional.) The decimal number or name of a TCP or UDP port. A port number is a number from 0 to 65535. TCP and UDP port names are listed in the "Usage Guidelines" section of the **access-list (extended)** command. TCP port names can only be used when filtering TCP. UDP port names can only be used when filtering UDP.
established	(Optional.) For the TCP protocol only; indicates an established connection. A match occurs if the TCP datagram has the ACK or RST bits set. The nonmatching case is that of the initial TCP datagram to form a connection.
log	(Optional.) Causes an informational logging message about the packet that matches the entry to be sent to the console. (The level of messages logged to the console is controlled by the **logging console** command.)
	The message includes the access list number, whether the packet was permitted or denied; the protocol, whether it was TCP, UDP, ICMP, or a number; and, if appropriate, the source and destination addresses and source and destination port numbers. The message is generated for the first packet that matches, and then at 5-minute intervals, including the number of packets permitted or denied in the prior 5-minute interval.

Default

An extended access list defaults to a list that denies everything. An extended access list is terminated by an implicit deny statement.

Command Mode

Access-list configuration

Usage Guidelines

This command first appeared in Cisco IOS Release 11.2.

You can use named access lists to control the transmission of packets on an interface and restrict contents of routing updates. The Cisco IOS software stops checking the extended access list after a match occurs.

Fragmented IP packets, other than the initial fragment, are immediately accepted by any extended IP access list. Extended access lists used to control virtual terminal line access or restrict contents of routing updates must not match against the TCP source port, the type of service value, or the packet's precedence.

NOTES

After an access list is created initially, any subsequent additions (possibly entered from the terminal) are placed at the end of the list. In other words, you cannot selectively add or remove access list command lines from a specific access list.

The following list contains precedence names:

- critical
- flash
- flash-override
- immediate
- internet
- network
- priority
- routine

Type of Service (ToS) names include the following:

- max-reliability
- max-throughput
- min-delay
- min-monetary-cost
- normal

ICMP message type names and ICMP message type and code names are the following:

- administratively-prohibited
- alternate-address
- conversion-error

- dod-host-prohibited
- dod-net-prohibited
- echo
- echo-reply
- general-parameter-problem
- host-isolated
- host-precedence-unreachable
- host-redirect
- host-tos-redirect
- host-tos-unreachable
- host-unknown
- host-unreachable
- information-reply
- information-request
- mask-reply
- mask-request
- mobile-redirect
- net-redirect
- net-tos-redirect
- net-tos-unreachable
- net-unreachable
- network-unknown
- no-room-for-option
- option-missing
- packet-too-big
- parameter-problem
- port-unreachable
- precedence-unreachable
- protocol-unreachable
- reassembly-timeout
- redirect
- router-advertisement

- router-solicitation
- source-quench
- source-route-failed
- time-exceeded
- timestamp-reply
- timestamp-request
- traceroute
- ttl-exceeded
- unreachable

IGMP message names are the following:

- dvmrp
- host-query
- host-report
- pim
- trace

The following list contains TCP port names that can be used instead of port numbers. Refer to the current Assigned Numbers RFC to find a reference to these protocols. Port numbers corresponding to these protocols can also be found by typing a **?** in the place of a port number.

- bgp
- chargen
- daytime
- discard
- domain
- echo
- finger
- ftp
- ftp-data
- gopher
- hostname
- irc
- klogin
- kshell
- lpd

- nntp
- pop2
- pop3
- smtp
- sunrpc
- syslog
- tacacs-ds
- talk
- telnet
- time
- uucp
- whois
- www

The following UDP port names can be used instead of port numbers. Refer to the current Assigned Numbers RFC to find a reference to these protocols. Port numbers corresponding to these protocols can also be found by typing a **?** in the place of a port number.

- biff
- bootpc
- bootps
- discard
- dns
- dnsix
- echo
- mobile-ip
- nameserver
- netbios-dgm
- netbios-ns
- ntp
- rip
- snmp
- snmptrap
- sunrpc
- syslog

- tacacs-ds
- talk
- tftp
- time
- who
- xdmcp

Example

In the following example, the access list named washington is a dynamic access list:

```
ip access-group washington in
!
ip access-list extended washington
 dynamic testlist timeout 5
 permit ip any any
 permit tcp any host 185.302.21.2 eq 23
```

Related Commands

clear access-temp
distribute-list in
distribute-list out
ip access-group
ip access-list
logging console
priority-list
queue-list
show access-lists
show ip access-list

IP ACCESS-GROUP

To control access to an interface, use the **ip access-group** interface configuration command. To remove the specified access group, use the **no** form of this command.

    ip access-group {*access-list-number* | *name*}{**in** | **out**}
    no ip access-group {*access-list-number* | *name*}{**in** | **out**}

Syntax	Description
access-list-number	Number of an access list. This is a decimal number from 1 to 199.
name	Name of an IP access list as specified by an **ip access-list** command.
in	Filters on inbound packets.
out	Filters on outbound packets.

Default

Entering a keyword is strongly recommended, but if a keyword is not specified, **out** is the default.

Command Mode

Interface configuration

Usage Guidelines

This command first appeared in Cisco IOS Release 10.0. The *name* argument first appeared in Cisco IOS Release 11.2.

Access lists are applied on either outbound or inbound interfaces. For standard inbound access lists, after receiving a packet, the Cisco IOS software checks the source address of the packet against the access list. For extended access lists, the router also checks the destination access list. If the access list permits the address, the software continues to process the packet. If the access list rejects the address, the software discards the packet and returns an ICMP Host Unreachable message.

For standard outbound access lists, after receiving and routing a packet to a controlled interface, the software checks the source address of the packet against the access list. For extended access lists, the router also checks the destination access list. If the access list permits the address, the software transmits the packet. If the access list rejects the address, the software discards the packet and returns an ICMP Host Unreachable message.

If the specified access list does not exist, all packets are passed.

When you enable outbound access lists, you automatically disable autonomous switching for that interface. When you enable input access lists on any cBus or CxBus interface, you automatically disable autonomous switching for all interfaces (with one exception—an SSE configured with simple access lists can still switch packets on output only).

Example

The following example applies list 101 on packets outbound from Ethernet interface 0:

```
interface ethernet 0
  ip access-group 101 out
```

Related Commands

access-list (extended)
access-list (standard)
ip access-list
show access-lists

IP ACCESS-LIST

To define an IP access list by name, use the **ip access-list** global configuration command. To remove a named IP access list use the **no** form of this command.

ip access-list {standard | extended} *name*
no ip access-list {standard | extended} *name*

CAUTION

Named access lists will not be recognized by any software release prior to Cisco IOS Release 11.2.

Syntax	Description
standard	Specifies a standard IP access list.
extended	Specifies an extended IP access list.
name	Name of the access list. Names cannot contain a space or quotation mark, and must begin with an alphabetic character to prevent ambiguity with numbered access lists.

Default

There is no named IP access list.

Command Mode

Global configuration

Usage Guidelines

This command first appeared in Cisco IOS Release 11.2.

Use this command to configure a named IP access list as opposed to a numbered IP access list. This command will take you into the access-list configuration mode, where you must define the denied or permitted access conditions with the **deny** and **permit** commands. Specifying **standard** or **extended** with the **ip access-list** command determines the prompt you get when you enter access-list configuration mode.

Use the **ip access-group** command to apply the access-list to an interface.

Named access lists are not compatible with Cisco IOS releases prior to Release 11.2.

Example

The following example defines a standard access list named Internetfilter:

```
ip access-list standard Internetfilter
 permit 192.5.34.0  0.0.0.255
 permit 128.88.0.0  0.0.255.255
 permit 36.0.0.0  0.255.255.255
 ! (Note: all other access implicitly denied)
```

Related Commands

deny
ip access-group
permit
show ip access-list

IP ACCOUNTING

To enable IP accounting on an interface, use the **ip accounting** interface configuration command. To disable IP accounting, use the **no** form of this command.

> **ip accounting [access-violations]**
> **no ip accounting [access-violations]**

Syntax	*Description*
access-violations	(Optional.) Enables IP accounting with the ability to identify IP traffic that fails IP access lists.

Default

Disabled

Command Mode

Interface configuration

Usage Guidelines

This command first appeared in Cisco IOS Release 10.0.

IP accounting records the number of bytes (IP header and data) and packets switched through the system on a source and destination IP address basis. Only transit IP traffic is measured and only on an outbound basis; traffic generated by the router access server or terminating in this device is not included in the accounting statistics.

The **access-violations** option first appeared in IOS Release 10.3. If you specify the **access-violations** keyword, **ip accounting** provides information identifying IP traffic that fails IP access lists. Identifying IP source addresses that violate IP access lists alerts you to possible attempts to breach security. The data might also indicate that you should verify IP access list configurations. To receive a logging message on the console when an extended access list entry denies a packet access (to log violations), include the **log** keyword in the **access-list (extended)** command.

Statistics are accurate even if IP fast switching or IP access lists are being used on the interface.

IP accounting disables autonomous switching and SSE switching on the interface.

Example

The following example enables IP accounting on Ethernet interface 0:

```
interface ethernet 0
 ip accounting
```

Related Commands

access-list (extended)
clear ip accounting
ip accounting-list
ip accounting-threshold
ip accounting-transits
show ip accounting

IP ACCOUNTING-LIST

To define filters to control the hosts for which IP accounting information is kept, use the **ip accounting-list** global configuration command. To remove a filter definition, use the **no** form of this command.

>   **ip accounting-list** *ip-address wildcard*
>   **no ip accounting-list** *ip-address wildcard*

Syntax	Description
ip-address	IP address in dotted-decimal format.
wildcard	Wildcard bits to be applied to *ip-address*.

Default

No filters are defined.

Command Mode

Global configuration

Usage Guidelines

This command first appeared in Cisco IOS Release 10.0.

The source and destination address of each IP datagram is logically ANDed with the wildcard bits and compared with the *ip-address*. If there is a match, the information about the IP datagram will be entered into the accounting database. If there is no match, the IP datagram is considered a *transit* datagram and will be counted according to the setting of the **ip accounting-transits** global configuration command.

Example

The following example adds all hosts with IP addresses beginning with 192.31 to the list of hosts for which accounting information will be kept:

```
ip accounting-list 192.31.0.0 0.0.255.255
```

Related Commands

clear ip accounting
ip accounting
ip accounting-threshold
ip accounting-transits
show ip accounting

IP ACCOUNTING-THRESHOLD

To set the maximum number of accounting entries to be created, use the **ip accounting-threshold** global configuration command. To restore the default number of entries, use the **no** form of this command.

> **ip accounting-threshold** *threshold*
> **no ip accounting-threshold** *threshold*

Syntax	Description
threshold	Maximum number of entries (source and destination address pairs) that the Cisco IOS software accumulates.

Default

512 entries

Command Mode

Global configuration

Usage Guidelines

This command first appeared in Cisco IOS Release 10.0.

The accounting threshold defines the maximum number of entries (source and destination address pairs) that the software accumulates, preventing IP accounting from possibly consuming all available free memory. This level of memory consumption could occur in a router that is switching traffic for many hosts. Overflows will be recorded; see the monitoring commands for display formats.

The default accounting threshold of 512 entries results in a maximum table size of 12,928 bytes. Active and checkpointed tables can reach this size independently.

Example

The following example sets the IP accounting threshold to only 500 entries:

```
ip accounting-threshold 500
```

Related Commands

clear ip accounting
ip accounting
ip accounting-list
ip accounting-transits
show ip accounting

IP ACCOUNTING-TRANSITS

To control the number of transit records that are stored in the IP accounting database, use the **ip accounting-transits** global configuration command. To return to the default number of records, use the **no** form of this command.

    ip accounting-transits *count*
    no ip accounting-transits

Syntax	Description
count	Number of transit records to store in the IP accounting database.

Default

0

Command Mode

Global configuration

Usage Guidelines

This command first appeared in Cisco IOS Release 10.0.

Transit entries are those that do not match any of the filters specified by **ip accounting-list** global configuration commands. If no filters are defined, no transit entries are possible.

To maintain accurate accounting totals, the Cisco IOS software maintains two accounting databases: an active and a checkpointed database.

Example

The following example specifies that no more than 100 transit records are stored:

```
ip accounting-transits 100
```

Related Commands

clear ip accounting
ip accounting
ip accounting-list
ip accounting-threshold
show ip accounting

IP DRP ACCESS-GROUP

To control the sources of DRP queries to the DRP Server Agent, use the **ip drp access-group** global configuration command. To remove the access list, use the **no** form of this command.

    ip drp access-group *access-list-number*
    no ip drp access-group *access-list-number*

Syntax	*Description*
access-list-number	Number of a standard IP access list in the range 1 to 99.

Default

The DRP Server Agent will answer all queries.

Command Mode

Global configuration

Usage Guidelines

This command first appeared in Cisco IOS Release 11.2 F.

This command applies an access list to the interface, thereby controlling who can send queries to the DRP Server Agent.

If both an authentication key chain and an access group have been specified, both security measures must permit access before a request is processed.

Example

The following example configures access list 1, which permits only queries from the host at 33.45.12.4:

```
access-list 1 permit 33.45.12.4
ip drp access-group 1
```

Related Commands

ip drp authentication key-chain
show ip drp

IP DRP AUTHENTICATION KEY-CHAIN

To configure authentication on the DRP Server Agent for DistributedDirector, use the **ip drp authentication key-chain** global configuration command. To remove the key chain, use the **no** form of this command.

> **ip drp authentication key-chain** *name-of-chain*
> **no ip drp authentication key-chain** *name-of-chain*

Syntax	Description
name-of-chain	Name of the key chain containing one or more authentication keys.

Default

No authentication is configured for the DRP Server Agent.

Command Mode

Global configuration

Usage Guidelines

This command first appeared in Cisco IOS Release 11.2 F.

When a key chain and key are configured, the key is used to authenticate all Director Response Protocol requests and responses. The active key on the DRP Server Agent must match the active key on the primary agent. Use the **key** and **key-string** commands to configure the key.

Example

The following example configures a key chain named *ddchain*:

```
ip drp authentication key-chain ddchain
```

Related Commands

accept-lifetime
ip drp access-group
key
key chain
key-string
send-lifetime
show ip drp
show key chain

IP DRP SERVER

To enable the DRP Server Agent that works with DistributedDirector, use the **ip drp server** global configuration command. To disable the DRP Server Agent, use the **no** form of this command.

ip drp server
no ip drp server

Syntax   Description

This command has no arguments or keywords.

Default

Disabled

Command Mode

Global configuration

Usage Guidelines

This command first appeared in Cisco IOS Release 11.2 F.

Example

The following example enables the DRP Server Agent:

```
ip drp server
```

Related Commands

ip drp access-group
ip drp authentication key-chain
show ip drp

IP MASK-REPLY

To have the Cisco IOS software respond to ICMP mask requests by sending ICMP Mask Reply messages, use the **ip mask-reply** interface configuration command. To disable this function, use the **no** form of this command.

ip mask-reply
no ip mask-reply

Syntax   Description

This command has no arguments or keywords.

Default

Disabled

Command Mode

Interface configuration

Usage Guidelines

This command first appeared in Cisco IOS Release 10.0.

Example

The following example enables the sending of ICMP Mask Reply messages on Ethernet interface 0:

```
interface ethernet 0
  ip address 131.108.1.0 255.255.255.0
  ip mask-reply
```

IP MTU

To set the Maximum Transmission Unit (MTU) size of IP packets sent on an interface, use the **ip mtu** interface configuration command. To restore the default MTU size, use the **no** form of this command.

> **ip mtu** *bytes*
> **no ip mtu**

Syntax	Description
bytes	MTU in bytes.

Default

Minimum is 128 bytes; maximum depends on interface medium.

Command Mode

Interface configuration

Usage Guidelines

This command first appeared in Cisco IOS Release 10.0.

If an IP packet exceeds the MTU set for the interface, the Cisco IOS software will fragment it.

All devices on a physical medium must have the same protocol MTU in order to operate.

NOTES

Changing the MTU value (with the **mtu** interface configuration command) can affect the IP MTU value. If the current IP MTU value is the same as the MTU value, and you change the MTU value, the IP MTU value will be modified automatically to match the new MTU. However, the reverse is not true; changing the IP MTU value has no effect on the value for the **mtu** command.

Example

The following example sets the maximum IP packet size for the first serial interface to 300 bytes:

```
interface serial 0
  ip mtu 300
```

Related Commands

mtu

IP SOURCE-ROUTE

To allow the Cisco IOS software to handle IP datagrams with source routing header options, use the **ip source-route** global configuration command. To have the software discard any IP datagram containing a source-route option, use the **no** form of this command.

ip source-route
no ip source-route

Syntax   Description

This command has no arguments or keywords.

Default

Enabled

Command Mode

Global configuration

Usage Guidelines

This command first appeared in Cisco IOS Release 10.0.

Example

The following example enables the handling of IP datagrams with source routing header options:

```
ip source-route
```

Related Commands

ping (privileged)
ping (user)

IP TCP CHUNK-SIZE

To alter the TCP maximum read size for Telnet or rlogin, use the **ip tcp chunk-size** global configuration command. To restore the default value, use the **no** form of this command.

ip tcp chunk-size *characters*
no ip tcp chunk-size

Syntax

characters

Description

Maximum number of characters that Telnet or rlogin can read in one read instruction. The default value is 0, which Telnet and rlogin interpret as the largest possible 32-bit positive number.

Default

0

Command Mode

Global configuration

Usage Guidelines

This command first appeared in Cisco IOS Release 9.1.

It is unlikely you will need to change the default value.

Example

The following example sets the maximum TCP read size to 64000 bytes:

```
ip tcp chunk-size 64000
```

IP TCP COMPRESSION-CONNECTIONS

To specify the total number of header compression connections that can exist on an interface, use the **ip tcp compression-connections** interface configuration command. To restore the default, use the no form of this command.

ip tcp compression-connections *number*
no ip tcp compression-connections *number*

Syntax

number

Description

Number of connections the cache supports. It can be a number from 3 to 256.

Default

16 connections

Command Mode

Interface configuration

Usage Guidelines

This command first appeared in Cisco IOS Release 10.0.

You should configure one connection for each TCP connection through the specified interface. Each connection sets up a compression cache entry, so you are in effect specifying the maximum number of cache entries and the size of the cache. Too few cache entries for the specified interface can lead to degraded performance, while too many cache entries can lead to wasted memory.

NOTES

Both ends of the serial connection must use the same number of cache entries.

Example

In the following example, the first serial interface is set for header compression with a maximum of ten cache entries:

```
interface serial 0
  ip tcp header-compression
  ip tcp compression-connections 10
```

Related Commands

ip tcp header-compression
show ip tcp header-compression

IP TCP HEADER-COMPRESSION

To enable TCP header compression, use the **ip tcp header-compression** interface configuration command. To disable compression, use the **no** form of this command.

ip tcp header-compression [passive]
no ip tcp header-compression [passive]

Syntax	Description
passive	(Optional.) Compresses outgoing TCP packets only if incoming TCP packets on the same interface are compressed. If you do not specify the **passive** keyword, the Cisco IOS software compresses all traffic.

Default

Disabled

Command Mode

Interface configuration

Usage Guidelines

This command first appeared in Cisco IOS Release 10.0.

You can compress the headers of your TCP/IP packets in order to reduce the size of those packets. TCP header compression is supported on serial lines using Frame Relay, HDLC, or Point-to-Point (PPP) encapsulation. You must enable compression on both ends of a serial connection; RFC 1144 specifies the compression process. Compressing the TCP header can speed up Telnet connections dramatically. In general, TCP header compression is advantageous when your traffic consists of many small packets, but not for traffic that consists of large packets. Transaction processing (usually using terminals) tends to use small packets while file transfers use large packets. This feature only compresses the TCP header, so it has no effect on UDP packets or other protocol headers.

When compression is enabled, fast switching is disabled. This means that fast interfaces like T1 can overload the router. Consider your network's traffic characteristics before using this command.

Example

In the following example, the first serial interface is set for header compression with a maximum of ten cache entries:

```
interface serial 0
 ip tcp header-compression
 ip tcp compression-connections 10
```

Related Commands

ip tcp compression-connections

IP TCP PATH-MTU-DISCOVERY

To enable Path MTU Discovery for all new TCP connections from the router, use the **ip tcp path-mtu-discovery** interface configuration command. To disable the feature, use the **no** form of this command.

ip tcp path-mtu-discovery [age-timer {*minutes* | infinite}]
no ip tcp path-mtu-discovery [age-timer {*minutes* | infinite}]

Syntax	Description
age-timer *minutes*	(Optional.) Time interval, in minutes, after which TCP re-estimates the Path MTU with a larger Maximum Segment Size (MSS). The maximum is 30 minutes; the default is 10 minutes.
infinite	(Optional.) Turns off the age-timer.

Default

Disabled. If enabled, *minutes* defaults to 10 minutes.

Command Mode

Interface configuration

Usage Guidelines

This command first appeared in Cisco IOS Release 10.3. The **age-timer** and **infinite** keywords first appeared in Cisco IOS Release 11.2.

Path MTU Discovery is a method for maximizing the use of available bandwidth in the network between the end points of a TCP connection. It is described in RFC 1191. Existing connections are not affected when this feature is turned on or off.

Customers using TCP connections to move bulk data between systems on distinct subnets would benefit most by enabling this feature. This might include customers using RSRB with TCP encapsulation, STUN, X.25 Remote Switching (also known as XOT, or X.25 over TCP), and some protocol translation configurations.

The age timer is a time interval for how often TCP re-estimates the Path MTU with a larger MSS. By using the age timer, TCP Path MTU becomes a dynamic process. If MSS used for the connection is smaller than what the peer connection can handle, a larger MSS is tried every time the age timer expires. The discovery process is stopped when either the send MSS is as large as the peer negotiated, or the user has disabled the timer on the router. You can turn off the age-timer by setting it to infinite.

Example

The following example enables Path MTU Discovery:

```
ip tcp path-mtu-discovery
```

IP TCP QUEUEMAX

To alter the maximum TCP outgoing queue per connection, use the **ip tcp queuemax** global configuration command. To restore the default value, use the **no** form of this command.

ip tcp queuemax *packets*
no ip tcp queuemax

Syntax	Description
packets	Outgoing queue size of TCP packets. The default value is 5 segments if the connection has a TTY associated with it. If there is no TTY associated with it, the default value is 20 segments.

Default

The default value is 5 segments if the connection has a TTY associated with it. If there is no TTY associated with it, the default value is 20 segments.

Command Mode

Global configuration

Usage Guidelines

This command first appeared in Cisco IOS Release 10.0.

Changing the default value changes the 5 segments, not the 20 segments.

Example

The following example sets the maximum TCP outgoing queue to 10 packets:

```
ip tcp queuemax 10
```

IP TCP SELECTIVE-ACK

To enable TCP selective acknowledgment, use the **ip tcp selective-ack** global configuration command. To disable TCP selective acknowledgment, use the **no** form of this command.

     ip tcp selective-ack
     no ip tcp selective-ack

Syntax   Description

This command has no arguments or keywords.

Default

Disabled

Command Mode

Global configuration

Usage Guidelines

This command first appeared in Cisco IOS Release 11.2 F.

TCP might not experience optimal performance if multiple packets are lost from one window of data. With the limited information available from cumulative acknowledgments, a TCP sender can learn about only one lost packet per round trip time. An aggressive sender could retransmit packets early, but such retransmitted segments might have already been successfully received.

The TCP selective acknowledgment mechanism helps overcome these limitations. The receiving TCP returns selective acknowledgment packets to the sender, informing the sender about data that has been received. The sender can then retransmit only the missing data segments.

TCP selective acknowledgment improves overall performance. The feature is used only when multiple packets drop from a TCP window. There is no performance impact when the feature is enabled, but not used.

This command becomes effective only on new TCP connections opened after the feature is enabled.

This feature must be disabled if you want TCP header compression. You might disable this feature if you have severe TCP problems.

Refer to RFC 2018 for more detailed information on TCP selective acknowledgment.

Example

The following example enables the router to send and receive TCP selective acknowledgments:

```
ip tcp selective-ack
```

Related Commands

ip tcp header-compression

IP TCP SYNWAIT-TIME

To set a period of time that the Cisco IOS software waits while attempting to establish a TCP connection before it times out, use the **ip tcp synwait-time** global configuration command. To restore the default time, use the **no** form of this command.

ip tcp synwait-time *seconds*
no ip tcp synwait-time *seconds*

Syntax	Description
seconds	Time, in seconds, that the software waits while attempting to establish a TCP connection. It can be any integer from 5 to 300 seconds. The default is 30 seconds.

Default

30 seconds

Command Mode

Global configuration

Usage Guidelines

This command first appeared in Cisco IOS Release 10.0.

In previous versions of Cisco IOS software, the system would wait a fixed 30 seconds when attempting to establish a TCP connection. If your network contains Public Switched Telephone Network (PSTN) Dial-on-Demand Routing (DDR), the call setup time may exceed 30 seconds. This amount of time is not sufficient in networks that have dial-up asynchronous connections because it will affect your ability to Telnet over the link (from the router) if the link must be brought up. If you have this type of network, you might want to set this to the UNIX value of 75.

Because this is a host parameter, it does not pertain to traffic going *through* the router, just for traffic originated *at* this device. Because UNIX has a fixed 75-second timeout, hosts are unlikely to see this problem.

Example

The following example configures the Cisco IOS software to continue attempting to establish a TCP connection for 180 seconds:

```
ip tcp synwait-time 180
```

IP TCP TIMESTAMP

To enable TCP timestamp, use the **ip tcp timestamp** global configuration command. To disable TCP timestamp, use the **no** form of this command.

ip tcp timestamp
no ip tcp timestamp

Syntax   Description

This command has no arguments or keywords.

Default

Disabled

Command Mode

Global configuration

Usage Guidelines

This command first appeared in Cisco IOS Release 11.2 F.

TCP timestamp improves round-trip time estimates. Refer to RFC 1323 for more detailed information on TCP timestamp.

This feature must be disabled if you want to use TCP header compression.

Example

The following example enables the router to send TCP timestamps:

```
ip tcp timestamp
```

Related Commands

ip tcp header-compression

IP TCP WINDOW-SIZE

To alter the TCP window size, use the **ip tcp window-size** global configuration command. To restore the default value, use the **no** form of this command.

    ip tcp window-size *bytes*
    no ip tcp window-size

Syntax	*Description*
bytes	Window size in bytes. The maximum is 65535 bytes. The default value is 2144 bytes.

Default

2144 bytes

Command Mode

Global configuration

Usage Guidelines

This command first appeared in Cisco IOS Release 9.1.

Do not use this command unless you clearly understand why you want to change the default value.

If your TCP window size is set to 1000 bytes, for example, you can have 1 packet of 1000 bytes or 2 packets of 500 bytes, and so on. However, there is also a limit on the number of packets allowed in the window. There can be a maximum of 5 packets if the connection has TTY; otherwise there can be 20 packets.

Example

The following example sets the TCP window size to 1000 bytes:

```
ip tcp window-size 1000
```

IP UNREACHABLES

To enable the generation of ICMP Unreachable messages, use the **ip unreachables** interface configuration command. To disable this function, use the **no** form of this command.

    ip unreachables
    no ip unreachables

Syntax   Description

This command has no arguments or keywords.

Default

Enabled

Command Mode

Interface configuration

Usage Guidelines

This command first appeared in Cisco IOS Release 10.0.

If the Cisco IOS software receives a nonbroadcast packet destined for itself that uses a protocol it does not recognize, it sends an ICMP Protocol Unreachable message to the source.

If the software receives a datagram that it cannot deliver to its ultimate destination because it knows of no route to the destination address, it replies to the originator of that datagram with an ICMP Host Unreachable message.

This command affects all kinds of ICMP unreachable messages.

Example

The following example enables the generation of ICMP Unreachable messages, as appropriate, on an interface:

```
interface ethernet 0
  ip unreachables
```

PERMIT

To set conditions for a named IP access list, use the **permit** access-list configuration command. To remove a condition from an access list, use the **no** form of this command.

> **permit** *source* [*source-wildcard*]
> **no permit** *source* [*source-wildcard*]
> **permit** *protocol source source-wildcard destination destination-wildcard* [**precedence** *precedence*] [**tos** *tos*] [**log**]
> **no permit** *protocol source source-wildcard destination destination-wildcard* [**precedence** *precedence*] [**tos** *tos*] [**log**]

For ICMP, you can also use the following syntax:

> **permit icmp** *source source-wildcard destination destination-wildcard* [*icmp-type* [*icmp-code*] | *icmp-message*] [**precedence** *precedence*] [**tos** *tos*] [**log**]

For IGMP, you can also use the following syntax:

> **permit igmp** *source source-wildcard destination destination-wildcard* [*igmp-type*] [**precedence** *precedence*] [**tos** *tos*] [**log**]

For TCP, you can also use the following syntax:

> **permit tcp** *source source-wildcard* [*operator port* [*port*]] *destination destination-wildcard* [*operator port* [*port*]] [**established**] [**precedence** *precedence*] [**tos** *tos*] [**log**]

For UDP, you can also use the following syntax:

> **permit udp** *source source-wildcard* [*operator port* [*port*]] *destination destination-wildcard* [*operator port* [*port*]] [**precedence** *precedence*] [**tos** *tos*] [**log**]

Syntax	Description
source	Number of the network or host from which the packet is being sent. There are two ways to specify the source: • Use a 32-bit quantity in four-part, dotted-decimal format. • Use the keyword **any** as an abbreviation for a *source* and *source-wildcard* of 0.0.0.0 255.255.255.255.
source-wildcard	(Optional.) Wildcard bits to be applied to the source. There are two ways to specify the source wildcard: • Use a 32-bit quantity in four-part, dotted-decimal format. Place ones in the bit positions you want to ignore. • Use the keyword **any** as an abbreviation for a *source* and *source-wildcard* of 0.0.0.0 255.255.255.255.
protocol	Name or number of an IP protocol. It can be one of the keywords **eigrp, gre, icmp, igmp, igrp, ip, ipinip, nos, ospf, tcp,** or **udp,** or an integer in the range 0 to 255 representing an IP protocol number. To match any Internet protocol (including ICMP, TCP, and UDP), use the keyword **ip.** Some protocols allow further qualifiers, which will be described later.
source	Number of the network or host from which the packet is being sent. There are three ways to specify the source: • Use a 32-bit quantity in four-part, dotted-decimal format. • Use the keyword **any** as an abbreviation for a *source* and *source-wildcard* of 0.0.0.0 255.255.255.255. • Use **host** *source* as an abbreviation for a *source* and *source-wildcard* of *source* 0.0.0.0.

Syntax	*Description*
source-wildcard	Wildcard bits to be applied to source. There are three ways to specify the source wildcard:
	• Use a 32-bit quantity in four-part, dotted-decimal format. Place ones in the bit positions you want to ignore.
	• Use the keyword **any** as an abbreviation for a *source* and *source-wildcard* of 0.0.0.0 255.255.255.255.
	• Use **host** *source* as an abbreviation for a *source* and *source-wildcard* of *source* 0.0.0.0.
destination	Number of the network or host to which the packet is being sent. There are three ways to specify the destination:
	• Use a 32-bit quantity in four-part, dotted-decimal format.
	• Use the keyword **any** as an abbreviation for the *destination* and *destination-wildcard* of 0.0.0.0 255.255.255.255.
	• Use **host** *destination* as an abbreviation for a *destination* and *destination-wildcard* of *destination* 0.0.0.0.
destination-wildcard	Wildcard bits to be applied to the destination. There are three ways to specify the destination wildcard:
	• Use a 32-bit quantity in four-part, dotted-decimal format. Place ones in the bit positions you want to ignore.
	• Use the keyword **any** as an abbreviation for a *destination* and *destination-wildcard* of 0.0.0.0 255.255.255.255.
	• Use **host** *destination* as an abbreviation for a *destination* and *destination-wildcard* of *destination* 0.0.0.0.
precedence *precedence*	(Optional.) Packets can be filtered by precedence level, as specified by a number from 0 to 7 or by name as listed in the section "Usage Guidelines."
tos *tos*	(Optional.) Packets can be filtered by type of service level, as specified by a number from 0 to 15 or by name as listed in the "Usage Guidelines" section of the **access-list (extended)** command.
icmp-type	(Optional.) ICMP packets can be filtered by ICMP message type. The type is a number from 0 to 255.
icmp-code	(Optional.) ICMP packets which are filtered by ICMP message type can also be filtered by the ICMP message code. The code is a number from 0 to 255.

Syntax	Description
icmp-message	(Optional.) ICMP packets can be filtered by an ICMP message type name or ICMP message type and code name. The possible names are found in the "Usage Guidelines" section of the **access-list (extended)** command.
igmp-type	(Optional.) IGMP packets can be filtered by IGMP message type or message name. A message type is a number from 0 to 15. IGMP message names are listed in the "Usage Guidelines" section of the **access-list (extended)** command.
operator	(Optional.) Compares source or destination ports. Possible operands include **lt** (less than), **gt** (greater than), **eq** (equal), **neq** (not equal), and **range** (inclusive range).
	If the operator is positioned after the *source* and *source-wildcard*, it must match the source port.
	If the operator is positioned after the *destination* and *destination-wildcard*, it must match the destination port.
	The **range** operator requires two port numbers. All other operators require one port number.
port	(Optional.) The decimal number or name of a TCP or UDP port. A port number is a number from 0 to 65535. TCP and UDP port names are listed in the "Usage Guidelines" section of the **access-list (extended)** command. TCP port names can only be used when filtering TCP. UDP port names can only be used when filtering UDP.
established	(Optional.) For the TCP protocol only; indicates an established connection. A match occurs if the TCP datagram has the ACK or RST bits set. The nonmatching case is that of the initial TCP datagram to form a connection.
log	(Optional.) Causes an informational logging message about the packet that matches the entry to be sent to the console. (The level of messages logged to the console is controlled by the **logging console** command.)
	The message includes the access list number, whether the packet was permitted or denied; the protocol, whether it was TCP, UDP, ICMP, or a number; and, if appropriate, the source and destination addresses and source and destination port numbers. The message is generated for the first packet that matches, and then at 5-minute intervals, including the number of packets permitted or denied in the prior 5-minute interval.

Default

There are no specific conditions under which a packet passes the named access list.

Command Mode

Access-list configuration

Usage Guidelines

This command first appeared in Cisco IOS Release 11.2.

Use this command following the **ip access-list** command to define the conditions under which a packet passes the access list.

Example

The following example sets conditions for a standard access list named Internetfilter:

```
ip access-list standard Internetfilter
  deny 192.5.34.0  0.0.0.255
  permit 128.88.0.0  0.0.255.255
  permit 36.0.0.0  0.255.255.255
  ! (Note: all other access implicitly denied)
```

Related Commands

deny
ip access-group
ip access-list
show ip access-list

SHOW ACCESS-LISTS

To display the contents of current access lists, use the **show access-lists** privileged EXEC command.

    show access-lists [*access-list-number* | *name*]

Syntax	Description
access-list-number	(Optional.) Access list number to display. The range is 0 to 1199. The system displays all access lists by default.
name	(Optional.) Name of the IP access list to display.

Default

The system displays all access lists.

Command Mode

Privileged EXEC

Sample Display

The following is sample output from the **show access-lists** command when access list 101 is specified:

```
Router# show access-lists 101
Extended IP access list 101
    permit tcp host 198.92.32.130 any established (4304 matches)
    permit udp host 198.92.32.130 any eq domain (129 matches)
    permit icmp host 198.92.32.130 any
    permit tcp host 198.92.32.130 host 171.69.2.141 gt 1023
    permit tcp host 198.92.32.130 host 171.69.2.135 eq smtp (2 matches)
    permit tcp host 198.92.32.130 host 198.92.30.32 eq smtp
    permit tcp host 198.92.32.130 host 171.69.108.33 eq smtp
    permit udp host 198.92.32.130 host 171.68.225.190 eq syslog
    permit udp host 198.92.32.130 host 171.68.225.126 eq syslog
    deny   ip 150.136.0.0 0.0.255.255 224.0.0.0 15.255.255.255
    deny   ip 171.68.0.0 0.1.255.255 224.0.0.0 15.255.255.255 (2 matches)
    deny   ip 172.24.24.0 0.0.1.255 224.0.0.0 15.255.255.255
    deny   ip 192.82.152.0 0.0.0.255 224.0.0.0 15.255.255.255
    deny   ip 192.122.173.0 0.0.0.255 224.0.0.0 15.255.255.255
    deny   ip 192.122.174.0 0.0.0.255 224.0.0.0 15.255.255.255
    deny   ip 192.135.239.0 0.0.0.255 224.0.0.0 15.255.255.255
    deny   ip 192.135.240.0 0.0.7.255 224.0.0.0 15.255.255.255
    deny   ip 192.135.248.0 0.0.3.255 224.0.0.0 15.255.255.255
    deny   ip 192.150.42.0 0.0.0.255 224.0.0.0 15.255.255.255
```

An access list counter counts how many packets are allowed by each line of the access list. This number is displayed as the number of matches.

Related Commands

access-list (extended)
access-list (standard)
clear access-list counters
clear access-temp
ip access-list
show ip access-list

SHOW IP ACCESS-LIST

To display the contents of all current IP access lists, use the **show ip access-list** EXEC command.

> **show ip access-list** [*access-list-number* | *name*]

Syntax	Description
access-list-number	(Optional.) Number of the IP access list to display. This is a decimal number from 1 to 199.
name	(Optional.) Name of the IP access list to display.

Default

Displays all standard and extended IP access lists.

Command Mode

EXEC

Usage Guidelines

This command first appeared in Cisco IOS Release 10.3.

The **show ip access-list** command provides output identical to the **show access-lists** command, except that it is IP-specific and allows you to specify a particular access list.

Sample Displays

The following is sample output from the **show ip access-list** command when all are requested:

```
Router# show ip access-list

Extended IP access list 101
    deny udp any any eq ntp
    permit tcp any any
    permit udp any any eq tftp
    permit icmp any any
    permit udp any any eq domain
```

The following is sample output from the **show ip access-list** command when the name of a specific access list is requested:

```
Router# show ip access-list Internetfilter
Extended IP access list Internetfilter
    permit tcp any 171.69.0.0 0.0.255.255 eq telnet
    deny tcp any any
    deny udp any 171.69.0.0 0.0.255.255 lt 1024
    deny ip any any log
```

SHOW IP ACCOUNTING

To display the active accounting or checkpointed database or to display access list violations, use the **show ip accounting** EXEC command.

show ip accounting [checkpoint] [output-packets | access-violations]

Syntax	Description
checkpoint	(Optional.) Indicates that the checkpointed database should be displayed.
output-packets	(Optional.) Indicates that information pertaining to packets that passed access control and were successfully routed should be displayed. If neither the **output-packets** nor **access-violations** keyword is specified, **output-packets** is the default.
access-violations	(Optional.) Indicates that information pertaining to packets that failed access lists and were not routed should be displayed. If neither the **output-packets** nor **access-violations** keyword is specified, **output-packets** is the default.

Default

If neither the **output-packets** nor **access-violations** keyword is specified, **show ip accounting** displays information pertaining to packets that passed access control and were successfully routed.

Command Mode

EXEC

Usage Guidelines

This command first appeared in Cisco IOS Release 10.0. The **output-packets** and **access-violations** keywords first appeared in Cisco IOS Release 10.3.

If you do not specify any keywords, the **show ip accounting** command displays information about the active accounting database.

To display IP access violations, you must give the **access-violations** keyword on the command. If you do not specify the keyword, the command defaults to displaying the number of packets that have passed access lists and were routed.

To use this command, you must first enable IP accounting on a per-interface basis.

Sample Displays

Following is sample output from the **show ip accounting** command:

```
Router# show ip accounting

     Source          Destination        Packets         Bytes
  131.108.19.40    192.67.67.20            7              306
  131.108.13.55    192.67.67.20           67             2749
  131.108.2.50     192.12.33.51           17             1111
  131.108.2.50     130.93.2.1              5              319
  131.108.2.50     130.93.1.2            463            30991
  131.108.19.40    130.93.2.1              4              262
  131.108.19.40    130.93.1.2             28             2552
```

131.108.20.2	128.18.6.100	39	2184
131.108.13.55	130.93.1.2	35	3020
131.108.19.40	192.12.33.51	1986	95091
131.108.2.50	192.67.67.20	233	14908
131.108.13.28	192.67.67.53	390	24817
131.108.13.55	192.12.33.51	214669	9806659
131.108.13.111	128.18.6.23	27739	1126607
131.108.13.44	192.12.33.51	35412	1523980
192.31.7.21	130.93.1.2	11	824
131.108.13.28	192.12.33.2	21	1762
131.108.2.166	192.31.7.130	797	141054
131.108.3.11	192.67.67.53	4	246
192.31.7.21	192.12.33.51	15696	695635
192.31.7.24	192.67.67.20	21	916
131.108.13.111	128.18.10.1	16	1137

The following is sample output from the **show ip accounting access-violations** command; the output pertains to packets that failed access lists and were not routed:

```
Router# show ip accounting access-violations

   Source           Destination      Packets      Bytes      ACL
131.108.19.40     192.67.67.20          7          306        77
131.108.13.55     192.67.67.20         67         2749       185
131.108.2.50      192.12.33.51         17         1111       140
131.108.2.50      130.93.2.1            5          319       140
131.108.19.40     130.93.2.1            4          262        77
Accounting data age is 41
```

Table 5–1 describes the fields shown in the displays.

Table 5–1 *Show IP Accounting (and Access-Violation) Field Descriptions*

Field	Description
Source	Source address of the packet.
Destination	Destination address of the packet.
Packets	Number of packets transmitted from the source address to the destination address.
	With the **access-violations** keyword, the number of packets transmitted from the source address to the destination address that violated an access control list.
Bytes	Sum of the total number of bytes (IP header and data) of all IP packets transmitted from the source address to the destination address.
	With the **access-violations** keyword, the total number of bytes transmitted from the source address to the destination address that violated an access-control list.
ACL	Number of the access list of the last packet transmitted from the source to the destination that failed an access list filter.

Related Commands

clear ip accounting
ip accounting
ip accounting-list
ip accounting-threshold
ip accounting-transits

SHOW IP DRP

To display information about the DRP Server Agent for DistributedDirector, use the **show ip drp** EXEC command.

show ip drp

Syntax Description

This command has no arguments or keywords.

Command Mode

EXEC

Usage Guidelines

This command first appeared in Cisco IOS Release 11.2 F.

Sample Display

The following is sample output from the **show ip drp** command:

```
Router# show ip drp
Director Responder Protocol Agent is enabled
717 director requests, 712 successful lookups, 5 failures, 0 no route
Authentication is enabled, using "test" key-chain
```

Table 5–2 describes the significant fields in the display.

Table 5–2 *Show IP DRP Field Descriptions*

Field	Description
director requests	Number of DRP requests that have been received (including any using authentication key-chain encryption that failed).
successful lookups	Number of successful DRP lookups that produced responses.
failures	Number of DRP failures (for various reasons including authentication key-chain encryption failures).

Related Commands

ip drp access-group
ip drp authentication key-chain

SHOW IP TCP HEADER-COMPRESSION

To display statistics about TCP header compression, use the **show ip tcp header-compression** EXEC command.

 show ip tcp header-compression

Syntax   Description

This command has no arguments or keywords.

Command Mode

EXEC

Usage Guidelines

This command first appeared in Cisco IOS Release 10.0.

Sample Display

The following is sample output from the **show ip tcp header-compression** command:

```
Router# show ip tcp header-compression

TCP/IP header compression statistics:
  Interface Serial1: (passive, compressing)
    Rcvd:    4060 total, 2891 compressed, 0 errors
             0 dropped, 1 buffer copies, 0 buffer failures
    Sent:    4284 total, 3224 compressed,
             105295 bytes saved, 661973 bytes sent
             1.15 efficiency improvement factor
    Connect: 16 slots, 1543 long searches, 2 misses, 99% hit ratio
             Five minute miss rate 0 misses/sec, 0 max misses/sec
```

Table 5–3 describes the significant fields shown in the display.

Table 5–3   *Show IP TCP Header-Compression Field Descriptions*

Field	Description
Rcvd:	
total	Total number of TCP packets received.
compressed	Total number of TCP packets compressed.
errors	Unknown packets.

Table 5–3 *Show IP TCP Header-Compression Field Descriptions, Continued*

Field	Description
dropped	Number of packets dropped due to invalid compression.
buffer copies	Number of packets that had to be copied into bigger buffers for decompression.
buffer failures	Number of packets dropped due to a lack of buffers.
Sent:	
total	Total number of TCP packets sent.
compressed	Total number of TCP packets compressed.
bytes saved	Number of bytes reduced.
bytes sent	Number of bytes sent.
efficiency improvement factor	Improvement in line efficiency because of TCP header compression.
Connect:	
slots	Size of the cache.
long searches	Indicates the number of times the software had to look to find a match.
misses	Indicates the number of times a match could not be made. If your output shows a large miss rate, then the number of allowable simultaneous compression connections may be too small.
hit ratio	Percentage of times the software found a match and was able to compress the header.
Five minute miss rate	Calculates the miss rate over the previous 5 minutes for a longer-term (and more accurate) look at miss rate trends.
max misses/sec	Maximum value of the previous field.

Related Commands
ip tcp header-compression

SHOW IP TRAFFIC

To display statistics about IP traffic, use the **show ip traffic** EXEC command.

show ip traffic

Syntax *Description*

This command has no arguments or keywords.

Command Mode

EXEC

Usage Guidelines

This command first appeared in Cisco IOS Release 10.0.

Sample Display

The following is sample output from the **show ip traffic** command:

```
Router# show ip traffic

IP statistics:
  Rcvd: 98 total, 98 local destination
        0 format errors, 0 checksum errors, 0 bad hop count
        0 unknown protocol, 0 not a gateway
        0 security failures, 0 bad options
  Frags:0 reassembled, 0 timeouts, 0 too big
        0 fragmented, 0 couldn't fragment
  Bcast:38 received, 52 sent
  Sent: 44 generated, 0 forwarded
        0 encapsulation failed, 0 no route
ICMP statistics:
  Rcvd: 0 format errors, 0 checksum errors, 0 redirects, 0 unreachable
        0 echo, 0 echo reply, 0 mask requests, 0 mask replies, 0 quench
        0 parameter, 0 timestamp, 0 info request, 0 other
  Sent: 0 redirects, 3 unreachable, 0 echo, 0 echo reply
        0 mask requests, 0 mask replies, 0 quench, 0 timestamp
        0 info reply, 0 time exceeded, 0 parameter problem
UDP statistics:
  Rcvd: 56 total, 0 checksum errors, 55 no port
  Sent: 18 total, 0 forwarded broadcasts
TCP statistics:
  Rcvd: 0 total, 0 checksum errors, 0 no port
  Sent: 0 total
EGP statistics:
  Rcvd: 0 total, 0 format errors, 0 checksum errors, 0 no listener
  Sent: 0 total
IGRP statistics:
  Rcvd: 73 total, 0 checksum errors
  Sent: 26 total
HELLO statistics:
  Rcvd: 0 total, 0 checksum errors
```

```
      Sent: 0 total
  ARP statistics:
    Rcvd: 20 requests, 17 replies, 0 reverse, 0 other
    Sent: 0 requests, 9 replies (0 proxy), 0 reverse
  Probe statistics:
    Rcvd: 6 address requests, 0 address replies
  0 proxy name requests, 0 other
    Sent: 0 address requests, 4 address replies (0 proxy)
         0 proxy name replies
```

Table 5–4 describes the significant fields shown in the display.

Table 5–4 *Show IP Traffic Field Descriptions*

Field	Description
format errors	A gross error in the packet format, such as an impossible Internet header length.
bad hop count	Occurs when a packet is discarded because its TTL field was decremented to zero.
encapsulation failed	Usually indicates that the router had no ARP request entry and therefore did not send a datagram.
no route	Counted when the Cisco IOS software discards a datagram that it was unable to route.
proxy name reply	Counted when the Cisco IOS software sends an ARP or Probe Reply on behalf of another host. The display shows the number of probe proxy requests that have been received and the number of responses that have been sent.

SHOW STANDBY

To display Hot Standby Router Protocol (HSRP) information, use the **show standby** EXEC command.

show standby [*type number* [*group*]] [**brief**]

Syntax	Description
type number	(Optional.) Interface type and number for which output is displayed.
group	(Optional.) Group number on the interface for which output is displayed.
brief	(Optional.) A single line of output summarizes each standby group.

Command Mode

EXEC

Usage Guidelines

This command first appeared in Cisco IOS Release 10.0.

If you want to specify a *group*, you must also specify an interface *type* and *number*.

Sample Displays

The following is sample output from the **show standby** command:

```
Router# show standby

Ethernet0 - Group 0
  Local state is Active, priority 100, may preempt
  Hellotime 3 holdtime 10
  Next hello sent in 0:00:00
  Hot standby IP address is 198.92.72.29 configured
  Active router is local
  Standby router is 198.92.72.21 expires in 0:00:07
  Tracking interface states for 2 interfaces, 2 up:
    Up    Ethernet0
    Up    Serial0
```

The following is sample output from the **show standby** command with a specific interface and the **brief** keyword:

```
Router# show standby ethernet0 brief

Interface  Grp Prio P State   Active addr    Standby addr  Group addr
Et0         0   100   Standby 171.69.232.33  local         172.19.48.254
```

Table 5–5 describes the fields in the display.

Table 5–5 *Show Standby Field Descriptions*

Field	Description
Ethernet0 - Group 0	Interface type and number and Hot Standby group number for the interface.
Local state is ...	State of local router, which can be one of the following: • Active—Current Hot Standby router. • Standby—Router next in line to be the Hot Standby router.
priority	Priority value of the router based on the **standby priority, standby preempt** command.
may preempt (indicated by P in the **brief** output)	Indicates that the router will attempt to assume control as the active router if its priority is greater than the current active router.
Hellotime	Time between hello packets, in seconds, based on the **standby timers** command.

Table 5-5 *Show Standby Field Descriptions, Continued*

Field	Description
holdtime	Time, in seconds, before other routers declare the active or standby router to be down, based on the **standby timers** command.
Next hello sent in ...	Time in which the Cisco IOS software will send the next hello packet (in hours:minutes:seconds).
Hot Standby IP address is ... configured	IP address of the current Hot Standby router. The word "configured" indicates that this address is known through the **standby ip** command. Otherwise, the address was learned dynamically through HSRP hello packets from other routers that do have the HSRP IP address configured.
Active router is ...	Value can be "local" or an IP address; this is the address of the current active Hot Standby router.
Standby router is ...	Value can be "local" or an IP address; this is the address of the "standby" router (the router that is next in line to be the Hot Standby router).
expires in	Time, in hours:minutes:seconds, in which the standby router will no longer be the standby router if the local router receives no hello packets from it.
Tracking interface states for ...	List of interfaces that are being tracked and their corresponding states. Based on the **standby track** command.

Related Commands

standby authentication
standby ip
standby priority, standby preempt
standby timers
standby track
standby use-bia

SHOW TCP STATISTICS

To display TCP statistics, use the **show tcp statistics** EXEC command.

    show tcp statistics

Syntax   Description

This command has no arguments or keywords.

Command Mode

EXEC

Usage Guidelines

This command first appeared in Cisco IOS Release 11.3.

Sample Display

The following is sample output from the **show tcp statistics** command:

```
Router# show tcp statistics

Rcvd: 210 Total, 0 no port
        0 checksum error, 0 bad offset, 0 too short
        132 packets (26640 bytes) in sequence
        5 dup packets (502 bytes)
        0 partially dup packets (0 bytes)
        0 out-of-order packets (0 bytes)
        0 packets (0 bytes) with data after window
        0 packets after close
        0 window probe packets, 0 window update packets
        0 dup ack packets, 0 ack packets with unsend data
        69 ack packets (3044 bytes)
Sent: 175 Total, 0 urgent packets
        16 control packets (including 1 retransmitted)
        69 data packets (3029 bytes)
        0 data packets (0 bytes) retransmitted
        73 ack only packets (49 delayed)
        0 window probe packets, 17 window update packets
    7 Connections initiated, 1 connections accepted, 8 connections established
    8 Connections closed (including 0 dropped, 0 embryonic dropped)
    1 Total rxmt timeout, 0 connections dropped in rxmt timeout
    0 Keepalive timeout, 0 keepalive probe, 0 Connections dropped in keepalive
```

Table 5–6 describes the significant fields shown in the display.

Table 5–6   *Show TCP Statistics Field Descriptions*

Field	Description
Rcvd:	Statistics in this section refer to packets received by the router.
Total	Total packets received.
no port	Number of packets received with no port.
checksum error	Number of packets received with checksum error.
bad offset	Number of packets received with bad offset to data.
too short	Number of packets received that were too short.

Table 5–6 *Show TCP Statistics Field Descriptions, Continued*

Field	Description
packets in sequence	Number of data packets received in sequence.
dup packets	Number of duplicate packets received.
partially dup packets	Number of packets received with partially duplicated data.
out-of-order packets	Number of out-of-order packets received.
packets with data after window	Number of packets received with data that exceeded the receiver's window size.
packets after close	Number of packets received after the connection had closed.
window probe packets	Number of window probe packets received.
window update packets	Number of window update packets received.
dup ack packets	Number of duplicate acknowledgment packets received.
ack packets with unsent data	Number of acknowledgment packets with unsent data received.
ack packets	Number of acknowledgment packets received.
Sent	Statistics in this section refer to packets sent by the router.
Total	Total number of packets sent.
urgent packets	Number of urgent packets sent.
control packets	Number of control packets (SYN, FIN, or RST) sent.
data packets	Number of data packets sent.
data packets retransmitted	Number of data packets retransmitted.
ack only packets	Number of packets sent that are acknowledgments only.
window probe packets	Number of window probe packets sent.
window update packets	Number of window update packets sent.
Connections initiated	Number of connections initiated.
connections accepted	Number of connections accepted.
connections established	Number of connections established.
Connections closed	Number of connections closed.

Table 5–6 *Show TCP Statistics Field Descriptions, Continued*

Field	Description
Total rxmt timeout	Number of times the router tried to retransmit, but timed out.
Connections dropped in rxmit timeout	Number of connections dropped in retransmit timeout.
Keepalive timeout	Number of keepalive packets in timeout.
Keepalive probe	Number of keepalive probes.
Connections dropped in keepalive	Number of connections dropped in keepalive.

Related Commands

clear tcp statistics

STANDBY AUTHENTICATION

To configure an authentication string for the HSRP, use the **standby authentication** interface configuration command. To delete an authentication string, use the **no** form of this command.

> **standby** [*group-number*] **authentication** *string*
> **no standby** [*group-number*] **authentication** *string*

Syntax	Description
group-number	(Optional.) Group number on the interface to which this authentication string applies.
string	Authentication string. It can be up to eight characters in length. The default string is **cisco**.

Defaults

The defaults are the following:

- *group-number*: 0
- *string*: **cisco**

Command Mode

Interface configuration

Usage Guidelines

This command first appeared in Cisco IOS Release 10.0.

The authentication string is transmitted unencrypted in all HSRP messages. The same authentication string must be configured on all routers and access servers on a cable to ensure interoperation. Authentication mismatch prevents a device from learning the designated Hot Standby IP address and the Hot Standby timer values from other routers configured with HSRP. Authentication mismatch does not prevent protocol events such as one router taking over as the designated router.

When group number 0 is used, no group number is written to NVRAM, providing backward compatibility.

Example

In the following example, "word" is configured as the authentication string required to allow Hot Standby routers in group 1 to interoperate:

```
interface ethernet 0
 standby 1 authentication word
```

STANDBY IP

To activate HSRP, use the **standby ip** interface configuration command. To disable HSRP, use the **no** form of this command.

> **standby** [*group-number*] **ip** [*ip-address* [**secondary**]]
> **no standby** [*group-number*] **ip** [*ip-address*]

Syntax	Description
group-number	(Optional.) Group number on the interface for which HSRP is being activated. Default is 0.
ip-address	(Optional.) IP address of the Hot Standby Router interface.
secondary	(Optional.) Indicates that the IP address is a secondary Hot Standby Router interface. Useful on interfaces with primary and secondary addresses; you can configure primary and secondary HSRP addresses.

Defaults

The defaults are the following:

- *group-number*: 0.
- HSRP is disabled.

Command Mode

Interface configuration

Usage Guidelines

This command first appeared in Cisco IOS Release 10.0. The *group-number* argument first appeared in IOS 10.3. The **secondary** keyword first appeared in Cisco IOS 11.1.

The **standby ip** command activates HSRP on the configured interface. If an IP address is specified, that address is used as the designated address for the Hot Standby group. If no IP address is specified, the designated address is learned through the standby function. For HSRP to elect a designated router, at least one router on the cable must have been configured with, or have learned, the designated address. Configuring the designated address on the active router always overrides a designated address that is currently in use.

When the **standby ip** command is enabled on an interface, the handling of proxy ARP requests is changed (unless proxy ARP was disabled). If the interface's Hot Standby state is active, proxy ARP requests are answered using the Hot Standby group's MAC address. If the interface is in a different state, proxy ARP responses are suppressed.

When group number 0 is used, no group number is written to NVRAM, providing backward compatibility.

Examples

In the following example, HSRP is enabled for group 1 on Ethernet interface 0; the IP address used by the Hot Standby group will be learned using HSRP:

```
interface ethernet 0
  standby 1 ip
```

In the following example, all three virtual IP addresses appear in the ARP table using the same (single) virtual MAC address. All three virtual IP addresses are using the same HSRP group (group 0).

```
ip address 1.1.1.1. 255.255.255.0
ip address 1.2.2.2. 255.255.255.0 secondary
ip address 1.3.3.3. 255.255.255.0 secondary
ip address 1.4.4.4. 255.255.255.0 secondary
standby ip 1.1.1.254
standby ip 1.2.2.254 secondary
standby ip 1.3.3.254 secondary
```

STANDBY PRIORITY, STANDBY PREEMPT

To configure HSRP priority, preemption, and preemption delay, use the **standby** interface configuration command. To restore the default values, use the **no** form of this command.

> **standby** [*group-number*] **priority** *priority* [**preempt** [**delay** *delay*]]
> **standby** [*group-number*] [**priority** *priority*] **preempt** [**delay** *delay*]

> **no standby** [*group-number*] **priority** *priority* [**preempt** [**delay** *delay*]]
> **no standby** [*group-number*] [**priority** *priority*] **preempt** [**delay** *delay*]

Syntax	Description
group-number	(Optional.) Group number on the interface to which the other arguments in this command apply.
priority *priority*	(Optional.) Priority value that prioritizes a potential Hot Standby router. The range is 1 to 255; the default is 100.
preempt	(Optional.) The router is configured to preempt, which means that when the local router has a Hot Standby priority higher than the current active router, the local router should attempt to assume control as the active router. If **preempt** is not configured, the local router assumes control as the active router only if it receives information indicating that there is no router currently in the active state (acting as the designated router).
delay *delay*	(Optional.) Time in seconds. The *delay* argument causes the local router to postpone taking over the active role for *delay* seconds since that router was last restarted. The range is 0 to 3600 seconds (1 hour). The default is 0 seconds (no delay).

Defaults

The defaults are the following:

- *group-number*: 0.
- *priority*: 100.
- *delay*: 0 seconds; if the router wants to preempt, it will do so immediately.

Command Mode

Interface configuration

Usage Guidelines

This command first appeared in Cisco IOS Release 11.3.

When using this command, you must specify at least one keyword (**priority** or **preempt**), or you can specify both. When group number 0 is used, no group number is written to NVRAM, providing backward compatibility.

The assigned priority is used to help select the active and standby routers. Assuming preemption is enabled, the router with the highest priority becomes the designated active router. In case of ties, the primary IP addresses are compared, and the higher IP address has priority.

Note that the device's priority can change dynamically if an interface is configured with the **standby track** command and another interface on the router goes down.

When a router first comes up, it does not have a complete routing table. If it is configured to preempt, it will become the active router, yet it is unable to provide adequate routing services. This problem is solved by configuring a delay before the preempting router actually preempts the currently active router.

Example

In the following example, the router has a priority of 120 (higher than the default value) and will wait for 300 seconds (5 minutes) before attempting to become the active router:

```
interface ethernet 0
  standby ip 172.19.108.254
  standby priority 120 preempt delay 300
```

Related Commands

standby track

STANDBY TIMERS

To configure the time between hellos and the time before other routers declare the active Hot Standby or standby router to be down, use the **standby timers** interface configuration command. To restore the timers to their default values, use the **no** form of this command.

> **standby** [*group-number*] **timers** *hellotime holdtime*
> **no standby** [*group-number*] **timers** *hellotime holdtime*

Syntax	Description
group-number	(Optional.) Group number on the interface to which the timers apply. The default is 0.
hellotime	Hello interval in seconds; it is an integer from 1 to 255. The default is 3 seconds.
holdtime	Time in seconds before the active or standby router is declared to be down; it is an integer from 1 to 255. The default is 10 seconds.

Defaults

The defaults are the following:

- *group-number*: 0
- *hellotime*: 3 second
- *holdtime*: 10 seconds

Command Mode

Interface configuration

Usage Guidelines

This command first appeared in Cisco IOS Release 10.0.

The **standby timers** command configures the time between standby hellos and the time before other routers declare the active or standby router to be down. Routers or access servers on which timer values are not configured can learn timer values from the active or standby router. The timers configured on the active router always override any other timer settings. All routers in a Hot Standby group should use the same timer values. Normally, holdtime is greater than or equal to 3 times *hellotime* (*holdtime* $\geq$ 3 * *hellotime*).

When group number 0 is used, no group number is written to NVRAM, providing backward compatibility.

Example

In the following example, for group number 1 on Ethernet interface 0, the time between hello packets is set to 5 seconds, and the time after which a router is considered to be down is set to 15 seconds:

```
interface ethernet 0
  standby 1 ip
  standby 1 timers 5 15
```

STANDBY TRACK

To configure an interface so that the Hot Standby priority changes based on the availability of other interfaces, use the **standby track** interface configuration command. To remove the tracking, use the **no** form of this command.

> **standby** [*group-number*] **track** *type number* [*interface-priority*]
> **no standby** [*group-number*] **track** *type number* [*interface-priority*]

Syntax	Description
group-number	(Optional.) Group number on the interface to which the tracking applies.
type	Interface type (combined with interface number) that will be tracked.
number	Interface number (combined with interface type) that will be tracked.
interface-priority	(Optional.) Amount by which the Hot Standby priority for the router is decremented (or incremented) when the interface goes down (or comes back up). The default value is 10.

Defaults

The defaults are the following:

- *group-number*: 0
- *interface-priority*: 10

Command Mode

Interface configuration

Usage Guidelines

This command first appeared in Cisco IOS Release 10.3.

This command ties the router's Hot Standby priority to the availability of its interfaces. It is useful for tracking interfaces that are not configured for the Hot Standby Router Protocol.

When a tracked interface goes down, the Hot Standby priority decreases by 10. If an interface is not tracked, its state changes do not affect the Hot Standby priority. For each interface configured for Hot Standby, you can configure a separate list of interfaces to be tracked.

The optional argument *interface-priority* specifies how much to decrement the Hot Standby priority by when a tracked interface goes down. When the tracked interface comes back up, the priority is incremented by the same amount.

When multiple tracked interfaces are down and *interface-priority* values have been configured, these configured priority decrements are cumulative. If tracked interfaces are down, but none of them were configured with priority decrements, the default decrement is 10 and it is noncumulative.

When group number 0 is used, no group number is written to NVRAM, providing backward compatibility.

Example

In the following example, Ethernet interface 1 tracks Ethernet interface 0 and serial interface 0. If one or both of these two interfaces go down, the Hot Standby priority of the router decreases by 10. Because the default Hot Standby priority is 100, the priority becomes 90 when one or both of the tracked interfaces go down.

```
interface ethernet 1
  ip address 198.92.72.37 255.255.255.240
  no ip redirects
  standby track ethernet 0
  standby track serial 0
  standby preempt
  standby ip 198.92.72.46
```

Related Commands

standby priority, standby preempt

STANDBY USE-BIA

To configure HSRP to use the interface's burned-in address as its virtual MAC address, instead of the preassigned MAC address (on Ethernet and FDDI) or the functional address (on Token Ring), use the **standby use-bia** interface configuration command. To restore the default virtual MAC address, use the **no** form of this command.

standby use-bia
no standby use-bia

Syntax   Description

This command has no arguments or keywords.

Default

HSRP uses the preassigned MAC address on Ethernet and FDDI, or the functional address on Token Ring.

Command Mode

Interface configuration

Usage Guidelines

This command first appeared in Cisco IOS Release 11.2.

For an interface with this command configured, only one standby group can be configured. Multiple groups need to be removed before this command is configured. Hosts on the interface need to have a default gateway configured. It is recommended you set the **no ip proxy-arp** command on the interface. It is desirable to configure the **standby use-bia** command on a Token Ring interface if there are devices that reject ARP replies with source hardware addresses set to a functional address.

When HSRP runs on a multiple-ring, source-routed bridging environment and the HRSP routers reside on different rings, configuring the **standby use-bia** command can prevent RIF confusion.

Example

In the following example, the burned-in address of Token Ring interface 4/0 will be the virtual MAC address mapped to the virtual IP address:

```
interface token4/0
  standby use-bia
```

TRANSMIT-INTERFACE

To assign a transmit interface to a receive-only interface, use the **transmit-interface** interface configuration command. To return to normal duplex Ethernet interfaces, use the **no** form of this command.

transmit-interface *type number*
no transmit-interface

Syntax	Description
type	Transmit interface type to be linked with the (current) receive-only interface.
number	Transmit interface number to be linked with the (current) receive-only interface.

Default

Disabled

Command Mode

Interface configuration

Usage Guidelines

This command first appeared in Cisco IOS Release 10.0.

Receive-only interfaces are used commonly with microwave Ethernet links.

Example

The following example specifies Ethernet interface 0 as a simplex Ethernet interface:

```
interface ethernet 1
 ip address 128.9.1.2
 transmit-interface ethernet 0
```

CHAPTER 6

Configuring RSVP

This chapter describes how to configure Resource Reservation Protocol (RSVP), which is an IP service. For a complete description of the RSVP commands in this chapter, refer to Chapter 7, "RSVP Commands."

RSVP enables end systems to request Quality of Service (QoS) guarantees from the network. The need for network resource reservations differs for data traffic versus real-time traffic in the following ways:

- Data traffic seldom needs reserved bandwidth because internetworks provide datagram services for data traffic. This asynchronous packet switching may not need guarantees of service quality. Routers can operate in a First-In, First Out (FIFO) manner for data traffic packets. End-to-end controls between data traffic senders and receivers help ensure adequate transmission of bursts of information.

- Real-time traffic (that is, voice or video information) experiences problems when operating over datagram services. Because real-time traffic sends an almost constant flow of information, the network "pipes" must be consistent. Some guarantee must be provided that service between real-time hosts will not vary. Routers operating on a FIFO basis risk unrecoverable disruption of the real-time information that is being transmitted.

Data applications (with little need for resource guarantees) frequently demand relatively lower bandwidth than real-time traffic. The almost constant, high bit-rate demands of a video conference application, and the bursty, low bit-rate demands of an interactive data application share available network resources.

RSVP prevents the demands of real-time traffic from impairing the bandwidth resources necessary for bursty data traffic. To do this, the routers sort and prioritize packets much like a statistical time division multiplexor would sort and prioritize several signal sources that share a single channel.

RSVP mechanisms enable real-time traffic to reserve the resources necessary for consistent latency. A video conferencing application can use settings in the router to propagate a request for a path with the required bandwidth and delay for video conferencing destinations. RSVP will check and repeat reservations at regular intervals. By this process, RSVP can adjust and alter the path between RSVP end systems to recover from router changes.

Real-time traffic (unlike data traffic) requires a guaranteed network consistency. Without consistent QoS, real-time traffic faces the following problems:

- Jitter—A slight time or phase movement in a transmission signal can introduce loss of synchronization or other errors.

- Insufficient bandwidth—Voice calls use a digital signal level 0 (DS0 at 64 Kbps); video conferencing uses T1/E1 (1.544 Mbs or 2.048 Mbps); and higher-fidelity video uses even more.

- Delay variations—If the wait time between the time when signal elements are sent and when they arrive varies, the real-time traffic will no longer be synchronized and may fail.

- Information loss—When signal elements drop or arrive too late, lost audio causes distortions with noise or crackle sounds. The lost video causes image blurring, distortions, or blackouts.

RSVP works in conjunction with Weighted Fair Queuing (WFQ) or Random Early Detection (RED). This combination of reservation setting with packet queuing uses two key concepts: end-to-end flows with RSVP and router-to-router conversations with WFQ. These concepts are implemented in the following ways:

- RSVP Flow—This is a stream that operates "multidestination simplex," since data travels across it in only one direction (from the origin to the targets). Flows travel from a set of senders to a set of receivers. The flows can be merged or left unmerged, and the method of merging them varies according to the attributes of the application using the flow.

- WFQ Conversation—This is the traffic for a single transport layer session or network layer flow that crosses a given interface. This conversation is called from the source and destination address, protocol type, port number, or other attributes in the relevant communications layer.

RSVP allows for hosts to send packets to a subset of all hosts (*multicasting*). RSVP assumes that resource reservation applies primarily to multicast applications (such as video conferencing). Although the primary target for RSVP is multimedia traffic, a clear interest exists for the reservation of bandwidth for unicast traffic (such as NFS and virtual private network management). A *unicast* transmission involves a host sending packets to a single host.

RSVP RESERVATION TYPES

Two types of multicast flows are a flow that originates from exactly one sender (called a *distinct reservation*), and a flow that originates from one or more senders (called a *shared reservation*). RSVP describes these reservations as having certain algorithmic attributes.

Understanding Distinct Reservation

An example of a distinct reservation is a video application, in which each sender emits a distinct data stream that requires admission and management in a queue. Such a flow, therefore, requires a separate reservation per sender on each transmission facility it crosses (such as Ethernet, an HDLC line, a Frame Relay DLCI, or an ATM virtual channel). RSVP refers to this distinct reservation as explicit and installs it using a Fixed Filter style of reservation.

Use of RSVP for unicast applications is generally a degenerate case of a distinct flow.

Understanding Shared Reservation

An example of a shared reservation is an audio application, in which each sender also emits a distinct data stream that requires admission and management in a queue. However, because of the nature of the application, a limited number of senders are transmitting data at any given time. Such a flow, therefore, does not require a separate reservation per sender. Instead, a single reservation that can be applied to any sender within a set is needed.

RSVP installs a shared reservation using a Wild Card or Shared Explicit style of reservation, with the difference between the two being determined by the scope of application (which is either wild or explicit). These filters operate in the following ways:

- The Wild Card Filter reserves bandwidth and delay characteristics for any sender and is limited by the list of source addresses carried in the reservation message.

- The Shared Explicit reservation style identifies the flows for specific network resources.

PLANNING FOR RSVP CONFIGURATION

You must plan carefully to successfully configure and use RSVP on your network. At a minimum, RSVP must reflect your assessment of bandwidth needs on router interfaces. Consider the following questions as you plan for RSVP configuration:

- How much bandwidth should RSVP allow per end-user application flow? You must understand the "feeds and speeds" of your applications. By default, the amount that can be reserved by a single flow can be the entire reservable bandwidth. You can, however, limit individual reservations to smaller amounts using the single flow bandwidth parameter. This value may not exceed the interface reservation limit, and no one flow may reserve more than the amount specified.

- How much bandwidth is available for RSVP? By default, 75 percent of the bandwidth available on an interface can be reserved. If you are using a tunnel interface, RSVP can make a reservation for the tunnel the bandwidth of which is the sum of the bandwidths reserved within the tunnel.

- How much bandwidth must be excluded from RSVP so that it can fairly provide the timely service required by low-volume data conversations? End-to-end controls for data traffic assumes that all sessions will behave so as to avoid congestion dynamically.

Real-time demands do not follow this behavior. Determine the bandwidth to set aside so bursty data traffic will not be deprived as a side effect of the RSVP QoS configuration.

Plan for RSVP before entering the details needed as RSVP configuration parameters.

Understanding RSVP Implementation Considerations

You should be aware of RSVP implementation considerations as you design your reservation system. RSVP does not model all data links that are likely to be present on the internetwork. RSVP models an interface as having a queuing system that completely determines the mix of traffic on the interface; bandwidth or delay characteristics are only deterministic to the extent that this model holds. Unfortunately, data links are often imperfectly modeled this way. Use the following guidelines:

- Serial line interfaces—PPP, HDLC, LAPB, HSSI, and similar serial line interfaces are well modeled by RSVP. The device can, therefore, make guarantees on these interfaces. Along with NBMA interfaces, these serial line interfaces are also the most in need of reservations.

- Multiaccess LANs—These data links are not modeled well by RSVP interfaces, because the LAN itself represents a queuing system that is not under the control of the device making the guarantees. The device guarantees what load it will offer, but it cannot guarantee what competing loads or timings of loads that neighboring LAN systems will offer. The network administrator can use admission controls to control how much traffic is placed on the LAN. The network administrator, however, should focus on the use of admission in network design in order to use RSVP effectively.

- Public X.25 networks—It is not clear that rate or delay reservations can be usefully made on public X.25 networks.

You must use a specialized configuration on Frame Relay and ATM networks, as discussed in the next sections.

Understanding Considerations for a Frame Relay Internetwork

The following RSVP implementation considerations apply as you design your reservation system for a Frame Relay internetwork:

- Reservations are made for an interface or subinterface. If subinterfaces contain more than one DLC, the bandwidth required and the bandwidth reserved may differ. Therefore, to operate correctly, RSVP subinterfaces of frame relay circuits must contain exactly one DLC.

- In addition, Frame Relay DLCs have rates (CIR) and burst controls (Bc and Be) that may not be reflected in the configuration, and may differ markedly from the interface speed (either adding up to exceed it or being significantly smaller). Therefore, the **ip rsvp bandwidth** interface configuration command must be entered for both the interface and the subinterface. Both bandwidths are used as admission criteria.

For example, suppose that a Frame Relay interface runs at a T1 rate (1.544 Mbps) and supports several DLCs to remote offices served by 128 and 56 Kbps lines. One must configure the amount of the total interface (75 percent of which is 1.158 Mbps) and the amount of each receiving interface (75 percent of which would be 96 and 42 Kbps, respectively) that may be reserved. Admission succeeds if, and only if, enough bandwidth is available on the DLC (the subinterface) and on the aggregate interface.

Knowing the Considerations for an ATM Internetwork

The following RSVP implementation considerations apply as you design your reservation system for an ATM internetwork:

- When ATM is configured, it most likely uses a Usable Bit Rate (UBR) or an Available Bit Rate (ABR) Virtual Channel (VC) connecting individual routers. With these classes of service, the ATM network makes a "best effort" to meet the traffic's bit-rate requirements, and assumes that the end-stations are responsible for information that does not get through the network.

- This ATM service has the capability of opening separate channels for reserved traffic having the necessary characteristics. RSVP should open these VCs and adjust the cache to make effective use of the VC for this purpose.

RSVP Task List

After you have planned your RSVP configuration, enter the Cisco IOS commands that implement your configuration plan. The following sections discuss how to configure RSVP. You must enable RSVP on an interface in order to use it; the other tasks in the following list are optional:

- Enabling RSVP
- Entering Senders in the RSVP Database
- Entering Receivers in the RSVP Database
- Entering Multicast Addresses
- Controlling Which RSVP Neighbor Can Offer a Reservation
- Monitoring RSVP

Enabling RSVP

By default, RSVP is disabled so that it is backward compatible with systems that do not implement RSVP. To enable RSVP on an interface, perform the following task in global configuration mode:

Task	Command
Enable RSVP for IP on an interface.	ip rsvp bandwidth [*interface-Kbps*] [*single-flow-Kbps*]

This command starts RSVP and sets the bandwidth and single-flow limits. The default maximum bandwidth is up to 75 percent of the bandwidth available on the interface. By default, the amount reservable by a flow can be up to the entire reservable bandwidth.

On subinterfaces, this applies the more restrictive of the available bandwidths of the physical interface and the subinterface. For example, a Frame Relay interface might have a T1 connector nominally capable of 1.536 Mbps, and 64 subinterfaces on 128 Kbps circuits (64K CIR), with 1,200 and 100 Kbps, respectively.

Reservations on individual circuits that do not exceed 100 Kbps normally succeed. If, however, reservations have been made on other circuits adding up to 1.2 Mbps, and a reservation is made on a subinterface which itself has enough remaining bandwidth, it will still be refused because the physical interface lacks supporting bandwidth.

ENTERING SENDERS IN THE RSVP DATABASE

You can configure the router to behave as though it is periodically receiving an RSVP PATH message from the sender or previous hop routes containing the indicated attributes. To enter senders in the RSVP database, perform the following task in global configuration mode:

Task	Command
Enter the senders in the RSVP database.	**ip rsvp sender** *session-ip-address sender-ip-address* [**tcp** | **udp** | *ip-protocol*] *session-dport sender-sport previous-hop-ip-address previous-hop-interface*

ENTERING RECEIVERS IN THE RSVP DATABASE

You can configure the router to behave as though it is continuously receiving an RSVP RESV message from the originator containing the indicated attributes. To enter receivers in the RSVP database, perform the following task in global configuration mode:

Task	Command
Enter the receivers in the RSVP database.	**ip rsvp reservation** *session-ip-address sender-ip-address* [**tcp** | **udp** | *ip-protocol*] *session-dport sender-sport next-hop-ip-address next-hop-interface* {**ff** | **se** | **wf**} {**rate** | **load**} [*bandwidth*] [*burst-size*]

Entering Multicast Addresses

If RSVP neighbors are discovered to be using UDP encapsulation, the router will automatically generate UDP-encapsulated messages for consumption by the neighbors.

To enter multicast addresses, perform the following task in global configuration mode:

Task	Command
Enter any multicast addresses necessary, if you use UDP.	ip rsvp udp-multicast [*multicast-address*]

However, in some cases, a host will not originate such a message until it has first heard from the router, which it can only do via UDP. You must instruct the router to generate UDP-encapsulated RSVP multicasts whenever it generates an IP-encapsulated multicast.

Controlling Which RSVP Neighbor Can Offer a Reservation

By default, any RSVP neighbor may offer a reservation. To control which RSVP neighbors can offer a reservation, perform the following task in global configuration mode:

Task	Command
Limit which routers may offer reservations.	ip rsvp neighbors *access-list-number*

When this command is configured, only neighbors conforming to the access list are accepted. The access list is applied to the IP header.

Monitoring RSVP

After you configure the RSVP reservations that reflect your network resource policy, you can verify the resulting RSVP operations. To do so, perform the following tasks in EXEC mode:

Task	Command
Display RSVP-related interface information.	show ip rsvp interface [*type number*]
Display RSVP-related filters and bandwidth information.	show ip rsvp installed [*type number*]
Display current RSVP neighbors.	show ip rsvp neighbor [*type number*]
Display RSVP sender information.	show ip rsvp sender [*type number*]
Display RSVP request information.	show ip rsvp request [*type number*]
Display RSVP receiver information.	show ip rsvp reservation [*type number*]

CHAPTER 7

RSVP Commands

Use the commands in this chapter to configure and monitor the Resource Reservation Protocol (RSVP), which is a signalling protocol. For RSVP configuration information and examples, refer to Chapter 6, "Configuring RSVP."

IP RSVP BANDWIDTH

To enable RSVP for IP on an interface, use the **ip rsvp bandwidth** interface configuration command. To disable RSVP, use the **no** form of the command.

> **ip rsvp bandwidth** [*interface-kbps*] [*single-flow-kbps*]
> **no ip rsvp bandwidth** [*interface-kbps*] [*single-flow-kbps*]

Syntax	Description
interface-kbps	(Optional.) Amount of bandwidth (in Kbps) on interface to be reserved. The range is 1 to 10,000,000.
single-flow-kbps	(Optional.) Amount of bandwidth (in Kbps) allocated to a single flow. The range is 1 to 10,000,000.

Default
Disabled

Command Mode
Interface configuration

Usage Guidelines
This command first appeared in Cisco IOS Release 11.2.

RSVP is disabled by default to allow backward compatibility with systems that do not implement RSVP.

Example

The following example shows a T1 (1536 Kbps) link configured to permit RSVP reservation of up to 1158 Kbps, but no more than 100 Kbps for any given flow on Ethernet 0 and serial 0 interfaces. Fair queuing is configured with 15 reservable queues to support those reserved flows, should they be required.

```
interface Ethernet 0
 ip rsvp bandwidth 1158 100
interface serial 0
 fair-queue 64 256 15
```

Related Commands

ip rsvp neighbors
ip rsvp reservation
ip rsvp sender
ip rsvp udp-multicast

IP RSVP NEIGHBORS

To enable neighbors to request a reservation, use the **ip rsvp neighbors** interface configuration command. To disable this feature, use the **no** form of the command.

> **ip rsvp neighbors** *access-list-number*
> **no ip rsvp neighbors** *access-list-number*

Syntax	Description
access-list-number	Number of a standard or extended access list. This can be any integer from 1 to 199.

Default

The router accepts messages from any neighbor.

Command Mode

Interface configuration

Usage Guidelines

This command first appeared in Cisco IOS Release 11.2.

Use this command to allow only specific RSVP neighbors to make a reservation. If no limits are specified, any neighbor can request a reservation. If an access list is specified, only neighbors meeting the specified access list requirements can make a reservation.

Example

The following example allows neighbors meeting access list 1 requirements to request a reservation:

```
interface ethernet 0
  ip rsvp neighbors 1
```

Related Commands

ip rsvp bandwidth
ip rsvp reservation
ip rsvp sender
ip rsvp udp-multicast

IP RSVP RESERVATION

To enable a router to simulate a RSVP RESV message reception from the sender, use the **ip rsvp reservation** interface configuration command. To disable this feature, use the **no** form of the command.

> **ip rsvp reservation** *session-ip-address sender-ip-address* [**tcp** | **udp** | *ip-protocol*]
> *session-dport sender-sport next-hop-ip address nexthop-interface* {**ff** | **se** | **wf**}
> {**rate** | **load**} [*bandwidth*] [*burst-size*]

> **no ip rsvp reservation** *session-ip-address sender-ip-address* [**tcp** | **udp** | *ip-protocol*]
> *session-dport sender-sport next-hop-ip address nexthop-interface* {**ff** | **se** | **wf**}
> {**rate** | **load**} [*bandwidth*] [*burst-size*]

Syntax	Description
session-ip-address	For unicast sessions, this is the address of the intended receiver; for multicast sessions, it is the IP multicast address of the session.
sender-ip-address	For unicast sessions, this is the address of the sender; for multicast sessions, it is the IP multicast address of the session.
tcp | **udp** | *ip-protocol*	(Optional.) TCP, UDP, or IP protocol in the range 0 to 255.
session-dport *sender-sport*	*Session-dport* is the destination port. *Sender-sport* is the source port. Port numbers are specified in all cases, as the use of 16-bit ports following the IP header which is not limited to UDP or TCP. If destination is zero, the source must be zero, and the implication is that ports are not checked. If destination is non-zero, the source must also be non-zero.
next-hop-ip-address	Host name or address of the receiver or the router closest to the receiver.
next-hop-interface	Next hop interface or subinterface type and number. Interface type can be **ethernet, loopback, null,** or **serial.**

Syntax	Description
**ff	se	wf**	Reservation style:
	• Fixed Filter (**ff**) is single reservation.
	• Shared Explicit (**se**) is shared reservation, limited scope.
	• Wild Card (**wf**) is shared reservation, unlimited scope.
**rate	load**	QoS: guaranteed bit **rate** service or controlled **load** service.
bandwidth	(Optional.) Average bit rate (Kbps) to reserve up to 75 percent of total on interface. The range is 1 to 10,000,000.
burst-size	(Optional.) Maximum burst size (Kilobytes of data in queue). The range is 1 to 65,535.

Default

The router cannot simulate receiving an RSVP RESV Message.

Command Mode

Interface configuration

Usage Guidelines

This command first appeared in Cisco IOS Release 11.2.

Use this command to force the router to act like it is receiving RSVP RESV messages from the sender.

Examples

The following example specifies the use of a Shared Explicit Filter style of reservation and the Controlled Load Service, with token buckets of 100 or 150 Kbps and 60 or 65K maximum queue depth:

```
ip rsvp reservation 224.250.0.2 132.240.1.1 UDP 20 30 132.240.4.1 Et1 se load 100 60
ip rsvp reservation 224.250.0.2 132.240.2.1 TCP 20 30 132.240.4.1 Et1 se load 150 65
```

The following example specifies the use of a Wild Card Filter style of reservation and the Guaranteed Bit Rate Service, with token buckets of 300 or 350 Kbps and 60 or 65K maximum queue depth:

```
ip rsvp reservation 224.250.0.3 0.0.0.0 UDP 20 0 132.240.4.1  Et1 wf rate 300 60
ip rsvp reservation 224.250.0.3 0.0.0.0 UDP 20 0 132.240.4.1  Et1 wf rate 350 65
```

Note that the Wild Card Filter does not admit the specification of the sender; it accepts all senders. This is denoted by setting the source address and port to zero. If, in any filter style, the destination port is specified to be zero, RSVP does not permit the source port to be anything else; it understands that such protocols do not use ports or that the specification applies to all ports.

Related Commands

ip rsvp bandwidth
ip rsvp neighbors
ip rsvp sender
ip rsvp udp-multicast

IP RSVP SENDER

To enable a router to simulate RSVP PATH message reception from the sender, use the **ip rsvp sender** interface configuration command. To disable this feature, use the **no** form of the command.

> **ip rsvp sender** *session-ip-address sender-ip-address* [**tcp** | **udp** | *ip-protocol*]
> *session-dport sender-sport previous-hop-ip-address previous-hop-interface*
> [*bandwidth*] [*burst-size*]

> **no ip rsvp sender** *session-ip-address sender-ip-address* [**tcp** | **udp** | *ip-protocol*]
> *session-dport sender-sport previous-hop-ip-address previous-hop-interface*
> [*bandwidth*] [*burst-size*]

Syntax	Description
session-ip-address	For unicast sessions, this is the address of the intended receiver; for multicast sessions, it is the IP multicast address of the session.
sender-ip-address	For unicast sessions, this is the address of the sender; for multicast sessions, it is the IP multicast address of the session.
tcp | **udp** | *ip-protocol*	TCP, UDP, or IP protocol in the range 0 to 255.
session-dport *sender-sport*	Destination/source ports. Port numbers are specified in all cases, as the use of 16-bit ports following the IP header which is not limited to UDP or TCP. If the destination is zero, the source must be zero, and the implication is that ports are not checked. If the destination is non-zero, the source must be non-zero.
previous-hop-ip-address	Address of the sender or the router closest to the sender.
previous-hop-interface	Address of the previous hop interface or subinterface. Interface type can be **ethernet, loopback, null,** or **serial.**
bandwidth	Average bit rate (Kbps) to reserve up to 75 percent of total on interface.
burst-size	Maximum burst size (kilobytes of data in queue).

Default

The router cannot simulate RSVP Path message reception.

Command Mode

Interface configuration

Usage Guidelines

This command first appeared in Cisco IOS Release 11.2.

Use this command to force the router to act like it is receiving RSVP PATH messages from the sender.

Example

The following example sets up the router to act like it is receiving RSVP messages using UDP over the Loopback 1 interface:

```
ip rsvp sender 224.250.0.1 132.240.2.1 udp 20 30 132.240.2.1 loopback 1 50 5
ip rsvp sender 224.250.0.2 132.240.2.1 udp 20 30 132.240.2.1 loopback 1 50 5
ip rsvp sender 224.250.0.2 132.240.2.28 udp 20 30 132.240.2.28 loopback 1 50 5
```

Related Commands

ip rsvp bandwidth
ip rsvp neighbors
ip rsvp reservation
ip rsvp udp-multicast

IP RSVP UDP-MULTICAST

To instruct the router to generate UDP-encapsulated RSVP multicasts whenever it generates an IP multicast, use the **ip rsvp udp-multicast** interface configuration command. To disable this feature, use the **no** form of the command.

> **ip rsvp udp-multicast** [*multicast-address*]
> **no ip rsvp udp-multicast** [*multicast-address*]

Syntax	Description
multicast-address	(Optional.) Host name or UDP multicast address of router.

Default

The generation of UDP multicasts is disabled. If a system sends a UDP-encapsulated RSVP message to the router, the router starts using UDP for contact with the neighboring system. The router uses multicast address 224.0.0.14 and starts sending to UDP port 1699. If the command is entered without specifying a multicast address, the router uses the same multicast address.

Command Mode

Interface configuration

Usage Guidelines

This command first appeared in Cisco IOS Release 11.2.

Use this command to instruct a router to generate UDP-encapsulated RSVP multicasts whenever it generates an IP-encapsulated multicast packet. Some hosts require this trigger from the router.

Example

The following example reserves up to 7500 Kbps on the Ethernet 2, with up to 1 Mbps per flow. The router is configured to use UDP encapsulation with the multicast address 224.0.0.14.

```
interface ethernet 2
 ip rsvp bandwidth 7500 1000
 ip rsvp udp-multicast 224.0.0.14
```

Related Commands

ip rsvp bandwidth
ip rsvp neighbors
ip rsvp reservation
ip rsvp sender

SHOW IP RSVP INTERFACE

To display RSVP-related interface information, use the **show ip rsvp interface** EXEC command.

> **show ip rsvp interface** [*type number*]

Syntax	Description
type number	(Optional.) Interface type and number.

Command Mode

EXEC

Usage Guidelines

This command first appeared in Cisco IOS Release 11.2.

Use this command to show the current allocation budget and maximum allocatable bandwidth.

Sample Display

The following is sample output from the **show ip rsvp interface** command:

```
Router# show ip rsvp interface
interfac allocate i/f max  flow max per/255 UDP  IP   UDP_IP  UDP M/C
Et1      0M       7500K    7500K    0  /255 0    0    0       0
Se0      0M       1158K    1158K    0  /255 0    0    0       0
Se1      30K      1158K    1158K    6  /255 0    1    0       0
```

Table 7–1 describes the significant fields shown in the display.

Table 7–1   *Show IP RSVP Interface Field Descriptions*

Field	Description
interface	Interface name.
allocate	Current allocation budget.
i/f max	Maximum allocatable bandwidth.
flow max	Maximum flow possible on this interface.
per /255	Percent of bandwidth utilized.
UDP	Number of neighbors sending UDP-encapsulated RSVP.
IP	Number of neighbors sending IP-encapsulated RSVP.
UDP_IP	Number of neighbors sending both.
UDP M/C	Is router configured for UDP on this interface?

SHOW IP RSVP INSTALLED

To display RSVP-related installed filters and corresponding bandwidth information, use the **show ip rsvp installed** EXEC command.

    show ip rsvp installed [*type number*]

Syntax	*Description*
type number	(Optional.) Interface type and number.

Command Mode

EXEC

Usage Guidelines

This command first appeared in Cisco IOS Release 11.2.

Use this command to show the current installed RSVP filters and the corresponding bandwidth information for a specified interface or all interfaces.

Sample Display

The following is sample output from the **show ip rsvp installed** command:

```
Router# show ip rsvp installed
RSVP:
RSVP: Ethernet1: has no installed reservations
RSVP: Serial0:
```

```
  kbps   To                   From         Protocol DPort Sport Weight Conversation
  0      224.250.250.1        132.240.2.28     UDP 20    30    128    270
  150    224.250.250.1        132.240.2.1      UDP 20    30    128    268
  100    224.250.250.1        132.240.1.1      UDP 20    30    128    267
  200    224.250.250.1        132.240.1.25     UDP 20    30    256    265
  200    224.250.250.2        132.240.1.25     UDP 20    30    128    271
  0      224.250.250.2        132.240.2.28     UDP 20    30    128    269
  150    224.250.250.2        132.240.2.1      UDP 20    30    128    266
  350    224.250.250.3        0.0.0.0          UDP 20     0    128    26
```

Table 7–2 describes significant fields shown in the display.

Table 7–2 *Show IP RSVP Installed Field Descriptions*

Field	Description
kbps	Reserved rate.
To	IP address of source device.
From	IP address of destination device.
Protocol DPort	Protocol type of destination UDP/TCP port (no longer the usual protocol).
Sport	Source UDP/TCP port.
Weight	Weight used in Weighted Fair Queuing (WFQ).
Conversation	WFQ conversation number. If the WFQ is not configured on the interface, weight and conversation will be zero.

SHOW IP RSVP NEIGHBOR

To display current RSVP neighbors, use the **show ip rsvp neighbor** EXEC command.

show ip rsvp neighbor [*type number*]

Syntax	*Description*
type number	(Optional.) Interface type and number.

Command Mode

EXEC

Usage Guidelines

This command first appeared in Cisco IOS Release 11.2.

Use this command to show the current RSVP neighbors and identify if the neighbor is using IP or UDP encapsulation for a specified interface or all interfaces.

Sample Display

The following is sample output from the **show ip rsvp neighbor** command:

```
Router# show ip rsvp neighbor

Interfac Neighbor       Encapsulation
Se1      132.240.1.49   RSVP
```

SHOW IP RSVP REQUEST

To display RSVP-related request information being requested upstream, use the **show ip rsvp request** EXEC command.

> **show ip rsvp request** [*type number*]

Syntax	*Description*
type number	(Optional.) Interface type and number.

Command Mode

EXEC

Usage Guidelines

This command first appeared in Cisco IOS Release 11.2.

Use this command to show the RSVP reservations currently being requested upstream for a specified interface or all interfaces. The received reservations may differ from requests because of aggregated or refused reservations.

Sample Display

The following is sample output from the **show ip rsvp request** command:

```
Router# show ip rsvp request
To            From         Pro DPort Sport Next Hop      I/F   Fi Serv BPS Bytes
132.240.1.49  132.240.4.53 1   0     0     132.240.3.53  Et1   FF LOAD 30K 3K
```

Table 7–3 describes the significant fields shown in the display.

Table 7–3 *Show IP RSVP Request Field Descriptions*

Field	Description
To	IP address of the receiver.
From	IP address of the sender.
Pro	Protocol code. Code 1 indicates ICMP.
DPort	Destination port number.

Table 7–3 *Show IP RSVP Request Field Descriptions, Continued*

Field	Description
Sport	Source port number.
Next Hop	IP address of the next hop.
I/F	Interface of the next hop.
Fi	Filter (Wildcard filter, Shared Explicit filter, or Fixed Format filter).
Serv	Service (value can be **rate** or **load**).
BPS	Requested rate of the reservation in bits per second.
Bytes	Bytes of burst size requested.

SHOW IP RSVP RESERVATION

To display RSVP-related receiver information currently in the database, use the **show ip rsvp reservation** EXEC command.

> **show ip rsvp reservation** [*type number*]

Syntax	*Description*
type number	(Optional.) Interface type and number.

Command Mode

EXEC

Usage Guidelines

This command first appeared in Cisco IOS Release 11.2.

Use this command to show the current receiver (RESV) information in the database for a specified interface or for all interfaces. This information includes reservations aggregated and forwarded from other RSVP routers.

Sample Display

The following is sample output from the **show ip rsvp reservation** command:

```
Router# show ip rsvp reservation

To            From          Pro DPort Sport Next Hop      I/F   Fi Serv BPS Bytes
132.240.1.49  132.240.4.53   1    0     0    132.240.1.49  Se1   FF LOAD 30K 3K
```

Table 7–4 describes the significant fields shown in the display.

Table 7–4   *Show IP RSVP Reservation Field Descriptions*

Field	Descriptions
To	IP address of the receiver.
From	IP address of the sender.
Pro	Protocol code.
DPort	Destination port number.
Sport	Source port number.
Next Hop	IP address of the next hop.
I/F	Interface of the next hop.
Fi	Filter (Wildcard filter, Shared Explicit filter, or Fixed Format filter).
Serv	Service (value can be **rate** or **load**).
BPS	Reservation rate in bits per second
Bytes	Bytes of burst size.

SHOW IP RSVP SENDER

To display RSVP-related sender information currently in the database, use the **show ip rsvp sender** EXEC command.

> **show ip rsvp sender** [*type number*]

Syntax	Description
type number	(Optional.) Interface type and number.

Command Mode

EXEC

Usage Guidelines

This command first appeared in Cisco IOS Release 11.2.

Use this command to show the current RSVP sender (PATH) information in the database for a specified interface or for all interfaces.

Sample Display

The following is sample output from the **show ip rsvp sender** command:

```
Router# show ip rsvp sender

To                From           Pro DPort Sport Prev Hop      I/F  BPS  Bytes
132.240.1.49      132.240.4.53   1   0     0     132.240.3.53  Et1  30K  3K
132.240.2.51      132.240.5.54   1   0     0     132.240.3.54  Et1  30K  3K
```

Table 7–5 describes the fields shown in the display.

Table 7–5 *Show IP RSVP Sender Field Descriptions*

Field	Description
To	IP address of the receiver.
From	IP address of the sender.
Pro	Protocol code.
DPort	Destination port number.
Sport	Source port number.
Prev Hop	IP address of previous hop.
I/F	Interface of previous hop.
BPS	Reservation rate in bits per second that the application is advertising it might achieve.
Bytes	Bytes of burst size that the application is advertising that it might achieve.

PART 2

IP Routing

CHAPTER 8

Configuring On-Demand Routing

This chapter describes how to configure On-Demand Routing (ODR). For a complete description of the ODR commands in this chapter, see Chapter 9, "On-Demand Routing Commands."

ODR is a feature that provides IP routing for stub sites, with minimum overhead. The overhead of a general, dynamic routing protocol is avoided without incurring the configuration and management overhead of static routing.

A *stub router* can be thought of as a spoke router in a hub-and-spoke network topology, where the only router to which the spoke is adjacent is the hub router. In such a network topology, the IP routing information required to represent this topology is fairly simple. These stub routers commonly have a WAN connection to the hub router, and a small number of LAN network segments (*stub networks*) are directly connected to the stub router.

These stub networks might consist only of end systems and the stub router, and thus do not require the stub router to learn any dynamic IP routing information. The stub routers can then be configured with a default route that directs IP traffic to the hub router.

To provide full connectivity, the hub router can be statically configured to know that a particular stub network is reachable via a particular stub router. However, if there are multiple hub routers, many stub networks, or asynchronous connections between hubs and spokes, statically configuring the stub networks on the hub routers becomes a problem.

ON-DEMAND ROUTING TASK LIST

Of the following tasks, the first three are required to configure ODR, and the remaining tasks are optional:

- Enabling ODR
- Filtering ODR Information
- Configuring the Default Route

283

- Redistributing ODR Information into the Hub's Dynamic Routing Protocol
- Reconfiguring CDP/ODR Timers
- Using ODR with Dialer Mappings

ENABLING ODR

ODR allows you to easily install IP stub networks where the hubs dynamically maintain routes to the stub networks. This is accomplished without requiring the configuration of an IP routing protocol on the stubs.

On stub routers that support the ODR feature, the stub router advertises IP prefixes corresponding to the IP networks configured on all directly connected interfaces. If the interface has multiple logical IP networks configured (via the **ip secondary** command), only the primary IP network is advertised through ODR. Because ODR advertises IP prefixes and not simply IP network numbers, ODR is able to carry Variable Length Subnet Mask (VLSM) information.

To enable ODR, perform the following task in global configuration mode:

Task	Command
Enable ODR on the hub router.	**router odr** *process-id*

Once ODR is enabled on a hub router, the hub router begins installing stub network routes in the IP forwarding table. The hub router can additionally be configured to redistribute these routes into any configured dynamic IP routing protocols.

On the stub router, no IP routing protocol must be configured. In fact, from the standpoint of ODR, a router is automatically considered to be a stub when no IP routing protocols have been configured.

The routing information that ODR generates is propagated between routers using the Cisco Discovery Protocol (CDP). This means that the operation of ODR is partially controlled by the configuration of CDP.

Using the global configuration command **no cdp run** disables the propagation of ODR stub routing information entirely. Using the interface configuration command **no cdp enable** disables the propagation of ODR information on a particular interface.

FILTERING ODR INFORMATION

The hub router will attempt to populate the IP routing table with ODR routes, as they are learned dynamically from stub routers. The IP next hop for these routes is the IP address of the neighboring router, as advertised through CDP.

Use IP filtering to limit the network prefixes that the hub router will permit to be learned dynamically through ODR.

To filter ODR information, perform the following task in router configuration mode:

Task	Command
Filter ODR information on the hub router.	**distribute-list** {*access-list-number*	*name*} **in**	**out** [*type number*]

For example, the following configuration causes the hub router to only accept advertisements for IP prefixes about (or subnets of) the class C network 198.92.110.0:

```
router odr
 distribute-list 101 in
access-list 101 permit ip any 198.92.110.0 255.255.255.0
```

CONFIGURING THE DEFAULT ROUTE

Although no IP routing protocol must be configured on the stub router, it is still necessary to configure the default route for IP traffic. You can optionally cause traffic for unknown subsets to follow the default route.

To configure the default route for IP traffic, perform the following tasks in global configuration mode:

Task	Command
Configure the default route on the stub router.	**ip route 0.0.0.0 0.0.0.0** *interface-name*
Cause traffic for unknown subnets of directly connected networks to also follow the default route.	**ip classless**

REDISTRIBUTING ODR INFORMATION INTO THE HUB'S DYNAMIC ROUTING PROTOCOL

This task may be performed by using the **redistribute** router configuration command. The exact syntax depends upon the routing protocol into which ODR is being redistributed.

RECONFIGURING CDP/ODR TIMERS

By default, CDP sends updates every 60 seconds. This update interval may not be frequent enough to provide speedy reconvergence of IP routes on the hub router side of the network. A faster reconvergence rate may be necessary if the stub connects to one of several hub routers via asynchronous interfaces (such as modem lines).

ODR expects to receive periodic CDP updates containing IP prefix information. When ODR fails to receive such updates for routes that it has installed in the routing table, these ODR routes are first marked invalid and are eventually removed from the routing table. (By default, ODR routes are marked invalid after 180 seconds and are removed from the routing table after 240 seconds.) These defaults are based on the default CDP update interval. Configuration changes made to either the CDP or ODR timers should be reflected through changes made to both.

To configure CDP/ODR timers, perform the following tasks beginning in global configuration mode:

Task	Command
Change the rate at which CDP updates are sent.	**cdp timer** *seconds*
Enable ODR.	**router odr**
Change the rate at which ODR routes are expired from the routing table.	**timers basic** *update invalid holddown flush* [*sleeptime*]

USING ODR WITH DIALER MAPPINGS

For interfaces that specify dialer mappings, CDP packets will make use of dialer map configuration statements that pertain to the IP protocol. Because CDP packets are always broadcast packets, these dialer map statements must handle broadcast packets, typically through the use of the dialer map **broadcast** keyword. The **dialer string** interface configuration command may also be used.

On DDR interfaces, certain kinds of packets can be classified as interesting. These interesting packets can cause a DDR connection to be made or cause the idle timer of a DDR interface to be reset. For the purposes of DDR classification, CDP packets are considered uninteresting. This is true even while CDP is making use of dialer-map statements for IP, where IP packets are classified as interesting.

CHAPTER 9

On-Demand Routing Commands

Use the commands in this chapter to configure On-Demand Routing (ODR). For ODR configuration information and examples, see Chapter 8, "Configuring On-Demand Routing."

ROUTER ODR

To configure a router to accept On-Demand Routing (ODR) routes from stub routers, use the **router odr** global configuration command. To disable ODR, use the **no** form of this command.

> **router odr** *process-id*
> **no router odr** *process-id*

Syntax	Description
process-id	Number of a process that identifies the routes to the other ODR routers.

Default

The router ignores any received ODR information.

Command Mode

Global configuration

Usage Guidelines

This command first appeared in Cisco IOS Release 11.2.

Use this command on hub routers to enable ODR to update the routing table with information learned via ODR stub routers.

Example

The following example sets up the routers in the distribution list to accept ODR routes from the specified access list:

```
router odr
 distribute-list 101 in
access-list 101 permit ip host 10.0.0.1 198.92.110.0 255.255.255.0
access-list 101 permit ip 11.1.1.1 255.0.0.0 198.92.111.0 255.255.255.0
router ospf 1
 redistribute odr subnets
```

Related Commands

Search online to find documentation for related commands.

distance
distribute-list in
distribute-list out
maximum-paths

TIMERS BASIC

To adjust ODR network timers, use the **timers basic** router configuration command. To restore the default timers, use the **no** form of this command.

> **timers basic** *update invalid holddown flush* [*sleeptime*]
> **no timers basic**

Syntax	Description
update	Rate in seconds at which updates are sent. This is the fundamental timing parameter of the routing protocol.
invalid	Interval of time in seconds after which a route is declared invalid; it should be at least three times the value of *update*. A route becomes invalid when there is an absence of updates that refresh the route. The route then enters holddown. The route is marked inaccessible and advertised as unreachable. However, the route is still used for forwarding packets.
holddown	Interval in seconds during which routing information regarding better paths is suppressed. It should be at least three times the value of *update*. A route enters into a holddown state when an update packet is received that indicates the route is unreachable. The route is marked inaccessible and advertised as unreachable. However, the route is still used for forwarding packets. When holddown expires, routes advertised by other sources are accepted and the route is no longer inaccessible.

Syntax	Description
flush	Amount of time in seconds that must pass before the route is removed from the routing table; the interval specified must be at least the sum of *invalid* and *holddown*. If it is less than this sum, the proper holddown interval cannot elapse, which results in a new route being accepted before the holddown interval expires.
sleeptime	(Optional.) Interval in milliseconds for postponing routing updates in the event of a flash update. The *sleeptime* value should be less than the *update* time. If the *sleeptime* is greater than the *update* time, routing tables will become unsynchronized.

Defaults

update is 90 seconds
invalid is 270 seconds
holddown is 280 seconds
flush is 630 seconds
sleeptime is 0 milliseconds

Command Mode

Router configuration

Usage Guidelines

This command first appeared in Cisco IOS Release 10.0.

The basic timing parameters for ODR are adjustable. Since this routing protocol is executing a distributed, asynchronous routing algorithm, it is important that these timers be the same for all routers and access servers in the network.

NOTES

The current and default timer values can be seen by inspecting the output of the **show ip protocols** EXEC command. The relationships of the various timers should be preserved as described previously.

Example

In the following example, updates are broadcast every 5 seconds. If a router is not heard from in 15 seconds, the route is declared unusable. Further information is suppressed for an additional 15 seconds. At the end of the suppression period, the route is flushed from the routing table.

```
router odr 109
 timers basic 5  15  15  30
```

Note that by setting a short update period, you run the risk of congesting slow-speed serial lines; however, this is not a big concern on faster-speed Ethernets and T1-rate serial lines. Also, if you have many routes in your updates, you can cause the routers to spend an excessive amount of time processing updates.

CHAPTER 10

Configuring RIP

This chapter describes how to configure RIP. For a complete description of the RIP commands that appear in this chapter, see Chapter 11, "RIP Commands."

The Routing Information Protocol (RIP) is a relatively old, but still commonly used, Interior Gateway Protocol (IGP) created for use in small, homogeneous networks. It is a classical distance-vector routing protocol. RIP is documented in RFC 1058.

RIP uses broadcast User Datagram Protocol (UDP) data packets to exchange routing information. The Cisco IOS software sends routing information updates every 30 seconds; this process is termed *advertising*. If a router does not receive an update from another router for 180 seconds or more, it marks the routes served by the router from which it has not received an update as being unusable. If there is still no update after 240 seconds, the router removes all routing table entries for such a router.

The metric that RIP uses to rate the value of different routes is *hop count*; the hop count is the number of routers that can be traversed in a route. A directly connected network has a metric of zero; an unreachable network has a metric of 16. This small range of metrics makes RIP an unsuitable routing protocol for large networks.

If the router has a default network path, RIP advertises a route that links the router to the pseudo-network 0.0.0.0. The network 0.0.0.0 does not exist; RIP treats 0.0.0.0 as a network to implement the default routing feature. The Cisco IOS software will advertise the default network if a default was learned by RIP, or if the router has a gateway of last resort and RIP is configured with a default metric.

RIP sends updates to the interfaces in the specified networks. If an interface's network is not specified, it is not advertised in any RIP update. Cisco's implementation of RIP Version 2 supports plain text and MD5 authentication, route summarization, Classless Interdomain Routing (CIDR), and Variable-Length Subnet Masks (VLSMs).

For protocol-independent features, which also apply to RIP, see Chapter 22, "Configuring IP Routing Protocol-Independent Features."

RIP CONFIGURATION TASK LIST

To configure RIP, complete the tasks in the following sections. You must enable RIP; the other tasks in the following list are optional:

- Enabling RIP
- Allowing Unicast Updates for RIP
- Applying Offsets to Routing Metrics
- Adjusting Timers
- Specifying a RIP Version
- Enabling RIP Authentication
- Disabling Route Summarization
- Running IGRP and RIP Concurrently
- Disabling the Validation of Source IP Addresses
- Enabling or Disabling Split Horizon
- Configuring Interpacket Delay

For information about the following topics, see Chapter 22:

- Filtering RIP information
- Key management (available in RIP Version 2)
- VLSM

ENABLING RIP

To enable RIP, perform the following tasks, starting in global configuration mode:

Task	Command
Step 1 Enable a RIP routing process, which places you in router configuration mode.	**router rip**
Step 2 Associate a network with a RIP routing process.	**network** *network-number*

ALLOWING UNICAST UPDATES FOR RIP

Because RIP is normally a broadcast protocol, in order for RIP routing updates to reach nonbroadcast networks, you must configure the Cisco IOS software to permit this exchange of routing information. To do so, perform the following task in router configuration mode:

Task	Command
Define a neighboring router with which to exchange routing information.	**neighbor** *ip-address*

To control the set of interfaces with which you want to exchange routing updates, you can disable the sending of routing updates on specified interfaces by configuring the **passive-interface** command.

APPLYING OFFSETS TO ROUTING METRICS

An offset list is the mechanism for increasing incoming and outgoing metrics to routes learned via RIP. This is done to provide a local mechanism for increasing the value of routing metrics. Optionally, you can limit the offset list with either an access list or an interface. To increase the value of routing metrics, perform the following task in router configuration mode:

Task	Command
Apply an offset to routing metrics.	**offset-list** [*access-list-number* | *name*] {**in** | **out**} *offset* [*type number*]

ADJUSTING TIMERS

Routing protocols use several timers that determine such variables as the frequency of routing updates, the length of time before a route becomes invalid, and other parameters. You can adjust these timers to tune routing protocol performance to better suit your internetwork needs. You can make the following timer adjustments:

- The rate (time in seconds between updates) at which routing updates are sent.
- The interval of time (in seconds) after which a route is declared invalid.
- The interval (in seconds) during which routing information regarding better paths is suppressed.
- The amount of time (in seconds) that must pass before a route is removed from the routing table.
- The amount of time for which routing updates will be postponed.

It also is possible to tune the IP routing support in the software to enable faster convergence of the various IP routing algorithms, and, hence, quicker fallback to redundant routers. The total effect is to minimize disruptions to end users of the network in situations where quick recovery is essential.

To adjust the timers, perform the following task in router configuration mode:

Task	Command
Adjust routing protocol timers.	**timers basic** *update invalid holddown flush* [*sleeptime*]

SPECIFYING A RIP VERSION

Cisco's implementation of RIP Version 2 supports authentication, key management, route summarization, CIDR, and VLSMs.

By default, the software receives RIP Version 1 and Version 2 packets, but sends only Version 1 packets. You can configure the software to receive and send only Version 1 packets. Alternatively, you can configure the software to receive and send only Version 2 packets. To do so, perform the following task in router configuration mode:

Task	Command
Configure the software to receive and send only RIP Version 1 or only RIP Version 2 packets.	**version** {1	2}

The preceding task controls the default behavior of RIP. You can override that behavior by configuring a particular interface to behave differently. To control which RIP version an interface sends, perform one of the following tasks in interface configuration mode:

Task	Command
Configure an interface to send only RIP Version 1 packets.	**ip rip send version 1**
Configure an interface to send only RIP Version 2 packets.	**ip rip send version 2**
Configure an interface to send RIP Version 1 and Version 2 packets.	**ip rip send version 1 2**

Similarly, to control how packets received from an interface are processed, perform one of the following tasks in interface configuration mode:

Task	Command
Configure an interface to accept only RIP Version 1 packets.	ip rip receive version 1
Configure an interface to accept only RIP Version 2 packets.	ip rip receive version 2
Configure an interface to accept either RIP Version 1 or 2 packets.	ip rip receive version 1 2

ENABLING RIP AUTHENTICATION

RIP Version 1 does not support authentication. If you are sending and receiving RIP Version 2 packets, you can enable RIP authentication on an interface.

The key chain determines the set of keys that can be used on the interface. If a key chain is not configured, no authentication is performed on that interface, not even the default authentication. Therefore, you must also perform the tasks in the section "Managing Authentication Keys" in Chapter 22.

Cisco supports two modes of authentication on an interface for which RIP authentication is enabled: plain text authentication and MD5 authentication. The default authentication in every RIP Version 2 packet is plain text authentication.

— **NOTES** ————————————————————————————

Do not use plain text authentication in RIP packets for security purposes because the unencrypted authentication key is sent in every RIP Version 2 packet. Use plain text authentication when security is not an issue—for example, to ensure that misconfigured hosts do not participate in routing.

To configure RIP authentication, perform the following tasks in interface configuration mode:

Task		Command
Step 1	Enable RIP authentication.	ip rip authentication key-chain *name-of-chain*
Step 2	Configure the interface to use MD5 digest authentication (or let it default to plain text authentication).	ip rip authentication mode {text | md5}

Task	Command
Step 3 Perform the authentication key management tasks.	See the section "Manage Authentication Keys" in Chapter 22.

See the "Key Management Examples" section of Chapter 22 for key management examples.

DISABLING ROUTE SUMMARIZATION

RIP Version 2 supports automatic route summarization by default. The software summarizes subprefixes to the classful network boundary when crossing classful network boundaries.

If you have disconnected subnets, disable automatic route summarization to advertise the subnets. When route summarization is disabled, the software transmits subnet and host routing information across classful network boundaries. To disable automatic summarization, perform the following task in router configuration mode:

Task	Command
Disable automatic summarization.	**no auto-summary**

RUNNING IGRP AND RIP CONCURRENTLY

It is possible to run IGRP and RIP concurrently. The IGRP information overrides the RIP information by default because of IGRP's administrative distance.

However, running IGRP and RIP concurrently does not work well when the network topology changes. Because IGRP and RIP have different update timers and because they require different amounts of time to propagate routing updates, one part of the network ends up believing IGRP routes and another part ends up believing RIP routes. This results in routing loops. Even though these loops do not exist for very long, the Time-to-Live (TTL) quickly reaches zero, and ICMP sends a "TTL exceeded" message. This message causes most applications to stop attempting network connections.

DISABLING THE VALIDATION OF SOURCE IP ADDRESSES

By default, the software validates the source IP address of incoming RIP routing updates. If that source address is not valid, the software discards the routing update.

You might want to disable this feature if you have a router that is "off network" and you want to receive its updates. However, disabling this feature is not recommended under normal circumstances. To disable the default function that validates the source IP addresses of incoming routing updates, perform the following task in router configuration mode:

Task	Command
Disable the validation of the source IP address of incoming RIP routing updates.	no validate-update-source

ENABLING OR DISABLING SPLIT HORIZON

Normally, routers that are connected to broadcast-type IP networks and that use distance-vector routing protocols employ the *split horizon* mechanism to reduce the possibility of routing loops. Split horizon blocks information about routes from being advertised by a router out of any interface from which that information originated. This behavior usually optimizes communications among multiple routers, particularly when links are broken. However, with nonbroadcast networks (such as Frame Relay and SMDS), situations can arise for which this behavior is less than ideal. For these situations, you might want to disable split horizon. This applies to both IGRP and RIP.

If an interface is configured with secondary IP addresses and split horizon is enabled, updates might not be sourced by every secondary address. One routing update is sourced per network number unless split horizon is disabled.

To enable or disable split horizon, perform the following tasks in interface configuration mode:

Task	Command
Enable split horizon.	ip split-horizon
Disable split horizon.	no ip split-horizon

Split horizon for Frame Relay and SMDS encapsulation is disabled by default. Split horizon is not disabled by default for interfaces using any of the X.25 encapsulations. For all other encapsulations, split horizon is enabled by default.

See the "Split Horizon Examples" section at the end of this chapter for examples of using split horizon.

NOTES

In general, changing the state of the default is not recommended unless you are certain that your application requires making a change in order to advertise routes properly. Remember this: If split horizon is disabled on a serial interface (and that interface is attached to a packet-switched network), you *must* disable split horizon for all routers in any relevant multicast groups on that network.

CONFIGURING INTERPACKET DELAY

By default, the software adds no delay between packets in a multiple-packet RIP update that is being sent. If you have a high-end router sending to a low-speed router, you might want to add such interpacket delay to RIP updates, in the range of 8 to 50 milliseconds. To do so, perform the following task in router configuration mode:

Task	Command
Add interpacket delay for RIP updates sent.	**output-delay** *delay*

SPLIT HORIZON EXAMPLES

In this section, two examples of configuring split horizon are provided.

Example 1

The following sample configuration illustrates a simple example of disabling split horizon on a serial link. In this example, the serial link is connected to an X.25 network.

```
interface serial 0
encapsulation x25
no ip split-horizon
```

Example 2

Figure 10–1 illustrates a typical situation in which the **no ip split-horizon** interface configuration command would be useful. This figure depicts two IP subnets that are both accessible via a serial interface on Router C (connected to Frame Relay network). In this example, the serial interface on Router C accommodates one of the subnets via the assignment of a secondary IP address.

The Ethernet interfaces for Router A, Router B, and Router C (connected to IP networks 12.13.50.0, 10.20.40.0, and 20.155.120.0) all have split horizon *enabled* by default, while the serial interfaces connected to networks 128.125.1.0 and 131.108.1.0 all have split horizon *disabled* by default. The partial interface configuration specifications for each router which follow illustrate that the **ip split-horizon** command is *not* explicitly configured under normal conditions for any of the interfaces.

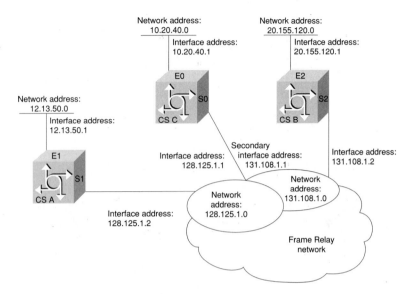

Figure 10–1
Disabled Split Horizon example for Frame Relay network.

In this example, split horizon must be disabled in order for network 128.125.0.0 to be advertised into network 131.108.0.0, and vice versa. These subnets overlap at Router C, interface S0. If split horizon were enabled on serial interface S0, it would not advertise a route back into the Frame Relay network for either of these networks.

Configuration for Router A

```
interface ethernet 1
 ip address 12.13.50.1
!
interface serial 1
 ip address 128.125.1.2
 encapsulation frame-relay
 no ip split-horizon
```

Configuration for Router B

```
interface ethernet 2
 ip address 20.155.120.1
!
interface serial 2
 ip address 131.108.1.2
 encapsulation frame-relay
 no ip split-horizon
```

Configuration for Router C

```
interface ethernet 0
 ip address 10.20.40.1
!
interface serial 0
 ip address 128.124.1.1
 ip address 131.108.1.1 secondary
 encapsulation frame-relay
```

CHAPTER 11

RIP Commands

Use the commands in this chapter to configure and monitor Routing Information Protocol (RIP). For RIP configuration information and examples, see Chapter 10, "Configuring RIP."

AUTO-SUMMARY

To restore the default behavior of automatic summarization of subnet routes into network-level routes, use the **auto-summary** router configuration command. To disable this feature and transmit subprefix routing information across classful network boundaries, use the **no** form of this command.

> **auto-summary**
> **no auto-summary**

Syntax   Description

This command has no arguments or keywords.

Default

Enabled (the software summarizes subprefixes to the classful network boundary when crossing classful network boundaries).

Command Mode

Router configuration

Usage Guidelines

This command first appeared in Cisco IOS Release 10.0.

Route summarization reduces the amount of routing information in the routing tables.

RIP Version 1 always uses automatic summarization. If you are using RIP Version 2, you can turn off automatic summarization by specifying **no auto-summary**. Disable automatic summarization if you must perform routing between disconnected subnets. When automatic summarization is off, subnets are advertised.

Example

In the following example, network numbers are not summarized automatically:

```
router rip
 version 2
 no auto-summary
```

DEFAULT-INFORMATION ORIGINATE

To generate a default route into RIP, use the **default-information originate** router configuration command. To disable this feature, use the **no** form of this command.

> **default-information originate [route-map** *mapname*]
> **no default-information originate**

Syntax	Description
route-map *mapname*	(Optional.) Routing process will generate the default route if the route map is satisfied.

Default

Disabled

Command Mode

Router configuration

Usage Guidelines

This command first appeared in Cisco IOS Release 11.1.

Example

The following example originates a   default route (0.0.0.0/0) over a certain interface when 172.68.0.0/16 is present. This is called "conditional default origination."

```
router rip
 version 2
 network 172.68.16.0
 default-information originate route-map condition
 !
 route-map condition permit 10
 match ip address 10
 set interface s1/0
```

```
!
access-list 10 permit 172.68.16.0 0.0.0.255
!
```

DEFAULT-METRIC

To set default metric values for RIP, use this form of the **default-metric** router configuration command. To return to the default state, use the **no** form of this command.

> **default-metric** *number*
> **no default-metric** [*number*]

Syntax	Description
number	Default metric value.

Default

Built-in, automatic metric translations, as appropriate for each routing protocol

Command Mode

Router configuration

Usage Guidelines

This command first appeared in Cisco IOS Release 10.0.

The **default-metric** command is used in conjunction with the **redistribute** router configuration command to cause the current routing protocol to use the same metric value for all redistributed routes. A default metric helps solve the problem of redistributing routes with incompatible metrics. Whenever metrics do not convert, using a default metric provides a reasonable substitute and enables the redistribution to proceed.

Example

The following example shows a router in autonomous system 109 using both the RIP and the OSPF routing protocols. The example advertises OSPF-derived routes using the RIP protocol and assigns the OSPF-derived routes a RIP metric of 10.

```
router rip
 default-metric 10
 redistribute ospf 109
```

Related Commands

Search online to find documentation for related commands.

redistribute

IP RIP AUTHENTICATION KEY-CHAIN

To enable authentication for RIP Version 2 packets and to specify the set of keys that can be used on an interface, use the **ip rip authentication key-chain** interface configuration command. Use the **no** form of this command to prevent authentication.

> ip rip authentication key-chain *name-of-chain*
> no ip rip authentication key-chain [*name-of-chain*]

Syntax

name-of-chain

Description

Enables authentication and specifies the group of keys that are valid.

Default

No authentication is provided for RIP packets.

Command Mode

Interface configuration

Usage Guidelines

This command first appeared in Cisco IOS Release 11.1.

If no key chain is configured with the **key-chain** command, no authentication is performed on the interface (not even the default authentication).

Example

The following example configures the interface to accept and send any key belonging to the key chain named *trees*:

```
ip rip authentication key-chain trees
```

Related Commands

Search online to find documentation for related commands.

key chain

IP RIP AUTHENTICATION MODE

To specify the type of authentication used in RIP Version 2 packets, use the **ip rip authentication mode** interface configuration command. Use the **no** form of this command to restore clear text authentication.

> ip rip authentication mode {text | md5}
> no ip rip authentication mode

Syntax	Description
text	Clear text authentication.
md5	Keyed MD5 authentication.

Default

Clear text authentication is provided for RIP packets.

Command Mode

Interface configuration

Usage Guidelines

This command first appeared in Cisco IOS Release 11.1.

RIP Version 1 does not support authentication.

Example

The following example configures the interface to use MD5 authentication:

```
ip rip authentication mode md5
```

Related Commands

Search online to find documentation for related commands.

ip rip authentication key-chain
key chain

IP RIP RECEIVE VERSION

To specify a RIP version to receive on an interface basis, use the **ip rip receive version** interface configuration command. Use the **no** form of this command to follow the global **version** rules.

ip rip receive version [1] [2]
no ip rip receive version

Syntax	Description
1	(Optional.) Accepts only RIP Version 1 packets on the interface.
2	(Optional.) Accepts only RIP Version 2 packets on the interface.

Default

The software behaves according to the **version** command.

Command Mode

Interface configuration

Usage Guidelines

This command first appeared in Cisco IOS Release 11.1.

Use this command to override the default behavior of RIP as specified by the **version** command. This command applies only to the interface being configured. You can configure the interface to accept both RIP versions.

Examples

The following example configures the interface to receive both RIP Version 1 and Version 2 packets:

```
ip rip receive version 1 2
```

The following example configures the interface to receive only RIP Version 1 packets:

```
ip rip receive version 1
```

Related Commands

Search online to find documentation for related commands.

ip rip send version
version

IP RIP SEND VERSION

To specify a RIP version to send on an interface basis, use the **ip rip send version** interface configuration command. Use the **no** form of this command to follow the global **version** rules.

> **ip rip send version** [1] [2]
> **no ip rip send version**

Syntax	Description
1	(Optional.) Sends only RIP Version 1 packets out the interface.
2	(Optional.) Sends only RIP Version 2 packets out the interface.

Default

The software behaves according to the router **version** command.

Command Mode

Interface configuration

Usage Guidelines

This command first appeared in Cisco IOS Release 11.1.

Use this command to override the default behavior of RIP as specified by the router **version** command. This command applies only to the interface being configured.

Examples

The following example configures the interface to send both RIP Version 1 and Version 2 packets out the interface:

```
ip rip send version 1 2
```

The following example configures the interface to send only RIP Version 2 packets out the interface:

```
ip rip send version 2
```

Related Commands

Search online to find documentation for related commands.

ip rip receive version
version

IP SPLIT-HORIZON

To enable the split horizon mechanism, use the **ip split-horizon** interface configuration command. To disable the split horizon mechanism, use the **no** form of this command.

> **ip split-horizon**
> **no ip split-horizon**

Syntax   Description

This command has no arguments or keywords.

Default

Varies with media

Command Mode

Interface configuration

Usage Guidelines

This command first appeared in Cisco IOS Release 10.0.

For all interfaces except those for which either Frame Relay or SMDS encapsulation is enabled, the default condition for this command is **ip split-horizon**; in other words, the split horizon feature is active. If the interface configuration includes either the **encapsulation frame-relay** or **encapsulation smds** commands, then the default is for split horizon to be disabled. Split horizon is not disabled by default for interfaces using any of the X.25 encapsulations.

— NOTES —

For networks that include links over X.25 PSNs, the **neighbor** router configuration command can be used to defeat the split horizon feature. You can as an alternative *explicitly* specify the **no ip split-horizon** command in your configuration. However, if you do so you *must* similarly disable split horizon for all routers in any relevant multicast groups on that network.

If split horizon has been disabled on an interface and you wish to enable it, use the **ip split-horizon** command to restore the split horizon mechanism.

— NOTES —

In general, changing the state of the default for the **ip split-horizon** command is not recommended, unless you are certain that your application requires a change in order to properly advertise routes. If split horizon is disabled on a serial interface (and that interface is attached to a packet-switched network), you *must* disable split horizon for all routers and access servers in any relevant multicast groups on that network.

Example

The following simple example disables split horizon on a serial link. The serial link is connected to an X.25 network:

```
interface serial 0
encapsulation x25
no ip split-horizon
```

Related Commands

Search online to find documentation for related commands.

neighbor

NEIGHBOR (IGRP AND RIP)

To define a neighboring router with which to exchange routing information, use this form of the **neighbor** router configuration command. To remove an entry, use the **no** form of this command.

> **neighbor** *ip-address*
> **no neighbor** *ip-address*

Syntax	Description
ip-address	IP address of a peer router with which routing information will be exchanged.

Default

No neighboring routers are defined.

Command Mode

Router configuration

Usage Guidelines

This command first appeared in Cisco IOS Release 10.0.

This command permits the point-to-point (nonbroadcast) exchange of routing information. When used in combination with the **passive-interface** router configuration command, routing information can be exchanged between a subset of routers and access servers on a LAN.

Multiple **neighbor** commands can be used to specify additional neighbors or peers.

Example

In the following example, RIP updates are sent to all interfaces on network 131.108.0.0 except interface Ethernet 1. However, in this case a **neighbor** router configuration command is included. This command permits the sending of routing updates to specific neighbors. One copy of the routing update is generated per neighbor.

```
router rip
 network 131.108.0.0
 passive-interface ethernet 1
 neighbor 131.108.20.4
```

Related Commands

Search online to find documentation for related commands.

passive-interface

NETWORK (RIP)

To specify a list of networks for the Routing Information Protocol (RIP) routing process, use this form of the **network** router configuration command. To remove an entry, use the **no** form of this command.

network *network-number*
no network *network-number*

Syntax	Description
network-number	IP address of the network of directly connected networks.

Default

No networks are specified.

Command Mode

Router configuration

Usage Guidelines

This command first appeared in Cisco IOS Release 10.0.

The network number specified must not contain any subnet information. You can specify multiple **network** commands. RIP routing updates will be sent and received only through interfaces on this network.

RIP sends updates to the interfaces in the specified networks. Also, if an interface's network is not specified, it will not be advertised in any RIP update.

Example

The following example defines RIP as the routing protocol to be used on all interfaces connected to networks 128.99.0.0 and 192.31.7.0:

```
router rip
  network 128.99.0.0
  network 192.31.7.0
```

Related Commands

Search online to find documentation for related commands.

router rip

OFFSET-LIST

To add an offset to incoming and outgoing metrics to routes learned via RIP, use the **offset-list** router configuration command. To remove an offset list, use the **no** form of this command.

offset-list {*access-list-number* | *name*} {**in** | **out**} *offset* [*type number*]
no offset-list {*access-list-number* | *name*} {**in** | **out**} *offset* [*type number*]

Syntax	Description
access-list-number | *name*	Standard access list number or name to be applied. Access list number 0 indicates all access lists. If *offset* is 0, no action is taken. For IGRP, the offset is added to the delay component only.
in	Applies the access list to incoming metrics.
out	Applies the access list to outgoing metrics.
offset	Positive offset to be applied to metrics for networks matching the access list. If the offset is 0, no action is taken.
type	(Optional.) Interface type to which the offset-list is applied.
number	(Optional.) Interface number to which the offset-list is applied.

Default

Disabled

Command Mode

Router configuration

Usage Guidelines

This command first appeared in Cisco IOS Release 10.0. The *type* and *number* arguments first appeared in Cisco IOS Release 10.3. The *name* argument first appeared in Cisco IOS Release 11.2.

The offset value is added to the routing metric. An offset-list with an interface type and interface number is considered extended and takes precedence over an offset-list that is not extended. Therefore, if an entry passes the extended offset-list and the normal offset-list, the extended offset-list's offset is added to the metric.

Examples

In the following example, the router applies an offset of 10 to the router's delay component only to access list 21:

```
offset-list 21 out 10
```

In the following example, the router applies an offset of 10 to routes learned from Ethernet interface 0:

```
offset-list 21 in 10 ethernet 0
```

OUTPUT-DELAY

To change the interpacket delay for RIP updates sent, use the **output-delay** router configuration command. To remove the delay, use the **no** form of this command.

output-delay *delay*
no output-delay [*delay*]

Syntax	Description
delay	Delay, in milliseconds, between packets in a multiple-packet RIP update. The range is 8 to 50 milliseconds. The default is no delay.

Default

0 milliseconds

Command Mode

Router configuration

Usage Guidelines

Consider using this command if you have a high-end router sending at high speed to a low-speed router that might not be able to receive at that fast a rate. Configuring this command will help prevent the routing table from losing information.

Example

In the following example, the interpacket delay is set to 10 milliseconds:

```
output-delay 10
```

ROUTER RIP

To configure the Routing Information Protocol (RIP) routing process, use the **router rip** global configuration command. To turn off the RIP routing process, use the **no** form of this command.

> **router rip**
> **no router rip**

Syntax   Description

This command has no arguments or keywords.

Default

No RIP routing process is defined.

Command Mode

Global configuration

Usage Guidelines

This command first appeared in Cisco IOS Release 10.0.

Example

The following example shows how to begin the RIP routing process:

```
router rip
```

Related Commands

Search online to find documentation for related commands.

network (RIP)

TIMERS BASIC

To adjust RIP network timers, use the **timers basic** router configuration command. To restore the default timers, use the **no** form of this command.

timers basic *update invalid holddown flush*
no timers basic

Syntax	Description
update	Rate in seconds at which updates are sent. This is the fundamental timing parameter of the routing protocol. The default is 30 seconds.
invalid	Interval of time in seconds after which a route is declared invalid; it should be at least three times the value of *update*. A route becomes invalid when there is an absence of updates that refresh the route. The route then enters holddown. The route is marked inaccessible and advertised as unreachable. However, the route is still used for forwarding packets. The default is 180 seconds.
holddown	Interval in seconds during which routing information regarding better paths is suppressed. It should be at least three times the value of *update*. A route enters into a holddown state when an update packet is received that indicates the route is unreachable. The route is marked inaccessible and advertised as unreachable. However, the route is still used for forwarding packets. When holddown expires, routes advertised by other sources are accepted and the route is no longer inaccessible. The default is 180 seconds.
flush	Amount of time in seconds that must pass before the route is removed from the routing table; the interval specified should be greater than the *invalid* value. If it is less than this sum, the proper holddown interval cannot elapse, which results in a new route being accepted before the holddown interval expires. The default is 240 seconds.

Defaults

update is 30 seconds
invalid is 180 seconds
holddown is 180 seconds
flush is 240 seconds

Command Mode

Router configuration

Usage Guidelines

This command first appeared in Cisco IOS Release 10.0.

The basic timing parameters for RIP are adjustable. Since RIP is executing a distributed, asynchronous routing algorithm, it is important that these timers be the same for all routers and access servers in the network.

NOTES

The current and default timer values can be seen by inspecting the output of the **show ip protocols** EXEC command. The relationships of the various timers should be preserved as described previously.

Example

In the following example, updates are broadcast every 5 seconds. If a router is not heard from in 15 seconds, the route is declared unusable. Further information is suppressed for an additional 15 seconds. At the end of the suppression period, the route is flushed from the routing table.

```
router rip
 timers basic 5  15  15  30
```

Note that by setting a short update period, you run the risk of congesting slow-speed serial lines; however, this is not a big concern on faster-speed Ethernets and T1-rate serial lines. Also, if you have many routes in your updates, you can cause the routers to spend an excessive amount of time processing updates.

VALIDATE-UPDATE-SOURCE

To have the Cisco IOS software validate the source IP address of incoming routing updates for RIP and IGRP routing protocols, use the **validate-update-source** router configuration command. To disable this function, use the **no** form of this command.

    validate-update-source
    no validate-update-source

Syntax   Description

This command has no arguments or keywords.

Default

Enabled

Command Mode

Router configuration

Usage Guidelines

This command first appeared in Cisco IOS Release 10.0.

This command is only applicable to RIP and IGRP. The software ensures that the source IP address of incoming routing updates is on the same IP network as one of the addresses defined for the receiving interface.

Disabling split horizon on the incoming interface will also cause the system to perform this validation check.

For unnumbered IP interfaces (interfaces configured as **ip unnumbered**), no checking is performed.

Example

In the following example, a router is configured to not perform validation checks on the source IP address of incoming RIP updates:

```
router rip
 network 128.105.0.0
 no validate-update-source
```

VERSION

To specify a RIP version used globally by the router, use the **version** router configuration command. Use the **no** form of this command to restore the default value.

> **version {1 | 2}**
> **no version**

Syntax	Description
1	Specifies RIP Version 1.
2	Specifies RIP Version 2.

Default

The software receives RIP Version 1 and Version 2 packets, but sends only Version 1 packets.

Command Mode

Router configuration

Usage Guidelines

This command first appeared in Cisco IOS Release 11.1.

To specify RIP versions used on an interface basis, use the **ip rip receive version** and **ip rip send version** commands.

Example

The following example enables the software to send and receive RIP Version 2 packets:

```
version 2
```

Related Commands

Search online to find documentation for related commands.

ip rip receive version
ip rip send version
show ip protocols

CHAPTER 12

Configuring IGRP

This chapter describes how to configure the Interior Gateway Routing Protocol (IGRP). For a complete description of the IGRP commands in this chapter, see Chapter 13, "IGRP Commands."

IGRP is a dynamic distance-vector routing protocol designed by Cisco in the mid-1980s for routing in an autonomous system that contains large, arbitrarily complex networks with diverse bandwidth and delay characteristics.

For protocol-independent features, see Chapter 22, "Configuring IP Routing Protocol-Independent Features."

UNDERSTANDING CISCO'S IGRP IMPLEMENTATION

IGRP uses a combination of user-configurable metrics, including internetwork delay, bandwidth, reliability, and load.

IGRP also advertises three types of routes: interior, system, and exterior (as shown in Figure 12–1). *Interior routes* are routes between subnets in the network attached to a router interface. If the network attached to a router is not subnetted, IGRP does not advertise interior routes.

System routes are routes to networks within an autonomous system. The Cisco IOS software derives system routes from directly connected network interfaces and system route information provided by other IGRP-speaking routers or access servers. System routes do not include subnet information.

Exterior routes are routes to networks outside the autonomous system that are considered when identifying a *gateway of last resort*. The Cisco IOS software chooses a gateway of last resort from the list of exterior routes that IGRP provides. The software uses the gateway (router) of last resort if it does not have a better route for a packet and the destination is not on a connected network. If the autonomous system has more than one connection to an external network, different routers can choose different exterior routers as the gateway of last resort.

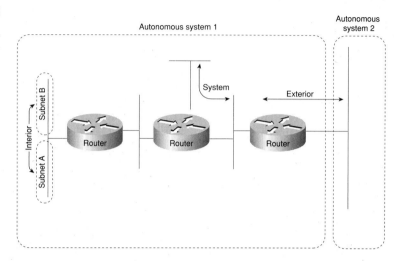

Figure 12–1
Interior, system, and exterior routes.

Understanding IGRP Updates

By default, a router running IGRP sends an update broadcast every 90 seconds. It declares a route inaccessible if it does not receive an update from the first router in the route within 3 update periods (270 seconds). After 7 update periods (630 seconds), the Cisco IOS software removes the route from the routing table.

IGRP uses *flash update* and *poison reverse updates* to speed up the convergence of the routing algorithm. A flash update occurs when an update notifying other routers of a metric change is sent sooner than the standard periodic update interval.

Poison reverse updates are sent to remove a route and place it in *holddown*, which keeps new routing information from being used for a certain period of time. Poison reverse updates are intended to defeat larger routing loops caused by increases in routing metrics.

IGRP CONFIGURATION TASK LIST

To configure IGRP, perform the tasks in the following sections. The first task in the following list, creating the IGRP routing process, is mandatory; the other tasks are optional:

- Creating the IGRP Routing Process
- Applying Offsets to Routing Metrics
- Allowing Unicast Updates for IGRP
- Defining Unequal-Cost Load Balancing
- Controlling Traffic Distribution
- Adjusting the IGRP Metric Weights
- Adjusting Timers

- Disabling Holddown
- Enforcing a Maximum Network Diameter
- Validating Source IP Addresses
- Enabling or Disabling Split Horizon

Also see the examples in the "IGRP Configuration Examples" section at the end of this chapter.

CREATING THE IGRP ROUTING PROCESS

To create the IGRP routing process, perform the following tasks starting in global configuration mode:

Task	Command
Step 1 Enable an IGRP routing process, which places you in router configuration mode.	router igrp *process-id*
Step 2 Associate networks with an IGRP routing process.	network *network-number*

IGRP sends updates to the interfaces in the specified networks. If an interface's network is not specified, it will not be advertised in any IGRP update.

It is not necessary to have a registered autonomous system number to use IGRP. If you do not have a registered number, you are free to create your own. Cisco recommends that if you do have a registered number, you use it to identify the IGRP process.

APPLYING OFFSETS TO ROUTING METRICS

An offset list is the mechanism for increasing incoming and outgoing metrics to routes learned via IGRP. This is done to provide a local mechanism for increasing the value of routing metrics. Optionally, you can limit the offset list with either an access list or an interface. To increase the value of routing metrics, perform the following task in router configuration mode:

Task	Command
Apply an offset to routing metrics.	offset-list [*access-list-number*	*name*] {in	out} *offset* [*type number*]

ALLOWING UNICAST UPDATES FOR IGRP

Because IGRP is normally a broadcast protocol, in order for IGRP routing updates to reach non-broadcast networks, you must configure the Cisco IOS software to permit this exchange of routing information.

To permit information exchange, perform the following task in router configuration mode:

Task	Command
Define a neighboring router with which to exchange routing information.	**neighbor** *ip-address*

To control the set of interfaces with which you want to exchange routing updates, you can disable the sending of routing updates on specified interfaces by configuring the **passive-interface** command. See the discussion on filtering in the "Filtering Routing Information" section in Chapter 22.

DEFINING UNEQUAL-COST LOAD BALANCING

IGRP can simultaneously use an asymmetric set of paths for a given destination. This feature is known as *unequal-cost load balancing*. Unequal-cost load balancing allows traffic to be distributed among multiple (up to four) unequal-cost paths to provide greater overall throughput and reliability. Alternate *path variance* (that is, the difference in desirability between the primary and alternate paths) is used to determine the feasibility of a potential route. An alternate route is *feasible* if the next router in the path is *closer* to the destination (has a lower metric value) than the current router and if the metric for the entire alternate path is *within* the variance. Only paths that are feasible can be used for load balancing and included in the routing table. While these conditions limit the number of cases in which load balancing can occur, they do ensure that the dynamics of the network remain stable.

The following general rules apply to IGRP unequal-cost load balancing:

- IGRP will accept up to four paths for a given destination network.
- The local best metric must be greater than the metric learned from the next router; that is, the next-hop router must be closer (have a smaller metric value) to the destination than the local best metric.
- The alternative path metric must be within the specified *variance* of the local best metric. The multiplier times the local best metric for the destination must be greater than or equal to the metric through the next router.

If these conditions are met, the route is deemed feasible and can be added to the routing table.

By default, the amount of variance is set to one (equal-cost load balancing). You can define how much worse an alternate path can be before that path is disallowed by performing the following task in router configuration mode:

Task	Command
Define the variance associated with a particular path.	**variance** *multiplier*

> **NOTES**
>
> By using the variance feature, the Cisco IOS software can balance traffic across all feasible paths and can immediately converge to a new path if one of the paths should fail.

See the "IGRP Feasible Successor Relationship Example" at the end of this chapter.

CONTROLLING TRAFFIC DISTRIBUTION

If variance is configured as described in the preceding section, IGRP or Enhanced IGRP will distribute traffic among multiple routes of unequal cost to the same destination. If you want to have faster convergence to alternate routes, but you do not want to send traffic across inferior routes in the normal case, you might prefer to have no traffic flow along routes with higher metrics.

To control how traffic is distributed among multiple routes of unequal cost, perform the following task in router configuration mode:

Task	Command
Distribute traffic proportionately to the ratios of metrics, or by the minimum-cost route.	**traffic-share** {**balanced**	**min**}

ADJUSTING THE IGRP METRIC WEIGHTS

You have the option of altering the default behavior of IGRP routing and metric computations. This allows, for example, tuning system behavior to allow for transmissions via satellite. Although IGRP metric defaults were carefully selected to provide excellent operation in most networks, you can adjust the IGRP metric. Adjusting IGRP metric weights can dramatically affect network performance, however, so ensure that you make all metric adjustments carefully.

To adjust the IGRP metric weights, perform the following task in router configuration mode.

> **CAUTION**
>
> Because of the complexity of this task, we recommend that you only perform it with guidance from an experienced system designer.

Task	Command
Adjust the IGRP metric.	**metric weights** *tos k1 k2 k3 k4 k5*

By default, the IGRP composite metric is a 24-bit quantity that is the sum of the segment delays and the lowest segment bandwidth (scaled and inverted) for a given route. For a network of homogeneous media, this metric reduces to a hop count. For a network of mixed media (FDDI, Ethernet, and serial lines running from 9600 Kbps to T1 rates), the route with the lowest metric reflects the most desirable path to a destination.

ADJUSTING TIMERS

Routing protocols use several timers that determine such variables as the frequency of routing updates, the length of time before a route becomes invalid, and other parameters. You can adjust these timers to tune routing protocol performance to better suit your internetwork needs. You can make the following timer adjustments:

- The rate (time in seconds between updates) at which routing updates are sent.
- The interval of time (in seconds) after which a route is declared invalid.
- The interval (in seconds) during which routing information regarding better paths is suppressed.
- The amount of time (in seconds) that must pass before a route is removed from the routing table.
- The amount of time for which routing updates will be postponed.

It also is possible to tune the IP routing support in the software to enable faster convergence of the various IP routing algorithms, and, hence, quicker fallback to redundant routers. The total effect is to minimize disruptions to end users of the network in situations where quick recovery is essential.

To adjust the timers, perform the following task in router configuration mode:

Task	Command
Adjust routing protocol timers.	**timers basic** *update invalid holddown flush* [*sleeptime*]

DISABLING HOLDDOWN

When the Cisco IOS software learns that a network is at a greater distance than was previously known, or it learns that the network is down, the route to that network is placed in holddown. During the holddown period, the route is advertised, but incoming advertisements about that network from any router other than the one that originally advertised the network's new metric will be ignored. This mechanism is often used to help avoid routing loops in the network, but it has the effect of increasing the topology convergence time.

To disable holddowns with IGRP, perform the following task in router configuration mode. All devices in an IGRP autonomous system must be consistent in the use of holddowns.

Task	Command
Disable the IGRP holddown period.	**no metric holddown**

ENFORCING A MAXIMUM NETWORK DIAMETER

The Cisco IOS software enforces a maximum diameter to the IGRP network. Routes whose hop counts exceed this diameter are not advertised. The default maximum diameter is 100 hops. The maximum diameter is 255 hops.

To configure the maximum diameter, perform the following task in router configuration mode:

Task	Command
Configure the maximum network diameter.	**metric maximum-hops** *hops*

VALIDATING SOURCE IP ADDRESSES

To disable the default function that validates the source IP addresses of incoming routing updates, perform the following task in router configuration mode:

Task	Command
Disable validation of the source IP address of incoming routing updates.	**no validate-update-source**

ENABLING OR DISABLING SPLIT HORIZON

Normally, routers that are connected to broadcast-type IP networks and that use distance-vector routing protocols employ the *split horizon* mechanism to reduce the possibility of routing loops. Split horizon blocks information about routes from being advertised by a router out of any interface from which that information originated. This behavior usually optimizes communications among multiple routers, particularly when links are broken. However, with nonbroadcast networks (such as Frame Relay and SMDS), situations can arise for which this behavior is less than ideal. For these situations, you might want to disable split horizon. This applies to both IGRP and RIP.

If an interface is configured with secondary IP addresses and split horizon is enabled, updates might not be sourced by every secondary address. One routing update is sourced per network number unless split horizon is disabled.

To enable or disable split horizon, perform the following tasks in interface configuration mode:

Task	Command
Step 1 Enable split horizon.	ip split-horizon
Step 2 Disable split horizon.	no ip split-horizon

Split horizon for Frame Relay and SMDS encapsulation is disabled by default. Split horizon is not disabled by default for interfaces using any of the X.25 encapsulations. For all other encapsulations, split horizon is enabled by default.

See the "Split Horizon Examples" section at the end of this chapter for examples of using split horizon.

--- NOTES ---

In general, changing the state of the default is not recommended unless you are certain that your application requires making a change in order to advertise routes properly. Remember that if split horizon is disabled on a serial interface (and that interface is attached to a packet-switched network), you *must* disable split horizon for all routers in any relevant multicast groups on that network.

IGRP CONFIGURATION EXAMPLES

This section contains the following IGRP configuration examples:

- IGRP Feasible Successor Relationship Example
- Split Horizon Examples

IGRP Feasible Successor Relationship Example

In Figure 12–2, the assigned metrics meet the conditions required for a feasible successor relationship, so the paths in this example can be included in routing tables and used for load balancing.

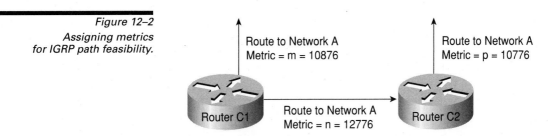

Figure 12–2
Assigning metrics for IGRP path feasibility.

The feasibility test would work in the following ways:

- Assume that Router C1 already has a route to Network A with metric *m* and has just received an update about Network A from C2. The best metric at C2 is *p*. The metric that C1 would use through C2 is *n*.
- If both of the following two conditions are met, the route to network A through C2 will be included in C1's routing table:
  - If *m* is greater than *p*.
  - If the *multiplier* (value specified by the **variance** router configuration command) times *m* is greater than or equal to *n*.
- The configuration for Router C1 would be as follows:

```
router igrp 109
 variance 10
```

A maximum of four paths can be in the routing table for a single destination. If there are more than four feasible paths, the four best feasible paths are used.

Split Horizon Examples

The following sample configuration illustrates a simple example of disabling split horizon on a serial link. In this example, the serial link is connected to an X.25 network.

```
interface serial 0
 encapsulation x25
 no ip split-horizon
```

Figure 12–3 illustrates a typical situation in which the **no ip split-horizon** interface configuration command would be useful. This figure depicts two IP subnets that are both accessible via a serial interface on Router C (connected to Frame Relay network). In this example, the serial interface on Router C accommodates one of the subnets via the assignment of a secondary IP address.

The Ethernet interfaces for Router A, Router B, and Router C (connected to IP networks 12.13.50.0, 10.20.40.0, and 20.155.120.0) all have split horizon *enabled* by default, while the serial interfaces connected to networks 128.125.1.0 and 131.108.1.0 all have split horizon *disabled* by default. The partial interface configuration specifications for each router that follow Figure 12–3 illustrate that the **ip split-horizon** command is *not* explicitly configured under normal conditions for any of the interfaces.

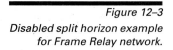

Figure 12–3

Disabled split horizon example for Frame Relay network.

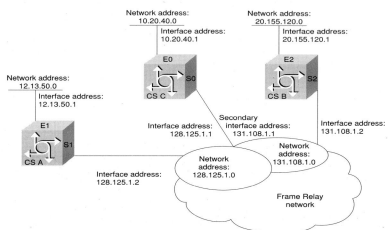

In this example, split horizon must be disabled in order for network 128.125.0.0 to be advertised into network 131.108.0.0, and vice versa. These subnets overlap at Router C, interface S0. If split horizon were enabled on serial interface S0, it would not advertise a route back into the Frame Relay network for either of these networks.

Configuration for Router A

```
interface ethernet 1
 ip address 12.13.50.1
!
interface serial 1
 ip address 128.125.1.2
 encapsulation frame-relay
```

Configuration for Router B

```
interface ethernet 2
 ip address 20.155.120.1
!
interface serial 2
 ip address 131.108.1.2
 encapsulation frame-relay
```

Configuration for Router C

```
interface ethernet 0
 ip address 10.20.40.1
 !
interface serial 0
 ip address 128.124.1.1
 ip address 131.108.1.1 secondary
 encapsulation frame-relay
```

CHAPTER 13

IGRP Commands

Use the commands in this chapter to configure and monitor Internet Gateway Routing Protocol (IGRP). For IGRP configuration information and examples, see Chapter 12, "Configuring IGRP."

DEFAULT-INFORMATION

To control the candidate default routing information between IGRP or Enhanced IGRP processes, use the **default-information** router configuration command. To suppress IGRP or Enhanced IGRP candidate information in incoming updates, use the **no default-information in** command. To suppress IGRP or Enhanced IGRP candidate information in outbound updates, use the **no default-information out** command.

default-information {in | out} {*access-list-number* | *name*}
no default-information {in | out}

Syntax	Description
in	Allows IGRP or Enhanced IGRP exterior or default routes to be received by an IGRP process.
out	Allows IGRP or Enhanced IGRP exterior routes to be advertised in updates.
access-list-number	*name*	Number or name of an access list. It can be a number in the range from 1 to 99 or an access list name.

Default

Normally, exterior routes are always accepted and default information is passed between IGRP or Enhanced IGRP processes when doing redistribution.

Command Mode

Router configuration

Usage Guidelines

This command first appeared in Cisco IOS Release 10.0. The *access-list-number* and *name* arguments first appeared in Cisco IOS Release 11.2.

The default network of 0.0.0.0 used by RIP cannot be redistributed by IGRP or Enhanced IGRP.

Examples

The following example allows IGRP exterior or default routes to be received by the IGRP process in autonomous system 23:

```
router igrp 23
  default-information in
```

The following example allows IP Enhanced IGRP exterior or default routes to be received by the IP Enhanced IGRP process in autonomous system 23:

```
router eigrp 23
  default-information in
```

DEFAULT-METRIC (IGRP AND ENHANCED IGRP ONLY)

To set metrics for IGRP or Enhanced IGRP, use this form of the **default-metric** router configuration command. To remove the metric value and restore the default state, use the **no** form of this command.

> **default-metric** *bandwidth delay reliability loading mtu*
> **no default-metric** *bandwidth delay reliability loading mtu*

Syntax	Description
bandwidth	Minimum bandwidth of the route in kilobits per second. It can be 0 or any positive integer.
delay	Route delay in tens of microseconds. It can be 0 or any positive number that is a multiple of 39.1 nanoseconds.
reliability	Likelihood of successful packet transmission expressed as a number between 0 and 255. The value 255 means 100 percent reliability; 0 means no reliability.
loading	Effective bandwidth of the route expressed as a number from 0 to 255 (255 is 100 percent loading).
mtu	Minimum maximum transmission unit (MTU) size of the route in bytes. It can be 0 or any positive integer.

Default

Only connected routes and interface static routes can be redistributed without a default metric.

Command Mode

Router configuration

Usage Guidelines

This command first appeared in Cisco IOS Release 10.0.

A default metric is required to redistribute a protocol into IGRP or Enhanced IGRP unless you use the **redistribute** command. Automatic metric translations occur between IGRP and Enhanced IGRP. You do not need default metrics to redistribute IGRP or Enhanced IGRP into itself.

Metric defaults have been carefully set to work for a wide variety of networks. Take great care in changing these values.

Keeping the same metrics is supported only when redistributing from IGRP, Enhanced IGRP, or static routes.

Example

The following example takes redistributed RIP metrics and translates them into IGRP metrics with values as follows: bandwidth = 1000, delay = 100, reliability = 250, loading = 100, and mtu =1500.

```
router igrp 109
  network 131.108.0.0
  redistribute rip
  default-metric 1000 100 250 100 1500
```

Related Commands

Search online to find documentation for related commands.

redistribute

IP SPLIT-HORIZON

To enable the split horizon mechanism, use the **ip split-horizon** interface configuration command. To disable the split horizon mechanism, use the **no** form of this command.

> **ip split-horizon**
> **no ip split-horizon**

Syntax   Description

This command has no arguments or keywords.

Default

Varies with media

Command Mode

Interface configuration

Usage Guidelines

This command first appeared in Cisco IOS Release 10.0.

For all interfaces except those for which either Frame Relay or SMDS encapsulation is enabled, the default condition for this command is **ip split-horizon**; in other words, the split horizon feature is active. If the interface configuration includes either the **encapsulation frame-relay** or **encapsulation smds** commands, then the default is for split horizon to be disabled. Split horizon is not disabled by default for interfaces using any of the X.25 encapsulations.

NOTES

For networks that include links over X.25 PSNs, the **neighbor** router configuration command can be used to defeat the split horizon feature. You can as an alternative *explicitly* specify the **no ip split-horizon** command in your configuration. However, if you do so, you *must* similarly disable split horizon for all routers in any relevant multicast groups on that network.

If split horizon has been disabled on an interface and you want to enable it, use the **ip split-horizon** command to restore the split horizon mechanism.

NOTES

In general, changing the state of the default for the **ip split-horizon** command is not recommended unless you are certain that your application requires a change in order to properly advertise routes. If split horizon is disabled on a serial interface (and that interface is attached to a packet-switched network), you *must* disable split horizon for all routers and access servers in any relevant multicast groups on that network.

Example

The following simple example disables split horizon on a serial link. The serial link is connected to an X.25 network:

```
interface serial 0
  encapsulation x25
  no ip split-horizon
```

Related Commands

Search online to find documentation for related commands.

neighbor

METRIC HOLDDOWN

To keep new IGRP routing information from being used for a certain period of time, use the **metric holddown** router configuration command. To disable this feature, use the **no** form of this command.

> **metric holddown**
> **no metric holddown**

Syntax   Description

This command has no arguments or keywords.

Default

Disabled

Command Mode

Router configuration

Usage Guidelines

This command first appeared in Cisco IOS Release 10.0.

Holddown keeps new routing information from being used for a certain period of time. This can prevent routing loops caused by slow convergence. It is sometimes advantageous to disable holddown to increase the network's capability to quickly respond to topology changes; this command provides this function.

Use the **metric holddown** command if other routers or access servers within the IGRP autonomous system are not configured with **no metric holddown**. If all routers are not configured the same way, you increase the possibility of routing loops.

Example

The following example disables metric holddown:

```
router igrp 15
 network 131.108.0.0
 network 192.31.7.0
 no metric holddown
```

Related Commands

Search online to find documentation for related commands.

metric maximum-hops
metric weights
timers basic

METRIC MAXIMUM-HOPS

To have the IP routing software advertise as unreachable those routes with a hop count higher than is specified by the command (IGRP only), use the **metric maximum-hops** router configuration command. To reset the value to the default, use the **no** form of this command.

> **metric maximum-hops** *hops*
> **no metric maximum-hops** *hops*

Syntax	*Description*
hops	Maximum hop count (in decimal). The default value is 100 hops; the maximum number of hops that can be specified is 255.

Default

100 hops

Command Mode

Router configuration

Usage Guidelines

This command first appeared in Cisco IOS Release 10.0.

This command provides a safety mechanism that breaks any potential *count-to-infinity* problems. It causes the IP routing software to advertise as unreachable routes with hop counts greater than the value assigned to the *hops* argument.

Example

In the following example, a router in autonomous system 71 attached to network 15.0.0.0 wants a maximum hop count of 200, doubling the default. The network administrators decided to do this because they have a complex WAN that can generate a large hop count under normal (nonlooping) operations.

```
router igrp 71
 network 15.0.0.0
 metric maximum-hops 200
```

Related Commands

Search online to find documentation for related commands.

metric holddown
metric weights

METRIC WEIGHTS

To allow the tuning of the IGRP or Enhanced IGRP metric calculations, use the **metric weights** router configuration command. To reset the values to their defaults, use the **no** form of this command.

> **metric weights** *tos k1 k2 k3 k4 k5*
> **no metric weights**

Syntax

Syntax	Description
tos	Type of service. Currently, it must always be zero.
k1–k5	Constants that convert an IGRP or Enhanced IGRP metric vector into a scalar quantity.

Defaults

tos: 0
k1: 1
k2: 0
k3: 1
k4: 0
k5: 0

Command Mode

Router configuration

Usage Guidelines

This command first appeared in Cisco IOS Release 10.0.

Use this command to alter the default behavior of IGRP routing and metric computation and allow the tuning of the IGRP metric calculation for a particular type of service (TOS).

If k5 equals 0, the composite IGRP or enhanced IGRP metric is computed according to the following formula:

```
metric = [k1 * bandwidth + (k2 * bandwidth)/(256 - load) + k3 * delay]
```

If k5 does not equal zero, an additional operation is performed:

```
metric = metric * [k5 / (reliability + k4)]
```

Bandwidth is the inverse minimum bandwidth of the path in bits per second scaled by a factor of 2.56×10^{12}. The range is from a 1200-bps line to 10 terabits per second.

Delay is in units of 10 microseconds. This gives a range of 10 microseconds to 168 seconds. A delay of all ones indicates that the network is unreachable.

The delay parameter is stored in a 32-bit field, in increments of 39.1 nanoseconds. This gives a range of 1 (39.1 nanoseconds) to hexadecimal FFFFFFFF (decimal 4,294,967,040 nanoseconds). A delay of all ones (that is, a delay of hexadecimal FFFFFFFF) indicates that the network is unreachable.

Table 13–1 lists the default values used for several common media.

Table 13–1   *Bandwidth Values by Media Type*

Media Type	Delay	Bandwidth
Satellite	5120 (2 seconds)	5120 (500 Mb)
Ethernet	25600 (1 ms)	256000 (10 Mb)
1.544 Mbps	512000 (20,000 ms)	1,657,856 bits
64 Kbps	512000 (20,000 ms)	40,000,000 bits
56 Kbps	512000 (20,000 ms)	45,714,176 bits
10 Kbps	512000 (20,000 ms)	256,000,000 bits
1 Kbps	512000 (20,000 ms)	2,560,000,000 bits

Reliability is given as a fraction of 255. That is, 255 is 100 percent reliability or a perfectly stable link.

Load is given as a fraction of 255. A load of 255 indicates a completely saturated link.

Example

The following example sets the metric weights to slightly different values than the defaults:

```
router igrp 109
 network 131.108.0.0
 metric weights 0 2 0 2 0 0
```

Related Commands

Search online to find documentation for related commands.

bandwidth
delay
metric holddown
metric maximum-hops

NEIGHBOR (IGRP AND RIP)

To define a neighboring router with which to exchange routing information, use this form of the **neighbor** router configuration command. To remove an entry, use the **no** form of this command.

> **neighbor** *ip-address*
> **no neighbor** *ip-address*

Syntax	Description
ip-address	IP address of a peer router with which routing information is exchanged.

Default

No neighboring routers are defined.

Command Mode

Router configuration

Usage Guidelines

This command first appeared in Cisco IOS Release 10.0.

This command permits the point-to-point (nonbroadcast) exchange of routing information. When used in combination with the **passive-interface** router configuration command, routing information can be exchanged between a subset of routers and access servers on a LAN.

Multiple **neighbor** commands can be used to specify additional neighbors or peers.

Example

In the following example, IGRP updates are sent to all interfaces on network 131.108.0.0 except interface Ethernet 1. However, in this case a **neighbor** router configuration command is included. This command permits the sending of routing updates to specific neighbors. One copy of the routing update is generated per neighbor.

```
router igrp 109
  network 131.108.0.0
  passive-interface ethernet 1
  neighbor 131.108.20.4
```

Related Commands

Search online to find documentation for related commands.

passive-interface

NETWORK (IGRP AND ENHANCED IGRP)

To specify a list of networks for the Enhanced IGRP routing process, use this form of the **network** router configuration command. To remove an entry, use the **no** form of this command.

> **network** *network-number*
> **no network** *network-number*

Syntax	Description
network-number	IP address of the directly connected networks.

Default

No networks are specified.

Command Mode

Router configuration

Usage Guidelines

This command first appeared in Cisco IOS Release 10.0.

The network number specified must not contain any subnet information. You can specify multiple **network** commands.

IGRP or Enhanced IGRP sends updates to the interfaces in the specified network(s). Also, if an interface's network is not specified, it is not advertised in any IGRP or Enhanced IGRP update.

Example

The following example configures a router for IGRP and assigns autonomous system 109. The **network** commands indicate the networks directly connected to the router.

```
router igrp 109
 network 131.108.0.0
 network 192.31.7.0
```

Related Commands

Search online to find documentation for related commands.

router igrp

OFFSET-LIST

To add an offset to incoming and outgoing metrics to routes learned via IGRP, use the **offset-list** router configuration command. To remove an offset list, use the **no** form of this command.

offset-list {*access-list-number* | *name*} {**in** | **out**} *offset* [*type number*]
no offset-list {*access-list-number* | *name*} {**in** | **out**} *offset* [*type number*]

Syntax	Description
access-list-number	*name*	Standard access list number or name to be applied. Access list number 0 indicates all access lists. If *offset* is 0, no action is taken. For IGRP, the offset is added to the delay component only.
in	Applies the access list to incoming metrics.
out	Applies the access list to outgoing metrics.
offset	Positive offset to be applied to metrics for networks matching the access list. If the offset is 0, no action is taken.
type	(Optional.) Interface type to which the offset-list is applied.
number	(Optional.) Interface number to which the offset-list is applied.

Default

Disabled

Command Mode

Router configuration

Usage Guidelines

This command first appeared in Cisco IOS Release 10.0. The *type* and *number* arguments first appeared in Cisco IOS Release 10.3. The *name* argument first appeared in Cisco IOS Release 11.2.

The offset value is added to the routing metric. An offset-list with an interface type and interface number is considered extended and takes precedence over an offset-list that is not extended. Therefore, if an entry passes the extended offset-list and the normal offset-list, the extended offset-list's offset is added to the metric.

Examples

In the following example, the router applies an offset of 10 to the router's delay component only to access list 121:

```
offset-list 21 out 10
```

In the following example, the router applies an offset of 10 to routes learned from Ethernet interface 0:

```
offset-list 21 in 10 ethernet 0
```

ROUTER IGRP

To configure the Interior Gateway Routing Protocol (IGRP) routing process, use the **router igrp** global configuration command. To shut down an IGRP routing process, use the **no** form of this command.

> **router igrp** *autonomous-system*
> **no router igrp** *autonomous-system*

Syntax	Description
autonomous-system	Autonomous system number that identifies the routes to the other IGRP routers. It is also used to tag the routing information.

Default

No IGRP routing process is defined.

Command Mode

Global configuration

Usage Guidelines

This command first appeared in Cisco IOS Release 10.0.

It is not necessary to have a registered autonomous system number to use IGRP. If you do not have a registered number, you are free to create your own. We recommend that if you do have a registered number, you use it to identify the IGRP process.

Example

The following example configures an IGRP routing process and assigns process number 109:

```
router igrp 109
```

Related Commands

Search online to find documentation for related commands.

network (IGRP and Enhanced IGRP)

SET METRIC

To set the metric value for IGRP in a route-map, use the **set metric** route-map configuration command. To return to the default metric value, use the **no** form of this command.

set metric *bandwidth delay reliability loading mtu*
no set metric *bandwidth delay reliability loading mtu*

Syntax	Description
bandwidth	Metric value or IGRP bandwidth of the route in kilobits per second. It can be in the range 0 to 4294967295.
delay	Route delay in tens of microseconds. It can be in the range from 0 to 4294967295.
reliability	Likelihood of successful packet transmission expressed as a number between 0 and 255. The value 255 means 100 percent reliability; 0 means no reliability.
loading	Effective bandwidth of the route expressed as a number from 0 to 255 (255 is 100 percent loading).
mtu	Minimum maximum transmission unit (MTU) size of the route in bytes. It can be in the range from 0 to 4294967295.

Default

No metric is set in the route-map.

Command Mode

Route-map configuration

Usage Guidelines

This command first appeared in Cisco IOS Release 10.0.

NOTES

We recommend that you consult your Cisco technical support representative before changing the default value.

Use the **route-map** global configuration command and the **match** and **set** route-map configuration commands to define the conditions for redistributing routes from one routing protocol into another. Each **route-map** command has a list of **match** and **set** commands associated with it. The **match** commands specify the *match criteria*—the conditions under which redistribution is allowed for the current **route-map** command. The **set** commands specify the *set actions*—the particular redistribution actions to perform if the criteria enforced by the **match** commands are met. The **no route-map** command deletes the route map.

The **set** route-map configuration commands specify the redistribution *set actions* to be performed when all of a route map's match criteria are met. When all match criteria are met, all set actions are performed.

Example

In the following example, the bandwidth is set to 10,000, the delay is set to 10, the reliability is set to 255, the loading is set to 1, and the MTU is set to 1500:

```
set metric 10000 10 255 1 1500
```

TIMERS BASIC

To adjust IGRP network timers, use the **timers basic** router configuration command. To restore the default timers, use the **no** form of this command.

> **timers basic** *update invalid holddown flush* [*sleeptime*]
> **no timers basic**

Syntax	Description
update	Rate in seconds at which updates are sent. This is the fundamental timing parameter of the routing protocol.
invalid	Interval of time in seconds after which a route is declared invalid; it should be at least three times the value of *update*. A route becomes invalid when there is an absence of updates that refresh the route. The route then enters holddown. The route is marked inaccessible and is advertised as unreachable. However, the route is still used for forwarding packets.
holddown	Interval in seconds during which routing information regarding better paths is suppressed. It should be at least three times the value of *update*. A route enters into a holddown state when an update packet is received that indicates that the route is unreachable. The route is marked inaccessible and advertised as unreachable. However, the route is still used for forwarding packets. When holddown expires, routes advertised by other sources are accepted and the route is no longer inaccessible.

Syntax	Description
flush	Amount of time in seconds that must pass before the route is removed from the routing table; the interval specified must be at least the sum of *invalid* and *holddown*. If it is less than this sum, the proper holddown interval cannot elapse, which results in a new route being accepted before the holddown interval expires.
sleeptime	(Optional.) Interval in milliseconds for postponing routing updates in the event of a flash update. The *sleeptime* value should be less than the *update* time. If the *sleeptime* is greater than the *update* time, routing tables become unsynchronized.

Defaults

update is 90 seconds
invalid is 270 seconds
holddown is 280 seconds
flush is 630 seconds
sleeptime is 0 milliseconds

Command Mode

Router configuration

Usage Guidelines

This command first appeared in Cisco IOS Release 10.0.

The basic timing parameters for IGRP are adjustable. Because this routing protocol is executing a distributed, asynchronous routing algorithm, it is important that these timers be the same for all routers and access servers in the network.

NOTES

The current and default timer values can be seen by inspecting the output of the **show ip protocols** EXEC command. The relationships of the various timers should be preserved, as described previously.

Example

In the following example, updates are broadcast every 5 seconds. If a router is not heard from in 15 seconds, the route is declared unusable. Further information is suppressed for an additional 15 seconds. At the end of the suppression period, the route is flushed from the routing table.

```
router igrp 109
  timers basic 5  15  15  30
```

Note that by setting a short update period, you run the risk of congesting slow-speed serial lines; however, this is not a big concern on faster-speed Ethernets and T1-rate serial lines. Also, if you have many routes in your updates, you can cause the routers to spend an excessive amount of time processing updates.

TRAFFIC-SHARE

To control how traffic is distributed among routes when there are multiple routes for the same destination network that have different costs, use the **traffic-share** router configuration command. To disable this function, use the **no** form of the command.

     traffic-share {balanced | min}
     [no] traffic share {balanced | min}

Syntax	Description
balanced	Distributes traffic proportionately to the ratios of the metrics.
min	Uses routes that have minimum costs.

Default

Traffic is distributed proportionately to the ratios of the metrics.

Command Mode

Router configuration

Usage Guidelines

This command first appeared in Cisco IOS Release 10.0.

This command applies to IGRP and Enhanced IGRP routing protocols only. With the default setting, routes that have higher metrics represent less-preferable routes and get less traffic. Configuring **traffic-share min** causes the Cisco IOS software to only divide traffic among the routes with the best metric. Other routes remain in the routing table but receive no traffic.

Example

In the following example, only routes of minimum cost are used:

```
router igrp 5
  traffic-share min
```

VALIDATE-UPDATE-SOURCE

To have the Cisco IOS software validate the source IP address of incoming routing updates for RIP and IGRP routing protocols, use the **validate-update-source** router configuration command. To disable this function, use the **no** form of this command.

validate-update-source
no validate-update-source

Syntax   *Description*

This command has no arguments or keywords.

Default

Enabled

Command Mode

Router configuration

Usage Guidelines

This command first appeared in Cisco IOS Release 10.0.

This command is only applicable to RIP and IGRP. The software ensures that the source IP address of incoming routing updates is on the same IP network as one of the addresses defined for the receiving interface.

Disabling split horizon on the incoming interface also causes the system to perform this validation check.

For unnumbered IP interfaces (interfaces configured as **ip unnumbered**), no checking is performed.

Example

In the following example, a router is configured to not perform validation checks on the source IP address of incoming RIP updates:

```
router rip
 network 128.105.0.0
 no validate-update-source
```

CHAPTER 14

Configuring OSPF

This chapter describes how to configure Open Shortest Path First (OSPF). For a complete description of the OSPF commands in this chapter, see Chapter 15, "OSPF Commands."

OSPF is an IGP developed by the OSPF working group of the Internet Engineering Task Force (IETF). Designed expressly for IP networks, OSPF supports IP subnetting and tagging of externally derived routing information. OSPF also allows packet authentication and uses IP multicast when sending and receiving packets.

Cisco supports RFC 1253, OSPF MIB, August 1991; the OSPF MIB defines an IP routing protocol that provides management information related to OSPF and is supported by Cisco routers.

For protocol-independent features, see Chapter 22, "Configuring IP Routing Protocol-Independent Features."

CISCO'S OSPF IMPLEMENTATION

Cisco's implementation conforms to the OSPF Version 2 specifications as detailed in the Internet RFC 1583. The following key features are supported in Cisco's OSPF implementation:

- Stub areas—Definition of stub areas is supported.

- Route redistribution—Routes learned via any IP routing protocol can be redistributed into any other IP routing protocol. At the intradomain level, this means that OSPF can import routes learned via IGRP, RIP, and IS-IS. OSPF routes can also be exported into IGRP, RIP, and IS-IS. At the interdomain level, OSPF can import routes learned via EGP and BGP. OSPF routes can also be exported into EGP and BGP.

- Authentication—Plain text and MD5 authentication among neighboring routers within an area is supported.

347

- Routing interface parameters—Configurable parameters supported include interface output cost, retransmission interval, interface transmit delay, router priority, router "dead" and hello intervals, and authentication key.
- Virtual links—Virtual links are supported.
- NSSA areas—RFC 1587.
- OSPF over demand circuit—RFC 1793.

NOTES

To take advantage of the OSPF stub area support, *default routing* must be used in the stub area.

OSPF CONFIGURATION TASK LIST

OSPF typically requires coordination among many internal routers, *area border routers* (routers connected to multiple areas), and autonomous system boundary routers. At a minimum, OSPF-based routers or access servers can be configured with all default parameter values, no authentication, and interfaces assigned to areas. If you intend to customize your environment, you must ensure that the configuration of all routers is coordinated.

To configure OSPF, complete the tasks in the following sections. The first task in the following list is mandatory; the other tasks are optional, but might be required for your particular application:

- Enabling OSPF
- Configuring OSPF Interface Parameters
- Configuring OSPF Over Different Physical Networks
- Configuring OSPF Area Parameters
- Configuring OSPF Not So Stubby Area (NSSA)
- Configuring Route Summarization Between OSPF Areas
- Configuring Route Summarization when Redistributing Routes into OSPF
- Creating Virtual Links
- Generating a Default Route
- Configuring Lookup of DNS Names
- Forcing the Router ID Choice with a Loopback Interface
- Controlling Default Metrics
- Configuring OSPF on Simplex Ethernet Interfaces
- Configuring Route Calculation Timers
- Configuring OSPF over On-Demand Circuits
- Logging Neighbor Changes
- Monitoring and Maintaining OSPF

In addition, you can specify route redistribution; see the task "Redistributing Routing Information" in Chapter 22, "Configuring IP Routing Protocol-Independent Features" for information on how to configure route redistribution.

ENABLING OSPF

As with other routing protocols, enabling OSPF requires that you create an OSPF routing process, specify the range of IP addresses to be associated with the routing process, and assign area IDs to be associated with that range of IP addresses. Perform the following tasks, starting in global configuration mode:

Task	Command
Step 1 Enable OSPF routing, which places you in router configuration mode.	**router ospf** *process-id*
Step 2 Define an interface on which OSPF runs and define the area ID for that interface.	**network** *address wildcard-mask* **area** *area-id*

CONFIGURING OSPF INTERFACE PARAMETERS

Cisco's OSPF implementation allows you to alter certain interface-specific OSPF parameters, as needed. You are not required to alter any of these parameters, but some interface parameters must be consistent across all routers in an attached network. Those parameters are controlled by the **ip ospf hello-interval, ip ospf dead-interval,** and **ip ospf authentication-key** commands. Therefore, be sure that if you do configure any of these parameters, the configurations for all routers on your network have compatible values.

In interface configuration mode, specify any of the following interface parameters as needed for your network:

Task	Command
Explicitly specify the cost of sending a packet on an OSPF interface.	**ip ospf cost** *cost*
Specify the number of seconds between link state advertisement retransmissions for adjacencies belonging to an OSPF interface.	**ip ospf retransmit-interval** *seconds*
Set the estimated number of seconds it takes to transmit a link state update packet on an OSPF interface.	**ip ospf transmit-delay** *seconds*

Task	Command
Set priority to help determine the OSPF designated router for a network.	**ip ospf priority** *number*
Specify the length of time, in seconds, between the hello packets that the Cisco IOS software sends on an OSPF interface.	**ip ospf hello-interval** *seconds*
Set the number of seconds that a device's hello packets must not have been seen before its neighbors declare the OSPF router down.	**ip ospf dead-interval** *seconds*
Assign a specific password to be used by neighboring OSPF routers on a network segment that is using OSPF's simple password authentication.	**ip ospf authentication-key** *key*
Enable OSPF MD5 authentication.	**ip ospf message-digest-key** *keyid* **md5** *key*

CONFIGURING OSPF OVER DIFFERENT PHYSICAL NETWORKS

By default, OSPF classifies different media into the following three types of networks:

- Broadcast networks (Ethernet, Token Ring, FDDI)
- Nonbroadcast multiaccess networks (SMDS, Frame Relay, X.25)
- Point-to-point networks (HDLC, PPP)

You can configure your network as either a broadcast or a nonbroadcast multiaccess network.

X.25 and Frame Relay provide an optional broadcast capability that can be configured in the map to allow OSPF to run as a broadcast network.

Configuring Your OSPF Network Type

You have the choice of configuring your OSPF network type as either broadcast or nonbroadcast multiaccess, regardless of the default media type. Using this feature, you can configure broadcast networks as nonbroadcast multiaccess networks when, for example, you have routers in your network that do not support multicast addressing. You also can configure nonbroadcast multiaccess networks (such as X.25, Frame Relay, and SMDS) as broadcast networks. This feature prevents you from having to configure neighbors, as described in the section "Configuring OSPF for Nonbroadcast Networks."

Configuring nonbroadcast, multiaccess networks as either broadcast or nonbroadcast assumes that there are virtual circuits from every router to every other router, or a fully meshed network. This is not true in some cases, for example, because of cost constraints or when you have only a partially meshed network. In these cases, you can configure the OSPF network type as a point-to-multipoint network. Routing between two routers not directly connected will go through the router that has virtual circuits to both routers. Note that you must not configure neighbors when using this feature.

An OSPF point-to-multipoint interface is defined as a numbered point-to-point interface having one or more neighbors. This creates multiple host routes. An OSPF point-to-multipoint network has the following benefits compared to nonbroadcast multiaccess and point-to-point networks:

- Point-to-multipoint is easier to configure because it requires no configuration of neighbor commands, it consumes only one IP subnet, and it requires no designated router election.
- It costs less because it does not require a fully meshed topology.
- It is more reliable because it maintains connectivity in the event of virtual circuit failure.

To configure your OSPF network type, perform the following task in interface configuration mode:

Task	Command
Configure the OSPF network type for a specified interface.	**ip ospf network** {**broadcast** | **non-broadcast** | **point-to-multipoint**}

See the "OSPF Point-to-Multipoint Example" section at the end of this chapter for an example of an OSPF point-to-multipoint network.

Configuring OSPF for Nonbroadcast Networks

Because there might be many routers attached to an OSPF network, a *designated router* is selected for the network. It is necessary to use special configuration parameters in the designated router selection if broadcast capability is not configured.

These parameters need only be configured in those devices that are themselves eligible to become the designated router or backup designated router (in other words, routers or access servers with a nonzero router priority value).

To configure routers that interconnect to nonbroadcast networks, perform the following task in router configuration mode:

Task	Command
Configure routers or access servers interconnecting to nonbroadcast networks.	**neighbor** *ip-address* [**priority** *number*] [**poll-interval** *seconds*]

You can specify the following neighbor parameters, as required:

- Priority for a neighboring router
- Nonbroadcast poll interval
- Interface through which the neighbor is reachable

CONFIGURING OSPF AREA PARAMETERS

Cisco's OSPF software allows you to configure several area parameters. These area parameters, shown in the following table, include authentication, defining stub areas, and assigning specific costs to the default summary route. *Authentication* allows password-based protection against unauthorized access to an area. *Stub areas* are areas into which information on external routes is not sent; instead, there is a default external route generated by the area border router into the stub area for destinations outside the autonomous system. To further reduce the number of link state advertisements sent into a stub area, you can configure **no-summary** on the Area Border Router (ABR) to prevent it from sending summary link advertisement (link state advertisements Type 3) into the stub area.

In router configuration mode, specify any of the following area parameters as needed for your network:

Task	Command
Step 1 Enable authentication for an OSPF area.	**area** *area-id* **authentication**
Step 2 Enable MD5 authentication for an OSPF area.	**area** *area-id* **authentication message-digest**
Step 3 Define an area to be a stub area.	**area** *area-id* **stub** [**no-summary**]
Step 4 Assign a specific cost to the default summary route used for the stub area.	**area** *area-id* **default-cost** *cost*

CONFIGURING OSPF NOT SO STUBBY AREA (NSSA)

NSSA area is similar to OSPF stub area. NSSA does not flood Type 5 external Link State Advertisements (LSAs) from the core into the area, but it has the ability to import AS external routes in a limited fashion within the area.

NSSA can import Type 7 AS external routes within NSSA area by redistribution. These Type 7 LSAs are translated into Type 5 LSAs by NSSA ABR which are flooded throughout the whole routing domain. Summarization and filtering are supported during the translation.

Use NSSA to simplify administration if you are an Internet Service Provider (ISP), or a network administrator that must connect a central site using OSPF to a remote site that is using a different routing protocol.

Prior to NSSA, the connection between the corporate site border router and the remote router could not be run as an OSPF stub area because routes for the remote site cannot be redistributed into stub area. A simple protocol like RIP was usually used, and it handled the redistribution. This meant maintaining two routing protocols.

With NSSA, you can extend OSPF to cover the remote connection by defining the area between the corporate router and the remote router as an NSSA. In router configuration mode, specify the following area parameters as needed to configure OSPF NSSA:

Task	Command
Define an area to be NSSA.	area *area-id* nssa [no-redistribution] [default-information-originate]

In router configuration mode on the ABR, specify the following command to control summarization and filtering of Type 7 LSA into Type 5 LSA:

Task	Command
Control the summarization and filtering during the translation. (Optional.)	**summary address** *prefix mask* [not advertise] [tag tag]

Understanding Implementation Considerations

Evaluate the following considerations before implementing this feature:

- You can set a Type 7 default route that can be used to reach external destinations. When configured, the router generates a Type 7 default into the NSSA by the NSSA ABR.

- Every router within the same area must agree that the area is NSSA; otherwise, the routers will not be able to communicate with each other.

NOTES

If possible, avoid using explicit redistribution on NSSA ABR because confusion may result over which packets are being translated by which router.

CONFIGURING ROUTE SUMMARIZATION BETWEEN OSPF AREAS

Route summarization is the consolidation of advertised addresses. This feature causes a single summary route to be advertised to other areas by an ABR. In OSPF, an ABR will advertise networks in one area into another area. If the network numbers in an area are assigned such that they are contiguous, you can configure the ABR to advertise a summary route that covers all the individual networks within the area that fall into the specified range.

To specify an address range, perform the following task in router configuration mode:

Task	Command
Specify an address range for which a single route will be advertised.	**area** *area-id* **range** *address mask*

CONFIGURING ROUTE SUMMARIZATION WHEN REDISTRIBUTING ROUTES INTO OSPF

When redistributing routes from other protocols into OSPF, each route is advertised individually in an external LSA. However, you can configure the Cisco IOS software to advertise a single route for all the redistributed routes that are covered by a specified network address and mask. Doing so helps decrease the size of the OSPF link state database.

To have the software advertise one summary route for all redistributed routes covered by a network address and mask, perform the following task in router configuration mode:

Task	Command
Specify an address and mask that covers redistributed routes, so only one summary route is advertised.	**summary-address** *address mask*

CREATING VIRTUAL LINKS

In OSPF, all areas must be connected to a backbone area. If there is a break in backbone continuity, or the backbone is purposefully partitioned, you can establish a *virtual link*. The two end points of a virtual link are Area Border Routers. The virtual link must be configured in both routers. The configuration information in each router consists of the other virtual endpoint (the other ABR), and the nonbackbone area that the two routers have in common (the *transit area*). Note that virtual links cannot be configured through stub areas.

To establish a virtual link, perform the following task in router configuration mode:

Task	Command
Establish a virtual link.	**area** *area-id* **virtual-link** *router-id* [**hello-interval** *seconds*] [**retransmit-interval** *seconds*] [**transmit-delay** *seconds*] [**dead-interval** *seconds*] [[**authentication-key** *key*] | [**message-digest-key** *keyid* **md5** *key*]]

To display information about virtual links, use the **show ip ospf virtual-links** EXEC command. To display the router ID of an OSPF router, use the **show ip ospf** EXEC command.

GENERATING A DEFAULT ROUTE

You can force an autonomous system boundary router to generate a default route into an OSPF routing domain. Whenever you specifically configure redistribution of routes into an OSPF routing domain, the router automatically becomes an autonomous system boundary router. However, an autonomous system boundary router does not, by default, generate a *default route* into the OSPF routing domain.

To force the autonomous system boundary router to generate a default route, perform the following task in router configuration mode:

Task	Command
Force the autonomous system boundary router to generate a default route into the OSPF routing domain.	**default-information originate** [**always**] [**metric** *metric-value*] [**metric-type** *type-value*] [**route-map** *map-name*]

CONFIGURING LOOKUP OF DNS NAMES

You can configure OSPF to look up Domain Naming System (DNS) names for use in all OSPF **show** command displays. This feature makes it easier to identify a router, because it is displayed by name rather than by its router ID or neighbor ID.

To configure DNS name lookup, perform the following task in global configuration mode:

Task	Command
Configure DNS name lookup.	**ip ospf name-lookup**

FORCING THE ROUTER ID CHOICE WITH A LOOPBACK INTERFACE

OSPF uses the largest IP address configured on the interfaces as its router ID. If the interface associated with this IP address is ever brought down, or if the address is removed, the OSPF process must recalculate a new router ID and resend all its routing information out its interfaces.

If a loopback interface is configured with an IP address, the Cisco IOS software will use this IP address as its router ID, even if other interfaces have larger IP addresses. Since loopback interfaces never go down, greater stability in the routing table is achieved.

OSPF automatically prefers a loopback interface over any other kind, and it chooses the highest IP address among all loopback interfaces. If no loopback interfaces are present, the highest IP address in the router is chosen. You cannot configure OSPF to use any particular interface.

To configure an IP address on a loopback interface, perform the following tasks, starting in global configuration mode:

Task	Command
Step 1 Create a loopback interface, which places you in interface configuration mode.	**interface loopback 0**
Step 2 Assign an IP address to this interface.	**ip address** *address mask*

CONTROLLING DEFAULT METRICS

In Cisco IOS Release 10.3 and later, by default, OSPF calculates the OSPF metric for an interface according to the bandwidth of the interface. For example, a 64K link gets a metric of 1562, while a T1 link gets a metric of 64.

The OSPF metric is calculated as *ref-bw* divided by *bandwidth*, with *ref-bw* equal to 10^8 by default, and *bandwidth* determined by the **bandwidth** command. The calculation gives FDDI a metric of 1. If you have multiple links with high bandwidth, you might want to specify a larger number to differentiate the cost on those links. To do so, perform the following task in router configuration mode:

Task	Command
Differentiate high bandwidth links.	**ospf auto-cost reference-bandwidth** *ref-bw*

CONFIGURING OSPF ON SIMPLEX ETHERNET INTERFACES

Because simplex interfaces between two devices on an Ethernet represent only one network segment, for OSPF you must configure the transmitting interface to be a passive interface. This prevents OSPF from sending hello packets for the transmitting interface. Both devices are able to see each other via the hello packet generated for the receiving interface.

To configure OSPF on simplex Ethernet interfaces, perform the following task in router configuration mode:

Task	Command
Suppress the sending of hello packets through the specified interface.	**passive-interface** *type number*

CONFIGURING ROUTE CALCULATION TIMERS

You can configure the delay between the time when OSPF receives a topology change and when it starts a Shortest Path First (SPF) calculation. You can also configure the hold time between two consecutive SPF calculations. To do this, perform the following task in router configuration mode:

Task	Command
Configure route calculation timers.	timers spf *spf-delay spf-holdtime*

CONFIGURING OSPF OVER ON-DEMAND CIRCUITS

The OSPF on-demand circuit is an enhancement to the OSPF protocol that allows efficient operation over on-demand circuits like ISDN, X.25 SVCs, and dial-up lines. This feature supports RFC 1793, *Extending OSPF to Support Demand Circuits.*

Prior to this feature, OSPF periodic hello and LSA updates would be exchanged between routers that connected on the demand link, even when no changes occurred in the hello or LSA information.

With this feature, periodic hellos are suppressed and the periodic refreshes of LSAs are not flooded over the demand circuit. These packets bring up the link only when they are exchanged for the first time, or when a change occurs in the information they contain. This operation allows the underlying datalink layer to be closed when the network topology is stable.

This feature is useful when you want to connect telecommuters or branch offices to an OSPF backbone at a central site. In this case, OSPF for on-demand circuits allows the benefits of OSPF over the entire domain while minimizing connection costs. Periodic refreshes of hello updates, LSA updates, and other protocol overhead are prevented from enabling the on-demand circuit when there is no "real" data to transmit.

Overhead protocols such as hellos and LSAs are transferred over the on-demand circuit only upon initial setup and when they reflect a change in the topology. This means that critical changes to the topology that require new SPF calculations are transmitted in order to maintain network topology integrity. Periodic refreshes that do not include changes, however, are not transmitted across the link.

To configure OSPF for on demand circuits, perform the following tasks, beginning in global configuration mode:

Task	Command
Step 1 Enable OSPF operation.	router ospf *process-id*
Step 2 Configure OSPF on an on demand circuit.	ip ospf demand-circuit

If the router is part of a point-to-point topology, then only one end of the demand circuit must be configured with this command. However, all routers must have this feature loaded.

If the router is part of a point-to-multipoint topology, only the multipoint end must be configured with this command.

Understanding Implementation Considerations

Evaluate the following considerations before implementing this feature:

- Because LSAs that include topology changes are flooded over an on-demand circuit, it is advised to put demand circuits within OSPF stub areas, or within NSSAs to isolate the demand circuits from as many topology changes as possible.

- To take advantage of the on-demand circuit functionality within a stub area or NSSA, every router in the area must have this feature loaded. If this feature is deployed within a regular area, all other regular areas must also support this feature before the demand circuit functionality can take effect. This is because type 5 external LSAs are flooded throughout all areas.

- You should not implement this on a broadcast-based network topology because the overhead protocols (such as hellos and LSAs) cannot be successfully suppressed, which means the link will remain up.

LOGGING NEIGHBOR CHANGES

To configure the router to send a syslog message when an OSPF neighbor state changes, perform the following task in router configuration mode:

Task	Command
Send a syslog message when a neighbor state changes.	ospf log-adj-changes

Configure this command if you want to know about OSPF neighbor changes without turning on the debugging command **debug ip ospf adjacency**. The **ospf log-adj-changes** command provides a higher level view of changes to the state of the peer relationship with less output.

MONITORING AND MAINTAINING OSPF

You can display specific statistics such as the contents of IP routing tables, caches, and databases. The information provided can be used to determine resource utilization and solve network problems. You can also display information about node reachability and discover the routing path your device's packets are taking through the network.

To display various routing statistics, perform the following tasks in EXEC mode:

Task	Command
Display general information about OSPF routing processes.	**show ip ospf** [*process-id*]
Display lists of information related to the OSPF database.	**show ip ospf** [*process-id area-id*] **database**
	show ip ospf [*process-id area-id*] **database** [**router**] [*link-state-id*]
	show ip ospf [*process-id area-id*] **database** [**network**] [*link-state-id*]
	show ip ospf [*process-id area-id*] **database** [**summary**] [*link-state-id*]
	show ip ospf [*process-id area-id*] **database** [**asb-summary**] [*link-state-id*]
	show ip ospf [*process-id*] **database** [**external**] [*link-state-id*]
	show ip ospf [*process-id area-id*] **database** [**database-summary**]
Display the internal OSPF routing table entries to ABR and Autonomous System Boundary Router (ASBR).	**show ip ospf border-routers**
Display OSPF-related interface information.	**show ip ospf interface** [*interface-name*]
Display OSPF-neighbor information on a per-interface basis.	**show ip ospf neighbor** [*interface-name*] [*neighbor-id*] **detail**
Display OSPF-related virtual links information.	**show ip ospf virtual-links**

OSPF Configuration Examples

The next sections provide OSPF configuration examples that include the following:

- OSPF Point-to-Multipoint Example
- Variable-Length Subnet Masks Example
- OSPF Routing and Route Redistribution Examples
- Route Map Examples

OSPF Point-to-Multipoint Example

In Figure 14–1, Mollie uses DLCI 201 to communicate with Neon, DLCI 202 to Jelly, and DLCI 203 to Platty. Neon uses DLCI 101 to communicate with Mollie and DLCI 102 to communicate with Platty. Platty communicates with Neon (DLCI 401) and Mollie (DLCI 402). Jelly communicates with Mollie (DLCI 301).

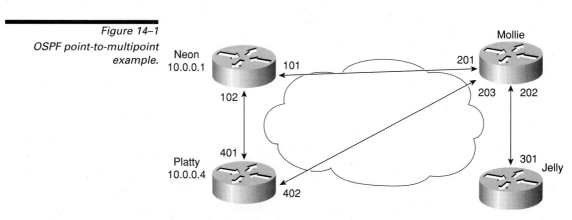

Figure 14–1
OSPF point-to-multipoint example.

Mollie's Configuration

```
hostname mollie
!
interface serial 1
 ip address 10.0.0.2 255.0.0.0
 ip ospf network point-to-multipoint
 encapsulation frame-relay
 frame-relay map ip 10.0.0.1 201 broadcast
 frame-relay map ip 10.0.0.3 202 broadcast
 frame-relay map ip 10.0.0.4 203 broadcast
!
router ospf 1
 network 10.0.0.0 0.0.0.255 area 0
```

Neon's Configuration

```
hostname neon
!
interface serial 0
 ip address 10.0.0.1 255.0.0.0
 ip ospf network point-to-multipoint
 encapsulation frame-relay
 frame-relay map ip 10.0.0.2 101 broadcast
 frame-relay map ip 10.0.0.4 102 broadcast
!
router ospf 1
 network 10.0.0.0 0.0.0.255 area 0
```

Platty's Configuration

```
hostname platty
!
interface serial 3
 ip address 10.0.0.4 255.0.0.0
 ip ospf network point-to-multipoint
 encapsulation frame-relay
 clock rate 1000000
 frame-relay map ip 10.0.0.1 401 broadcast
 frame-relay map ip 10.0.0.2 402 broadcast
!
router ospf 1
 network 10.0.0.0 0.0.0.255 area 0
```

Jelly's Configuration

```
hostname jelly
!
interface serial 2
 ip address 10.0.0.3 255.0.0.0
 ip ospf network point-to-multipoint
 encapsulation frame-relay
 clock rate 2000000
 frame-relay map ip 10.0.0.2 301 broadcast
!
router ospf 1
 network 10.0.0.0 0.0.0.255 area 0
```

Variable-Length Subnet Masks Example

OSPF, static routes, and IS-IS support Variable-Length Subnet Masks (VLSMs). With VLSMs, you can use different masks for the same network number on different interfaces, which allows you to conserve IP addresses and more efficiently use available address space.

In the following example, a 30-bit subnet mask is used, leaving two bits of address space reserved for serial line host addresses. There is sufficient host address space for two host endpoints on a point-to-point serial link.

```
interface ethernet 0
 ip address 131.107.1.1 255.255.255.0
! 8 bits of host address space reserved for ethernets

interface serial 0
 ip address 131.107.254.1 255.255.255.252
! 2 bits of address space reserved for serial lines

! Router is configured for OSPF and assigned AS 107
router ospf 107
! Specifies network directly connected to the router
 network 131.107.0.0 0.0.255.255 area 0.0.0.0
```

OSPF Routing and Route Redistribution Examples

OSPF typically requires coordination among many internal routers, area border routers, and autonomous system boundary routers. At a minimum, OSPF-based routers can be configured with all default parameter values, with no authentication, and with interfaces assigned to areas.

The three examples in the following list demonstrate this for specific situations:

- The first is a simple configuration illustrating basic OSPF commands.
- The second example illustrates a configuration for an internal router, ABR, and ASBRs within a single, arbitrarily assigned, OSPF autonomous system.
- The third example illustrates a more complex configuration and the application of various tools available for controlling OSPF-based routing environments.

Basic OSPF Configuration Example

The following example illustrates a simple OSPF configuration that enables OSPF routing process 9000, attaches Ethernet 0 to area 0.0.0.0, and redistributes RIP into OSPF and OSPF into RIP:

```
interface ethernet 0
 ip address 130.93.1.1 255.255.255.0
 ip ospf cost 1
!
interface ethernet 1
 ip address 130.94.1.1 255.255.255.0
!
router ospf 9000
 network 130.93.0.0 0.0.255.255 area 0.0.0.0
 redistribute rip metric 1 subnets
!
router rip
 network 130.94.0.0
 redistribute ospf 9000
 default-metric 1
```

Basic OSPF Configuration Example for Internal Router, ABR, and ASBRs

The following example illustrates the assignment of four area IDs to four IP address ranges. In the example, OSPF routing process 109 is initialized, and four OSPF areas are defined: 10.9.50.0, 2, 3, and 0. Areas 10.9.50.0, 2, and 3 mask specific address ranges, while Area 0 enables OSPF for *all other* networks.

```
router ospf 109
 network 131.108.20.0 0.0.0.255 area 10.9.50.0
 network 131.108.0.0 0.0.255.255 area 2
 network 131.109.10.0 0.0.0.255 area 3
 network 0.0.0.0 255.255.255.255 area 0
!
! Interface Ethernet0 is in area 10.9.50.0:
interface ethernet 0
 ip address 131.108.20.5 255.255.255.0
```

```
!
! Interface Ethernet1 is in area 2:
interface ethernet 1
 ip address 131.108.1.5 255.255.255.0
!
! Interface Ethernet2 is in area 2:
interface ethernet 2
 ip address 131.108.2.5 255.255.255.0
!
! Interface Ethernet3 is in area 3:
interface ethernet 3
 ip address 131.109.10.5 255.255.255.0
!
! Interface Ethernet4 is in area 0:
interface ethernet 4
 ip address 131.109.1.1 255.255.255.0
!
! Interface Ethernet5 is in area 0:
interface ethernet 5
 ip address 10.1.0.1 255.255.0.0
```

Each **network area** router configuration command is evaluated sequentially, so the order of these commands in the configuration is important. The Cisco IOS software sequentially evaluates the *address/wildcard-mask* pair for each interface. See Chapter 15 for more information.

Consider the first **network area** command. Area ID 10.9.50.0 is configured for the interface on which subnet 131.108.20.0 is located. Assume that a match is determined for interface Ethernet 0. Interface Ethernet 0 is attached to Area 10.9.50.0 only.

The second **network area** command is evaluated next. For Area 2, the same process is then applied to all interfaces (except interface Ethernet 0). Assume that a match is determined for interface Ethernet 1. OSPF is then enabled for that interface and Ethernet 1 is attached to Area 2.

This process of attaching interfaces to OSPF areas continues for all **network area** commands. Note that the last **network area** command in this example is a special case. With this command, all available interfaces (not explicitly attached to another area) are attached to Area 0.

Complex Internal Router, ABR, and ASBRs Example

The following example outlines a configuration for several routers within a single OSPF autonomous system. Figure 14–2 provides a general network map that illustrates this example configuration.

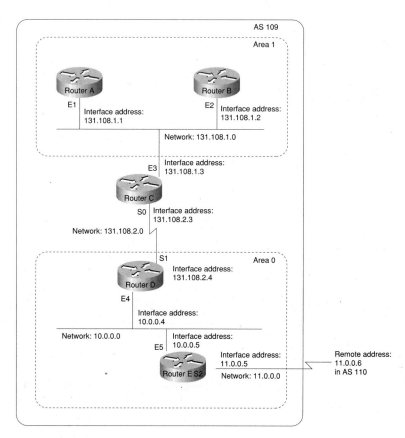

Figure 14–2
Sample OSPF autonomous system network map.

In this configuration, five routers are configured in OSPF autonomous system 109:

- Router A and Router B are both internal routers within Area 1.

- Router C is an OSPF area border router. Note that for Router C, Area 1 is assigned to E3 and Area 0 is assigned to S0.

- Router D is an internal router in Area 0 (backbone area). In this case, both **network** router configuration commands specify the same area (Area 0, which is the backbone area).

- Router E is an OSPF autonomous system boundary router. Note that BGP routes are redistributed into OSPF and that these routes are advertised by OSPF.

NOTES

It is not necessary to include definitions of all areas in an OSPF autonomous system in the configuration of all routers in the autonomous system. You must only define the *directly* connected areas. In the example that follows, routes in Area 0 are learned by the routers in Area 1 (Router A and Router B) when the area border router (Router C) injects summary link state advertisements into Area 1.

Autonomous system 109 is connected to the outside world via the BGP link to the external peer at IP address 11.0.0.6.

Router A—Internal Router

```
interface ethernet 1
 ip address 131.108.1.1 255.255.255.0

router ospf 109
 network 131.108.0.0 0.0.255.255 area 1
```

Router B—Internal Router

```
interface ethernet 2
 ip address 131.108.1.2 255.255.255.0

router ospf 109
 network 131.108.0.0 0.0.255.255 area 1
```

Router C—ABR

```
interface ethernet 3
 ip address 131.108.1.3 255.255.255.0

interface serial 0
 ip address 131.108.2.3 255.255.255.0

router ospf 109
 network 131.108.1.0 0.0.0.255 area 1
 network 131.108.2.0 0.0.0.255 area 0
```

Router D—Internal Router

```
interface ethernet 4
 ip address 10.0.0.4 255.0.0.0

interface serial 1
 ip address 131.108.2.4 255.255.255.0

router ospf 109
 network 131.108.2.0 0.0.0.255 area 0
 network 10.0.0.0 0.255.255.255 area 0
```

Router E—ASBR

```
interface ethernet 5
 ip address 10.0.0.5 255.0.0.0

interface serial 2
 ip address 11.0.0.5 255.0.0.0
```

```
router ospf 109
 network 10.0.0.0 0.255.255.255 area 0
 redistribute bgp 109 metric 1 metric-type 1

router bgp 109
 network 131.108.0.0
 network 10.0.0.0
 neighbor 11.0.0.6 remote-as 110
```

Complex OSPF Configuration for ABR Examples

The next example configuration accomplishes several tasks needed to set up an ABR. These tasks can be split into the following two general categories:

- Basic OSPF configuration
- Route redistribution

The specific tasks outlined in this configuration are detailed briefly in the following descriptions. Figure 14–3 illustrates the network address ranges and area assignments for the interfaces.

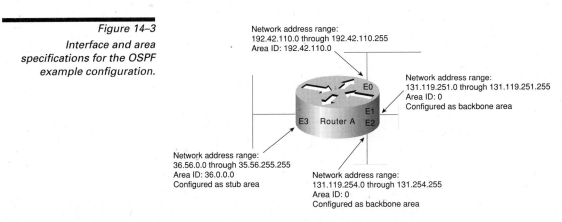

Figure 14–3

Interface and area specifications for the OSPF example configuration.

Network address range:
192.42.110.0 through 192.42.110.255
Area ID: 192.42.110.0

Network address range:
131.119.251.0 through 131.119.251.255
Area ID: 0
Configured as backbone area

Network address range:
36.56.0.0 through 35.56.255.255
Area ID: 36.0.0.0
Configured as stub area

Network address range:
131.119.254.0 through 131.254.255
Area ID: 0
Configured as backbone area

The basic configuration tasks in this example are the following:

- Configure address ranges for Ethernet 0 through Ethernet 3 interfaces.
- Enable OSPF on each interface.
- Set up an OSPF authentication password for each area and network.
- Assign link state metrics and other OSPF interface configuration options.
- Create a stub area with area id 36.0.0.0. (Note that although the **authentication** and **stub** options of the **area** router configuration command are specified with separate **area** command entries, they can be merged into a single **area** command.)
- Specify the backbone area (Area 0).

Configuration tasks associated with redistribution are the following:

- Redistribute IGRP and RIP into OSPF with various options set (including **metric-type, metric, tag,** and **subnet**).
- Redistribute IGRP and OSPF into RIP.

The following is an example OSPF configuration:

```
interface ethernet 0
 ip address 192.42.110.201 255.255.255.0
 ip ospf authentication-key abcdefgh
 ip ospf cost 10
!
interface ethernet 1
 ip address 131.119.251.201 255.255.255.0
 ip ospf authentication-key ijklmnop
 ip ospf cost 20
 ip ospf retransmit-interval 10
 ip ospf transmit-delay 2
 ip ospf priority 4
!
interface ethernet 2
 ip address 131.119.254.201 255.255.255.0
 ip ospf authentication-key abcdefgh
 ip ospf cost 10
!
interface ethernet 3
 ip address 36.56.0.201 255.255.0.0
 ip ospf authentication-key ijklmnop
 ip ospf cost 20
 ip ospf dead-interval 80
```

OSPF is on network 131.119.0.0:

```
router ospf 201
 network 36.0.0.0 0.255.255.255 area 36.0.0.0
 network 192.42.110.0 0.0.0.255 area 192.42.110.0
 network 131.119.0.0 0.0.255.255 area 0
 area 0 authentication
 area 36.0.0.0 stub
 area 36.0.0.0 authentication
 area 36.0.0.0 default-cost 20
 area 192.42.110.0 authentication
 area 36.0.0.0 range 36.0.0.0 255.0.0.0
 area 192.42.110.0 range 192.42.110.0 255.255.255.0
 area 0 range 131.119.251.0 255.255.255.0
 area 0 range 131.119.254.0 255.255.255.0

 redistribute igrp 200 metric-type 2 metric 1 tag 200 subnets
 redistribute rip metric-type 2 metric 1 tag 200
```

IGRP autonomous system 200 is on 131.119.0.0:

```
router igrp 200
 network 131.119.0.0
!
! RIP for 192.42.110
!
router rip
 network 192.42.110.0
 redistribute igrp 200 metric 1
 redistribute ospf 201 metric 1
```

Route Map Examples

The examples in this section illustrate the use of redistribution, with and without route maps. Examples from both the IP and CLNS routing protocols are given.

The following example redistributes all OSPF routes into IGRP:

```
router igrp 109
 redistribute ospf 110
```

The following example redistributes RIP routes with a hop count equal to 1 into OSPF. These routes will be redistributed into OSPF as external LSAs with a metric of 5, metric type of Type 1, and a tag equal to 1.

```
router ospf 109
 redistribute rip route-map rip-to-ospf
!
route-map rip-to-ospf permit
 match metric 1
 set metric 5
 set metric-type type1
 set tag 1
```

The following example redistributes OSPF learned routes with tag 7 as a RIP metric of 15:

```
router rip
 redistribute ospf 109 route-map 5
!
route-map 5 permit
 match tag 7
 set metric 15
```

The following example redistributes OSPF intra-area and interarea routes with next-hop routers on serial interface 0 into BGP with an INTER_AS metric of 5:

```
router bgp 109
 redistribute ospf 109 route-map 10
!
route-map 10 permit
 match route-type internal
 match interface serial 0
 set metric 5
```

The following example redistributes two types of routes into the integrated IS-IS routing table (supporting both IP and CLNS). The first routes are OSPF external IP routes with tag 5; these are inserted into Level 2 IS-IS LSPs with a metric of 5. The second routes are ISO-IGRP derived CLNS prefix routes that match CLNS access list 2000. These will be redistributed into IS-IS as Level 2 LSPs with a metric of 30.

```
router isis
 redistribute ospf 109 route-map 2
 redistribute iso-igrp nsfnet route-map 3
!
route-map 2 permit
 match route-type external
 match tag 5
 set metric 5
 set level level-2
!
route-map 3 permit
 match address 2000
 set metric 30
```

With the following configuration, OSPF external routes with tags 1, 2, 3, and 5 are redistributed into RIP with metrics of 1, 1, 5, and 5, respectively. The OSPF routes with a tag of 4 are not redistributed.

```
router rip
 redistribute ospf 109 route-map 1
!
route-map 1 permit
 match tag 1 2
 set metric 1
!
route-map 1 permit
 match tag 3
 set metric 5
!
route-map 1 deny
 match tag 4
!
route map 1 permit
 match tag 5
 set metric 5
```

The following configuration sets the condition that if there is an OSPF route to network 140.222.0.0, the default network 0.0.0.0 is generated into RIP with a metric of 1:

```
router rip
 redistribute ospf 109 route-map default
!
route-map default permit
 match ip address 1
 set metric 1
!
 access-list 1 permit 140.222.0.0 0.0.255.255
 access-list 2 permit 0.0.0.0 0.0.0.0
```

In the following configuration, a RIP learned route for network 160.89.0.0 and an ISO-IGRP learned route with prefix 49.0001.0002 will be redistributed into an IS-IS Level 2 LSP with a metric of 5:

```
router isis
 redistribute rip route-map 1
 redistribute iso-igrp remote route-map 1
!
route-map 1 permit
 match ip address 1
 match clns address 2
 set metric 5
 set level level-2
!
 access-list 1 permit 160.89.0.0 0.0.255.255
 clns filter-set 2 permit 49.0001.0002...
```

The following configuration example illustrates how a route map is referenced by the **default-information** router configuration command. This is called *conditional default origination*. OSPF will originate the default route (network 0.0.0.0) with a Type 2 metric of 5 based on 140.222.0.0, with network 0.0.0.0 in the routing table.

```
route-map ospf-default permit
 match ip address 1
 set metric 5
 set metric-type type-2
!
 access-list 1 140.222.0.0 0.0.255.255
!
router ospf 109
 default-information originate route-map ospf-default
```

CHAPTER 15

OSPF Commands

Use the commands in this chapter to configure and monitor the Open Shortest Path First (OSPF) routing protocol. For OSPF configuration information and examples, see Chapter 14, "Configuring OSPF."

AREA AUTHENTICATION

To enable authentication for an OSPF area, use the **area authentication** router configuration command. To remove an area's authentication specification or a specified area from the configuration, use the **no** form of this command.

> **area** *area-id* **authentication** [message-digest]
> **no area** *area-id* **authentication**
> **no area** *area-id*

Syntax	Description
area-id	Identifier of the area for which authentication is to be enabled. The identifier can be specified as either a decimal value or an IP address.
message-digest	(Optional.) Enables MD5 authentication on the area specified by *area-id*.

Default

Type 0 authentication (no authentication)

Command Mode

Router configuration

Usage Guidelines

This command first appeared in Cisco IOS Release 10.0. The **message-digest** keyword first appeared in Cisco IOS Release 11.0.

Specifying authentication for an area sets the authentication to Type 1 (simple password) as specified in RFC 1247. If this command is not included in the configuration file, authentication of Type 0 (no authentication) is assumed.

The authentication type must be the same for all routers and access servers in an area. The authentication password for all OSPF routers on a network must be the same if they are to communicate with each other via OSPF. Use the **ip ospf authentication-key** command to specify this password.

If you enable MD5 authentication with the **message-digest** keyword, you must configure a password with the **ip ospf message-digest-key** command.

To remove the area's authentication specification, use the **no** form of this command with the **authentication** keyword.

NOTES

To remove the specified area from the software configuration, use the command **no area** *area-id* (with no other keywords). That is, **no area** *area-id* removes all area options, such as **area authentication**, **area default-cost**, **area nssa**, **area range**, **area stub**, and **area virtual-link**.

Example

The following example mandates authentication for areas 0 and 36.0.0.0 of OSPF routing process 201. Authentication keys are also provided.

```
interface ethernet 0
 ip address 131.119.251.201 255.255.255.0
 ip ospf authentication-key adcdefgh
!
interface ethernet 1
 ip address 36.56.0.201 255.255.0.0
 ip ospf authentication-key ijklmnop
!
router ospf 201
 network 36.0.0.0 0.255.255.255 area 36.0.0.0
 network 131.119.0.0 0.0.255.255 area 0
 area 36.0.0.0 authentication
 area 0 authentication
```

Related Commands

Search online to find documentation for related commands.

area default-cost
area stub

ip ospf authentication-key
ip ospf message-digest-key

AREA DEFAULT-COST

To specify a cost for the default summary route sent into a stub area, use the **area default-cost** router configuration command. To remove the assigned default route cost, use the **no** form of this command.

> **area** *area-id* **default-cost** *cost*
> **no area** *area-id* **default-cost** *cost*
> **no area** *area-id*

Syntax	Description
area-id	Identifier for the stub area. The identifier can be specified as either a decimal value or as an IP address.
cost	Cost for the default summary route used for a stub area. The acceptable value is a 24-bit number.

Default
Cost of 1

Command Mode
Router configuration

Usage Guidelines
This command first appeared in Cisco IOS Release 10.0.

The command is used only on an area border router attached to a stub area.

There are two stub area router configuration commands: the **stub** and **default-cost** options of the **area** command. In all routers and access servers attached to the stub area, the area should be configured as a stub area using the **stub** option of the **area** command. Use the **default-cost** option only on an area border router attached to the stub area. The **default-cost** option provides the metric for the summary default route generated by the area border router into the stub area.

NOTES

To remove the specified area from the software configuration, use the command **no area** *area-id* (with no other keywords). That is, **no area** *area-id* removes all area options, such as **area authentication**, **area default-cost**, **area nssa**, **area range**, **area stub**, and **area virtual-link**.

Example

The following example assigns a default-cost of 20 to stub network 36.0.0.0:

```
interface ethernet 0
 ip address 36.56.0.201 255.255.0.0
!
router ospf 201
 network 36.0.0.0 0.255.255.255 area 36.0.0.0
 area 36.0.0.0 stub
 area 36.0.0.0 default-cost 20
```

Related Commands

Search online to find documentation for related commands.

area authentication
area stub

AREA NSSA

To configure an area as a not so stubby area (NSSA), use the **area nssa** router configuration command. To remove the nssa distinction from the area, use the **no** form of this command.

> **area** *area-id* **nssa** [**no-redistribution**] [*default-information-originate*]
> **no area** *area-id* **nssa**
> **no area** *area-id*

Syntax	Description
area-id	Identifier of the area for which authentication is to be enabled. The identifier can be specified as either a decimal value or an IP address.
no-redistribution	(Optional.) Used when the router is a NSSA ABR and you want the **redistribute** command to import routes only into the normal areas, but not into the NSSA area.
default-information-originate	(Optional.) Used to generate a Type 7 default into the NSSA area. This argument only takes effect on NSSA ABR.

Default

No NSSA area is defined.

Command Mode

Router configuration

Usage Guidelines

This command first appeared in Cisco IOS Release 10.0.

To remove the specified area from the software configuration, use the command**no area** *area-id* (with no other keywords). That is, **no area** *area-id* removes all area options, such as **area authentication, area default-cost**, **area nssa**, **area range**, **area stub**, and **area virtual-link**.

Example

In the following example, NSSA authentication is enabled on area 1:

```
router ospf1
  redistribute rip subnets
  network 172.19.92.0.0.0.0.255 area 1
  area 1 nssa
```

AREA RANGE

To consolidate and summarize routes at an area boundary, use the **area range** router configuration command. To disable this function, use the **no** form of this command.

area *area-id* **range** *address mask*
no area *area-id* **range** *address mask*
no area *area-id*

Syntax	Description
area-id	Identifier of the area about which routes are to be summarized. It can be specified as either a decimal value or as an IP address.
address	IP address.
mask	IP mask.

Default

Disabled

Command Mode

Router configuration

Usage Guidelines

This command first appeared in Cisco IOS Release 10.0.

The **area range** command is used only with area border routers (ABRs). It is used to consolidate or summarize routes for an area. The result is that a single summary route is advertised to other areas by the ABR. Routing information is condensed at area boundaries. External to the area, a single route is advertised for each address range. This is called *route summarization*.

Multiple **area** router configuration commands specifying the **range** option can be configured. Thus, OSPF can summarize addresses for many different sets of address ranges.

NOTES

To remove the specified area from the software configuration, use the command**no area** *area-id* (with no other keywords). That is, **no area** *area-id* removes all area options, such as **area authentication**, **area default-cost**, **area nssa**, **area range**, **area stub**, and **area virtual-link**.

Example

The following example specifies one summary route to be advertised by the ABR to other areas for all subnets on network 36.0.0.0 and for all hosts on network 192.42.110.0:

```
interface ethernet 0
 ip address 192.42.110.201 255.255.255.0
!
interface ethernet 1
 ip address 36.56.0.201 255.255.0.0
!
router ospf 201
 network 36.0.0.0 0.255.255.255 area 36.0.0.0
 network 192.42.110.0 0.0.0.255 area 0
 area 36.0.0.0 range 36.0.0.0 255.0.0.0
 area 0 range 192.42.110.0 255.255.255.0
```

AREA STUB

To define an area as a stub area, use the **area stub** router configuration command. To disable this function, use the **no** form of this command.

> **area** *area-id* **stub** [**no-summary**]
> **no area** *area-id* **stub**
> **no area** *area-id*

Syntax	Description
area-id	Identifier for the stub area; either a decimal value or an IP address.
no-summary	(Optional.) Prevents an ABR from sending summary link advertisements into the stub area.

Default

No stub area is defined.

Command Mode

Router configuration

Usage Guidelines

This command first appeared in Cisco IOS Release 10.0.

You must configure the **area stub** command on all routers and access servers in the stub area. Use the **area** router configuration command with the **default-cost** option to specify the cost of a default internal router sent into a stub area by an area border router.

There are two stub area router configuration commands: the **stub** and **default-cost** options of the **area** router configuration command. In all routers attached to the stub area, the area should be configured as a stub area using the **stub** option of the **area** command. Use the **default-cost** option only on an ABR attached to the stub area. The **default-cost** option provides the metric for the summary default route generated by the area border router into the stub area.

To further reduce the number of link state advertisements (LSA) sent into a stub area, you can configure **no-summary** on the ABR to prevent it from sending summary LSAs (LSA type 3) into the stub area.

Part II

Command Reference

— **NOTES** —————————————————————————

To remove the specified area from the software configuration, use the command **no area** *area-id* (with no other keywords). That is, **no area** *area-id* removes all area options, such as **area authentication**, **area default-cost**, **area nssa**, **area range**, **area stub**, and **area virtual-link**.

Example

The following example assigns a default cost of 20 to stub network 36.0.0.0:

```
interface ethernet 0
 ip address 36.56.0.201 255.255.0.0
 !
router ospf 201
 network 36.0.0.0 0.255.255.255 area 36.0.0.0
 area 36.0.0.0 stub
 area 36.0.0.0 default-cost 20
```

Related Commands

Search online to find documentation for related commands.

area authentication
area default-cost

AREA VIRTUAL-LINK

To define an OSPF virtual link, use the **area virtual-link** router configuration command with the optional parameters. To remove a virtual link, use the **no** form of this command.

> area *area-id* **virtual-link** *router-id* [**hello-interval** *seconds*] [**retransmit-interval** *seconds*] [**transmit-delay** *seconds*] [**dead-interval** *seconds*] [[**authentication-key** *key*] | [**message-digest-key** *keyid* **md5** *key*]]

no area *area-id* **virtual-link** *router-id* [**hello-interval** *seconds*] [**retransmit-interval**
   seconds] [**transmit-delay** *seconds*] [**dead-interval** *seconds*] [[**authentication-key** *key*] |
   [**message-digest-key** *keyid* **md5** *key*]]
no area *area-id*

Syntax	Description
area-id	Area ID assigned to the transit area for the virtual link. This can be either a decimal value or a valid IP address. There is no default.
router-id	Router ID associated with the virtual link neighbor. The router ID appears in the **show ip ospf** display. It is internally derived by each router from the router's interface IP addresses. This value must be entered in the format of an IP address. There is no default.
hello-interval *seconds*	(Optional.) Time in seconds between the hello packets that the Cisco IOS software sends on an interface. Unsigned integer value to be advertised in the software's hello packets. The value must be the same for all routers and access servers attached to a common network. The default is 10 seconds.
retransmit-interval *seconds*	(Optional.) Time in seconds between link state advertisement retransmissions for adjacencies belonging to the interface. Expected round-trip delay between any two routers on the attached network. The value must be greater than the expected round-trip delay. The default is 5 seconds.
transmit-delay *seconds*	(Optional.) Estimated time in seconds it takes to transmit a link state update packet on the interface. Integer value that must be greater than zero. Link state advertisements in the update packet have their age incremented by this amount before transmission. The default value is 1 second.
dead-interval *seconds*	(Optional.) Time in seconds that a software's hello packets are not seen before its neighbors declare the router down. Unsigned integer value. The default is four times the hello interval, or 40 seconds. As with the hello interval, this value must be the same for all routers and access servers attached to a common network.

Syntax	Description
authentication-key *key*	(Optional.) Password to be used by neighboring routers. Any continuous string of characters that you can enter from the keyboard up to 8 bytes long. This string acts as a key that will allow the authentication procedure to generate or verify the authentication field in the OSPF header. This key is inserted directly into the OSPF header when originating routing protocol packets. A separate password can be assigned to each network on a per-interface basis. All neighboring routers on the same network must have the same password to be able to route OSPF traffic. The password is encrypted in the configuration file if the **service password-encryption** command is enabled. There is no default value.
message-digest-key *keyid* **md5** *key*	(Optional.) Key identifier and password to be used by neighboring routers and this router for MD5 authentication. The *keyid* is a number in the range 1 to 255. The *key* is an alphanumeric string of up to 16 characters. All neighboring routers on the same network must have the same key identifier and key to be able to route OSPF traffic. There is no default value.

Part II

Command Reference

Defaults

area-id: No area ID is predefined.
router-id: No router ID is predefined.
hello-interval *seconds*: 10 seconds
retransmit-interval *seconds*: 5 seconds
transmit-delay *seconds*: 1 second
dead-interval *seconds*: 40 seconds
authentication-key *key*: No key is predefined.
message-digest-key *keyid* **md5** *key*: No key is predefined.

Command Mode

Router configuration

Usage Guidelines

This command first appeared in Cisco IOS Release 10.0. The following keywords and arguments first appeared in Cisco IOS Release 11.0: **message-digest-key** *keyid* **md5** *key*.

In OSPF, all areas must be connected to a backbone area. If the connection to the backbone is lost, it can be repaired by establishing a virtual link.

The smaller the hello interval, the faster topological changes will be detected, but more routing traffic will ensue.

The setting of the retransmit interval should be conservative, or needless retransmissions will result. The value should be larger for serial lines and virtual links.

The transmit delay value should take into account the transmission and propagation delays for the interface.

The Cisco IOS software will use the specified authentication key only when authentication is enabled for the backbone with the **area** *area-id* **authentication** router configuration command.

The two authentication schemes, simple text and MD5 authentication, are mutually exclusive. You can specify one or the other or neither. Any keywords and arguments you specify after **authentication-key** *key* or **message-digest-key** *keyid* **md5** *key* are ignored. Therefore, specify any optional arguments before such a keyword-argument combination.

— **NOTES** ──

Each virtual link neighbor must include the transit area ID and the corresponding virtual link neighbor's router ID in order for a virtual link to be properly configured. Use the **show ip ospf** EXEC command to see the router ID.

— **NOTES** ──

To remove the specified area from the software configuration, use the command **no area** *area-id* (with no other keywords). That is, **no area** *area-id* removes all area options, such as **area authentication**, **area default-cost**, **area nssa**, **area range**, **area stub**, and **area virtual-link**.

Examples

The following example establishes a virtual link with default values for all optional parameters:

```
router ospf 201
 network 36.0.0.0 0.255.255.255 area 36.0.0.0
 area 36.0.0.0 virtual-link 36.3.4.5
```

The following example establishes a virtual link with MD5 authentication:

```
router ospf 201
 network 36.0.0.0 0.255.255.255 area 36.0.0.0
 area 36.0.0.0 virtual-link 36.3.4.5 message-digest-key 3 md5 sa5721bk47
```

Related Commands

Search online to find documentation for related commands.

area authentication
service password-encryption
show ip ospf

DEFAULT-INFORMATION ORIGINATE (OSPF)

To generate a default route into an OSPF routing domain, use the **default-information originate** router configuration command. To disable this feature, use the **no** form of this command.

> **default-information originate** [**always**] [**metric** *metric-value*] [**metric-type** *type-value*]
> {**level-1** | **level-1-2** | **level-2**} [**route-map** *map-name*]
> **no default-information originate** [**always**] [**metric** *metric-value*] [**metric-type** *type-value*]
> {**level-1** | **level-1-2** | **level-2**} [**route-map** *map-name*]

Syntax	Description
originate	Causes the Cisco IOS software to generate a default external route into an OSPF domain if the software already has a default route and you want to propagate to other routers.
always	(Optional.) Always advertises the default route regardless of whether the software has a default route.
metric *metric-value*	(Optional.) Metric used for generating the default route. If you omit a value and do not specify a value using the **default-metric** router configuration command, the default metric value is 10. The value used is specific to the protocol.
metric-type *type-value*	(Optional.) External link type associated with the default route advertised into the OSPF routing domain. It can be one of the following values: 1—Type 1 external route 2—Type 2 external route The default is Type 2 external route.
level-1	Level 1 routes are redistributed into other IP routing protocols independently. It specifies if IS-IS advertises network 0.0.0.0 into the Level 1 area.
level-1-2	Both Level 1 and Level 2 routes are redistributed into other IP routing protocols. It specifies if IS-IS advertises network 0.0.0.0 into both levels in a single command.
level-2	Level 2 routes are redistributed into other IP routing protocols independently. It specifies if IS-IS advertises network 0.0.0.0 into the Level 2 subdomain.
route-map *map-name*	(Optional.) Routing process will generate the default route if the route map is satisfied.

Default

Disabled

Command Mode

Router configuration

Usage Guidelines

This command first appeared in Cisco IOS Release 10.0.

Whenever you use the **redistribute** or the **default-information** router configuration commands to redistribute routes into an OSPF routing domain, the Cisco IOS software automatically becomes an autonomous system boundary router (ASBR). However, an ASBR does not, by default, generate a *default route* into the OSPF routing domain. The software still must have a default route for itself before it generates one, except when you have specified the **always** keyword.

When you use this command for the OSPF process, the default network must reside in the routing table and you must satisfy the **route-map** *map-name* keyword. Use the **default-information originate always route-map** *map-name* form of the command when you do not want the dependency on the default network in the routing table.

Example

The following example specifies a metric of 100 for the default route redistributed into the OSPF routing domain and an external metric type of Type 1:

```
router ospf 109
  redistribute igrp 108 metric 100 subnets
  default-information originate metric 100 metric-type 1
```

Related Commands

Search online to find documentation for related commands.

redistribute

DEFAULT-METRIC

To set default metric values for the OSPF routing protocol, use this form of the **default-metric** router configuration command. To return to the default state, use the **no** form of this command.

> **default-metric** *number*
> **no default-metric** *number*

Syntax	Description
number	Default metric value appropriate for the specified routing protocol.

Default

Built-in, automatic metric translations, as appropriate for each routing protocol.

Command Mode

Router configuration

Usage Guidelines

This command first appeared in Cisco IOS Release 10.0.

The **default-metric** command is used in conjunction with the **redistribute** router configuration command to cause the current routing protocol to use the same metric value for all redistributed routes. A default metric helps solve the problem of redistributing routes with incompatible metrics. Whenever metrics do not convert, using a default metric provides a reasonable substitute and enables the redistribution to proceed.

Example

The following example shows a router in autonomous system 109 using both the RIP and the OSPF routing protocols. The example advertises OSPF-derived routes using the RIP protocol and assigns the IGRP-derived routes a RIP metric of 10.

```
router rip
 default-metric 10
 redistribute ospf 109
```

Related Commands

Search online to find documentation for related commands.

redistribute

IP OSPF AUTHENTICATION-KEY

To assign a password to be used by neighboring routers that are using OSPF's simple password authentication, use the **ip ospf authentication-key** interface configuration command. To remove a previously assigned OSPF password, use the **no** form of this command.

ip ospf authentication-key *password*
no ip ospf authentication-key

Syntax	Description
password	Any continuous string of characters that can be entered from the keyboard up to 8 bytes in length.

Default

No password is specified.

Command Mode

Interface configuration

Usage Guidelines

This command first appeared in Cisco IOS Release 10.0.

The password created by this command is used as a "key" that is inserted directly into the OSPF header when the Cisco IOS software originates routing protocol packets. A separate password can be assigned to each network on a per-interface basis. All neighboring routers on the same network must have the same password to be able to exchange OSPF information.

NOTES ——————————————————————————————————

The Cisco IOS software will use this key only when authentication is enabled for an area with the **area authentication** router configuration command.

Example

In the following example, the authentication key is enabled with the string *yourpass*:

```
ip ospf authentication-key yourpass
```

Related Commands

Search online to find documentation for related commands.

area authentication

IP OSPF COST

To explicitly specify the cost of sending a packet on an interface, use the **ip ospf cost** interface configuration command. To reset the path cost to the default value, use the **no** form of this command.

ip ospf cost *cost*
no ip ospf cost

Syntax	Description
cost	Unsigned integer value expressed as the link state metric. It can be a value in the range 1 to 65535.

Default

No default cost is predefined.

Command Mode

Interface configuration

Usage Guidelines

This command first appeared in Cisco IOS Release 10.0.

You can set the metric manually using this command, if you need to change the default. Using the **bandwidth** command changes the link cost as long as this command is not used.

The link state metric is advertised as the link cost in the router link advertisement. We do not support type of service (TOS), so you can assign only one cost per interface.

In general, the path cost is calculated using the following formula:

$$10^8 \div Bandwidth$$

Using this formula, the default path costs were calculated as noted in the following list. If these values do not suit your network, you can use your own method of calculating path costs.

- 56-kbps serial link—Default cost is 1785
- 64-kbps serial link—Default cost is 1562
- T1 (1.544-Mbps serial link)—Default cost is 65
- E1 (2.048-Mbps serial link)—Default cost is 48
- 4-Mbps Token Ring—Default cost is 25
- Ethernet—Default cost is 10
- 16-Mbps Token Ring—Default cost is 6
- FDDI—Default cost is 1

Example

The following example sets the interface cost value to 65:

```
ip ospf cost 65
```

IP OSPF DEAD-INTERVAL

To set how long hello packets must not have been seen before its neighbors declare the router down, use the **ip ospf dead-interval** interface configuration command. To return to the default time, use the **no** form of this command.

> **ip ospf dead-interval** *seconds*
> **no ip ospf dead-interval**

Syntax	Description
seconds	Unsigned integer that specifies the interval in seconds; the value must be the same for all nodes on the network.

Default

Four times the interval set by the **ip ospf hello-interval** command

Command Mode

Interface configuration

Usage Guidelines

This command first appeared in Cisco IOS Release 10.0.

The interval is advertised in the router's hello packets. This value must be the same for all routers and access servers on a specific network.

Example

The following example sets the OSPF dead interval to 60 seconds:

```
interface ethernet 1
 ip ospf dead-interval 60
```

Related Commands

Search online to find documentation for related commands.

ip ospf hello-interval

IP OSPF DEMAND-CIRCUIT

To configure OSPF to treat the interface as an OSPF demand circuit, use the **ip ospf demand-circuit** interface configuration command. To remove the demand circuit designation from the interface, use the **no** form of this command.

> **ip ospf demand-circuit**
> **no ip ospf demand-circuit**

Syntax   Description

This command has no arguments or keywords.

Default

The circuit is not a demand circuit.

Command Mode

Interface configuration

Usage Guidelines

This command first appeared in Cisco IOS Release 11.2.

On point-to-point interfaces, only one end of the demand circuit must be configured with this command. Periodic hellos are suppressed and periodic refreshes of LSAs do not flood the demand circuit. It allows the underlying datalink layer to be closed when the topology is stable. In point-to-multipoint topology, only the multipoint end must configured with this command.

Example

The following example sets the configures an ISDN on demand circuit:

```
router ospf1
  network 18.0.3.0.0.0.0.25 area 0
interface BRIO
  ip ospf demand-circuit
```

IP OSPF HELLO-INTERVAL

To specify the interval between hello packets that the Cisco IOS software sends on the interface, use the **ip ospf hello-interval** interface configuration command. To return to the default time, use the **no** form of this command.

>**ip ospf hello-interval** *seconds*
>**no ip ospf hello-interval**

Syntax	Description
seconds	Unsigned integer that specifies the interval in seconds. The value must be the same for all nodes on a specific network.

Default

10 seconds

Command Mode

Interface configuration

Usage Guidelines

This command first appeared in Cisco IOS Release 10.0.

This value is advertised in the hello packets. The smaller the hello interval, the faster topological changes will be detected, but more routing traffic will ensue. This value must be the same for all routers and access servers on a specific network.

Example

The following example sets the interval between hello packets to 15 seconds:

```
interface ethernet 1
  ip ospf hello-interval 15
```

Related Commands

Search online to find documentation for related commands.

ip ospf dead-interval

Part II

Command Reference

IP OSPF MESSAGE-DIGEST-KEY

To enable OSPF MD5 authentication, use the **ip ospf message-digest-key** interface configuration command. To remove an old MD5 key, use the **no** form of this command.

> **ip ospf message-digest-key** *keyid* **md5** *key*
> **no ip ospf message-digest-key** *keyid*

Syntax	Description
keyid	An identifier in the range 1 to 255.
key	Alphanumeric password of up to 16 bytes.

Default

OSPF MD5 authentication is disabled.

Command Mode

Interface configuration

Usage Guidelines

This command first appeared in Cisco IOS Release 11.0.

Usually, one key per interface is used to generate authentication information when sending packets and to authenticate incoming packets. The same key identifier on the neighbor router must have the same *key* value.

The process of changing keys is as follows. Suppose the current configuration is as follows:

```
interface ethernet 1
  ip ospf message-digest-key 100 md5 OLD
```

You change the configuration to the following:

```
interface ethernet 1
  ip ospf message-digest-key 101 md5 NEW
```

The system assumes its neighbors do not have the new key yet, so it begins a rollover process. It sends multiple copies of the same packet, each authenticated by different keys. In this example, the system sends out two copies of the same packet—the first one authenticated by key 100 and the second one authenticated by key 101.

Rollover allows neighboring routers to continue communication while the network administrator is updating them with the new key. Rollover stops once the local system finds that all its neighbors know the new key. The system detects that a neighbor has the new key when it receives packets from the neighbor authenticated by the new key.

After all neighbors have been updated with the new key, the old key should be removed. In this example, you would enter the following:

```
interface ethernet 1
  no ip ospf message-digest-key 100
```

Then, only key 101 is used for authentication on Ethernet interface 1.

We recommend that you not keep more than one key per interface. Every time you add a new key, you should remove the old key to prevent the local system from continuing to communicate with a hostile system that knows the old key. Removing the old key also reduces overhead during rollover.

Example

The following example sets a new key 19 with the password *8ry4222*:

```
interface ethernet 1
  ip ospf message-digest-key 10 md5 xvv560qle
  ip ospf message-digest-key 19 md5 8ry4222
```

Related Commands

Search online to find documentation for related commands.

area authentication

IP OSPF NAME-LOOKUP

To configure OSPF to look up Domain Name System (DNS) names for use in all OSPF **show** EXEC command displays, use the **ip ospf name-lookup** global configuration command. To disable this feature, use the **no** form of this command.

> **ip ospf name-lookup**
> **no ip ospf name-lookup**

Syntax   Description

This command has no arguments or keywords.

Default

Disabled

Command Mode

Global configuration

Usage Guidelines

This command first appeared in Cisco IOS Release 10.0.

This feature makes it easier to identify a router because it is displayed by name rather than by its router ID or neighbor ID.

Example

The following example configures OSPF to look up DNS names for use in all OSPF **show** EXEC command displays:

```
ip ospf name-lookup
```

Sample Display

The following is sample output from the **show ip ospf database** EXEC command, for example, once you have enabled the DNS name lookup feature:

```
Router# show ip ospf database

        OSPF Router with id (160.89.41.1) (Autonomous system 109)


                Router Link States (Area 0.0.0.0)

    Link ID         ADV Router      Age     Seq#        Checksum Link count
    160.89.41.1     router          381     0x80000003 0x93BB    4
    160.89.34.2     neon            380     0x80000003 0xD5C8    2

                Net Link States (Area 0.0.0.0)

    Link ID         ADV Router      Age     Seq#        Checksum
    160.89.32.1     router          381     0x80000001 0xC117
```

IP OSPF NETWORK

To configure the OSPF network type to a type other than the default for a given media, use the **ip ospf network** interface configuration command. To return to the default value, use the **no** form of this command.

> **ip ospf network {broadcast | non-broadcast | point-to-multipoint}**
> **no ip ospf network**

Syntax	Description
broadcast	Sets the network type to broadcast.
non-broadcast	Sets the network type to nonbroadcast.
point-to-multipoint	Sets the network type to point-to-multipoint.

Default

Depends on the network type.

Command Mode

Interface configuration

Usage Guidelines

This command first appeared in Cisco IOS Release 10.0. The **point-to-multipoint** keyword first appeared in Cisco IOS Release 10.3.

Using this feature, you can configure broadcast networks as nonbroadcast multiaccess (NBMA) networks when, for example, you have routers in your network that do not support multicast addressing. You can also configure nonbroadcast multiaccess networks (such as X.25, Frame Relay, and SMDS) as broadcast networks. This feature saves you from having to configure neighbors.

Configuring NBMA networks as either broadcast or nonbroadcast assumes that there are virtual circuits from every router to every router or fully meshed network. This is not true for some cases, for example, because of cost constraints or when you have only a partially meshed network. In these cases, you can configure the OSPF network type as a point-to-multipoint network. Routing between two routers that are not directly connected will go through the router that has virtual circuits to both routers. Note that you do not need to configure neighbors when using this feature.

If this command is issued on an interface that does not allow it, it will be ignored.

Example

The following example sets your OSPF network as a broadcast network:

```
interface serial 0
 ip address 160.89.77.17 255.255.255.0
 ip ospf network broadcast
 encapsulation frame-relay
```

Related Commands

Search online to find documentation for related commands.

frame-relay map
neighbor (OSPF)
x25 map

IP OSPF PRIORITY

To set the router priority, which helps determine the designated router for this network, use the **ip ospf priority** interface configuration command. To return to the default value, use the **no** form of this command.

> **ip ospf priority** *number*
> **no ip ospf priority**

Syntax	Description
number	8-bit unsigned integer that specifies the priority. The range is from 0 to 255.

Default

Priority of 1

Command Mode

Interface configuration

Usage Guidelines

This command first appeared in Cisco IOS Release 10.0.

When two routers attached to a network both attempt to become the designated router, the one with the higher router priority takes precedence. If there is a tie, the router with the higher router ID takes precedence. A router with a router priority set to zero is ineligible to become the designated router or backup designated router. Router priority is only configured for interfaces to multiaccess networks (in other words, not point-to-point networks).

This priority value is used when you configure OSPF for nonbroadcast networks using the **neighbor** router configuration command for OSPF.

Example

The following example sets the router priority value to 4:

```
interface ethernet 0
  ip ospf priority 4
```

Related Commands

Search online to find documentation for related commands.

ip ospf network
neighbor (OSPF)

IP OSPF RETRANSMIT-INTERVAL

To specify the time between link state advertisement retransmissions for adjacencies belonging to the interface, use the **ip ospf retransmit-interval** interface configuration command. To return to the default value, use the **no** form of this command.

> **ip ospf retransmit-interval** *seconds*
> **no ip ospf retransmit-interval**

Syntax	Description
seconds	Time in seconds between retransmissions. It must be greater than the expected round-trip delay between any two routers on the attached network. The range is 1 to 65535 seconds. The default is 5 seconds.

Default

5 seconds

Command Mode

Interface configuration

Usage Guidelines

This command first appeared in Cisco IOS Release 10.0.

When a router sends a link state advertisement (LSA) to its neighbor, it keeps the LSA until it receives back the acknowledgment. If it receives no acknowledgment in *seconds*, it will retransmit the LSA.

The setting of this parameter should be conservative, or needless retransmission will result. The value should be larger for serial lines and virtual links.

Example

The following example sets the retransmit-interval value to 8 seconds:

```
interface ethernet 2
  ip ospf retransmit-interval 8
```

IP OSPF TRANSMIT-DELAY

To set the estimated time it takes to transmit a link state update packet on the interface, use the **ip ospf transmit-delay** interface configuration command. To return to the default value, use the **no** form of this command.

> **ip ospf transmit-delay** *seconds*
> **no ip ospf transmit-delay**

Syntax	Description
seconds	Time in seconds that it takes to transmit a link state update. The range is 1 to 65535 seconds. The default is 1 second.

Default

1 second

Command Mode

Interface configuration

Usage Guidelines

This command first appeared in Cisco IOS Release 10.0.

Link state advertisements in the update packet must have their ages incremented by the amount specified in the *seconds* argument before transmission. The value assigned should take into account the transmission and propagation delays for the interface.

If the delay is not added before transmission over a link, the time in which the LSA propagates over the link is not considered. This setting has more significance on very low speed links.

Example

The following example sets the retransmit-delay value to 3 seconds:

```
interface ethernet 0
 ip ospf transmit-delay 3
```

NEIGHBOR (OSPF)

To configure OSPF routers interconnecting to nonbroadcast networks, use this form of the **neighbor** router configuration command. To remove a configuration, use the **no** form of this command.

> **neighbor** *ip-address* [**priority** *number*] [**poll-interval** *seconds*]
> **no neighbor** *ip-address* [**priority** *number*] [**poll-interval** *seconds*]

Syntax	Description
ip-address	Interface IP address of the neighbor.
priority *number*	(Optional.) 8-bit number indicating the router priority value of the nonbroadcast neighbor associated with the IP address specified. The default is 0.
poll-interval *seconds*	(Optional.) Unsigned integer value reflecting the poll interval. RFC 1247 recommends that this value be much larger than the hello interval. The default is 2 minutes (120 seconds).

Default

No configuration is specified.

Command Mode

Router configuration

Usage Guidelines

This command first appeared in Cisco IOS Release 10.0.

The X.25 and Frame Relay provide an optional broadcast capability that can be configured in the map to allow OSPF to run as a broadcast network. At the OSPF level you can configure the router as a broadcast network.

One neighbor entry must be included in the Cisco IOS software configuration for each known non-broadcast network neighbor. The neighbor address has to be on the primary address of the interface.

If a neighboring router has become inactive (hello packets have not been seen for the Router Dead Interval period), it may still be necessary to send hello packets to the dead neighbor. These hello packets will be sent at a reduced rate called *Poll Interval*.

When the router first starts up, it sends only hello packets to those routers with non-zero priority, that is, routers which are eligible to become designated routers (DR) and backup designated routers (BDR). After DR and BDR are selected, DR and BDR will then start sending hello packets to all neighbors in order to form adjacencies.

Example

The following example declares a router at address 131.108.3.4 on a nonbroadcast network, with a priority of 1 and a poll-interval of 180:

```
router ospf
   neighbor 131.108.3.4 priority 1 poll-interval 180
```

Related Commands

Search online to find documentation for related commands.

ip ospf priority

NETWORK AREA

To define the interfaces on which OSPF runs and to define the area ID for those interfaces, use the **network area** router configuration command. To disable OSPF routing for interfaces defined with the *address wildcard-mask* pair, use the **no** form of this command.

> **network** *address wildcard-mask* **area** *area-id*
> **no network** *address wildcard-mask* **area** *area-id*

Syntax	Description
address	IP address.
wildcard-mask	IP-address-type mask that includes "don't care" bits.
area-id	Area that is to be associated with the OSPF address range. It can be specified as either a decimal value or as an IP address. If you intend to associate areas with IP subnets, you can specify a subnet address as the *area-id*.

Default

Disabled

Command Mode

Router configuration

Usage Guidelines

This command first appeared in Cisco IOS Release 10.0.

The *address* and *wildcard-mask* arguments together allow you to define one or multiple interfaces to be associated with a specific OSPF area using a single command. Using the *wildcard-mask* allows you to define one or multiple interfaces to be associated with a specific OSPF area using a single command. If you intend to associate areas with IP subnets, you can specify a subnet address as the *area-id*.

For OSPF to operate on the interface, that interface's primary address must be covered by the **network area** command. If the **network area** command covers only the secondary address, it will not enable OSPF over that interface.

The Cisco IOS software sequentially evaluates the *address/wildcard-mask* pair for each interface as follows:

1. The *wildcard-mask* is logically ORed with the interface IP address.

2. The *wildcard-mask* is logically ORed with *address* in the **network** command.

3. The software compares the two resulting values.

4. If they match, OSPF is enabled on the associated interface, and this interface is attached to the OSPF area specified.

NOTES

Any individual interface can only be attached to a single area. If the address ranges specified for different areas overlap, the software will adopt the first area in the **network** command list and ignore the subsequent overlapping portions. In general, it is recommended that you devise address ranges that do not overlap in order to avoid inadvertent conflicts.

Example

In the following partial example, OSPF routing process 109 is initialized, and four OSPF areas are defined: 10.9.50.0, 2, 3, and 0. Areas 10.9.50.0, 2, and 3 mask specific address ranges, while area 0 enables OSPF for all other networks.

```
interface ethernet 0
 ip address 131.108.20.1 255.255.255.0
router ospf 109
 network 131.108.20.0  0.0.0.255 area 10.9.50.0
 network 131.108.0.0  0.0.255.255 area 2
 network 131.109.10.0  0.0.0.255 area 3
 network 0.0.0.0  255.255.255.255 area 0
```

Related Commands

Search online to find documentation for related commands.

router ospf

OSPF AUTO-COST

To control how OSPF calculates default metrics for the interface, use the **ospf auto-cost** router configuration command. To assign cost based only on the interface type, use the **no** form of this command.

> **ospf auto-cost reference-bandwidth** *ref-bw*
> **no ospf auto-cost reference-bandwidth**

Syntax	Description
ref-bw	Rate in megabits per second (bandwidth). The range is 1 to 4294967; the default is 100.

Part II Command Reference

Default

100 Mbits

Command Mode

Router configuration

Usage Guidelines

This command first appeared in Cisco IOS Release 11.2.

In Cisco IOS Release 10.3 and later, by default OSPF will calculate the OSPF metric for an interface according to the bandwidth of the interface. For example, a 64K link will get a metric of 1562, while a T1 link will have a metric of 64.

The OSPF metric is calculated as *ref-bw* divided by *bandwidth*, with *ref-bw* equal to 10^8 by default, and *bandwidth* determined by the **bandwidth** command. The calculation gives FDDI a metric of 1.

If you have multiple links with high bandwidth (such as FDDI or ATM), you might want to use a larger number to differentiate the cost on those links.

The value set by the **ip ospf cost** command overrides the cost resulting from the **ospf auto-cost** command.

Example

The following example changes the cost of the FDDI link to 10, while the gigabit Ethernet link remains at a cost of 1. Thus, the link costs are differentiated.

```
router ospf 1
  ospf auto-cost reference-bandwidth 1000
```

Related Commands

Search online to find documentation for related commands.

ip ospf cost

OSPF LOG-ADJ-CHANGES

To configure the router to send a syslog message when the state of an OSPF neighbor changes, use the **ospf log-adj-changes** router configuration command. To turn off this feature, use the **no** form of this command.

> **ospf log-adj-changes**
> **no ospf log-adj-changes**

Syntax   Description

This command has no arguments or keywords.

Default

No such syslog message is sent.

Command Mode

Router configuration

Usage Guidelines

This command first appeared in Cisco IOS Release 11.2.

Configure this command if you want to know about OSPF neighbor changes without turning on the debugging command **debug ip ospf adjacency**. The **ospf log-adj-changes** command provides a higher level view of changes to the state of the peer relationship with less output.

Example

The following example configures the router to send a syslog message for any neighbor state changes:

```
ospf log-adj-changes
```

ROUTER OSPF

To configure an OSPF routing process, use the **router ospf** global configuration command. To terminate an OSPF routing process, use the **no** form of this command.

> **router ospf** *process-id*
> **no router ospf** *process-id*

Syntax   *Description*

process-id   Internally used identification parameter for an OSPF routing process. It is locally assigned and can be any positive integer. A unique value is assigned for each OSPF routing process.

Default

No OSPF routing process is defined.

Command Mode

Global configuration

Usage Guidelines

This command first appeared in Cisco IOS Release 10.0.

You can specify multiple OSPF routing processes in each router.

Example

The following example shows how to configure an OSPF routing process and assign a process number of 109:

```
router ospf 109
```

Related Commands

Search online to find documentation for related commands.

network area

SHOW IP OSPF

To display general information about OSPF routing processes, use the **show ip ospf** EXEC command.

   show ip ospf [*process-id*]

Syntax	Description
process-id	(Optional.) Process ID. If this argument is included, only information for the specified routing process is included.

Command Mode

EXEC

Usage Guidelines

This command first appeared in Cisco IOS Release 10.0.

Sample Display

The following is sample output from the **show ip ospf** command when entered without a specific OSPF process ID:

```
Router# show ip ospf

Routing Process "ospf 201" with ID 192.42.110.200
Supports only single TOS(TOS0) route
It is an area border and autonomous system boundary router
Summary Link update interval is 0:30:00 and the update due in 0:16:26
External Link update interval is 0:30:00 and the update due in 0:16:27
Redistributing External Routes from,
    igrp 200 with metric mapped to 2, includes subnets in redistribution
    rip with metric mapped to 2
    igrp 2 with metric mapped to 100
    igrp 32 with metric mapped to 1
Number of areas in this router is 3
Area 192.42.110.0
    Number of interfaces in this area is 1
    Area has simple password authentication
    SPF algorithm executed 6 times
    Area ranges are
    Link State Update Interval is 0:30:00 and due in 0:16:55
    Link State Age Interval is 0:20:00 and due in 0:06:55
```

Table 15–1 describes significant fields shown in the display.

Table 15–1   *Show IP OSPF Field Descriptions*

Field	Description
Routing process "ospf 201" with ID 192.42.110.200	Process ID and OSPF router ID.
Supports ...	Number of Types of service supported (Type 0 only).
It is ...	Possible types are internal, area border, or autonomous system boundary.
Summary Link update interval	Specify summary update interval in hours:minutes:seconds, and time to next update.
External Link update interval	Specify external update interval in hours:minutes:seconds, and time to next update.
Redistributing External Routes from	Lists of redistributed routes, by protocol.
Number of areas	Number of areas in router, area addresses, and so on.

Table 15–1 *Show IP OSPF Field Descriptions, Continued*

Field	Description
Link State Update Interval	Specify router and network link state update interval in hours:minutes:seconds, and time to next update.
Link State Age Interval	Specify max-aged update deletion interval and time until next database cleanup in hours:minutes:seconds.

SHOW IP OSPF BORDER-ROUTERS

To display the internal OSPF routing table entries to an area border router (ABR) and autonomous system boundary router (ASBR), use the **show ip ospf border-routers** privileged EXEC command.

show ip ospf border-routers

Syntax   Description

This command has no arguments or keywords.

Command Mode

Privileged EXEC

Usage Guidelines

This command first appeared in Cisco IOS Release 10.0.

Sample Display

The following is sample output from the **show ip ospf border-routers** command:

```
Router# show ip ospf border-routers

OSPF Process 109 internal Routing Table

Destination      Next Hop       Cost   Type   Rte Type Area      SPF No

160.89.97.53     144.144.1.53   10     ABR    INTRA    0.0.0.3   3
160.89.103.51    160.89.96.51   10     ABR    INTRA    0.0.0.3   3
160.89.103.52    160.89.96.51   20     ASBR   INTER    0.0.0.3   3
160.89.103.52    144.144.1.53   22     ASBR   INTER    0.0.0.3   3
```

Table 15–2 describes the fields shown in the display.

Table 15–2   *Show IP OSPF Border-Routers Field Descriptions*

Field	Description
Destination	Destination's router ID.
Next Hop	Next hop toward the destination.
Cost	Cost of using this route.
Type	The router type of the destination; it is either an area border router (ABR) or autonomous system boundary router (ASBR) or both.
Rte Type	The type of this route, it is either an intra-area or interarea route.
Area	The area ID of the area that this route is learned from.
SPF No	The internal number of SPF calculation that installs this route.

SHOW IP OSPF DATABASE

Use the **show ip ospf database** EXEC command to display lists of information related to the OSPF database for a specific router. The various forms of this command deliver information about different OSPF link state advertisements.

> **show ip ospf** [*process-id area-id*] **database**
> **show ip ospf** [*process-id area-id*] **database** [**router**] [*link-state-id*]
> **show ip ospf** [*process-id area-id*] **database** [**network**] [*link-state-id*]
> **show ip ospf** [*process-id area-id*] **database** [**summary**] [*link-state-id*]
> **show ip ospf** [*process-id area-id*] **database** [**asb-summary**] [*link-state-id*]
> **show ip ospf** [*process-id area-id*] **database** [**nssa-external**] [*link-state-id*]
> **show ip ospf** [*process-id*] **database** [**external**] [*link-state-id*]
> **show ip ospf** [*process-id area-id*] **database** [**database-summary**]

Syntax	*Description*
process-id	(Optional.) Internally used identification parameter. It is locally assigned and can be any positive integer number. The number used here is the number assigned administratively when enabling the OSPF routing process.
area-id	(Optional.) Area number associated with the OSPF address range defined in the **network** router configuration command used to define the particular area.

Syntax	*Description*
link-state-id	(Optional.) Identifies the portion of the Internet environment that is being described by the advertisement. The value entered depends on the advertisement's LS type. It must be entered in the form of an IP address.

When the link state advertisement is describing a network, the *link-state-id* can take one of two forms:

- The network's IP address (as in type 3 summary link advertisements and in autonomous system external link advertisements).

- A derived address obtained from the link state ID. (Note that masking a network links advertisement's link state ID with the network's subnet mask yields the network's IP address.)

When the link state advertisement is describing a router, the link state ID is always the described router's OSPF router ID.

When an autonomous system external advertisement (LS Type = 5) is describing a default route, its link state ID is set to Default Destination (0.0.0.0).

Syntax Description

When entered with the optional keyword **asb-summary, external, network, router, summary,** or **database-summary**, different displays result. Examples and brief descriptions of each form follow.

Command Mode

EXEC

Usage Guidelines

This command first appeared in Cisco IOS Release 10.0. The following form of the command first appeared in Cisco IOS Release 11.0:

> **show ip ospf** [*process-id area-id*] **database** [**database-summary**].

Sample Display of Show IP OSPF Database with No Arguments or Keywords

The following is sample output from the **show ip ospf database** command when no arguments or keywords are used:

```
Router# show ip ospf database

OSPF Router with id(190.20.239.66) (Process ID 300)

          Displaying Router Link States(Area 0.0.0.0)
```

```
       Link ID        ADV Router       Age      Seq#        Checksum  Link count
     155.187.21.6    155.187.21.6     1731    0x80002CFB    0x69BC        8
     155.187.21.5    155.187.21.5     1112    0x800009D2    0xA2B8        5
     155.187.1.2     155.187.1.2      1662    0x80000A98    0x4CB6        9
     155.187.1.1     155.187.1.1      1115    0x800009B6    0x5F2C        1
     155.187.1.5     155.187.1.5      1691    0x80002BC     0x2A1A        5
     155.187.65.6    155.187.65.6     1395    0x80001947    0xEEE1        4
     155.187.241.5   155.187.241.5    1161    0x8000007C    0x7C70        1
     155.187.27.6    155.187.27.6     1723    0x80000548    0x8641        4
     155.187.70.6    155.187.70.6     1485    0x80000B97    0xEB84        6

               Displaying Net Link States(Area 0.0.0.0)

       Link ID        ADV Router       Age      Seq#        Checksum
     155.187.1.3    192.20.239.66     1245    0x800000EC    0x82E

           Displaying Summary Net Link States(Area 0.0.0.0)

       Link ID        ADV Router       Age      Seq#        Checksum
     155.187.240.0   155.187.241.5    1152    0x80000077     0x7A05
     155.187.241.0   155.187.241.5    1152    0x80000070     0xAEB7
     155.187.244.0   155.187.241.5    1152    0x80000071     0x95CB
```

Table 15–3 describes significant fields shown in the display.

Table 15–3 *Show IP OSPF Database Field Descriptions*

Field	Description
Link ID	Router ID number.
ADV Router	Advertising router's ID.
Age	Link state age.
Seq#	Link state sequence number (detects old or duplicate link state advertisements).
Checksum	Fletcher checksum of the complete contents of the link state advertisement.
Link count	Number of interfaces detected for router.

Sample Display Using Show IP OSPF Database ASB-Summary

The following is sample output from the **show ip ospf database asb-summary** command when no optional arguments are specified:

```
Router# show ip ospf database asb-summary

OSPF Router with id(190.20.239.66) (Process ID 300)

          Displaying Summary ASB Link States(Area 0.0.0.0)
```

```
LS age: 1463
Options: (No TOS-capability)
LS Type: Summary Links(AS Boundary Router)
Link State ID: 155.187.245.1 (AS Boundary Router address)
Advertising Router: 155.187.241.5
LS Seq Number: 80000072
Checksum: 0x3548
Length: 28
Network Mask: 0.0.0.0 TOS: 0  Metric: 1
```

Table 15–4 describes significant fields shown in the display.

Table 15–4 *Show IP OSPF Database ASB-Summary Field Descriptions*

Field	Description
OSPF Router with id	Router ID number.
Process ID	OSPF process ID.
LS age	Link state age.
Options	Type of service options (Type 0 only).
LS Type	Link state type.
Link State ID	Link state ID (autonomous system boundary router).
Advertising Router	Advertising router's ID.
LS Seq Number	Link state sequence (detects old or duplicate link state advertisements).
Checksum	LS checksum (Fletcher checksum of the complete contents of the link state advertisement).
Length	Length in bytes of the link state advertisement.
Network Mask	Network mask implemented.
TOS	Type of service.
Metric	Link state metric.

Sample Display Using Show IP OSPF Database External

The following is sample output from the **show ip ospf database external** command when no optional arguments are specified:

```
Router# show ip ospf database external

OSPF Router with id(190.20.239.66) (Autonomous system 300)

          Displaying AS External Link States
```

```
LS age: 280
Options: (No TOS-capability)
LS Type: AS External Link
Link State ID: 143.105.0.0 (External Network Number)
Advertising Router: 155.187.70.6
LS Seq Number: 80000AFD
Checksum: 0xC3A
Length: 36
Network Mask: 255.255.0.0
        Metric Type: 2 (Larger than any link state path)
        TOS: 0
        Metric: 1
        Forward Address: 0.0.0.0
        External Route Tag: 0
```

Table 15–5 describes significant fields shown in the display.

Table 15–5 *Show IP OSPF Database External Field Descriptions*

Field	Description
OSPF Router with id	Router ID number.
Autonomous system	OSPF autonomous system number (OSPF process ID).
LS age	Link state age.
Options	Type of service options (Type 0 only).
LS Type	Link state type.
Link State ID	Link state ID (External Network Number).
Advertising Router	Advertising router's ID.
LS Seq Number	Link state sequence number (detects old or duplicate link state advertisements).
Checksum	LS checksum (Fletcher checksum of the complete contents of the link state advertisement).
Length	Length in bytes of the link state advertisement.
Network Mask	Network mask implemented.
Metric Type	External Type.
TOS	Type of service.
Metric	Link state metric.

Table 15–5 *Show IP OSPF Database External Field Descriptions, Continued*

Field	Description
Forward Address	Forwarding address. Data traffic for the advertised destination will be forwarded to this address. If the forwarding address is set to 0.0.0.0, data traffic will be forwarded instead to the advertisement's originator.
External Route Tag	External route tag, a 32-bit field attached to each external route. This is not used by the OSPF protocol itself.

Sample Display Using Show IP OSPF Database Network

The following is sample output from the **show ip ospf database network** command when no optional arguments are specified:

```
Router# show ip ospf database network
 OSPF Router with id(190.20.239.66) (Process ID 300)

                 Displaying Net Link States(Area 0.0.0.0)

 LS age: 1367
 Options: (No TOS-capability)
 LS Type: Network Links
 Link State ID: 155.187.1.3 (address of Designated Router)
 Advertising Router: 190.20.239.66
 LS Seq Number: 800000E7
 Checksum: 0x1229
 Length: 52
 Network Mask: 255.255.255.0
         Attached Router: 190.20.239.66
         Attached Router: 155.187.241.5
         Attached Router: 155.187.1.1
         Attached Router: 155.187.54.5
         Attached Router: 155.187.1.5
```

Table 15–6 describes significant fields shown in the display.

Table 15–6 *Show IP OSPF Database Network Field Descriptions*

Field	Description
OSPF Router with id	Router ID number.
Process ID 300	OSPF process ID.
LS age	Link state age.
Options	Type of service options (Type 0 only).
LS Type:	Link state type.

Table 15–6 *Show IP OSPF Database Network Field Descriptions, Continued*

Field	Description
Link State ID	Link state ID of designated router.
Advertising Router	Advertising router's ID.
LS Seq Number	Link state sequence (detects old or duplicate link state advertisements).
Checksum	LS checksum (Fletcher checksum of the complete contents of the link state advertisement).
Length	Length in bytes of the link state advertisement.
Network Mask	Network mask implemented.
AS Boundary Router	Definition of router type.
Attached Router	List of routers attached to the network, by IP address.

Sample Display Using Show IP OSPF Database Router

The following is sample output from the **show ip ospf database router** command when no optional arguments are specified:

```
Router# show ip ospf database router

OSPF Router with id(190.20.239.66) (Process ID 300)


                Displaying Router Link States(Area 0.0.0.0)

LS age: 1176
Options: (No TOS-capability)
LS Type: Router Links
Link State ID: 155.187.21.6
Advertising Router: 155.187.21.6
LS Seq Number: 80002CF6
Checksum: 0x73B7
Length: 120
AS Boundary Router
155    Number of Links: 8

Link connected to: another Router (point-to-point)
(link ID) Neighboring Router ID: 155.187.21.5
(Link Data) Router Interface address: 155.187.21.6
Number of TOS metrics: 0
TOS 0 Metrics: 2
```

Table 15–7 describes significant fields shown in the display.

Table 15–7 *Show IP OSPF Database Router Field Descriptions*

Field	Description
OSPF Router with id	Router ID number.
Process ID	OSPF process ID.
LS age	Link state age.
Options	Type of service options (Type 0 only).
LS Type	Link state type.
Link State ID	Link state ID.
Advertising Router	Advertising router's ID.
LS Seq Number	Link state sequence (detects old or duplicate link state advertisements).
Checksum	LS checksum (Fletcher checksum of the complete contents of the link state advertisement).
Length	Length in bytes of the link state advertisement.
AS Boundary Router	Definition of router type.
Number of Links	Number of active links.
link ID	Link type.
Link Data	Router interface address.
TOS	Type of service metric (Type 0 only).

Sample Display Using Show IP OSPF Database Summary

The following is sample output from **show ip ospf database summary** command when no optional arguments are specified:

```
Router# show ip ospf database summary

        OSPF Router with id(190.20.239.66) (Process ID 300)

            Displaying Summary Net Link States(Area 0.0.0.0)

LS age: 1401
Options: (No TOS-capability)
LS Type: Summary Links(Network)
Link State ID: 155.187.240.0 (summary Network Number)
Advertising Router: 155.187.241.5
```

```
LS Seq Number: 80000072
Checksum: 0x84FF
Length: 28
Network Mask: 255.255.255.0   TOS: 0  Metric: 1
```

Table 15–8 describes significant fields shown in the display.

Table 15–8 *Show IP OSPF Database Summary Field Descriptions*

Field	Description
OSPF Router with id	Router ID number.
Process ID	OSPF process ID.
LS age	Link state age.
Options	Type of service options (Type 0 only).
LS Type	Link state type.
Link State ID	Link state ID (summary network number).
Advertising Router	Advertising router's ID.
LS Seq Number	Link state sequence (detects old or duplicate link state advertisements).
Checksum	LS checksum (Fletcher checksum of the complete contents of the link state advertisement).
Length	Length in bytes of the link state advertisement.
Network Mask	Network mask implemented.
TOS	Type of service.
Metric	Link state metric.

Sample Display Using Show IP OSPF Database Database-Summary

The following is sample output from **show ip ospf database database-summary** command when no optional arguments are specified:

```
Router# show ip ospf database database-summary

        OSPF Router with ID (172.19.65.21) (Process ID 1)


Area ID     Router   Network  Sum-Net   Sum-ASBR   Subtotal   Delete   Maxage
202         1        0        0         0          1          0        0
AS External                                        0          0        0
Total       1        0        0         0          1
```

Table 15–9 describes significant fields shown in the display.

Table 15–9 *Show IP OSPF Database Database-Summary Field Descriptions*

Field	Description
Area ID	Area number.
Router	Number of router link state advertisements in that area.
Network	Number of network link state advertisements in that area.
Sum-Net	Number of summary link state advertisements in that area.
Sum-ASBR	Number of summary autonomous system boundary router (ASBR) link state advertisements in that area.
Subtotal	Sum of Router, Network, Sum-Net, and Sum-ASBR for that area.
Delete	Number of link state advertisements that are marked "Deleted" in that area.
Maxage	Number of link state advertisements that are marked "Maxaged" in that area.
AS External	Number of external link state advertisements.

SHOW IP OSPF INTERFACE

To display OSPF-related interface information, use the **show ip ospf interface** EXEC command.

> **show ip ospf interface** [*type number*]

Syntax	Description
type	(Optional.) Interface type.
number	(Optional.) Interface number.

Command Mode

EXEC

Usage Guidelines

This command first appeared in Cisco IOS Release 10.0.

Sample Display

The following is sample output of the **show ip ospf interface** command when Ethernet 0 is specified:

```
Router# show ip ospf interface ethernet 0

Ethernet 0 is up, line protocol is up
Internet Address 131.119.254.202, Mask 255.255.255.0, Area 0.0.0.0
```

Part II

Command Reference

```
AS 201, Router ID 192.77.99.1, Network Type BROADCAST, Cost: 10
Transmit Delay is 1 sec, State OTHER, Priority 1
Designated Router id 131.119.254.10, Interface address 131.119.254.10
Backup Designated router id 131.119.254.28, Interface addr 131.119.254.28
Timer intervals configured, Hello 10, Dead 60, Wait 40, Retransmit 5
Hello due in 0:00:05
Neighbor Count is 8, Adjacent neighbor count is 2
  Adjacent with neighbor 131.119.254.28  (Backup Designated Router)
  Adjacent with neighbor 131.119.254.10  (Designated Router)
```

Table 15–10 describes significant fields shown in the display.

Table 15–10 *Show IP OSPF Interface Ethernet 0 Field Descriptions*

Field	Description
Ethernet	Status of physical link and operational status of protocol.
Internet Address	Interface IP address, subnet mask, and area address.
AS	Autonomous system number (OSPF process ID), router ID, network type, link state cost.
Transmit Delay	Transmit delay, interface state, and router priority.
Designated Router	Designated router ID and respective interface IP address.
Backup Designated router	Backup designated router ID and respective interface IP address.
Timer intervals configured	Configuration of timer intervals.
Hello	Number of seconds until next hello packet is sent out this interface.
Neighbor Count	Count of network neighbors and list of adjacent neighbors.

SHOW IP OSPF NEIGHBOR

To display OSPF-neighbor information on a per-interface basis, use the **show ip ospf neighbor** EXEC command.

> **show ip ospf neighbor** [*type number*] [*neighbor-id*] [**detail**]

Syntax	Description
type	(Optional.) Interface type.
number	(Optional.) Interface number.
neighbor-id	(Optional.) Neighbor ID.
detail	(Optional.) Displays all neighbors given in detail (list all neighbors).

Command Mode

EXEC

Usage Guidelines

This command first appeared in Cisco IOS Release 10.0.

Sample Displays

The following is sample output from the **show ip ospf neighbor** command showing a single line of summary information for each neighbor:

```
Router# show ip ospf neighbor

    ID        Pri  State         Dead Time   Address         Interface
199.199.199.137 1  FULL/DR        0:00:31    160.89.80.37    Ethernet0
192.31.48.1    1   FULL/DROTHER   0:00:33    192.31.48.1     Fddi0
192.31.48.200  1   FULL/DROTHER   0:00:33    192.31.48.200   Fddi0
199.199.199.137 5  FULL/DR        0:00:33    192.31.48.189   Fddi0
```

The following is sample output showing summary information about the neighbor that matches the neighbor ID:

```
Router# show ip ospf neighbor 199.199.199.137

Neighbor 199.199.199.137, interface address 160.89.80.37
    In the area 0.0.0.0 via interface Ethernet0
    Neighbor priority is 1, State is FULL
    Options 2
    Dead timer due in 0:00:32
    Link State retransmission due in 0:00:04
 Neighbor 199.199.199.137, interface address 192.31.48.189
    In the area 0.0.0.0 via interface Fddi0
    Neighbor priority is 5, State is FULL
    Options 2
    Dead timer due in 0:00:32
    Link State retransmission due in 0:00:03
```

If you specify the interface along with the Neighbor ID, the Cisco IOS software displays the neighbors that match the neighbor ID on the interface, as in the following sample display:

```
Router# show ip ospf neighbor ethernet 0 199.199.199.137

Neighbor 199.199.199.137, interface address 160.89.80.37
    In the area 0.0.0.0 via interface Ethernet0
    Neighbor priority is 1, State is FULL
    Options 2
    Dead timer due in 0:00:37
    Link State retransmission due in 0:00:04
```

Part
II

Command Reference

You can also specify the interface without the neighbor ID to show all neighbors on the specified interface, as in the following sample display:

```
Router# show ip ospf neighbor fddi 0

    ID          Pri   State          Dead Time    Address         Interface
192.31.48.1      1    FULL/DROTHER   0:00:33      192.31.48.1     Fddi0
192.31.48.200    1    FULL/DROTHER   0:00:32      192.31.48.200   Fddi0
199.199.199.137  5    FULL/DR        0:00:32      192.31.48.189   Fddi0
```

The following is sample output from the **show ip ospf neighbor detail** command:

```
Router# show ip ospf neighbor detail

Neighbor 160.89.96.54, interface address 160.89.96.54
    In the area 0.0.0.3 via interface Ethernet0
    Neighbor priority is 1, State is FULL
    Options 2
    Dead timer due in 0:00:38
 Neighbor 160.89.103.52, interface address 160.89.103.52
    In the area 0.0.0.0 via interface Serial0
    Neighbor priority is 1, State is FULL
    Options 2
    Dead timer due in 0:00:31
```

Table 15–11 describes the fields shown in the displays.

Table 15–11 *Show IP OSPF Neighbor Field Descriptions*

Field	Description
Neighbor	Neighbor router ID.
interface address	IP address of the interface.
In the area	Area and interface through which OSPF neighbor is known.
Neighbor priority	Router priority of neighbor, neighbor state.
State	OSPF state.
Options	Hello packet options field contents (E-bit only; possible values are 0 and 2; 2 indicates area is not a stub; 0 indicates area is a stub.
Dead timer	Expected time before Cisco IOS software will declare neighbor dead.

SHOW IP OSPF VIRTUAL-LINKS

To display parameters about and the current state of OSPF virtual links, use the **show ip ospf virtual-links** EXEC command.

show ip ospf virtual-links

Syntax   Description

This command has no arguments or keywords.

Command Mode

EXEC

Usage Guidelines

This command first appeared in Cisco IOS Release 10.0.

The information displayed by the **show ip ospf virtual-links** command is useful in debugging OSPF routing operations.

Sample Display

The following is sample output from the **show ip ospf virtual-links** command:

```
Router# show ip ospf virtual-links

Virtual Link to router 160.89.101.2 is up
Transit area 0.0.0.1, via interface Ethernet0, Cost of using 10
Transmit Delay is 1 sec, State POINT_TO_POINT
Timer intervals configured, Hello 10, Dead 40, Wait 40, Retransmit 5
Hello due in 0:00:08
Adjacency State FULL
```

Table 15–12 describes significant fields shown in the display.

Table 15–12 *Show IP OSPF Virtual-Links Field Descriptions*

Field	Description
Virtual Link to router 160.89.101.2 is up	Specifies the OSPF neighbor, and if the link to that neighbor is up or down.
Transit area 0.0.0.1	The transit area through which the virtual link is formed.
via interface Ethernet0	The interface through which the virtual link is formed.
Cost of using 10	The cost of reaching the OSPF neighbor through the virtual link.
Transmit Delay is 1 sec	The transmit delay on the virtual link.
State POINT_TO_POINT	The state of the OSPF neighbor.
Timer intervals...	The various timer intervals configured for the link.
Hello due in 0:00:08	When the next hello is expected from the neighbor.
Adjacency State FULL	The adjacency state between the neighbors.

SUMMARY-ADDRESS

Use the **summary-address** router configuration command to create aggregate addresses for OSPF. The **no summary-address** command restores the default.

> **summary-address** *address mask* {**level-1** | **level-1-2** | **level-2**} *prefix mask* [**not-advertise**] [**tag** *tag*]
>
> **no summary-address** *address mask* {**level-1** | **level-1-2** | **level-2**}

Syntax	Description
address	Summary address designated for a range of addresses.
mask	IP subnet mask used for the summary route.
level-1	Only routes redistributed into Level 1 are summarized with the configured address/mask value. This keyword applies to IS-IS only.
level-1-2	The summary router is injected into both a Level 1 area and a Level 2 subdomain. This keyword applies to IS-IS only.
level-2	Routes learned by Level 1 routing will be summarized into the Level 2 backbone with the configured address/mask value. This keyword applies to IS-IS only.
prefix	IP route prefix for the destination.
mask	IP subnet mask used for the summary route.
not-advertise	(Optional.) Used to suppress routes that match the prefix/mask pair. This keyword applies to OSPF only.
tag *tag*	(Optional.) Tag value that can be used as a "match" value for controlling redistribution via route maps. This keyword applies to OSPF only.

Default

Disabled

Command Mode

Router configuration

Usage Guidelines

This command first appeared in Cisco IOS Release 10.0.

Multiple groups of addresses can be summarized for a given level. Routes learned from other routing protocols can also be summarized. The metric used to advertise the summary is the smallest metric of all the more specific routes. This command helps reduce the size of the routing table.

Using this command for OSPF causes an OSPF autonomous system boundary router (ASBR) to advertise one external route as an aggregate for all redistributed routes that are covered by the address. For OSPF, this command summarizes only routes from other routing protocols that are being redistributed into OSPF. Use the **area range** command for route summarization between OSPF areas.

Example

In the following example, summary address 10.1.0.0 includes address 10.1.1.0, 10.1.2.0, 10.1.3.0, and so forth. Only the address 10.1.0.0 is advertised in an external link state advertisement.

```
summary-address 10.1.0.0 255.255.0.0
```

Related Commands

Search online to find documentation for related commands.

area range
ip ospf authentication-key
ip ospf message-digest-key

TIMERS SPF

To configure the delay time between when OSPF receives a topology change and when it starts a shortest path first (SPF) calculation, and the hold time between two consecutive SPF calculations, use the **timers spf** router configuration command. To return to the default timer values, use the **no** form of this command.

timers spf *spf-delay spf-holdtime*
no timers spf *spf-delay spf-holdtime*

Syntax	Description
spf-delay	Delay time, in seconds, between when OSPF receives a topology change and when it starts a SPF calculation. It can be an integer from 0 to 65535. The default time is 5 seconds. A value of 0 means that there is no delay; that is, the SPF calculation is started immediately.
spf-holdtime	Minimum time, in seconds, between two consecutive SPF calculations. It can be an integer from 0 to 65535. The default time is 10 seconds. A value of 0 means that there is no delay; that is, two consecutive SPF calculations can be done one immediately after the other.

Defaults

spf-delay: 5 seconds
spf-holdtime: 10 seconds

Command Mode

Router configuration

Usage Guidelines

This command first appeared in Cisco IOS Release 10.3.

Setting the delay and hold time low causes routing to switch to the alternate path more quickly in the event of a failure. However, it consumes more CPU processing time.

Example

The following example changes the delay to 10 seconds and the hold time to 20 seconds:

```
timers spf 10 20
```

CHAPTER 16

Configuring IP Enhanced IGRP

This chapter describes how to configure IP Enhanced Interior Gateway Routing Protocol (IGRP). For a complete description of the IP Enhanced IGRP commands listed in this chapter, see Chapter 17, "IP Enhanced IGRP Commands."

For protocol-independent features that work with IP Enhanced IGRP, see Chapter 22, "Configuring IP Routing Protocol-Independent Features."

Enhanced IGRP is an enhanced version of the IGRP developed by Cisco Systems, Inc. Enhanced IGRP uses the same distance vector algorithm and distance information as IGRP. However, the convergence properties and the operating efficiency of Enhanced IGRP have improved significantly over IGRP.

The convergence technology is based on research conducted at SRI International. It employs an algorithm referred to as the Diffusing Update Algorithm (DUAL). This algorithm guarantees loop-free operation at every instant throughout a route computation and allows all devices involved in a topology change to synchronize at the same time. Routers that are not affected by topology changes are not involved in recomputations. The convergence time with DUAL rivals that of any other existing routing protocol.

CISCO'S IP ENHANCED IGRP IMPLEMENTATION

IP Enhanced IGRP provides the following features:

- Automatic redistribution—IP IGRP routes can be automatically redistributed into Enhanced IGRP, and IP Enhanced IGRP routes can be automatically redistributed into IGRP. If desired, you can turn off redistribution. You can also completely turn off IP Enhanced IGRP and IP IGRP on the router or on individual interfaces.

- Increased network width—With IP RIP, the largest possible width of your network is 15 hops. When IP Enhanced IGRP is enabled, the largest possible width is 224 hops. Because the Enhanced IGRP metric is large enough to support thousands of hops, the only barrier to expanding the network is the transport layer hop counter. Cisco works around this problem by incrementing the transport control field only when an IP packet has traversed 15 routers and the next hop to the destination was learned by way of Enhanced IGRP. When a RIP route is being used as the next hop to the destination, the transport control field is incremented as usual.

Enhanced IGRP offers the following features:

- Fast convergence—The DUAL algorithm allows routing information to converge as quickly as any currently available routing protocol.

- Partial updates—Enhanced IGRP sends incremental updates when the state of a destination changes instead of sending the entire contents of the routing table. This feature minimizes the bandwidth required for Enhanced IGRP packets.

- Less CPU usage than IGRP—This occurs because full update packets do not have to be processed each time they are received.

- Neighbor discovery mechanism—This is a simple hello mechanism used to learn about neighboring routers. It is protocol independent.

- Variable-length subnet masks.

- Arbitrary route summarization.

- Scaling—Enhanced IGRP scales to large networks.

Enhanced IGRP has the following four basic components:

- Neighbor discovery/recovery

- Reliable transport protocol

- DUAL finite state machine

- Protocol-dependent modules

Neighbor discovery/recovery is the process that routers use to dynamically learn of other routers on their directly attached networks. Routers must also discover when their neighbors become unreachable or inoperative. Neighbor discovery/recovery is achieved with low overhead by periodically sending small hello packets. As long as hello packets are received, the Cisco IOS software can determine that a neighbor is alive and functioning. After this status is determined, the neighboring routers can exchange routing information.

The reliable transport protocol is responsible for guaranteed, ordered delivery of Enhanced IGRP packets to all neighbors. It supports intermixed transmission of multicast and unicast packets. Some Enhanced IGRP packets must be transmitted reliably and others need not be. For efficiency, reliability is provided only when necessary. For example, on a multiaccess network that has multicast capabilities (such as Ethernet), it is not necessary to send hellos reliably to all neighbors individually. Therefore, Enhanced IGRP sends a single multicast hello with an indication in the packet informing the receivers that the packet need not be acknowledged. Other types of packets (such as updates) require acknowledgment; this is indicated in the packet. The reliable transport has a provision to send multicast packets quickly when there are unacknowledged packets pending. Doing so helps ensure that convergence time remains low in the presence of varying speed links.

The DUAL finite state machine embodies the decision process for all route computations. It tracks all routes advertised by all neighbors. DUAL uses the distance information (known as a metric) to select efficient, loop-free paths. DUAL selects routes to be inserted into a routing table based on feasible successors; a successor is a neighboring router used for packet forwarding that has a least-cost path to a destination that is guaranteed not to be part of a routing loop. When there are no feasible successors, but there are neighbors advertising the destination, a recomputation must occur. This is the process whereby a new successor is determined. The amount of time it takes to recompute the route affects the convergence time. Even though the recomputation is not processor intensive, it is advantageous to avoid recomputation if it is not necessary. When a topology change occurs, DUAL tests for feasible successors. If there are feasible successors, it will use any it finds in order to avoid unnecessary recomputation.

The protocol-dependent modules are responsible for network layer protocol-specific tasks. An example is the IP Enhanced IGRP module, which is responsible for sending and receiving Enhanced IGRP packets that are encapsulated in IP. It is also responsible for parsing Enhanced IGRP packets and informing DUAL of the new information received. IP Enhanced IGRP asks DUAL to make routing decisions, but the results are stored in the IP routing table. Also, IP Enhanced IGRP is responsible for redistributing routes learned by other IP routing protocols.

ENHANCED IGRP CONFIGURATION TASK LIST

To configure IP Enhanced IGRP, complete the tasks in the following sections. At a minimum, you must enable IP Enhanced IGRP. The remaining tasks in the following list are optional:

- Enabling IP Enhanced IGRP
- Transitioning from IGRP to Enhanced IGRP
- Logging Enhanced IGRP Neighbor Adjacency Changes
- Configuring the Percentage of Link Bandwidth Used
- Adjusting the IP Enhanced IGRP Metric Weights
- Applying Offsets to Routing Metrics
- Disabling Route Summarization
- Configuring Summary Aggregate Addresses
- Configuring Enhanced IGRP Route Authentication
- Configuring Enhanced IGRP's Protocol-Independent Parameters
- Monitoring and Maintaining Enhanced IGRP

See the section "IP Enhanced IGRP Configuration Examples" at the end of this chapter for configuration examples.

ENABLING IP ENHANCED IGRP

To create an IP Enhanced IGRP routing process, perform the following tasks, beginning in global configuration mode:

Task	Command
Step 1 Enable an IP Enhanced IGRP routing process in global configuration mode.	**router eigrp** *autonomous-system*
Step 2 Associate networks with an IP Enhanced IGRP routing process in router configuration mode.	**network** *network-number*

IP Enhanced IGRP sends updates to the interfaces in the specified networks. If you do not specify an interface's network, it will not be advertised in any IP Enhanced IGRP update.

TRANSITIONING FROM IGRP TO ENHANCED IGRP

If you have routers on your network that are configured for IGRP, and you want to make a transition to routing Enhanced IGRP, you must designate transition routers on which both IGRP and Enhanced IGRP are configured. In these cases, perform the tasks as noted in the previous section, "Enabling IP Enhanced IGRP," and read the Chapter 12, "Configuring IGRP." You must use the same autonomous system number in order for routes to be redistributed automatically.

LOGGING ENHANCED IGRP NEIGHBOR ADJACENCY CHANGES

You can enable the logging of neighbor adjacency changes to monitor the stability of the routing system and to help you detect problems. By default, adjacency changes are not logged. To enable such logging, perform the following task in global configuration mode:

Task	Command
Enable logging of Enhanced IGRP neighbor adjacency changes.	**log-neighbor-changes**

CONFIGURING THE PERCENTAGE OF LINK BANDWIDTH USED

By default, Enhanced IGRP packets consume a maximum of 50 percent of the link bandwidth, as configured with the **bandwidth** interface configuration command. You might want to change that value if a different level of link utilization is required or if the configured bandwidth does not match the actual link bandwidth (it may have been configured to influence route metric calculations).

To configure the percentage of bandwidth that may be used by Enhanced IGRP on an interface, perform the following task in interface configuration mode:

Task	Command
Configure the percentage of bandwidth that may be used by Enhanced IGRP on an interface.	**ip bandwidth-percent eigrp** *percent*

ADJUSTING THE IP ENHANCED IGRP METRIC WEIGHTS

You can adjust the default behavior of IP Enhanced IGRP routing and metric computations. For example, this adjustment allows you to tune system behavior to allow for satellite transmission. Although IP Enhanced IGRP metric defaults have been carefully selected to provide excellent operation in most networks, you can adjust the IP Enhanced IGRP metric. Adjusting IP Enhanced IGRP metric weights can dramatically affect network performance, so be careful if you adjust them.

To adjust the IP Enhanced IGRP metric weights, perform the following task in router configuration mode:

Task	Command
Adjust the IP Enhanced IGRP metric.	**metric weights** *tos k1 k2 k3 k4 k5*

— **NOTES** ————————————————————————————————

Because of the complexity of this task, it is not recommended unless it is done with guidance from an experienced network designer.

———————————————————————————————————————

By default, the IP Enhanced IGRP composite metric is a 32-bit quantity that is a sum of the segment delays and the lowest segment bandwidth (scaled and inverted) for a given route. For a network of homogeneous media, this metric reduces to a hop count. For a network of mixed media (FDDI, Ethernet, and serial lines running from 9600 Kbps to T1 rates), the route with the lowest metric reflects the most desirable path to a destination.

APPLYING OFFSETS TO ROUTING METRICS

An offset list is the mechanism for increasing incoming and outgoing metrics to routes learned via Enhanced IGRP. This is done to provide a local mechanism for increasing the value of routing metrics. Optionally, you can limit the offset list with either an access list or an interface. To increase the value of routing metrics, perform the following task in router configuration mode:

Task	Command
Apply an offset to routing metrics.	**offset-list** [*access-list-number*	*name*] {**in**	**out**} *offset* [*type number*]

DISABLING ROUTE SUMMARIZATION

You can configure IP Enhanced IGRP to perform automatic summarization of subnet routes into network-level routes. For example, you can configure subnet 131.108.1.0 to be advertised as 131.108.0.0 over interfaces that have subnets of 192.31.7.0 configured. Automatic summarization is performed when there are two or more **network** router configuration commands configured for the IP Enhanced IGRP process. By default, this feature is enabled.

To disable automatic summarization, perform the following task in router configuration mode:

Task	Command
Disable automatic summarization.	**no auto-summary**

Route summarization works in conjunction with the **ip summary-address eigrp** interface configuration command, in which additional summarization can be performed. If automatic summarization is in effect, there is usually no need to configure network level summaries using the **ip summary-address eigrp** command.

CONFIGURING SUMMARY AGGREGATE ADDRESSES

You can configure a summary aggregate address for a specified interface. If there are any more specific routes in the routing table, IP Enhanced IGRP will advertise the summary address out the interface with a metric equal to the minimum of all more specific routes.

To configure a summary aggregate address, perform the following task in interface configuration mode:

Task	Command
Configure a summary aggregate address.	**ip summary-address eigrp** *autonomous-system-number address mask*

See the "Route Summarization Example" at the end of this chapter for an example of summarizing aggregate addresses.

CONFIGURING ENHANCED IGRP ROUTE AUTHENTICATION

IP Enhanced IGRP route authentication provides MD5 authentication of routing updates from the IP Enhanced IGRP routing protocol. The MD5 keyed digest in each Enhanced IGRP packet prevents the introduction of unauthorized or false routing messages from unapproved sources.

Before you can enable Enhanced IGRP route authentication, you must enable IP Enhanced IGRP.

To enable authentication of IP Enhanced IGRP packets, perform the following tasks, beginning in interface configuration mode:

Task	Command
Step 1 Enable MD5 authentication in IP Enhanced IGRP packets.	**ip authentication mode eigrp** *autonomous-system* **md5**
Step 2 Enable authentication of IP Enhanced IGRP packets.	**ip authentication key-chain eigrp** *autonomous-system key-chain*
Step 3 Exit to global configuration mode.	**exit**
Step 4 Identify a key chain. (Match the name configured in Step 1.)	**key chain** *name-of-chain*
Step 5 In key chain configuration mode, identify the key number.	**key** *number*
Step 6 In key chain key configuration mode, identify the key string.	**key-string** *text*
Step 7 Optionally, specify the time period during which the key can be received.	**accept-lifetime** *start-time* {**infinite** | *end-time* | **duration** *seconds*}
Step 8 Optionally, specify the time period during which the key can be sent.	**send-lifetime** *start-time* {**infinite** | *end-time* | **duration** *seconds*}

Each key has its own key identifier (specified with the **key** *number* command), which is stored locally. The combination of the key identifier and the interface associated with the message uniquely identifies the authentication algorithm and MD5 authentication key in use.

You can configure multiple keys with lifetimes. Only one authentication packet is sent, regardless of how many valid keys exist. The software examines the key numbers in order from lowest to highest and uses the first valid key it encounters. Note that the router needs to know the time.

For an example of route authentication, see the section "Route Authentication Example" at the end of this chapter.

CONFIGURING ENHANCED IGRP'S PROTOCOL-INDEPENDENT PARAMETERS

Enhanced IGRP works with AppleTalk, IP, and IPX. The bulk of this chapter describes IP Enhanced IGRP. However, this section describes Enhanced IGRP features that work for Apple-Talk, IP, and IPX. To configure such protocol-independent parameters, perform one or both of the tasks in the following list:

- Adjusting the Interval between Hello Packets and the Hold Time
- Disabling Split Horizon

For more protocol-independent features that work with IP Enhanced IGRP, see Chapter 22.

Adjusting the Interval between Hello Packets and the Hold Time

You can adjust the interval between hello packets and the hold time.

Routing devices periodically send hello packets to each other to dynamically learn of other routers on their directly attached networks. This information is used to discover who their neighbors are and to learn when their neighbors become unreachable or inoperative.

By default, hello packets are sent every 5 seconds. The exception is on low-speed, nonbroadcast, multiaccess (NBMA) media, on which the default hello interval is 60 seconds. (Low speed is considered to be a rate of T1 or slower, as specified with the **bandwidth** interface configuration command.) The default hello interval remains 5 seconds for high-speed NBMA networks. Note that for the purposes of Enhanced IGRP, Frame Relay and SMDS networks may or may not be considered to be NBMA. These networks are considered NBMA if the interface has not been configured to use physical multicasting; otherwise, they are not considered NBMA.

You can configure the hold time on a specified interface for a particular IP Enhanced IGRP routing process designated by the autonomous system number. The hold time, which is advertised in hello packets, indicates to neighbors the length of time they should consider the sender valid. The default hold time is three times the hello interval, or 15 seconds. For slow-speed NBMA networks, the default hold time is 180 seconds.

To change the interval between hello packets, perform the following task in interface configuration mode:

Task	Command
Configure the hello interval for an IP Enhanced IGRP routing process.	**ip hello-interval eigrp** *autonomous-system-number seconds*

On very congested and large networks, the default hold time might not be sufficient time for all routers to receive hello packets from their neighbors. In this case, you may want to increase the hold time.

To change the hold time, perform the following task in interface configuration mode:

Task	Command
Configure the hold time for an IP Enhanced IGRP routing process.	**ip hold-time eigrp** *autonomous-system-number seconds*

NOTES

Do not adjust the hold time without advising technical support.

Disabling Split Horizon

Split horizon controls IP Enhanced IGRP update and query packets. When split horizon is enabled on an interface, these packets are not sent to destinations for which this interface is the next hop. This reduces the possibility of routing loops.

By default, split horizon is enabled on all interfaces.

Split horizon blocks route information from being advertised by a router out of any interface from which that information originated. This behavior usually optimizes communications among multiple routing devices, particularly when links are broken. However, with nonbroadcast networks (such as Frame Relay and SMDS), situations can arise for which this behavior is less than ideal. For these situations, you may want to disable split horizon.

To disable split horizon, perform the following task in interface configuration mode:

Task	Command
Disable split horizon.	**no ip split-horizon eigrp** *autonomous-system-number*

MONITORING AND MAINTAINING ENHANCED IGRP

To delete neighbors from the neighbor table, perform the following task in EXEC mode:

Task	Command
Delete neighbors from the neighbor table.	**clear ip eigrp neighbors** [*ip-address*	*interface*]

To display various routing statistics, perform the following tasks in EXEC mode:

Task		Command
Step 1	Display information about interfaces configured for Enhanced IGRP.	show ip eigrp interfaces [*interface*] [*as-number*]
Step 2	Display the IP Enhanced IGRP discovered neighbors.	show ip eigrp neighbors [*type number*]
Step 3	Display the IP Enhanced IGRP topology table for a given process.	show ip eigrp topology [*autonomous-system-number* | [[*ip-address*] *mask*]]
Step 4	Display the number of packets sent and received for all or a specified IP Enhanced IGRP process.	show ip eigrp traffic [*autonomous-system-number*]

IP ENHANCED IGRP CONFIGURATION EXAMPLES

This section contains the following examples:

- Route Summarization Example
- Route Authentication Example

Route Summarization Example

The following example configures route summarization on the interface and also configures the auto-summary feature. This configuration causes IP Enhanced IGRP to summarize network 10.0.0.0 out Ethernet interface 0 only. In addition, this example disables auto-summarization.

```
interface Ethernet 0
 ip summary-address eigrp 1 10.0.0.0 255.0.0.0
 !
router eigrp 1
 network 172.16.0.0
 no auto-summary
```

Route Authentication Example

The following example enables MD5 authentication on IP Enhanced IGRP packets in autonomous system 1. Figure 16–1 shows the scenario.

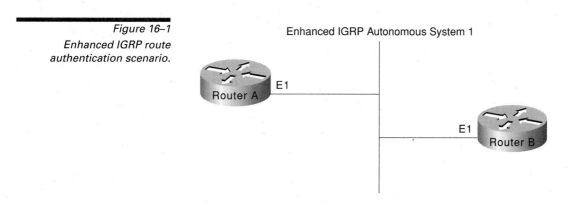

Figure 16–1
Enhanced IGRP route
authentication scenario.

Enhanced IGRP Autonomous System 1

Router A

```
ip authentication mode eigrp 1 md5
ip authentication key-chain eigrp 1 holly
key chain holly
key 1
 key-string 0987654321
 accept-lifetime infinite
 send-lifetime 04:00:00 Dec 4 1996 04:48:00 Dec 4 1996
exit
key 2
 key-string 1234567890
 accept-lifetime infinite
 send-lifetime 04:45:00 Dec 4 1996 infinite
```

Router B

```
ip authentication mode eigrp 1 md5
ip authentication key-chain eigrp 1 mikel
key chain mikel
key 1
 key-string 0987654321
 accept-lifetime infinite
 send-lifetime 04:00:00 Dec 4 1996 infinite
exit
key 2
 key-string 1234567890
 accept-lifetime infinite
 send-lifetime 04:45:00 Dec 4 1996 infinite
```

Router A accepts and attempts to verify the MD5 digest of any Enhanced IGRP packet with a key equal to 1. It also accepts a packet with a key equal to 2. All other MD5 packets are dropped. Router A sends all Enhanced IGRP packets with key 2.

Router B accepts key 1 or key 2 and sends key 1. In this scenario, MD5 authenticates.

CHAPTER 17

IP Enhanced IGRP Commands

Use the commands in this chapter to configure and monitor IP Enhanced IGRP. For configuration information and examples, see Chapter 16, "Configuring IP Enhanced IGRP."

AUTO-SUMMARY

To restore the default behavior of automatic summarization of subnet routes into network-level routes, use the **auto-summary** router configuration command. To disable this feature and transmit subprefix routing information across classful network boundaries, use the **no** form of this command.

> **auto-summary**
> **no auto-summary**

Syntax   Description

This command has no arguments or keywords.

Default

Enabled (the software summarizes subprefixes to the classful network boundary when crossing classful network boundaries).

Command Mode

Router configuration

Usage Guidelines

This command first appeared in Cisco IOS Release 10.0.

Route summarization reduces the amount of routing information in the routing tables.

431

By default, BGP does not accept subnets redistributed from IGP. To advertise and carry subnet routes in BGP, use an explicit **network** command or the **no auto-summary** command. If you disable auto-summarization and have not entered a **network** command, you will not advertise network routes for networks with subnet routes unless they contain a summary route.

IP Enhanced IGRP summary routes are given an administrative distance value of 5. You cannot configure this value.

RIP Version 1 always uses automatic summarization. If you are using RIP Version 2, you can turn off automatic summarization by specifying **no auto-summary**. Disable automatic summarization if you must perform routing between disconnected subnets. When automatic summarization is off, subnets are advertised.

Example

The following example disables automatic summarization for process eigrp 109:

```
router eigrp 109
  no auto-summary
```

Related Commands

Search online to find documentation for related commands.

ip summary-address eigrp

CLEAR IP EIGRP NEIGHBORS

To delete entries from the neighbor table, use the **clear ip eigrp neighbors** EXEC command.

   clear ip eigrp neighbors [*ip-address* | *type number*]

Syntax	Description
ip-address	(Optional.) Address of the neighbor.
type number	(Optional.) Interface type and number. Specifying these arguments removes from the neighbor table all entries learned via this interface.

Command Mode
EXEC

Usage Guidelines
This command first appeared in Cisco IOS Release 10.0.

Example

The following example removes the neighbor whose address is 160.20.8.3:

```
clear ip eigrp neighbors 160.20.8.3
```

Related Commands

Search online to find documentation for related commands.

show ip eigrp interfaces

DEFAULT-INFORMATION

To control the candidate default routing information between IGRP or Enhanced IGRP processes, use the **default-information** router configuration command. To suppress IGRP or Enhanced IGRP candidate information in incoming updates, use the **no default-information in** command. To suppress IGRP or Enhanced IGRP candidate information in outbound updates, use the **no default-information out** command.

> **default-information** {**in** | **out**} {*access-list-number* | *name*}
> **no default-information** {**in** | **out**}

**Part
II**

Command Reference

Syntax	*Description*
in	Allows IGRP or Enhanced IGRP exterior or default routes to be received by an IGRP process.
out	Allows IGRP or Enhanced IGRP exterior routes to be advertised in updates.
access-list-number	*name*	Number or name of an access list. It can be a number in the range 1 to 99 or an access list name.

Default

Normally, exterior routes are always accepted and default information is passed between IGRP or Enhanced IGRP processes when doing redistribution.

Command Mode

Router configuration

Usage Guidelines

This command first appeared in Cisco IOS Release 10.0. The *access-list-number* and *name* arguments first appeared in Cisco IOS Release 11.2.

The default network of 0.0.0.0 used by RIP cannot be redistributed by IGRP or Enhanced IGRP.

Examples

The following example allows IGRP exterior or default routes to be received by the IGRP process in autonomous system 23:

```
router igrp 23
  default-information in
```

The following example allows IP Enhanced IGRP exterior or default routes to be received by the IP Enhanced IGRP process in autonomous system 23:

```
router eigrp 23
  default-information in
```

DEFAULT-METRIC (IGRP AND ENHANCED IGRP)

To set metrics for IGRP or Enhanced IGRP, use this form of the **default-metric** router configuration command. To remove the metric value and restore the default state, use the **no** form of this command.

> **default-metric** *bandwidth delay reliability loading mtu*
> **no default-metric** *bandwidth delay reliability loading mtu*

Syntax	Description
bandwidth	Minimum bandwidth of the route in kilobits per second. It can be 0 or any positive integer.
delay	Route delay in tens of microseconds. It can be 0 or any positive number that is a multiple of 39.1 nanoseconds.
reliability	Likelihood of successful packet transmission expressed as a number between 0 and 255. The value 255 means 100 percent reliability; 0 means no reliability.
loading	Effective bandwidth of the route expressed as a number from 0 to 255 (255 is 100 percent loading).
mtu	Minimum maximum transmission unit (MTU) size of the route in bytes. It can be 0 or any positive integer.

Default

Only connected routes and interface static routes can be redistributed without a default metric.

Command Mode

Router configuration

Usage Guidelines

This command first appeared in Cisco IOS Release 10.0.

A default metric is required to redistribute a protocol into IGRP or Enhanced IGRP, unless you use the **redistribute** command. Automatic metric translations occur between IGRP and Enhanced IGRP. You do not need default metrics to redistribute IGRP or Enhanced IGRP into itself.

Metric defaults have been carefully set to work for a wide variety of networks. Take great care in changing these values.

Keeping the same metrics is supported only when redistributing from IGRP, Enhanced IGRP, or static routes.

Example

The following example takes redistributed RIP metrics and translates them into IGRP metrics with values as follows: bandwidth = 1000, delay = 100, reliability = 250, loading = 100, and mtu =1500.

```
router igrp 109
  network 131.108.0.0
  redistribute rip
  default-metric 1000 100 250 100 1500
```

Related Commands

Search online to find documentation for related commands.

redistribute

DISTANCE EIGRP

To allow the use of two administrative distances—internal and external—that could be a better route to a node, use the **distance eigrp** router configuration command. To reset these values to their defaults, use the **no** form of this command.

distance eigrp *internal-distance external-distance*
no distance eigrp

Syntax	Description
internal-distance	Administrative distance for Enhanced IGRP internal routes. Internal routes are those that are learned from another entity within the same autonomous system. It can be a value from 1 to 255.
external-distance	Administrative distance for Enhanced IGRP external routes. External routes are those for which the best path is learned from a neighbor external to the autonomous system. It can be a value from 1 to 255.

Default

internal-distance: 90
external-distance: 170

Command Mode

Router configuration

Usage Guidelines

This command first appeared in Cisco IOS Release 10.0.

An administrative distance is a rating of the trustworthiness of a routing information source, such as an individual router or a group of routers. Numerically, an administrative distance is an integer between 0 and 255. In general, the higher the value, the lower the trust rating. An administrative distance of 255 means the routing information source cannot be trusted at all and should be ignored.

Use the **distance eigrp** command if another protocol is known to be able to provide a better route to a node than was actually learned via external Enhanced IGRP or if some internal routes should really be preferred by Enhanced IGRP.

Table 17–1 lists the default administrative distances.

Table 17–1 *Default Administrative Distances*

Route Source	Default Distance
Connected interface	0
Static route	1
Enhanced IGRP summary route	5
External BGP	20
Internal Enhanced IGRP	90
IGRP	100
OSPF	110
IS-IS	115
RIP	120
EGP	140
Internal BGP	200
Unknown	255

To display the default administrative distance for a specified routing process, use the **show ip protocols** EXEC command.

Example

In the following example, the **router eigrp** global configuration command sets up Enhanced IGRP routing in autonomous system number 109. The **network** router configuration commands specify Enhanced IGRP routing on networks 192.31.7.0 and 128.88.0.0. The first **distance** router configuration command sets the default administrative distance to 255, which instructs the Cisco IOS software to ignore all routing updates from routers for which an explicit distance has not been set. The second **distance** router configuration command sets the administrative distance for all routers on the Class C network 192.31.7.0 to 90. The third **distance** router configuration command sets the administrative distance for the router with the address 128.88.1.3 to 120.

```
router eigrp 109
 network 192.31.7.0
 network 128.88.0.0
 distance 255
!
! use caution when executing the next two commands!
!
 distance 90 192.31.7.0 0.0.0.255
 distance 120 128.88.1.3 0.0.0.0
```

Related Commands

Search online to find documentation for related commands.

show ip protocols

IP AUTHENTICATION KEY-CHAIN EIGRP

To enable authentication of IP Enhanced IGRP packets, use the **ip authentication key-chain eigrp** interface configuration command. To disable such authentication, use the **no** form of this command.

> **ip authentication key-chain eigrp** *autonomous-system key-chain*
> **no ip authentication key-chain eigrp** *autonomous-system key-chain*

Syntax	Description
autonomous-system	Autonomous system to which the authentication applies.
key-chain	Name of the authentication key chain.

Default

No authentication is provided for Enhanced IGRP packets.

Command Mode

Interface configuration

Usage Guidelines

This command first appeared in Cisco IOS Release 11.2 F.

Example

The following example applies authentication to autonomous system 2 and identifies a key chain named *sports*:

```
ip authentication key-chain eigrp 2 sports
```

Related Commands

Search online to find documentation for related commands.

accept-lifetime
ip authentication mode eigrp
key
key chain
key-string
send-lifetime

IP AUTHENTICATION MODE EIGRP

To specify the type of authentication used in IP Enhanced IGRP packets, use the **ip authentication mode eigrp** interface configuration command. To disable that type of authentication, use the **no** form of this command.

> **ip authentication mode eigrp** *autonomous-system* **md5**
> **no ip authentication mode eigrp** *autonomous-system* **md5**

Syntax	Description
autonomous-system	Autonomous system number.
md5	Keyed MD5 authentication.

Default

No authentication is provided for IP Enhanced IGRP packets.

Command Mode

Interface configuration

Usage Guidelines

This command first appeared in Cisco IOS Release 11.2 F.

Configure authentication to prevent unapproved sources from introducing unauthorized or false routing messages. When authentication is configured, an MD5 keyed digest is added to each Enhanced IGRP packet in the specified autonomous system.

Example

The following example configures the interface to use MD5 authentication in Enhanced IGRP packets in autonomous system 10:

```
ip authentication mode eigrp 10 md5
```

Related Commands

Search online to find documentation for related commands.

accept-lifetime
ip authentication key-chain eigrp
key
key chain
key-string
send-lifetime

IP BANDWIDTH-PERCENT EIGRP

To configure the percentage of bandwidth that may be used by Enhanced IGRP on an interface, use the **ip bandwidth-percent eigrp** interface configuration command. To restore the default value, use the **no** form of this command.

> **ip bandwidth-percent eigrp** *as-number percent*
> **no ip bandwidth-percent eigrp** *as-number percent*

Syntax	Description
as-number	Autonomous system number.
percent	Percent of bandwidth that Enhanced IGRP may use.

Default

50 percent

Command Mode

Interface configuration

Usage Guidelines

This command first appeared in Cisco IOS Release 11.2.

Enhanced IGRP will use up to 50 percent of the bandwidth of a link, as defined by the **bandwidth** interface configuration command. This command may be used if some other fraction of the bandwidth is desired. Note that values greater than 100 percent may be configured; this may be useful if the bandwidth is set artificially low for other reasons.

Example

The following example allows Enhanced IGRP to use up to 75 percent (42 Kbps) of a 56-Kbps serial link in autonomous system 209:

```
interface serial 0
  bandwidth 56
  ip bandwidth-percent eigrp 209 75
```

Related Commands

Search online to find documentation for related commands.

bandwidth

IP HELLO-INTERVAL EIGRP

To configure the hello interval for the Enhanced IGRP routing process designated by an autonomous system number, use the **ip hello-interval eigrp** interface configuration command. To restore the default value, use the **no** form of this command.

ip hello-interval eigrp *autonomous-system-number seconds*
no ip hello-interval eigrp *autonomous-system-number seconds*

Syntax	Description
autonomous-system-number	Autonomous system number.
seconds	Hello interval, in seconds.

Defaults

For low-speed, NBMA networks: 60 seconds
For all other networks: 5 seconds

Command Mode

Interface configuration

Usage Guidelines

This command first appeared in Cisco IOS Release 10.0.

The default of 60 seconds applies only to low-speed, nonbroadcast, multiaccess (NBMA) media. Low speed is considered to be a rate of T1 or slower, as specified with the **bandwidth** interface configuration command. Note that for the purposes of Enhanced IGRP, Frame Relay and SMDS networks may or may not be considered to be NBMA. These networks are considered NBMA if the interface has not been configured to use physical multicasting; otherwise, they are considered not to be NBMA.

Example

The following example sets the hello interval for Ethernet interface 0 to 10 seconds:

```
interface ethernet 0
  ip hello-interval eigrp 109 10
```

Related Commands

Search online to find documentation for related commands.

ip hold-time eigrp

IP HOLD-TIME EIGRP

To configure the hold time for a particular Enhanced IGRP routing process designated by the autonomous system number, use the **ip hold-time eigrp** interface configuration command. To restore the default value, use the **no** form of this command.

ip hold-time eigrp *autonomous-system-number seconds*
no ip hold-time eigrp *autonomous-system-number seconds*

Syntax	Description
autonomous-system-number	Autonomous system number.
seconds	Hold time, in seconds.

Defaults

For low-speed, NBMA networks: 180 seconds
For all other networks: 15 seconds

Command Mode

Interface configuration

Usage Guidelines

This command first appeared in Cisco IOS Release 10.0.

On very congested and large networks, the default hold time might not be sufficient time for all routers and access servers to receive hello packets from their neighbors. In this case, you may want to increase the hold time.

We recommend that the hold time be at least three times the hello interval. If a router does not receive a hello packet within the specified hold time, routes through this router are considered unavailable.

Part II

Command Reference

Increasing the hold time delays route convergence across the network.

The default of 180 seconds hold time and 60 seconds hello interval apply only to low-speed, non-broadcast, multiaccess (NBMA) media. Low speed is considered to be a rate of T1 or slower, as specified with the **bandwidth** interface configuration command.

Example

The following example sets the hold time for Ethernet interface 0 to 40 seconds:

```
interface ethernet 0
  ip hold-time eigrp 109 40
```

Related Commands

Search online to find documentation for related commands.

ip hello-interval eigrp

IP SPLIT-HORIZON EIGRP

To enable Enhanced IGRP split horizon, use the **ip split-horizon eigrp** interface configuration command. To disable split horizon, use the **no** form of this command.

> **ip split-horizon eigrp** *autonomous-system-number*
> **no ip split-horizon eigrp** *autonomous-system-number*

Syntax	Description
autonomous-system-number	Autonomous system number.

Default

Enabled

Command Mode

Interface configuration

Usage Guidelines

This command first appeared in Cisco IOS Release 10.0.

For networks that include links over X.25 PSNs, you can use the **neighbor** router configuration command to defeat the split horizon feature. As an alternative, you can explicitly specify the **no ip split-horizon eigrp** command in your configuration. However, if you do so, you must similarly disable split horizon for all routers and access servers in any relevant multicast groups on that network.

NOTES

In general, it is recommended that you not change the default state of split horizon unless you are certain that your application requires the change in order to properly advertise routes. Remember that if split horizon is disabled on a serial interface and that interface is attached to a packet-switched network, you must disable split horizon for all routers and access servers in any relevant multicast groups on that network.

Example

The following example disables split horizon on a serial link connected to an X.25 network:

```
interface serial 0
 encapsulation x25
 no ip split-horizon eigrp
```

Related Commands

Search online to find documentation for related commands.

ip split-horizon
neighbor (IGRP, RIP)

IP SUMMARY-ADDRESS EIGRP

To configure a summary aggregate address for a specified interface, use the **ip summary-address eigrp** interface configuration command. To disable a configuration, use the **no** form of this command.

ip summary-address eigrp *autonomous-system-number address mask*
no ip summary-address eigrp *autonomous-system-number address mask*

Syntax	Description
autonomous-system-number	Autonomous system number.
address	IP summary aggregate address to apply to an interface.
mask	Subnet mask.

Default

No summary aggregate addresses are predefined.

Command Mode

Interface configuration

Usage Guidelines

This command first appeared in Cisco IOS Release 10.0.

Enhanced IGRP summary routes are given an administrative distance value of 5. You cannot configure this value.

Example

The following example sets the IP summary aggregate address for Ethernet interface 0:

```
interface ethernet 0
 ip summary-address eigrp 109 192.1.0.0 255.255.0.0
```

Related Commands

Search online to find documentation for related commands.

auto-summary

LOG-NEIGHBOR-CHANGES

To enable the logging of changes in Enhanced IGRP neighbor adjacencies, use the **log-neighbor-change** router configuration command. To disable the logging of changes in Enhanced IGRP neighbor adjacencies, use the **no** form of this command.

> **log-neighbor-changes**
> **no log-neighbor-changes**

Syntax   Description

This command has no arguments or keywords.

Default

No adjacency changes are logged.

Command Mode

Router configuration

Usage Guidelines

This command first appeared in Cisco IOS Release 11.2.

Enables the logging of neighbor adjacency changes to monitor the stability of the routing system and to help detect problems.

Example

The following configuration will log neighbor changes for Enhanced IGRP process 209:

```
ip router eigrp 209
 log-neighbor-changes
```

METRIC WEIGHTS

To allow the tuning of the IGRP or Enhanced IGRP metric calculations, use the **metric weights** router configuration command. To reset the values to their defaults, use the **no** form of this command.

metric weights *tos k1 k2 k3 k4 k5*
no metric weights

Syntax	Description
tos	Type of service. Currently, it must always be zero.
k1–k5	Constants that convert an IGRP or enhanced IGRP metric vector into a scalar quantity.

Defaults

tos: 0
k1: 1
k2: 0
k3: 1
k4: 0
k5: 0

Command Mode

Router configuration

Usage Guidelines

This command first appeared in Cisco IOS Release 10.0.

Use this command to alter the default behavior of IGRP routing and metric computation and allow the tuning of the IGRP metric calculation for a particular type of service (TOS).

If k5 equals 0, the composite IGRP or Enhanced IGRP metric is computed according to the following formula:

```
metric = [k1 * bandwidth + (k2 * bandwidth)/(256 - load) + k3 * delay]
```

If k5 does not equal zero, an additional operation is done:

```
metric = metric * [k5 / (reliability + k4)]
```

Bandwidth is inverse minimum bandwidth of the path in bits per second scaled by a factor of 2.56×10^{12}. The range is from a 1200-bps line to 10 terabits per second.

Delay is in units of 10 microseconds. This gives a range of 10 microseconds to 168 seconds. A delay of all ones indicates that the network is unreachable.

The delay parameter is stored in a 32-bit field, in increments of 39.1 nanoseconds. This gives a range of 1 (39.1 nanoseconds) to hexadecimal FFFFFFFF (decimal 4,294,967,040 nanoseconds). A delay of all ones (that is, a delay of hexadecimal FFFFFFFF) indicates that the network is unreachable.

Table 17–2 lists the default values used for several common media.

Table 17–2   *Bandwidth Values by Media Type*

Media Type	Delay	Bandwidth
Satellite	5120 (2 seconds)	5120 (500 Mbits)
Ethernet	25600 (1 ms)	256000 (10 Mbits)
1.544 Mbps	512000 (20,000 ms)	1,657,856 bits
64 Kbps	512000 (20,000 ms)	40,000,000 bits
56 Kbps	512000 (20,000 ms)	45,714,176 bits
10 Kbps	512000 (20,000 ms)	256,000,000 bits
1 Kbps	512000 (20,000 ms)	2,560,000,000 bits

Reliability is given as a fraction of 255. That is, 255 is 100 percent reliability or a perfectly stable link.

Load is given as a fraction of 255. A load of 255 indicates a completely saturated link.

Example

The following example sets the metric weights to slightly different values than the defaults:

```
router igrp 109
 network 131.108.0.0
 metric weights 0 2 0 2 0 0
```

Related Commands

Search online to find documentation for related commands.

bandwidth
delay
metric holddown
metric maximum-hops

NETWORK (IGRP AND ENHANCED IGRP)

To specify a list of networks for the Enhanced IGRP routing process, use this form of the **network** router configuration command. To remove an entry, use the **no** form of this command.

network *network-number*
no network *network-number*

Syntax	*Description*
network-number	IP address of the directly connected networks.

Default

No networks are specified.

Command Mode

Router configuration

Usage Guidelines

This command first appeared in Cisco IOS Release 10.0.

The network number specified must not contain any subnet information. You can specify multiple **network** commands.

IGRP or Enhanced IGRP sends updates to the interfaces in the specified network(s). Also, if an interface's network is not specified, it will not be advertised in any IGRP or Enhanced IGRP update.

Example

The following example configures a router for IGRP and assigns autonomous system 109. The **network** commands indicate the networks directly connected to the router.

```
router igrp 109
network 131.108.0.0
network 192.31.7.0
```

Related Commands

Search online to find documentation for related commands.

router igrp
router eigrp

OFFSET-LIST

To add an offset to incoming and outgoing metrics to routes learned via Enhanced IGRP, use the **offset-list** router configuration command. To remove an offset list, use the **no** form of this command.

offset-list {*access-list-number* | *name*} {**in** | **out**} *offset* [*type number*]
no offset-list {*access-list-number* | *name*} {**in** | **out**} *offset* [*type number*]

Syntax	Description
access-list-number	*name*	Standard access list number or name to be applied. Access list number 0 indicates all access lists. If *offset* is 0, no action is taken. For IGRP, the offset is added to the delay component only.
in	Applies the access list to incoming metrics.
out	Applies the access list to outgoing metrics.
offset	Positive offset to be applied to metrics for networks matching the access list. If the offset is 0, no action is taken.
type	(Optional.) Interface type to which the offset-list is applied.
number	(Optional.) Interface number to which the offset-list is applied.

Default

Disabled

Command Mode

Router configuration

Usage Guidelines

This command first appeared in Cisco IOS Release 10.0. The *type* and *number* arguments first appeared in Cisco IOS Release 10.3. The *name* argument first appeared in Cisco IOS Release 11.2.

The offset value is added to the routing metric. An offset-list with an interface type and interface number is considered extended and takes precedence over an offset-list that is not extended. Therefore, if an entry passes the extended offset-list and the normal offset-list, the extended offset-list's offset is added to the metric.

Examples

In the following example, the router applies an offset of 10 to the router's delay component only to access list 21:

```
offset-list 21 out 10
```

In the following example, the router applies an offset of 10 to routes learned from Ethernet interface 0:

```
offset-list 21 in 10 ethernet 0
```

ROUTER EIGRP

To configure the Enhanced IGRP routing process, use the **router eigrp** global configuration command. To shut down a routing process, use the **no** form of this command.

> **router eigrp** *autonomous-system*
> **no router eigrp** *autonomous-system*

Syntax	*Description*
autonomous-system	Autonomous system number that identifies the routes to the other Enhanced IGRP routers. It is also used to tag the routing information.

Default
Disabled

Command Mode
Global configuration

Usage Guidelines
This command first appeared in Cisco IOS Release 10.0.

Example
The following example shows how to configure an Enhanced IGRP routing process and assign process number 109:

```
router eigrp 109
```

Related Commands
Search online to find documentation for related commands.

network (IGRP and Enhanced IGRP)

SET METRIC

To set the metric value for IP Enhanced IGRP in a route-map, use the **set metric** route-map configuration command. To return to the default metric value, use the **no** form of this command.

> **set metric** *bandwidth delay reliability loading mtu*
> **no set metric** *bandwidth delay reliability loading mtu*

Syntax	Description
bandwidth	Metric value or IGRP bandwidth of the route in kilobits per second. It can be in the range 0 to 4294967295.
delay	Route delay in tens of microseconds. It can be in the range 0 to 4294967295.
reliability	Likelihood of successful packet transmission expressed as a number between 0 and 255. The value 255 means 100 percent reliability; 0 means no reliability.
loading	Effective bandwidth of the route expressed as a number from 0 to 255 (255 is 100 percent loading).
mtu	Minimum maximum transmission unit (MTU) size of the route in bytes. It can be in the range 0 to 4294967295.

Default

No metric will be set in the route-map. .

Command Mode

Route-map configuration

Usage Guidelines

This command first appeared in Cisco IOS Release 10.0.

NOTES ————————————————————————————————

We recommend you consult your Cisco technical support representative before changing the default value.

Use the **route-map** global configuration command, and the **match** and **set** route-map configuration commands, to define the conditions for redistributing routes from one routing protocol into another. Each **route-map** command has a list of **match** and **set** commands associated with it. The **match** commands specify the *match criteria*—the conditions under which redistribution is allowed for the current **route-map** command. The **set** commands specify the *set actions*—the particular redistribution actions to perform if the criteria enforced by the **match** commands are met. The **no route-map** command deletes the route map.

The **set** route-map configuration commands specify the redistribution *set actions* to be performed when all of a route map's match criteria are met. When all match criteria are met, all set actions are performed.

Example

In the following example, the bandwidth is set to 10,000, the delay is set to 10, the reliability is set to 255, the loading is set to 1, and the MTU is set to 1500:

```
set metric 10000 10 255 1 1500
```

SHOW IP EIGRP INTERFACES

To display information about interfaces configured for Enhanced IGRP, use the **show ip eigrp interfaces** EXEC command.

show ip eigrp interfaces [*type number*] [*as-number*]

Syntax	Description
type	(Optional.) Interface type.
number	(Optional.) Interface number.
as-number	(Optional.) Autonomous system number.

Command Mode

EXEC

Usage Guidelines

This command first appeared in Cisco IOS Release 11.2.

Use the **show ip eigrp** interfaces command to determine on which interfaces Enhanced IGRP is active, and to find out information about Enhanced IGRP relating to those interfaces.

If an interface is specified, only that interface is displayed. Otherwise, all interfaces on which Enhanced IGRP is running are displayed.

If an autonomous system is specified, only the routing process for the specified autonomous system is displayed. Otherwise, all Enhanced IGRP processes are displayed.

Sample Display

The following is sample output from the **show ip eigrp interfaces** command:

```
Router> show ip eigrp interfaces

IP EIGRP interfaces for process 109

                    Xmit Queue   Mean   Pacing Time   Multicast    Pending
Interface   Peers   Un/Reliable  SRTT   Un/Reliable   Flow Timer   Routes
Di0         0       0/0          0      11/434        0            0
Et0         1       0/0          337    0/10          0            0
SE0:1.16    1       0/0          10     1/63          103          0
Tu0         1       0/0          330    0/16          0            0
```

Table 17–3 describes the fields in the display.

Table 17–3 .Show IP EIGRP Interfaces Field Descriptions

Field	Description
Interface	Interface over which Enhanced IGRP is configured.
Peers	Number of directly connected Enhanced IGRP neighbors.
Xmit Queue Un/Reliable	Number of packets remaining in the Unreliable and Reliable transmit queues.
Mean SRTT	Mean SRTT in seconds.
Pacing Time Un/Reliable	Pacing time used to determine when Enhanced IGRP packets should be sent out the interface (Unreliable and Reliable packets).
Multicast Flow Timer	Maximum number of seconds in which router will send multicast Enhanced IGRP packets.
Pending Routes	Number of routes in the packets sitting in the transmit queue waiting to be sent.

Related Commands

Search online to find documentation for related commands.

show ip eigrp neighbors

SHOW IP EIGRP NEIGHBORS

To display the neighbors discovered by Enhanced IGRP, use the **show ip eigrp neighbors** EXEC command.

> **show ip eigrp neighbors** [*type number*]

Syntax	Description
type	(Optional.) Interface type.
number	(Optional.) Interface number.

Command Mode

EXEC

Usage Guidelines

This command first appeared in Cisco IOS Release 10.3.

Use the **show ip eigrp neighbors** command to determine when neighbors become active and inactive. It is also useful for debugging certain types of transport problems.

Sample Display

The following is sample output from the **show ip eigrp neighbors** command:

```
Router# show ip eigrp neighbors

IP-EIGRP Neighbors for process 77
Address              Interface      Holdtime Uptime   Q     Seq  SRTT RTO
                                    (secs)   (h:m:s)  Count Num  (ms) (ms)
160.89.81.28         Ethernet1      13       0:00:41  0     11   4    20
160.89.80.28         Ethernet0      14       0:02:01  0     10   12   24
160.89.80.31         Ethernet0      12       0:02:02  0     4    5    20
```

Table 17–4 explains the fields in the output.

Table 17–4   *Show IP Enhanced IGRP Neighbors Field Descriptions*

Field	Description
process 77	Autonomous system number specified in the **router** configuration command.
Address	IP address of the enhanced IGRP peer.
Interface	Interface on which the router is receiving hello packets from the peer.
Holdtime	Length of time, in seconds, that the Cisco IOS software will wait to hear from the peer before declaring it down. If the peer is using the default hold time, this number will be less than 15. If the peer configures a nondefault hold time, it will be reflected here.
Uptime	Elapsed time, in hours, minutes, and seconds, since the local router first heard from this neighbor.
Q Count	Number of Enhanced IGRP packets (Update, Query, and Reply) that the software is waiting to send.
Seq Num	Sequence number of the last update, query, or reply packet that was received from this neighbor.
SRTT	Smooth round-trip time. This is the number of milliseconds it takes for an Enhanced IGRP packet to be sent to this neighbor and for the local router to receive an acknowledgment of that packet.
RTO	Retransmission timeout, in milliseconds. This is the amount of time the software waits before retransmitting a packet from the retransmission queue to a neighbor.

Part II

Command Reference

SHOW IP EIGRP TOPOLOGY

To display the Enhanced IGRP topology table, use the **show ip eigrp topology** EXEC command.

show ip eigrp topology [*autonomous-system-number* | [[*ip-address*] *mask*]]

Syntax	*Description*
autonomous-system-number	(Optional.) Autonomous system number.
ip-address	(Optional.) IP address. When specified with a mask, a detailed description of the entry is provided.
mask	(Optional.) Subnet mask.

Command Mode

EXEC

Usage Guidelines

This command first appeared in Cisco IOS Release 10.0.

Use the **show ip eigrp topology** command to determine Diffusing Update Algorithm (DUAL) states and to debug possible DUAL problems.

Sample Display

The following is sample output from the **show ip eigrp topology** command:

```
Router# show ip eigrp topology

IP-EIGRP Topology Table for process 77

Codes: P - Passive, A - Active, U - Update, Q - Query, R - Reply,
       r - Reply status

P 160.89.90.0 255.255.255.0, 2 successors, FD is 0
         via 160.89.80.28 (46251776/46226176), Ethernet0
         via 160.89.81.28 (46251776/46226176), Ethernet1
         via 160.89.80.31 (46277376/46251776), Ethernet0
P 160.89.81.0 255.255.255.0, 1 successors, FD is 307200
         via Connected, Ethernet1
         via 160.89.81.28 (307200/281600), Ethernet1
         via 160.89.80.28 (307200/281600), Ethernet0
         via 160.89.80.31 (332800/307200), Ethernet0
```

Table 17–5 explains the fields in the output.

Table 17–5   *Show IP Enhanced IGRP Topology Field Descriptions*

Field	Description
Codes	State of this topology table entry. Passive and Active refer to the Enhanced IGRP state with respect to this destination; Update, Query, and Reply refer to the type of packet that is being sent.
P – Passive	No Enhanced IGRP computations are being performed for this destination.
A – Active	Enhanced IGRP computations are being performed for this destination.
U – Update	Indicates that an update packet was sent to this destination.
Q – Query	Indicates that a query packet was sent to this destination.
R – Reply	Indicates that a reply packet was sent to this destination.
r – Reply status	Flag that is set when after the software has sent a query and is waiting for a reply.
160.89.90.0 and so on	Destination IP network number.
255.255.255.0	Destination subnet mask.
successors	Number of successors. This number corresponds to the number of next hops in the IP routing table.
FD	Feasible distance. This value is used in the feasibility condition check. If the neighbor's reported distance (the metric after the slash) is less than the feasible distance, the feasibility condition is met and that path is a feasible successor. Once the software determines it has a feasible successor, it does not have to send a query for that destination.
replies	Number of replies that are still outstanding (have not been received) with respect to this destination. This information appears only when the destination is in Active state.
state	Exact Enhanced IGRP state that this destination is in. It can be the number 0, 1, 2, or 3. This information appears only when the destination is Active.
via	IP address of the peer who told the software about this destination. The first N of these entries, where N is the number of successors, are the current successors. The remaining entries on the list are feasible successors.

Table 17–5   *Show IP Enhanced IGRP Topology Field Descriptions, Continued*

Field	Description
(46251776/46226176)	The first number is the Enhanced IGRP metric that represents the cost to the destination. The second number is the Enhanced IGRP metric that this peer advertised.
Ethernet0	Interface from which this information was learned.

SHOW IP EIGRP TRAFFIC

To display the number of Enhanced IGRP packets sent and received, use the **show ip eigrp traffic** EXEC command.

> **show ip eigrp traffic** [*autonomous-system-number*]

Syntax	*Description*
autonomous-system-number	(Optional.) Autonomous system number.

Command Mode

EXEC

Usage Guidelines

This command first appeared in Cisco IOS Release 10.0.

Sample Display

The following is sample output from the **show ip eigrp traffic** command:

```
Router# show ip eigrp traffic

IP-EIGRP Traffic Statistics for process 77
   Hellos sent/received: 218/205
   Updates sent/received: 7/23
   Queries sent/received: 2/0
   Replies sent/received: 0/2
   Acks sent/received: 21/14
```

Table 17–6 describes the fields that might be shown in the display.

Table 17–6   *Show IP Enhanced IGRP Traffic Field Descriptions*

Field	Description
process 77	Autonomous system number specified in the **ip router** command.
Hellos sent/received	Number of hello packets that were sent and received.
Updates sent/received	Number of update packets that were sent and received.

Table 17–6 *Show IP Enhanced IGRP Traffic Field Descriptions, Continued*

Field	Description
Queries sent/received	Number of query packets that were sent and received.
Replies sent/received	Number of reply packets that were sent and received.
Acks sent/received	Number of acknowledgment packets that were sent and received.

TRAFFIC-SHARE

To control how traffic is distributed among routes when there are multiple routes for the same destination network that have different costs, use the **traffic-share** router configuration command. To disable this function, use the **no** form of the command.

> **traffic-share** {balanced | min}
> **no traffic share** {balanced | min}

Syntax	*Description*
balanced	Distributes traffic proportionately to the ratios of the metrics.
min	Uses routes that have minimum costs.

Default

Traffic is distributed proportionately to the ratios of the metrics.

Command Mode

Router configuration

Usage Guidelines

This command first appeared in Cisco IOS Release 10.0.

This command applies to IGRP and Enhanced IGRP routing protocols only. With the default setting, routes that have higher metrics represent less-preferable routes and get less traffic. Configuring **traffic-share min** causes the Cisco IOS software to only divide traffic among the routes with the best metric. Other routes will remain in the routing table, but will receive no traffic.

Example

In the following example, only routes of minimum cost will be used:

```
router igrp 5
  traffic-share min
```

Part II

Command Reference

VARIANCE

To control load balancing in an Enhanced IGRP-based internetwork, use the **variance** router configuration command. To reset the variance to the default value, use the **no** form of this command.

> **variance** *multiplier*
> **no variance**

Syntax	Description
multiplier	Metric value used for load balancing. It can be a value from 1 to 128. The default is 1, which means equal-cost load balancing.

Default

1 (equal-cost load balancing)

Command Mode

Router configuration

Usage Guidelines

This command first appeared in Cisco IOS Release 10.0.

Setting a variance value lets the Cisco IOS software determine the feasibility of a potential route. A route is feasible if the next router in the path is closer to the destination than the current router and if the metric for the entire path is within the variance. Only paths that are feasible can be used for load balancing and included in the routing table.

If the following two conditions are met, the route is deemed feasible and can be added to the routing table:

1. The local best metric must be greater than the metric learned from the next router.

2. The multiplier times the local best metric for the destination must be greater than or equal to the metric through the next router.

Example

The following example sets a variance value of 4:

```
router igrp 109
  variance 4
```

CHAPTER 18

Configuring
Integrated IS-IS

This chapter describes how to configure Integrated Intermediate System-to-Intermediate System (IS-IS). For a complete description of the integrated IS-IS commands listed in this chapter, see Chapter 19, "Integrated IS-IS Commands."

IS-IS is an International Organization for Standardization (ISO) dynamic routing specification; IS-IS is described in ISO 10589. Cisco's implementation of IS-IS allows you to configure IS-IS as an IP routing protocol.

IS-IS CONFIGURATION TASK LIST

To configure IS-IS, complete the tasks in the following sections. Enabling IS-IS is required; the remainder of the tasks in the following list are optional (although you might need to perform them, depending upon your specific application):

- Enabling IS-IS
- Configuring IS-IS Interface Parameters
- Configuring Miscellaneous IS-IS Parameters
- Monitoring IS-IS

In addition, you can filter routing information and specify route redistribution. See the "Filtering Routing Information" and "Redistributing Routing Information" sections, respectively, in Chapter 22, "Configuring IP Routing Protocol-Independent Features" for information on how to do this.

See the end of this chapter for an IS-IS configuration example.

ENABLING IS-IS

Unlike for other routing protocols, enabling IS-IS requires that you create an IS-IS routing process and assign it to specific interfaces (rather than to networks). You can specify *only one* IS-IS process per router. Only one IS-IS process is allowed whether you run it in integrated mode, ISO CLNS only, or IP only.

Network Entity Titles (NETs) define the area addresses for the IS-IS area and the system ID of the router.

To enable IS-IS, perform the following tasks, starting in global configuration mode:

Task	Command
Step 1 Enable IS-IS routing and specify an IS-IS process for IP, which places you in router configuration mode.	**router isis**
Step 2 Configure NETs for the routing process; you can specify a name for a NET as well as an address.	**net** *network-entity-title*
Step 3 Enter interface configuration mode.	**interface** *type number*
Step 4 Specify the interfaces that should be actively routing IS-IS.	**ip router isis** [*tag*]

See the "IS-IS as an IP Routing Protocol Example" section at the end of this chapter for an example of configuring IS-IS as an IP routing protocol.

CONFIGURING IS-IS INTERFACE PARAMETERS

Cisco Systems' IS-IS implementation allows you to alter certain interface-specific IS-IS parameters. Most interface configuration commands can be configured independently from other attached routers. The **isis password** command should configure the same password on all routers on a network. The settings of other commands (**isis hello-interval, isis hello-multiplier, isis retransmit-interval, isis retransmit-throttle-interval, isis csnp-interval,** and so on) can be different on different routers or interfaces. However, if you decide to change certain values from the defaults, it makes sense to configure them similarly on multiple routers and interfaces.

You can perform the following tasks, which are described in the next sections:

- Configuring IS-IS Link-State Metrics
- Setting the Advertised Hello Interval
- Setting the Advertised CSNP Interval
- Setting the Retransmission Interval
- Setting the LSP Transmissions Interval

- Setting the Retransmission Throttle Interval
- Setting the Hello Multiplier
- Specifying Designated Router Election
- Specifying the Interface Circuit Type
- Assigning a Password for an Interface

Configuring IS-IS Link-State Metrics

You can configure a cost for a specified interface. You can configure the *default-metric* for Level 1 or Level 2 routing. To configure the metric for the specified interface, perform the following task in interface configuration mode:

Task	Command
Configure the metric (or cost) for the specified interface.	**isis metric** *default-metric* {**level-1** | **level-2**}

Setting the Advertised Hello Interval

You can specify the length of time (in seconds) between hello packets that the Cisco IOS software sends on the interface. To do so, perform the following task in interface configuration mode:

Task	Command
Specify the length of time, in seconds, between hello packets that the Cisco IOS software sends on the specified interface.	**isis hello-interval** *seconds* {**level-1** | **level-2**}

The hello interval can be configured independently for Level 1 and Level 2, except on serial point-to-point interfaces. (Because there is only a single type of hello packet sent on serial links, it is independent of Level 1 or Level 2.) Specify an optional level for X.25, SMDS, and Frame Relay multiaccess networks. X25, SMDS, ATM, and Frame Relay networks should be configured with point-to-point subinterfaces.

Setting the Advertised CSNP Interval

Complete Sequence Number PDUs (CSNPs) are sent by the designated router to maintain database synchronization. You can configure the IS-IS CSNP interval for the interface.

To configure the CSNP interval for the specified interface, perform the following task in interface configuration mode:

Task	Command
Configure the IS-IS CSNP interval for the specified interface.	**isis csnp-interval** *seconds* {**level-1**	**level-2**}

This feature does not apply to serial point-to-point interfaces. It does apply to WAN connections if the WAN is viewed as a multiaccess meshed network.

Setting the Retransmission Interval

You can configure the number of seconds between retransmission of IS-IS Link State PDUs (LSPs) for point-to-point links. To set the retransmission level, perform the following task in interface configuration mode:

Task	Command
Configure the number of seconds between retransmission of IS-IS LSPs for point-to-point links.	**isis retransmit-interval** *seconds*

The value you specify should be an integer greater than the expected round-trip delay between any two routers on the attached network. The setting of this parameter should be conservative, or needless retransmission results. The value should be larger for serial lines.

Setting the LSP Transmissions Interval

To configure the delay between successive IS-IS link state packet transmissions, perform the following tasks in interface configuration mode:

Task	Command
Configure the delay between successive IS-IS link state packet transmissions.	**isis lsp-interval** *milliseconds*

Setting the Retransmission Throttle Interval

You can configure the maximum rate at which IS-IS LSPs are retransmitted on point-to-point links in terms of the number of milliseconds between packets. This is different than the retransmission interval, which is the amount of time between successive retransmissions of the *same* LSP.

The retransmission throttle interval is typically not necessary, except in cases of very large networks with high point-to-point neighbor counts. To set the retransmission throttle interval, perform the following task in interface configuration mode:

Task	Command
Configure the IS-IS LSP retransmission throttle interval.	isis retransmit-throttle-interval *milliseconds*

Setting the Hello Multiplier

To specify the number of IS-IS hello packets a neighbor must miss before the router should declare the adjacency as down, perform the following task in interface configuration mode. The default value is 3.

Task	Command
Set the hello multiplier.	isis hello-multiplier *multiplier* {level-1 I level-2}

Specifying Designated Router Election

You can configure the priority to use for designated router election. Priorities can be configured for Level 1 and Level 2 individually.

To specify the designated router election, perform the following task in interface configuration mode:

Task	Command
Configure the priority to use for designated router election.	isis priority *value* {level-1 I level-2}

Specifying the Interface Circuit Type

You can specify adjacency levels on a specified interface. This parameter is also referred to as the *interface circuit type*.

To specify the interface circuit type, perform the following task in interface configuration mode:

Task	Command
Configure the type of adjacency desired for neighbors on the specified interface (the interface circuit type).	isis circuit-type {level-1 I level-1-2 I level-2-only}

Assigning a Password for an Interface

You can assign different passwords for different routing levels. Specifying Level 1 or Level 2 configures the password for only Level 1 or Level 2 routing, respectively. If you do not specify a level, the default is Level 1. By default, authentication is disabled.

To configure a password for the specified level, perform the following task in interface configuration mode:

Task	Command
Configure the authentication password for a specified interface.	**isis password** *password* {**level-1** | **level-2**}

CONFIGURING MISCELLANEOUS IS-IS PARAMETERS

These tasks differ from the preceding interface-specific IS-IS tasks because they configure IS-IS itself, rather than the interface.

You can configure the optional IS-IS parameters in the following list:

- Generating a Default Route
- Specifying the System Type
- Configuring IS-IS Authentication Passwords
- Summarizing Address Ranges
- Setting the Overload Bit

Generating a Default Route

You can force a default route into an IS-IS routing domain. Whenever you specifically configure redistribution of routes into an IS-IS routing domain, the Cisco IOS software does not, by default, redistribute the *default route* into the IS-IS routing domain. The following feature allows you to force the boundary router to redistribute the default route or generate a default route into its L2 LSP. You can use a route-map to conditionally advertise the default route, depending on the existence of another route in the router's routing table.

To generate a default route, perform the following task in router configuration mode:

Task	Command
Force a default route into the IS-IS routing domain.	**default-information originate** [**route-map** *map-name*]

See the discussion of redistribution of routes in Chapter 22.

Specifying the System Type

You can configure the router to act as a Level 1 (intra-area) router, as both a Level 1 router and a Level 2 (interarea) router, or as an interarea router only.

To specify router level support, perform the following task in router configuration mode:

Task	Command
Configure the system type (area or backbone router).	**is-type** {**level-1**	**level-1-2**	**level-2-only**}

Configuring IS-IS Authentication Passwords

You can assign passwords to areas and domains.

The area authentication password is inserted in Level 1 (station router level) LSPs, CSNPs, and PSNPs. The routing domain authentication password is inserted in Level 2 (the area router level) LSP, CSNP, and PSNPs.

To configure either area or domain authentication passwords, perform the following tasks in router configuration mode:

Task	Command
Step 1 Configure the area authentication password.	**area-password** *password*
Step 2 Configure the routing domain authentication password.	**domain-password** *password*

Summarizing Address Ranges

You can create aggregate addresses that are represented in the routing table by a summary address. This process is called *route summarization*. One summary address can include multiple groups of addresses for a given level. Routes learned from other routing protocols also can be summarized. The metric used to advertise the summary is the smallest metric of all the more-specific routes.

To create a summary of addresses for a given level, perform the following task in router configuration mode:

Task	Command
Create a summary of addresses for a given level.	**summary-address** *address mask* {**level-1**	**level-1-2**	**level-2**}

Setting the Overload Bit

You can configure the router to set the overload bit (also known as the hippity bit) in its non-pseudo-node LSPs. Normally, setting the overload bit is allowed only when a router runs into problems. For example, when a router is experiencing a memory shortage, it might be because the Link State database is not complete, resulting in an incomplete or inaccurate routing table. By setting the overload bit in its LSPs, other routers can ignore the unreliable router in their SPF calculations until the router has recovered from its problems.

The result is that no paths through this router are seen by other routers in the IS-IS area. However, IP and CLNS prefixes directly connected to this router are still reachable.

This command can be useful when you want to connect a router to an ISIS network, but don't want real traffic flowing through it under any circumstances. Examples of this include the following:

- A test router in the lab, connected to a production network.
- A router configured as an LSP flooding server—for example, on an NBMA network in combination with the mesh-group feature.
- A router that is aggregating VCs used only for network management. In this case, the network management stations must be on a network directly connected to the router with the **set-overload-bit** command configured.

To set the overload bit, perform the following task in router configuration mode:

Task	Command
Set the overload bit.	**set-overload-bit**

MONITORING IS-IS

You can display the IS-IS link state database by performing the following commands in EXEC mode:

Task	Command
Step 1 Display the IS-IS link state database.	**show isis database** [level-1] [level-2] [l1] [l2] [detail] [lspid]
Step 2 Display how often and why the router has run a full SPF calculation	**show isis spf-log**

IS-IS CONFIGURATION EXAMPLE

This section contains an IS-IS configuration example.

IS-IS as an IP Routing Protocol Example

The following example shows how to configure three routers to run IS-IS as an IP routing protocol. Figure 18–1 illustrates the example configuration.

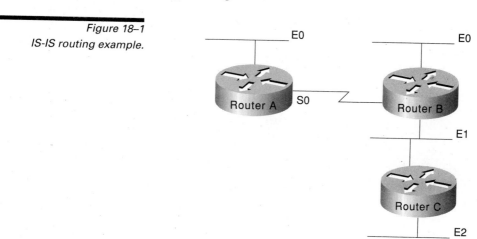

Figure 18–1
IS-IS routing example.

Configuration for Router A

```
router isis
 net 49.0001.0000.0000.000a.00
interface ethernet 0
 ip router isis
interface serial 0
 ip router isis
```

Configuration for Router B

```
router isis
 net 49.0001.0000.0000.000b.00
interface ethernet 0
 ip router isis
interface ethernet 1
 ip router isis
interface serial 0
 ip router isis
```

Configuration for Router C

```
router isis
 net 49.0001.0000.0000.000c.00
interface ethernet 1
 ip router isis
interface ethernet 2
 ip router isis
```

CHAPTER 19

Integrated IS-IS Commands

Use the commands in this chapter to configure and monitor IS-IS. For IS-IS configuration information and examples, see Chapter 18, "Configuring Integrated IS-IS."

AREA-PASSWORD

To configure the IS-IS area authentication password, use the **area-password** router configuration command. To disable the password, use the **no** form of this command.

> **area-password** *password*
> **no area-password** [*password*]

Syntax	Description
password	Password you assign.

Default

No area password is defined and area password authentication is disabled.

Command Mode

Router configuration

Usage Guidelines

This command first appeared in Cisco IOS Release 10.0.

Using the **area-password** command on all routers in an area will prevent unauthorized routers from injecting false routing information into the linkstate database.

This password is exchanged as plain text and thus this feature provides only limited security.

This password is inserted in Level 1 (station router level) link state PDUs (LSPs), complete sequence number PDUs (CSNPs), and partial sequence number PDUs (PSNP).

Example

The following example assigns an area authentication password:

```
router isis
  area-password angel
```

Related Commands

Search online to find documentation for related commands.

domain-password
isis password

DEFAULT-INFORMATION ORIGINATE (IS-IS)

To generate a default route into an IS-IS routing domain, use the **default-information originate** router configuration command. To disable this feature, use the **no** form of this command.

> **default-information originate** [route-map *map-name*]
> **no default-information originate** [route-map *map-name*]

Syntax	Description
route-map *map-name*	(Optional.) Routing process will generate the default route if the route map is satisfied.

Default

Disabled

Command Mode

Router configuration

Usage Guidelines

This command first appeared in Cisco IOS Release 10.0.

If a router configured with this command has a route to 0.0.0.0 in the routing table, IS-IS will originate an advertisement for 0.0.0.0 in its LSPs.

Without a route-map, the default is only advertised in L2 LSPs. For L1 routing, there is another mechanism to find the default route, which is to look for the closest L1L2 router. The closest L1L2 router can be found by looking at the attached-bit (ATT) in L1 LSPs.

A route-map can be used for two things: 1) make the router generate default in its L1 LSPs. 2) advertise 0/0 conditionally. With a **match ip address** *standard-access-list* command, you can specify one or more IP routes that must exist before the router will advertise 0/0.

Example

In the following example, the software is forced to generate a default external route into an IS-IS domain:

```
router isis
! BGP routes will be distributed into IS-IS
redistribute bgp 120
! access list 2 is applied to outgoing routing updates
distribute-list 2 out
default-information originate
! access list 2 defined as giving access to network 100.105.0.0
access-list 2 permit 100.105.0.0 0.0.255.255
```

Related Commands

Search online to find documentation for related commands.

redistribute
show isis database

DOMAIN-PASSWORD

To configure the IS-IS routing domain authentication password, use the **domain-password** router configuration command. To disable a password, use the **no** form of this command.

> **domain-password** *password*
> **no domain-password** [*password*]

Syntax	Description
password	Password you assign.

Default

No password is specified and no authentication is enabled for exchange of L2 routing information.

Command Mode

Router configuration

Usage Guidelines

This command first appeared in Cisco IOS Release 10.0.

This password is exchanged as plain text and thus this feature provides only limited security.

This password is inserted in Level 2 (area router level) link state PDUs (LSPs), complete sequence number PDUs (CSNPs), and partial sequence number PDUs (PSNPs).

Example

The following example assigns an authentication password to the routing domain:

```
router isis
  domain-password flower
```

Related Commands

Search online to find documentation for related commands.

area-password
isis password

IP ROUTER ISIS

To configure an IS-IS routing process for IP on an interface, use the **ip router isis** interface configuration command. To disable IS-IS for IP, use the **no** form of this command.

> **ip router isis** [*tag*]
> **no ip router isis** [*tag*]

Syntax	Description
tag	(Optional.) Defines a meaningful name for a routing process. If not specified, a null tag is assumed. It must be unique among all IP router processes for a given router. Use the same text for the argument *tag* as specified in the **router isis** global configuration command.

Default

No routing processes are specified.

Command Mode

Interface configuration

Usage Guidelines

This command first appeared in Cisco IOS Release 10.0.

Before the IS-IS router process is useful, a NET must be assigned with the **net** command and some interfaces must be enabled with IS-IS.

If you have IS-IS running and at least one ISO-IGRP process, the IS-IS process and the ISO-IGRP process cannot both be configured without a tag. The null tag can be used by only one process. Therefore, if you do not use ISO-IGRP, the IS-IS tag should be null. If you run ISO-IGRP and IS-IS, a null tag can still be used for IS-IS, but not for ISO-IGRP at the same time.

Example

The following example specifies IS-IS as an IP routing protocol for a process named *Finance*, and specifies that the *Finance* process will be routed on interfaces Ethernet 0 and serial 0:

```
router isis Finance
 net 49.0001.aaaa.aaaa.aaaa.00
interface Ethernet 0
 ip router isis Finance
interface serial 0
 ip router isis Finance
```

Related Commands

Search online to find documentation for related commands.

net
router isis

ISIS CIRCUIT-TYPE

To configure the type of adjacency, use the **isis circuit-type** interface configuration command. To reset the circuit type to Level 1 and Level 2, use the **no** form of this command.

isis circuit-type {level-1 | level-1-2 | level-2-only}
no isis circuit-type

Syntax	Description
level-1	A Level 1 adjacency may be established if there is at least one area address in common between this system and its neighbors. Level 2 adjacencies will never be established over this interface.
level-1-2	A Level 1 and Level 2 adjacency is established if the neighbor is also configured as **level-1-2** and there is at least one area in common. If there is no area in common, a Level 2 adjacency is established. This is the default.
level-2-only	Level 2 adjacencies are established if the other routers are L2 or L1L2 routers and their interfaces are configured for L1L2 or L2. Level 1 adjacencies will never be established over this interface.

Default

A Level 1 and Level 2 adjacency is established.

Command Mode

Interface configuration

Usage Guidelines

This command first appeared in Cisco IOS Release 10.0.

Normally, this command does not need to be configured. The proper way is to configure a router as an L1-only, L1L2 or L2-only system. Only on routers that are between areas (L1L2 routers) should you configure some interfaces to be L2-only to prevent wasting bandwidth by sending out unused L1 hellos. Note that on point-to-point interfaces, the L1 and L2 hellos are in the same packet.

Example

In the following example, other routers on Ethernet interface 0 are in the same area. Other routers on Ethernet interface 1 are in other areas, so the router will stop sending L1 hellos.

```
interface ethernet 0
ip router isis
interface ethernet 1
 isis circuit-type level-2-only
```

ISIS CSNP-INTERVAL

To configure the IS-IS complete sequence number PDUs (CSNP) interval, use the **isis csnp-interval** interface configuration command. To restore the default value, use the **no** form of this command.

> **isis csnp-interval** *seconds* {level-1 | level-2}
> **no isis csnp-interval** {level-1 | level-2}

Syntax	Description
seconds	Interval of time between transmission of CSNPs on multiaccess networks. This interval only applies for the designated router. The default is 10 seconds.
level-1	Configures the interval of time between transmission of CSNPs for Level 1 independently.
level-2	Configures the interval of time between transmission of CSNPs for Level 2 independently.

Default

10 seconds

Command Mode

Interface configuration

Usage Guidelines

This command first appeared in Cisco IOS Release 10.0.

It is very unlikely you will need to change the default value of this command.

This command only applies for the designated router (DR) for a specified interface. Only DRs send CSNP packets in order to maintain database synchronization. The CSNP interval can be configured independently for Level 1 and Level 2. This feature does not apply to serial point-to-point interfaces. It does apply to WAN connections if the WAN is viewed as a multiaccess meshed network.

For multi-access WAN interfaces (such as ATM, Frame Relay, and X.25), it is highly recommended you configure the NBMA cloud as multiple point-to-point subinterfaces. Doing so will make routing much more robust if one or more PVCs fail.

The **isis csnp-interval** command on point-to-point subinterfaces only makes sense when using it in combination with the IS-IS mesh-group feature.

Example

In the following example, Ethernet interface 0 is configured for transmitting CSN PDUs every 30 seconds.

```
interface ethernet 0
  isis csnp-interval 30 level-1
```

ISIS HELLO-INTERVAL

To specify the length of time between hello packets that the Cisco IOS software sends, use the **isis hello-interval** interface configuration command. To restore the default value, use the **no** form of this command.

> **isis hello-interval** *seconds* {level-1 | level-2}
> **no isis hello-interval** {level-1 | level-2}

Syntax	Description
seconds	An integer value. By default, a value three times the hello interval *seconds* is advertised as the *holdtime* in the hello packets transmitted. (That multiplier of 3 can be changed by specifying the **isis hello-multiplier** command.) With smaller hello intervals, topological changes are detected faster, but there is more routing traffic. The default is 10 seconds.
level-1	Configures the hello interval for Level 1 independently. Use this on X.25, SMDS, and Frame Relay multiaccess networks.
level-2	Configures the hello interval for Level 2 independently. Use this on X.25, SMDS, and Frame Relay multiaccess networks.

Default

10 seconds

Command Mode

Interface configuration

Usage Guidelines

This command first appeared in Cisco IOS Release 10.0.

The hello interval can be configured independently for Level 1 and Level 2, except on serial point-to-point interfaces. (Because there is only a single type of hello packet sent on serial links, it is independent of Level 1 or Level 2.) The **level-1** and **level-2** keywords are used on X.25, SMDS, and Frame Relay multiaccess networks or LAN interfaces.

A faster hello interval gives faster convergence, but increases bandwidth and CPU usage. It might also add to instability in the network. A slower hello interval saves bandwidth and CPU. Especially when used in combination with a higher hello multiplier, this may increase overall network stability.

It makes more sense to tune the hello interval and hello multiplier on point-to-point interfaces than on LAN interfaces.

Example

In the following example, serial interface 0 is configured to advertise hello packets every 5 seconds. The router is configured to act as a station router. This will cause more traffic than configuring a longer interval, but topological changes will be detected faster.

```
interface serial 0
  isis hello-interval 5 level-1
```

Related Commands

Search online to find documentation for related commands.

isis hello-multiplier

ISIS HELLO-MULTIPLIER

To specify the number of IS-IS hello packets a neighbor must miss before the router should declare the adjacency as down, use the **isis hello-multiplier** interface configuration command. To restore the default value, use the **no** form of this command.

> isis hello-multiplier *multiplier* {level-1 | level-2}
> no isis hello-multiplier {level-1 | level-2}

Syntax	Description
multiplier	Integer value. The advertised holdtime in IS-IS hellos will be set to the hello-multiplier times the hello-interval. Neighbors will declare an adjacency to this router down after not having received any IS-IS hellos during the advertised holdtime. The holdtime (and thus the hello-multiplier and the hello-interval) can be set on a per interface basis, and can be different between different routers in one area.
	Using a smaller hello-multiplier will give fast convergence, but can result in more routing instability. Increment the hello-multiplier to a larger value to help network stability when needed. Never configure a hello-multiplier lower then the default value of 3.
level-1	Configures the hello multiplier independently for Level 1 adjacencies.
level-2	Configures the hello multiplier independently for Level 2 adjacencies.

Default

multiplier is 3

Command Mode

Interface configuration

Usage Guidelines

On point-to-point links, there is only one hello for both Level 1 and Level 2. So configuring different hello-multipliers only make sense for multi-access networks, such as Ethernet, FDDI, etc. Separate Level 1 and Level 2 hellos are also sent over NBMA networks in multipoint mode, such as X.25, Frame Relay and ATM. However, it is recommended to run IS-IS over point-to-point subinterfaces over WAN NBMA media.

Example

In the following example, the network administrator wants to increase network stability by making sure an adjacency will go down only when many (10) hellos are missed. The total time to detect link failure is 60 seconds. This will ensure that the network remains stable, even when the link is fully congested.

```
interface serial 1
 ip router isis
 isis hello-interval 6 level-1
 isis hello-multiplier 10 level-1
```

ISIS LSP-INTERVAL

To configure the time delay between successive IS-IS link state packet transmissions, use the **isis lsp-interval** interface configuration command. To restore the default value, use the **no** form of this command.

>   isis lsp-interval *milliseconds*
>   no isis lsp-interval

Syntax	Description
milliseconds	Interval between successive link state packets, in milliseconds.

Default

33 milliseconds

Command Mode

Interface configuration

Usage Guidelines

This command first appeared in Cisco IOS Release 11.1.

In topologies with a large number of IS-IS neighbors and interfaces, a router may have difficulty with the CPU load imposed by link state packet (LSP) transmission and reception. This command allows the LSP transmission rate (and by implication the reception rate of other systems) to be reduced.

Example

The following example causes the system to transmit LSPs every 100 milliseconds (10 packets per second) on serial interface 0:

```
interface serial 0
  isis lsp-interval 100
```

Related Commands

Search online to find documentation for related commands.

isis retransmit-interval

ISIS METRIC

To configure the metric for an interface, use the **isis metric** interface configuration command. To restore the default metric value, use the **no** form of this command.

>   isis metric *default-metric* {level-1 | level-2}
>   no isis metric {level-1 | level-2}

Syntax	Description
default-metric	Metric assigned to the link and used to calculate the cost from each other router via the links in the network to other destinations. You can configure this metric for Level 1 or Level 2 routing. The range is from 0 to 63. The default value is 10.
level-1	This metric should be used only in the SPF calculation for L1 (intra-area) routing.
level-2	This metric should be used only in the SPF calculation for L2 (inter-area) routing.

Default

default-metric = 10
If **level-1** or **level-2** is not specified, **level-1** is assumed.

Command Mode

Interface configuration

Usage Guidelines

This command first appeared in Cisco IOS Release 10.0.

Specifying the **level-1** or **level-2** keywords resets the metric only for Level 1 or Level 2 routing, respectively.

It is highly recommended to configure metrics on all interfaces. If you do not do so, the IS-IS metrics are simply hop-count like metrics.

Example

In the following example, serial interface 0 is configured for a default link-state metric cost of 15 for Level 1:

```
interface serial 0
  isis metric 15 level-1
```

ISIS PASSWORD

To configure the authentication password for an interface, use the **isis password** interface configuration command. To disable authentication for IS-IS, use the **no** form of this command.

isis password *password* {level-1 | level-2}
no isis password {level-1 | level-2}

Syntax	Description
password	Authentication password you assign for an interface.
level-1	Configures the authentication password for Level 1 independently. For Level 1 routing, the router acts as a station router only.
level-2	Configures the authentication password for Level 2 independently. For Level 2 routing, the router acts as an area router only.

Default

Disabled
If no keyword is specified, the default is **level-1**.

Command Mode

Interface configuration

Usage Guidelines

This command first appeared in Cisco IOS Release 10.0.

This command enables you to prevent unauthorized routers from forming adjacencies with this router, and thus protects the network from intruders.

The password is exchanged as plain text and thus provides only limited security.

Different passwords can be assigned for different routing levels using the **level-1** and **level-2** keyword arguments.

Specifying the **level-1** or **level-2** keywords disables the password only for Level 1 or Level 2 routing, respectively.

Example

The following example configures a password for Ethernet interface 0 at Level 1:

```
interface ethernet 0
  isis password frank level-1
```

ISIS PRIORITY

To configure the priority of designated routers, use the **isis priority** interface configuration command. To reset the default priority, use the **no** form of this command.

> **isis priority** *value* {level-1 | level-2}
> **no isis priority** {level-1 | level-2}

Syntax	Description
value	Sets the priority of a router and is a number from 0 to 127. The default value is 64.
level-1	Sets the priority for Level 1 independently.
level-2	Sets the priority for Level 2 independently.

Default

Priority of 64

Command Mode

Interface configuration

Usage Guidelines

This command first appeared in Cisco IOS Release 10.0.

Priorities can be configured for Level 1 and Level 2 independently. Specifying the **level-1** or **level-2** keywords resets priority only for Level 1 or Level 2 routing, respectively.

The priority is used to determine which router on a LAN will be the designated router or Designated Intermediate System (DIS). The priorities are advertised in the hellos. The router with the highest priority will become the DIS.

In IS-IS, there is no backup designated router. Setting the priority to 0 lowers the chance of this system becoming the DIS, but does not prevent it. If a router with a higher priority comes on line, it will take over the role from the current DIS. In the case of equal priorities, the highest MAC address breaks the tie.

Example

The following example shows Level 1 routing given priority by setting the priority level to 50. This router is now more likely to become the DIS.

```
interface ethernet 0
  isis priority 80 level-1
```

ISIS RETRANSMIT-INTERVAL

To configure the time between retransmission of each LSP (IS-IS link-state PDU) over point-to-point links, use the **isis retransmit-interval** interface configuration command. To restore the default value, use the **no** form of this command.

isis retransmit-interval *seconds*
no isis retransmit-interval *seconds*

Syntax	Description
seconds	Time in seconds between retransmission of each LSP. It is an integer that should be greater than the expected round-trip delay between any two routers on the attached network. The default is 5 seconds.

Default

5 seconds

Command Mode

Interface configuration

Usage Guidelines

This command first appeared in Cisco IOS Release 10.0.

The setting of the *seconds* argument should be conservative, or needless retransmission will result.

This command has no effect on LAN (multipoint) interfaces. On point-to-point links, the value can be increased to enhance network stability.

Retransmissions only occur when LSPs are dropped. So setting this to a higher value has little effect on reconvergence. The more neighbors routers have, and the more paths over which LSPs can be flooded, the higher this value can be made.

The value should be larger for serial lines.

Example

The following example configures serial interface 0 for retransmission of IS-IS LSP every 10 seconds for a large serial line:

```
interface serial 0
  isis retransmit-interval 60
```

Related Commands

Search online to find documentation for related commands.

isis lsp-interval
isis retransmit-throttle-interval

ISIS RETRANSMIT-THROTTLE-INTERVAL

To configure the amount of time between retransmissions of any IS-IS link-state PDUs (LSPs) on a point-to-point interface, use the **isis retransmit-throttle-interval** interface configuration command. To restore the default value, use the **no** form of this command.

> isis retransmit-throttle-interval *milliseconds*
> no isis lsp-interval

Syntax	Description
milliseconds	Minimum delay (in milliseconds) between LSP retransmissions on the interface.

Default

The delay is determined by the **isis lsp-interval** command.

Command Mode

Interface configuration

Usage Guidelines

This command first appeared in Cisco IOS Release 11.1.

This command may be useful in very large networks with many LSPs and many interfaces as a way of controlling LSP retransmission traffic. This command controls the rate at which LSPs can be retransmitted on the interface.

The **isis retransmit-throttle-interval** command is distinct from the rate at which LSPs are transmitted on the interface (controlled by the **isis lsp-interval** command) and the period between retransmissions of a single LSP (controlled by the **isis retransmit-interval** command). These commands may all be used in combination to control the offered load of routing traffic from one router to its neighbors.

Example

The following example configures serial interface 0 to limit the rate of LSP retransmissions to one every 300 milliseconds:

```
interface serial 0
  isis retransmit-throttle-interval 300
```

Related Commands

Search online to find documentation for related commands.

isis lsp-interval
isis retransmit-interval

IS-TYPE

To configure the IS-IS level at which the Cisco IOS software operates, use the **is-type** router configuration command. To reset the default value, use the **no** form of this command.

is-type {level-1 | level-1-2 | level-2-only}
no is-type {level-1 | level-1-2 | level-2-only}

Syntax	Description
level-1	Router acts as a station router. This router will only learn about destinations inside its area. For inter-area routing, it depends on the closest L1L2 router.
level-1-2	Router acts as both a station router and an area router. This router will run two instances of the routing algorithm. It will have one linkstate database (LSDB) for destinations inside the area (L1 routing) and run an SPF calculation to discover the area topology. It will also have another LSDB with LSPs of all other backbone (L2) routers and run another SPF calculation to discover the topology of the backbone, and the existence of all other areas.
level-2-only	Router acts as an area router only. This router is part of the backbone, and does not talk to L1-only routers in its own area.

Default

Router acts as both a station router and an area router.

Command Mode

Router configuration

Usage Guidelines

This command first appeared in Cisco IOS Release 10.3.

It is highly recommended that you configure the type of an IS-IS router.

If there is only one area, there is no need to run two copies of the same algorithm. You have the option to run L1-only or L2-only everywhere. If IS-IS is used for CLNS routing, L1-only must be used everywhere. If IS-IS is used for IP routing, only, it is slightly preferred to run L2-only everywhere, as this allows easy addition of other areas later.

Example

The following example specifies an area router:

```
router isis
  is-type level-2-only
```

NET

To configure an IS-IS network entity title (NET) for the routing process, use the **net** router configuration command. To remove a NET, use the **no** form of this command.

net *network-entity-title*
no net *network-entity-title*

Syntax	*Description*
network-entity-title	NET that specifies the area address and the system ID for an IS-IS routing process. This argument can be either an address or a name.

Default

No NET is configured and the IS-IS process will not start. A NET is mandatory.

Command Mode

Router configuration

Usage Guidelines

This command first appeared in Cisco IOS Release 10.0.

Under most circumstances, one and only one NET must be configured.

A NET is an NSAP where the last byte is always zero. On a Cisco router running IS-IS, a NET can be 8 to 20 bytes. The last byte is always the n-selector and must be zero.

The six bytes in front of the n-selector are the system ID. The system ID length is a fixed size and cannot be changed. The system ID must be unique throughout each area (L1) and throughout the backbone (L2).

All bytes in front of the system ID are the area ID.

Even when IS-IS is used to do IP routing only (no CLNS routing enabled), a NET must still be configured. This is needed to instruct the router about its system ID and area ID.

Multiple NETs per router are allowed, with a maximum of three. In rare circumstances, it is possible to configure two or three NETs. In such a case, the area this router is in will have three area addresses. There will still be only one area, but it will have more area addresses.

Configuring multiple NETs can be temporarily useful in the case of network reconfiguration where multiple areas are merged, or where one area is in the process of being split into more areas. Multiple area addresses enable you to renumber an area slowly, without the need of a flag day.

Example

The following example configures a router with system ID 0000.0c11.11 and area ID 47.0004.004d.0001:

```
router isis Pieinthesky
 net 47.0004.004d.0001.0000.0c11.1111.00
```

ROUTER ISIS

To enable the IS-IS routing protocol and to specify an IS-IS process for IP, use the **router isis** global configuration command. To disable IS-IS routing, use the **no** form of this command.

router isis [*tag*]
no router isis [*tag*]

Syntax	Description
tag	(Optional.) Meaningful name for a routing process. If it is not specified, a null tag is assumed and the process is referenced with a null tag. This name must be unique among all IP router processes for a given router.

Default

Disabled

Command Mode

Global configuration

Usage Guidelines

This command first appeared in Cisco IOS Release 10.0.

This command is needed to configure a NET and configure an interface with **clns router isis** or ip router isis.

You can specify only one IS-IS process per router. Only one IS-IS process is allowed whether you run it in integrated mode, ISO CLNS only, or IP only.

Example

The following example configures IS-IS for IP routing, with system ID 0000.0000.0002 and area ID 01.0001, and enables IS-IS to form adjacencies on Ethernet 0 and serial 0 interfaces. The IP prefix assigned to Ethernet 0 will be advertised to other IS-IS routers:

```
router isis
 net 01.0001.0000.0000.0002.00
 is-type level-1
!
interface ethernet 0
 ip address 10.1.1.1 255.255.255.0
 ip router isis
!
interface serial 0
 ip unnumbered ethernet0
 ip router isis
```

Related Commands

Search online to find documentation for related commands.

clns router isis
ip router isis
net

SET-OVERLOAD-BIT

To configure the router to signal other routers not to use it as intermediate hop in their SPF calculations, use the **set-overload-bit** router configuration command. To remove the designation, use the **no** form of this command.

> **set-overload-bit**
> **no set-overload-bit**

Syntax   Description

This command has no arguments or keywords.

Default

The overload bit is not set.

Command Mode

Router configuration

Usage Guidelines

This command first appeared in Cisco IOS Release 11.2.

This command forces the router to set the overload bit (also known as the hippity bit) in its non-pseudonode LSPs. Normally the setting of the overload bit is allowed only when a router runs into problems. For example, when a router is experiencing a memory shortage, it might be that the Link State database is not complete, resulting in an incomplete or inaccurate routing table. By setting the overload bit in its LSPs, other routers can ignore the unreliable router in their SPF calculations until the router has recovered from its problems.

The result will be that no paths through this router are seen by other routers in the IS-IS area. However, IP and CLNS prefixes directly connected to this router will be still be reachable.

This command can be useful when you want to connect a router to an ISIS network, but don't want real traffic flowing through it under any circumstances. Examples are:

- A test router in the lab, connected to a production network.
- A router configured as an LSP flooding server, e.g. on an NBMA network, in combination with the mesh-group feature.
- A router that is aggregating VCs used only for network management. In this case, the network management stations must be on a network directly connected to the router with the **set-overload-bit** command configured.

Example

The following example configures the set-over-load bit:

```
router isis
 set-overload-bit
```

SHOW ISIS DATABASE

To display the IS-IS link state database, use the **show isis database** EXEC command.

   show isis database [level-1] [level-2] [l1] [l2] [detail] [lspid]

Syntax	Description
level-1	(Optional.) Displays the IS-IS link state database for Level 1.
level-2	(Optional.) Displays the IS-IS link state database for Level 2.
l1	(Optional.) Abbreviation for the option **level-1**.
l2	(Optional.) Abbreviation for the option **level-2**.
detail	(Optional.) When specified, the contents of each LSP are displayed. Otherwise, a summary display is provided.
lspid	(Optional.) Link-state PDU identifier. When specified, the contents of a single LSP is displayed by its ID number.

Command Mode

EXEC

Usage Guidelines

This command first appeared in Cisco IOS Release 10.0.

Each of the options shown in brackets for this command can be entered in an arbitrary string within the same command entry. For example, the following are both valid command specifications and provide the same output: **show isis database detail l2** and **show isis database l2 detail**.

Sample Display

The following is sample output from the **show isis database** command when it is specified with no options or as **show isis database l1 l2**:

```
Router# show isis database

IS-IS Level-1 Link State Database
LSPID                   LSP Seq Num   LSP Checksum   LSP Holdtime   ATT/P/OL
0000.0C00.0C35.00-00    0x0000000C    0x5696         792            0/0/0
0000.0C00.40AF.00-00*   0x00000009    0x8452         1077           1/0/0
0000.0C00.62E6.00-00    0x0000000A    0x38E7         383            0/0/0
0000.0C00.62E6.03-00    0x00000006    0x82BC         384            0/0/0
0800.2B16.24EA.00-00    0x00001D9F    0x8864         1188           1/0/0
0800.2B16.24EA.01-00    0x00001E36    0x0935         1198           1/0/0

IS-IS Level-2 Link State Database
LSPID                   LSP Seq Num   LSP Checksum   LSP Holdtime   ATT/P/OL
0000.0C00.0C35.03-00    0x00000005    0x04C8         792            0/0/0
0000.0C00.3E51.00-00    0x00000007    0xAF96         758            0/0/0
0000.0C00.40AF.00-00*   0x0000000A    0x3AA9         1077           0/0/0
```

Table 19–1 describes significant fields shown in the display.

Table 19–1 *Show IS-IS Database Field Descriptions*

Field	Description
LSPID	The LSP identifier. The first six octets form the System ID of the router that originated the LSP. The next octet is the pseudonode ID. When this byte is zero, the LSP describes links from the system. When it is nonzero, the LSP is a so called non-pseudonode LSP. This is similar to a router LSA in OSPF. The LSP will describe the state of the originating router. For each LAN, the designated router for that LAN will create and flood a pseudonode LSP, describing all systems attached to that LAN. The last octet is the LSP number. If there is more data than can fit in a single LSP, the LSP will be divided into multiple LSP fragments. Each fragment will have a different LSP number. An asterisk (*) indicates that the LSP was originated by the system on which this command is issued.
LSP Seq Num	Sequence number for the LSP that allows other systems to determine if they have received the latest information from the source.
LSP Checksum	Checksum of the entire LSP packet.
LSP Holdtime	Amount of time the LSP remains valid, in seconds. An LSP holdtime of zero indicates that this LSP was purged and is being removed from all routers' LSDB. The value between brackets indicates how long the purged LSP will stay in the LSDB before being completely removed.
ATT	The Attach bit. This indicates that the router is also a Level 2 router, and it can reach other areas. L1-only routers and L1L2 routers that have lost connection to other L2 routers will use the attached bit to find the closest L2 router. They will point a default route to the closest L2 router.
P	The P bit. Detects if the IS is area partition repair capable. Cisco and other vendors do not support area partition repair.
OL	The Overload bit. Determines if the IS is congested. If the Overload bit is set, other routers will not use this system as a transit router when calculating routers. Only packets for destinations directly connected to the overloaded router will be sent to this router.

Sample Display Using Show IS-IS Database Detail

The following is sample output from the **show isis database detail** command.

```
Router# show isis database detail

IS-IS Level-1 Link State Database
LSPID                    LSP Seq Num  LSP Checksum  LSP Holdtime  ATT/P/OL
0000.0C00.0C35.00-00  0x0000000C    0x5696        325           0/0/0
  Area Address: 47.0004.004D.0001
  Area Address: 39.0001
  Metric: 10   IS 0000.0C00.62E6.03
  Metric: 0    ES 0000.0C00.0C35
  --More--
0000.0C00.40AF.00-00* 0x00000009    0x8452        608           1/0/0
  Area Address: 47.0004.004D.0001
  Metric: 10   IS 0800.2B16.24EA.01
  Metric: 10   IS 0000.0C00.62E6.03
  Metric: 0    ES 0000.0C00.40AF

IS-IS Level-2 Link State Database
LSPID                    LSP Seq Num  LSP Checksum  LSP Holdtime  ATT/P/OL
0000.0C00.0C35.03-00  0x00000005    0x04C8        317           0/0/0
  Metric: 0    IS 0000.0C00.0C35.00
  --More--
0000.0C00.3E51.00-00  0x00000009    0xAB98        1182          0/0/0
  Area Address: 39.0004
  Metric: 10   IS 0000.0C00.40AF.00
  Metric: 10   IS 0000.0C00.3E51.05
```

As the output shows, in addition to the information displayed with **show isis database**, the **show isis database detail** command displays the contents of each LSP.

Table 19–2 describes the additional fields shown in the display.

Table 19–2   *Show IS-IS Database Detail Field Descriptions*

Field	Description
Area Address:	Reachable area addresses from the router. For L1 LSPs, these are the area addresses configured manually on the originating router. For L2 LSPs, these are all the area addresses for the area this route belongs to.
Metric:	IS-IS metric for the cost of the adjacency between the originating router and the advertised neighbor, or the metric of the cost to get from the advertising router to the advertised destination (which can be an IP address, an ES or a CLNS prefix).

Sample Display Using Show IS-IS Database Detail Displaying IP Addresses

The following is additional sample output from the **show isis database detail** command. This is a Level 2 LSP. The area address 39.0001 is the address of the area in which the router resides.

```
Router# show isis database detail l2

IS-IS Level-2 Link State Database
LSPID                   LSP Seq Num  LSP Checksum  LSP Holdtime  ATT/P/OL
0000.0C00.1111.00-00* 0x00000006    0x4DB3        1194          0/0/0
   Area Address: 39.0001
   NLPID:        0x81 0xCC
   IP Address:   160.89.64.17
   Metric: 10    IS 0000.0C00.1111.09
   Metric: 10    IS 0000.0C00.1111.08
   Metric: 10    IP 160.89.65.0 255.255.255.0
   Metric: 10    IP 160.89.64.0 255.255.255.0
   Metric: 0     IP-External 10.0.0.0 255.0.0.0
```

Table 19–3 describes the additional field shown in the display.

Table 19–3 *Show IS-IS Database Detail Field Descriptions Displaying IP Addresses*

Field	Description
Various addresses	The "IP" entries are the directly connected IP subnets the router is advertising (with associated metrics). The "IP-External" is a redistribute route.

SHOW ISIS SPF-LOG

To display how often and why the router has run a full SPF calculation, use the **show isis spf-log** EXEC command.

> **show isis spf-log**

Syntax   Description

This command has no arguments or keywords.

Command Mode

User EXEC

Usage Guidelines

This command first appeared in Cisco IOS Release 10.0.

Sample Display

The following is sample output from the **show isis spf-log** command:

```
Router# show isis spf-log
                 Level 1 SPF log
   When    Duration  Nodes  Count   Last trigger LSP   Triggers
00:15:46   3124      40     1         milles.00-00     TLVCODE
00:15:24   3216      41     5         milles.00-00     TLVCODE NEWLSP
00:15:19   3096      41     1         deurze.00-00     TLVCODE
```

```
00:14:54    3004    41    2        milles.00-00    ATTACHFLAG LSPHEADER
00:14:49    3384    41    1        milles.00-01    TLVCODE
00:14:23    2932    41    3        milles.00-00    TLVCODE
00:05:18    3140    41    1                        PERIODIC
00:03:54    3144    41    1        milles.01-00    TLVCODE
00:03:49    2908    41    1        milles.01-00    TLVCODE
00:03:28    3148    41    3         bakel.00-00    TLVCODE TLVCONTENT
00:03:15    3054    41    1        milles.00-00    TLVCODE
00:02:53    2958    41    1        mortel.00-00    TLVCODE
00:02:48    3632    41    2        milles.00-00    NEWADJ TLVCODE
00:02:23    2988    41    1        milles.00-01    TLVCODE
00:02:18    3016    41    1        gemert.00-00    TLVCODE
00:02:14    2932    41    1         bakel.00-00    TLVCONTENT
00:02:09    2988    41    2         bakel.00-00    TLVCONTENT
00:01:54    3228    41    1        milles.00-00    TLVCODE
00:01:38    3120    41    3          rips.03-00    TLVCONTENT
```

Table 19–4 describes the fields in the display.

Table 19–4   *Show IS-IS SPF-Log Field Descriptions*

Field	Description
When	How long ago (hh:mm:ss) a full SPF calculation occurred. The last 20 occurrences are logged.
Duration	Number of milliseconds it took to complete this SPF run. Elapsed time is wall clock time, not CPU time.
Nodes	Number of routers and pseudonodes (LANs) that make up the topology calculated in this SPF run.
Count	Number of events that triggered this SPF run. When there is a topology change, often multiple LSPs are received in a short time. A router waits 5 seconds before running a full SPF run, so it can include all new information. This count denotes the number of events (such as receiving new LSPs) that occurred while the router was waiting its 5 seconds before running full SPF.
Last trigger LSP	Whenever a full SPF calculation is triggered by the arrival of a new LSP, the router stores the LSP id. The LSP id can give a clue as to the source of routing instability in an area. If multiple LSPs are causing an SPF run, only the LSP id of the last received LSP is remembered.

Table 19-4 *Show IS-IS SPF-Log Field Descriptions, Continued*

Field	Description
Triggers	A list of all reasons that triggered a full SPF calculation. Possible triggers are:
	• PERIODIC—Typically, every 15 minutes a router runs a periodic full SPF calculation.
	• NEWSYSID—A new system ID (via NET) was configured on this router.
	• NEWAREA—A new area (via NET) was configured on this router.
	• NEWLEVEL—A new level (via is-type) was configured on this router.
	• RTCLEARED—A **clear clns route** command was issued on this router.
	• NEWMETRIC—A new metric was configured on an interface of this router.
	• IPBACKUP—An IP route disappeared, which was not learned via IS-IS, but via another protocol with better administrative distance. IS-IS will run a full SPF to install an IS-IS route for the disappeared IP prefix.
	• IPQUERY—A **clear ip route** command was issued on this router.
	• ATTACHFLAG—This router is now attached to the L2 backbone or it has just lost contact to the L2 backbone.
	• ADMINDIST—Another administrative distance was configured for the IS-IS process on this router.
	• AREASET—Set of learned area-addresses in this area changed.
	• NEWADJ—This router has created a new adjacency to another router.
	• DBCHANGED—A **clear isis *** command was issued on this router.
	• BACKUPOVFL—An IP prefix disappeared. The router knows there is another way to reach that prefix, but has not stored that backup route. The only way to find the alternative route is to run a full SPF run.
	• NEWLSP—A new router or pseudonode appeared in the topology.
	• LSPEXPIRED—Some LSP in the LSDB has expired.
	• LSPHEADER—ATT/P/OL bits or is-type in an LSP header changed.
	• TLVCODE—TLV code mismatch, indicating that different TLVs are included in the newest version of an LSP.
	• TLVCONTENT—TLV contents changed. This normally indicates that an adjacency somewhere in the area has come up or gone down. Look at the "Last trigger LSP" to get an indication of where the instability may have occurred.

Part
II

Command Reference

SUMMARY-ADDRESS

Use the **summary-address** router configuration command to create aggregate addresses for IS-IS or OSPF. The **no summary-address** command restores the default.

summary-address *address mask* {level-1 | level-1-2 | level-2} *prefix mask*
no summary-address *address mask* {level-1 | level-1-2 | level-2}

Syntax	Description
address	Summary address designated for a range of addresses.
mask	IP subnet mask used for the summary route.
level-1	Only routes redistributed into Level 1 are summarized with the configured address/mask value.
level-1-2	The summary router will be applied both when redistributing routes into L1 and L2 IS-IS, and when L2 IS-IS advertised L1 routes reachable in its area.
level-2	Routes learned by Level 1 routing will be summarized into the Level 2 backbone with the configured address/mask value, and redistributed routes into L2 IS-IS will be summarized also.
prefix	IP route prefix for the destination.
mask	IP subnet mask used for the summary route.

Default

All redistributed routes are advertised individually.

Command Mode

Router configuration

Usage Guidelines

This command first appeared in Cisco IOS Release 10.0.

Multiple groups of addresses can be summarized for a given level. Routes learned from other routing protocols can also be summarized. The metric used to advertise the summary is the smallest metric of all the more specific routes. This command helps reduce the size of the routing table.

This command also reduces the size of the LSPs and thus the Link State Database. It also helps stability because a summary advertisement is depending on many more specific routes. If one more specific route flaps, in most cases this does not cause a flap of the summary advertisement.

The drawback of summary addresses is that other routes might have less information to calculate the most optimal routing table for all individual destinations.

Example

In the following example, we redistribute RIP routes into IS-IS. In the RIP world, there are IP routes for 10.1.1, 10.1.2, 10.1.3, 10.1.4, and so forth. We want to advertise only 10.1.0.0 into our IS-IS Level 1 Link State PDU.

```
router isis
net 01.0000.0000.0001.00
redistribute rip level-1 metric 40
summary-address 10.1.0.0 255.255.0.0 level-1
```

CHAPTER 20

Configuring BGP

This chapter describes how to configure Border Gateway Protocol (BGP). For a complete description of the BGP commands in this chapter, see Chapter 21, "BGP Commands."

The Border Gateway Protocol, as defined in RFCs 1163 and 1267, is an Exterior Gateway Protocol (EGP). It allows you to set up an interdomain routing system that automatically guarantees the loop-free exchange of routing information between autonomous systems.

For protocol-independent features, see Chapter 22, "Configuring IP Routing Protocol-Independent Features."

CISCO'S BGP IMPLEMENTATION

In BGP, each route consists of a network number, a list of autonomous systems that information has passed through (called the *autonomous system path*), and a list of other *path attributes*. Cisco supports BGP Versions 2, 3, and 4, as defined in RFCs 1163, 1267, and 1771, respectively.

The primary function of a BGP system is to exchange network reachability information with other BGP systems, including information about the list of autonomous system paths. This information can be used to construct a graph of autonomous system connectivity from which routing loops can be pruned and with which autonomous system-level policy decisions can be enforced.

You can configure the value for the Multi Exit Discriminator (MED) metric attribute using route maps. (The name of this metric for BGP Versions 2 and 3 is *INTER_AS_METRIC*.) When an update is sent to an IBGP peer, the MED is passed along without any change. This action enables all the peers in the same autonomous system to make a consistent path selection.

A third-party next-hop router address is used in the *NEXT_HOP* attribute, regardless of the autonomous system of that third-party router. The Cisco IOS software automatically calculates the value for this attribute. Transitive, optional path attributes are passed along to other BGP-speaking routers.

BGP Version 4 supports Classless Interdomain Routing (CIDR), which lets you reduce the size of your routing tables by creating aggregate routes, resulting in *supernets*. CIDR eliminates the concept of network classes within BGP and supports the advertising of IP prefixes. CIDR routes can be carried by OSPF, Enhanced IGRP, ISIS-IP, and RIP.

See the "BGP Route Map Examples" section at the end of this chapter for examples of how to use route maps to redistribute BGP Version 4 routes.

Understanding How BGP Selects Paths

The BGP process selects a single autonomous system path to use and to pass along to other BGP-speaking routers. Cisco's BGP implementation has a reasonable set of factory defaults that can be overridden by administrative weights. The algorithm for path selection is as follows:

- If the next hop is inaccessible, do not consider it.
- Consider larger BGP administrative weights first.
- If the routers have the same weight, consider the route with higher local preference.
- If the routes have the same local preference, prefer the route that the local router originated.
- If no route was originated, prefer the shorter autonomous system path.
- If all paths are of the same autonomous system path length, prefer the lowest origin code (IGP < EGP < INCOMPLETE).
- If origin codes are the same and all the paths are from the same autonomous system, prefer the path with the lowest Multi Exit Discriminator (MED) metric. A missing metric is treated as zero.
- If the MEDs are the same, prefer external paths over internal paths.
- If IGP synchronization is disabled and only internal paths remain, prefer the path through the closest neighbor.
- Prefer the route with the lowest IP address value for the BGP router ID.

Understanding BGP Multipath Support

When a BGP speaker learns two identical EBGP paths for a prefix from a neighboring AS, it will choose the path with the lowest route-id as the best path. This best path is installed in the IP routing table. If BGP multipath support is enabled and the EBGP paths are learned from the same neighboring AS, instead of picking one best path, multiple paths are installed in the IP routing table.

During packet switching, depending on the switching mode, either per-packet or per-destination load balancing is performed among the multiple paths. A maximum of six paths is supported. The **maximum-paths** router configuration command controls the number of paths allowed. By default, BGP will install only one path to the IP routing table.

Basic BGP Configuration Tasks

The BGP configuration tasks are divided into basic and advanced tasks. The first three basic tasks are required to configure BGP; the remaining basic and advanced tasks are optional.

Basic BGP configuration tasks are the following:

- Enabling BGP Routing
- Configuring BGP Neighbors
- Configuring BGP Soft Reconfiguration
- Resetting BGP Connections
- Configuring BGP Interactions with IGPs
- Configuring BGP Administrative Weights
- Configuring BGP Route Filtering by Neighbor
- Configuring BGP Path Filtering by Neighbor
- Disabling Next-Hop Processing on BGP Updates
- Configuring the BGP Version
- Setting the Network Weight
- Configuring the Multi Exit Discriminator Metric
- Monitoring and Maintaining BGP

Advanced BGP Configuration Tasks

Advanced, optional BGP configuration tasks are shown in the following list:

- Using Route Maps To Modify Updates
- Resetting EBGP Connections Immediately upon Link Failure
- Configuring Aggregate Addresses
- Disabling Automatic Summarization of Network Numbers
- Configuring BGP Community Filtering
- Configuring a Routing Domain Confederation
- Configuring a Route Reflector
- Configuring Neighbor Options
- Configuring BGP Peer Groups
- Indicating Backdoor Routes
- Modifying Parameters While Updating the IP Routing Table
- Setting Administrative Distance
- Adjusting BGP Timers

- Changing the Local Preference Value
- Redistributing Network 0.0.0.0
- Selecting a Path Based on MEDs from Other Autonomous Systems
- Configuring Route Dampening

For information on configuring features that apply to multiple IP routing protocols (such as redistributing routing information), see Chapter 22.

ENABLING BGP ROUTING

To enable BGP routing, establish a BGP routing process by performing the following steps starting in global configuration mode:

Task	Command
Step 1 Enable a BGP routing process, which places you in router configuration mode.	**router bgp** *autonomous-system*
Step 2 Flag a network as local to this autonomous system and enter it into the BGP table.	**network** *network-number* [**mask** *network-mask*] [**route-map** *route-map-name*]

— NOTES

For exterior protocols, a reference to an IP network from the **network** router configuration command controls only which networks are advertised. This is in contrast to Interior Gateway Protocols (IGP), such as IGRP, which also use the **network** command to determine where to send updates.

— NOTES

The **network** command is used to inject IGP routes into the BGP table. The *network-mask* portion of the command allows supernetting and subnetting. A maximum of 200 entries of the command are accepted. Alternatively, you can use the **redistribute** command to achieve the same result.

CONFIGURING BGP NEIGHBORS

Like other EGPs, with BGP the relationships it has with its neighbors must be completely defined. BGP supports two kinds of neighbors: internal and external. *Internal neighbors* are in the same autonomous system; *external neighbors* are in different autonomous systems. Normally, external neighbors are adjacent to each other and share a subnet, while internal neighbors may be anywhere in the same autonomous system.

To configure BGP neighbors, perform the following task in router configuration mode:

Task	Command
Specify a BGP neighbor.	**neighbor** {*ip-address* | *peer-group-name*} **remote-as** *number*

See the "BGP Neighbor Configuration Examples" section at the end of this chapter for an example of configuring BGP neighbors.

CONFIGURING BGP SOFT RECONFIGURATION

Whenever there is a change in the policy, the BGP session has to be cleared for the new policy to take effect. Clearing a BGP session causes cache invalidation and results in a tremendous impact on the operation of networks.

Soft reconfiguration allows policies to be configured and activated without clearing the BGP session. Soft reconfiguration can be done on a per-neighbor basis in the following situations:

- When soft reconfiguration is used to generate inbound updates from a neighbor, it is called *inbound soft reconfiguration.*
- When soft reconfiguration is used to send a new set of updates to a neighbor, it is called *outbound soft reconfiguration.*

Performing inbound reconfiguration enables the new inbound policy to take effect. Performing outbound reconfiguration causes the new local outbound policy to take effect without resetting the BGP session. As a new set of updates is sent during outbound policy reconfiguration, a new inbound policy of the neighbor can also take effect.

In order to generate new inbound updates without resetting the BGP session, the local BGP speaker should store all the received updates without modification, regardless of whether it is accepted or denied by the current inbound policy. This is memory intensive and should be avoided. On the other hand, outbound soft reconfiguration does not have any memory overhead. One could trigger an outbound reconfiguration in the other side of the BGP session to make the new inbound policy take effect.

To allow inbound reconfiguration, BGP should be configured to store all received updates. Outbound reconfiguration does not require preconfiguration.

You can configure the Cisco IOS software to start storing received updates, which is required for inbound BGP soft reconfiguration. Outbound reconfiguration does not require inbound soft reconfiguration to be enabled.

To configure BGP soft configuration, perform the following task in router configuration mode:

Task	Command
Configure BGP soft reconfiguration.	neighbor {*ip-address*	*peer-group-name*} soft-reconfiguration inbound

Cisco's implementation of BGP supports BGP Versions 2, 3, and 4. If the neighbor does not accept default Version 4, dynamic version negotiation is implemented to negotiate down to Version 2.

If you specify a BGP peer group by using the *peer-group-name* argument, all members of the peer group will inherit the characteristic configured with this command.

RESETTING BGP CONNECTIONS

Once you have defined two routers to be BGP neighbors, they will form a BGP connection and exchange routing information. If you subsequently change a BGP filter, weight, distance, version, or timer, or make a similar configuration change, you must reset BGP connections for the configuration change to take effect. Perform either of the following tasks in EXEC mode to reset BGP connections:

Task	Command
Reset a particular BGP connection.	clear ip bgp *address*
Reset all BGP connections.	clear ip bgp *

CONFIGURING BGP INTERACTIONS WITH IGPs

If your autonomous system will be passing traffic through it from another autonomous system to a third autonomous system, it is very important that your autonomous system be consistent about the routes that it advertises. For example, if your BGP were to advertise a route before all routers in your network had learned about the route through your IGP, your autonomous system could receive traffic that some routers cannot yet route. To prevent this from happening, BGP must wait until the IGP has propagated routing information across your autonomous system. This causes BGP to be *synchronized* with the IGP. Synchronization is enabled by default.

In some cases, you do not need synchronization. If you will not be passing traffic from a different autonomous system through your autonomous system, or if all routers in your autonomous system will be running BGP, you can disable synchronization. Disabling this feature can allow you to carry fewer routes in your IGP and allow BGP to converge more quickly. To disable synchronization, perform the following task in router configuration mode:

Task	Command
Disable synchronization between BGP and an IGP.	**no synchronization**

When you disable synchronization, you should also clear BGP sessions using the **clear ip bgp** command.

See the "BGP Path Filtering by Neighbor Example" section at the end of this chapter for an example of BGP synchronization.

In general, you will not want to redistribute most BGP routes into your IGP. A common design is to redistribute one or two routes and to make them exterior routes in IGRP, or have your BGP speaker generate a default route for your autonomous system. When redistributing from BGP into IGP, only the routes learned using EBGP are redistributed.

In most circumstances, you also will not want to redistribute your IGP into BGP. Just list the networks in your autonomous system with **network** router configuration commands and your networks will be advertised. Networks that are listed this way are referred to as *local networks* and have a BGP origin attribute of "IGP." They must appear in the main IP routing table and can have any source; for example, they can be directly connected or learned via an IGP. The BGP routing process periodically scans the main IP routing table to detect the presence or absence of local networks, updating the BGP routing table as appropriate.

If you do perform redistribution into BGP, you must be very careful about the routes that can be in your IGP, especially if the routes were redistributed from BGP into the IGP elsewhere. This creates a situation where BGP is potentially injecting information into the IGP and then sending such information back into BGP, and vice versa.

Networks that are redistributed into BGP from the EGP protocol will be given the BGP origin attribute "EGP." Other networks that are redistributed into BGP will have the BGP origin attribute of "incomplete." The origin attribute in Cisco's implementation is only used in the path selection process.

CONFIGURING BGP ADMINISTRATIVE WEIGHTS

An administrative weight is a number that you can assign to a path so that you can control the path selection process. The administrative weight is local to the router. A weight can be a number from 0 to 65535. Paths that the Cisco IOS software originates have weight 32768 by default; other paths have weight 0. If you have particular neighbors that you want to prefer for most of your traffic, you can assign a higher weight to all routes learned from that neighbor.

Perform the following task in router configuration mode to configure BGP administrative weights:

Task	Command
Specify a weight for all routes from a neighbor.	**neighbor** {*ip-address* ǀ *peer-group-name*} **weight** *weight*

In addition, you can assign weights based on autonomous system path access lists. A given weight becomes the weight of the route if the autonomous system path is accepted by the access list. Any number of weight filters are allowed.

To assign weights based on autonomous system path access lists, perform the following tasks starting in global configuration mode:

	Task	Command
Step 1	Define a BGP-related access list.	**ip as-path access-list** *access-list-number* {**permit** ǀ **deny**} *as-regular-expression*
Step 2	Enter router configuration mode.	**router bgp** *autonomous-system*
Step 3	Configure administrative weight on all incoming routes matching an autonomous system path filter.	**neighbor** *ip-address* **filter-list** *access-list-number* **weight** *weight*

CONFIGURING BGP ROUTE FILTERING BY NEIGHBOR

If you want to restrict the routing information that the Cisco IOS software learns or advertises, you can filter BGP routing updates to and from particular neighbors. To do this, define an access list and apply it to the updates. Distribute-list filters are applied to network numbers and not autonomous system paths.

To filter BGP routing updates, perform the following task in router configuration mode:

Task	Command
Filter BGP routing updates to and from neighbors as specified in an access list.	**neighbor** {*ip-address* ǀ *peer-group-name*} **distribute-list** *access-list-number* ǀ *name* {**in** ǀ **out**}

CONFIGURING BGP PATH FILTERING BY NEIGHBOR

In addition to filtering routing updates based on network numbers, you can specify an access list filter on both incoming and outbound updates based on the BGP autonomous system paths.

Each filter is an access list based on regular expressions. To do this, define an autonomous system path access list and apply it to updates to and from particular neighbors.

To configure BGP path filtering, perform the following tasks starting in global configuration mode:

Task	Command
Step 1 Define a BGP-related access list.	**ip as-path access-list** *access-list-number* {**permit** I **deny**} *as-regular-expression*
Step 2 Enter router configuration mode.	**router bgp** *autonomous-system*
Step 3 Establish a BGP filter.	**neighbor** {*ip-address* I *peer-group-name*} **filter-list** *access-list-number* {**in** I **out** I **weight** *weight*}

See the "BGP Path Filtering by Neighbor Example" section at the end of this chapter for an example of BGP path filtering by neighbor.

DISABLING NEXT-HOP PROCESSING ON BGP UPDATES

You can configure the Cisco IOS software to disable next-hop processing for BGP updates to a neighbor. This might be useful in nonmeshed networks such as Frame Relay or X.25, where BGP neighbors might not have direct access to all other neighbors on the same IP subnet.

To disable next-hop processing, perform the following task in router configuration mode:

Task	Command
Disable next-hop processing on BGP updates to a neighbor.	**neighbor** {*ip-address* I *peer-group-name*} **next-hop-self**

Configuring this command causes the current router to advertise itself as the next hop for the specified neighbor. Therefore, other BGP neighbors will forward to it packets for that address. This is useful in a nonmeshed environment, because you know that a path exists from the present router to that address. In a fully meshed environment, this is not useful, as it will result in unnecessary extra hops and there might be a direct access through the fully meshed cloud that requires fewer hops.

CONFIGURING THE BGP VERSION

By default, BGP sessions begin using BGP Version 4 and negotiating downward to earlier versions if necessary. To prevent negotiation and force the BGP version used to communicate with a neighbor, perform the following task in router configuration mode:

Task	Command
Specify the BGP version to use when communicating with a neighbor.	**neighbor** {*ip-address* I *peer-group-name*} **version** *value*

SETTING THE NETWORK WEIGHT

Weight is a parameter that affects the best path selection process. To set the absolute weight for a network, perform the following task in router configuration mode:

Task	Command
Set the weight for a network.	**network** *address mask* **weight** *weight* [**route-map** *map-name*]

CONFIGURING THE MULTI EXIT DISCRIMINATOR METRIC

BGP uses the MED metric as a hint to external neighbors about preferred paths. (The name of this metric for BGP Versions 2 and 3 is *INTER_AS_METRIC*.) You can set the MED of the redistributed routes by performing the following task; all the routes without a MED will also be set to this value. Perform the following task in router configuration mode:

Task	Command
Set a multi exit discriminator.	**default-metric** *number*

Alternatively, you can set the MED using the **route-map** command. See the "BGP Route Map Examples" section at the end of this chapter for examples of using BGP route maps.

ADVANCED BGP CONFIGURATION TASKS

This section contains advanced BGP configuration tasks.

USING ROUTE MAPS TO MODIFY UPDATES

You can use a route map on a per-neighbor basis to filter updates and modify various attributes. A route map can be applied to either inbound or outbound updates. Only the routes that pass the route map are sent or accepted in updates.

On both the inbound and the outbound updates, Cisco supports matching based on autonomous system path, community, and network numbers. Autonomous system path matching requires the **as-path access-list** command, community based matching requires the **community-list** command, and network-based matching requires the **ip access-list** command. Perform the following task in router configuration mode:

Task	Command
Apply a route map to incoming or outgoing routes.	**neighbor** {*ip-address* I *peer-group-name*} **route-map** *route-map-name* {**in** I **out**}

See the "BGP Route Map Examples" section at the end of this chapter for BGP route map examples.

RESETTING EBGP CONNECTIONS IMMEDIATELY UPON LINK FAILURE

Normally, when a link between external neighbors goes down, the BGP session will not be reset immediately. If you want the EBGP session to be reset as soon as an interface goes down, perform the following task in router configuration mode:

Task	Command
Automatically reset EBGP sessions.	**bgp fast-external-fallover**

CONFIGURING AGGREGATE ADDRESSES

Classless interdomain routing enables you to create aggregate routes (or *supernets*) to minimize the size of routing tables. You can configure aggregate routes in BGP either by redistributing an aggregate route into BGP or by using the conditional aggregation feature described in the following task table. An aggregate address will be added to the BGP table if there is at least one more specific entry in the BGP table.

To create an aggregate address in the routing table, perform one or more of the following tasks in router configuration mode:

Task	Command
Create an aggregate entry in the BGP routing table.	**aggregate-address** *address mask*
Generate an aggregate with AS-SET.	**aggregate-address** *address mask* **as-set**

Task	Command
Advertise summary addresses only.	**aggregate-address** *address-mask* **summary-only**
Suppress selected, more specific routes.	**aggregate-address** *address mask* **suppress-map** *map-name*
Generate an aggregate based on conditions specified by the route map.	**aggregate-address** *address mask* **advertise-map** *map-name*
Generate an aggregate with attributes specified in the route map.	**aggregate-address** *address mask* **attribute-map** *map-name*

See the "BGP Aggregate Route Examples" section at the end of this chapter for examples of using BGP aggregate routes.

DISABLING AUTOMATIC SUMMARIZATION OF NETWORK NUMBERS

In BGP Version 3, when a subnet is redistributed from an IGP into BGP, only the network route is injected into the BGP table. By default, this automatic summarization is enabled. To disable automatic network number summarization, perform the following task in router configuration mode:

Task	Command
Disable automatic network summarization.	**no auto-summary**

CONFIGURING BGP COMMUNITY FILTERING

BGP supports transit policies via controlled distribution of routing information. The distribution of routing information is based on one of the following three values:

- IP address (see the "Configuring BGP Route Filtering by Neighbor" section earlier in this chapter).
- The value of the *AS_PATH* attribute (see the "Configuring BGP Path Filtering by Neighbor" section earlier in this chapter).
- The value of the *COMMUNITIES* attribute (as described in this section).

The *COMMUNITIES* attribute is a way to group destinations into communities and apply routing decisions based on those communities. This method simplifies a BGP speaker's configuration that controls distribution of routing information.

A *community* is a group of destinations that share some common attributes. Each destination can belong to multiple communities. Autonomous system administrators can define to which communities a destination belongs. By default, all destinations belong to the general Internet community; the community is carried as the *COMMUNITIES* attribute.

The *COMMUNITIES* attribute is an optional, transitive, global attribute in the numerical range from 1 to 4,294,967,200. Along with the Internet community, there are a few predefined, well-known communities, as shown in the following list:

- **internet**—Advertise this route to the Internet community. All routers belong to it.

- **no-export**—Do not advertise this route to EBGP peers.

- **no-advertise**—Do not advertise this route to any peer (internal or external).

Based on the community, you can control which routing information to accept, prefer, or distribute to other neighbors. A BGP speaker can set, append, or modify the community of a route when you learn, advertise, or redistribute routes. When routes are aggregated, the resulting aggregate has a *COMMUNITIES* attribute that contains all communities from all the initial routes.

You can use community lists to create groups of communities to use in a match clause of a route map. Just like an access list, a series of community lists can be created. Statements are checked until a match is found. As soon as one statement is satisfied, the test is concluded.

To create a community list, perform the following task in global configuration mode:

Task	Command
Create a community list.	**ip community-list** *community-list-number* {**permit** | **deny**} *community-number*

To set the *COMMUNITIES* attribute and match clauses based on communities, see the **match community-list** and **set community** commands in the "Redistributing Routing Information" section in Chapter 22.

By default, no *COMMUNITIES* attribute is sent to a neighbor. You can specify that the *COMMUNITIES* attribute be sent to the neighbor at an IP address by performing the following task in router configuration mode:

Task	Command
Specify that the *COMMUNITIES* attribute be sent to the neighbor at this IP address.	**neighbor** {*ip-address* | *peer-group-name*} **send-community**

CONFIGURING A ROUTING DOMAIN CONFEDERATION

One way to reduce the IBGP mesh is to divide an autonomous system into multiple autonomous systems and group them into a single confederation. To the outside world, the confederation looks like a single autonomous system. Each autonomous system is fully meshed within itself, and has a few connections to other autonomous systems in the same confederation. Even though the peers in different autonomous systems have EBGP sessions, they exchange routing information as if they were IBGP peers. Specifically, the next-hop, MED, and local preference information is preserved. This enables to you to retain a single IGP for all of the autonomous systems.

To configure a BGP confederation, you must specify a confederation identifier. To the outside world, the group of autonomous systems will look like a single autonomous system with the confederation identifier as the autonomous system number. To configure a BGP confederation identifier, perform the following task in router configuration mode:

Task	Command
Configure a BGP confederation.	**bgp confederation identifier** *autonomous-system*

In order to treat the neighbors from other autonomous systems within the confederation as special EBGP peers, perform the following task in router configuration mode:

Task	Command
Specify the autonomous systems that belong to the confederation.	**bgp confederation peers** *autonomous-system* [*autonomous-system ...*]

See the "BGP Confederation Example" section at the end of this chapter for an example configuration of several peers in a confederation.

For an alternative way to reduce the IBGP mesh, see the next section, "Configuring a Route Reflector."

CONFIGURING A ROUTE REFLECTOR

BGP requires that all of the IBGP speakers be fully meshed. However, this requirement does not scale when there are many IBGP speakers. Instead of configuring a confederation, another way to reduce the IBGP mesh is to configure a *route reflector*.

Figure 20–1 illustrates a simple IBGP configuration with three IBGP speakers (Routers A, B, and C). Without route reflectors, when Router A receives a route from an external neighbor, it must advertise it to both Routers B and C. Routers B and C do not readvertise the IBGP learned route to other IBGP speakers because the routers do not pass routes learned from internal neighbors on to other internal neighbors, thus preventing a routing information loop.

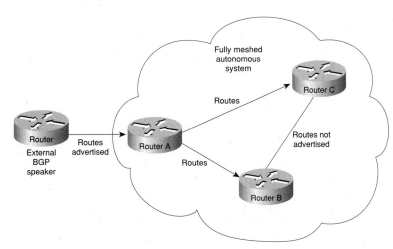

Figure 20–1
Three fully meshed
IBGP speakers.

With route reflectors, all IBGP speakers need not be fully meshed because there is a method to pass learned routes to neighbors. In this model, an internal BGP peer is configured to be a route reflector responsible for passing IBGP learned routes to a set of IBGP neighbors. In Figure 20–2, Router B is configured as a route reflector. When the route reflector receives routes advertised from Router A, it advertises them to Router C, and vice versa. This scheme eliminates the need for the IBGP session between Routers A and C.

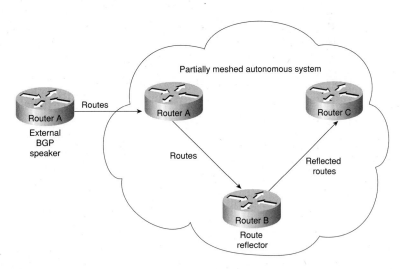

Figure 20–2
Simple BGP model with a
route reflector.

The internal peers of the route reflector are divided into two groups: client peers and all the other routers in the autonomous system (nonclient peers). A route reflector reflects routes between these two groups. The route reflector and its client peers form a *cluster*. The nonclient peers must be fully meshed with each other, but the client peers need not be fully meshed. The clients in the cluster do not communicate with IBGP speakers outside their cluster.

Figure 20–3 illustrates a more complex route reflector scheme. Router A is the route reflector in a cluster with Routers B, C, and D. Routers E, F, and G are fully meshed, nonclient routers.

Figure 20–3

More complex BGP route reflector model.

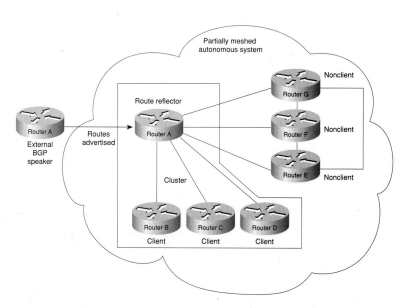

When the route reflector receives an advertised route, depending on the neighbor, it does the following:

- A route from an external BGP speaker is advertised to all clients and nonclient peers.

- A route from a nonclient peer is advertised to all clients.

- A route from a client is advertised to all clients and nonclient peers. Hence, the clients need not be fully meshed.

To configure a route reflector and its clients, perform the following task in router configuration mode:

Task	Command
Configure the local router as a BGP route reflector and the specified neighbor as a client.	**neighbor** *ip-address* **route-reflector-client**

Along with route reflector-aware BGP speakers, it is possible to have BGP speakers that do not understand the concept of route reflectors. They can be members of either client or nonclient groups. This allows easy, gradual migration from the old BGP model to the route reflector model.

Initially, you can create a single cluster with a route reflector and a few clients. All the other IBGP speakers can be nonclient peers to the route reflector and then more clusters can be created gradually.

An autonomous system can have multiple route reflectors. A route reflector treats other route reflectors just like other IBGP speakers. A route reflector can be configured to have other route reflectors in a client group or nonclient group. In a simple configuration, the backbone can be divided into many clusters. Each route reflector would then be configured with other route reflectors as nonclient peers (thus, all the route reflectors will be fully meshed). The clients are configured to maintain IBGP sessions with only the route reflector in their cluster.

Usually a cluster of clients will have a single route reflector. In that case, the cluster is identified by the router ID of the route reflector. To increase redundancy and avoid a single point of failure, a cluster might have more than one route reflector. In this case, all route reflectors in the cluster must be configured with the 4-byte cluster ID so that a route reflector can recognize updates from route reflectors in the same cluster. All the route reflectors serving a cluster should be fully meshed and all of them should have identical sets of client and nonclient peers.

If the cluster has more than one route reflector, configure the cluster ID by performing the following task in router configuration mode:

Task	Command
Configure the cluster ID.	bgp cluster-id *cluster-id*

Use the **show ip bgp** command to display the originator ID and the cluster-list attributes.

By default, the clients of a route reflector are not required to be fully meshed and the routes from a client are reflected to other clients. However, if the clients are fully meshed, the route reflector does not need to reflect routes to clients. To disable client-to-client route reflection, perform the following task in router configuration mode:

Task	Command
Disable client-to-client route reflection.	no bgp client-to-client reflection

— **NOTES**

If client-to-client reflection is enabled, the clients of a route reflector cannot be members of a peer group.

As the IBGP learned routes are reflected, it is possible for routing information to loop. The route reflector model has the following mechanisms to avoid routing loops:

- Originator-ID is an optional, nontransitive BGP attribute. This is a 4-byte attribute created by a route reflector. The attribute carries the router ID of the originator of the route in the local autonomous system. Therefore, if a misconfiguration causes routing information to come back to the originator, the information is ignored.

- Cluster-list is an optional, nontransitive BGP attribute. It is a sequence of cluster IDs that the route has passed. When a route reflector reflects a route from its clients to nonclient peers, it appends the local cluster ID to the cluster-list. If the cluster-list is empty, it creates a new one. Using this attribute, a route reflector can identify whether routing information is looped back to the same cluster due to misconfiguration. If the local cluster ID is found in the cluster-list, the advertisement is ignored.

- Using **set** clauses in outbound route maps modifies attributes, possibly creating routing loops. To avoid this, **set** clauses of outbound route maps are ignored for routes reflected to IBGP peers.

CONFIGURING NEIGHBOR OPTIONS

There are many ways to customize a BGP neighbor, and these customized features can also be applied to a peer group. To avoid documenting each option twice (for both neighbors and peer groups), all of the supported neighbor options appear in the next section, "Configuring BGP Peer Groups" under "Assigning Options to the Peer Group."

To provide BGP routing information to a large number of neighbors, you can configure BGP to accept neighbors based on an access list. If a neighbor attempts to initiate a BGP connection, its address must be accepted by the access list for the connection to be accepted. If you do this, the router will not attempt to initiate a BGP connection to these neighbors, so the neighbors must be explicitly configured to initiate the BGP connection. If no access list is specified, all connections are accepted.

Specify an access list of BGP neighbors by performing the following task in router configuration mode:

Task	Command
Specify an access list of BGP neighbors.	**neighbor any** [*access-list-number*	*name*]

CONFIGURING BGP PEER GROUPS

Often, in a BGP speaker, many neighbors are configured with the same update policies (that is, the same outbound route maps, distribute lists, filter lists, update source, and so on). Neighbors with the same update policies can be grouped into peer groups to simplify configuration and, more importantly, to make updating more efficient. When you have many peers, this approach is highly recommended.

The three steps to configure a BGP peer group are the following:

1. Creating the Peer Group
2. Assigning Options to the Peer Group
3. Making Neighbors Members of the Peer Group

Creating the Peer Group

To create a BGP peer group, perform the following task in router configuration mode:

Task	Command
Create a BGP peer group.	neighbor *peer-group-name* **peer-group**

Assigning Options to the Peer Group

After you create a peer group, you configure the peer group with **neighbor** commands. By default, members of the peer group inherit all the configuration options of the peer group. Members can also be configured to override the options that do not affect outbound updates.

Peer group members will always inherit the following: remote-as (if configured), version, update-source, out-route-map, out-filter-list, out-dist-list, minimum-advertisement-interval, and next-hop-self. All the peer group members will inherit changes made to the peer group.

NOTES

A limitation on EBGP peer group is that all members of a peer group each receive one identical copy of an update, so all the members (peering addresses) must be in the same logical IP subnet (lis) to prevent the update from being invalidated or dropped.

To assign configuration options to an individual neighbor, specify any of the following commands using the IP address. To assign the options to a peer group, specify any of the commands using the peer group name. Perform any of these tasks in router configuration mode.

Task	Command
Specify a BGP neighbor.	neighbor {*ip-address* I *peer-group-name*} **remote-as** *number*
Associate a description with a neighbor.	neighbor {*ip-address* I *peer-group-name*} **description** *text*
Allow a BGP speaker (the local router) to send the default route 0.0.0.0 to a neighbor for use as a default route.	neighbor {*ip-address* I *peer-group-name*} **default-originate** [**route-map** *map-name*]
Specify that the *COMMUNITIES* attribute be sent to the neighbor at this IP address.	neighbor {*ip-address* I *peer-group-name*} **send-community**

Task	Command
Allow internal BGP sessions to use any operational interface for TCP connections.	**neighbor** {*ip-address* | *peer-group-name*} **update-source** *interface*
Allow BGP sessions, even when the neighbor is not on a directly connected segment.	**neighbor** {*ip-address* | *peer-group-name*} **ebgp-multihop**
Set the minimum interval between sending BGP routing updates.	**neighbor** {*ip-address* | *peer-group-name*} **advertisement-interval** *seconds*
Limit the number of prefixes allowed from a neighbor.	**neighbor** {*ip-address* | *peer-group-name*} **maximum-prefix** *maximum* [*threshold*] [**warning-only**]
Invoke MD5 authentication on a TCP connection to a BGP peer.	**neighbor** {*ip-address* | *peer-group-name*} **password** *string*
Specify a weight for all routes from a neighbor.	**neighbor** {*ip-address* | *peer-group-name*} **weight** *weight*
Filter BGP routing updates to and from neighbors, as specified in an access list.	**neighbor** {*ip-address* | *peer-group-name*} **distribute-list** {*access-list-number* | *name*} {**in** | **out**}
Establish a BGP filter.	**neighbor** {*ip-address* | *peer-group-name*} **filter-list** *access-list-number* {**in** | **out** | **weight** *weight*}
Disable next-hop processing on the BGP updates to a neighbor.	**neighbor** {*ip-address* | *peer-group-name*} **next-hop-self**
Specify the BGP version to use when communicating with a neighbor.	**neighbor** {*ip-address* | *peer-group-name*} **version** *value*
Apply a route map to incoming or outgoing routes.	**neighbor** {*ip-address* | *peer-group-name*} **route-map** *map-name* {**in** | **out**}
Configure the software to start storing received updates.	**neighbor** {*ip-address* | *peer-group-name*} **soft-reconfiguration inbound**

If a peer group is not configured with a remote-as, the members can be configured with the **neighbor remote-as** command. This allows you to create peer groups containing EBGP neighbors.

You can customize inbound policies for peer group members, (using, for example, a distribute list, route map, or filter list) because one identical copy of an update is sent to every member of a group. Therefore, neighbor options related to outgoing updates cannot be customized for peer group members.

External BGP peers normally must reside on a directly connected network. Sometimes it is useful to relax this restriction in order to test BGP; do so by specifying the **neighbor ebgp-multihop** command.

For internal BGP, you might want to allow your BGP connections to stay up regardless of which interface is used to reach a neighbor. To do this, you first configure a *loopback* interface and assign it an IP address. Next, configure the BGP update source to be the loopback interface. Finally, configure your neighbor to use the address on the loopback interface. Now the IBGP session will be up as long as there is a route, regardless of any interface.

You can set the minimum interval of time between BGP routing updates.

You can invoke MD5 authentication between two BGP peers, meaning that each segment sent on the TCP connection between them is verified. This feature must be configured with the same password on both BGP peers; otherwise, the connection between them will not be made. The authentication feature uses the MD5 algorithm. Invoking authentication causes the Cisco IOS software to generate and check the MD5 digest of every segment sent on the TCP connection. If authentication is invoked and a segment fails authentication, then a message appears on the console.

See the "TCP MD5 Authentication for BGP Example" at the end of this chapter for an example of enabling MD5 authentication.

Making Neighbors Members of the Peer Group

Finally, to configure a BGP neighbor to be a member of that BGP peer group, perform the following task in router configuration mode, using the same peer group name:

Task	Command
Make a BGP neighbor a member of the peer group.	**neighbor** *ip-address* **peer-group** *peer-group-name*

See the "BGP Peer Group Examples" section at the end of this chapter for examples of IBGP and EBGP peer groups.

INDICATING BACKDOOR ROUTES

You can indicate which networks are reachable by using a *backdoor* route that the border router should use. A backdoor network is treated as a local network, except that it is not advertised. To configure backdoor routes, perform the following task in router configuration mode:

Task	Command
Indicate reachable networks through backdoor routes.	**network** *address* **backdoor**

Modifying Parameters While Updating the IP Routing Table

By default, when a BGP route is put into the IP routing table, the MED is converted to an IP route metric, the BGP next hop is used as the next hop for the IP route, and the tag is not set. However, you can use a route map to perform mapping. To modify metric and tag information when the IP routing table is updated with BGP learned routes, perform the following task in router configuration mode:

Task	Command
Apply a route map to routes when updating the IP routing table.	**table-map** *route-map name*

Setting Administrative Distance

Administrative distance is a measure of the preference of different routing protocols. BGP uses three different administrative distances: external, internal, and local. Routes learned through external BGP are given the external distance, routes learned with internal BGP are given the internal distance, and routes that are part of this autonomous system are given the local distance. To assign a BGP administrative distance, perform the following task in router configuration mode:

Task	Command
Assign a BGP administrative distance.	**distance bgp** *external-distance internal-distance local-distance*

Changing the administrative distance of BGP routes is considered dangerous and generally is not recommended. The external distance should be lower than any other dynamic routing protocol, and the internal and local distances should be higher than any other dynamic routing protocol.

Adjusting BGP Timers

BGP uses certain timers to control periodic activities such as the sending of keepalive messages, and the interval after not receiving a keepalive message after which the Cisco IOS software declares a peer dead. You can adjust these timers. When a connection is started, BGP will negotiate the hold time with the neighbor. The smaller of the two hold times will be chosen. The keepalive timer is then set based on the negotiated hold time and the configured keepalive time. To adjust BGP timers, perform the following task in router configuration mode:

Task	Command
Adjust BGP timers.	**timers bgp** *keepalive holdtime*

CHANGING THE LOCAL PREFERENCE VALUE

You can define a particular path as more preferable or less preferable than other paths by changing the default local preference value of 100. To assign a different default local preference value, perform the following task in router configuration mode:

Task	Command
Change the default local preference value.	bgp default local-preference *value*

You can use route maps to change the default local preference of specific paths. See the "BGP Route Map Examples" section at the end of this chapter for examples using BGP route maps.

REDISTRIBUTING NETWORK 0.0.0.0

By default, you are not allowed to redistribute network 0.0.0.0. To permit the redistribution of network 0.0.0.0, perform the following task in router configuration mode:

Task	Command
Allow the redistribution of network 0.0.0.0 into BGP.	default-information originate

SELECTING A PATH BASED ON MEDs FROM OTHER AUTONOMOUS SYSTEMS

The MED is one of the parameters that is considered when selecting the best path among many alternative paths. A path with a lower MED is preferred over a path with a higher MED.

By default, during the best-path selection process, MED comparison is done only among paths from the same autonomous system. You can allow comparison of MEDs among paths regardless of the autonomous system from which the paths are received. To do so, perform the following task in router configuration mode:

Task	Command
Allow the comparison of MEDs for paths from neighbors in different autonomous systems.	bgp always-compare-med

CONFIGURING ROUTE DAMPENING

Route dampening is a BGP feature designed to minimize the propagation of flapping routes across an internetwork. A route is considered to be flapping when it continually cycles between being available and unavailable.

For example, consider a network with three BGP autonomous systems: AS 1, AS 2, and AS 3. Suppose the route to network A in AS 1 flaps (it becomes unavailable). Under circumstances without route dampening, AS 1's EBGP neighbor to AS 2 sends a Withdraw message to AS 2. The border router in AS 2, in turn, propagates the Withdraw to AS 3. When the route to network A reappears, AS 1 sends an Advertisement to AS 2, which sends it to AS 3. If the route to network A repeatedly becomes unavailable, then available (it flaps), many Withdrawals and Advertisements are sent. This is a problem in an internetwork connected to the Internet because a route flap in the Internet backbone usually involves many routes.

Minimizing Flapping

The route dampening feature minimizes the flapping problem as follows. Suppose again that the route to network A flaps. The router in AS 2 (where route dampening is enabled) assigns network A a penalty of 1000 and moves it to "history" state. The router in AS 2 continues to advertise the status of the route to neighbors. The penalties are cumulative. When the route flaps so often that the penalty exceeds a configurable suppress limit, the router stops advertising the route to network A, regardless of how many times it flaps. Thus, the route is dampened.

The penalty placed on network A is decayed until the reuse limit is reached, upon which the route is once again advertised. At half of the reuse limit, the dampening information for the route to network A is removed.

Understanding Route Dampening Terms

The following terms are used when describing route dampening:

- Flap—A route cycles between availability and unavailability.
- History state—After a route flaps once, it is assigned a penalty and put into "history state," meaning that the router does not have the best path, based on historical information.
- Penalty—Each time a route flaps, the router configured for route dampening in another AS assigns the route a penalty of 1000. Penalties are cumulative. The penalty for the route is stored in the BGP routing table until the penalty exceeds the suppress limit. At that point, the route state changes from "history" to "damp."
- Damp state—In this state, the route has flapped so often that the router will not advertise this route to BGP neighbors.
- Suppress limit—A route is suppressed when its penalty exceeds this limit. The default value is 2000.
- Half-life—Once the route has been assigned a penalty, the penalty is decreased by half after the half-life period (which is 15 minutes by default). The process of reducing the penalty happens every 5 seconds.
- Reuse limit—As the penalty for a flapping route decreases and falls below this reuse limit, the route is unsuppressed. That is, the route is added back to the BGP table and once again used for forwarding. The default reuse limit is 750. The process of unsuppressing routes

occurs at 10-second increments. Every 10 seconds, the router finds out which routes are now unsuppressed and advertises them to the world.

- Maximum suppress limit—This value is the maximum amount of time a route can be suppressed. The default value is 4 times the half-life.

The routes external to an AS learned via IBGP are not dampened. This policy prevents the IBGP peers from having a higher penalty for routes external to the AS.

Enabling Route Dampening

To enable BGP route dampening, perform the following task in global configuration mode:

Task	Command
Enable BGP route dampening.	bgp dampening

To change the default values of various dampening factors, perform the following task in global configuration mode:

Task	Command
Change the default values of route dampening factors.	bgp dampening *half-life reuse suppress max-suppress* [route-map *map*]

Monitoring and Maintaining BGP Route Dampening

You can monitor the flaps of all flapping paths. The statistics will be deleted once the route is not suppressed and is stable for at least one half-life. To display flap statistics, perform the following tasks in EXEC mode:

	Task	Command
Step 1	Display BGP flap statistics for all paths.	show ip bgp flap-statistics
Step 2	Display BGP flap statistics for all paths that match the regular expression.	show ip bgp flap-statistics regexp *regexp*
Step 3	Display BGP flap statistics for all paths that pass the filter.	show ip bgp flap-statistics filter-list *list*
Step 4	Display BGP flap statistics for a single entry.	show ip bgp flap-statistics *address mask*
Step 5	Display BGP flap statistics for more specific entries.	show ip bgp flap-statistics *address mask* longer-prefix

To clear BGP flap statistics (thus making it less likely that the route will be dampened), perform the following tasks in EXEC mode:

Task		Command
Step 1	Clear BGP flap statistics for all routes.	**clear ip bgp flap-statistics**
Step 2	Clear BGP flap statistics for all paths that match the regular expression.	**clear ip bgp flap-statistics regexp** *regexp*
Step 3	Clear BGP flap statistics for all paths that pass the filter.	**clear ip bgp flap-statistics filter-list** *list*
Step 4	Clear BGP flap statistics for a single entry.	**clear ip bgp flap-statistics** *address mask*
Step 5	Clear BGP flap statistics for all paths from a neighbor.	**clear ip bgp** *address* **flap-statistics**

Once a route is dampened, you can display BGP route dampening information, including the time remaining before the dampened routes will be unsuppressed. To display this information, perform the following task in EXEC mode:

Task	Command
Display the dampened routes, including the time remaining before they will be unsuppressed.	**show ip bgp dampened-paths**

You can clear BGP route dampening information and unsuppress any suppressed routes by performing the following task in EXEC mode:

Task	Command
Clear route dampening information and unsuppress the suppressed routes.	**clear ip bgp dampening** [*address mask*]

MONITORING AND MAINTAINING BGP

You can remove all contents of a particular cache, table, or database. You also can display specific statistics. The following sections describe each of these tasks.

Clearing Caches, Tables, and Databases

You can remove all contents of a particular cache, table, or database. Clearing a cache, table, or database can become necessary when the contents of the particular structure have become, or are suspected to be, invalid.

The following table lists the tasks associated with clearing caches, tables, and databases for BGP. Perform these tasks in EXEC mode:

Task		Command
Step 1	Reset a particular BGP connection.	clear ip bgp *address*
Step 2	Reset all BGP connections.	clear ip bgp *
Step 3	Remove all members of a BGP peer group.	clear ip bgp peer-group *tag*

Displaying System and Network Statistics

You can display specific statistics such as the contents of BGP routing tables, caches, and databases. This information can be used to determine resource utilization and solve network problems. You can also display information about node reachability and discover the routing path your device's packets are taking through the network.

To display various routing statistics, perform the following tasks in EXEC mode:

Task		Command
Step 1	Display all BGP routes that contain subnet and supernet network masks.	show ip bgp cidr-only
Step 2	Display routes that belong to the specified communities.	show ip bgp community *community-number* [exact]
Step 3	Display routes that are permitted by the community list.	show ip bgp community-list *community-list-number* [exact]
Step 4	Display routes that are matched by the specified autonomous system path access list.	show ip bgp filter-list *access-list-number*
Step 5	Display the routes with inconsistent originating autonomous systems.	show ip bgp inconsistent-as
Step 6	Display the routes that match the specified regular expression entered on the command line.	show ip bgp regexp *regular-expression*

Task		Command
Step 7	Display the contents of the BGP routing table.	show ip bgp [*network*] [*network-mask*] [subnets]
Step 8	Display detailed information on the TCP and BGP connections to individual neighbors.	show ip bgp neighbors [*address*]
Step 9	Display routes learned from a particular BGP neighbor.	show ip bgp neighbors [*address*] [received-routes I routes I advertised-routes I paths *regular-expression* I dampened-routes]
Step 10	Display all BGP paths in the database.	show ip bgp paths
Step 11	Display information about BGP peer groups.	show ip bgp peer-group [*tag*] [summary]
Step 12	Display the status of all BGP connections.	show ip bgp summary

BGP CONFIGURATION EXAMPLES

The next sections provide the following BGP configuration examples:

- BGP Route Map Examples
- BGP Neighbor Configuration Examples
- BGP Synchronization Example
- BGP Path Filtering by Neighbor Example
- BGP Aggregate Route Examples
- BGP Confederation Example
- TCP MD5 Authentication for BGP Example
- BGP Peer Group Examples
- BGP Community with Route Maps Examples

BGP Route Map Examples

The following example shows how you can use route maps to modify incoming data from a neighbor. Any route received from 140.222.1.1 that matches the filter parameters set in autonomous system access list 200 will have its weight set to 200 and its local preference set to 250, and it will be accepted.

```
router bgp 100
!
 neighbor 140.222.1.1 route-map fix-weight in
 neighbor 140.222.1.1 remote-as 1
!
route-map fix-weight permit 10
 match as-path 200
 set local-preference 250
 set weight 200
!
ip as-path access-list 200 permit ^690$
ip as-path access-list 200 permit ^1800
```

In the following example, route map *freddy* marks all paths originating from autonomous system 690 with a MED metric attribute of 127. The second permit clause is required so that routes not matching autonomous system path list 1 will still be sent to neighbor 1.1.1.1.

```
router bgp 100
 neighbor 1.1.1.1 route-map freddy out
!
ip as-path access-list 1 permit ^690_
ip as-path access-list 2 permit .*
!
route-map freddy permit 10
 match as-path 1
 set metric 127
!
route-map freddy permit 20
 match as-path 2
```

The following example shows how you can use route maps to modify incoming data from the IP forwarding table:

```
router bgp 100
 redistribute igrp 109 route-map igrp2bgp
!
route-map igrp2bgp
 match ip address 1
 set local-preference 25
 set metric 127
 set weight 30000
 set next-hop 192.92.68.24
 set origin igp
!
access-list 1 permit 131.108.0.0 0.0.255.255
access-list 1 permit 160.89.0.0 0.0.255.255
access-list 1 permit 198.112.0.0 0.0.127.255
```

It is proper behavior not to accept any autonomous system path not matching the **match** clause of the route map. This means that you will not set the metric and the Cisco IOS software will not accept the route. However, you can configure the software to accept autonomous system paths not matched in the **match** clause of the route map command by using multiple maps of the same name, some without accompanying **set** commands.

```
route-map fnord permit 10
 match as-path 1
 set local-preference 5
!
route-map fnord permit 20
 match as-path 2
```

The following example shows how you can use route maps in a reverse operation to set the route tag (as defined by the BGP/OSPF interaction document, RFC 1403) when exporting routes from BGP into the main IP routing table:

```
router bgp 100
 table-map set_ospf_tag
!
route-map set_ospf_tag
 match as-path 1
 set automatic-tag
!
ip as-path access-list 1 permit .*
```

In the following example, the route map called *set-as-path* is applied to outbound updates to the neighbor 200.69.232.70. The route map will prepend the autonomous system path "100 100" to routes that pass access list 1. The second part of the route map is to permit the advertisement of other routes.

```
router bgp 100
 network 171.60.0.0
 network 172.60.0.0
 neighbor 200.69.232.70 remote-as 200
 neighbor 200.69.232.70 route-map set-as-path out
!
route-map set-as-path 10 permit
 match address 1
 set as-path prepend 100 100
!
route-map set-as-path 20 permit
 match address 2
!
access-list 1 permit 171.60.0.0 0.0.255.255
access-list 1 permit 172.60.0.0 0.0.255.255
!
access-list 2 permit 0.0.0.0 255.255.255.255
```

Inbound route-maps can do prefix-based matching and set various parameters of the update. Inbound prefix matching is available in addition to as-path and community-list matching. In the following example, the **set local preference** command sets the local preference of the inbound prefix 140.10.0.0/16 to 120.

```
!
router bgp 100
 network 131.108.0.0
 neighbor 131.108.1.1 remote-as 200
 neighbor 131.108.1.1 route-map set-local-pref in !
```

```
route-map set-local-pref permit 10
 match ip address 2
 set local preference 120
!
route-map set-local-pref permit 20
!
access-list 2 permit 140.10.0.0 0.0.255.255 access-list 2 deny any
```

BGP Neighbor Configuration Examples

In the following example, a BGP router is assigned to autonomous system 109, and two networks are listed as originating in the autonomous system. Then the addresses of three remote routers (and their autonomous systems) are listed. The router being configured will share information about networks 131.108.0.0 and 192.31.7.0 with the neighbor routers. The first router listed is in a different autonomous system; the second **neighbor** command specifies an internal neighbor (with the same autonomous system number) at address 131.108.234.2; and the third **neighbor** command specifies a neighbor on a different autonomous system.

```
router bgp 109
 network 131.108.0.0
 network 192.31.7.0
 neighbor 131.108.200.1 remote-as 167
 neighbor 131.108.234.2 remote-as 109
 neighbor 150.136.64.19 remote-as 99
```

In Figure 20–4, Router A is being configured; the internal BGP neighbor is not directly linked to Router A. External neighbors (in autonomous system 167 and autonomous system 99) must be linked directly to Router A.

Figure 20–4

Assigning internal and external BGP neighbors.

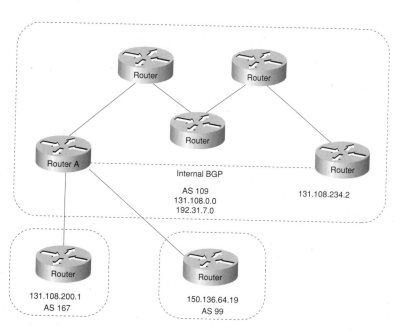

BGP Synchronization Example

In the configuration shown in Figure 20–5 with synchronization on, Router B does not advertise network 198.92.68.0 to Router A until an IGRP route for network 198.92.68.0 exists. If you specify the **no synchronization** router configuration command, Router B advertises network 198.92.68.0 as soon as possible. However, because routing information still must be sent to interior peers, you must configure a full internal BGP mesh.

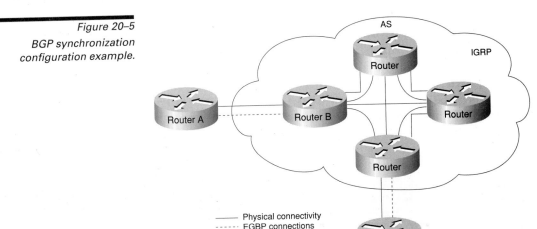

Figure 20–5
BGP synchronization configuration example.

BGP Path Filtering by Neighbor Example

The following is an example of BGP path filtering by neighbor. The routes that pass as-path access list 1 will get weight 100. Only the routes that pass as-path access list 2 will be sent to 193.1.12.10. Similarly, only routes passing access list 3 will be accepted from 193.1.12.10.

```
router bgp 200
 neighbor 193.1.12.10 remote-as 100
 neighbor 193.1.12.10 filter-list 1 weight 100
 neighbor 193.1.12.10 filter-list 2 out
 neighbor 193.1.12.10 filter-list 3 in
ip as-path access-list 1 permit _109_
ip as-path access-list 2 permit _200$
ip as-path access-list 2 permit ^100$
ip as-path access-list 3 deny _690$
ip as-path access-list 3 permit .*
```

BGP Aggregate Route Examples

The following examples show how you can use aggregate routes in BGP either by redistributing an aggregate route into BGP or by using the conditional aggregate routing feature.

In the following example, the **redistribute static** command is used to redistribute aggregate route 193.*.*.*:

```
ip route 193.0.0.0 255.0.0.0 null 0
!
router bgp 100
  redistribute static
```

The following configuration creates an aggregate entry in the BGP routing table when there is at least one specific route that falls into the specified range. The aggregate route will be advertised as coming from your autonomous system and has the atomic aggregate attribute set to show that information might be missing. (By default, atomic aggregate is set unless you use the **as-set** keyword in the **aggregate-address** command.)

```
router bgp 100
  aggregate-address 193.0.0.0 255.0.0.0
```

The following example creates an aggregate entry using the same rules as in the previous example, but the path advertised for this route will be an AS_SET consisting of all elements contained in all paths that are being summarized:

```
router bgp 100
  aggregate-address 193.0.0.0 255.0.0.0 as-set
```

The following example not only creates the aggregate route for 193.*.*.*, but also suppresses advertisements of more specific routes to all neighbors:

```
router bgp 100
  aggregate-address 193.0.0.0 255.0.0.0 summary-only
```

BGP Confederation Example

The following is a sample configuration from several peers in a confederation. The confederation consists of three internal autonomous systems with autonomous system numbers 6001, 6002, and 6003. To the BGP speakers outside the confederation, the confederation looks like a normal autonomous system with autonomous system number 666 (specified via the **bgp confederation identifier** command).

In a BGP speaker in autonomous system 6001, the **bgp confederation peers** command marks the peers from autonomous systems 6002 and 6003 as special EBGP peers. Hence peers 171.69.232.55 and 171.69.232.56 will get the local-preference, next-hop, and MED unmodified in the updates. The router at 160.69.69.1 is a normal EBGP speaker and the updates received by it from this peer will be just like a normal EBGP update from a peer in autonomous system 666.

```
router bgp 6001
  bgp confederation identifier 666
  bgp confederation peers 6002 6003
  neighbor 171.69.232.55 remote-as 6002
  neighbor 171.69.232.56 remote-as 6003
  neighbor 160.69.69.1 remote-as 777
```

In a BGP speaker in autonomous system 6002, the peers from autonomous systems 6001 and 6003 are configured as special EBGP peers. So, 170.70.70.1 is a normal IBGP peer and 199.99.99.2 is a normal EBGP peer from autonomous system 700.

```
router bgp 6002
  bgp confederation identifier 666
  bgp confederation peers 6001 6003
  neighbor 170.70.70.1 remote-as 6002
  neighbor 171.69.232.57 remote-as 6001
  neighbor 171.69.232.56 remote-as 6003
  neighbor 199.99.99.2 remote-as 700
```

In a BGP speaker in autonomous system 6003, the peers from autonomous systems 6001 and 6002 are configured as special EBGP peers. Hence, 200.200.200.200.200 is a normal EBGP peer from autonomous system 701.

```
router bgp 6003
  bgp confederation identifier 666
  bgp confederation peers 6001 6002
  neighbor 171.69.232.57 remote-as 6001
  neighbor 171.69.232.55 remote-as 6002
  neighbor 200.200.200.200 remote-as 701
```

The following is a part of the configuration from the BGP speaker 200.200.200.205 from autonomous system 701. Neighbor 171.69.232.56 is configured as a normal EBGP speaker from autonomous system 666. The internal division of the autonomous system into multiple autonomous systems is not known to the peers external to the confederation.

```
router bgp 701
  neighbor 171.69.232.56 remote-as 666
  neighbor 200.200.200.205 remote-as 701
```

TCP MD5 Authentication for BGP Example

The following example specifies that the router and its BGP peer at 145.2.2.2 invoke MD5 authentication on the TCP connection between them:

```
router bgp 109
  neighbor 145.2.2.2 password v61ne0qkel33&
```

BGP Peer Group Examples

This section contains an IBGP peer group example and an EBGP peer group example.

IBGP Peer Group Example

In the following example, the peer group named *internal* configures the members of the peer group to be IBGP neighbors. By definition, this is an IBGP peer group because the **router bgp** command and the **neighbor remote-as** command indicate the same autonomous system (in this case, AS 100). All the peer group members use loopback 0 as the update source and use *set-med* as the outbound route-map. The example also shows that, except for the neighbor at address 171.69.232.55, all the neighbors have filter-list 2 as the inbound filter list.

```
router bgp 100
 neighbor internal peer-group
 neighbor internal remote-as 100
 neighbor internal update-source loopback 0
 neighbor internal route-map set-med out
 neighbor internal filter-list 1 out
 neighbor internal filter-list 2 in
 neighbor 171.69.232.53 peer-group internal
 neighbor 171.69.232.54 peer-group internal
 neighbor 171.69.232.55 peer-group internal
 neighbor 171.69.232.55 filter-list 3 in
```

EBGP Peer Group Example

In the following example, the peer group *external-peers* is defined without the **neighbor remote-as** command. This is what makes it an EBGP peer group. Each member of the peer group is configured with its respective autonomous system number separately. Thus, the peer group consists of members from autonomous systems 200, 300, and 400. All the peer group members have *set-metric* route map as an outbound route map and filter-list 99 as an outbound filter list. Except for neighbor 171.69.232.110, all have 101 as the inbound filter list.

```
router bgp 100
 neighbor external-peers peer-group
 neighbor external-peers route-map set-metric out
 neighbor external-peers filter-list 99 out
 neighbor external-peers filter-list 101 in
 neighbor 171.69.232.90 remote-as 200
 neighbor 171.69.232.90 peer-group external-peers
 neighbor 171.69.232.100 remote-as 300
 neighbor 171.69.232.100 peer-group external-peers
 neighbor 171.69.232.110 remote-as 400
 neighbor 171.69.232.110 peer-group external-peers
 neighbor 171.69.232.110 filter-list 400 in
```

BGP Community with Route Maps Examples

This section contains three examples of the use of BGP communities with route maps.

In the first example, the route map *set-community* is applied to the outbound updates to the neighbor 171.69.232.50. The routes that pass access list 1 have the special community attribute value "no-export." The remaining routes are advertised normally. This special community value automatically prevents the advertisement of those routes by the BGP speakers in autonomous system 200.

```
router bgp 100
 neighbor 171.69.232.50 remote-as 200
 neighbor 171.69.232.50 send-community
 neighbor 171.69.232.50 route-map set-community out
 !
```

```
route-map set-community 10 permit
 match address 1
 set community no-export
 !
route-map set-community 20 permit
 match address 2
```

In the second example, the route map *set-community* is applied to the outbound updates to neighbor 171.69.232.90. All the routes that originate from AS 70 have the community values 200 200 added to their already existing values. All other routes are advertised as normal.

```
route-map bgp 200
 neighbor 171.69.232.90 remote-as 100
 neighbor 171.69.232.90 send-community
 neighbor 171.69.232.90 route-map set-community out
 !
route-map set-community 10 permit
 match as-path 1
 set community 200 200 additive
 !
route-map set-community 20 permit
 match as-path 2
 !
ip as-path access-list 1 permit 70$
ip as-path access-list 2 permit .*
```

In the third example, community-based matching is used to set selectively MED and local-preference for routes from neighbor 171.69.232.55. All the routes that match community list 1 get the MED set to 8000. This includes any routes that have the communities "100 200 300" or "900 901." These routes could have other community values also.

All the routes that pass community list 2 get the local preference set to 500. This includes the routes that have community values 88 or 90. If they belong to any other community, they will not be matched by community list 2.

All the routes that match community list 3 get the local-preference set to 50. Community list 3 will match all the routes, because all the routes are members of the Internet community. Thus, all the remaining routes from neighbor 171.69.232.55 get a local preference 50.

```
router bgp 200
 neighbor 171.69.232.55 remote-as 100
 neighbor 171.69.232.55 route-map filter-on-community in
 !
route-map filter-on-community 10 permit
 match community 1
 set metric 8000
 !
route-map filter-on-community 20 permit
 match community 2 exact-match
 set local-preference 500
 !
```

```
route-map filter-on-community 30 permit
 match community 3
 set local-preference 50
!
ip community-list 1 permit 100 200 300
ip community-list 1 permit 900 901
!
ip community-list 2 permit 88
ip community-list 2 permit 90
!
ip community-list 3 permit internet
```

CHAPTER 21

BGP Commands

Use the commands in this chapter to configure and monitor Border Gateway Protocol (BGP). For BGP configuration information and examples, see Chapter 20, "Configuring BGP."

AGGREGATE-ADDRESS

To create an aggregate entry in a BGP routing table, use the **aggregate-address** router configuration command. To disable this feature, use the **no** form of this command.

> **aggregate-address** *address mask* [**as-set**] [**summary-only**] [**suppress-map** *map-name*]
>   [**advertise-map** *map-name*] [**attribute-map** *map-name*]
> **no aggregate-address** *address mask* [**as-set**] [**summary-only**] [**suppress-map** *map-name*]
>   [**advertise-map** *map-name*] [**attribute-map** *map-name*]

Syntax	Description
address	Aggregate address.
mask	Aggregate mask.
as-set	(Optional.) Generates autonomous system set path information.
summary-only	(Optional.) Filters all more specific routes from updates.
suppress-map *map-name*	(Optional.) Name of route map used to select the routes to be suppressed.
advertise-map *map-name*	(Optional.) Name of route map used to select the routes to create AS-SET origin communities.
attribute-map *map-name*	(Optional.) Name of route map used to set the attribute of the aggregate route.

Default

Disabled

Command Mode

Router configuration

Usage Guidelines

This command first appeared in Cisco IOS Release 10.0.

You can implement aggregate routing in BGP either by redistributing an aggregate route into BGP or by using this conditional aggregate routing feature.

Using the **aggregate-address** command with no arguments will create an aggregate entry in the BGP routing table if there are any more-specific BGP routes available that fall in the specified range. The aggregate route will be advertised as coming from your autonomous system and has the atomic aggregate attribute set to show that information might be missing. (By default, the atomic aggregate attribute is set unless you specify the **as-set** keyword.)

Using the **as-set** keyword creates an aggregate entry using the same rules that the command follows without this keyword, but the path advertised for this route will be an AS_SET consisting of all elements contained in all paths that are being summarized. Do not use this form of **aggregate-address** when aggregating many paths, because this route must be continually withdrawn and re-updated as autonomous system path reachability information for the summarized routes changes.

Using the **summary-only** keyword not only creates the aggregate route (for example, 193.*.*.*) but will also suppress advertisements of more-specific routes to all neighbors. If you only want to suppress advertisements to certain neighbors, you may use the **neighbor distribute-list** command, with caution. If a more specific route leaks out, all BGP speakers will prefer that route over the less-specific aggregate you are generating (using longest-match routing).

Using the **suppress-map** keyword creates the aggregate route but suppresses advertisement of specified routes. You can use the **match** clauses of route maps to selectively suppress some more specific routes of the aggregate and leave others unsuppressed. IP access lists and autonomous system path access lists match clauses are supported.

Example

In the following example, an aggregate address is created. The path advertised for this route will be an AS_SET consisting of all elements contained in all paths that are being summarized.

```
router bgp 5
 aggregate-address 193.0.0.0 255.0.0.0 as-set
```

Related Commands

Search online to find documentation for related commands.

match as-path
match ip address
route-map

AUTO-SUMMARY

To restore the default behavior of automatic summarization of subnet routes into network-level routes, use the **auto-summary** router configuration command. To disable this feature and transmit subprefix routing information across classful network boundaries, use the **no** form of this command.

> **auto-summary**
> **no auto-summary**

Syntax   Description

This command has no arguments or keywords.

Default

Enabled (the software summarizes subprefixes to the classful network boundary when crossing classful network boundaries).

Command Mode

Router configuration

Usage Guidelines

This command first appeared in Cisco IOS Release 10.0.

Route summarization reduces the amount of routing information in the routing tables.

By default, BGP does not accept subnets redistributed from IGP. To advertise and carry subnet routes in BGP, use an explicit **network** command or the **no auto-summary** command. If you disable auto-summarization and have not entered a **network** command, you will not advertise network routes for networks with subnet routes unless they contain a summary route.

Example

In the following example, network numbers are not summarized automatically:

```
router bgp 6
  no auto-summary
```

BGP ALWAYS-COMPARE-MED

To allow the comparison of the Multi Exit Discriminator (MED) for paths from neighbors in different autonomous systems, use the **bgp always-compare-med** router configuration command. To disallow the comparison, use the **no** form of this command.

> **bgp always-compare-med**
> **no bgp always-compare-med**

Syntax   Description

This command has no arguments or keywords.

Default

The Cisco IOS software does not compare MEDs for paths from neighbors in different autonomous systems.

Command Mode

Router configuration

Usage Guidelines

This command first appeared in Cisco IOS Release 11.0.

The MED is one of the parameters that is considered when selecting the best path among many alternative paths. The path with a lower MED is preferred over a path with a higher MED.

By default, during the best-path selection process, MED comparison is done only among paths from the same autonomous system. This command changes the default behavior by allowing comparison of MEDs among paths regardless of the autonomous system from which the paths are received.

Example

In the following example, the BGP speaker in autonomous system 100 is configured to compare MEDs among alternative paths, regardless of the autonomous system from which the paths are received:

```
router bgp 109
 bgp always-compare-med
```

BGP CLIENT-TO-CLIENT REFLECTION

To restore route reflection from a BGP route reflector to clients, use the **bgp client-to-client reflection** router configuration command. To disable client-to-client reflection, use the **no** form of this command.

> **bgp client-to-client reflection**
> **no bgp client-to-client reflection**

Syntax   Description

This command has no arguments or keywords.

Default

When a route reflector is configured, the route reflector reflects routes from a client to other clients.

Command Mode

Router configuration

Usage Guidelines

This command first appeared in Cisco IOS Release 11.1.

By default, the clients of a route reflector are not required to be fully meshed and the routes from a client are reflected to other clients. However, if the clients are fully meshed, route reflection is not required. Use the **no bgp client-to-client reflection** command to disable client-to-client reflection.

If client-to-client reflection is enabled, the clients of a route reflector cannot be members of a peer group.

Example

In the following example, the local router is a route reflector. The three neighbors are fully meshed, so client-to-client reflection is disabled.

```
router bgp 5
 neighbor 155.24.95.22 route-reflector-client
 neighbor 155.24.95.23 route-reflector-client
 neighbor 155.24.95.24 route-reflector-client
 no bgp client-to-client reflection
```

Related Commands

Search online to find documentation for related commands.

bgp cluster-id
neighbor route-reflector-client
show ip bgp

BGP CLUSTER-ID

To configure the cluster ID if the BGP cluster has more than one route reflector, use the **bgp cluster-id** router configuration command. To remove the cluster ID, use the **no** form of this command.

> **bgp cluster-id** *cluster-id*
> **no bgp cluster-id** *cluster-id*

Part II

Command Reference

Syntax	Description
cluster-id	Cluster ID of this router acting as a route reflector; maximum of 4 bytes.

Default

The router ID of the single route reflector in a cluster

Command Mode

Router configuration

Usage Guidelines

This command first appeared in Cisco IOS Release 11.0.

Together, a route reflector and its clients form a *cluster*.

Usually a cluster of clients will have a single route reflector. In that case, the cluster is identified by the router ID of the route reflector. In order to increase redundancy and avoid a single point of failure, a cluster might have more than one route reflector. In this case, all route reflectors in the cluster must be configured with the 4-byte cluster ID so that a route reflector can recognize updates from route reflectors in the same cluster.

If the cluster has more than one route reflector, use this command to configure the cluster ID.

Example

In the following example, the local router is one of the route reflectors serving the cluster. It is configured with the cluster ID to identify the cluster.

```
router bgp 5
  neighbor 198.92.70.24 route-reflector-client
  bgp cluster-id 50000
```

Related Commands

Search online to find documentation for related commands.

bgp client-to-client reflection
neighbor route-reflector-client
show ip bgp

BGP CONFEDERATION IDENTIFIER

To specify a BGP confederation identifier, use the **bgp confederation identifier** router configuration command. To remove the confederation identifier, use the **no** form of this command.

bgp confederation identifier *autonomous-system*
no bgp confederation identifier *autonomous-system*

Syntax

autonomous-system

Description

Autonomous system number that internally includes multiple autonomous systems.

Default

No confederation identifier is configured.

Command Mode

Router configuration

Usage Guidelines

This command first appeared in Cisco IOS Release 10.3.

Another way to reduce the IBGP mesh is to divide an autonomous system into multiple autonomous systems and group them into a single confederation. Each autonomous system is fully meshed within itself, and has a few connections to another autonomous system in the same confederation. Even though the peers in different autonomous systems have EBGP sessions, they exchange routing information as if they are IBGP peers. Specifically, the next-hop and local preference information is preserved. This enables to you to retain a single Interior Gateway Protocol (IGP) for all the autonomous systems. To the outside world, the confederation looks like a single autonomous system.

Example

In the following example, the autonomous system is divided into autonomous systems 4001, 4002, 4003, 4004, 4005, 4006, and 4007 and identified by the confederation identifier 5. Neighbor 1.2.3.4 is someone inside your routing domain confederation. Neighbor 3.4.5.6 is someone outside your routing domain confederation. To the outside world, there appears to be a single autonomous system with the number 5.

```
router bgp 4001
 bgp confederation identifier 5
 bgp confederation peers 4002 4003 4004 4005 4006 4007
 neighbor 1.2.3.4 remote-as 4002
 neighbor 3.4.5.6 remote-as 510
```

Related Commands

Search online to find documentation for related commands.

bgp confederation peers

BGP CONFEDERATION PEERS

To configure the autonomous systems that belong to the confederation, use the **bgp confederation peers** router configuration command. To remove an autonomous system from the confederation, use the **no** form of this command.

bgp confederation peers *autonomous-system* [*autonomous-system*]
no bgp confederation peers *autonomous-system* [*autonomous-system*]

Syntax	Description
autonomous-system	Autonomous system number.

Default

No confederation peers are configured.

Command Mode

Router configuration

Usage Guidelines

This command first appeared in Cisco IOS Release 10.3.

The autonomous systems specified in this command are visible internally to a confederation. Each autonomous system is fully meshed within itself. The **bgp confederation identifier** command specifies the confederation to which the autonomous systems belong.

Example

The following example specifies that autonomous systems 1090, 1091, 1092, and 1093 belong to a single confederation:

```
router bgp 1090
  bgp confederation peers 1091 1092 1093
```

Related Commands

Search online to find documentation for related commands.

bgp confederation identifier

BGP DAMPENING

To enable BGP route dampening or change various BGP route dampening factors, use the **bgp dampening** global configuration command. To disable the feature or restore the default values, use the **no** form of this command.

bgp dampening [*half-life reuse suppress max-suppress-time*] [**route-map** *map*]
no bgp dampening [*half-life reuse suppress max-suppress-time*] [**route-map** *map*]

Syntax	Description
half-life	(Optional.) Time (in minutes) after which a penalty is decreased. Once the route has been assigned a penalty, the penalty is decreased by half after the half-life period (which is 15 minutes by default). The process of reducing the penalty happens every 5 seconds. The range of the half-life period is 1 to 45 minutes. The default is 15 minutes.
reuse	(Optional.) If the penalty for a flapping route decreases enough to fall below this value, the route is unsuppressed. The process of unsuppressing routes occurs at 10-second increments. The range of the reuse value is 1 to 20000; the default is 750.
suppress	(Optional.) A route is suppressed when its penalty exceeds this limit. The range is 1 to 20000; the default is 2000.
max-suppress-time	(Optional.) Maximum time (in minutes) a route can be suppressed. The range is 1 to 20000; the default is 4 times the *half-life*. If the *half-life* value is allowed to default, the maximum suppress time defaults to 60 minutes.
route-map *map*	(Optional.) Name of route map that controls where BGP route dampening is enabled.

Default

Disabled by default.

half-life is 15 minutes
reuse is 750
suppress is 2000
max-suppress-time is 4 times *half-life*

Command Mode

Global configuration

Usage Guidelines

This command first appeared in Cisco IOS Release 11.0.

If this command is used with no arguments, it enables BGP route dampening. The arguments *half-life*, *reuse*, *suppress*, and *max-suppress-time* are position-dependent. Therefore, if any of them are used, they must all be specified.

Example

The following example sets the half-life to 30 minutes, the reuse value to 1500, the suppress value to 10000; and the maximum suppress time to 120 minutes:

```
bgp dampening 30 1500 10000 120
```

Related Commands

Search online to find documentation for related commands.

clear ip bgp dampening
clear ip bgp flap-statistics
show ip bgp dampened-paths
show ip bgp flap-statistics

BGP DEFAULT LOCAL-PREFERENCE

To change the default local preference value, use the **bgp default local-preference** router configuration command. To return to the default setting, use the **no** form of this command.

> **bgp default local-preference** *value*
> **no bgp default local-preference** *value*

Syntax	Description
value	Local preference value from 0 to 4294967295. Higher is more preferred.

Default

Local preference value of 100

Command Mode

Router configuration

Usage Guidelines

This command first appeared in Cisco IOS Release 10.0.

Generally, the default value of 100 allows you to easily define a particular path as less preferable than paths with no local preference attribute. The preference is sent to all routers and access servers in the local autonomous system.

Example

In the following example, the default local preference value is raised from the default of 100 to 200:

```
router bgp 200
  bgp default local-preference 200
```

Related Commands

Search online to find documentation for related commands.

set local-preference

BGP FAST-EXTERNAL-FALLOVER

To immediately reset the BGP sessions of any directly adjacent external peers if the link used to reach them goes down, use the **bgp fast-external-fallover** router configuration command. To disable this feature, use the **no** form of this command.

bgp fast-external-fallover
no bgp fast-external-fallover

Syntax   Description

This command has no arguments or keywords.

Default

Enabled

Command Mode

Router configuration

Usage Guidelines

This command first appeared in Cisco IOS Release 10.0.

Example

In the following example, the automatic resetting of BGP sessions is disabled:

```
router bgp 109
  no bgp fast-external-fallover
```

CLEAR IP BGP

To reset a BGP connection using BGP soft reconfiguration, use the **clear ip bgp** EXEC command at the system prompt.

clear ip bgp {* | *address* | *peer-group name*} [**soft** [**in** | **out**]]

Syntax	Description
*	Resets all current BGP sessions.
address	Resets only the identified BGP neighbor.
peer-group-name	Resets the specified BGP peer group.
soft	(Optional.) Soft reconfiguration.
in | **out**	(Optional.) Triggers inbound or outbound soft reconfiguration. If the **in** or **out** option is not specified, both inbound and outbound soft reconfiguration are triggered.

Part II

Command Reference

Command Mode

EXEC

Usage Guidelines

This command first appeared in Cisco IOS Release 10.0.

If you specify BGP soft reconfiguration, by including the **soft** keyword, the sessions are not reset and the router sends all routing updates again. To generate new inbound updates without resetting the BGP session, the local BGP speaker should store all received updates without modification regardless of whether it is accepted by the inbound policy. This process is memory intensive and should be avoided if possible. Outbound BGP soft configuration does not have any memory overhead. You can trigger an outbound reconfiguration on the other side of the BGP session to make the new inbound policy take effect.

Use this command whenever any of the following changes occur:

- Additions or changes to the BGP-related access lists
- Changes to BGP-related weights
- Changes to BGP-related distribution lists
- Changes in the BGP timer's specifications
- Changes to the BGP administrative distance
- Changes to BGP-related route maps

Example

The following example resets all current BGP sessions:

```
clear ip bgp *
```

Related Commands

Search online to find documentation for related commands.

show ip bgp
timers bgp

CLEAR IP BGP DAMPENING

To clear BGP route dampening information and unsuppress the suppressed routes, use the **clear ip bgp dampening** EXEC command.

clear ip bgp dampening [*address mask*]

Syntax	Description
address	(Optional.) IP address of the network about which to clear dampening information.
mask	(Optional.) Network mask applied to the *address*.

Command Mode

EXEC

Usage Guidelines

This command first appeared in Cisco IOS Release 11.0.

Example

The following example clears route dampening information about the route to network 150.0.0.0 and unsuppresses its suppressed routes:

```
clear ip bgp dampening 150.0.0.0 255.255.0.0
```

Related Commands

Search online to find documentation for related commands.

bgp dampening
show ip bgp dampened-paths

CLEAR IP BGP FLAP-STATISTICS

To clear BGP flap statistics, use the **clear ip bgp flap-statistics** EXEC command.

> **clear ip bgp flap-statistics** [{**regexp** *regexp*} | {**filter-list** *list*} | {*address mask*}]
> **clear ip bgp** *address* **flap-statistics**

Syntax	Description
regexp *regexp*	(Optional.) Clears flap statistics for all the paths that match the regular expression.
filter-list *list*	(Optional.) Clears flap statistics for all the paths that pass the access list.
address	(Optional.) Clears flap statistics for a single entry at this IP address. If this argument is placed before **flap-statistics**, the router clears flap statistics for all paths from the neighbor at this address.
mask	(Optional.) Network mask applied to the *address*.

Command Mode

EXEC

Part II

Command Reference

Usage Guidelines

This command first appeared in Cisco IOS Release 11.0.

If no arguments or keywords are specified, the router clears flap statistics for all routes.

Example

The following example clears all of the flap statistics for paths that pass access list 3:

```
clear ip bgp flap-statistics filter-list 3
```

Related Commands

Search online to find documentation for related commands.

bgp dampening

CLEAR IP BGP PEER-GROUP

To remove all the members of a BGP peer group, use the **clear ip bgp peer-group** EXEC command.

> **clear ip bgp peer-group** *tag*

Syntax	Description
tag	Name of the BGP peer group to clear

Command Mode

EXEC

Usage Guidelines

This command first appeared in Cisco IOS Release 11.0.

Example

The following example removes all members from the BGP peer group *internal*:

```
clear ip bgp peer-group internal
```

Related Commands

Search online to find documentation for related commands.

neighbor peer-group (assigning members)

DEFAULT-INFORMATION ORIGINATE (BGP)

To allow the redistribution of network 0.0.0.0 into BGP, use the **default-information originate** router configuration command. To disable this feature, use the **no** form of this command.

> **default-information originate**
> **no default-information originate**

Syntax   Description

This command has no arguments or keywords.

Default

Disabled

Command Mode

Router configuration

Usage Guidelines

This command first appeared in Cisco IOS Release 10.0.

The same functionality will result from the **network 0.0.0.0** command, using the **network** router configuration command.

Example

The following example configures BGP to redistribute network 0.0.0.0 into BGP:

```
router bgp 164
  default-information originate
```

DEFAULT-METRIC (BGP, OSPF, AND RIP)

To set default metric values for the BGP, OSPF, and RIP routing protocols, use this form of the **default-metric** router configuration command. To return to the default state, use the **no** form of this command.

> **default-metric** *number*
> **no default-metric** *number*

Syntax   *Description*

number   Default metric value appropriate for the specified routing protocol.

Default

Built-in, automatic metric translations, as appropriate for each routing protocol

Command Mode

Router configuration

Usage Guidelines

This command first appeared in Cisco IOS Release 10.0.

The **default-metric** command is used in conjunction with the **redistribute** router configuration command to cause the current routing protocol to use the same metric value for all redistributed routes. A default metric helps solve the problem of redistributing routes with incompatible metrics. Whenever metrics do not convert, using a default metric provides a reasonable substitute and enables the redistribution to proceed.

In BGP, this sets the Multi Exit Discriminator (MED) metric. (The name of this metric for BGP Versions 2 and 3 is INTER_AS.)

Example

The following example shows a router in autonomous system 109 using both the RIP and the OSPF routing protocols. The example advertises OSPF-derived routes using the RIP protocol and assigns the IGRP-derived routes a RIP metric of 10.

```
router rip
 default-metric 10
 redistribute ospf 109
```

Related Commands

Search online to find documentation for related commands.

redistribute

DISTANCE BGP

To allow the use of external, internal, and local administrative distances that could be a better route to a node, use the **distance bgp** router configuration command. To return to the default values, use the **no** form of this command.

> **distance bgp** *external-distance internal-distance local-distance*
> **no distance bgp**

Syntax	Description
external-distance	Administrative distance for BGP external routes. External routes are routes for which the best path is learned from a neighbor external to the autonomous system. Acceptable values are from 1 to 255. The default is 20. Routes with a distance of 255 are not installed in the routing table.
internal-distance	Administrative distance for BGP internal routes. Internal routes are those routes that are learned from another BGP entity within the same autonomous system. Acceptable values are from 1 to 255. The default is 200. Routes with a distance of 255 are not installed in the routing table.
local-distance	Administrative distance for BGP local routes. Local routes are those networks listed with a **network** router configuration command, often as back doors, for that router or for networks that are being redistributed from another process. Acceptable values are from 1 to 255. The default is 200. Routes with a distance of 255 are not installed in the routing table.

Defaults

external-distance: 20
internal-distance: 200
local-distance: 200

Command Mode

Router configuration

Usage Guidelines

This command first appeared in Cisco IOS Release 10.0.

An administrative distance is a rating of the trustworthiness of a routing information source, such as an individual router or a group of routers. Numerically, an administrative distance is an integer between 0 and 255. In general, the higher the value, the lower the trust rating. An administrative distance of 255 means the routing information source cannot be trusted at all and should be ignored.

Use this command if another protocol is known to be able to provide a better route to a node than was actually learned via external BGP, or if some internal routes should really be preferred by BGP.

— **NOTES** —————————————————————

Changing the administrative distance of BGP internal routes is considered dangerous and is not recommended. One problem that can arise is the accumulation of routing table inconsistencies, which can break routing.

Example

In the following example, internal routes are known to be preferable to those learned through the IGP, so the administrative distance values are set accordingly:

```
router bgp 109
 network 131.108.0.0
 neighbor 129.140.6.6 remote-as 123
 neighbor 128.125.1.1 remote-as 47
 distance bgp 20 20 200
```

IP AS-PATH ACCESS-LIST

To define a BGP-related access list, use the **ip as-path access-list** global configuration command. To disable use of the access list, use the **no** form of this command.

ip as-path access-list *access-list-number* {**permit** | **deny**} *as-regular-expression*
no ip as-path access-list *access-list-number* {**permit** | **deny**} *as-regular-expression*

Syntax	Description
access-list-number	Integer from 1 to 199 that indicates the regular expression access list number.
permit	Permits access for matching conditions.
deny	Denies access to matching conditions.
as-regular-expression	Autonomous system in the access list using a regular expression. See Appendix C, "Regular Expressions" in the *Cisco IOS Dial Solutions* book for information about forming regular expressions.

Default

No access lists are defined.

Command Mode

Global configuration

Usage Guidelines

This command first appeared in Cisco IOS Release 10.0.

You can specify an access list filter on both inbound and outbound BGP routes. In addition, you can assign *weights* based on a set of filters. Each filter is an access list based on regular expressions. If the regular expression matches the representation of the autonomous system path of the route as an ASCII string, then the **permit** or **deny** condition applies. The autonomous system path does not contain the local autonomous system number. Use the **ip as-path access-list** global configuration command to define a BGP access list, and the **neighbor** router configuration command to apply a specific access list.

Example

The following example specifies that the BGP neighbor with IP address 128.125.1.1 is not sent advertisements about any path through or from the adjacent autonomous system 123:

```
ip as-path access-list 1 deny _123_
ip as-path access-list 1 deny ^123$

router bgp 109
 network 131.108.0.0
 neighbor 129.140.6.6 remote-as 123
 neighbor 128.125.1.1 remote-as 47
 neighbor 128.125.1.1 filter-list 1 out
```

Related Commands

Search online to find documentation for related commands.

neighbor distribute-list
neighbor filter-list

IP COMMUNITY-LIST

To create a community list for BGP and control access to it, use the **ip community-list** global configuration command. To delete the community list, use the **no** form of this command.

ip community-list *community-list-number* {**permit** | **deny**} *community-number*
no ip community-list *community-list-number*

Syntax	Description
community-list-number	Integer from 1 to 99 that identifies one or more permit or deny groups of communities.
permit	Permits access for a matching condition.
deny	Denies access for a matching condition.
community-number	Community number configured by a **set community** command. Valid value is one of the following:

- A number from 1 to 4294967200. You can specify a single number or multiple numbers separated by a space.
- **internet**—The Internet community.
- **no-export**—Do not advertise this route to an EBGP peer.
- **no-advertise**—Do not advertise this route to any peer (internal or external).

Default

Once you permit a value for the community number, the community list defaults to an implicit deny for everything else.

Command Mode

Global configuration

Usage Guidelines

This command first appeared in Cisco IOS Release 10.3.

Example

In the following example, the Cisco IOS software permits all routes except the routes with the communities 5 and 10 or 10 and 15:

```
ip community-list 1 deny 5 10
ip community-list 1 deny 10 15
ip community-list 1 permit internet
```

Related Commands

Search online to find documentation for related commands.

set community

MATCH AS-PATH

To match a BGP autonomous system path access list, use the **match as-path** route-map configuration command. To remove a path list entry, use the **no** form of this command.

> **match as-path** *path-list-number*
> **no match as-path** *path-list-number*

Syntax	Description
path-list-number	Autonomous system path access list. An integer from 1 to 199.

Default

No path lists are defined.

Command Mode

Route-map configuration

Usage Guidelines

This command first appeared in Cisco IOS Release 10.0.

The values set by the **match** and **set** commands override global values. For example, the weights assigned with the **match as-path** and **set weight** route-map commands override the weights assigned using the **neighbor weight** and **neighbor filter-list** commands.

A route map can have several parts. Any route that does not match at least one **match** clause relating to a **route-map** command will be ignored; that is, the route will not be advertised for outbound route maps and will not be accepted for inbound route maps. If you want to modify only some data, you must configure a second route-map section with an explicit match specified.

The implemented weight is based on the first matched autonomous system path.

Example

In the following example, the autonomous system path is set to match BGP autonomous system path access list 20:

```
route-map igp2bgp
  match as-path 20
```

Related Commands

Search online to find documentation for related commands.

match community-list
match interface
match ip address
match ip next-hop
match ip route-source
match metric
match route-type
match tag
route-map
set as-path
set automatic-tag
set community
set level
set local-preference
set metric
set metric-type
set next-hop
set origin
set tag
set weight

MATCH COMMUNITY-LIST

To match a BGP community, use the **match community-list** route-map configuration command. To remove the community list entry, use the **no** form of this command.

> **match community-list** *community-list-number* [**exact**]
> **no match community-list** *community-list-number* [**exact**]

Syntax	*Description*
community-list-number	Community list number in the range 1 to 99.
exact	(Optional.) Indicates an exact match is required. All of the communities and only those communities in the community list must be present.

Default

No community list is defined.

Command Mode

Route-map configuration

Usage Guidelines

This command first appeared in Cisco IOS Release 10.3.

A route map can have several parts. Any route that does not match at least one **match** clause relating to a **route-map** command will be ignored; that is, the route will not be advertised for outbound route maps and will not be accepted for inbound route maps. If you want to modify only some data, you must configure a second route-map section with an explicit match specified.

Matching based on community list is one of the types of match clauses applicable to BGP.

Examples

In the following example, the routes that match community list 1 will have the weight set to 100. Any route that has community 109 will have the weight set to 100.

```
ip community-list 1 permit 109
!
route-map set_weight
 match community-list 1
 set weight 100
```

In the following example, the routes that match community list 1 will have the weight set to 200. Any route that has community 109 alone will have the weight set to 200.

```
ip community-list 1 permit 109
!
route-map set_weight
 match community-list 1 exact
 set weight 200
```

Related Commands

Search online to find documentation for related commands.

route-map
set weight

NEIGHBOR ADVERTISEMENT-INTERVAL

To set the minimum interval between the sending of BGP routing updates, use the **neighbor advertisement-interval** router configuration command. To remove an entry, use the **no** form of this command.

> **neighbor** {*ip-address* | *peer-group-name*} **advertisement-interval** *seconds*
> **no neighbor** {*ip-address* | *peer-group-name*} **advertisement-interval** *seconds*

Syntax	Description
ip-address	Neighbor's IP address.
peer-group-name	Name of a BGP peer group.
seconds	Time in seconds. Integer from 0 to 600.

Default

30 seconds for external peers and 5 seconds for internal peers.

Command Mode

Router configuration

Usage Guidelines

This command first appeared in Cisco IOS Release 10.0.

If you specify a BGP peer group by using the *peer-group-name* argument, all the members of the peer group will inherit the characteristic configured with this command.

Part
II

Command Reference

Example

In the following example, the minimum time between sending BGP routing updates is set to 10 seconds:

```
router bgp 5
  neighbor 4.4.4.4 advertisement-interval 10
```

Related Commands

Search online to find documentation for related commands.

neighbor peer-group (creating)

NEIGHBOR DEFAULT-ORIGINATE

To allow a BGP speaker (the local router) to send the default route 0.0.0.0 to a neighbor for use as a default route, use the **neighbor default-originate** router configuration command. To remove the default route, use the **no** form of this command.

neighbor {*ip-address* | *peer-group-name*} **default-originate** [**route-map** *map-name*]
no neighbor {*ip-address* | *peer-group-name*} **default-originate** [**route-map** *map-name*]

Syntax	Description
ip-address	Neighbor's IP address.
peer-group-name	Name of a BGP peer group.
route-map *map-name*	(Optional.) Name of the route map. The route map allows route 0.0.0.0 to be injected conditionally.

Default

No default route is sent to the neighbor.

Command Mode

Router configuration

Usage Guidelines

This command first appeared in Cisco IOS Release 11.0.

This command does not require the presence of 0.0.0.0 in the local router. When used with a route map, the default route 0.0.0.0 is injected if the route map contains a **match ip address** clause and there is a route that matches the IP access list exactly. The route map can contain other match clauses also.

Examples

In the following example, the local router injects route 0.0.0.0 to the neighbor 160.89.2.3 unconditionally:

```
router bgp 109
 network 160.89.0.0
 neighbor 160.89.2.3 remote-as 200
 neighbor 160.89.2.3 default-originate
```

In the following example, the local router injects route 0.0.0.0 to the neighbor 160.89.2.3 only if there is a route to 198.92.68.0:

```
router bgp 109
 network 160.89.0.0
 neighbor 160.89.2.3 remote-as 200
 neighbor 160.89.2.3 default-originate route-map default-map
 !
route-map default-map 10 permit
 match ip address 1
 !
access-list 1 permit 198.92.68.0
```

NEIGHBOR DESCRIPTION

To associate a description with a neighbor, use the **neighbor description** router configuration command. To remove the description, use the **no** form of this command.

> **neighbor** {*ip-address* | *peer-group-name*} **description** *text*
> **no neighbor** {*ip-address* | *peer-group-name*} **description** [*text*]

Syntax	Description
text	Text (up to 80 characters) that describes the neighbor.

Default

There is no description of the neighbor.

Command Mode

Router configuration

Usage Guidelines

This command first appeared in Cisco IOS Release 11.3.

Example

In the following example, the description of the neighbor is "peer with abc.com":

```
router bgp 109
 network 160.89.0.0
 neighbor 160.89.2.3 description peer with abc.com
```

NEIGHBOR DISTRIBUTE-LIST

To distribute BGP neighbor information as specified in an access list, use the **neighbor distribute-list** router configuration command. To remove an entry, use the **no** form of this command.

neighbor {*ip-address* | *peer-group-name*} **distribute-list** {*access-list-number* | *name*} {**in** | **out**}
no neighbor {*ip-address* | *peer-group-name*} **distribute-list** {*access-list-number* | *name*} {**in** | **out**}

Syntax	Description
ip-address	Neighbor's IP address.
peer-group-name	Name of a BGP peer group.
access-list-number | *name*	Number or name of a standard or extended access list. It can be an integer from 1 to 199.
in	Access list is applied to incoming advertisements to that neighbor.
out	Access list is applied to outgoing advertisements from that neighbor.

Default

No BGP neighbor is specified.

Command Mode

Router configuration

Usage Guidelines

This command first appeared in Cisco IOS Release 10.0. The *peer-group-name* argument first appeared in Cisco IOS Release 11.0. The *access-list-name* argument first appeared in Cisco IOS Release 11.2.

Using distribute lists is one of two ways to filter BGP advertisements. The other way is to use AS-path filters, as with the **ip as-path access-list** global configuration command and the **neighbor filter-list** command.

If you specify a BGP peer group by using the *peer-group-name* argument, all the members of the peer group will inherit the characteristic configured with this command. Specifying the command with an IP address will override the value inherited from the peer group.

Example

The following example applies list 39 to incoming advertisements to neighbor 120.23.4.1:

```
router bgp 109
 network 131.108.0.0
 neighbor 120.23.4.1 distribute-list 39 in
```

Related Commands

Search online to find documentation for related commands.

ip as-path access-list
neighbor filter-list
neighbor peer-group (creating)

NEIGHBOR EBGP-MULTIHOP

To accept and attempt BGP connections to external peers residing on networks that are not directly connected, use the **neighbor ebgp-multihop** router configuration command. To return to the default, use the **no** form of this command.

> **neighbor** {*ip-address* | *peer-group-name*} **ebgp-multihop** [*ttl*]
> **no neighbor** {*ip-address* | *peer-group-name*} **ebgp-multihop**

Syntax	Description
ip-address	IP address of the BGP-speaking neighbor.
peer-group-name	Name of a BGP peer group.
ttl	(Optional.) Time-to-live in the range 1 to 255 hops.

Default

Only directly connected neighbors are allowed.

Command Mode

Router configuration

Usage Guidelines

This command first appeared in Cisco IOS Release 10.0. The *peer-group-name* argument first appeared in Cisco IOS Release 11.0.

This feature should only be used under the guidance of technical support staff.

If you specify a BGP peer group by using the *peer-group-name* argument, all the members of the peer group will inherit the characteristic configured with this command.

Example

The following example allows connections to or from neighbor 131.108.1.1, which resides on a network that is not directly connected:

```
router bgp 109
  neighbor 131.108.1.1 ebgp-multihop
```

Related Commands

Search online to find documentation for related commands.

neighbor peer-group (creating)

NEIGHBOR FILTER-LIST

To set up a BGP filter, use the **neighbor filter-list** router configuration command. To disable this function, use the **no** form of this command.

> **neighbor** {*ip-address* | *peer-group-name*} **filter-list** *access-list-number* {**in** | **out** |
> **weight** *weight*}
> **no neighbor** {*ip-address* | *peer-group-name*} **filter-list** *access-list-number* {**in** | **out** |
> **weight** *weight*}

Syntax	Description
ip-address	IP address of the neighbor.
peer-group-name	Name of a BGP peer group.
access-list-number	Number of an autonomous system path access list. You define this access list with the **ip as-path access-list** command.
in	Access list to incoming routes.
out	Access list to outgoing routes.
weight *weight*	Assigns a relative importance to incoming routes matching autonomous system paths. Acceptable values are 0 to 65535.

Default

Disabled

Command Mode

Router configuration

Usage Guidelines

This command first appeared in Cisco IOS Release 10.0.

This command establishes filters on both inbound and outbound BGP routes. Any number of weight filters are allowed on a per-neighbor basis, but only one in or out filter is allowed. The weight of a route affects BGP's route-selection rules.

The implemented weight is based on the first matched autonomous system path. Weights indicated when an autonomous system path is matched override the weights assigned by global **neighbor** commands. In other words, the weights assigned with the **match as-path** and **set weight** route-map commands override the weights assigned using the **neighbor weight** and **neighbor filter-list** commands.

See the "Regular Expressions" appendix in the *Dial Solutions Command Reference* for information on forming regular expressions.

If you specify a BGP peer group by using the *peer-group-name* argument, all the members of the peer group will inherit the characteristic configured with this command. Specifying the command with an IP address will override the value inherited from the peer group.

Example

In the following example, the BGP neighbor with IP address 128.125.1.1 is not sent advertisements about any path through or from the adjacent autonomous system 123:

```
ip as-path access-list 1 deny _123_
ip as-path access-list 1 deny ^123$

router bgp 109
 network 131.108.0.0
 neighbor 129.140.6.6 remote-as 123
 neighbor 128.125.1.1 remote-as 47
 neighbor 128.125.1.1 filter-list 1 out
```

Related Commands

Search online to find documentation for related commands.

ip as-path access-list
neighbor distribute-list
neighbor peer-group (creating)
neighbor weight

NEIGHBOR MAXIMUM-PREFIX

To control how many prefixes can be received from a neighbor, use the **neighbor maximum-prefix** router configuration command. To disable this function, use the **no** form of this command.

> **neighbor** {*ip-address* | *peer-group-name*} **maximum-prefix** *maximum* [*threshold*]
> [**warning-only**]
> **no neighbor** {*ip-address* | *peer-group-name*} **maximum-prefix** *maximum*

Syntax	Description
ip-address	IP address of the neighbor.
peer-group-name	Name of a BGP peer group.
maximum	Maximum number of prefixes allowed from this neighbor.
threshold	(Optional.) Integer specifying at what percentage of *maximum* the router starts to generate a warning message. The range is 1 to 100; the default is 75 (percent).
warning-only	(Optional.) Allows the router to generate log message when the *maximum* is exceeded, instead of terminating the peering.

Default

Disabled; there is no limit on the number of prefixes.

Command Mode

Router configuration

Usage Guidelines

This command first appeared in Cisco IOS Release 11.3.

This command allows you to configure a maximum number of prefixes a BGP router is allowed to receive from a peer. It adds another mechanism (in addition to distribute lists, filter lists, and route maps) to control prefixes received from a peer.

When the number of received prefixes exceeds the *maximum* number configured, the router terminates the peering (by default). However, if the keyword **warning-only** is configured, the router instead only sends a log message, but continues peering with the sender. If the peer is terminated, the peer stays down until the **clear ip bgp** command is issued.

Example

In the following example, the maximum number of prefixes allowed from the neighbor at 129.140.6.6 is set to 1000:

```
router bgp 109
 network 131.108.0.0
 neighbor 129.140.6.6 maximum-prefix 1000
```

Part
II

Command Reference

Related Commands

Search online to find documentation for related commands.

clear ip bgp

NEIGHBOR NEXT-HOP-SELF

To disable next-hop processing of BGP updates on the router, use the **neighbor next-hop-self** router configuration command. To disable this feature, use the **no** form of this command.

> **neighbor** {*ip-address* | *peer-group-name*} **next-hop-self**
> **no neighbor** {*ip-address* | *peer-group-name*} **next-hop-self**

Syntax	Description
ip-address	IP address of the BGP-speaking neighbor.
peer-group-name	Name of a BGP peer group.

Default

Disabled

Command Mode

Router configuration

Usage Guidelines

This command first appeared in Cisco IOS Release 10.0. The *peer-group-name* argument first appeared in Cisco IOS Release 11.0.

This command is useful in nonmeshed networks (such as Frame Relay or X.25) where BGP neighbors may not have direct access to all other neighbors on the same IP subnet.

If you specify a BGP peer group by using the *peer-group-name* argument, all the members of the peer group will inherit the characteristic configured with this command. Specifying the command with an IP address will override the value inherited from the peer group.

Example

The following example forces all updates destined for 131.108.1.1 to advertise this router as the next hop:

```
router bgp 109
 neighbor 131.108.1.1 next-hop-self
```

Related Commands

Search online to find documentation for related commands.

neighbor peer-group (creating)

NEIGHBOR PASSWORD

To enable MD5 authentication on a TCP connection between two BGP peers, use the **neighbor password** router configuration command. To disable this feature, use the **no** form of this command.

neighbor {*ip-address* | *peer-group-name*} **password** *string*
no neighbor {*ip-address* | *peer-group-name*} **password**

Syntax	Description
ip-address	IP address of the BGP-speaking neighbor.
peer-group-name	Name of a BGP peer group.
string	Case-sensitive password of up to 80 characters. The first character cannot be a number. The string can contain any alphanumeric characters, including spaces. You cannot specify a password in the format *number-space-anything*. The space after the number causes problems.

Part II

Command Reference

Default

Disabled

Command Mode

Router configuration

Usage Guidelines

This command first appeared in Cisco IOS Release 11.0.

You can invoke authentication between two BGP peers, causing each segment sent on the TCP connection between them to be verified. This feature must be configured with the same password on both BGP peers; otherwise, the connection between them will not be made. The authentication feature uses the MD5 algorithm. Specifying this command causes the generation and checking of the MD5 digest on every segment sent on the TCP connection.

Configuring a password for a neighbor will cause an existing session to be torn down and a new one established.

If you specify a BGP peer group by using the *peer-group-name* argument, all the members of the peer group will inherit the characteristic configured with this command.

If a router has a password configured for a neighbor, but the neighbor router does not, a message such as the following will appear on the console while the routers attempt to establish a BGP session between them:

```
%TCP-6-BADAUTH: No MD5 digest from [peer's IP address]:11003 to [local router's
IP address]:179
```

Similarly, if the two routers have different passwords configured, a message such as the following will appear on the console:

```
%TCP-6-BADAUTH: Invalid MD5 digest from [peer's IP address]:11004 to [local router's
IP address]:179
```

Example

The following example enables the authentication feature between this router and the BGP neighbor at 131.102.1.1. The password that must also be configured for the neighbor is *bla4u00=2nkq*.

```
router bgp 109
  neighbor 131.108.1.1 password bla4u00=2nkq
```

Related Commands

Search online to find documentation for related commands.

neighbor peer-group (creating)

NEIGHBOR PEER-GROUP (ASSIGNING MEMBERS)

To configure a BGP neighbor to be a member of a peer group, use the **neighbor peer-group** router configuration command. To remove the neighbor from the peer group, use the **no** form of this command.

> **neighbor** *ip-address* **peer-group** *peer-group-name*
> **no neighbor** *ip-address* **peer-group** *peer-group-name*

Syntax

Syntax	Description
ip-address	IP address of the BGP neighbor who belongs to the peer group specified by the *tag*.
peer-group-name	Name of the BGP peer group to which this neighbor belongs.

Default

There are no BGP neighbors in a peer group.

Command Mode

Router configuration

Usage Guidelines

This command first appeared in Cisco IOS Release 11.0.

The neighbor at the IP address indicated inherits all the configured options of the peer group.

Example

In the following example, three neighbors are assigned to the peer group called *internal*.

```
router bgp 100
 neighbor internal peer-group
 neighbor internal remote-as 100
 neighbor internal update-source loopback 0
 neighbor internal route-map set-med out
 neighbor internal filter-list 1 out
 neighbor internal filter-list 2 in
 neighbor 171.69.232.53 peer-group internal
 neighbor 171.69.232.54 peer-group internal
 neighbor 171.69.232.55 peer-group internal
 neighbor 171.69.232.55 filter-list 3 in
```

Related Commands

Search online to find documentation for related commands.

neighbor peer-group (creating)

NEIGHBOR PEER-GROUP (CREATING)

To create a BGP peer group, use the **neighbor peer-group** router configuration command. To remove the peer group and all of its members, use the **no** form of this command.

neighbor *peer-group-name* **peer-group**
no neighbor *peer-group-name* **peer-group**

Syntax

peer-group-name

Description

Name of the BGP peer group.

Default

There is no BGP peer group.

Command Mode

Router configuration

Usage Guidelines

This command first appeared in Cisco IOS Release 11.0.

Often in a BGP speaker, there are many neighbors configured with the same update policies (that is, same outbound route maps, distribute lists, filter lists, update source, and so on). Neighbors with the same update policies can be grouped into peer groups to simplify configuration and make update calculation more efficient.

Once a peer group is created with the **neighbor peer-group** command, it can be configured with the **neighbor** commands. By default, members of the peer group inherit all the configuration options of the peer group. Members can also be configured to override the options that do not affect outbound updates.

Peer group members will always inherit the following configuration options: remote-as (if configured), version, update-source, out-route-map, out-filter-list, out-dist-list, minimum-advertisement-interval, and next-hop-self. All the peer group members will inherit changes made to the peer group.

If a peer group is not configured with a remote-as, the members can be configured with the **neighbor** {*ip-address* | *peer-group-name*} **remote-as** command. This command allows you to create peer groups containing EBGP neighbors.

Example for an IBGP Peer Group

In the following example, the peer group named *internal* configures the members of the peer group to be IBGP neighbors. By definition, this is an IBGP peer group because the **router bgp** command and the **neighbor remote-as** command indicate the same autonomous system (in this case, AS 100). All the peer group members use loopback 0 as the update source and use *set-med* as the outbound route-map. The **neighbor internal filter-list 2 in** command shows that, except for 171.69.232.55, all the neighbors have filter-list 2 as the inbound filter list.

```
router bgp 100
 neighbor internal peer-group
 neighbor internal remote-as 100
 neighbor internal update-source loopback 0
 neighbor internal route-map set-med out
 neighbor internal filter-list 1 out
 neighbor internal filter-list 2 in
 neighbor 171.69.232.53 peer-group internal
 neighbor 171.69.232.54 peer-group internal
 neighbor 171.69.232.55 peer-group internal
 neighbor 171.69.232.55 filter-list 3 in
```

Example for an EBGP Peer Group

In the following example, the peer group *external-peers* is defined without the **neighbor remote-as** command. This is what makes it an EBGP peer group. Each individual member of the peer group is configured with its respective AS-number separately. Thus the peer group consists of members from autonomous systems 200, 300, and 400. All the peer group members have *set-metric* route map as an outbound route map and filter-list 99 as an outbound filter list. Except for neighbor 171.69.232.110, all of them have 101 as the inbound filter list.

```
router bgp 100
 neighbor external-peers peer-group
 neighbor external-peers route-map set-metric out
 neighbor external-peers filter-list 99 out
 neighbor external-peers filter-list 101 in
 neighbor 171.69.232.90 remote-as 200
 neighbor 171.69.232.90 peer-group external-peers
 neighbor 171.69.232.100 remote-as 300
 neighbor 171.69.232.100 peer-group external-peers
 neighbor 171.69.232.110 remote-as 400
 neighbor 171.69.232.110 peer-group external-peers
 neighbor 171.69.232.110 filter-list 400 in
```

Related Commands

Search online to find documentation for related commands.

clear ip bgp peer-group
neighbor peer-group (assigning members)
show ip bgp peer-group

NEIGHBOR REMOTE-AS

To add an entry to the BGP neighbor table, use the **neighbor remote-as** router configuration command. To remove an entry from the table, use the **no** form of this command.

neighbor {*ip-address* | *peer-group-name*} **remote-as** *number*
no neighbor {*ip-address* | *peer-group-name*} **remote-as** *number*

Syntax	*Description*
ip-address	Neighbor's IP address.
peer-group-name	Name of a BGP peer group.
number	Autonomous system to which the neighbor belongs.

Default

There are no BGP neighbor peers.

Command Mode

Router configuration

Usage Guidelines

This command first appeared in Cisco IOS Release 10.0. The *peer-group-name* argument first appeared in Cisco IOS Release 11.0.

Specifying a neighbor with an autonomous system number that matches the autonomous system number specified in the **router bgp** global configuration command identifies the neighbor as internal to the local autonomous system. Otherwise, the neighbor is considered external.

If you specify a BGP peer group by using the *peer-group-name* argument, all the members of the peer group will inherit the characteristic configured with this command.

Examples

The following example specifies that a router at the address 131.108.1.2 is a neighbor in autonomous system number 109:

```
router bgp 110
 network 131.108.0.0
 neighbor 131.108.1.2 remote-as 109
```

In the following example, a BGP router is assigned to autonomous system 109, and two networks are listed as originating in the autonomous system. Then the addresses of three remote routers (and their autonomous systems) are listed. The router being configured will share information about networks 131.108.0.0 and 192.31.7.0 with the neighbor routers. The first router listed is in the same Class B network address space, but in a different autonomous system; the second **neighbor** command illustrates specification of an internal neighbor (with the same autonomous system number) at address 131.108.234.2; and the last **neighbor** command specifies a neighbor on a different network.

```
router bgp 109
  network 131.108.0.0
  network 192.31.7.0
  neighbor 131.108.200.1  remote-as 167
  neighbor 131.108.234.2  remote-as 109
  neighbor 150.136.64.19  remote-as  99
```

Related Commands

Search online to find documentation for related commands.

neighbor peer-group (creating)

NEIGHBOR ROUTE-MAP

To apply a route map to incoming or outgoing routes, use the **neighbor route-map** router configuration command. To remove a route map, use the **no** form of this command.

> **neighbor** {*ip-address* | *peer-group-name*} **route-map** *map-name* {**in** | **out**}
> **no neighbor** {*ip-address* | *peer-group-name*} **route-map** *map-name* {**in** | **out**}

Syntax	Description
ip-address	Neighbor's IP address.
peer-group-name	Name of a BGP peer group.
map-name	Name of route map.
in	Apply to incoming routes.
out	Apply to outgoing routes.

Default

No route maps are applied to a peer.

Command Mode

Router configuration

Usage Guidelines

This command first appeared in Cisco IOS Release 10.0.

If an outbound route map is specified, it is proper behavior to only advertise routes that match at least one section of the route map.

If you specify a BGP peer group by using the *peer-group-name* argument, all the members of the peer group will inherit the characteristic configured with this command. Specifying the command with an IP address will override the value inherited from the peer group.

Example

In the following example, route map *internal-map* is applied to incoming route from 198.92.70.24:

```
router bgp 5
 neighbor 198.92.70.24 route-map internal-map in
 !
route-map internal-map
 match as-path 1
 set local-preference 100
```

Related Commands

Search online to find documentation for related commands.

neighbor peer-group (creating)

NEIGHBOR ROUTE-REFLECTOR-CLIENT

To configure the router as a BGP route reflector and configure the specified neighbor as its client, use the **neighbor route-reflector-client** router configuration command. To indicate that the neighbor is not a client, use the **no** form of this command. When all the clients are disabled, the local router is no longer a route reflector.

> **neighbor** *ip-address* **route-reflector-client**
> **no neighbor** *ip-address* **route-reflector-client**

Syntax	Description
ip-address	IP address of the BGP neighbor being identified as a client.

Default

There is no route reflector in the autonomous system.

Command Mode

Router configuration

Usage Guidelines

This command first appeared in Cisco IOS Release 11.1.

By default, all IBGP speakers in an autonomous system must be fully meshed, and neighbors do not readvertise IBGP learned routes to neighbors, thus preventing a routing information loop.

If you use route reflectors, all IBGP speakers need not be fully meshed. In the route reflector model, an internal BGP peer is configured to be a *route reflector* responsible for passing IBGP learned routes to IBGP neighbors. This scheme eliminates the need for each router to talk to every other router.

Use the **neighbor route-reflector-client** command to configure the local router as the route reflector and the specified neighbor as one of its clients. All the neighbors configured with this command will be members of the client group and the remaining IBGP peers will be members of the nonclient group for the local route reflector.

If client-to-client reflection is enabled (by default it is enabled), clients of a route reflector cannot be members of a peer group. The **bgp client-to-client reflection** command controls client-to-client reflection.

Example

In the following example, the local router is a route reflector. It passes learned IBGP routes to the neighbor at 198.92.70.24.

```
router bgp 5
  neighbor 198.92.70.24 route-reflector-client
```

Related Commands

Search online to find documentation for related commands.

bgp client-to-client reflection
bgp cluster-id
show ip bgp

NEIGHBOR SEND-COMMUNITY

To specify that a COMMUNITIES attribute should be sent to a BGP neighbor, use the **neighbor send-community** router configuration command. To remove the entry, use the **no** form of this command.

> **neighbor** {*ip-address* | *peer-group-name*} **send-community**
> **no neighbor** {*ip-address* | *peer-group-name*} **send-community**

Syntax	Description
ip-address	Neighbor's IP address.
peer-group-name	Name of a BGP peer group.

Default

No COMMUNITIES attribute is sent to any neighbor.

Command Mode

Router configuration

Usage Guidelines

This command first appeared in Cisco IOS Release 10.3. The *peer-group-name* argument first appeared in Cisco IOS Release 11.0.

If you specify a BGP peer group by using the *peer-group-name* argument, all the members of the peer group will inherit the characteristic configured with this command.

Example

In the following example, the router belongs to autonomous system 109 and is configured to send the COMMUNITIES attribute to its neighbor at IP address 198.92.70.23:

```
router bgp 109
 neighbor 198.92.70.23 send-community
```

Related Commands

Search online to find documentation for related commands.

match community-list
neighbor peer-group (creating)
set community

NEIGHBOR SOFT-RECONFIGURATION INBOUND

To configure the Cisco IOS software to start storing received updates, use the **neighbor soft-reconfiguration inbound** router configuration command. To not store received updates, use the **no** form of this command.

  neighbor {*ip-address* | *peer-group-name*} **soft-reconfiguration inbound**
  no neighbor {*ip-address* | *peer-group-name*} **soft-reconfiguration inbound**

Syntax	Description
ip-address	IP address of the BGP-speaking neighbor.
peer-group-name	Name of a BGP peer group.

Default

None

Command Mode

Router configuration

Usage Guidelines

This command first appeared in Cisco IOS Release 11.2.

Entering this command starts the storage of received updates. This is required to do inbound soft reconfiguration. Outbound BGP soft reconfiguration does not require inbound soft reconfiguration to be enabled.

If you specify a BGP peer group by using the *peer-group-name* argument, all the members of the peer group will inherit the characteristic configured with this command.

Example

In the following example, inbound soft-reconfiguration is enabled for the neighbor 131.108.1.1. All the updates received from this neighbor will be stored unmodified, regardless of the inbound policy. When inbound soft reconfiguration is done later, the stored information will be used to generate a new set of inbound updates.

```
router bgp 100
  neighbor 131.108.1.1 remote-as 200
  neighbor 131.108.1.1 soft-reconfiguration inbound
```

Related Commands

Search online to find documentation for related commands.

neighbor peer-group (creating)

NEIGHBOR UPDATE-SOURCE

To have the Cisco IOS software allow internal BGP sessions to use any operational interface for TCP connections, use the **neighbor update-source** router configuration command. To restore the interface assignment to the closest interface, which is called the *best local address*, use the **no** form of this command

> **neighbor** {*ip-address* | *peer-group-name*} **update-source** *interface*
> **no neighbor** {*ip-address* | *peer-group-name*} **update-source** *interface*

Syntax	Description
ip-address	IP address of the BGP-speaking neighbor.
peer-group-name	Name of a BGP peer group.
interface	Loopback interface.

Default

Best local address

Command Mode

Router configuration

Usage Guidelines

This command first appeared in Cisco IOS Release 10.0.

If you specify a BGP peer group by using the *peer-group-name* argument, all the members of the peer group will inherit the characteristic configured with this command.

Example

In the following example, BGP TCP connections for the specified neighbor will be sourced with loopback interface's IP address rather than the best local address:

```
router bgp 110
  network 160.89.0.0
  neighbor 160.89.2.3 remote-as 110
  neighbor 160.89.2.3 update-source Loopback0
```

Related Commands

Search online to find documentation for related commands.

neighbor peer-group (creating)

NEIGHBOR VERSION

To configure the Cisco IOS software to accept only a particular BGP version, use the **neighbor version** router configuration command. To use the default version level of a neighbor, use the **no** form of this command.

neighbor {*ip-address* | *peer-group-name*} **version** *value*
no neighbor {*ip-address* | *peer-group-name*} **version** *value*

Syntax	Description
ip-address	IP address of the BGP-speaking neighbor.
peer-group-name	Name of a BGP peer group.
value	BGP version number. The version can be set to 2 to force the software to only use Version 2 with the specified neighbor. The default is to use Version 4 and dynamically negotiate down to Version 2 if requested.

Default

BGP Version 4

Command Mode

Router configuration

Usage Guidelines

This command first appeared in Cisco IOS Release 10.0.

Entering this command disables dynamic version negotiation.

Our implementation of BGP supports BGP Versions 2, 3, and 4. If the neighbor does not accept default Version 4, dynamic version negotiation is implemented to negotiate down to Version 2.

If you specify a BGP peer group by using the *peer-group-name* argument, all the members of the peer group will inherit the characteristic configured with this command.

Example

The following example locks down to Version 4 of the BGP protocol:

```
router bgp 109
  neighbor 131.104.27.2 version 4
```

Related Commands

Search online to find documentation for related commands.

neighbor peer-group (creating)

NEIGHBOR WEIGHT

To assign a weight to a neighbor connection, use the **neighbor weight** router configuration command. To remove a weight assignment, use the **no** form of this command.

> **neighbor** {*ip-address* | *peer-group-name*} **weight** *weight*
> **no neighbor** {*ip-address* | *peer-group-name*} **weight** *weight*

Syntax	Description
ip-address	Neighbor's IP address.
peer-group-name	Name of a BGP peer group.
weight	Weight to assign. Acceptable values are 0 to 65535.

Default

Routes learned through another BGP peer have a default weight of 0 and routes sourced by the local router have a default weight of 32768.

Command Mode

Router configuration

Usage Guidelines

This command first appeared in Cisco IOS Release 10.0.

All routes learned from this neighbor will have the assigned weight initially. The route with the highest weight will be chosen as the preferred route when multiple routes are available to a particular network.

The weights assigned with the **match as-path** and **set weight** route-map commands override the weights assigned using the **neighbor weight** and **neighbor filter-list** commands.

NOTES

For weight changes to take effect, it may be necessary to use **clear ip bgp peer-group ***.

If you specify a BGP peer group by using the *peer-group-name* argument, all the members of the peer group will inherit the characteristic configured with this command.

Example

The following example sets the weight of all routes learned via 151.23.12.1 to 50:

```
router bgp 109
 neighbor 151.23.12.1 weight 50
```

Related Commands

Search online to find documentation for related commands.

neighbor distribute-list
neighbor filter-list
neighbor peer-group (creating)

NETWORK (BGP)

To specify the list of networks for the BGP routing process, use this form of the **network** router configuration command. To remove an entry, use the **no** form of this command.

> **network** *network-number* [**mask** *network-mask*]
> **no network** *network-number* [**mask** *network-mask*]

Syntax	Description
network-number	Network that BGP will advertise.
mask	Network or subnetwork mask.
network-mask	(Optional.) Network mask address.

Default

No networks are specified.

Command Mode

Router configuration

Usage Guidelines

This command first appeared in Cisco IOS Release 10.0.

These types of networks can be learned from connected routes, dynamic routing, and from static route sources.

A maximum of 200 **network** commands may be specified for a single BGP process.

Example

The following example sets up network 131.108.0.0 to be included in the BGP updates:

```
router bgp 120
  network 131.108.0.0
```

Related Commands

Search online to find documentation for related commands.

network backdoor
network mask
network weight
router bgp

NETWORK BACKDOOR

To specify a backdoor route to a BGP border router that will provide better information about the network, use the **network backdoor** router configuration command. To remove an address from the list, use the **no** form of this command.

> **network** *address* **backdoor**
> **no network** *address* **backdoor**

Syntax	Description
address	IP address of the network to which you want a backdoor route.

Default

No network is advertised.

Command Mode

Router configuration

Usage Guidelines

This command first appeared in Cisco IOS Release 10.0.

A backdoor network is treated as a local network, except that it is not advertised.

Example

The following example configures network 131.108.0.0 as a local network and network 192.31.7.0 as a backdoor network:

```
router bgp 109
 network 131.108.0.0
 network 192.31.7.0 backdoor
```

NETWORK WEIGHT

To assign an absolute weight to a BGP network, use the **network weight** router configuration command. To delete an entry, use the **no** form of the command.

network *address mask* **weight** *weight* [**route-map** *map-name*]
no network *address mask* **weight** *weight* [**route-map** *map-name*]

Syntax	Description
address	IP address of the network.
mask	Network mask of the network.
weight	Absolute weight, or importance. It can be an integer from 0 to 65535.
route-map *map-name*	(Optional.) Name of route-map.

Default

Weight is unmodified. Weight is zero if the original default weight has not been modified by other router configuration commands.

Command Mode

Router configuration

Usage Guidelines

This command first appeared in Cisco IOS Release 10.0.

The weight specified by this command overrides a weight assigned by the **redistribute** command.

Example

In the following example, the BGP network has a weight of 100:

```
router bgp 5
 network 193.0.0.0 255.0.0.0 weight 100
```

ROUTER BGP

To configure the Border Gateway Protocol (BGP) routing process, use the **router bgp** global configuration command. To remove a routing process, use the **no** form of this command.

router bgp *autonomous-system*
no router bgp *autonomous-system*

Syntax	Description
autonomous-system	Number of an autonomous system that identifies the router to other BGP routers and tags the routing information passed along.

Default

No BGP routing process is enabled by default.

Command Mode

Global configuration

Usage Guidelines

This command first appeared in Cisco IOS Release 10.0.

This command allows you to set up a distributed routing core that automatically guarantees the loop-free exchange of routing information between autonomous systems.

Example

The following example configures a BGP process for autonomous system 120:

```
router bgp 120
```

Related Commands

Search online to find documentation for related commands.

network (BGP)
timers bgp

SET AS-PATH

To modify an autonomous system path for BGP routes, use the **set as-path** route map configuration command. To not modify the autonomous system path, use the **no** form of this command.

set as-path {**tag** | **prepend** *as-path-string*}
no set as-path {**tag** | **prepend** *as-path-string*}

Syntax	Description
tag	Converts the tag of a route into an autonomous system path. Applies only when redistributing routes into BGP.
prepend *as-path-string*	Appends the string following the keyword **prepend** to the as-path of the route that is matched by the route map. Applies to inbound and outbound BGP route maps.

Default

Autonomous system path is not modified.

Command Mode

Route map configuration

Usage Guidelines

This command first appeared in Cisco IOS Release 11.0.

The only global BGP metric available to influence the best path selection is the AS-PATH length. By varying the length of the AS-PATH, a BGP speaker can influence the best path selection by a peer further away.

By allowing you to convert the tag into an autonomous system path, the **set as-path tag** variation of this command modifies the autonomous system length. The **set as-path prepend** variation allows you to "prepend" an arbitrary autonomous system path string to BGP routes. Usually the local autonomous system number is prepended multiple times. This increases the autonomous system path length.

Examples

The following example converts the tag of a redistributed route into an autonomous system path:

```
route-map set-as-path-from-tag
 match as-path 2
 set as-path prepend 100 100 100
 !
router bgp 100
 redistribute ospf 109 route-map set-as-path-from-tag
```

The following example prepends 100 100 100 to all the routes advertised to 131.108.1.1:

```
route-map set-as-path
 match as-path 1
 set as-path prepend 100 100 100
 !
router bgp 100
 neighbor 131.108.1.1 route-map set-as-path out
```

Related Commands

Search online to find documentation for related commands.

match as-path
match community-list
match interface
match ip address
match ip next-hop
match ip route-source
match metric
match route-type
match tag
route-map
set automatic-tag
set community
set level
set local-preference
set metric
set metric-type
set next-hop
set origin
set tag
set weight

SET COMMUNITY

To set the BGP COMMUNITIES attribute, use the **set community** route-map configuration command. To delete the entry, use the **no** form of this command.

> **set community** {*community-number* [**additive**]} | **none**
> **no set community** {*community-number* [**additive**]} | **none**

Syntax	Description
community-number	Valid values are 1 to 4294967200, **no-export**, or **no-advertise**.
additive	(Optional.) Adds the community to the already existing communities.
none	Removes the COMMUNITY attribute from the prefixes that pass the route-map.

Default

No BGP COMMUNITIES attributes exist.

Command Mode

Route-map configuration

Usage Guidelines

This command first appeared in Cisco IOS Release 10.3.

You must have a match clause (even if it points to a "permit everything" list) if you want to set tags.

Use the **route-map** global configuration command, and the **match** and **set** route-map configuration commands, to define the conditions for redistributing routes from one routing protocol into another. Each **route-map** command has a list of **match** and **set** commands associated with it. The **match** commands specify the *match criteria*—the conditions under which redistribution is allowed for the current **route-map** command. The **set** commands specify the *set actions*—the particular redistribution actions to perform if the criteria enforced by the **match** commands are met. The **no route-map** command deletes the route map.

The **set** route-map configuration commands specify the redistribution *set actions* to be performed when all of a route map's match criteria are met. When all match criteria are met, all set actions are performed.

Example

In the following example, routes that pass the autonomous system path access list 1 have the community set to 109. Routes that pass the autonomous system path access list 2 have the community set to no-export (these routes will not be advertised to any EBGP peers).

```
route-map set_community 10 permit
 match as-path 1
 set community 109

route-map set_community 20 permit
 match as-path 2
 set community no-export
```

Related Commands

Search online to find documentation for related commands.

match community-list
route-map

SET DAMPENING

To set the BGP route dampening factors, use the **set dampening** route-map configuration command. To disable this function, use the **no** form of this command.

set dampening *half-life reuse suppress max-suppress-time*
no set dampening

Syntax	Description
half-life	Time (in minutes) after which a penalty is decreased. Once the route has been assigned a penalty, the penalty is decreased by half after the half-life period (which is 15 minutes by default). The process of reducing the penalty happens every 5 seconds. The range of the half-life period is 1 to 45 minutes. The default is 15 minutes.
reuse	If the penalty for a flapping route decreases enough to fall below this value, the route is unsuppressed. The process of unsuppressing routes occurs at 10-second increments. The range of the reuse value is 1 to 20000; the default is 750.
suppress	A route is suppressed when its penalty exceeds this limit. The range is 1 to 20000; the default is 2000.
max-suppress-time	Maximum time (in minutes) a route can be suppressed. The range is 1 to 20000; the default is 4 times the *half-life*. If the *half-life* value is allowed to default, the maximum suppress time defaults to 60 minutes.

Default

Disabled

Command Mode

Route-map configuration

Usage Guidelines

This command first appeared in Cisco IOS Release 11.0.

You must have a match clause (even if it points to a "permit everything" list) if you want to set tags.

Use the **route-map** global configuration command, and the **match** and **set** route-map configuration commands, to define the conditions for redistributing routes from one routing protocol into another. Each **route-map** command has a list of **match** and **set** commands associated with it. The **match** commands specify the *match criteria*—the conditions under which redistribution is allowed for the current **route-map** command. The **set** commands specify the *set actions*—the particular redistribution actions to perform if the criteria enforced by the **match** commands are met. The **no route-map** command deletes the route map.

The **set** route-map configuration commands specify the redistribution *set actions* to be performed when all of a route map's match criteria are met. When all match criteria are met, all set actions are performed.

Example

The following example sets the half-life to 30 minutes, the reuse value to 1500, the suppress value to 10000; and the maximum suppress time to 120 minutes:

```
route-map tag
 match as path 10
 set dampening 30 1500 10000 120
 !
router bgp 100
 neighbor 171.69.233.52 route-map tag in
```

Related Commands

Search online to find documentation for related commands.

match as-path
match community-list
match interface
match ip address
match ip next-hop
match ip route-source
match metric
match route-type
match tag
route-map
set as-path
set automatic-tag
set community
set level
set local-preference
set metric
set metric-type
set next-hop
set origin
set tag
set weight
show route-map

SET METRIC-TYPE INTERNAL

To set the MED value on prefixes advertised to EBGP neighbors to match the IGP metric of the next hop, use the **set metric internal** route-map configuration command. To return to the default, use the **no** form of this command.

set metric-type internal
no set metric-type internal

Syntax   Description

This command has no arguments or keywords.

Default

Disabled

Command Mode

Route-map configuration

Usage Guidelines

This command first appeared in Cisco IOS Release 10.3.

This command will cause BGP to advertise a MED that corresponds to the IGP metric associated with the NEXT HOP of the route. This command applies to generated, iBGP-, and eBGP-derived routes.

If this command is used, multiple BGP speakers in a common AS can advertise different MEDs for a particular prefix. Also, note that if the IGP metric changes, BGP will not readvertise the route.

You must have a match clause (even if it points to a "permit everything" list) if you want to set tags.

Use the **route-map** global configuration command, and the **match** and **set** route-map configuration commands, to define the conditions for redistributing routes from one routing protocol into another. Each **route-map** command has a list of **match** and **set** commands associated with it. The **match** commands specify the *match criteria*—the conditions under which redistribution is allowed for the current **route-map** command. The **set** commands specify the *set actions*—the particular redistribution actions to perform if the criteria enforced by the **match** commands are met. The **no route-map** command deletes the route map.

The **set** route-map configuration commands specify the redistribution *set actions* to be performed when all of a route map's match criteria are met. When all match criteria are met, all set actions are performed.

Example

In the following example, the MED for all the advertised routes to neighbor 160.89.2.3 is set to the corresponding IGP metric of the nexthop:

```
router bgp 109
 network 160.89.0.0
 neighbor 160.89.2.3 remote-as 200
 neighbor 160.89.2.3 route-map setMED out
!
route-map setMED permit 10
 match as-path 1
 set metric-type internal
!
 ip as-path access-list 1 permit .*
```

Related Commands

Search online to find documentation for related commands.

route-map

SET ORIGIN

To set the BGP origin code, use the **set origin** route-map configuration command. To delete an entry, use the **no** form of this command.

> **set origin** {**igp** | **egp** *autonomous-system* | **incomplete**}

Syntax	Description
igp	Remote IGP.
egp	Local EGP.
autonomous-system	Remote autonomous system. This is an integer from 0 to 65535.
incomplete	Unknown heritage.

Default

Default origin, based on route in main IP routing table.

Command Mode

Route-map configuration

Usage Guidelines

This command first appeared in Cisco IOS Release 10.0.

You must have a match clause (even if it points to a "permit everything" list) if you want to set tags.

Use the **route-map** global configuration command with **match** and **set** route-map configuration commands to define the conditions for redistributing routes from one routing protocol into another. Each **route-map** command has a list of **match** and **set** commands associated with it. The **match** commands specify the *match criteria*—the conditions under which redistribution is allowed for the current **route-map** command. The **set** commands specify the *set actions*—the particular redistribution actions to perform if the criteria enforced by the **match** commands are met. The **no route-map** command deletes the route map.

The **set** route-map configuration commands specify the redistribution *set actions* to be performed when all of a route map's match criteria are met. When all match criteria are met, all set actions are performed.

Example

In the following example, routes that pass the route map have the origin set to IGP:

```
route-map set_origin
 match as-path 10
 set origin igp
```

Related Commands

Search online to find documentation for related commands.

match as-path
match community-list
match interface
match ip address
match ip next-hop
match ip route-source
match metric
match route-type
match tag
route-map
set as-path
set automatic tag
set community
set level
set local-preference
set metric
set metric-type
set next-hop
set tag
set weight

SET WEIGHT

To specify the BGP weight for the routing table, use the **set weight** route-map configuration command. To delete an entry, use the **no** form of this command.

> **set weight** *weight*
> **no set weight** *weight*

Syntax	Description
weight	Weight value. It can be an integer from 0 to 65535.

Default

The weight is not changed by the specified route map.

Command Mode

Route-map configuration

Usage Guidelines

This command first appeared in Cisco IOS Release 10.0.

You must have a match clause (even if it points to a "permit everything" list) if you want to set tags.

The implemented weight is based on the first matched autonomous system path. Weights indicated when an autonomous system path is matched override the weights assigned by global **neighbor** commands. In other words, the weights assigned with the **match as-path** and **set weight** route-map commands override the weights assigned using the **neighbor weight** and **neighbor filter-list** commands.

Example

In the following example, the BGP weight for the routes matching the autonomous system path access list is set to 200:

```
route-map set-weight
  match as-path 10
  set weight 200
```

Related Commands

Search online to find documentation for related commands.

match as-path
match community-list
match interface
match ip address
match ip next-hop
match ip route-source
match metric
match route-type
match tag
route-map
set as-path
set automatic-tag
set community
set level
set local-preference
set metric
set metric-type
set next-hop
set origin
set tag

SHOW IP BGP

To display entries in the BGP routing table, use the **show ip bgp** EXEC command.

show ip bgp [*network*] [*network-mask*] [**longer-prefixes**]

Syntax	Description
network	(Optional.) Network number, entered to display a particular network in the BGP routing table.
network-mask	(Optional.) Displays all BGP routes matching the address/mask pair.
longer-prefixes	(Optional.) Displays route and more specific routes.

Command Mode

EXEC

Usage Guidelines

This command first appeared in Cisco IOS Release 10.0.

Sample Displays

The following is sample output from the **show ip bgp** command:

```
Router# show ip bgp

BGP table version is 716977, local router ID is 193.0.32.1
Status codes: s suppressed, * valid, > best, i - internal
Origin codes: i - IGP, e - EGP, ? - incomplete

     Network          Next Hop          Metric LocPrf Weight Path
 *   i3.0.0.0         193.0.22.1             0    100      0 1800 1239 ?
 *>i                  193.0.16.1             0    100      0 1800 1239 ?
 *   i6.0.0.0         193.0.22.1             0    100      0 1800 690 568 ?
 *>i                  193.0.16.1             0    100      0 1800 690 568 ?
 *   i7.0.0.0         193.0.22.1             0    100      0 1800 701 35 ?
 *>i                  193.0.16.1             0    100      0 1800 701 35 ?
 *                    198.92.72.24                          0 1878 704 701 35 ?
 *   i8.0.0.0         193.0.22.1             0    100      0 1800 690 560 ?
 *>i                  193.0.16.1             0    100      0 1800 690 560 ?
 *                    198.92.72.24                          0 1878 704 701 560 ?
 *   i13.0.0.0        193.0.22.1             0    100      0 1800 690 200 ?
 *>i                  193.0.16.1             0    100      0 1800 690 200 ?
 *                    198.92.72.24                          0 1878 704 701 200 ?
 *   i15.0.0.0        193.0.22.1             0    100      0 1800 174 ?
 *>i                  193.0.16.1             0    100      0 1800 174 ?
 *   i16.0.0.0        193.0.22.1             0    100      0 1800 701 i
 *>i                  193.0.16.1             0    100      0 1800 701 i
 *                    198.92.72.24                          0 1878 704 701 i
```

Table 21–1 describes significant fields shown in the display.

Table 21–1 *Show IP BGP Field Descriptions*

Field	Description
BGP table version	Internal version number of the table. This number is incremented whenever the table changes.
local router ID	IP address of the router.
Status codes	Status of the table entry. The status is displayed at the beginning of each line in the table. It can be one of the following values: s—The table entry is suppressed. *—The table entry is valid. >—The table entry is the best entry to use for that network. i—The table entry was learned via an internal BGP session.
Origin codes	Indicates the origin of the entry. The origin code is placed at the end of each line in the table. It can be one of the following values: i—Entry originated from IGP and was advertised with a **network** router configuration command. e—Entry originated from EGP. ?—Origin of the path is not clear. Usually, this is a router that is redistributed into BGP from an IGP.
Network	IP address of a network entity.
Next Hop	IP address of the next system that is used when forwarding a packet to the destination network. An entry of 0.0.0.0 indicates that the router has some non-BGP routes to this network.
Metric	If shown, this is the value of the interautonomous system metric. This field is frequently not used.
LocPrf	Local preference value as set with the **set local-preference** route-map configuration command. The default value is 100.
Weight	Weight of the route as set via autonomous system filters.
Path	Autonomous system paths to the destination network. There can be one entry in this field for each autonomous system in the path.

The following is sample output from the **show ip bgp** command when you specify **longer-prefixes**:

```
Router# show ip bgp 198.92.0.0 255.255.0.0 longer-prefixes

BGP table version is 1738, local router ID is 198.92.72.24
Status codes: s suppressed, * valid, > best, i - internal
Origin codes: i - IGP, e - EGP, ? - incomplete

      Network          Next Hop          Metric LocPrf Weight Path
*> 198.92.0.0          198.92.72.30        8896         32768 ?
*                      198.92.72.30                         0 109 108 ?
*> 198.92.1.0          198.92.72.30        8796         32768 ?
*                      198.92.72.30                         0 109 108 ?
*> 198.92.11.0         198.92.72.30       42482         32768 ?
*                      198.92.72.30                         0 109 108 ?
*> 198.92.14.0         198.92.72.30        8796         32768 ?
*                      198.92.72.30                         0 109 108 ?
*> 198.92.15.0         198.92.72.30        8696         32768 ?
*                      198.92.72.30                         0 109 108 ?
*> 198.92.16.0         198.92.72.30        1400         32768 ?
*                      198.92.72.30                         0 109 108 ?
*> 198.92.17.0         198.92.72.30        1400         32768 ?
*                      198.92.72.30                         0 109 108 ?
*> 198.92.18.0         198.92.72.30        8876         32768 ?
*                      198.92.72.30                         0 109 108 ?
*> 198.92.19.0         198.92.72.30        8876         32768 ?
*                      198.92.72.30                         0 109 108 ?
```

SHOW IP BGP CIDR-ONLY

To display routes with nonnatural network masks (that is, classless interdomain routing, or CIDR), use the **show ip bgp cidr-only** privileged EXEC command.

show ip bgp cidr-only

Syntax   Description

This command has no arguments or keywords.

Command Mode

Privileged EXEC

Usage Guidelines

This command first appeared in Cisco IOS Release 10.0.

Sample Display

The following is sample output from the **show ip bgp cidr-only** command:

```
Router# show ip bgp cidr-only

BGP table version is 220, local router ID is 198.92.73.131
Status codes: s suppressed, * valid, > best, i - internal
Origin codes: i - IGP, e - EGP, ? - incomplete

   Network          Next Hop           Metric LocPrf Weight Path
*> 192.0.0.0/8      198.92.72.24                        0 1878 ?
*> 198.92.0.0/16    198.92.72.30                        0 108 ?
```

Table 21–2 describes significant fields shown in the display.

Part
II

Command Reference

Table 21–2   *Show IP BGP CIDR-Only Field Descriptions*

Field	Description
BGP table version is 220	Internal version number for the table. This number is incremented any time the table changes.
local router ID	An Internet address of the router.
Status codes	s—The table entry is suppressed.
	*—The table entry is valid.
	>—The table entry is the best entry to use for that network.
	i—The table entry was learned via an internal BGP session.
Origin codes	Indicates the origin of the entry. The origin code is placed at the end of each line in the table. It can be one of the following values:
	i—Entry originated from IGP and was advertised with a **network** router configuration command.
	e—Entry originated from EGP.
	?—Origin of the path is not clear. Usually, this is a router that is redistributed into BGP from an IGP.
Network	Internet address of the network the entry describes.
Next Hop	IP address of the next system to use when forwarding a packet to the destination network. An entry of 0.0.0.0 indicates that the access server has some non-BGP route to this network.
Metric	If shown, this is the value of the interautonomous system metric. This field is frequently not used.
LocPrf	Local preference value. Default is 100.

Table 21–2 *Show IP BGP CIDR-Only Field Descriptions, Continued*

Field	Description
Weight	Set through the use of autonomous system filters.
Path	Autonomous system paths to the destination network. There can be one entry in this field for each autonomous system in the path. At the end of the path is the origin code for the path.
	i—The entry was originated with the IGP and advertised with a **network** router configuration command.
	e—The route originated with EGP.
	?—The origin of the path is not clear. Usually this is a path that is redistributed into BGP from an IGP.

SHOW IP BGP COMMUNITY

To display routes that belong to specified BGP communities, use the **show ip bgp community** EXEC command.

> **show ip bgp community** *community-number* [**exact**]

Syntax	*Description*
community-number	Valid value is community number in the range 1 to 4294967200, **internet**, **no-export**, or **no-advertise**.
exact	(Optional.) Displays only routes that have exactly the same specified communities.

Command Mode

EXEC

Usage Guidelines

This command first appeared in Cisco IOS Release 10.3.

Sample Display

The following is sample output from the **show ip bgp community** command:

```
Router# show ip bgp community 10

BGP table version is 716977, local router ID is 193.0.32.1
Status codes: s suppressed, * valid, > best, i - internal
Origin codes: i - IGP, e - EGP, ? - incomplete
```

```
        Network          Next Hop        Metric LocPrf Weight Path
 * i3.0.0.0              193.0.22.1         0     100     0 1800 1239 ?
 *>i                     193.0.16.1         0     100     0 1800 1239 ?
 * i6.0.0.0              193.0.22.1         0     100     0 1800 690 568 ?
 *>i                     193.0.16.1         0     100     0 1800 690 568 ?
 * i7.0.0.0              193.0.22.1         0     100     0 1800 701 35 ?
 *>i                     193.0.16.1         0     100     0 1800 701 35 ?
 *                       198.92.72.24                     0 1878 704 701 35 ?
 * i8.0.0.0              193.0.22.1         0     100     0 1800 690 560 ?
 *>i                     193.0.16.1         0     100     0 1800 690 560 ?
 *                       198.92.72.24                     0 1878 704 701 560 ?
 * i13.0.0.0             193.0.22.1         0     100     0 1800 690 200 ?
 *>i                     193.0.16.1         0     100     0 1800 690 200 ?
 *                       198.92.72.24                     0 1878 704 701 200 ?
 * i15.0.0.0             193.0.22.1         0     100     0 1800 174 ?
 *>i                     193.0.16.1         0     100     0 1800 174 ?
 * i16.0.0.0             193.0.22.1         0     100     0 1800 701 i
 *>i                     193.0.16.1         0     100     0 1800 701 i
 *                       198.92.72.24                     0 1878 704 701 i
```

Table 21–3 describes significant fields shown in the display.

Table 21–3   *Show IP BGP Community Field Descriptions*

Field	Description
BGP table version	Internal version number of the table. This number is incremented whenever the table changes.
local router ID	IP address of the router.
Status codes	Status of the table entry. The status is displayed at the beginning of each line in the table. It can be one of the following values: s—The table entry is suppressed. *—The table entry is valid. >—The table entry is the best entry to use for that network. i—The table entry was learned via an internal BGP session.
Origin codes	Indicates the origin of the entry. The origin code is placed at the end of each line in the table. It can be one of the following values: i—Entry originated from IGP and was advertised with a **network** router configuration command. e—Entry originated from EGP. ?—Origin of the path is not clear. Usually, this is a router that is redistributed into BGP from an IGP.
Network	IP address of a network entity.

Table 21–3   *Show IP BGP Community Field Descriptions, Continued*

Field	Description
Next Hop	IP address of the next system that is used when forwarding a packet to the destination network. An entry of 0.0.0.0 indicates that the router has some non-BGP routes to this network.
Metric	If shown, this is the value of the interautonomous system metric. This field is frequently not used.
LocPrf	Local preference value as set with the **set local-preference** route-map configuration command. The default value is 100.
Weight	Weight of the route as set via autonomous system filters.
Path	Autonomous system paths to the destination network. There can be one entry in this field for each autonomous system in the path.

SHOW IP BGP COMMUNITY-LIST

To display routes that are permitted by the BGP community list, use the **show ip bgp community-list** EXEC command.

> **show ip bgp community-list** *community-list-number* [**exact**]

Syntax	Description
community-list-number	Community list number in the range 1 to 99.
exact	(Optional.) Displays only routes that have an exact match.

Command Mode

EXEC

Usage Guidelines

This command first appeared in Cisco IOS Release 10.3.

Sample Display

The following is sample output of the **show ip bgp community-list** command:

```
Router# show ip bgp community-list 20

BGP table version is 716977, local router ID is 193.0.32.1
Status codes: s suppressed, * valid, > best, i - internal
Origin codes: i - IGP, e - EGP, ? - incomplete

   Network          Next Hop         Metric LocPrf Weight Path
 * i3.0.0.0         193.0.22.1            0    100      0 1800 1239 ?
 *>i                193.0.16.1            0    100      0 1800 1239 ?
```

```
 * i6.0.0.0        193.0.22.1        0    100    0 1800 690 568 ?
 *>i               193.0.16.1        0    100    0 1800 690 568 ?
 * i7.0.0.0        193.0.22.1        0    100    0 1800 701 35 ?
 *>i               193.0.16.1        0    100    0 1800 701 35 ?
 *                 198.92.72.24                  0 1878 704 701 35 ?
 * i8.0.0.0        193.0.22.1        0    100    0 1800 690 560 ?
 *>i               193.0.16.1        0    100    0 1800 690 560 ?
 *                 198.92.72.24                  0 1878 704 701 560 ?
 * i13.0.0.0       193.0.22.1        0    100    0 1800 690 200 ?
 *>i               193.0.16.1        0    100    0 1800 690 200 ?
 *                 198.92.72.24                  0 1878 704 701 200 ?
 * i15.0.0.0       193.0.22.1        0    100    0 1800 174 ?
 *>i               193.0.16.1        0    100    0 1800 174 ?
 * i16.0.0.0       193.0.22.1        0    100    0 1800 701 i
 *>i               193.0.16.1        0    100    0 1800 701 i
 *                 198.92.72.24                  0 1878 704 701 i
```

Table 21–4 describes significant fields shown in the display.

Table 21–4   *Show IP BGP Community List Field Descriptions*

Field	Description
BGP table version	Internal version number of the table. This number is incremented whenever the table changes.
local router ID	IP address of the router.
Status codes	Status of the table entry. The status is displayed at the beginning of each line in the table. It can be one of the following values: s—The table entry is suppressed. *—The table entry is valid. >—The table entry is the best entry to use for that network. i—The table entry was learned via an internal BGP session.
Origin codes	Indicates the origin of the entry. The origin code is placed at the end of each line in the table. It can be one of the following values: i—Entry originated from IGP and was advertised with a **network** router configuration command. e—Entry originated from EGP. ?—Origin of the path is not clear Usually, this is a router that is redistributed into BGP from an IGP.
Network	IP address of a network entity.

Table 21–4 *Show IP BGP Community List Field Descriptions, Continued*

Field	Description
Next Hop	IP address of the next system that is used when forwarding a packet to the destination network. An entry of 0.0.0.0 indicates that the router has some non-BGP routes to this network.
Metric	If shown, this is the value of the interautonomous system metric. This field is frequently not used.
LocPrf	Local preference value as set with the **set local-preference** route-map configuration command. The default value is 100.
Weight	Weight of the route as set via autonomous system filters.
Path	Autonomous system paths to the destination network. There can be one entry in this field for each autonomous system in the path.

SHOW IP BGP DAMPENED-PATHS

To display BGP dampened routes, use the **show ip bgp dampened-paths** EXEC command.

> **show ip bgp dampened-paths**

Syntax   Description

This command has no arguments or keywords.

Command Mode

EXEC

Usage Guidelines

This command first appeared in Cisco IOS Release 11.0.

Sample Display

The following is sample output from the **show ip bgp dampened-paths** command:

```
Router# show ip bgp dampened-paths
BGP table version is 10, local router ID is 171.69.232.182
Status codes: s suppressed, d damped, h history, * valid, > best, i -
internal
Origin codes: i - IGP, e - EGP, ? - incomplete

   Network          From           Reuse    Path
*d 10.0.0.0         171.69.232.177  00:18:4 100 ?
*d 12.0.0.0         171.69.232.177  00:28:5 100 ?
```

Table 21–5 describes the fields in the display.

Table 21–5 *Show IP BGP Dampened-Paths Field Descriptions*

Field	Description
BGP table version	Internal version number for the table. This number is incremented any time the table changes.
local router	IP address of the router where route dampening is enabled.
*d Network	Route to the network indicated is dampened.
From	IP address of the peer that advertised this path.
Reuse	Time (in hours:minutes:seconds) after which the path will be made available.
Path	AS-path of the route that is being dampened.

Related Commands

Search online to find documentation for related commands.

bgp dampening
clear ip bgp dampening

SHOW IP BGP FILTER-LIST

To display routes that conform to a specified filter list, use the **show ip bgp filter-list** privileged EXEC command.

> **show ip bgp filter-list** *access-list-number*

Syntax | Description

access-list-number — Number of an autonomous system path access list. It can be a number from 1 to 199.

Command Mode

Privileged EXEC

Usage Guidelines

This command first appeared in Cisco IOS Release 10.0.

Sample Display

The following is sample output from the **show ip bgp filter-list** command:

```
Router# show ip bgp filter-list 2
```

```
BGP table version is 1738, local router ID is 198.92.72.24
Status codes: s suppressed, * valid, > best, i - internal
Origin codes: i - IGP, e - EGP, ? - incomplete

        Network           Next Hop         Metric LocPrf Weight Path
                                                         0 109 108 ?
    *   198.92.0.0        198.92.72.30                   0 109 108 ?
    *   198.92.1.0        198.92.72.30                   0 109 108 ?
    *   198.92.11.0       198.92.72.30                   0 109 108 ?
    *   198.92.14.0       198.92.72.30                   0 109 108 ?
    *   198.92.15.0       198.92.72.30                   0 109 108 ?
    *   198.92.16.0       198.92.72.30                   0 109 108 ?
    *   198.92.17.0       198.92.72.30                   0 109 108 ?
    *   198.92.18.0       198.92.72.30                   0 109 108 ?
    *   198.92.19.0       198.92.72.30                   0 109 108 ?
    *   198.92.24.0       198.92.72.30                   0 109 108 ?
    *   198.92.29.0       198.92.72.30                   0 109 108 ?
    *   198.92.30.0       198.92.72.30                   0 109 108 ?
    *   198.92.33.0       198.92.72.30                   0 109 108 ?
    *   198.92.35.0       198.92.72.30                   0 109 108 ?
    *   198.92.36.0       198.92.72.30                   0 109 108 ?
    *   198.92.37.0       198.92.72.30                   0 109 108 ?
    *   198.92.38.0       198.92.72.30                   0 109 108 ?
    *   198.92.39.0       198.92.72.30                   0 109 108 ?
```

Table 21–6 describes significant fields shown in the display.

Table 21–6   *Show IP BGP Filter-List Field Descriptions*

Field	Description
BGP table version	Internal version number for the table. This number is incremented any time the table changes.
local router ID	An Internet address of the access server.
Status codes	s—The table entry is suppressed. *—The table entry is valid. >—The table entry is the best entry to use for that network. i—The table entry was learned via an internal BGP session.
Origin codes	Indicates the origin of the entry. The origin code is placed at the end of each line in the table. It can be one of the following values: i—Entry originated from IGP and was advertised with a **network** router configuration command. e—Entry originated from EGP. ?—Origin of the path is not clear. Usually, this is a router that is redistributed into BGP from an IGP.
Network	Internet address of the network the entry describes.

Table 21–6 *Show IP BGP Filter-List Field Descriptions, Continued*

Field	Description
Next Hop	IP address of the next system to use when forwarding a packet to the destination network. An entry of 0.0.0.0 indicates that the access server has some non-BGP route to this network.
Metric	If shown, this is the value of the interautonomous system metric. This field is frequently not used.
LocPrf	Local preference value. Default is 100.
Weight	Set through the use of autonomous system filters.
Path	Autonomous system paths to the destination network. There can be one entry in this field for each autonomous system in the path. At the end of the path is the origin code for the path. i—The entry was originated with the IGP and advertised with a **network** router configuration command. e—The route originated with EGP. ?—The origin of the path is not clear. Usually this is a path that is redistributed into BGP from an IGP.

SHOW IP BGP FLAP-STATISTICS

To display BGP flap statistics, use the **show ip bgp flap-statistics** EXEC command.

show ip bgp flap-statistics [{**regexp** *regexp*} | {**filter-list** *list*} | {*address mask* [**longer-prefix**]}]

Syntax	*Description*
regexp *regexp*	(Optional.) Clears flap statistics for all the paths that match the regular expression.
filter-list *list*	(Optional.) Clears flap statistics for all the paths that pass the access list.
address	(Optional.) Clears flap statistics for a single entry at this IP address.
mask	(Optional.) Network mask applied to the *address*.
longer-prefix	(Optional.) Displays flap statistics for more specific entries.

Command Mode
EXEC

Usage Guidelines

This command first appeared in Cisco IOS Release 11.0.

If no arguments or keywords are specified, the router displays flap statistics for all routes.

Sample Display

The following is sample output from the **show ip bgp flap-statistics** command:

```
Router# show ip bgp flap-statistics
BGP table version is 10, local router ID is 171.69.232.182
Status codes: s suppressed, d damped, h history, * valid, > best, i -
internal
Origin codes: i - IGP, e - EGP, ? - incomplete

    Network          From          Flaps Duration Reuse    Path
*d 10.0.0.0          171.69.232.177  4      00:13:31 00:18:10 100
*d 12.0.0.0          171.69.232.177  4      00:02:45 00:28:20 100
```

Table 21–7 describes the significant fields in the display.

Table 21–7   *Show IP BGP Flap-Statistics Field Descriptions*

Field	Description
BGP table version	Internal version number for the table. This number is incremented any time the table changes.
local router ID	IP address of the router where route dampening is enabled.
Network	Route to the network indicated is dampened.
From	IP address of the peer that advertised this path.
Flaps	Number of times the route has flapped.
Duration	Time (in hours:minutes:seconds) since the router noticed the first flap.
Reuse	Time (in hours:minutes:seconds) after which the path will be made available.
Path	AS-path of the route that is being dampened.

Related Commands

Search online to find documentation for related commands.

bgp dampening
clear ip bgp flap-statistics

SHOW IP BGP INCONSISTENT-AS

To display routes with inconsistent originating autonomous systems, use the **show ip bgp inconsistent-as** privileged EXEC command.

> **show ip bgp inconsistent-as**

Syntax   *Description*

This command has no arguments or keywords.

Command Mode

Privileged EXEC

Part
II

Command Reference

Usage Guidelines

This command first appeared in Cisco IOS Release 11.0.

Sample Display

The following is sample output from the **show ip bgp inconsistent-as** command:

```
Router# show ip bgp inconsistent-as
BGP table version is 87, local router ID is 172.19.82.53
Status codes: s suppressed, * valid, > best, i - internal
Origin codes: i - IGP, e - EGP, ? - incomplete

   Network          Next Hop          Metric LocPrf Weight Path
*  11.0.0.0         171.69.232.55          0             0 300 88 90 99 ?
*>                  171.69.232.52       2222             0 400 ?
*  171.69.0.0       171.69.232.55          0             0 300 90 99 88 200 ?
*>                  171.69.232.52       2222             0 400 ?
*  200.200.199.0    171.69.232.55          0             0 300 88 90 99 ?
*>                  171.69.232.52       2222             0 400 ?
```

SHOW IP BGP NEIGHBORS

To display information about the TCP and BGP connections to neighbors, use the **show ip bgp neighbors** EXEC command.

> **show ip bgp neighbors** [*address*] [**received-routes** | **routes** | **advertised-routes** | {**paths** *regular-expression*} | **dampened-routes**]

Syntax	Description
address	(Optional.) Address of the neighbor whose routes you have learned from. If you omit this argument, all neighbors are displayed.
received-routes	(Optional.) Displays all received routes (both accepted and rejected) from the specified neighbor.

Syntax	Description
routes	(Optional.) Displays all routes that are received and accepted. This is a subset of the output from the **received-routes** keyword.
advertised-routes	(Optional.) Displays all the routes the router has advertised to the neighbor.
paths *regular-expression*	(Optional.) Regular expression that is used to match the paths received.
dampened-routes	(Optional.) Displays the dampened routes to the neighbor at the IP address specified.

Command Mode

EXEC

Usage Guidelines

This command first appeared in Cisco IOS Release 10.0. The **received-routes** keyword first appeared in Cisco IOS Release 11.2.

Sample Displays

The following is sample output from the **show ip bgp neighbors** command:

```
Router# show ip bgp neighbors 171.69.232.178

BGP neighbor is 171.69.232.178,  remote AS 10, external link
  Index 1, Offset 0, Mask 0x2
    Inbound soft reconfiguration allowed
    BGP version 4, remote router ID 171.69.232.178
    BGP state = Established, table version = 27, up for 00:06:12
    Last read 00:00:12, hold time is 180, keepalive interval is 60 seconds
    Minimum time between advertisement runs is 30 seconds
    Received 19 messages, 0 notifications, 0 in queue
    Sent 17 messages, 0 notifications, 0 in queue
    Inbound path policy configured
    Route map for incoming advertisements is testing
    Connections established 2; dropped 1
Connection state is ESTAB, I/O status: 1, unread input bytes: 0
Local host: 171.69.232.181, Local port: 11002
Foreign host: 171.69.232.178, Foreign port: 179

Enqueued packets for retransmit: 0, input: 0, saved: 0

Event Timers (current time is 0x530C294):
Timer          Starts    Wakeups          Next
Retrans          12         0             0x0
TimeWait          0         0             0x0
AckHold          12        10             0x0
SendWnd           0         0             0x0
```

```
KeepAlive          0         0           0x0
GiveUp             0         0           0x0
PmtuAger           0         0           0x0

iss:  133981889  snduna:  133982166  sndnxt:  133982166      sndwnd:  16108
irs: 3317025518  rcvnxt: 3317025810  rcvwnd:      16093  delrcvwnd:    291

SRTT: 441 ms, RTTO: 2784 ms, RTV: 951 ms, KRTT: 0 ms
minRTT: 0 ms, maxRTT: 300 ms, ACK hold: 300 ms
Flags: higher precedence, nagle

Datagrams (max data segment is 1460 bytes):
Rcvd: 15 (out of order: 0), with data: 12, total data bytes: 291
Sent: 23 (retransmit: 0), with data: 11, total data bytes: 276
```

Table 21–8 describes the fields shown in the display.

Table 21–8 *Show IP BGP Neighbors Field Descriptions*

Field	Description
BGP neighbor	IP address of the BGP neighbor and its autonomous system number. If the neighbor is in the same autonomous system as the router, then the link between them is internal; otherwise, it is considered external.
BGP version	BGP version being used to communicate with the remote router; the neighbor's router ID (an IP address) is also specified.
BGP state	Internal state of this BGP connection.
table version	Indicates that the neighbor has been updated with this version of the primary BGP routing table.
up for	Amount of time that the underlying TCP connection has been in existence.
Last read	Time that BGP last read a message from this neighbor.
hold time	Maximum amount of time that can elapse between messages from the peer.
keepalive interval	Time period between sending keepalive packets, which help ensure that the TCP connection is up.
Received	Number of total BGP messages received from this peer, including keepalives.
notifications	Number of error messages received from the peer.

Table 21–8 *Show IP BGP Neighbors Field Descriptions, Continued*

Field	Description
Sent	Total number of BGP messages that have been sent to this peer, including keepalives.
notifications	Number of error messages the router has sent to this peer.
Connections established	Number of times the router has established a TCP connection and the two peers have agreed to speak BGP with each other.
dropped	Number of times that a good connection has failed or been taken down.
Connection state	State of BGP peer.
unread input bytes	Number of bytes of packets still to be processed.
Local host, Local port	Peering address of local router, plus port.
Foreign host, Foreign port	Neighbor's peering address.
Event Timers	Table displays the number of starts and wakeups for each timer.
iss	Initial send sequence number.
snduna	Last send sequence number the local host sent but has not received an acknowledgment for.
sndnxt	Sequence number the local host will send next.
sndwnd	TCP window size of the remote host.
irs	Initial receive sequence number.
rcvnxt	Last receive sequence number the local host has acknowledged.
rcvwnd	Local host's TCP window size.
delrecvwnd	Delayed receive window—data the local host has read from the connection, but has not yet subtracted from the receive window the host has advertised to the remote host. The value in this field gradually increases until it is larger than a full-sized packet, at which point it is applied to the rcvwnd field.
SRTT	A calculated smoothed round-trip timeout.
RTTO	Round-trip timeout.
RTV	Variance of the round-trip time.

Table 21–8 *Show IP BGP Neighbors Field Descriptions, Continued*

Field	Description
KRTT	New round-trip timeout (using the Karn algorithm). This field separately tracks the round-trip time of packets that have been retransmitted.
minRTT	Smallest recorded round-trip timeout (hard wire value used for calculation).
maxRTT	Largest recorded round-trip timeout.
ACK hold	Time the local host will delay an acknowledgment in order to piggyback data on it.
Flags	IP precedence of the BGP packets.
Datagrams: Rcvd	Number of update packets received from neighbor.
with data	Number of update packets received with data.
total data bytes	Total bytes of data.
Sent	Number of update packets sent.
with data	Number of update packets with data sent.
total data bytes	Total number of data bytes.

The following is sample output from the **show ip bgp neighbors** command with **advertised-routes**:

```
Router# show ip bgp neighbors 171.69.232.178 advertised-routes

BGP table version is 27, local router ID is 171.69.232.181
Status codes: s suppressed, d damped, h history, * valid, > best, i -
internal
Origin codes: i - IGP, e - EGP, ? - incomplete

    Network          Next Hop          Metric LocPrf Weight Path
*>i110.0.0.0         171.69.232.179         0    100      0 ?
*> 200.2.2.0         0.0.0.0                0         32768 i
```

The following is sample output from the **show ip bgp neighbors** command with **routes**:

```
Router# show ip bgp neighbors 171.69.232.178 routes

BGP table version is 27, local router ID is 171.69.232.181
Status codes: s suppressed, d damped, h history, * valid, > best, i -
internal
Origin codes: i - IGP, e - EGP, ? - incomplete

    Network          Next Hop          Metric LocPrf Weight Path
*> 10.0.0.0          171.69.232.178        40            0 10 ?
*> 20.0.0.0          171.69.232.178        40            0 10 ?
```

Table 21–9 describes the fields shown in the display.

Table 21–9   *Show IP BGP Neighbors Advertised-Routes and Routes Field Descriptions*

Field	Description
BGP table version	Internal version number of the table. This number is incremented whenever the table changes.
local router ID	IP address of the router.
Status codes	s—The table entry is suppressed. *—The table entry is valid. >—The table entry is the best entry to use for that network. i—The table entry was learned via an internal BGP session.
Origin codes	Indicates the origin of the entry. The origin code is placed at the end of each line in the table. It can be one of the following values: i—Entry originated from IGP and was advertised with a **network** router configuration command. e—Entry originated from EGP. ?—Origin of the path is not clear. Usually, this is a router that is redistributed into BGP from an IGP.
Network	IP address of a network entity.
Next Hop	IP address of the next system that is used when forwarding a packet to the destination network. An entry of 0.0.0.0 indicates that the router has some non-BGP routes to this network.
Metric	If shown, this is the value of the interautonomous system metric. This field is frequently not used.
LocPrf	Local preference value as set with the **set local-preference** route-map configuration command. The default value is 100.
Weight	Weight of the route as set via autonomous system filters.
Path	Autonomous system paths to the destination network. There can be one entry in this field for each autonomous system in the path.

The following is sample output from the **show ip bgp neighbors** command with **paths**:

```
Router# show ip bgp neighbors 171.69.232.178 paths ^10

Address    Refcount Metric Path
0x60E577B0      2     40 10 ?
```

SHOW IP BGP PATHS

To display all the BGP paths in the database, use the **show ip bgp paths** EXEC command.

    show ip bgp paths

Syntax   Description

This command has no arguments or keywords.

Command Mode

EXEC

Usage Guidelines

This command first appeared in Cisco IOS Release 10.0.

Sample Display

The following is sample output from the **show ip bgp paths** command:

```
Router# show ip bgp paths
Address     Hash Refcount Metric Path
0x60E5742C   0        1      0 i
0x60E3D7AC   2        1      0 ?
0x60E5C6C0  11        3      0 10 ?
0x60E577B0  35        2     40 10 ?
```

Table 21–10 describes significant fields shown in the display.

Table 21–10 *Show IP BGP Paths Field Descriptions*

Field	Description
Address	Internal address where the path is stored.
Hash	Hash bucket where path is stored.
Refcount	Number of routes using that path.
Metric	The multiple exit discriminator (MED) metric for the path. (The name of this metric for BGP versions 2 and 3 is INTER_AS.)
Path	The AS_PATH for that route, followed by the origin code for that route.

SHOW IP BGP PEER-GROUP

To display information about BGP peer groups, use the **show ip bgp peer-group** EXEC command.

    show ip bgp peer-group [*tag*] [**summary**]

Syntax	Description
tag	(Optional.) Displays information about that specific peer group.
summary	(Optional.) Displays a summary of the status of all the members of a peer group.

Command Mode
EXEC

Usage Guidelines
This command first appeared in Cisco IOS Release 11.0.

Sample Display
The following is sample output from the **show ip bgp peer-group** command:

```
Router# show ip bgp peer-group0 internal
BGP neighbor is internal, peer-group leader
  BGP version 4
  Minimum time between advertisement runs is 5 seconds
  Incoming update AS path filter list is 2
  Outgoing update AS path filter list is 1
  Route map for outgoing advertisements is set-med
```

SHOW IP BGP REGEXP

To display routes matching the regular expression, use the **show ip bgp regexp** privileged EXEC command.

> **show ip bgp regexp** *regular-expression*

Syntax	Description
regular-expression	Regular expression to match the BGP autonomous system paths.

Command Mode
Privileged EXEC

Usage Guidelines
This command first appeared in Cisco IOS Release 10.0.

Sample Display

```
Router# show ip bgp regexp 108$

BGP table version is 1738, local router ID is 198.92.72.24
Status codes: s suppressed, * valid, > best, i - internal
Origin codes: i - IGP, e - EGP, ? - incomplete
```

```
      Network          Next Hop          Metric LocPrf Weight Path
*     198.92.0.0       198.92.72.30                       0 109 108 ?
*     198.92.1.0       198.92.72.30                       0 109 108 ?
*     198.92.11.0      198.92.72.30                       0 109 108 ?
*     198.92.14.0      198.92.72.30                       0 109 108 ?
*     198.92.15.0      198.92.72.30                       0 109 108 ?
*     198.92.16.0      198.92.72.30                       0 109 108 ?
*     198.92.17.0      198.92.72.30                       0 109 108 ?
*     198.92.18.0      198.92.72.30                       0 109 108 ?
*     198.92.19.0      198.92.72.30                       0 109 108 ?
*     198.92.24.0      198.92.72.30                       0 109 108 ?
*     198.92.29.0      198.92.72.30                       0 109 108 ?
*     198.92.30.0      198.92.72.30                       0 109 108 ?
*     198.92.33.0      198.92.72.30                       0 109 108 ?
*     198.92.35.0      198.92.72.30                       0 109 108 ?
*     198.92.36.0      198.92.72.30                       0 109 108 ?
*     198.92.37.0      198.92.72.30                       0 109 108 ?
*     198.92.38.0      198.92.72.30                       0 109 108 ?
*     198.92.39.0      198.92.72.30                       0 109 108 ?
```

SHOW IP BGP SUMMARY

To display the status of all BGP connections, use the **show ip bgp summary** EXEC command.

> **show ip bgp summary**

Syntax   Description

This command has no arguments or keywords.

Command Mode

EXEC

Usage Guidelines

This command first appeared in Cisco IOS Release 10.0.

Sample Display

The following is sample output from the **show ip bgp summary** command:

```
Router# show ip bgp summary

BGP table version is 717029, main routing table version 717029
19073 network entries (37544 paths) using 3542756 bytes of memory
691 BGP path attribute entries using 57200 bytes of memory

Neighbor        V    AS MsgRcvd MsgSent   TblVer  InQ OutQ Up/Down  State
193.0.16.1      4  1755   32642    2973   717029    0    0 1:27:11
193.0.17.1      4  1755    4790    2973   717029    0    0 1:27:51
193.0.18.1      4  1755    7722    3024   717029    0    0 1:28:13
```

```
193.0.19.1      4  1755      0        0         0       0    0 2d02      Active
193.0.20.1      4  1755   3673     3049    717029       0    0 2:50:10
193.0.21.1      4  1755   3741     3048    717029       0    0 12:24:43
193.0.22.1      4  1755  33129     3051    717029       0    0 12:24:48
193.0.23.1      4  1755      0        0         0       0    0 2d02      Active
193.0.24.1      4  1755      0        0         0       0    0 2d02      Active
193.0.25.1      4  1755      0        0         0       0    0 2d02      Active
193.0.26.1      4  1755      0        0         0       0    0 2d02      Active
193.0.27.1      4  1755   4269     3049    717029       0    0 12:39:33
193.0.28.1      4  1755   3037     3050    717029       0    0 2:08:15
198.92.72.24    4  1878  11635    13300    717028       0    0 0:50:39
```

Table 21–11 describes significant fields shown in the display.

Table 21–11　*Show IP BGP Summary Field Descriptions*

Field	Description
BGP table version	Internal version number of BGP database.
main routing table version	Last version of BGP database that was injected into main routing table.
Neighbor	IP address of a neighbor.
V	BGP version number spoken to that neighbor.
AS	Autonomous system.
MsgRcvd	BGP messages received from that neighbor.
MsgSent	BGP messages sent to that neighbor.
TblVer	Last version of the BGP database that was sent to that neighbor.
InQ	Number of messages from that neighbor waiting to be processed.
OutQ	Number of messages waiting to be sent to that neighbor.
Up/Down	The length of time that the BGP session has been in state Established, or the current state if it is not Established.
State	Current state of the BGP session.

SYNCHRONIZATION

To enable the synchronization between BGP and your IGP, use the **synchronization** router configuration command. To enable the Cisco IOS software to advertise a network route without waiting for the IGP, use the **no** form of this command.

> **synchronization**
> **no synchronization**

Syntax   Description

This command has no arguments or keywords.

Default
Enabled

Command Mode
Router configuration

Usage Guidelines
This command first appeared in Cisco IOS Release 10.0.

Usually, a BGP speaker does not advertise a route to an external neighbor unless that route is local or exists in the IGP. The **no synchronization** command allows the Cisco IOS software to advertise a network route without waiting for the IGP. This feature allows routers and access servers within an autonomous system to have the route before BGP makes it available to other autonomous systems.

Use **synchronization** if there are routers in the autonomous system that do not speak BGP.

Example
The following example enables a router to advertise a network route without waiting for the IGP:

```
router bgp 120
  no synchronization
```

TABLE-MAP
To modify metric and tag values when the IP routing table is updated with BGP learned routes, use the **table-map** router configuration command. To disable this function, use the **no** form of the command.

table-map *route-map-name*
no table-map *route-map-name*

Syntax   *Description*
route-map-name   Route-map name, from the **route-map** command.

Default
Disabled

Command Mode
Router configuration

Usage Guidelines

This command first appeared in Cisco IOS Release 10.0.

This command adds the route-map name defined by the **route-map** command to the IP routing table. This command is used to set the tag name and the route metric to implement redistribution.

You can use **match** clauses of route maps in the **table-map** command. IP access list, autonomous system paths, and next-hop match clauses are supported.

Example

In the following example, the Cisco IOS software is configured to automatically compute the tag value for the BGP learned routes and to update the IP routing table.

```
route-map tag
 match as path 10
 set automatic-tag
 !
router bgp 100
 table-map tag
```

Related Commands

Search online to find documentation for related commands.

match as-path
match ip address
match ip next-hop
route-map

TIMERS BGP

To adjust BGP network timers, use the **timers bgp** router configuration command. To reset the BGP timing defaults, use the **no** form of this command.

> **timers bgp** *keepalive holdtime*
> **no timers bgp**

Syntax	Description
keepalive	Frequency, in seconds, with which the Cisco IOS software sends *keepalive* messages to its peer. The default is 60 seconds.
holdtime	Interval, in seconds, after not receiving a *keepalive* message that the software declares a peer dead. The default is 180 seconds.

Defaults

keepalive: 60 seconds
holdtime: 180 seconds

Command Mode

Router configuration

Usage Guidelines

This command first appeared in Cisco IOS Release 10.0.

Example

The following example changes the keepalive timer to 70 seconds and the holdtime timer to 210 seconds:

```
timers bgp 70 210
```

Related Commands

Search online to find documentation for related commands.

clear ip bgp peer-group
router bgp
show ip bgp

Configuring IP Routing Protocol-Independent Features

This chapter describes how to configure IP routing protocol-independent features. For a complete description of the IP routing protocol-independent commands in this chapter, see Chapter 23, "IP Routing Protocol-Independent Commands."

Previous chapters addressed configurations of specific routing protocols. The following list shows optional features that are protocol-independent; these features are explained in the subsequent sections:

- Using Variable-Length Subnet Masks
- Configuring Static Routes
- Specifying Default Routes
- Changing the Maximum Number of Paths
- Redistributing Routing Information
- Filtering Routing Information
- Enabling Policy Routing
- Managing Authentication Keys
- Monitoring and Maintaining the IP Network

See the section "IP Routing Protocol-Independent Configuration Examples" at end of this chapter for configuration examples.

USING VARIABLE-LENGTH SUBNET MASKS

Enhanced IGRP, IS-IS, OSPF, RIP Version 2, and static routes support Variable-Length Subnet Masks (VLSMs). With VLSMs, you can use different masks for the same network number on different interfaces, which allows you to conserve IP addresses and more efficiently use available address space. However, using VLSMs also presents address assignment challenges for the network administrator as well as ongoing administrative challenges.

Refer to RFC 1219 for detailed information about VLSMs and how to assign addresses correctly.

NOTES

Consider your decision to use VLSMs carefully. You can easily make mistakes in address assignments and you will generally find it more difficult to monitor your network using VLSMs.

The best way to implement VLSMs is to keep your existing numbering plan in place and gradually migrate some networks to VLSMs to recover address space. See the "Variable-Length Subnet Mask Example" section at the end of this chapter for an example of using VLSMs.

CONFIGURING STATIC ROUTES

Static routes are user-defined routes that cause packets moving between a source and a destination to take a specified path. Static routes can be important if the Cisco IOS software cannot build a route to a particular destination. They are also useful for specifying a gateway of last resort to which all unroutable packets will be sent.

To configure a static route, perform the following task in global configuration mode:

Task	Command
Establish a static route.	**ip route** *prefix mask* {*address* | *interface*} [*distance*] [**tag** *tag*] [**permanent**]

See the "Overriding Static Routes with Dynamic Protocols Example" section at the end of this chapter for an example of configuring static routes.

The software remembers static routes until you remove them (using the **no** form of the **ip route** global configuration command). However, you can override static routes with dynamic routing information through prudent assignment of administrative distance values. Each dynamic routing protocol has a default administrative distance, as listed in Table 22–1. If you would like a static route to be overridden by information from a dynamic routing protocol, simply ensure that the administrative distance of the static route is higher than that of the dynamic protocol.

Table 22–1 *Dynamic Routing Protocol Default Administrative Distances*

Route Source	Default Distance
Connected interface	0
Static route	1
Enhanced IGRP summary route	5

Table 22–1 *Dynamic Routing Protocol Default Administrative Distances, Continued*

Route Source	Default Distance
External BGP	20
Internal Enhanced IGRP	90
IGRP	100
OSPF	110
IS-IS	115
RIP	120
Internal BGP	200
Unknown	255

Static routes that point to an interface will be advertised via RIP, IGRP, and other dynamic routing protocols, regardless of whether **redistribute static** commands were specified for those routing protocols. This is because static routes that point to an interface are considered in the routing table to be connected and hence lose their static nature. However, if you define a static route to an interface that is not one of the networks defined in a **network** command, no dynamic routing protocols will advertise the route unless a **redistribute static** command is specified for these protocols.

When an interface goes down, all static routes through that interface are removed from the IP routing table. Also, when the software can no longer find a valid next hop for the address specified as the forwarding router's address in a static route, the static route is removed from the IP routing table.

SPECIFYING DEFAULT ROUTES

A router might not be able to determine the routes to all other networks. To provide complete routing capability, the common practice is to use some routers as *smart routers* and give the remaining routers default routes to the smart router. (Smart routers have routing table information for the entire internetwork.) These default routes can be passed along dynamically or can be configured into the individual routers.

Most dynamic interior routing protocols include a mechanism for causing a smart router to generate dynamic default information that is then passed along to other routers.

Specifying a Default Network

If a router has a directly connected interface onto the specified default network, the dynamic routing protocols running on that device will generate or source a default route. In the case of RIP, it will advertise the pseudonetwork 0.0.0.0. In the case of IGRP, the network itself is advertised and flagged as an exterior route.

A router that is generating the default for a network also may need a default of its own. One way of doing this is to specify a static route to the network 0.0.0.0 through the appropriate device.

To define a static route to a network as the static default route, perform the following task in global configuration mode:

Task	Command
Specify a default network.	ip default-network *network-number*

Understanding the Gateway of Last Resort

When default information is being passed along through a dynamic routing protocol, no further configuration is required. The system periodically scans its routing table to choose the optimal default network as its default route. In the case of RIP, there is only one choice, network 0.0.0.0. In the case of IGRP, there might be several networks that can be candidates for the system default. The Cisco IOS software uses both administrative distance and metric information to determine the default route (*gateway of last resort*). The selected default route appears in the gateway of last resort display of the **show ip route** EXEC command.

If dynamic default information is not being passed to the software, candidates for the default route are specified with the **ip default-network** command. In this usage, **ip default-network** takes an unconnected network as an argument. If this network appears in the routing table from any source (dynamic or static), it is flagged as a candidate default route.

If the router has no interface on the default network, but does have a route to it, it considers this network as a candidate default path. The route candidates are examined and the best one is chosen, based on administrative distance and metric. The gateway to the best default path becomes the gateway of last resort.

CHANGING THE MAXIMUM NUMBER OF PATHS

By default, most IP routing protocols install a maximum of four parallel routes in a routing table. The exception is BGP, which by default allows only one path to a destination.

The range of maximum paths is 1 to 6 paths. To change the maximum number of parallel paths allowed, perform the following task in router configuration mode:

Task	Command
Configure the maximum number of parallel paths allowed in a routing table.	**maximum-paths** *maximum*

REDISTRIBUTING ROUTING INFORMATION

In addition to running multiple routing protocols simultaneously, the Cisco IOS software can redistribute information from one routing protocol to another. For example, you can instruct the software to readvertise IGRP-derived routes using the RIP protocol or to re-advertise static routes using the IGRP protocol. This applies to all of the IP-based routing protocols.

You also can conditionally control the redistribution of routes between routing domains by defining a method known as *route maps* between the two domains.

The following five tables list tasks associated with route redistribution. Although redistribution is a protocol-independent feature, some of the **match** and **set** commands are specific to a particular protocol.

To define a route map for redistribution, perform the following task in global configuration mode:

Task	Command
Define any route maps needed to control redistribution.	**route-map** *map-tag* [**permit** I **deny**] [*sequence-number*]

One or more **match** commands and one or more **set** commands typically follow a **route-map** command. If there are no **match** commands, then everything matches. If there are no **set** commands, nothing is done (other than the match). Therefore, you need at least one **match** or **set** command. To define conditions for redistributing routes from one routing protocol into another, perform at least one of the following tasks in route-map configuration mode:

Task		Command
Step 1	Match a BGP autonomous system path access list.	**match as-path** *path-list-number*
Step 2	Match a BGP community list.	**match community-list** *community-list-number* [**exact**]
Step 3	Match a standard access list.	**match ip address** {*access-list-number* I *name* ...*access-list-number* I *name*...*name*}
Step 4	Match the specified metric.	**match metric** *metric-value*
Step 5	Match a next-hop router address passed by one of the access lists specified.	**match ip next-hop** {*access-list-number* I *name* ...*access-list-number* I *name*...*name*}
Step 6	Match the specified tag value.	**match tag** *tag-value*...*tag-value*
Step 7	Match the specified next-hop route out of one of the interfaces specified.	**match interface** *type number*...*type number*

Task	Command
Step 8 Match the address specified by the specified advertised access lists.	**match ip route-source** {*access-list-number* | *name ...access-list-number* | *name...name*}
Step 9 Match the specified route type.	**match route-type** {**local** | **internal** | **external** [**type-1** | **type-2**] | **level-1** | **level-2**}

One or more **match** commands and one or more **set** commands must follow a **route-map** command. To define conditions for redistributing routes from one routing protocol into another, perform at least one of the following tasks in route-map configuration mode:

Task	Command
Set the *COMMUNITIES* attribute.	**set community** {*community-number* [**additive**]} | **none**
Set BGP route dampening factors.	**set dampening** *halflife reuse suppress max-suppress-time*
Assign a value to a local BGP path.	**set local-preference** *value*
Specify the BGP weight for the routing table.	**set weight** *weight*
Set the BGP origin code.	**set origin** {**igp** | **egp** *as* | **incomplete**}
Modify the BGP autonomous system path.	**set as-path** {**tag** | **prepend** *as-path-string*}
Specify the address of the next hop.	**set next-hop** *next-hop*
Enable automatic computing of the tag table.	**set automatic-tag**
Set the level of routes that are advertised into the specified area of the routing domain.	**set level** {**level-1** | **level-2** | **level-1-2** | **stub-area** | **backbone**}
Set the metric value to give the redistributed routes (for any protocol except IGRP or IP Enhanced IGRP).	**set metric** *metric-value*
Set the metric value to give the redistributed routes (for IGRP or IP Enhanced IGRP only).	**set metric** *bandwidth delay reliability loading mtu*
Set the metric type to give redistributed routes.	**set metric-type** {**internal** | **external** | **type-1** | **type-2**}

Task	Command
Set the MED value on prefixes advertised to EBGP neighbor to match the IGP metric of the next hop.	**set metric-type internal**
Set the tag value to associate with the redistributed routes.	**set tag** *tag-value*

See the "BGP Route Map Examples" section in Chapter 20, "Configuring BGP," for examples of BGP route maps. See the "BGP Community with Route Maps Examples" section in Chapter 20 for examples of BGP communities and route maps.

To distribute routes from one routing domain into another and to control route redistribution, perform the following tasks in router configuration mode:

Task		Command
Step 1	Redistribute routes from one routing protocol to another routing protocol.	**redistribute** *protocol* [*process-id*] {**level-1** | **level-1-2** | **level-2**} [**metric** *metric-value*] [**metric-type** *type-value*] [**match internal** | **external** *type-value*] [**tag** *tag-value*] [**route-map** *map-tag*] [**weight** *weight*] [**subnets**]
Step 2	Cause the current routing protocol to use the same metric value for all redistributed routes (BGP, OSPF, RIP).	**default-metric** *number*
Step 3	Cause the IGRP or Enhanced IGRP routing protocol to use the same metric value for all non-IGRP redistributed routes.	**default-metric** *bandwidth delay reliability loading mtu*
Step 4	Disable the redistribution of default information between IGRP processes. This is enabled by default.	**no default-information** {**in** | **out**}

The metrics of one routing protocol do not necessarily translate into the metrics of another. For example, the RIP metric is hop count and the IGRP metric is a combination of five quantities. In such situations, an artificial metric is assigned to the redistributed route. Because of this unavoidable tampering with dynamic information, carelessly exchanging routing information between different routing protocols can create routing loops, which can seriously degrade network operation.

Understanding Supported Metric Translations

This section describes supported automatic metric translations between the routing protocols. The following descriptions assume that you have not defined a default redistribution metric that replaces metric conversions:

- RIP can automatically redistribute static routes. It assigns static routes a metric of 1 (directly connected).

- BGP does not normally send metrics in its routing updates.

- IGRP can automatically redistribute static routes and information from other IGRP-routed autonomous systems. IGRP assigns to static routes a metric that identifies them as directly connected. IGRP does not change the metrics of routes derived from IGRP updates from other autonomous systems.

- Note that any protocol can redistribute other routing protocols if a default metric is in effect.

FILTERING ROUTING INFORMATION

You can filter routing protocol information by performing the following tasks, each of which is described in this section:

- Preventing Routing Updates through an Interface
- Controlling the Advertising of Routes in Routing Updates
- Controlling the Processing of Routing Updates
- Filtering Sources of Routing Information

NOTES

When routes are redistributed between OSPF processes, no OSPF metrics are preserved.

Preventing Routing Updates through an Interface

To prevent other routers on a local network from learning about routes dynamically, you can keep routing update messages from being sent through a router interface. This is done to prevent other systems on an interface from learning about routes dynamically. This feature applies to all IP-based routing protocols except BGP.

OSPF and IS-IS behave somewhat differently. In OSPF, the interface address you specify as passive appears as a stub network in the OSPF domain. OSPF routing information is neither sent nor received through the specified router interface. In IS-IS, the specified IP addresses are advertised without actually running IS-IS on those interfaces.

To prevent routing updates through a specified interface, perform the following task in router configuration mode:

Task	Command
Suppress the sending of routing updates through the specified interface.	**passive-interface** *type number*

See the "Passive Interface Examples" section at the end of this chapter for examples of configuring passive interfaces.

Controlling the Advertising of Routes in Routing Updates

To prevent other routers from learning one or more routes, you can suppress routes from being advertised in routing updates. This is done to prevent other routers from learning a particular device's interpretation of one or more routes. You cannot specify an interface name in OSPF. When used for OSPF, this feature applies only to external routes.

To suppress routes from being advertised in routing updates, perform the following task in router configuration mode:

Task	Command
Permit or deny routes from being advertised in routing updates depending upon the action listed in the access list.	**distribute-list** {*access-list-number* | *name*} **out** [*interface-name*]

Controlling the Processing of Routing Updates

You might want to avoid processing certain routes listed in incoming updates. This feature does not apply to OSPF or IS-IS. Perform the following task in router configuration mode:

Task	Command
Suppress routes listed in updates from being processed.	**distribute-list** {*access-list-number* | *name*} **in** [*interface-name*]

Filtering Sources of Routing Information

This is done to prioritize routing information from different sources, because some pieces of routing information may be more accurate than others. An *administrative distance* is a rating of the trust-worthiness of a routing information source, such as an individual router or a group of routers. In a large network, some routing protocols and some routers can be more reliable than others as sources of routing information. Also, when multiple routing processes are running in the same router for IP, it is possible for the same route to be advertised by more than one routing process. By specifying administrative distance values, you enable the router to discriminate intelligently between sources of routing information. The router will always pick the route whose routing protocol has the lowest administrative distance.

To filter sources of routing information, perform the following task in router configuration mode:

Task	Command
Filter routing information sources.	**distance** *weight* [*address-mask* [*access-list-number* | *name*]] [**ip**]

There are no general guidelines for assigning administrative distances, because each network has its own requirements. You must determine a reasonable matrix of administrative distances for the network as a whole. Table 22–1 shows the default administrative distance for various routing information sources.

For example, consider a router using IGRP and RIP. Suppose you trust the IGRP-derived routing information more than the RIP-derived routing information. In this example, because the default IGRP administrative distance is lower than the default RIP administrative distance, the router uses the IGRP-derived information and ignores the RIP-derived information. However, if you lose the source of the IGRP-derived information (because of a power shutdown in another building, for example), the router uses the RIP-derived information until the IGRP-derived information reappears.

For an example of filtering on sources of routing information, see the section "Administrative Distance Examples" at the end of this chapter.

NOTES

You also can use administrative distance to rate the routing information from routers running the same routing protocol. This application is generally discouraged if you are unfamiliar with this particular use of administrative distance, because it can result in inconsistent routing information, including forwarding loops.

ENABLING POLICY ROUTING

Policy routing is a more flexible mechanism for routing packets than is destination routing. Policy routing is a process whereby the router puts packets through a route map before routing them. The route map determines which packets are routed to which router next. You might enable policy routing if you want certain packets to be routed some way other than the obvious shortest path. Some possible applications for policy routing are to provide equal access, protocol-sensitive routing, source-sensitive routing, routing based on interactive versus batch traffic, or routing based on dedicated links.

To enable policy routing, you must identify which route map to use for policy routing and create the route map. The route map itself specifies the match criteria and the resulting action if all of the match clauses are met. These steps are described in the following three task tables.

To enable policy routing on an interface, indicate which route map the router should use by performing the following task in interface configuration mode. All packets arriving on the specified interface will be subject to policy routing. This command disables fast switching of all packets arriving on this interface.

Task	Command
Identify the route map to use for policy routing.	**ip policy route-map** *map-tag*

You must also define the route map to be used for policy routing. Perform the following task in global configuration mode:

Task	Command
Define a route map to control where packets are output.	**route-map** *map-tag* [**permit** | **deny**] [*sequence-number*]

The next step is to define the criteria by which packets are examined to see if they will be policy-routed. No match clause in the route map indicates all packets. Perform one or more of the following tasks in route-map configuration mode:

Task	Command
Match the Level 3 length of the packet.	**match length** *min max*
Match the destination IP address that is permitted by one or more standard or extended access lists.	**match ip address** {*access-list-number* | *name*} [...*access-list-number* | *name*]

The last step is to specify where the packets that pass the match criteria are output. To do so, perform one or more of the following tasks in route-map configuration mode:

Task	Command
Specify the next hop to which to route the packet (it need not be adjacent).	**set ip next-hop** *ip-address* [... *ip-address*]
Specify the output interface for the packet.	**set interface** *type number* [... *type number*]
Specify the next hop to which to route the packet, if there is no explicit route for this destination.	**set ip default next-hop** *ip-address* [... *ip-address*]
Specify the output interface for the packet, if there is no explicit route for this destination.	**set default interface** *type number* [... *type number*]

The **set** commands can be used in conjunction with each other. They are evaluated in the order shown in the previous task table. A usable next hop implies an interface. Once the local router finds a next hop and a usable interface, it routes the packet.

To display the cache entries in the policy route-cache, use the **show ip cache policy** command.

If you want policy routing to be fast-switched, see the section "Enabling Fast-Switched Policy Routing," which follows.

See the "Policy Routing Example" section at the end of this chapter for an example of policy routing.

Enabling Fast-Switched Policy Routing

IP policy routing can now be fast-switched. Prior to this feature, policy routing could only be process switched, which meant that on most platforms, the switching rate was approximately 1,000 to 10,000 packets per second. This was not fast enough for many applications. Users who need policy routing to occur at faster speeds can now implement policy routing without slowing down the router.

Fast-switched policy routing supports all of the **match** commands and most of the **set** commands, except for the following restrictions:

- The **set ip default** command is not supported.

- The **set interface** command is supported only over point-to-point links, unless a route-cache entry exists using the same interface specified in the **set interface** command in the route map. Also, at the process level, the routing table is consulted to determine if the interface is on a reasonable path to the destination. During fast switching, the software does not make this check. Instead, if the packet matches, the software blindly forwards the packet to the specified interface.

Policy routing must be configured before you configure fast-switched policy routing. Fast switching of policy routing is disabled by default. To have policy routing be fast-switched, perform the following task in interface configuration mode:

Task	Command
Enable fast switching of policy routing.	**ip route-cache policy**

Enabling Local Policy Routing

Packets that are generated by the router are not normally policy-routed. To enable local policy routing for such packets, indicate which route map the router should use by performing the following task in global configuration mode. All packets originating on the router will then be subject to local policy routing.

Task	Command
Identify the route map to use for local policy routing.	**ip local policy route-map** *map-tag*

Use the **show ip local policy** command to display the route map used for local policy routing, if one exists.

MANAGING AUTHENTICATION KEYS

Key management is a method of controlling authentication keys used by routing protocols. Not all protocols can use key management. Authentication keys are available for Director Response Protocol (DRP) Agent, IP Enhanced IGRP, and RIP Version 2.

Before you manage authentication keys, authentication must be enabled. See the appropriate protocol chapter to see how to enable authentication for that protocol.

To manage authentication keys, define a key chain, identify the keys that belong to the key chain, and specify how long each key is valid. Each key has its own key identifier (specified with the **key** *number* command), which is stored locally. The combination of the key identifier and the interface associated with the message uniquely identifies the authentication algorithm and MD5 authentication key in use.

You can configure multiple keys with lifetimes. Only one authentication packet is sent, regardless of how many valid keys exist. The software examines the key numbers in order from lowest to highest, and uses the first valid key it encounters. The lifetimes allow for overlap during key changes; note that the router must know the time.

To manage authentication keys, perform the following tasks beginning in global configuration mode:

Task	Command
Step 1 Identify a key chain.	**key chain** *name-of-chain*
Step 2 In key chain configuration mode, identify the key number.	**key** *number*
Step 3 In key chain key configuration mode, identify the key string.	**key-string** *text*
Step 4 Specify the time period during which the key can be received.	**accept-lifetime** *start-time* {**infinite** | *end-time* | **duration** *seconds*}
Step 5 Specify the time period during which the key can be sent.	**send-lifetime** *start-time* {**infinite** | *end-time* | **duration** *seconds*}

Use the **show key chain** command to display key chain information. For examples of key management, see the "Managing Authentication Keys" section at the end of this chapter.

MONITORING AND MAINTAINING THE IP NETWORK

You can remove all contents of a particular cache, table, or database. You also can display specific statistics. The following sections describe each of these tasks.

Clearing Routes from the IP Routing Table

You can remove all contents of a particular table. This can become necessary when the contents of the particular structure have become, or are suspected to be, invalid.

To clear one or more routes from the IP routing table, perform the following task in EXEC mode:

Task	Command
Clear one or more routes from the IP routing table.	**clear ip route** {*network* [*mask*] | ***}

Displaying System and Network Statistics

You can display specific statistics such as the contents of IP routing tables, caches, and databases. This information can be used to determine resource utilization and solve network problems. You can also display information about node reachability and discover the routing path that your device's packets are taking through the network.

To display various routing statistics, perform the following tasks in EXEC mode:

Task	Command
Step 1 Display the cache entries in the policy route-cache.	**show ip cache policy**
Step 2 Display the local policy route map, if any.	**show ip local policy**
Step 3 Display policy route maps.	**show ip policy**
Step 4 Display the parameters and current state of the active routing protocol process.	**show ip protocols**
Step 5 Display the current state of the routing table.	**show ip route** [*address* [*mask*] [**longer-prefixes**]] | [*protocol* [*process-id*]]
Step 6 Display the current state of the routing table in summary form.	**show ip route summary**
Step 7 Display supernets.	**show ip route supernets-only**
Step 8 Display authentication key information.	**show key chain** [*name*]
Step 9 Display all route maps configured or only the one specified.	**show route-map** [*map-name*]

IP ROUTING PROTOCOL-INDEPENDENT CONFIGURATION EXAMPLES

The following sections provide routing protocol-independent configuration examples:

- Variable-Length Subnet Mask Example
- Overriding Static Routes with Dynamic Protocols Example
- Administrative Distance Examples
- Static Routing Redistribution Example
- IGRP Redistribution Example
- RIP and IGRP Redistribution Example
- IP Enhanced IGRP Redistribution Examples
- RIP and IP Enhanced IGRP Redistribution Examples
- OSPF Routing and Route Redistribution Examples
- Default Metric Values Redistribution Example
- Route Map Examples

- Passive Interface Examples
- Policy Routing Example
- Key Management Examples

Variable-Length Subnet Mask Example

In the following example, a 14-bit subnet mask is used, leaving two bits of address space reserved for serial line host addresses. There is sufficient host address space for two host endpoints on a point-to-point serial link.

```
interface ethernet 0
 ip address 131.107.1.1 255.255.255.0
! 8 bits of host address space reserved for ethernets

interface serial 0
 ip address 131.107.254.1 255.255.255.252
! 2 bits of address space reserved for serial lines

! Router is configured for OSPF and assigned AS 107
router ospf 107
! Specifies network directly connected to the router
 network 131.107.0.0 0.0.255.255 area 0.0.0.0
```

Overriding Static Routes with Dynamic Protocols Example

In the following example, packets for network 10.0.0.0 from Router B (where the static route is installed) will be routed through 131.108.3.4 if a route with an administrative distance less than 110 is not available. Figure 22–1 illustrates this point. The route learned by a protocol with an administrative distance of less than 110 might cause Router B to send traffic destined for network 10.0.0.0 via the alternate path—through Router D.

```
ip route 10.0.0.0 255.0.0.0 131.108.3.4 110
```

Figure 22–1
Overriding static routes.

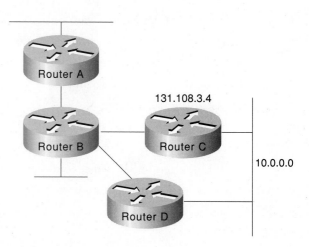

Administrative Distance Examples

In the following example, the **router igrp** global configuration command sets up IGRP routing in autonomous system 109. The **network** router configuration commands specify IGRP routing on networks 192.31.7.0 and 128.88.0.0. The first **distance** router configuration command sets the default administrative distance to 255, which instructs the router to ignore all routing updates from routers for which an explicit distance has not been set. The second **distance** command sets the administrative distance to 90 for all routers on the Class C network 192.31.7.0. The third **distance** command sets the administrative distance to 120 for the router with the address 128.88.1.3.

```
router igrp 109
 network 192.31.7.0
 network 128.88.0.0
 distance 255
 distance 90 192.31.7.0 0.0.0.255
 distance 120 128.88.1.3 0.0.0.0
```

The following example assigns the router with the address 192.31.7.18 an administrative distance of 100, and all other routers on subnet 192.31.7.0 an administrative distance of 200:

```
distance 100 192.31.7.18 0.0.0.0
distance 200 192.31.7.0 0.0.0.255
```

However, if you reverse the order of these commands, all routers on subnet 192.31.7.0 are assigned an administrative distance of 200, including the router at address 192.31.7.18. This is shown in the following example:

```
distance 200 192.31.7.0 0.0.0.255
distance 100 192.31.7.18 0.0.0.0
```

Assigning administrative distances is a problem unique to each network and is done in response to the greatest perceived threats to the connected network. Even when general guidelines exist, the network manager must ultimately determine a reasonable matrix of administrative distances for the network as a whole.

In the following example, the distance value for IP routes learned is 90. Preference is given to these IP routes rather than routes with the default administrative distance value of 110.

```
router isis
 distance 90 ip
```

Static Routing Redistribution Example

In the example that follows, three static routes are specified, two of which are to be advertised. Do this by specifying the **redistribute static** router configuration command, then specifying an access list that allows only those two networks to be passed to the IGRP process. Any redistributed static routes should be sourced by a single router to minimize the likelihood of creating a routing loop.

```
ip route 192.1.2.0 255.255.255.0 192.31.7.65
ip route 193.62.5.0 255.255.255.0 192.31.7.65
ip route 131.108.0.0 255.255.255.0 192.31.7.65
access-list 3 permit 192.1.2.0
access-list 3 permit 193.62.5.0
```

```
!
router igrp 109
 network 192.31.7.0
 default-metric 10000 100 255 1 1500
 redistribute static
 distribute-list 3 out static
```

IGRP Redistribution Example

Each IGRP routing process can provide routing information to only one autonomous system; the Cisco IOS software must run a separate IGRP process and maintain a separate routing database for each autonomous system it services. However, you can transfer routing information between these routing databases.

Suppose that the router has one IGRP routing process for network 15.0.0.0 in autonomous system 71 and another for network 192.31.7.0 in autonomous system 109, as the following commands specify:

```
router igrp 71
 network 15.0.0.0
router igrp 109
 network 192.31.7.0
```

To transfer a route to 192.31.7.0 into autonomous system 71 (without passing any other information about autonomous system 109), use the command in the following example:

```
router igrp 71
 redistribute igrp 109
 distribute-list 3 out igrp 109
access-list 3 permit 192.31.7.0
```

RIP and IGRP Redistribution Example

Consider a WAN at a university that uses RIP as an interior routing protocol. Assume that the university wants to connect its WAN to a regional network, 128.1.0.0, which uses IGRP as the routing protocol. The goal in this case is to advertise the networks in the university network to the routers on the regional network. The commands for the interconnecting router are listed in the following example:

```
router igrp 109
 network 128.1.0.0
 redistribute rip
 default-metric 10000 100 255 1 1500
 distribute-list 10 out rip
```

In this example, the **router** global configuration command starts an IGRP routing process. The **network** router configuration command specifies that network 128.1.0.0 (the regional network) is to receive IGRP routing information. The **redistribute** router configuration command specifies that RIP-derived routing information be advertised in the routing updates. The **default-metric** router configuration command assigns an IGRP metric to all RIP-derived routes.

The **distribute-list** router configuration command instructs the Cisco IOS software to use access list 10 (not defined in this example) to limit the entries in each outgoing update. The access list prevents unauthorized advertising of university routes to the regional network.

IP Enhanced IGRP Redistribution Examples

Each IP Enhanced IGRP routing process provides routing information to only one autonomous system. The Cisco IOS software must run a separate IP Enhanced IGRP process and maintain a separate routing database for each autonomous system it services. However, you can transfer routing information between these routing databases.

Suppose the software has one IP Enhanced IGRP routing process for network 15.0.0.0 in autonomous system 71 and another for network 192.31.7.0 in autonomous system 109, as in the following commands:

```
router eigrp 71
 network 15.0.0.0
router eigrp 109
 network 192.31.7.0
```

To transfer a route from 192.31.7.0 into autonomous system 71 (without passing any other information about autonomous system 109), use the command in the following example:

```
router eigrp 71
 redistribute eigrp 109 route-map 109-to-71
 route-map 109-to-71 permit
 match ip address 3
 set metric 10000 100 1 255 1500
access-list 3 permit 192.31.7.0
```

The following example is an alternative way to transfer a route to 192.31.7.0 into autonomous system 71. Unlike the previous configuration, this one does not allow you to set the metric arbitrarily.

```
router eigrp 71
 redistribute eigrp 109
 distribute-list 3 out eigrp 109
access-list 3 permit 192.31.7.0
```

RIP and IP Enhanced IGRP Redistribution Examples

This section provides a simple RIP redistribution example and a complex redistribution example between IP Enhanced IGRP and BGP.

Example 1: Simple Redistribution

Consider a WAN at a university that uses RIP as an interior routing protocol. Assume that the university wants to connect its WAN to a regional network, 128.1.0.0, which uses IP Enhanced IGRP as the routing protocol. The goal in this case is to advertise the networks in the university network to the routers on the regional network. The commands for the interconnecting router are the following:

```
router eigrp 109
 network 128.1.0.0
 redistribute rip
 default-metric 10000 100 255 1 1500
 distribute-list 10 out rip
```

In this example, the **router** global configuration command starts an IP Enhanced IGRP routing process. The **network** router configuration command specifies that network 128.1.0.0 (the regional network) is to send and receive IP Enhanced IGRP routing information. The **redistribute** router configuration command specifies that RIP-derived routing information be advertised in the routing updates. The **default-metric** router configuration command assigns an IP Enhanced IGRP metric to all RIP-derived routes.

The **distribute-list** router configuration command instructs the Cisco IOS software to use access list 10 (not defined in this example) to limit the entries in each outgoing update. The access list prevents unauthorized advertising of university routes to the regional network.

Example 2: Complex Redistribution

The most complex redistribution case is one in which *mutual* redistribution is required between an IGP (in this case IP Enhanced IGRP) and BGP.

Suppose that BGP is running on a router somewhere else in autonomous system 1, and that the BGP routes are injected into IP Enhanced IGRP routing process 1. You must use filters to ensure that the proper routes are advertised. The example configuration for router R1 illustrates the use of access filters and a distribution list to filter routes advertised to BGP neighbors. This example also illustrates configuration commands for redistribution between BGP and IP Enhanced IGRP.

```
! Configuration for router R1:
router bgp 1
 network 131.108.0.0
 neighbor 192.5.10.1 remote-as 2
 neighbor 192.5.10.15 remote-as 1
 neighbor 192.5.10.24 remote-as 3
 redistribute eigrp 1
 distribute-list 1 out eigrp 1
!
! All networks that should be advertised from R1 are controlled with access lists:
!
access-list 1 permit 131.108.0.0
access-list 1 permit 150.136.0.0
access-list 1 permit 128.125.0.0
!
router eigrp 1
 network 131.108.0.0
 network 192.5.10.0
 redistribute bgp 1
```

OSPF Routing and Route Redistribution Examples

OSPF typically requires coordination among many internal routers, area border routers, and autonomous system boundary routers. At a minimum, OSPF-based routers can be configured with all default parameter values, with no authentication, and with interfaces assigned to areas.

Three types of examples follow:

- The first examples are simple configurations illustrating basic OSPF commands.

- The second example illustrates a configuration for an internal router, ABR, and ASBRs within a single, arbitrarily assigned, OSPF autonomous system.

- The third example illustrates a more complex configuration and the application of various tools available for controlling OSPF-based routing environments.

Basic OSPF Configuration Examples

The following example illustrates a simple OSPF configuration that enables OSPF routing process 9000, attaches Ethernet 0 to area 0.0.0.0, and redistributes RIP into OSPF and OSPF into RIP:

```
interface ethernet 0
 ip address 130.93.1.1 255.255.255.0
 ip ospf cost 1
!
interface ethernet 1
 ip address 130.94.1.1 255.255.255.0
!
router ospf 9000
 network 130.93.0.0 0.0.255.255 area 0.0.0.0
 redistribute rip metric 1 subnets
!
router rip
 network 130.94.0.0
 redistribute ospf 9000
 default-metric 1
```

The following example illustrates the assignment of four area IDs to four IP address ranges. In the example, OSPF routing process 109 is initialized, and four OSPF areas are defined: 10.9.50.0, 2, 3, and 0. Areas 10.9.50.0, 2, and 3 mask specific address ranges, while Area 0 enables OSPF for *all other* networks.

```
router ospf 109
 network 131.108.20.0 0.0.0.255 area 10.9.50.0
 network 131.108.0.0 0.0.255.255 area 2
 network 131.109.10.0 0.0.0.255 area 3
 network 0.0.0.0 255.255.255.255 area 0
!
! Interface Ethernet0 is in area 10.9.50.0:
interface ethernet 0
 ip address 131.108.20.5 255.255.255.0
!
! Interface Ethernet1 is in area 2:
```

```
interface ethernet 1
 ip address 131.108.1.5 255.255.255.0
!
! Interface Ethernet2 is in area 2:
interface ethernet 2
 ip address 131.108.2.5 255.255.255.0
!
! Interface Ethernet3 is in area 3:
interface ethernet 3
 ip address 131.109.10.5 255.255.255.0
!
! Interface Ethernet4 is in area 0:
interface ethernet 4
 ip address 131.109.1.1 255.255.255.0
!
! Interface Ethernet5 is in area 0:
interface ethernet 5
 ip address 10.1.0.1 255.255.0.0
```

Each **network** router configuration command is evaluated sequentially, so the specific order of these commands in the configuration is important. The Cisco IOS software sequentially evaluates the *address/wildcard-mask* pair for each interface.

Consider the first **network** command. Area ID 10.9.50.0 is configured for the interface on which subnet 131.108.20.0 is located. Assume that a match is determined for interface Ethernet 0. Interface Ethernet 0 is attached to Area 10.9.50.0 only.

The second **network** command is evaluated next. For Area 2, the same process is then applied to all interfaces (except interface Ethernet 0). Assume that a match is determined for interface Ethernet 1. OSPF is then enabled for that interface and Ethernet 1 is attached to Area 2.

This process of attaching interfaces to OSPF areas continues for all **network** commands. Note that the last **network** command in this example is a special case. With this command, all available interfaces (not explicitly attached to another area) are attached to Area 0.

Internal Router, ABR, and ASBRs Configuration Example

The following example outlines a configuration for several routers within a single OSPF autonomous system. Figure 22–2 provides a general network map that illustrates this example configuration.

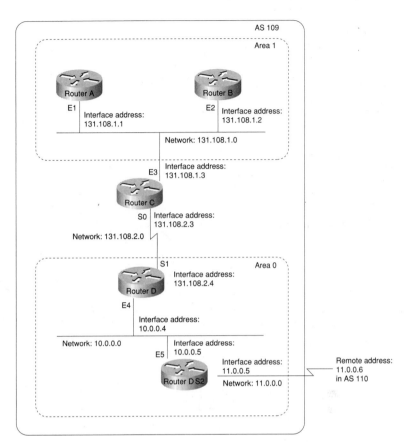

Figure 22–2
Sample OSPF autonomous system network map.

In this configuration, five routers are configured in OSPF autonomous system 109 as explained in the following points:

- Router A and Router B are both internal routers within Area 1.

- Router C is an OSPF area border router. Note that for Router C, Area 1 is assigned to E3 and Area 0 is assigned to S0.

- Router D is an internal router in Area 0 (backbone area). In this case, both **network** router configuration commands specify the same area (Area 0, or the backbone area).

- Router E is an OSPF autonomous system boundary router. Note that BGP routes are redistributed into OSPF and that these routes are advertised by OSPF.

NOTES

It is not necessary to include definitions of all areas in an OSPF autonomous system in the configuration of all routers in the autonomous system. You must only define the *directly* connected areas. In the example that follows, routes in Area 0 are learned by the routers in Area 1 (Router A and Router B) when the area border router (Router C) injects summary link state advertisements into Area 1.

Autonomous system 109 is connected to the outside world via the BGP link to the external peer at IP address 11.0.0.6.

Router A—Internal Router

```
    interface ethernet 1
      ip address 131.108.1.1 255.255.255.0

    router ospf 109
      network 131.108.0.0 0.0.255.255 area 1
```

Router B—Internal Router

```
    interface ethernet 2
      ip address 131.108.1.2 255.255.255.0

    router ospf 109
      network 131.108.0.0 0.0.255.255 area 1
```

Router C—ABR

```
    interface ethernet 3
      ip address 131.108.1.3 255.255.255.0

    interface serial 0
      ip address 131.108.2.3 255.255.255.0

    router ospf 109
      network 131.108.1.0 0.0.0.255 area 1
      network 131.108.2.0 0.0.0.255 area 0
```

Router D—Internal Router

```
    interface ethernet 4
      ip address 10.0.0.4 255.0.0.0

    interface serial 1
      ip address 131.108.2.4 255.255.255.0

    router ospf 109
      network 131.108.2.0 0.0.0.255 area 0
      network 10.0.0.0 0.255.255.255 area 0
```

Router E—ASBR

```
interface ethernet 5
 ip address 10.0.0.5 255.0.0.0

interface serial 2
 ip address 11.0.0.5 255.0.0.0

router ospf 109
 network 10.0.0.0 0.255.255.255 area 0
 redistribute bgp 109 metric 1 metric-type 1

router bgp 109
 network 131.108.0.0
 network 10.0.0.0
 neighbor 11.0.0.6 remote-as 110
```

Complex OSPF Configuration Example

The following example configuration accomplishes several tasks in setting up an ABR. These tasks can be split into the following two general categories:

- Basic OSPF configuration
- Route redistribution

The specific tasks outlined in this configuration are detailed briefly in the following descriptions. Figure 22–3 illustrates the network address ranges and area assignments for the interfaces.

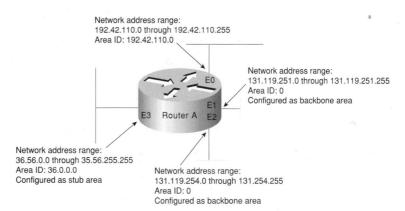

Figure 22–3
Interface and area specifications for OSPF example configuration.

Network address range:
192.42.110.0 through 192.42.110.255
Area ID: 192.42.110.0

Network address range:
131.119.251.0 through 131.119.251.255
Area ID: 0
Configured as backbone area

Network address range:
36.56.0.0 through 35.56.255.255
Area ID: 36.0.0.0
Configured as stub area

Network address range:
131.119.254.0 through 131.254.255
Area ID: 0
Configured as backbone area

The basic configuration tasks in this example are the following:

- Configure address ranges for Ethernet 0 through Ethernet 3 interfaces.
- Enable OSPF on each interface.
- Set up an OSPF authentication password for each area and network.
- Assign link state metrics and other OSPF interface configuration options.

- Create a stub area with area id 36.0.0.0. (Note that the **authentication** and **stub** options of the **area** router configuration command are specified with separate **area** command entries, but can be merged into a single **area** command.)
- Specify the backbone area (Area 0).

Configuration tasks associated with redistribution are the following:

- Redistribute IGRP and RIP into OSPF with various options set (including **metric-type, metric, tag,** and **subnet**).
- Redistribute IGRP and OSPF into RIP.

The following is an example OSPF configuration:

```
interface ethernet 0
 ip address 192.42.110.201 255.255.255.0
 ip ospf authentication-key abcdefgh
 ip ospf cost 10
!
interface ethernet 1
 ip address 131.119.251.201 255.255.255.0
 ip ospf authentication-key ijklmnop
 ip ospf cost 20
 ip ospf retransmit-interval 10
 ip ospf transmit-delay 2
 ip ospf priority 4
!
interface ethernet 2
 ip address 131.119.254.201 255.255.255.0
 ip ospf authentication-key abcdefgh
 ip ospf cost 10
!
interface ethernet 3
 ip address 36.56.0.201 255.255.0.0
 ip ospf authentication-key ijklmnop
 ip ospf cost 20
 ip ospf dead-interval 80
```

OSPF is on network 131.119.0.0:

```
router ospf 201
 network 36.0.0.0 0.255.255.255 area 36.0.0.0
 network 192.42.110.0 0.0.0.255 area 192.42.110.0
 network 131.119.0.0 0.0.255.255 area 0
 area 0 authentication
 area 36.0.0.0 stub
 area 36.0.0.0 authentication
 area 36.0.0.0 default-cost 20
 area 192.42.110.0 authentication
 area 36.0.0.0 range 36.0.0.0 255.0.0.0
 area 192.42.110.0 range 192.42.110.0 255.255.255.0
 area 0 range 131.119.251.0 255.255.255.0
 area 0 range 131.119.254.0 255.255.255.0
```

```
    redistribute igrp 200 metric-type 2 metric 1 tag 200 subnets
    redistribute rip metric-type 2 metric 1 tag 200
```

IGRP autonomous system 200 is on 131.119.0.0:

```
router igrp 200
 network 131.119.0.0
 !
 ! RIP for 192.42.110
 !
router rip
 network 192.42.110.0
 redistribute igrp 200 metric 1
 redistribute ospf 201 metric 1
```

Default Metric Values Redistribution Example

The following example shows a router in autonomous system 109 using both RIP and IGRP. The example advertises IGRP-derived routes using the RIP protocol and assigns the IGRP-derived routes a RIP metric of 10.

```
router rip
 default-metric 10
 redistribute igrp 109
```

Route Map Examples

The examples in this section illustrate the use of redistribution, with and without route maps. Examples from both the IP and CLNS routing protocols are provided.

The following example redistributes all OSPF routes into IGRP:

```
router igrp 109
 redistribute ospf 110
```

The following example redistributes RIP routes with a hop count equal to 1 into OSPF. These routes will be redistributed into OSPF as external link state advertisements with a metric of 5, metric type of Type 1, and a tag equal to 1.

```
router ospf 109
 redistribute rip route-map rip-to-ospf
 !
route-map rip-to-ospf permit
 match metric 1
 set metric 5
 set metric-type type1
 set tag 1
```

The following example redistributes OSPF learned routes with tag 7 as a RIP metric of 15:

```
router rip
 redistribute ospf 109 route-map 5
 !
route-map 5 permit
 match tag 7
 set metric 15
```

The following example redistributes OSPF intra-area and interarea routes with next-hop routers on serial interface 0 into BGP with an INTER_AS metric of 5:

```
router bgp 109
 redistribute ospf 109 route-map 10
 !
route-map 10 permit
 match route-type internal
 match interface serial 0
 set metric 5
```

The following example redistributes two types of routes into the integrated IS-IS routing table (supporting both IP and CLNS). The first are OSPF external IP routes with tag 5; these are inserted into Level 2 IS-IS LSPs with a metric of 5. The second are ISO-IGRP derived CLNS prefix routes that match CLNS access list 2000. These will be redistributed into IS-IS as Level 2 LSPs with a metric of 30.

```
router isis
 redistribute ospf 109 route-map 2
 redistribute iso-igrp nsfnet route-map 3
 !
route-map 2 permit
 match route-type external
 match tag 5
 set metric 5
 set level level-2
 !
route-map 3 permit
 match address 2000
 set metric 30
```

With the following configuration, OSPF external routes with tags 1, 2, 3, and 5 are redistributed into RIP with metrics of 1, 1, 5, and 5, respectively. The OSPF routes with a tag of 4 are not redistributed.

```
router rip
 redistribute ospf 109 route-map 1
 !
route-map 1 permit
 match tag 1 2
 set metric 1
 !
route-map 1 permit
 match tag 3
 set metric 5
 !
route-map 1 deny
 match tag 4
 !
route map 1 permit
 match tag 5
 set metric 5
```

Given the following configuration, a RIP learned route for network 160.89.0.0 and an ISO-IGRP learned route with prefix 49.0001.0002 will be redistributed into an IS-IS Level 2 LSP with a metric of 5:

```
router isis
 redistribute rip route-map 1
 redistribute iso-igrp remote route-map 1
 !
route-map 1 permit
 match ip address 1
 match clns address 2
 set metric 5
 set level level-2
 !
access-list 1 permit 160.89.0.0 0.0.255.255
 clns filter-set 2 permit 49.0001.0002...
```

The following configuration example illustrates how a route map is referenced by the **default-information** router configuration command. This is called *conditional default origination*. OSPF will originate the default route (network 0.0.0.0) with a Type 2 metric of 5 if 140.222.0.0 is in the routing table.

```
route-map ospf-default permit
 match ip address 1
 set metric 5
 set metric-type type-2
 !
access-list 1 140.222.0.0 0.0.255.255
 !
router ospf 109
 default-information originate route-map ospf-default
```

See more route map examples in the sections "BGP Route Map Examples" and "BGP Community with Route Maps Examples" in Chapter 20, "Configuring BGP."

Passive Interface Examples

The following example sends IGRP updates to all interfaces on network 131.108.0.0 except interface Ethernet 1. Figure 22–4 shows this configuration.

```
router igrp 109
 network 131.108.0.0
 passive-interface ethernet 1
```

In the following example, as in the first example, IGRP updates are sent to all interfaces on network 131.108.0.0 except interface Ethernet 1. However, in this case a **neighbor** router configuration command is included, which permits routing updates to be sent to specific neighbors. One copy of the routing update is generated per neighbor.

```
router igrp 109
 network 131.108.0.0
 passive-interface ethernet 1
 neighbor 131.108.20.4
```

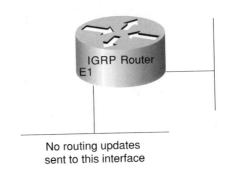

Figure 22–4
Filtering IGRP updates.

No routing updates
sent to this interface

In OSPF, hello packets are not sent on an interface that is specified as passive. Hence, the router will not be able to discover any neighbors, and none of the OSPF neighbors will be able to see the router on that network. In effect, this interface will appear as a stub network to the OSPF domain. This is useful if you want to import routes associated with a connected network into the OSPF domain without any OSPF activity on that interface.

The **passive-interface** router configuration command typically is used when the wildcard specification on the **network** router configuration command configures more interfaces than is desirable. The following configuration causes OSPF to run on all subnets of 131.108.0.0:

```
interface ethernet 0
 ip address 131.108.1.1 255.255.255.0
interface ethernet 1
 ip address 131.108.2.1 255.255.255.0
interface ethernet 2
 ip address 131.108.3.1 255.255.255.0
!
router ospf 109
 network 131.108.0.0 0.0.255.255 area 0
```

If you do not want OSPF to run on 131.108.3.0, enter the following commands:

```
router ospf 109
 network 131.108.0.0 0.0.255.255 area 0
 passive-interface ethernet 2
```

Policy Routing Example

The following example provides two sources with equal access to two different service providers. Packets arriving on async interface 1 from the source 1.1.1.1 are sent to the router at 6.6.6.6 if the router has no explicit route for the packet's destination. Packets arriving from the source 2.2.2.2 are sent to the router at 7.7.7.7 if the router has no explicit route for the packet's destination. All other packets for which the router has no explicit route to the destination are discarded.

```
access-list 1 permit ip 1.1.1.1
access-list 2 permit ip 2.2.2.2
!
interface async 1
 ip policy route-map equal-access
!
route-map equal-access permit 10
 match ip address 1
 set ip default next-hop 6.6.6.6
route-map equal-access permit 20
 match ip address 2
 set ip default next-hop 7.7.7.7
route-map equal-access permit 30
 set default interface null0
```

Key Management Examples

The following example configures a key chain called *trees*. In this example, the software will always accept and send *willow* as a valid key. The key *chestnut* will be accepted from 1:30 p.m. to 3:30 p.m. and will be sent from 2:00 p.m. to 3:00 p.m. The overlap allows for migration of keys or discrepancies in the router's time. Likewise, the key *birch* immediately follows *chestnut*, and there is a half hour leeway on each side to handle time-of-day differences.

```
interface ethernet 0
 ip rip authentication key-chain trees
 ip rip authentication mode md5
!
router rip
 network 172.19.0.0
 version 2
!
key chain trees
 key 1
 key-string willow
 key 2
 key-string chestnut
 accept-lifetime 13:30:00 Jan 25 1996 duration 7200
 send-lifetime 14:00:00 Jan 25 1996 duration 3600
 key 3
 key-string birch
 accept-lifetime 14:30:00 Jan 25 1996 duration 7200
 send-lifetime 15:00:00 Jan 25 1996 duration 3600
```

The following example configures a key chain called *flintstone*:

```
key chain flintstone
 key 1
 key-string fred
 key 2
 key-string barney
 accept-lifetime 00:00:00 Dec 5 1995 23:59:59 Dec 5 1995
 send-lifetime 06:00:00 Dec 5 1995 18:00:00 Dec 5 1995
```

```
!
interface Ethernet0
 ip address 172.19.104.75 255.255.255.0 secondary
 ip address 171.69.232.147 255.255.255.240
 ip rip authentication key-chain flintstone
 media-type 10BaseT
!
interface Ethernet1
 no ip address
 shutdown
 media-type 10BaseT
interface Fddi0
 ip address 2.1.1.1 255.255.255.0
 no keepalive
!
interface Fddi1
 ip address 3.1.1.1 255.255.255.0
 ip rip send version 1
 ip rip receive version 1
 no keepalive
!
router rip
 version 2
 network 172.19.0.0
 network 2.0.0.0
 network 3.0.0.0
```

CHAPTER 23

IP Routing Protocol-Independent Commands

Use the commands in this chapter to configure and monitor the features that are routing protocol-independent. For configuration information and examples on IP routing protocol-independent features, see Chapter 22, "Configuring IP Routing Protocol-Independent Features."

ACCEPT-LIFETIME

To set the time period during which the authentication key on a key chain is received as valid, use the **accept-lifetime** key chain key configuration command. To revert to the default value, use the **no** form of this command.

> **accept-lifetime** *start-time* {**infinite** | *end-time* | **duration** *seconds*}
> **no accept-lifetime** [*start-time* {**infinite** | *end-time* | **duration seconds**}]

Syntax	Description
start-time	Beginning time that the key specified by the key command is valid to be received. The syntax can be either of the following:

hh:mm:ss Month date year

hh:mm:ss date Month year

hh—hours

mm—minutes

ss—seconds

date—date (1-31)

Month—first three letters of the month

year—year (four digits)

The default start time and the earliest acceptable date is January 1, 1993.

Syntax	Description
infinite	Key is valid to be received from the *start-time* on.
end-time	Key is valid to be received from the *start-time* until *end-time*. The *end-time* must be after the *start-time*. The syntax is the same as that for *start-time*. The default end time is an infinite time period.
duration *seconds*	Length of time (in seconds) that the key is valid to be received.

Default

Forever (Starting time is January 1, 1993, and ending time is infinite.)

Command Mode

Key chain key configuration

Usage Guidelines

This command first appeared in Cisco IOS Release 11.1.

Only DRP Agent, IP Enhanced IGRP, and RIP Version 2 use key chains.

Specify a *start-time* and one of the following: **infinite**, *end-time*, or **duration** *seconds*.

We recommend running NTP or some other time synchronization method if you assign a lifetime to a key.

If the last key expires, authentication will continue and an error message will be generated. To disable authentication, you must manually delete the last valid key.

Example

In the following example, the key *chestnut* will be accepted from 1:30 p.m. to 3:30 p.m. and be sent from 2:00 p.m. to 3:00 p.m. The key *birch* will be accepted from 2:30 p.m. to 4:40 p.m. and be sent from 3:00 p.m. to 4:00 p.m. The overlap allows for migration of keys or discrepancies in the router's set time. There is a half-hour leeway on each side to handle time differences.

```
interface ethernet 0
 ip rip authentication key-chain trees
 ip rip authentication mode md5
!
router rip
 network 172.19.0.0
 version 2
!
key chain trees
 key 1
 key-string chestnut
 accept-lifetime 13:30:00 Jan 25 1996 duration 7200
 send-lifetime 14:00:00 Jan 25 1996 duration 3600
 key 2
```

```
key-string birch
accept-lifetime 14:30:00 Jan 25 1996 duration 7200
send-lifetime 15:00:00 Jan 25 1996 duration 3600
```

Related Commands

Search online to find documentation for related commands.

key
key chain
key-string
send-lifetime
show key chain

CLEAR IP ROUTE

To remove one or more routes from the IP routing table, use the **clear ip route** EXEC command.

clear ip route *{network [mask] | *}*

Syntax	Description
network	Network or subnet address to remove.
mask	(Optional.) Network mask associated with the IP address you wish to remove.
*	Removes all entries.

Command Mode

EXEC

Usage Guidelines

This command first appeared in Cisco IOS Release 10.0.

Example

The following example removes a route to network 132.5.0.0 from the IP routing table:

```
clear ip route 132.5.0.0
```

Related Commands

Search online to find documentation for related commands.

show ip route

DISTANCE

To define an administrative distance, use the **distance** router configuration command. To remove a distance definition, use the **no** form of this command.

> **distance** *weight* [*address mask* [*access-list-number* | *name*]] [**ip**]
> **no distance** *weight* [*address mask* [*access-list-number*]] [**ip**]

Syntax	Description
weight	Administrative distance. This can be an integer from 10 to 255. (The values 0 to 9 are reserved for internal use.) Used alone, the argument *weight* specifies a default administrative distance that the Cisco IOS software uses when no other specification exists for a routing information source. Routes with a distance of 255 are not installed in the routing table.
address	(Optional.) IP address in four-part, dotted notation.
mask	(Optional.) IP address mask in four-part, dotted-decimal format. A bit set to 1 in the *mask* argument instructs the software to ignore the corresponding bit in the address value.
access-list-number	*name*	(Optional.) Number or name of a standard IP access list to be applied to incoming routing updates.
ip	(Optional.) IP-derived routes for IS-IS. It can be applied independently for IP routes and ISO CLNS routes.

Default

Table 23–1 lists default administrative distances.

Table 23–1   *Default Administrative Distances*

Route Source	Default Distance
Connected interface	0
Static route	1
Enhanced IGRP summary route	5
External BGP	20
Internal Enhanced IGRP	90
IGRP	100
OSPF	110
IS-IS	115

Table 23-1 *Default Administrative Distances, Continued*

Route Source	Default Distance
RIP	120
EGP	140
Internal BGP	200
Unknown	255

Command Mode

Router configuration

Usage Guidelines

This command first appeared in Cisco IOS Release 10.0. The *access-list-name* argument first appeared in Cisco IOS Release 11.2.

Numerically, an administrative distance is an integer between 0 and 255. In general, the higher the value, the lower the trust rating. An administrative distance of 255 means the routing information source cannot be trusted at all and should be ignored.

When the optional access list number is used with this command, it is applied when a network is being inserted into the routing table. This behavior allows filtering of networks according to the IP address of the router supplying the routing information. This could be used, as an example, to filter out possibly incorrect routing information from routers not under your administrative control.

The order in which you enter **distance** commands can affect the assigned administrative distances in unexpected ways (see the "Example" section for further clarification).

Weight values are also subjective; there is no quantitative method for choosing weight values.

For BGP, the **distance** command sets the administrative distance of the External BGP route.

The **show ip protocols** EXEC command displays the default administrative distance for a specified routing process.

Example

In the following example, the **router igrp** global configuration command sets up IGRP routing in autonomous system number 109. The **network** router configuration commands specify IGRP routing on networks 192.31.7.0 and 128.88.0.0. The first **distance** router configuration command sets the default administrative distance to 255, which instructs the Cisco IOS software to ignore all routing updates from routers for which an explicit distance has not been set. The second **distance** command sets the administrative distance for all routers on the Class C network 192.31.7.0 to 90. The third **distance** command sets the administrative distance for the router with the address 128.88.1.3 to 120.

```
router igrp 109
 network 192.31.7.0
 network 128.88.0.0
 distance 255
 distance 90 192.31.7.0 0.0.0.255
 distance 120 128.88.1.3 0.0.0.0
```

Related Commands

Search online to find documentation for related commands.

distance bgp

DISTRIBUTE-LIST IN

To filter networks received in updates, use the **distribute-list in** router configuration command. To change or cancel the filter, use the **no** form of this command.

> **distribute-list** {*access-list-number* | *name*} **in** [*type number*]
> **no distribute-list** {*access-list-number* | *name*} **in** [*type number*]

Syntax	Description
access-list-number | *name*	Standard IP access list number or name. The list defines which networks are to be received and which are to be suppressed in routing updates.
in	Applies the access list to incoming routing updates.
type	(Optional.) Interface type.
number	(Optional.) Interface number on which the access list should be applied to incoming updates. If no interface is specified, the access list will be applied to all incoming updates.

Default

Disabled

Command Mode

Router configuration

Usage Guidelines

This command first appeared in Cisco IOS Release 10.0. The *access-list-name*, *type*, and *number* arguments first appeared in Cisco IOS Release 11.2.

This command is not supported in IS-IS or OSPF.

Example

In the following example, the Enhanced IGRP routing process accepts only two networks—network 0.0.0.0 and network 131.108.0.0:

```
access-list 1 permit 0.0.0.0
access-list 1 permit 131.108.0.0
access-list 1 deny 0.0.0.0 255.255.255.255
router eigrp
 network 131.108.0.0
 distribute-list 1 in
```

Related Commands

Search online to find documentation for related commands.

access-list (extended)
access-list (standard)
distribute-list out
redistribute

DISTRIBUTE-LIST OUT

To suppress networks from being advertised in updates, use the **distribute-list out** router configuration command. To cancel this function, use the **no** form of this command.

> **distribute-list** {*access-list-number* | *name*} **out** [*interface-name* | *routing-process* | *autonomous-system-number*]
> **no distribute-list** {*access-list-number* | *name*} **out** [*interface-name* | *routing-process* | *autonomous-system-number*]

Syntax	Description
access-list-number	*name*	Standard IP access list number or name. The list defines which networks are to be sent and which are to be suppressed in routing updates.
out	Applies the access list to outgoing routing updates.
interface-name	(Optional.) Name of a particular interface.
routing-process	(Optional.) Name of a particular routing process, or the keyword **static** or **connected**.
autonomous-system-number	(Optional.) Autonomous system number.

Default

Disabled

Command Mode

Router configuration

Usage Guidelines

This command first appeared in Cisco IOS Release 10.0. The *access-list-name* argument first appeared in Cisco IOS Release 11.2.

When redistributing networks, a routing process name can be specified as an optional trailing argument to the **distribute-list** command. This causes the access list to be applied to only those routes derived from the specified routing process. After the process-specific access list is applied, any access list specified by a **distribute-list** command without a process name argument will be applied. Addresses not specified in the **distribute-list** command will not be advertised in outgoing routing updates.

— **NOTES** ————————————————————————————————

To filter networks received in updates, use the **distribute-list in** command.

Examples

The following example would cause only one network to be advertised by a RIP routing process: network 131.108.0.0.

```
access-list 1 permit 131.108.0.0
access-list 1 deny 0.0.0.0 255.255.255.255
router rip
 network 131.108.0.0
 distribute-list 1 out
```

In the following example, access list 1 is applied to outgoing routing updates and IS-IS is enabled on Ethernet interface 0. Only network 131.131.101.0 will be advertised in outgoing IS-IS routing updates.

```
router isis
 redistribute ospf 109
 distribute-list 1 out
interface Ethernet 0
 ip router isis
access-list 1 permit 131.131.101.0 0.0.0.255
```

Related Commands

Search online to find documentation for related commands.

access-list (extended)
access-list (standard)
distribute-list in
redistribute

IP DEFAULT-NETWORK

To select a network as a candidate route for computing the gateway of last resort, use the **ip default-network** global configuration command. To remove a route, use the **no** form of this command.

> **ip default-network** *network-number*
> **no ip default-network** *network-number*

Syntax	Description
network-number	Number of the network.

Default

If the router has a directly connected interface onto the specified network, the dynamic routing protocols running on that router will generate (or source) a default route. For RIP, this is flagged as the pseudonetwork 0.0.0.0; for IGRP, it is the network itself, flagged as an exterior route.

Command Mode

Global configuration

Usage Guidelines

This command first appeared in Cisco IOS Release 10.0.

The Cisco IOS software uses both administrative distance and metric information to determine the default route. Multiple **ip default-network** commands can be given. All candidate default routes, both static (that is, flagged by **ip default-network**) and dynamic, appear in the routing table preceded by an asterisk.

If the IP routing table indicates that the specified network number is subnetted and a non-zero subnet number is specified, then the system will automatically configure a static summary route. This static summary route is configured instead of a default network. The effect of the static summary route is to cause traffic destined for subnets that are not explicitly listed in the IP routing table to be routed using the specified subnet.

Examples

The following example defines a static route to network 10.0.0.0 as the static default route:

```
ip route 10.0.0.0 255.0.0.0 131.108.3.4
ip default-network 10.0.0.0
```

If the following command was issued on a router not connected to network 129.140.0.0, the software might choose the path to that network as a default route when the network appeared in the routing table:

```
ip default-network 129.140.0.0
```

Related Commands

Search online to find documentation for related commands.

show ip route

IP LOCAL POLICY ROUTE-MAP

To identify a route map to use for local policy routing, use the **ip local policy route-map** global configuration command. To disable local policy routing, use the **no** form of this command.

> **ip local policy route-map** *map-tag*
> **no ip local policy route-map** *map-tag*

Syntax	Description
map-tag	Name of the route map to use for local policy routing. The name must match a *map-tag* specified by a **route-map** command.

Default

Packets that are generated by the router are not policy-routed.

Command Mode

Global configuration

Usage Guidelines

This command first appeared in Cisco IOS Release 11.1.

Packets that are generated by the router are not normally policy-routed. However, you can use this command to policy-route such packets. You might enable local policy routing if you want packets originated at the router to take a route other than the obvious shortest path.

The **ip local policy route-map** command identifies a route map to use for local policy routing. Each **route-map** command has a list of **match** and **set** commands associated with it. The **match** commands specify the *match criteria*—the conditions under which packets should be policy-routed. The **set** commands specify the *set actions*—the particular policy routing actions to perform if the criteria enforced by the **match** commands are met. The **no ip local policy route-map** command deletes the reference to the route map and disables local policy routing.

Example

In the following example, packets with a destination IP address matching that allowed by extended access list 131 are sent to the router at IP address 174.21.3.20:

```
ip local policy route-map xyz
!
route-map xyz
 match ip address 131
 set ip next-hop 174.21.3.20
```

Related Commands

Search online to find documentation for related commands.

match ip address
match length
route-map
set default interface
set interface
set ip default next-hop
set ip next-hop
show ip local policy

IP POLICY ROUTE-MAP

To identify a route map to use for policy routing on an interface, use the **ip policy route-map** interface configuration command. To disable policy routing on the interface, use the **no** form of this command.

> ip policy route-map *map-tag*
> no ip policy route-map *map-tag*

Syntax	Description
map-tag	Name of the route map to use for policy routing. Must match a *map-tag* specified by a **route-map** command.

Default

No policy routing occurs on the interface.

Command Mode

Interface configuration

Usage Guidelines

This command first appeared in Cisco IOS Release 11.0.

You might enable policy routing if you want your packets to take a route other than the obvious shortest path.

The **ip policy route-map** command identifies a route map to use for policy routing. Each **route-map** command has a list of **match** and **set** commands associated with it. The **match** commands specify the *match criteria*—the conditions under which policy routing is allowed for the interface. The **set** commands specify the *set actions*—the particular policy routing actions to perform if the criteria enforced by the **match** commands are met. The **no ip policy route-map** command deletes the pointer to the route map.

Example

In the following example, packets with the destination IP address of 174.95.16.18 are sent to a router at IP address 174.21.3.20:

```
interface serial 0
 ip policy route-map wethersfield
!
route-map wethersfield
 match ip address 174.95.16.18
 set ip next-hop 174.21.3.20
```

Related Commands

Search online to find documentation for related commands.

match ip address
match length
route-map
set default interface
set interface
set ip default next-hop
set ip next-hop

IP ROUTE

To establish static routes, use the **ip route** global configuration command. To remove static routes, use the **no** form of this command.

> **ip route** *prefix mask* {*address* | *interface*} [*distance*] [**tag** *tag*] [**permanent**]
> **no ip route** *prefix mask*

Syntax	Description
prefix	IP route prefix for the destination.
mask	Prefix mask for the destination.
address	IP address of the next hop that can be used to reach that network.
interface	Network interface to use.
distance	(Optional.) An administrative distance.
tag *tag*	(Optional.) Tag value that can be used as a "match" value for controlling redistribution via route maps.
permanent	(Optional.) Specifies that the route will not be removed, even if the interface shuts down.

Default

No static routes are established.

Command Mode

Global configuration

Usage Guidelines

This command first appeared in Cisco IOS Release 10.0.

A static route is appropriate when the Cisco IOS software cannot dynamically build a route to the destination.

If you specify an administrative distance, you are flagging a static route that can be overridden by dynamic information. For example, IGRP-derived routes have a default administrative distance of 100. To have a static route that would be overridden by an IGRP dynamic route, specify an administrative distance greater than 100. Static routes have a default administrative distance of 1.

Static routes that point to an interface will be advertised via RIP, IGRP, and other dynamic routing protocols, regardless of whether **redistribute static** commands were specified for those routing protocols. This is because static routes that point to an interface are considered in the routing table to be connected and hence lose their static nature. However, if you define a static route to an interface that is not one of the networks defined in a **network** command, no dynamic routing protocols will advertise the route unless a **redistribute static** command is specified for these protocols.

Examples

In the following example, an administrative distance of 110 was chosen. In this case, packets for network 10.0.0.0 will be routed through to a router at 131.108.3.4 if dynamic information with administrative distance less than 110 is not available.

```
ip route 10.0.0.0 255.0.0.0 131.108.3.4 110
```

In the following example, packets for network 131.108.0.0 will be routed to a router at 131.108.6.6:

```
ip route 131.108.0.0 255.255.0.0 131.108.6.6
```

KEY

To identify an authentication key on a key chain, use the **key** key chain configuration command. To remove the key from the key chain, use the **no** form of this command.

key *number*
no key *number*

Syntax	Description
number	Identification number of an authentication key on a key chain. The range of keys is 0 to 2147483647. The key identification numbers need not be consecutive.

Default

No key exists on the key chain.

Command Mode

Key chain configuration

Usage Guidelines

This command first appeared in Cisco IOS Release 11.1.

Only DRP Agent, IP Enhanced IGRP, and RIP Version 2 use key chains.

It is useful to have multiple keys on a key chain so that the software can sequence through the keys as they become invalid after time, based on the **accept-lifetime** and **send-lifetime** settings.

Each key has its own key identifier, which is stored locally. The combination of the key identifier and the interface associated with the message uniquely identifies the authentication algorithm and MD5 authentication key in use. Only one authentication packet is sent, regardless of the number of valid keys. The software starts looking at the lowest key identifier number and uses the first valid key.

If the last key expires, authentication will continue and an error message will be generated. To disable authentication, you must manually delete the last valid key.

To remove all keys, remove the key chain by using the **no key chain** command.

Example

The following example configures a key chain called *trees*. The key *chestnut* will be accepted from 1:30 p.m. to 3:30 p.m. and be sent from 2:00 p.m. to 3:00 p.m. The key *birch* will be accepted from 2:30 p.m. to 4:40 p.m. and be sent from 3:00 p.m. to 4:00 p.m. The overlap allows for migration of keys or a discrepancy in the router's set time. There is a half hour leeway on each side to handle time-of-day differences.

```
interface ethernet 0
 ip rip authentication key-chain trees
 ip rip authentication mode md5
!
router rip
 network 172.19.0.0
 version 2
!
key chain trees
 key 1
 key-string chestnut
 accept-lifetime 13:30:00 Jan 25 1996 duration 7200
 send-lifetime 14:00:00 Jan 25 1996 duration 3600
 key 2
 key-string birch
 accept-lifetime 14:30:00 Jan 25 1996 duration 7200
 send-lifetime 15:00:00 Jan 25 1996 duration 3600
```

Related Commands

Search online to find documentation for related commands.

accept-lifetime
key chain
key-string
send-lifetime
show key chain

KEY CHAIN

To enable authentication for routing protocols, identify a group of authentication keys by using the **key chain** global configuration command. To remove the key chain, use the **no** form of this command.

> **key chain** *name-of-chain*
> **no key chain** *name-of-chain*

Syntax	*Description*
name-of-chain	Name of a key chain. A key chain must have at least one key and can have up to 2147483647 keys.

Default

No key chain exists.

Command Mode

Global configuration

Usage Guidelines

This command first appeared in Cisco IOS Release 11.1.

Only DRP Agent, IP Enhanced IGRP, and RIP Version 2 use key chains.

You must configure a key chain with keys to enable authentication.

You can identify multiple key chains, but it makes sense to use one key chain per interface per routing protocol. Upon specifying the **key chain** command, you enter key chain mode.

Example

The following example configures a key chain called *trees*. The key *chestnut* will be accepted from 1:30 p.m. to 3:30 p.m. and be sent from 2:00 p.m. to 3:00 p.m. The key *birch* will be accepted from 2:30 p.m. to 4:40 p.m. and be sent from 3:00 p.m. to 4:00 p.m. The overlap allows for migration of keys or a discrepancy in the router's set time. There is a half-hour leeway on each side to handle time-of-day differences.

Part II

Command Reference

```
interface ethernet 0
 ip rip authentication key-chain trees
 ip rip authentication mode md5
 !
 router rip
 network 172.19.0.0
 version 2
 !
 key chain trees
 key 1
 key-string chestnut
 accept-lifetime 13:30:00 Jan 25 1996 duration 7200
 send-lifetime 14:00:00 Jan 25 1996 duration 3600
  key 2
  key-string birch
  accept-lifetime 14:30:00 Jan 25 1996 duration 7200
  send-lifetime 15:00:00 Jan 25 1996 duration 3600
```

Related Commands

Search online to find documentation for related commands.

accept-lifetime
ip rip authentication key-chain
key
key-string
send-lifetime
show key chain

KEY-STRING

To specify the authentication string for a key, use the **key-string** key chain key configuration command. To remove the authentication string, use the **no** form of this command.

> **key-string** *text*
> **no key-string** [*text*]

Syntax	Description
text	Authentication string that must be sent and received in the packets using the routing protocol being authenticated. The string can contain from 1 to 80 uppercase and lowercase alphanumeric characters, except that the first character cannot be a number.

Default

No key exists.

Command Mode

Key chain key configuration

Usage Guidelines

This command first appeared in Cisco IOS Release 11.1.

Only DRP Agent, IP Enhanced IGRP, and RIP Version 2 use key chains. Each key can have only one key string.

If password encryption is configured (with the **service password-encryption** command), the software saves the key string as encrypted text. When you write to the terminal with the **show running-config** command, the software displays `key-string 7` `encrypted text`.

Example

The following example configures a key chain called *trees*. The key *chestnut* will be accepted from 1:30 p.m. to 3:30 p.m. and be sent from 2:00 p.m. to 3:00 p.m. The key *birch* will be accepted from 2:30 p.m. to 4:40 p.m. and be sent from 3:00 p.m. to 4:00 p.m. The overlap allows for migration of keys or a discrepancy in the router's set time. There is a half-hour leeway on each side to handle time-of-day differences.

```
interface ethernet 0
 ip rip authentication key-chain trees
 ip rip authentication mode md5
!
router rip
 network 172.19.0.0
 version 2
!
key chain trees
 key 1
 key-string chestnut
 accept-lifetime 13:30:00 Jan 25 1996 duration 7200
 send-lifetime 14:00:00 Jan 25 1996 duration 3600
 key 2
 key-string birch
 accept-lifetime 14:30:00 Jan 25 1996 duration 7200
 send-lifetime 15:00:00 Jan 25 1996 duration 3600
```

Related Commands

Search online to find documentation for related commands.

accept-lifetime
key
key chain
send-lifetime
service password-encryption
show key chain

MATCH INTERFACE

To distribute any routes that have their next hop out one of the interfaces specified, use the **match interface** route-map configuration command. To remove the **match interface** entry, use the **no** form of this command.

> **match interface** *type number* [*...type number*]
> **no match interface** *type number* [*...type number*]

Syntax	Description
type	Interface type.
number	Interface number.

Default

No match interfaces are defined.

Command Mode

Route-map configuration

Usage Guidelines

This command first appeared in Cisco IOS Release 10.0.

Use the **route-map** global configuration command and the **match** and **set** route-map configuration commands to define the conditions for redistributing routes from one routing protocol into another. Each **route-map** command has a list of **match** and **set** commands associated with it. The **match** commands specify the *match criteria*—the conditions under which redistribution is allowed for the current **route-map** command. The **set** commands specify the *set actions*—the particular redistribution actions to perform if the criteria enforced by the **match** commands are met. The **no route-map** command deletes the route map.

The **match** route-map configuration command has multiple formats. The **match** commands may be given in any order, and all **match** commands must "pass" to cause the route to be redistributed according to the *set actions* given with the **set** commands. The **no** forms of the **match** commands remove the specified match criteria.

A route map can have several parts. Any route that does not match at least one **match** clause relating to a **route-map** command will be ignored; that is, the route will not be advertised for outbound route maps and will not be accepted for inbound route maps. If you want to modify only some data, you must configure a second route-map section with an explicit match specified.

Example

In the following example, routes that have their next hop out Ethernet interface 0 will be distributed:

```
route-map name
match interface ethernet 0
```

Related Commands

Search online to find documentation for related commands.

match as-path
match community-list
match ip address
match ip next-hop
match ip route-source
match metric
match route-type
match tag
route-map
set as-path
set automatic-tag
set community
set level
set local-preference
set metric
set metric-type
set next-hop
set origin
set tag
set weight

MATCH IP ADDRESS

To distribute any routes that have a destination network number address that is permitted by a standard or extended access list, or to perform policy routing on packets, use the **match ip address** route-map configuration command. To remove the **match ip address** entry, use the **no** form of this command.

> **match ip address** {*access-list-number* | *name*} [...*access-list-number* | *name*]
> **no match ip address** {*access-list-number* | *name*} [...*access-list-number* | *name*]

Syntax	Description
access-list-number	*name*	Number or name of a standard or extended access list. It can be an integer from 1 to 199.

Default

No access list numbers are specified.

Command Mode

Route-map configuration

Usage Guidelines

This command first appeared in Cisco IOS Release 10.0.

Use route maps to redistribute routes or to subject packets to policy routing. Both purposes are described in this section.

- Redistribution

  Use the **route-map** global configuration command and the **match** and **set** route-map configuration commands to define the conditions for redistributing routes from one routing protocol into another. Each **route-map** command has a list of **match** and **set** commands associated with it. The **match** commands specify the *match criteria*—the conditions under which redistribution is allowed for the current **route-map**. The **set** commands specify the *set actions*—the particular redistribution actions to perform if the criteria enforced by the **match** commands are met. The **no route-map** command deletes the route map.

  The **match** route-map configuration command has multiple formats. The related **match** commands are listed in the section "Related Commands for Redistribution." The **match** commands can be given in any order, and all **match** commands must "pass" to cause the route to be redistributed according to the *set actions* given with the **set** commands. The **no** forms of the **match** commands remove the specified match criteria.

  When you are passing routes through a route map, a route map can have several parts. Any route that does not match at least one **match** clause relating to a **route-map** command will be ignored; that is, the route will not be advertised for outbound route maps and will not be accepted for inbound route maps. If you want to modify only some data, you must configure a second route-map section with an explicit match specified.

- Policy Routing

  Another purpose of route maps is to enable policy routing. Use the **ip policy route-map** interface configuration command, in addition to the **route-map** global configuration command, and the **match** and **set** route-map configuration commands to define the conditions for policy routing packets. Each **route-map** command has a list of **match** and **set** commands associated with it. The related **match** and **set** commands are listed in the section "Related Commands for Policy Routing." The **match** commands specify the *match criteria*—the conditions under which policy routing occurs. The **set** commands specify the *set actions*—the particular routing actions to perform if the criteria enforced by the **match** commands are met. You might want to policy route packets based on their source, for example, using an access list.

Examples

In the following example, routes that have addresses specified by access list numbers 5 or 80 will be matched:

```
route-map name
 match ip address 5 80
```

In the following policy routing example, packets that have addresses specified by access list numbers 6 or 25 will be routed to Ethernet interface 0:

```
interface serial 0
 ip policy route-map chicago
!
route-map chicago
 match ip address 6 25
 set interface ethernet 0
```

Related Commands for Redistribution

Search online to find documentation for related commands.

match as-path
match community-list
match interface
match ip next-hop
match ip route-source
match metric
match route-type
match tag
route-map
set as-path
set automatic-tag
set community
set level
set local-preference
set metric
set metric-type
set next-hop
set origin
set tag
set weight

Related Commands for Policy Routing

Search online to find documentation for related commands.

ip policy route-map
match length
route-map
set default interface
set interface
set ip default next-hop
set ip next-hop

MATCH IP NEXT-HOP

To redistribute any routes that have a next-hop router address passed by one of the access lists specified, use the **match ip next-hop** route-map configuration command. To remove the next-hop entry, use the **no** form of this command.

> **match ip next-hop** {*access-list-number* | *name*}[...*access-list-number* | *name*]
> **no match ip next-hop** {*access-list-number* | *name*}[...*access-list-number* | *name*]

Syntax	Description
access-list-number | *name*	Number or name of a standard or extended access list. It can be an integer from 1 to 199.

Default

Routes are distributed freely, without being required to match a next-hop address.

Command Mode

Route-map configuration

Usage Guidelines

This command first appeared in Cisco IOS Release 10.0.

Use the **route-map** global configuration command and the **match** and **set** route-map configuration commands to define the conditions for redistributing routes from one routing protocol into another. Each **route-map** command has a list of **match** and **set** commands associated with it. The **match** commands specify the *match criteria*—the conditions under which redistribution is allowed for the current **route-map** command. The **set** commands specify the *set actions*—the particular redistribution actions to perform if the criteria enforced by the **match** commands are met. The **no route-map** command deletes the route map.

The **match** route-map configuration command has multiple formats. The **match** commands may be given in any order, and all **match** commands must "pass" to cause the route to be redistributed according to the *set actions* given with the **set** commands. The **no** forms of the **match** commands remove the specified match criteria.

A route map can have several parts. Any route that does not match at least one **match** clause relating to a **route-map** command will be ignored; that is, the route will not be advertised for outbound route maps and will not be accepted for inbound route maps. If you want to modify only some data, you must configure a second route-map section with an explicit match specified.

Example

In the following example, routes that have a next-hop router address passed by access list 5 or 80 will be distributed:

```
route-map name
 match ip next-hop 5 80
```

Related Commands

Search online to find documentation for related commands.

match as-path
match community-list
match interface
match ip address
match ip route-source
match metric
match route-type
match tag
route-map
set as-path
set automatic-tag
set community
set level
set local-preference
set metric
set metric-type
set next-hop
set origin
set tag
set weight

MATCH IP ROUTE-SOURCE

To redistribute routes that have been advertised by routers and access servers at the address specified by the access lists, use the **match ip route-source** route-map configuration command. To remove the route-source entry, use the **no** form of this command.

match ip route-source {*access-list-number* | *name*}[...*access-list-number* | *name*]
no match ip route-source {*access-list-number* | *name*}[...*access-list-number* | *name*]

Syntax	Description
access-list-number | *name*	Number or name of a standard or extended access list. It can be an integer from 1 to 199.

Default

No filtering on route source.

Command Mode

Route-map configuration

Usage Guidelines

This command first appeared in Cisco IOS Release 10.0.

Use the **route-map** global configuration command and the **match** and **set** route-map configuration commands to define the conditions for redistributing routes from one routing protocol into another. Each **route-map** command has a list of **match** and **set** commands associated with it. The **match** commands specify the *match criteria*—the conditions under which redistribution is allowed for the current **route-map**. The **set** commands specify the *set actions*—the particular redistribution actions to perform if the criteria enforced by the **match** commands are met. The **no route-map** command deletes the route map.

The **match** route-map configuration command has multiple formats. The **match** commands may be given in any order, and all **match** commands must "pass" to cause the route to be redistributed according to the *set actions* given with the **set** commands. The **no** forms of the **match** commands remove the specified match criteria.

A route map can have several parts. Any route that does not match at least one **match** clause relating to a **route-map** command will be ignored; that is, the route will not be advertised for outbound route maps and will not be accepted for inbound route maps. If you want to modify only some data, you must configure a second route-map section with an explicit match specified.

There are situations in which a route's next hop and source router address are not the same.

Example

In the following example, routes that have been advertised by routers and access servers at the addresses specified by access lists 5 and 80 will be distributed:

```
route-map name
  match ip route-source 5 80
```

Related Commands

Search online to find documentation for related commands.

match as-path
match community-list
match interface
match ip address
match ip next-hop
match metric
match route-type
match tag
route-map
set as-path
set automatic-tag
set community
set level

set local-preference
set metric
set metric-type
set next-hop
set origin
set tag
set weight

MATCH LENGTH

To base policy routing on the Level 3 length of a packet, use the **match length** route-map configuration command. To remove the entry, use the **no** form of this command.

> **match length** *min max*
> **no match length** *min max*

Part II

Command Reference

Syntax	Description
min	Minimum Level 3 length of the packet, inclusive, allowed for a match. Range is 0 to 0x7FFFFFFF.
max	Maximum Level 3 length of the packet, inclusive, allowed for a match. Range is 0 to 0x7FFFFFFF.

Default

No policy routing on the length of a packet.

Command Mode

Route-map configuration

Usage Guidelines

This command first appeared in Cisco IOS Release 11.0.

Use the **ip policy route-map** interface configuration command, the **route-map** global configuration command, and the **match** and **set** route-map configuration commands, to define the conditions for policy routing packets. The **ip policy route-map** command identifies a route map by name. Each **route-map** has a list of **match** and **set** commands associated with it. The **match** commands specify the *match criteria*—the conditions under which policy routing occurs. The **set** commands specify the *set actions*—the particular routing actions to perform if the criteria enforced by the **match** commands are met.

The **match** route-map configuration command has multiple formats. The **match** commands can be given in any order, and all **match** commands must "pass" to cause the packet to be routed according to the *set actions* given with the **set** commands. The **no** forms of the **match** commands remove the specified match criteria.

You might want to base your policy routing on the length of packets so that your interactive traffic and bulk traffic are directed to different routers.

Example

In the following example, packets 3 to 200 bytes long, inclusive, will be routed to FDDI interface 0:

```
interface serial 0
 ip policy route-map interactive
!
route-map interactive
 match length 3 200
 set interface fddi 0
```

Related Commands

Search online to find documentation for related commands.

ip policy route-map
match ip address
route-map
set default interface
set interface
set ip default next-hop
set ip next-hop

MATCH METRIC

To redistribute routes with the metric specified, use the **match metric** route-map configuration command. To remove the entry, use the **no** form of this command.

> **match metric** *metric-value*
> **no match metric** *metric-value*

Syntax	Description
metric-value	Route metric, which can be an IGRP five-part metric. It is a metric value from 0 to 4294967295.

Default

No filtering on a metric value.

Command Mode

Route-map configuration

Usage Guidelines

This command first appeared in Cisco IOS Release 11.2.

Use the **route-map** global configuration command and the **match** and **set** route-map configuration commands to define the conditions for redistributing routes from one routing protocol into another. Each **route-map** command has a list of **match** and **set** commands associated with it. The **match** commands specify the *match criteria*—the conditions under which redistribution is allowed for the current **route-map** command. The **set** commands specify the *set actions*—the particular redistribution actions to perform if the criteria enforced by the **match** commands are met. The **no route-map** command deletes the route map.

The **match** route-map configuration command has multiple formats. The **match** commands may be given in any order, and all **match** commands must "pass" to cause the route to be redistributed according to the *set actions* given with the **set** commands. The **no** forms of the **match** commands remove the specified match criteria.

A route map can have several parts. Any route that does not match at least one **match** clause relating to a **route-map** command will be ignored; that is, the route will not be advertised for outbound route maps and will not be accepted for inbound route maps. If you want to modify only some data, you must configure a second route-map section with an explicit match specified.

Example

In the following example, routes with the metric 5 will be redistributed:

```
route-map name
  match metric 5
```

Related Commands

Search online to find documentation for related commands.

match as-path
match community-list
match interface
match ip address
match ip next-hop
match ip route-source
match route-type
match tag
route-map
set as-path
set automatic-tag
set community
set level
set local-preference
set metric
set metric-type
set next-hop
set origin
set tag
set weight

MATCH ROUTE-TYPE

To redistribute routes of the specified type, use the **match route-type** route-map configuration command. To remove the route-type entry, use the **no** form of this command.

> **match route-type** {**local** | **internal** | **external** [**type-1** | **type-2**] | **level-1** | **level-2**}
> **no match route-type** {**local** | **internal** | **external** [**type-1** | **type-2**] | **level-1** | **level-2**}

Syntax	Description
local	Locally generated BGP routes.
internal	OSPF intra-area and interarea routes or enhanced IGRP internal routes.
external [**type-1**	**type-2**]	OSPF external routes, or enhanced IGRP external routes. For OSPF, **external type-1** matches only Type 1 external routes and **external type-2** matches only Type 2 external routes.
level-1	IS-IS Level 1 routes.
level-2	IS-IS Level 2 routes.

Default

Disabled

Command Mode

Route-map configuration

Usage Guidelines

This command first appeared in Cisco IOS Release 10.0. The following keywords first appeared in Cisco IOS Release 11.2: **local** and **external** [**type-1** | **type-2**].

Use the **route-map** global configuration command and the **match** and **set** route-map configuration commands to define the conditions for redistributing routes from one routing protocol into another. Each **route-map** command has a list of **match** and **set** commands associated with it. The **match** commands specify the *match criteria*—the conditions under which redistribution is allowed for the current **route-map** command. The **set** commands specify the *set actions*—the particular redistribution actions to perform if the criteria enforced by the **match** commands are met. The **no route-map** command deletes the route map.

The **match** route-map configuration command has multiple formats. The **match** commands may be given in any order, and all **match** commands must "pass" to cause the route to be redistributed according to the *set actions* given with the **set** commands. The **no** forms of the **match** commands remove the specified match criteria.

A route map can have several parts. Any route that does not match at least one **match** clause relating to a **route-map** command will be ignored; that is, the route will not be advertised for outbound route maps and will not be accepted for inbound route maps. If you want to modify only some data, you must configure a second route-map section with an explicit match specified.

Example

In the following example, internal routes will be redistributed:

```
route-map name
  match route-type internal
```

Related Commands

Search online to find documentation for related commands.

match as-path
match community-list
match interface
match ip address
match ip next-hop
match ip route-source
match metric
match tag
route-map
set as-path
set automatic-tag
set community
set level
set local-preference
set metric
set metric-type
set next-hop
set origin
set tag
set weight

MATCH TAG

To redistribute routes in the routing table that match the specified tags, use the **match tag** route-map configuration command. To remove the tag entry, use the **no** form of this command.

> **match tag** *tag-value* [...*tag-value*]
> **no match** tag *tag-value* [...*tag-value*]

Syntax	Description
tag-value	List of one or more route tag values. Each can be an integer from 0 to 4294967295.

Default

No match tag values are defined.

Command Mode

Route-map configuration

Usage Guidelines

This command first appeared in Cisco IOS Release 10.0.

Use the **route-map** global configuration command and the **match** and **set** route-map configuration commands to define the conditions for redistributing routes from one routing protocol into another. Each **route-map** command has a list of **match** and **set** commands associated with it. The **match** commands specify the *match criteria*—the conditions under which redistribution is allowed for the current **route-map** command. The **set** commands specify the *set actions*—the particular redistribution actions to perform if the criteria enforced by the **match** commands are met. The **no route-map** command deletes the route map.

The **match** route-map configuration command has multiple formats. The **match** commands may be given in any order, and all **match** commands must "pass" to cause the route to be redistributed according to the *set actions* given with the **set** commands. The **no** forms of the **match** commands remove the specified match criteria.

A route map can have several parts. Any route that does not match at least one **match** clause relating to a **route-map** command will be ignored; that is, the route will not be advertised for outbound route maps and will not be accepted for inbound route maps. If you want to modify only some data, you must configure second route-map section with an explicit match specified.

Example

In the following example, routes stored in the routing table with tag 5 will be redistributed:

```
route-map name
  match tag 5
```

Related Commands

Search online to find documentation for related commands.

match as-path
match community-list
match interface
match ip address
match ip next-hop
match ip route-source
match metric
match route-type
route-map
set as-path
set automatic-tag
set community

set level
set local-preference
set metric
set metric-type
set next-hop
set origin
set tag
set weight

MAXIMUM-PATHS

To control the maximum number of parallel routes an IP routing protocol can support, use the **maximum-paths** router configuration command. To restore the default value, use the **no** form of this command.

    maximum-paths *maximum*
    no maximum-paths

Syntax	*Description*
maximum	Maximum number of parallel routes an IP routing protocol installs in a routing table, in the range 1 to 6.

Defaults

The default for BGP is 1 path. The default for all other IP routing protocols is 4 paths.

Command Mode

Router configuration

Usage Guidelines

This command first appeared in Cisco IOS Release 11.2.

Example

The following example allows a maximum of 2 paths to a destination:

```
maximum-paths 2
```

PASSIVE-INTERFACE

To disable sending routing updates on an interface, use the **passive-interface** router configuration command. To reenable the sending of routing updates, use the **no** form of this command.

    passive-interface *type number*
    no passive-interface *type number*

Syntax	Description
type	Interface type.
number	Interface number.

Default

Routing updates are sent on the interface.

Command Mode

Router configuration

Usage Guidelines

This command first appeared in Cisco IOS Release 10.0.

If you disable the sending of routing updates on an interface, the particular subnet will continue to be advertised to other interfaces, and updates from other routers on that interface continue to be received and processed.

For OSPF, OSPF routing information is neither sent nor received through the specified router interface. The specified interface address appears as a stub network in the OSPF domain.

For IS-IS, this command instructs IS-IS to advertise the IP addresses for the specified interface without actually running IS-IS on that interface. The **no** form of this command for IS-IS disables advertising IP addresses for the specified address.

Enhanced IGRP is disabled on an interface that is configured as passive although it advertises the route.

Examples

The following example sends IGRP updates to all interfaces on network 131.108.0.0 except Ethernet interface 1:

```
router igrp 109
 network 131.108.0.0
 passive-interface ethernet 1
```

The following configuration enables IS-IS on interfaces Ethernet 1 and serial 0 and advertises the IP addresses of Ethernet 0 in its Link State PDUs:

```
router isis Finance
 passive-interface Ethernet 0
interface Ethernet 1
 ip router isis Finance
interface serial 0
 ip router isis Finance
```

REDISTRIBUTE

To redistribute routes from one routing domain into another routing domain, use the **redistribute** router configuration command. To disable redistribution, use the **no** form of this command.

> **redistribute** *protocol* [*process-id*] {**level-1** | **level-1-2** | **level-2**} [**metric** *metric-value*]
> [**metric-type** *type-value*] [**match** {**internal** | **external 1** | **external 2**}]
> [**tag** *tag-value*] [**route-map** *map-tag*] [**weight** *weight*] [**subnets**]
> **no redistribute** *protocol* [*process-id*] {**level-1** | **level-1-2** | **level-2**} [**metric**
> *metric-value*] [**metric-type** *type-value*] [**match** {**internal** | **external 1** | **external 2**}]
> [**tag** *tag-value*] [**route-map** *map-tag*] [**weight** *weight*] [**subnets**]

Part II

Command Reference

Syntax	Description
protocol	Source protocol from which routes are being redistributed. It can be one of the following keywords: **bgp**, **egp**, **igrp**, **isis**, **ospf**, **static** [**ip**], **connected**, and **rip**.
	The keyword **static** [**ip**] is used to redistribute IP static routes. The optional **ip** keyword is used when redistributing into IS-IS.
	The keyword **connected** refers to routes that are established automatically by virtue of having enabled IP on an interface. For routing protocols such as OSPF and IS-IS, these routes will be redistributed as external to the autonomous system.
process-id	(Optional.) For **bgp**, **egp**, or **igrp**, this is an autonomous system number, which is a 16-bit decimal number.
	For **isis**, this is an optional *tag* that defines a meaningful name for a routing process. You can specify only one IS-IS process per router. Creating a name for a routing process means that you use names when configuring routing.
	For **ospf**, this is an appropriate OSPF process ID from which routes are to be redistributed. This identifies the routing process. This value takes the form of a nonzero decimal number.
	For **rip**, no *process-id* value is needed.
level-1	For IS-IS, Level 1 routes are redistributed into other IP routing protocols independently.
level-1-2	For IS-IS, both Level 1 and Level 2 routes are redistributed into other IP routing protocols.
level-2	For IS-IS, Level 2 routes are redistributed into other IP routing protocols independently.

Syntax	*Description*
metric *metric-value*	(Optional.) Metric used for the redistributed route. If a value is not specified for this option, and no value is specified using the **default-metric** command, the default metric value is 0. Use a value consistent with the destination protocol.
metric-type *type-value*	(Optional.) For OSPF, the external link type associated with the default route advertised into the OSPF routing domain. It can be one of two values:
	1—Type 1 external route
	2—Type 2 external route
	If a **metric-type** is not specified, the Cisco IOS software adopts a Type 2 external route.
	For IS-IS, it can be one of two values:
	internal—IS-IS metric that is < 63.
	external—IS-IS metric that is > 64 < 128.
	The default is **internal**.
match {internal | external 1 | external 2}	(Optional.) For OPSF, the criteria by which OSPF routes are redistributed into other routing domains. It can be one of the following:
	internal—Routes that are internal to a specific autonomous system.
	external 1—Routes that are external to the autonomous system, but are imported into OSPF as type 1 external route.
	external 2—Routes that are external to the autonomous system, but are imported into OSPF as type 2 external route.
tag *tag-value*	(Optional.) 32-bit decimal value attached to each external route. This is not used by the OSPF protocol itself. It may be used to communicate information between Autonomous System Boundary Routers. If none is specified, then the remote autonomous system number is used for routes from BGP and EGP; for other protocols, zero (0) is used.
route-map	(Optional.) Route map should be interrogated to filter the importation of routes from this source routing protocol to the current routing protocol. If not specified, all routes are redistributed. If this keyword is specified, but no route map tags are listed, no routes will be imported.
map-tag	(Optional.) Identifier of a configured route map.
weight *weight*	(Optional.) Network weight when redistributing into BGP. An integer from 0 to 65535.
subnets	(Optional.) For redistributing routes into OSPF, the scope of redistribution for the specified protocol.

Defaults

Route redistribution is disabled.

protocol—No source protocol is defined.
process-id—No process ID is defined.
metric *metric-value*—0
metric-type *type-value*—Type 2 external route
match internal | external—internal, external 1, external 2
external *type-value*—internal
tag *tag-value*—If no value is specified, the remote autonomous system number is used for routes from BGP and EGP; for other protocols, the default is 0.
route-map *map-tag*—If the **route-map** argument is not entered, all routes are redistributed; if no *map-tag* value is entered, no routes are imported.
weight *weight*—No network weight is defined.
subnets—No subnets are defined.

Command Mode

Router configuration

Usage Guidelines

This command first appeared in Cisco IOS Release 10.0.

Changing or disabling any keyword will not affect the state of other keywords.

A router receiving a link-state protocol (LSP) with an internal metric will consider the cost of the route from itself to the redistributing router plus the advertised cost to reach the destination. An external metric only considers the advertised metric to reach the destination.

Routes learned from IP routing protocols can be redistributed at **level-1** into an attached area or at **level-2**. The keyword **level-1-2** allows both in a single command.

Redistributed routing information should always be filtered by the **distribute-list out** router configuration command. This ensures that only those routes intended by the administrator are passed along to the receiving routing protocol.

Whenever you use the **redistribute** or the **default-information** router configuration commands to redistribute routes into an OSPF routing domain, the router automatically becomes an Autonomous System Boundary Router (ASBR). However, an ASBR does not, by default, generate a *default route* into the OSPF routing domain.

When routes are redistributed between OSPF processes, no OSPF metrics are preserved.

When routes are redistributed into OSPF and no metric is specified in the **metric** keyword, the default metric that OSPF uses is 20 for routes from all protocols except BGP route, which gets a metric of 1.

When redistributing routes into OSPF, only routes that are not subnetted are redistributed if the **subnets** keyword is not specified.

The only **connected** routes affected by this **redistribute** command are the routes not specified by the **network** command.

You cannot use the **default-metric** command to affect the metric used to advertise **connected** routes.

NOTES

The **metric** value specified in the **redistribute** command supersedes the **metric** value specified using the **default-metric** command.

Default redistribution of IGPs or EGP into BGP is not allowed unless **default-information originate** is specified.

When routes are redistributed into OSPF and no metric is specified in the **metric** keyword, the default metric that OSPF uses is 20 for routes from all protocols except BGP route, which gets a metric of 1.

Examples

The following are examples of the various configurations you would use to redistribute one routing protocol into another routing protocol.

The following example configuration causes OSPF routes to be redistributed into a BGP domain:

```
router bgp 109
redistribute ospf...
```

The following example configuration causes IGRP routes to be redistributed into an OSPF domain:

```
router ospf 110
redistribute igrp...
```

The following example causes the specified IGRP process routes to be redistributed into an OSPF domain. The IGRP-derived metric will be remapped to 100 and RIP routes to 200.

```
router ospf 109
redistribute igrp 108 metric 100 subnets
redistribute rip metric 200 subnets
```

In the following example, BGP routes are configured to be redistributed into IS-IS. The link-state cost is specified as 5, and the metric type will be set to external, indicating that it has lower priority than internal metrics.

```
router isis
redistribute bgp 120 metric 5 metric-type external
```

Related Commands

Search online to find documentation for related commands.

default-information originate (BGP)
default-information originate (IS-IS)
default-information originate (OSPF)

distribute-list out
route-map
show route-map

ROUTE-MAP

To define the conditions for redistributing routes from one routing protocol into another, or to enable policy routing, use the **route-map** global configuration command and the **match** and **set** route-map configuration commands. To delete an entry, use the **no** form of this command.

    route-map *map-tag* [**permit** | **deny**] [*sequence-number*]
    no route-map *map-tag* [**permit** | **deny**] [*sequence-number*]

Syntax	Description
map-tag	Defines a meaningful name for the route map. The **redistribute** router configuration command uses this name to reference this route map. Multiple route maps may share the same map tag name.
permit	(Optional.) If the match criteria are met for this route map, and **permit** is specified, the route is redistributed as controlled by the set actions. In the case of policy routing, the packet is policy routed.
	If the match criteria are not met, and **permit** is specified, the next route map with the same map tag is tested. If a route passes none of the match criteria for the set of route maps sharing the same name, it is not redistributed by that set.
	The **permit** keyword is the default.
deny	(Optional.) If the match criteria are met for the route map, and **deny** is specified, the route is not redistributed. In the case of policy routing, the packet is not policy routed, and no further route maps sharing the same map tag name will be examined. If the packet is not policy-routed, it reverts to the normal forwarding algorithm.
sequence-number	(Optional.) Number that indicates the position a new route map is to have in the list of route maps already configured with the same name. If given with the **no** form of this command, it specifies the position of the route map that should be deleted.

Default

No default is available.

Command Mode

Global configuration

Usage Guidelines

This command first appeared in Cisco IOS Release 10.0.

Use route maps to redistribute routes or to subject packets to policy routing. Both purposes are described in this section.

- Redistribution

  Use the **route-map** global configuration command and the **match** and **set** route-map configuration commands to define the conditions for redistributing routes from one routing protocol into another. Each **route-map** command has a list of **match** and **set** commands associated with it. The **match** commands specify the *match criteria*—the conditions under which redistribution is allowed for the current **route-map** command. The **set** commands specify the *set actions*—the particular redistribution actions to perform if the criteria enforced by the **match** commands are met. The **no route-map** command deletes the route map.

  The **match** route-map configuration command has multiple formats. The related **match** commands are listed in the section "Related Commands for Redistribution." The **match** commands can be given in any order, and all **match** commands must "pass" to cause the route to be redistributed according to the *set actions* given with the **set** commands. The **no** forms of the **match** commands remove the specified match criteria.

  Use route maps when you want detailed control over how routes are redistributed between routing processes. The destination routing protocol is the one you specify with the **router** global configuration command. The source routing protocol is the one you specify with the **redistribute** router configuration command. See the following example as an illustration of how route maps are configured.

  When you are passing routes through a route map, a route map can have several parts. Any route that does not match at least one **match** clause relating to a **route-map** command will be ignored; that is, the route will not be advertised for outbound route maps and will not be accepted for inbound route maps. If you want to modify only some data, you must configure a second route-map section with an explicit match specified.

- Policy Routing

  Another purpose of route maps is to enable policy-routing. Use the **ip policy route-map** command, in addition to the **route-map** command, and the **match** and **set** commands to define the conditions for policy-routing packets. The related **match** and **set** commands are listed in the section "Related Commands for Policy Routing." The **match** commands specify the conditions under which policy routing occurs. The **set** commands specify the routing actions to perform if the criteria enforced by the **match** commands are met. You might want to policy-route packets some way other than the obvious shortest path.

The *sequence-number* works as follows:

1. If no entry is defined with the supplied tag, an entry is created with *sequence-number* set to 10.

2. If only one entry is defined with the supplied tag, that entry becomes the default entry for the following **route-map** command. The *sequence-number* of this entry is unchanged.

3. If more than one entry is defined with the supplied tag, an error message is printed to indicate that *sequence-number* is required.

If **no route-map** *map-tag* is specified (with no *sequence-number*), the whole route-map is deleted.

Example

The following example redistributes RIP routes with a hop count equal to 1 into OSPF. These routes will be redistributed into OSPF as external link state advertisements with a metric of 5, metric type of Type 1, and a tag equal to 1.

```
router ospf 109
 redistribute rip route-map rip-to-ospf

route-map rip-to-ospf permit
 match metric 1
 set metric 5
 set metric-type type1
 set tag 1
```

Related Commands for Redistribution

Search online to find documentation for related commands.

match as-path
match community-list
match interface
match ip address
match ip next-hop
match ip route-source
match metric
match route-type
match tag
set as-path
set automatic-tag
set community
set level
set local-preference
set metric
set metric-type
set next-hop
set origin
set tag
set weight
show route-map

Related Commands for Policy Routing

Search online to find documentation for related commands.

ip policy route-map
match ip address
match length
set default interface
set interface
set ip default next-hop
set ip next-hop

SEND-LIFETIME

To set the time period during which an authentication key on a key chain is valid to be sent, use the
send-lifetime key chain key configuration command. To revert to the default value, use the **no form**
of this command.

> send-lifetime *start-time* {**infinite** | *end-time* | **duration** *seconds*}
> no send-lifetime [*start-time* {**infinite** | *end-time* | **duration** *seconds*}]

Syntax	Description
start-time	Beginning time that the key specified by the **key** command is valid to be sent. The syntax can be either of the following:
	hh:mm:ss Month date year
	hh:mm:ss date Month year
	hh—hours
	mm—minutes
	ss—seconds
	date—date (1-31)
	Month—first three letters of the month
	year—year (four digits)
	The default start time and the earliest acceptable date is January 1, 1993.
infinite	Key is valid to be sent from the *start-time* on.
end-time	Key is valid to be sent from the *start-time* until *end-time*. The syntax is the same as that for *start-time*. The *end-time* must be after the *start-time*. The default end time is an infinite time period.
duration *seconds*	Length of time in seconds that the key is valid to be sent.

Default

Forever (The starting time is January 1, 1993, and the ending time is infinite.)

Command Mode

Key chain key configuration

Usage Guidelines

This command first appeared in Cisco IOS Release 11.1.

Specify a *start-time* and one of the following: **infinite**, *end-time*, or **duration** *seconds*.

We recommend running NTP or some other time synchronization method if you intend to set lifetimes on keys.

If the last key expires, authentication will continue and an error message will be generated. To disable authentication, you must manually delete the last valid key.

Example

The following example configures a key chain called *trees*. The key *chestnut* will be accepted from 1:30 p.m. to 3:30 p.m. and be sent from 2:00 p.m. to 3:00 p.m. The key *birch* will be accepted from 2:30 p.m. to 4:40 p.m. and be sent from 3:00 p.m. to 4:00 p.m. The overlap allows for migration of keys or a discrepancy in the router's set time. There is a half-hour leeway on each side to handle time-of-day differences.

```
interface ethernet 0
 ip rip authentication key-chain trees
 ip rip authentication mode md5
!
router rip
 network 172.19.0.0
 version 2
!
key chain trees
 key 1
 key-string chestnut
 accept-lifetime 13:30:00 Jan 25 1996 duration 7200
 send-lifetime 14:00:00 Jan 25 1996 duration 3600
 key 2
 key-string birch
 accept-lifetime 14:30:00 Jan 25 1996 duration 7200
 send-lifetime 15:00:00 Jan 25 1996 duration 3600
```

Related Commands

Search online to find documentation for related commands.

accept-lifetime
key

key chain
key-string
show key chain

SET AUTOMATIC-TAG

To automatically compute the tag value, use the **set automatic-tag** route-map configuration command. To disable this function, use the **no** form of this command.

> **set automatic-tag**
> **no set automatic-tag**

Syntax   Description

This command has no arguments or keywords.

Default

Disabled

Command Mode

Route-map configuration

Usage Guidelines

This command first appeared in Cisco IOS Release 10.0.

You must have a match clause (even if it points to a "permit everything" list) if you want to set tags.

Use the **route-map** global configuration command and the **match** and **set** route-map configuration commands to define the conditions for redistributing routes from one routing protocol into another. Each **route-map** command has a list of **match** and **set** commands associated with it. The **match** commands specify the *match criteria*—the conditions under which redistribution is allowed for the current **route-map** command. The **set** commands specify the *set actions*—the particular redistribution actions to perform if the criteria enforced by the **match** commands are met. The **no route-map** command deletes the route map.

The **set** route-map configuration commands specify the redistribution *set actions* to be performed when all of a route map's match criteria are met. When all match criteria are met, all set actions are performed.

Example

In the following example, the Cisco IOS software is configured to automatically compute the tag value for the BGP learned routes:

```
route-map tag
 match as path 10
 set automatic-tag
```

```
 !
 router bgp 100
  table-map tag
```

Related Commands

Search online to find documentation for related commands.

match as-path
match community-list
match interface
match ip address
match ip next-hop
match ip route-source
match metric
match route-type
match tag
route-map
set as-path
set community
set level
set local-preference
set metric
set metric-type
set next-hop
set origin
set tag
set weight
show route-map

SET DEFAULT INTERFACE

To indicate where to output packets that pass a match clause of a route map for policy routing and have no explicit route to the destination, use the **set default interface** route-map configuration command. To delete an entry, use the **no** form of this command.

set default interface *type number* [... *type number*]
no set default interface *type number* [... *type number*]

Syntax	Description
type	Interface type, used with the interface number, to which packets are output.
number	Interface number, used with the interface type, to which packets are output.

Default

Disabled

Command Mode

Route-map configuration

Usage Guidelines

This command first appeared in Cisco IOS Release 11.0.

Use this command to provide certain users a different default route. If the Cisco IOS software has no explicit route for the destination, then it routes the packet to this interface. The first interface specified with the **set default interface** command that is up is used. The optionally specified interfaces are tried in turn.

Use the **ip policy route-map** interface configuration command, the **route-map** global configuration command, and the **match** and **set** route-map configuration commands, to define the conditions for policy routing packets. The **ip policy route-map** command identifies a route map by name. Each **route-map** command has a list of **match** and **set** commands associated with it. The **match** commands specify the *match criteria*—the conditions under which policy routing occurs. The **set** commands specify the *set actions*—the particular routing actions to perform if the criteria enforced by the **match** commands are met.

The set clauses can be used in conjunction with one another. They are evaluated in the following order:

set ip next-hop
set interface
set ip default next-hop
set default interface

Example

In the following example, packets that have a Level 3 length of 3 to 50 bytes and for which the software has no explicit route to the destination are output to Ethernet interface 0:

```
interface serial 0
 ip policy route-map brighton
!
route-map brighton
 match length 3 50
 set default interface ethernet 0
```

Related Commands

Search online to find documentation for related commands.

ip policy route-map
match ip address

match length
route-map
set interface
set ip default next-hop
set ip next-hop

SET INTERFACE

To indicate where to output packets that pass a match clause of route map for policy routing, use the **set interface** route-map configuration command. To delete an entry, use the **no** form of this command.

    set interface *type number* [...*type number*]
    no set interface *type number* [...*type number*]

Part
II

Command Reference

Syntax	Description
type	Interface type, used with the interface number, to which packets are output.
number	Interface number, used with the interface type, to which packets are output.

Default

Disabled

Command Mode

Route-map configuration

Usage Guidelines

This command first appeared in Cisco IOS Release 11.0.

Use the **ip policy route-map** interface configuration command, the **route-map** global configuration command, and the **match** and **set** route-map configuration commands, to define the conditions for policy routing packets. The **ip policy route-map** command identifies a route map by name. Each **route-map** command has a list of **match** and **set** commands associated with it. The **match** commands specify the *match criteria*—the conditions under which policy routing occurs. The **set** commands specify the *set actions*—the particular routing actions to perform if the criteria enforced by the **match** commands are met.

If the first interface specified with the **set interface** command is down, the optionally specified interfaces are tried in turn.

The set clauses can be used in conjunction with one another. They are evaluated in the following order:

set ip next-hop
set interface
set ip default next-hop
set default interface

A useful next hop implies an interface. As soon as a next hop and an interface are found, the packet is routed.

Specifying **set interface null** 0 is a way to write a policy so that the packet is dropped and an "unreachable" message is generated.

Example

In the following example, packets with a Level 3 length of 3 to 50 bytes are output to Ethernet interface 0:

```
interface serial 0
 ip policy route-map testing
!
route-map testing
 match length 3 50
 set interface ethernet 0
```

Related Commands

Search online to find documentation for related commands.

ip policy route-map
match ip address
match length
route-map
set default interface
set ip default next-hop
set ip next-hop

SET IP DEFAULT NEXT-HOP

To indicate where to output packets that pass a match clause of a route map for policy routing and for which the Cisco IOS software has no explicit route to a destination, use the **set ip default next-hop** route-map configuration command. To delete an entry, use the **no** form of this command.

> **set ip default next-hop** *ip-address* [...*ip-address*]
> **no set ip default next-hop** *ip-address* [...*ip-address*]

Syntax	Description
ip-address	IP address of the next hop to which packets are output. It need not be an adjacent router.

Default
Disabled

Command Mode
Route-map configuration

Usage Guidelines
This command first appeared in Cisco IOS Release 11.0.

Use this command to provide certain users a different default route. If the software has no explicit route for the destination in the packet, then it routes the packet to this next hop. The first next hop specified with the **set ip default next-hop** command that appears to be adjacent to the router is used. The optional specified IP addresses are tried in turn.

Use the **ip policy route-map** interface configuration command, the **route-map** global configuration command, and the **match** and **set** route-map configuration commands, to define the conditions for policy routing packets. The **ip policy route-map** command identifies a route map by name. Each **route-map** command has a list of **match** and **set** commands associated with it. The **match** commands specify the *match criteria*—the conditions under which policy routing occurs. The **set** commands specify the *set actions*—the particular routing actions to perform if the criteria enforced by the **match** commands are met.

The set clauses can be used in conjunction with one another. They are evaluated in the following order:

set ip next-hop
set interface
set ip default next-hop
set default interface

Example
The following example provides two sources with equal access to two different service providers. Packets arriving on async interface 1 from the source 1.1.1.1 are sent to the router at 6.6.6.6 if the software has no explicit route for the packet's destination. Packets arriving from the source 2.2.2.2 are sent to the router at 7.7.7.7 if the software has no explicit route for the packet's destination. All other packets for which the software has no explicit route to the destination are discarded.

```
access-list 1 permit ip 1.1.1.1 0.0.0.0
access-list 2 permit ip 2.2.2.2 0.0.0.0
!
interface async 1
 ip policy route-map equal-access
!
route-map equal-access permit 10
 match ip address 1
 set ip default next-hop 6.6.6.6
```

Part II

Command Reference

```
route-map equal-access permit 20
 match ip address 2
 set ip default next-hop 7.7.7.7
 route-map equal-access permit 30
 set default interface null0
```

Related Commands

Search online to find documentation for related commands.

ip policy route-map
match ip address
match length
route-map
set default interface
set interface
set ip next-hop

SET IP NEXT-HOP

To indicate where to output packets that pass a match clause of a route map for policy routing, use the **set ip next-hop** route-map configuration command. To delete an entry, use the **no** form of this command.

> **set ip next-hop** *ip-address* [...*ip-address*]
> **no set ip next-hop** *ip-address* [...*ip-address*]

Syntax	Description
ip-address	IP address of the next hop to which packets are output. It need not be an adjacent router.

Default

Disabled

Command Mode

Route-map configuration

Usage Guidelines

This command first appeared in Cisco IOS Release 11.0.

Use the **ip policy route-map** interface configuration command, the **route-map** global configuration command, and the **match** and **set** route-map configuration commands, to define the conditions for policy routing packets. The **ip policy route-map** command identifies a route map by name. Each **route-map** command has a list of **match** and **set** commands associated with it. The **match** commands specify the *match criteria*—the conditions under which policy routing occurs. The **set** commands specify the *set actions*—the particular routing actions to perform if the criteria enforced by the **match** commands are met.

If the first next hop specified with the **set ip next-hop** command is down, the optionally specified IP addresses are tried in turn.

The set clauses can be used in conjunction with one another. They are evaluated in the following order:

set ip next-hop
set interface
set ip default next-hop
set default interface

Example

In the following example, packets with a Level 3 length of 3 to 50 bytes are output to the router at IP address 161.14.2.2:

```
interface serial 0
 ip policy route-map thataway
!
route-map thataway
 match length 3 50
 set ip next-hop 161.14.2.2
```

Related Commands

Search online to find documentation for related commands.

ip policy route-map
match ip address
match length
route-map
set default interface
set interface
set ip default next-hop

SET LEVEL

To indicate where to import routes, use the **set level** route-map configuration command. To delete an entry, use the **no** form of this command.

> **set level** {level-1 | level-2 | level-1-2 | stub-area | backbone}
> **no set level** {level-1 | level-2 | level-1-2 | stub-area | backbone}

Syntax	Description
level-1	Imports routes into a Level-1 area.
level-2	Imports routes into a Level-2 subdomain.

Syntax	*Description*
level-1-2	Imports routes into Level-1 and Level-2.
stub-area	Imports routes into OSPF NSSA area.
backbone	Imports routes into OSPF backbone area.

Defaults

Disabled

For IS-IS destinations, the default value is **level-2**. For OSPF destinations, the default value is **backbone**.

Command Mode

Route-map configuration

Usage Guidelines

This command first appeared in Cisco IOS Release 10.0.

Use the **route-map** global configuration command and the **match** and **set** route-map configuration commands to define the conditions for redistributing routes from one routing protocol into another. Each **route-map** command has a list of **match** and **set** commands associated with it. The **match** commands specify the *match criteria*—the conditions under which redistribution is allowed for the current **route-map** command. The **set** commands specify the *set actions*—the particular redistribution actions to perform if the criteria enforced by the **match** commands are met. The **no route-map** command deletes the route map.

The **set** route-map configuration commands specify the redistribution *set actions* to be performed when all of a route map's match criteria are met. When all match criteria are met, all set actions are performed.

Example

In the following example, routes will be imported into the Level 1 area:

```
route-map name
  set level level-1
```

Related Commands

Search online to find documentation for related commands.

match as-path
match community-list
match interface
match ip address
match ip next-hop

match ip route-source
match metric
match route-type
match tag
route-map
set as-path
set community
set local-preference
set metric
set metric-type
set next-hop
set origin
set tag
set weight
show route-map

SET LOCAL-PREFERENCE

To specify a preference value for the autonomous system path, use the **set local-preference** route-map configuration command. To delete an entry, use the **no** form of this command.

> **set local-preference** *value*
> **no set local-preference** *value*

Syntax	Description
value	Preference value. An integer from 0 to 4294967295.

Default

Preference value of 100

Command Mode

Route-map configuration

Usage Guidelines

This command first appeared in Cisco IOS Release 10.0.

The preference is sent only to all routers in the local autonomous system.

You must have a match clause (even if it points to a "permit everything" list) if you want to set tags.

Use the **route-map** global configuration command and the **match** and **set** route-map configuration commands to define the conditions for redistributing routes from one routing protocol into another. Each **route-map** command has a list of **match** and **set** commands associated with it. The **match** commands specify the *match criteria*—the conditions under which redistribution is allowed for the current **route-map** command. The **set** commands specify the *set actions*—the particular redistribution actions to perform if the criteria enforced by the **match** commands are met. The **no route-map** command deletes the route map.

The **set** route-map configuration commands specify the redistribution *set actions* to be performed when all of a route map's match criteria are met. When all match criteria are met, all set actions are performed.

You can change the default preference value with the **bgp default local-preference** command.

Example

In the following example, the local preference is set to 100 for all routes that are included in access list 1:

```
route-map map-preference
 match as-path 1
 set local-preference 100
```

Related Commands

Search online to find documentation for related commands.

bgp default local-preference
match as-path
match community-list
match interface
match ip address
match ip next-hop
match ip route-source
match metric
match route-type
match tag
route-map
set as-path
set automatic-tag
set community
set level
set metric
set metric-type
set next-hop
set origin
set tag
set weight

SET METRIC

To set the metric value for a routing protocol, use the **set metric** route-map configuration command. To return to the default metric value, use the **no** form of this command.

> **set metric** *metric-value*
> **no set metric** *metric-value*

Syntax	Description
metric-value	Metric value; an integer from -294967295 to 294967295. This argument applies to all routing protocols except IGRP and IP Enhanced IGRP.

Default

The dynamically learned metric value.

Command Mode

Route-map configuration

Usage Guidelines

This command first appeared in Cisco IOS Release 10.0.

— **NOTES** ────────────────────────────────

We recommend that you consult your Cisco technical support representative before changing the default value.

────────────────────────────────

Use the **route-map** global configuration command and the **match** and **set** route-map configuration commands to define the conditions for redistributing routes from one routing protocol into another. Each **route-map** command has a list of **match** and **set** commands associated with it. The **match** commands specify the *match criteria*—the conditions under which redistribution is allowed for the current **route-map** command. The **set** commands specify the *set actions*—the particular redistribution actions to perform if the criteria enforced by the **match** commands are met. The **no route-map** command deletes the route map.

The **set** route-map configuration commands specify the redistribution *set actions* to be performed when all of a route map's match criteria are met. When all match criteria are met, all set actions are performed.

Example

In the following example, the metric value for the routing protocol is set to 100:

```
route-map set-metric          •
  set metric 100
```

Related Commands

Search online to find documentation for related commands.

match as-path
match community-list
match interface
match ip address
match ip next-hop
match ip route-source
match metric
match route-type
match tag
route-map
set as-path
set community
set level
set local-preference
set metric-type
set next-hop
set origin
set tag
set weight
show route-map

SET METRIC-TYPE

To set the metric type for the destination routing protocol, use the **set metric-type** route-map configuration command. To return to the default, use the **no** form of this command.

> set metric-type {internal | external | type-1 | type-2}
> no set metric-type {internal | external | type-1 | type-2}

Syntax	Description
internal	IS-IS internal metric.
external	IS-IS external metric.
type-1	OSPF external type 1 metric.
type-2	OSPF external type 2 metric.

Default

Disabled

Command Mode

Route-map configuration

Usage Guidelines

This command first appeared in Cisco IOS Release 10.0.

Use the **route-map** global configuration command with **match** and **set** route-map configuration commands to define the conditions for redistributing routes from one routing protocol into another. Each **route-map** command has a list of **match** and **set** commands associated with it. The **match** commands specify the *match criteria*—the conditions under which redistribution is allowed for the current **route-map** command. The **set** commands specify the *set actions*—the particular redistribution actions to perform if the criteria enforced by the **match** commands are met. The **no route-map** command deletes the route map.

The **set** route-map configuration commands specify the redistribution *set actions* to be performed when all of a route map's match criteria are met. When all match criteria are met, all set actions are performed.

Example

In the following example, the metric type of the destination protocol is set to OSPF external type 1:

```
route-map map-type
    set metric-type type-1
```

Related Commands

Search online to find documentation for related commands.

match as-path
match community-list
match interface
match ip address
match ip next-hop
match ip route-source
match metric
match route-type
match tag
route-map
set as-path
set automatic-tag
set community
set level
set local-preference
set metric
set next-hop

set origin
set tag
set weight
show route-map

SET NEXT-HOP

To specify the address of the next hop, use the **set next-hop** route-map configuration command. To delete an entry, use the **no** form of this command.

> **set next-hop** *next-hop*
> **no set next-hop** *next-hop*

Syntax	*Description*
next-hop	IP address of the next hop router.

Default

Default next-hop address.

Command Mode

Route-map configuration

Usage Guidelines

This command first appeared in Cisco IOS Release 10.0.

You must have a match clause (even if it points to a "permit everything" list) if you want to set tags.

Use the **route-map** global configuration command with **match** and **set** route-map configuration commands to define the conditions for redistributing routes from one routing protocol into another. Each **route-map** command has a list of **match** and **set** commands associated with it. The **match** commands specify the *match criteria*—the conditions under which redistribution is allowed for the current **route-map** command. The **set** commands specify the *set actions*—the particular redistribution actions to perform if the criteria enforced by the **match** commands are met. The **no route-map** command deletes the route map.

The **set** route-map configuration commands specify the redistribution *set actions* to be performed when all of a route map's match criteria are met. When all match criteria are met, all set actions are performed.

Example

In the following example, routes that pass the access list have the next hop set to 198.92.70.24:

```
route-map map_hop
 match address 5
 set next-hop 198.92.70.24
```

Related Commands

Search online to find documentation for related commands.

match as-path
match community-list
match interface
match ip address
match ip next-hop
match ip route-source
match metric
match route-type
match tag
route-map
set as-path
set automatic-tag
set community
set level
set local-preference
set metric
set metric-type
set origin
set tag
set weight
show route-map

SET ORIGIN

To set the BGP origin code, use the **set origin** route-map configuration command. To delete an entry, use the **no** form of this command.

set origin {igp | egp *autonomous-system* | incomplete}

Syntax	Description
igp	Remote IGP.
egp	Local EGP.
autonomous-system	Remote autonomous system. This is an integer from 0 to 65535.
incomplete	Unknown heritage.

Default

Default origin, based on route in main IP routing table.

Command Mode

Route-map configuration

Usage Guidelines

This command first appeared in Cisco IOS Release 10.0.

You must have a match clause (even if it points to a "permit everything" list) if you want to set tags.

Use the **route-map** global configuration command with **match** and **set** route-map configuration commands to define the conditions for redistributing routes from one routing protocol into another. Each **route-map** command has a list of **match** and **set** commands associated with it. The **match** commands specify the *match criteria*—the conditions under which redistribution is allowed for the current **route-map** command. The **set** commands specify the *set actions*—the particular redistribution actions to perform if the criteria enforced by the **match** commands are met. The **no route-map** command deletes the route map.

The **set** route-map configuration commands specify the redistribution *set actions* to be performed when all of a route map's match criteria are met. When all match criteria are met, all set actions are performed.

Example

In the following example, routes that pass the route map have the origin set to IGP:

```
route-map set_origin
  match as-path 10
    set origin igp
```

Related Commands

Search online to find documentation for related commands.

match as-path
match community-list
match interface
match ip address
match ip next-hop
match ip route-source
match metric
match route-type
match tag
route-map
set as-path
set automatic-tag
set community
set level
set local-preference

set metric
set metric-type
set next-hop
set tag
set weight
show route-map

SET TAG

To set a tag value of the destination routing protocol, use the **set tag** route-map configuration command. To delete the entry, use the **no** form of this command.

> **set tag** *tag-value*
> **no set tag** *tag-value*

Part
II

Command Reference

Syntax	Description
tag-value	Name for the tag. Integer from 0 to 4294967295.

Default

If not specified, the default action is to *forward* the tag in the source routing protocol onto the new destination protocol.

Command Mode

Route-map configuration

Usage Guidelines

This command first appeared in Cisco IOS Release 10.0.

Use the **route-map** global configuration command with **match** and **set** route-map configuration commands to define the conditions for redistributing routes from one routing protocol into another. Each **route-map** command has a list of **match** and **set** commands associated with it. The **match** commands specify the *match criteria*—the conditions under which redistribution is allowed for the current **route-map** command. The **set** commands specify the *set actions*—the particular redistribution actions to perform if the criteria enforced by the **match** commands are met. The **no route-map** command deletes the route map.

The **set** route-map configuration commands specify the redistribution *set actions* to be performed when all of a route map's match criteria are met. When all match criteria are met, all set actions are performed.

Example

In the following example, the tag value of the destination routing protocol is set to 5:

```
route-map tag
 set tag 5
```

Related Commands

Search online to find documentation for related commands.

match as-path
match community-list
match interface
match ip address
match ip next-hop
match ip route-source
match metric
match route-type
match tag
route-map
set as-path
set automatic-tag
set community
set level
set local-preference
set metric
set metric-type
set next-hop
set origin
set weight
show route-map

SHOW IP CACHE POLICY

To display the cache entries in the policy route-cache, use the **show ip cache policy** EXEC command.

    show ip cache policy

Syntax   Description

This command has no arguments or keywords.

Command Mode

EXEC

Usage Guidelines

This command first appeared in Cisco IOS Release 11.3.

Sample Display

The following is sample output from the **show ip cache policy** command:

```
Router# show ip cache policy

Total adds 10, total deletes 10

Type Routemap/sequence    Age       Interface    Next Hop
NH   george/10            00:04:31  Ethernet0    171.69.1.2
Int  george/30            00:01:23  Serial4      171.69.5.129
```

Table 23–2 describes the significant fields in the display.

Table 23–2 *Show IP Cache Policy Field Descriptions*

Field	Description
Total adds	Number of times a cache entry was created.
total deletes	Number of times a cache entry or the entire cache was deleted.
Type	NH indicates **set ip nexthop** command. Int indicates **set interface** command.
Routemap	Name of route-map that created the entry; in this example, "george."
sequence	Route-map sequence number.
Age	Age of cache entry.
Interface	Output interface type and number.
Next Hop	IP address of the next hop.

Related Commands

Search online to find documentation for related commands.

ip route-cache

SHOW IP LOCAL POLICY

To display the route map used for local policy routing, if any, use the **show ip local policy** EXEC command.

> **show ip local policy**

Syntax   Description

This command has no arguments or keywords.

Command Mode

EXEC

Usage Guidelines

This command first appeared in Cisco IOS Release 11.1.

Sample Display

The following is sample output from the **show ip local policy** command:

```
Router# show ip local policy

Local policy routing is enabled, using route map equal
route-map equal, permit, sequence 10
  Match clauses:
    length 150 200
  Set clauses:
    ip next-hop 10.10.11.254
  Policy routing matches: 0 packets, 0 bytes
route-map equal, permit, sequence 20
  Match clauses:
    ip address (access-lists): 101
  Set clauses:
    ip next-hop 10.10.11.14
  Policy routing matches: 2 packets, 172 bytes
```

Table 23–3 describes the fields in the display.

Table 23–3   *Show IP Local Policy Field Descriptions*

Field	Description
route-map equal	The name of the route-map is "equal."
permit	The route-map contains permit statements.
sequence	The sequence number of the route map, which determines in what order it is processed among other route-maps.
Match clauses:	Clauses in the route-map that must be matched to satisfy the permit or deny action.
Set clauses:	Set clauses that will be put into place if the match clauses are met.
Policy routing matches: packets	Number of packets that meet the match clauses.
bytes	Number of bytes in the packets that meet the match clauses.

Related Commands

Search online to find documentation for related commands.

ip local policy route-map
match ip address
match length
route-map
set default interface
set interface
set ip default next-hop
set ip next-hop

SHOW IP POLICY

To display the route map used for policy routing, use the **show ip policy** EXEC command.

   show ip policy

Syntax   Description

This command has no arguments or keywords.

Command Mode

EXEC

Usage Guidelines

This command first appeared in Cisco IOS Release 11.1.

Sample Displays

The following is sample output from the **show ip policy** command:

```
Router# show ip policy

Interface      Route map
local          equal
Ethernet0      equal
```

The following is sample output from the **show route-map** command, which relates to the preceding sample display:

```
Router# show route-map

route-map equal, permit, sequence 10
  Match clauses:
    length 150 200
  Set clauses:
    ip next-hop 10.10.11.254
  Policy routing matches: 0 packets, 0 bytes
```

```
route-map equal, permit, sequence 20
  Match clauses:
    ip address (access-lists): 101
  Set clauses:
    ip next-hop 10.10.11.14
  Policy routing matches: 144 packets, 15190 bytes
```

Table 23–4 describes the fields in the display.

Table 23–4 *Show IP Policy Field Descriptions*

Field	Description
route-map equal	The name of the route-map is "equal."
permit	The route-map contains permit statements.
sequence	Sequence number of the route-map, which determines in what order it is processed among other route-maps.
Match clauses:	Clauses in the route-map that must be matched to satisfy the permit or deny action.
Set clauses:	Set clauses that will be put into place if the match clauses are met.
Policy routing matches: packets	Number of packets that meet the match clauses.
bytes	Number of bytes in the packets that meet the match clauses.

Related Commands

Search online to find documentation for related commands.

match ip address
match length
route-map
set default interface
set interface
set ip default next-hop
set ip next-hop

SHOW IP PROTOCOLS

To display the parameters and current state of the active routing protocol process, use the **show ip protocols** EXEC command.

show ip protocols

Syntax   Description

This command has no arguments or keywords.

Command Mode

EXEC

Usage Guidelines

This command first appeared in Cisco IOS Release 10.0.

The information displayed by **show ip protocols** is useful in debugging routing operations. Information in the Routing Information Sources field of the **show ip protocols** output can help you identify a router suspected of delivering bad routing information.

Sample Displays

The following is sample output from the **show ip protocols** command, showing IGRP processes:

```
Router# show ip protocols

Routing Protocol is "igrp 109"
  Sending updates every 90 seconds, next due in 44 seconds
  Invalid after 270 seconds, hold down 280, flushed after 630
  Outgoing update filter list for all interfaces is not set
  Incoming update filter list for all interfaces is not set
  Default networks flagged in outgoing updates
  Default networks accepted from incoming updates
  IGRP metric weight K1=1, K2=0, K3=1, K4=0, K5=0
  IGRP maximum hopcount 100
  IGRP maximum metric variance 1
  Redistributing: igrp 109
  Routing for Networks:
    198.92.72.0
  Routing Information Sources:
    Gateway         Distance      Last Update
    198.92.72.18         100      0:56:41
    198.92.72.19         100      6d19
    198.92.72.22         100      0:55:41
    198.92.72.20         100      0:01:04
    198.92.72.30         100      0:01:29
  Distance: (default is 100)

Routing Protocol is "bgp 1878"
  Sending updates every 60 seconds, next due in 0 seconds
  Outgoing update filter list for all interfaces is 1
  Incoming update filter list for all interfaces is not set
```

```
Redistributing: igrp 109
IGP synchronization is disabled
Automatic route summarization is enabled
Neighbor(s):
  Address            FiltIn FiltOut DistIn DistOut Weight RouteMap
  192.108.211.17            1
  192.108.213.89            1
  198.6.255.13              1
  198.92.72.18              1
  198.92.72.19
  198.92.84.17              1
Routing for Networks:
  192.108.209.0
  192.108.211.0
  198.6.254.0
Routing Information Sources:
  Gateway          Distance      Last Update
  198.92.72.19         20        0:05:28
Distance: external 20 internal 200 local 200
```

Table 23–5 describes significant fields shown in the display.

Table 23–5 *Show IP Protocols Field Descriptions for IGRP Processes*

Field	Description
Routing Protocol is "igrp 109"	Specifies the routing protocol used.
Sending updates every 90 seconds	Specifies the time between sending updates.
next due in 44 seconds	Precisely when the next update is due to be sent.
Invalid after 270 seconds	Specifies the value of the invalid parameter.
hold down for 280	Specifies the current value of the hold-down parameter.
flushed after 630	Specifies the time in seconds after which the individual routing information will be thrown (flushed) out.
Outgoing update...	Specifies whether the outgoing filtering list has been set.
Incoming update...	Specifies whether the incoming filtering list has been set.
Default networks	Specifies how these networks will be handled in both incoming and outgoing updates.
IGRP metric	Specifies the value of the K0-K5 metrics, as well as the maximum hopcount.
Redistributing	Lists the protocol that is being redistributed.
Routing	Specifies the networks for which the routing process is currently injecting routes.

Table 23–5 *Show IP Protocols Field Descriptions for IGRP Processes, Continued*

Field	Description
Routing Information Sources	Lists all the routing sources the Cisco IOS software is using to build its routing table. For each source, you will see the following displayed: • IP address • Administrative distance • Time the last update was received from this source.

The following is sample output from the **show ip protocols** command, showing Enhanced IGRP processes:

```
Router# show ip protocols

Routing Protocol is "eigrp 77"
  Outgoing update filter list for all interfaces is not set
  Incoming update filter list for all interfaces is not set
  Redistributing: eigrp 77
  Automatic network summarization is in effect
  Routing for Networks:
    160.89.0.0
  Routing Information Sources:
    Gateway          Distance      Last Update
    160.89.81.28        90         0:02:36
    160.89.80.28        90         0:03:04
    160.89.80.31        90         0:03:04
  Distance: internal 90 external 170
```

Table 23–6 describes the fields that might be shown in the display.

Table 23–6 *Show IP Protocols Field Descriptions for Enhanced IGRP Processes*

Field	Description
Routing Protocol is "eigrp 77"	Name and autonomous system number of the currently running routing protocol.
Outgoing update filter list for all interfaces...	Indicates whether a filter for outgoing routing updates has been specified with the **distribute-list out** command.
Incoming update filter list for all interfaces...	Indicates whether a filter for incoming routing updates has been specified with the **distribute-list in** command.
Redistributing: eigrp 77	Indicates whether route redistribution has been enabled with the **redistribute** command.
Automatic network summarization...	Indicates whether route summarization has been enabled with the **auto-summary** command.

Table 23–6   *Show IP Protocols Field Descriptions for Enhanced IGRP Processes, Continued*

Field	Description
Routing for Networks:	Networks for which the routing process is currently injecting routes.
Routing Information Sources:	Lists all the routing sources that the Cisco IOS software is using to build its routing table. The following is displayed for each source: IP address, administrative distance, and time the last update was received from this source.
Distance: internal 90 external 170	Internal and external distances of the router. Internal distance is the degree of preference given to Enhanced IGRP internal routes. External distance is the degree of preference given to Enhanced IGRP external routes.

The following is sample output from the **show ip protocols** command, showing IS-IS processes:

```
Router# show ip protocols

Routing Protocol is "isis"
  Sending updates every 0 seconds
  Invalid after 0 seconds, hold down 0, flushed after 0
  Outgoing update filter list for all interfaces is not set
  Incoming update filter list for all interfaces is not set
  Redistributing: isis
  Address Summarization:
    None
  Routing for Networks:
    Serial0
  Routing Information Sources:
  Distance: (default is 115)
```

The following is sample output from the **show ip protocols** command, showing RIP processes:

```
Router# show ip protocols

Routing Protocol is "rip"
  Sending updates every 30 seconds, next due in 2 seconds
  Invalid after 180 seconds, hold down 180, flushed after 240
  Outgoing update filter list for all interfaces is not set
  Incoming update filter list for all interfaces is not set
  Redistributing: rip
  Default version control: send version 2, receive version 2
    Interface        Send  Recv   Key-chain
    Ethernet0         2     2     trees
    Fddi0             2     2
  Routing for Networks:
    172.19.0.0
    2.0.0.0
    3.0.0.0
```

```
Routing Information Sources:
   Gateway         Distance      Last Update
   Distance: (default is 120)
```

SHOW IP ROUTE

Use the **show ip route** EXEC command to display the current state of the routing table.

show ip route [*address* [*mask*] [**longer-prefixes**]] | [*protocol* [*process-id*]]

Syntax	Description
address	(Optional.) Address about which routing information should be displayed.
mask	(Optional.) Argument for a subnet mask.
longer-prefixes	(Optional.) The *address* and *mask* pair becomes a prefix, and any routes that match that prefix are displayed.
protocol	(Optional.) Name of a routing protocol; or the keyword **connected**, **static**, or **summary**. If you specify a routing protocol, use one of the following keywords: **bgp, egp, eigrp, hello, igrp, isis, ospf,** or **rip**.
process-id	(Optional.) Number used to identify a process of the specified protocol.

Command Mode

EXEC

Usage Guidelines

This command first appeared in Cisco IOS Release 10.0. The **longer-prefixes** keyword first appeared in Cisco IOS Release 11.0. The *process-id* argument first appeared in Cisco IOS Release 10.3.

Sample Displays

The following is sample output from the **show ip route** command when entered without an address:

```
Router# show ip route

Codes: I - IGRP derived, R - RIP derived, O - OSPF derived
       C - connected, S - static, E - EGP derived, B - BGP derived
       * - candidate default route, IA - OSPF inter area route
       E1 - OSPF external type 1 route, E2 - OSPF external type 2 route

Gateway of last resort is 131.119.254.240 to network 129.140.0.0

O E2 150.150.0.0 [160/5] via 131.119.254.6, 0:01:00, Ethernet2
E      192.67.131.0 [200/128] via 131.119.254.244, 0:02:22, Ethernet2
O E2 192.68.132.0 [160/5] via 131.119.254.6, 0:00:59, Ethernet2
```

Part II

Command Reference

```
O E2 130.130.0.0 [160/5] via 131.119.254.6, 0:00:59, Ethernet2
E    128.128.0.0 [200/128] via 131.119.254.244, 0:02:22, Ethernet2
E    129.129.0.0 [200/129] via 131.119.254.240, 0:02:22, Ethernet2
E    192.65.129.0 [200/128] via 131.119.254.244, 0:02:22, Ethernet2
E    131.131.0.0 [200/128] via 131.119.254.244, 0:02:22, Ethernet2
E    192.75.139.0 [200/129] via 131.119.254.240, 0:02:23, Ethernet2
E    192.16.208.0 [200/128] via 131.119.254.244, 0:02:22, Ethernet2
E    192.84.148.0 [200/129] via 131.119.254.240, 0:02:23, Ethernet2
E    192.31.223.0 [200/128] via 131.119.254.244, 0:02:22, Ethernet2
E    192.44.236.0 [200/129] via 131.119.254.240, 0:02:23, Ethernet2
E    140.141.0.0 [200/129] via 131.119.254.240, 0:02:22, Ethernet2
E    141.140.0.0 [200/129] via 131.119.254.240, 0:02:23, Ethernet2
```

The following is sample output that includes some IS-IS Level 2 routes learned:

```
Router# show ip route

Codes: I - IGRP derived, R - RIP derived, O - OSPF derived
       C - connected, S - static, E - EGP derived, B - BGP derived
       i - IS-IS derived
       * - candidate default route, IA - OSPF inter area route
E1 - OSPF external type 1 route, E2 - OSPF external type 2 route
       L1 - IS-IS level-1 route, L2 - IS-IS level-2 route

Gateway of last resort is not set

       160.89.0.0 is subnetted (mask is 255.255.255.0), 3 subnets
C      160.89.64.0 255.255.255.0 is possibly down,
         routing via 0.0.0.0, Ethernet0
i L2   160.89.67.0 [115/20] via 160.89.64.240, 0:00:12, Ethernet0
i L2   160.89.66.0 [115/20] via 160.89.64.240, 0:00:12, Ethernet0
```

Table 23–7 describes significant fields shown in these two displays.

Table 23–7   *Show IP Route Field Descriptions*

Field	Description
O	Indicates protocol that derived the route. Possible values include the following:
	• I—IGRP derived
	• R—RIP derived
	• O—OSPF derived
	• C—connected
	• S—static
	• E—EGP derived
	• B—BGP derived
	• i—IS-IS derived

Table 23–7 *Show IP Route Field Descriptions, Continued*

Field	Description
E2	Type of route. Possible values include the following: • *—Indicates the last path used when a packet was forwarded. It pertains only to the non-fast-switched packets. However, it does not indicate what path will be used next when forwarding a non-fast-switched packet, except when the paths are equal cost. • IA—OSPF interarea route. • E1—OSPF external type 1 route. • E2—OSPF external type 2 route. • L1—IS-IS Level 1 route. • L2—IS-IS Level 2 route.
150.150.0.0	Indicates the address of the remote network.
[160/5]	The first number in the brackets is the administrative distance of the information source; the second number is the metric for the route.
via 131.119.254.6	Specifies the address of the next router to the remote network.
0:01:00	Specifies the last time the route was updated in hours:minutes:seconds.
Ethernet2	Specifies the interface through which the specified network can be reached.

When you specify that you want information about a specific network displayed, more detailed statistics are shown. The following is sample output from the **show ip route** command when entered with the address 131.119.0.0.

```
Router# show ip route 131.119.0.0

Routing entry for 131.119.0.0 (mask 255.255.0.0)
   Known via "igrp 109", distance 100, metric 10989
   Tag 0
   Redistributing via igrp 109
   Last update from 131.108.35.13 on TokenRing0, 0:00:58 ago
   Routing Descriptor Blocks:
 * 131.108.35.13, from 131.108.35.13, 0:00:58 ago, via TokenRing0
     Route metric is 10989, traffic share count is 1
     Total delay is 45130 microseconds, minimum bandwidth is 1544 Kbit
     Reliability 255/255, minimum MTU 1500 bytes
     Loading 2/255, Hops 4
```

Table 23–8 describes significant fields shown in the display.

Table 23–8 *Show IP Route with Address Field Descriptions*

Field	Description
Routing entry for 131.119.0.0 (mask 255.255.0.0)	Network number and mask.
Known via "igrp 109"	Indicates how the route was derived.
distance	Administrative distance of the information source.
Tag	Integer that is used to implement the route.
Redistributing via igrp	Indicates redistribution protocol.
Last update from 131.108.35.13 on TokenRing0	Indicates the IP address of a router that is the next hop to the remote network and the router interface on which the last update arrived.
0:00:58 ago	Specifies the last time the route was updated in hours:minutes:seconds.
131.108.35.13, from 131.108.35.13, 0:00:58 ago	Indicates the next hop address, the address of the gateway that sent the update, and the time that has elapsed since this update was received in hours:minutes:seconds.
via TokenRing0	Interface for this route.
Route metric	This value is the best metric for this routing descriptor block.
traffic share count	Number of uses for this routing descriptor block.
Total delay	Total propagation delay in microseconds.
minimum bandwidth	Minimum bandwidth encountered when transmitting data along this route.
Reliability 255/255	Likelihood of successful packet transmission expressed as a number between 0 and 255 (255 is 100 percent reliability).
minimum MTU	Smallest MTU along the path.
Loading 2/255	Effective bandwidth of the route in kilobits per second/255 is saturation.
Hops	Hops to the destination or to the router where the route first enters IGRP.

The following is sample output using the **longer-prefixes** keyword. When the **longer-prefixes** keyword is included, the address and mask pair become the prefix, and any address that matches that prefix is displayed. Therefore, multiple addresses are displayed.

In the following example, the logical AND operation is performed on the source address 128.0.0.0 and the mask 128.0.0.0, resulting in 128.0.0.0. Each destination in the routing table is also logically ANDed with the mask and compared to that result of 128.0.0.0. Any destinations that fall into that range are displayed in the output.

```
Router# show ip route 128.0.0.0 128.0.0.0 longer-prefixes

Codes: C - connected, S - static, I - IGRP, R - RIP, M - mobile, B - BGP
       D - EIGRP, EX - EIGRP external, O - OSPF, IA - OSPF inter area
       E1 - OSPF external type 1, E2 - OSPF external type 2, E - EGP
       i - IS-IS, L1 - IS-IS level-1, L2 - IS-IS level-2, * - candidate default

Gateway of last resort is not set

S    134.134.0.0 is directly connected, Ethernet0
S    131.131.0.0 is directly connected, Ethernet0
S    129.129.0.0 is directly connected, Ethernet0
S    128.128.0.0 is directly connected, Ethernet0
S    198.49.246.0 is directly connected, Ethernet0
S    192.160.97.0 is directly connected, Ethernet0
S    192.153.88.0 is directly connected, Ethernet0
S    192.76.141.0 is directly connected, Ethernet0
S    192.75.138.0 is directly connected, Ethernet0
S    192.44.237.0 is directly connected, Ethernet0
S    192.31.222.0 is directly connected, Ethernet0
S    192.16.209.0 is directly connected, Ethernet0
S    144.145.0.0 is directly connected, Ethernet0
S    140.141.0.0 is directly connected, Ethernet0
S    139.138.0.0 is directly connected, Ethernet0
S    129.128.0.0 is directly connected, Ethernet0
     172.19.0.0 255.255.255.0 is subnetted, 1 subnets
C       172.19.64.0 is directly connected, Ethernet0
     171.69.0.0 is variably subnetted, 2 subnets, 2 masks
C       171.69.232.32 255.255.255.240 is directly connected, Ethernet0
S       171.69.0.0 255.255.0.0 is directly connected, Ethernet0
Router#
```

Related Commands

Search online to find documentation for related commands.

show interfaces tunnel
show ip route summary

SHOW IP ROUTE SUMMARY

To display the current state of the routing table, use the **show ip route summary** EXEC command.

   show ip route summary

Syntax   Description

This command has no arguments or keywords.

Command Mode

EXEC

Usage Guidelines

This command first appeared in Cisco IOS Release 10.0.

Sample Display

The following is sample output from the **show ip route summary** command:

```
Router# show ip route summary

Route Source    Networks    Subnets    Overhead    Memory (bytes)
connected       0           3          126         360
static          1           2          126         360
igrp 109        747         12         31878       91080
internal        3                                  360
Total           751         17         32130       92160
Router#
```

Table 23–9 describes the fields shown in the display.

Table 23–9   *Show IP Route Summary Field Descriptions*

Field	Description
Route Source	Routing protocol name, or the keyword **connected, static,** or **internal.** Internal indicates those routes that are in the routing table that are not owned by any routing protocol.
Networks	Number of prefixes that are present in the routing table for each route source.
Subnets	Number of subnets that are present in the routing table for each route source, including host routes.
Overhead	Any additional memory involved in allocating the routes for the particular route source other than the memory specified in the Memory field.
Memory	Number of bytes allocated to maintain all the routes for the particular route source.

Related Commands

Search online to find documentation for related commands.

show ip route

SHOW IP ROUTE SUPERNETS-ONLY

To display information about supernets, use the **show ip route supernets-only** privileged EXEC command.

> **show ip route supernets-only**

Syntax   Description

This command has no arguments or keywords.

Command Mode

Privileged EXEC

Usage Guidelines

This command first appeared in Cisco IOS Release 10.0.

Sample Display

The following is sample output from the **show ip route supernets-only** command. This display shows supernets only; it does not show subnets.

```
Router# show ip route supernets-only

Codes: I - IGRP derived, R - RIP derived, O - OSPF derived
       C - connected, S - static, E - EGP derived, B - BGP derived
       i - IS-IS derived, D - EIGRP derived
       * - candidate default route, IA - OSPF inter area route
       E1 - OSPF external type 1 route, E2 - OSPF external type 2 route
       L1 - IS-IS level-1 route, L2 - IS-IS level-2 route
       EX - EIGRP external route

Gateway of last resort is not set

B    198.92.0.0 (mask is 255.255.0.0) [20/0] via 198.92.72.30, 0:00:50
B    192.0.0.0 (mask is 255.0.0.0) [20/0] via 198.92.72.24, 0:02:50
```

Table 23–10 describes the fields in the display.

Table 23–10   *Show IP Route Supernets-Only Field Descriptions*

Field	Description
B	BGP derived, as shown in list of codes.
198.92.0.0 (mask is 255.255.0.0)	Supernet IP address.
[20/0]	Administrative distance (external/internal).
via 198.92.72.30	Next hop IP address.
0:00:50	Age of the route (how long ago the update was received).

SHOW KEY CHAIN

To display authentication key information, use the **show key chain** EXEC command.

>   **show key chain** [*name-of-chain*]

Syntax	*Description*
name-of-chain	(Optional.) Name of the key chain to display, as named in the **key chain** command.

Default

Information about all key chains is displayed.

Command Mode

EXEC

Usage Guidelines

This command first appeared in Cisco IOS Release 11.1.

Sample Display

The following is sample output from the **show key chain** command:

```
Router#  show key chain

Key-chain flintstone:
    key 1 -- text "fred"
        accept lifetime (always valid) - (always valid) [valid now]
        send lifetime (always valid) - (always valid) [valid now]
    key 2 -- text "barney"
        accept lifetime (00:00:00 Dec 5 1995) - (23:59:59 Dec 5 1995)
        send lifetime (06:00:00 Dec 5 1995) - (18:00:00 Dec 5 1995)
```

Related Commands

Search online to find documentation for related commands.

accept-lifetime
key
key chain
key-string
send-lifetime

SHOW ROUTE-MAP

To display configured route-maps, use the **show route-map** EXEC command.

> **show route-map** [*map-name*]

Part
II

Command Reference

Syntax	Description
map-name	(Optional.) Name of a specific route-map.

Command Mode

EXEC

Usage Guidelines

This command first appeared in Cisco IOS Release 10.0.

Sample Display

The following is sample output from the **show route-map** command:

```
Router# show route-map

route-map abc, permit, sequence 10
  Match clauses:
    tag 1 2
  Set clauses:
    metric 5
route-map xyz, permit, sequence 20
  Match clauses:
    tag 3 4
  Set clauses:
    metric 6
```

Table 23–11 describes the fields shown in the display.

Table 23–11 *Show Route-Map Field Descriptions*

Field	Description
route-map	Name of the route map.
permit	Indicates that the route is redistributed as controlled by the set actions.
sequence	Number that indicates the position a new route map is to have in the list of route maps already configured with the same name.
Match clauses: tag	Match criteria—conditions under which redistribution is allowed for the current route map.
Set clauses: metric	Set actions—the particular redistribution actions to perform if the criteria enforced by the **match** commands are met.

Related Commands

Search online to find documentation for related commands.

redistribute
route-map

CHAPTER 24

Configuring IP Multicast Routing

This chapter describes how to configure IP multicast routing. For a complete description of the IP multicast routing commands in this chapter, see Chapter 25, "IP Multicast Routing Commands."

Traditional IP communication allows a host to send packets to a single host (*unicast transmission*) or to all hosts (*broadcast transmission*). IP multicast provides a third scheme, allowing a host to send packets to a subset of all hosts (*group transmission*). These hosts are known as group members. Packets delivered to group members are identified by a single multicast group address. Multicast packets are delivered to a group using best-effort reliability, just like IP unicast packets.

The multicast environment consists of senders and receivers. Any host, regardless of whether it is a member of a group, can send to a group. However, only the members of a group receive the message.

A multicast address is chosen for the receivers in a multicast group. Senders use that address as the destination address of a datagram to reach all members of the group.

Membership in a multicast group is dynamic; hosts can join and leave at any time. There is no restriction on the location or number of members in a multicast group. A host can be a member of more than one multicast group at a time.

The activity and membership of a multicast group can vary from group-to-group and from time-to-time. A multicast group can be active for a long time, or it may be very short-lived. Membership in a group can change constantly. A group that has members may have no activity.

Routers executing a multicast routing protocol, such as Protocol-Independent Multicast (PIM), maintain forwarding tables to forward multicast datagrams. Routers use the Internet Group Management Protocol (IGMP) to learn whether members of a group are present on their directly attached subnets. Hosts join multicast groups by sending IGMP report messages.

Many multimedia applications involve multiple participants; IP multicast is naturally suitable for this communication paradigm.

CISCO'S IMPLEMENTATION OF IP MULTICAST ROUTING

The Cisco IOS software supports the following protocols to implement IP multicast routing:

- Internet Group Management Protocol (IGMP) is used between hosts on a LAN and the router(s) on that LAN to track of which multicast groups the hosts are members.

- Protocol-Independent Multicast (PIM) is used between routers so that they can track which multicast packets to forward to each other and to their directly connected LANs.

- Distance Vector Multicast Routing Protocol (DVMRP) is the protocol used on the MBONE (the multicast backbone of the Internet). The Cisco IOS software supports PIM-to-DVMRP interaction.

- Cisco Group Management Protocol (CGMP) is a protocol used on routers connected to Cisco Catalyst switches to perform tasks similar to those performed by IGMP.

Figure 24–1 shows where these protocols operate within the IP multicast environment. The protocols are further described after the figure.

Figure 24–1
IP multicast routing protocols.

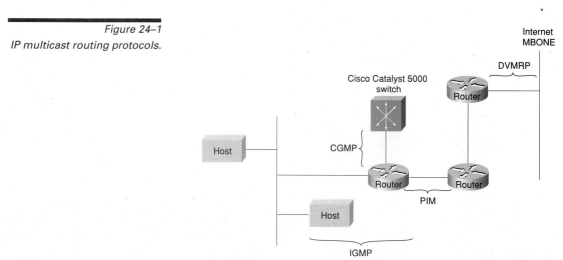

Internet Group Management Protocol

IP hosts use Internet Group Management Protocol to report their group membership to directly connected multicast routers. IGMP is an integral part of IP. IGMP is defined in RFC 1112, *Host Extensions for IP Multicasting.*

IGMP uses group addresses, which are Class D IP addresses. The high-order four bits of a Class D address are 1110. This means that host group addresses can be in the range 224.0.0.0 to 239.255.255.255. The address 224.0.0.0 is guaranteed not to be assigned to any group. The address 224.0.0.1 is assigned to all systems on a subnet. The address 224.0.0.2 is assigned to all routers on a subnet.

Protocol-Independent Multicast Protocol

The Protocol-Independent Multicast protocol maintains the current IP multicast service mode of receiver-initiated membership. It is not dependent on a specific unicast routing protocol.

PIM is defined in the following IETF Internet drafts:

- *Protocol Independent Multicast (PIM): Motivation and Architecture*
- *Protocol Independent Multicast (PIM), Dense Mode Protocol Specification*
- *Protocol Independent Multicast (PIM), Sparse Mode Protocol Specification*
- *IGMP Router Extensions for Routing to Dense Multicast Groups*
- *IGMP Router Extensions for Routing to Sparse Multicast Groups*

PIM can operate in dense mode, sparse mode, or sparse-dense mode.

In dense mode, a router assumes that all other routers will forward multicast packets for a group. If a router receives a multicast packet and has no directly connected members or PIM neighbors present, a Prune message is sent back to the source. Subsequent multicast packets are not flooded to the router on this pruned branch. PIM builds source-based multicast distribution trees.

In sparse mode, a router assumes that other routers do not want to forward multicast packets for a group, unless there is an explicit request for the traffic. When hosts join a multicast group, the directly connected routers send PIM Join messages toward the Rendezvous Point (RP). The RP keeps track of multicast groups. Hosts that send multicast packets are registered with the RP by that host's first-hop router. The RP then sends Join messages toward the source. At this point, packets are forwarded on a shared distribution tree. If the multicast traffic from a specific source is sufficient, the receiver's first-hop router may send Join messages toward the source to build a source-based distribution tree.

Distance Vector Multicast Routing Protocol

Cisco routers run PIM, and know enough about Distance Vector Multicast Routing Protocol to successfully forward multicast packets to and receive packets from a DVMRP neighbor. It is also possible to propagate DVMRP routes into and through a PIM cloud. However, PIM only uses this information. Cisco routers do not implement DVMRP to forward multicast packets.

DVMRP builds a parent-child database using a constrained multicast model to build a forwarding tree rooted at the source of the multicast packets. Multicast packets are initially flooded down this source tree. If redundant paths are on the source-tree, packets are not forwarded along those paths. Forwarding occurs until Prune messages are received on those parent-child links, which further constrain the broadcast of multicast packets.

DVMRP is implemented in the equipment of many vendors and is based on the public-domain mrouted program.

The Cisco IOS software supports dynamic discovery of DVMRP routers and can interoperate with them over traditional media (such as Ethernet and FDDI), or over DVMRP-specific tunnels.

Cisco Group Management Protocol

Cisco Group Management Protocol is a protocol used on routers connected to Cisco Catalyst switches to perform tasks similar to those performed by IGMP. CGMP is necessary because the Catalyst switch cannot tell the difference between IP multicast data packets and IGMP Report messages, which are both MAC-level addressed to the same group address.

BASIC IP MULTICAST ROUTING TASKS

IP multicast routing tasks are divided into basic and advanced tasks, which are discussed in the following sections. The first two basic tasks in the following are required to configure IP multicast routing; the remaining basic and advanced tasks are optional:

- Enabling IP Multicast Routing
- Enabling PIM on an Interface
- Configuring Auto-RP
- Configuring IGMP Features
- Configuring the TTL Threshold
- Disabling Fast Switching of IP Multicast
- Configuring sdr Listener Support
- Configuring Basic DVMRP Interoperability Features
- Enabling the Functional Address for IP Multicast over Token Ring LANs

ADVANCED IP MULTICAST ROUTING TASKS

Advanced, optional IP multicast routing tasks are the following:

- Configuring Advanced PIM Features
- Configuring Advanced DVMRP Interoperability Features
- Configuring an IP Multicast Static Route
- Controlling the Transmission Rate to a Multicast Group
- Configuring RTP Header Compression
- Configuring IP Multicast over ATM Point-to-Multipoint Virtual Circuits
- Configuring an IP Multicast Boundary
- Configuring an Intermediate IP Multicast Helper
- Storing IP Multicast Headers
- Enabling CGMP
- Configuring Stub IP Multicast Routing
- Loading Split IP Multicast Traffic across Equal-Cost Paths
- Monitoring and Maintaining IP Multicast Routing

See the "IP Multicast Configuration Examples" at the end of this chapter for examples of multicast routing configurations.

ENABLING IP MULTICAST ROUTING

Enabling IP multicast routing allows the Cisco IOS software to forward multicast packets. To enable IP multicast routing on the router, perform the following task in global configuration mode:

Task	Command
Enable IP multicast routing.	ip multicast-routing

ENABLING PIM ON AN INTERFACE

Enabling PIM on an interface also enables IGMP operation on that interface. An interface can be configured to be in dense mode, sparse mode, or sparse-dense mode. The mode determines how the router populates its multicast routing table and how the router forwards multicast packets that it receives from its directly connected LANs. You must enable PIM in one of these modes for an interface to perform IP multicast routing.

In populating the multicast routing table, dense-mode interfaces are always added to the table. Sparse-mode interfaces are added to the table only when periodic Join messages are received from downstream routers, or when there is a directly connected member on the interface. When forwarding from a LAN, sparse-mode operation occurs if there is an RP known for the group. If so, the packets are encapsulated and sent toward the RP. When no RP is known, the packet is flooded in a dense-mode fashion. If the multicast traffic from a specific source is sufficient, the receiver's first-hop router may send joins toward the source to build a source-based distribution tree.

There is no default mode setting. By default, multicast routing is disabled on an interface.

Enabling Dense Mode

To configure PIM on an interface to be in dense mode, perform the following task in interface configuration mode:

Task	Command
Enable dense-mode PIM on the interface.	ip pim dense-mode

See the "PIM Dense Mode Example" section at the end of this chapter for an example of how to configure a PIM interface in dense mode.

Enabling Sparse Mode

To configure PIM on an interface to be in sparse mode, perform the following task in interface configuration mode:

Task	Command
Enable sparse-mode PIM on the interface.	**ip pim sparse-mode**

See the "PIM Sparse Mode Example" section at the end of this chapter for an example of how to configure a PIM interface in sparse mode.

Enabling Sparse-Dense Mode

If you configure either **ip pim sparse-mode** or **ip pim dense-mode**, then sparseness or denseness is applied to the interface as a whole. However, some environments might require PIM to run in a single region in sparse mode for some groups and in dense mode for other groups.

An alternative to enabling only dense mode or only sparse mode is to enable sparse-dense mode. In this case, the interface is treated as dense mode if the group is in dense mode; the interface is treated in sparse mode if the group is in sparse mode. You must have an RP if the interface is in sparse-dense mode, and you want to treat the group as a sparse group.

If you configure sparse-dense mode, the idea of sparseness or denseness is applied to the group on the router, and the network manager should apply the same concept throughout the network.

Another benefit of sparse-dense mode is that Auto-RP information can be distributed in a dense-mode manner; yet, multicast groups for user groups can be used in a sparse-mode manner. Thus, there is no need to configure a default RP at the leaf routers.

When an interface is treated in dense mode, it is populated in a multicast routing table's outgoing interface list when either of the following is true:

- There are members or DVMRP neighbors on the interface.
- There are PIM neighbors and the group hasn't been pruned.

When an interface is treated in sparse mode, it is populated in a multicast routing table's outgoing interface list when either of the following is true:

- There are members or DVMRP neighbors on the interface.
- An explicit Join has been received by a PIM neighbor on the interface.

To enable PIM to operate in the same mode as the group, perform the following task in interface configuration mode:

Task	Command
Enable PIM to operate in sparse or dense mode, depending on the group.	**ip pim sparse-dense-mode**

Configuring a Rendezvous Point

If you configure PIM to operate in sparse mode, you must also choose one or more routers to be RPs. You do not have to configure the routers to be RPs; they learn this themselves. RPs are used by senders to a multicast group to announce their existence and by receivers of multicast packets to learn about new senders. The Cisco IOS software can be configured so that packets for a single multicast group can use one or more RPs.

You must configure the IP address of RPs in leaf routers only. *Leaf routers* are those routers that are directly connected either to a multicast group member or to a sender of multicast messages.

The RP address is used by first-hop routers to send PIM register messages on behalf of a host sending a packet to the group. The RP address is also used by last-hop routers to send PIM join/prune messages to the RP to inform it about group membership. The RP does not need to know it is an RP. You must configure the RP address only on first-hop and last-hop routers (leaf routers).

A PIM router can be an RP for more than one group; a group can have more than one RP. The conditions specified by the access list determine for which groups the router is an RP.

To configure the address of the RP, perform the following task on a leaf router in global configuration mode:

Task	Command
Configure the address of a PIM rendezvous point.	**ip pim rp-address** *ip-address* [*access-list-number*] [**override**]

CONFIGURING AUTO-RP

Auto-RP is a feature that automates the distribution of group-to-RP mappings in a PIM network. This feature has the following benefits:

- It is easy to use multiple RPs within a network to serve different group ranges.
- It allows load splitting among different RPs and arrangement of RPs according to the location of group participants.
- It avoids inconsistent, manual RP configurations that can cause connectivity problems.

Multiple RPs can be used to serve different group ranges or serve as hot backups of each other. To make Auto RP work, a router must be designated as an *RP-mapping agent*, which receives the RP-announcement messages from the RPs and arbitrates conflicts. The RP-mapping agent then sends the consistent group-to-RP mappings to all other routers. Thus, all routers automatically discover which RP to use for the groups they support.

One way to start is to place (preserve) the default RP for all global groups at or near the border router of your routing domain, while placing another RP in a more centrally located router for all local groups using the administratively scoped addresses (239.x.x.x).

NOTES

If you configure PIM in sparse mode or sparse-dense mode and do not configure Auto-RP, you must statically configure an RP as described in the section "Assigning an RP to Multicast Groups" later in this chapter.

Setting Up Auto-RP in a New Internetwork

You do not need a default RP in this case. Follow the process described in the section "Adding Auto-RP to an Existing Sparse-Mode Cloud," except that you should skip the first step of choosing a default RP.

Adding Auto-RP to an Existing Sparse-Mode Cloud

The following sections contain some suggestions for the initial deployment of Auto-RP into an existing sparse-mode cloud to provide experience and allow minimal disruption of the existing multicast infrastructure.

Choosing a Default RP

Sparse-mode environments need a default RP; sparse-dense-mode environments do not. If you have sparse-dense mode configured everywhere, you do not need to choose a default RP.

Adding Auto-RP to a sparse-mode cloud requires a default RP. In an existing PIM sparse mode region, at least one RP is defined across the network that has good connectivity and availability. That is, the **ip pim rp-address** command is already configured on all routers in this network.

Use that RP for the global groups (for example, 224.x.x.x and other global groups). There is no need to reconfigure the group address range that RP serves. RPs discovered dynamically through Auto-RP take precedence over statically configured RPs. Assume it is desirable to use a second RP for the local groups.

Announcing the RP and the Group Range it Serves

Find another router to serve as the RP for the local groups. The RP-mapping agent can double as an RP itself. Assign the whole range of 239.x.x.x to that RP, or assign a subrange of that (for example, 239.2.x.x).

To designate that a router is the RP, perform the following task in global configuration mode:

Task	Command
Configure a router to be the RP.	**ip pim send-rp-announce** *type number* **scope** *ttl* **group-list** *access-list-number*

To change the group ranges that this RP optimally serves in the future, change the announcement setting on the RP. If the change is valid, all other routers automatically adopt the new group-to-RP mapping.

The following example advertises the IP address of Ethernet 0 as the RP for the administratively scoped groups:

```
ip pim send-rp-announce ethernet0 scope 16 group-list 1
access-list 1 permit 239.0.0.0 0.255.255.255
```

Assigning the RP Mapping Agent

The RP mapping agent is the router that sends the authoritative Discovery packets telling other routers which group-to-RP mapping to use. Such a role is necessary in the event of conflicts (such as overlapping group-to-RP ranges).

Find a router whose connectivity is not likely to be interrupted and assign it the role of RP-mapping agent. All routers within *ttl* number of hops from the source router receive the Auto-RP Discovery messages. To assign the role of RP mapping agent, in that router perform the following task in global configuration mode:

Task	Command
Assign the RP mapping agent.	**ip pim send-rp-discovery scope** *ttl*

Verifying the Group-to-RP Mapping

To see if the group-to-RP mapping has arrived, perform one of the following tasks in EXEC mode on the designated routers:

Task	Command
Display active RPs that are cached with associated multicast routing entries. The information is learned by configuration or Auto-RP.	**show ip pim rp mapping**
Display information actually cached in the routing table.	**show ip pim rp** [*group-name* | *group-address*] [**mapping**]

Starting IP Multicast

Use your IP multicast application software to start joining and sending to a group.

Preventing Join Messages to False RPs

Note the **ip pim accept-rp** commands previously configured throughout the network. If that command is not configured on any router, this problem can be addressed later. In those routers already configured with **ip pim accept-rp** command, you must specify the command again to accept the newly advertised RP.

To accept all RPs advertised with Auto-RP and reject all other RPs by default, use the **ip pim accept-rp auto-rp** command.

If all interfaces are in sparse mode, a default configured RP to support the two well-known groups 224.0.1.39 and 224.0.1.40. Auto RP relies on these two well-known groups to collect and distribute RP-mapping information.When this is the case and the **ip pim accept-rp auto-rp** command is configured, another **ip pim accept-rp** command accepting the default RP must be configured, as in the following:

```
ip pim accept-rp default RP address 1
access-list 1 permit 224.0.1.39
access-list 1 permit 224.0.1.40
```

Filtering Incoming RP Announcement Messages

To filter incoming RP announcement messages, perform the following task in global configuration mode:

Task	Command
Filter incoming RP announcement messages.	**ip pim rp-announce-filter rp-list** *access-list-number* **group-list** *access-list-number*

CONFIGURING IGMP FEATURES

To configure IGMP features, perform the tasks in the following list:

- Configuring a Router to be a Member of a Group
- Controlling Access to IP Multicast Groups
- Modifying the IGMP Host-Query Message Interval
- Changing the IGMP Version
- Changing the IGMP Query Timeout
- Changing the Maximum Query Response Time
- Configuring the Router as a Statically Connected Member

Configuring a Router to be a Member of a Group

Cisco routers can be configured to be members of a multicast group. This is useful for determining multicast reachability in a network. If a device is configured to be a group member and supports the protocol that is being transmitted to the group, it can respond (for example, the **ping** command). The device responds to ICMP echo request packets addressed to a group of which it is a member. Another example is the multicast traceroute tools provided in the Cisco IOS software.

To have the router join a multicast group and enable IGMP, perform the following task in interface configuration mode:

Task	Command
Join a multicast group.	**ip igmp join-group** *group-address*

Controlling Access to IP Multicast Groups

Multicast routers send IGMP host-query messages to determine which multicast groups have members of the router's attached local networks. The routers then forward to these group members all packets addressed to the multicast group. You can place a filter on each interface that restricts the multicast groups that the hosts on the subnet serviced by the interface can join.

To filter multicast groups allowed on an interface, perform the following task in interface configuration mode:

Task	Command
Control the multicast groups that hosts on the subnet serviced by an interface can join.	**ip igmp access-group** *access-list-number*

Modifying the IGMP Host-Query Message Interval

Multicast routers send IGMP host-query messages to discover which multicast groups are present on attached networks. These messages are sent to the all-systems group address of 224.0.0.1 with a Time-to-Live (TTL) of 1.

Multicast routers send host-query messages periodically to refresh their knowledge of memberships present on their networks. If, after some number of queries, the Cisco IOS software discovers that no local hosts are members of a multicast group, the software stops forwarding onto the local network multicast packets from remote origins for that group and sends a prune message upstream toward the source.

Multicast routers elect a PIM designated router for the LAN (subnet). This is the router with the highest IP address. The designated router is responsible for sending IGMP host-query messages to all hosts on the LAN. In sparse mode, the designated router also sends PIM register and PIM join messages toward the RP router.

By default, the designated router sends IGMP host-query messages once per minute in order to keep the IGMP overhead on hosts and networks very low. To modify this interval, perform the following task in interface configuration mode:

Task	Command
Configure the frequency at which the designated router sends IGMP host-query messages.	**ip igmp query-interval** *seconds*

Changing the IGMP Version

By default, the router uses IGMP Version 2, which allows such features as the IGMP query timeout and the maximum query response time.

All systems on the subnet must support the same version. The router does not automatically detect Version 1 systems and switch to Version 1, as did earlier releases of the Cisco IOS software.

Configure the router for Version 1 if your hosts do not support Version 2.

To control which version of IGMP the router uses, perform the following task in interface configuration mode:

Task	Command
Select the IGMP version that the router uses.	**ip igmp version** {**2**	**1**}

Changing the IGMP Query Timeout

You can specify the period of time before the router takes over as the querier for the interface, after the previous querier has stopped doing so. By default, the router waits 2 times the query interval controlled by the **ip igmp query-interval** command. After that time, if the router has received no queries, it becomes the querier. This feature requires IGMP Version 2.

To change the query timeout, perform the following task in interface configuration mode:

Task	Command
Set the IGMP query timeout.	**ip igmp query-timeout** *seconds*

Changing the Maximum Query Response Time

By default, the maximum query response time advertised in IGMP queries is 10 seconds. If the router is using IGMP Version 2, you can change this value. The maximum query response time allows a router to quickly detect that there are no more directly connected group members on a LAN. Decreasing the value allows the router to *prune* groups faster.

To change the maximum query response time, perform the following task in interface configuration mode:

Task	Command
Set the maximum query response time advertised in IGMP queries.	**ip igmp query-max-response-time** *seconds*

Configuring the Router as a Statically Connected Member

Sometimes either there is no group member on a network segment or a host cannot report its group membership using IGMP. However, you may want multicast traffic to go to that network segment. Following are two ways to pull multicast traffic down to a network segment:

- Use the **ip igmp join-group** command. With this method, the router accepts the multicast packets in addition to forwarding them. Accepting the multicast packets prevents the router from fast switching.

- Use the **ip igmp static-group** command. With this method, the router does not accept the packets itself, but only forwards them. Hence, this method allows fast switching. The outgoing interface appears in the IGMP cache, but the router itself is not a member, as evidenced by lack of an "L" (local) flag in the multicast route entry.

To configure the router itself to be a statically connected member of a group (and allow fast switching), perform the following task in interface configuration mode:

Task	Command
Configure the router as a statically connected member of a group.	**ip igmp static-group** *group-address*

CONFIGURING THE TTL THRESHOLD

The TTL value controls whether packets are forwarded out of an interface. You specify the TTL value in hops. Only multicast packets with a TTL greater than the interface TTL threshold are forwarded on the interface. The default value is 0, which means that all multicast packets are forwarded on the interface. To change the default TTL threshold value, perform the following task in interface configuration mode:

Task	Command
Configure the TTL threshold of packets being forwarded out of an interface.	**ip multicast ttl-threshold** *ttl*

DISABLING FAST SWITCHING OF IP MULTICAST

Fast switching of IP multicast packets is enabled by default on all interfaces (including GRE and DVMRP tunnels), with the following exception: It is disabled and not supported over X.25 encapsulated interfaces. Keep the following conditions in mind:

- If fast switching is disabled on an *incoming* interface for a multicast routing table entry, the packet is sent at process level for all interfaces in the outgoing interface list.
- If fast switching is disabled on an *outgoing* interface for a multicast routing table entry, the packet is process-level switched for that interface, but may be fast switched for other interfaces in the outgoing interface list.

Disable fast switching if you want to log debug messages, because when fast switching is enabled, debug messages are not logged.

To disable fast switching of IP multicast, perform the following task in interface configuration mode:

Task	Command
Disable fast switching of IP multicast.	no ip mroute-cache

CONFIGURING SDR LISTENER SUPPORT

The tasks in the following list configure Session Directory Protocol (sdr) listener support:

- Enabling sdr Listener Support
- Limiting How Long an sdr Cache Entry Exists

Enabling sdr Listener Support

The multicast backbone (MBONE) allows efficient, many-to-many communication and is widely used for multimedia conferencing. To help announce multimedia conference sessions and provide the necessary conference setup information to potential participants, the Session Directory Protocol Version 2 tool is available. A session directory client announcing a conference session periodically multicasts an announcement packet on a well-known multicast address and port.

To enable session directory listener support, perform the following task in interface configuration mode:

Task	Command
Enable sdr listener support.	ip sdr listen

Limiting How Long an sdr Cache Entry Exists

By default, entries are never deleted from the sdr cache. However, you can limit how long an sdr cache entry stays active in the cache. To do so, perform the following task in global configuration mode:

Task	Command
Limit how long an sdr cache entry stays active in the cache.	ip sdr cache-timeout *minutes*

CONFIGURING BASIC DVMRP INTEROPERABILITY FEATURES

The following list shows some basic tasks that allow interoperability with DVMRP machines:

- Configuring DVMRP Interoperability
- Configuring a DVMRP Tunnel
- Advertising Network 0.0.0.0 to DVMRP Neighbors

For more advanced DVMRP features, see the section "Configuring Advanced DVMRP Interoperability Features" later in this chapter.

Configuring DVMRP Interoperability

Cisco multicast routers using PIM can interoperate with non-Cisco multicast routers that use the Distance Vector Multicast Routing Protocol (DVMRP).

PIM routers dynamically discover DVMRP multicast routers on attached networks. Once a DVMRP neighbor has been discovered, the router periodically transmits DVMRP Report messages advertising the unicast sources reachable in the PIM domain. By default, directly connected subnets and networks are advertised. The router forwards multicast packets that have been forwarded by DVMRP routers and, in turn, forwards multicast packets to DVMRP routers.

You can configure what sources are advertised and what metrics are used by configuring the **ip dvmrp metric** command. You can also direct all sources learned via a particular unicast routing process to be advertised into DVMRP.

The mrouted protocol is a public-domain implementation of DVMRP. It is necessary to use mrouted Version 3.8 (which implements a nonpruning version of DVMRP) when Cisco routers are directly connected to DVMRP routers or interoperate with DVMRP routers over an MBONE tunnel. DVMRP advertisements produced by the Cisco IOS software can cause older versions of mrouted to corrupt their routing tables and those of their neighbors. Any router connected to the MBONE should have an access-list to limit the number of unicast routes that are advertised via DVMRP.

To configure the sources that are advertised and the metrics that are used when transmitting DVMRP Report messages, perform the following task in interface configuration mode:

Task	Command
Configure the metric associated with a set of destinations for DVMRP reports.	**ip dvmrp metric** *metric* [**list** *access-list-number*] [[*protocol process-id*]	[**dvmrp**]]

A more sophisticated way to achieve the same results as the preceding command is to use a route map instead of an access list. This gives you a finer granularity of control. To subject unicast routes to route-map conditions before being injected into DVMRP, perform the following task in interface configuration mode:

Task	Command
Subject unicast routes to route-map conditions before being injected into DVMRP.	**ip dvmrp metric** *metric* **route-map** *map-name*

Responding to MRINFO Requests

The Cisco IOS software answers mrinfo requests sent by mrouted systems and Cisco routers. The software returns information about neighbors on DVMRP tunnels and all of the router's interfaces. This information includes the metric (which is always set to 1), the configured TTL threshold, the status of the interface, and various flags. The **mrinfo** command can also be used to query the router itself, as in the following example:

```
mm1-7kd# mrinfo
    171.69.214.27 (mm1-7kd.cisco.com) [version cisco 11.1] [flags: PMS]:
    171.69.214.27 -> 171.69.214.26 (mm1-r7kb.cisco.com) [1/0/pim/querier]
    171.69.214.27 -> 171.69.214.25 (mm1-45a.cisco.com) [1/0/pim/querier]
    171.69.214.33 -> 171.69.214.34 (mm1-45c.cisco.com) [1/0/pim]
    171.69.214.137 -> 0.0.0.0 [1/0/pim/querier/down/leaf]
    171.69.214.203 -> 0.0.0.0 [1/0/pim/querier/down/leaf]
    171.69.214.18 -> 171.69.214.20 (mm1-45e.cisco.com) [1/0/pim]
    171.69.214.18 -> 171.69.214.19 (mm1-45c.cisco.com) [1/0/pim]
    171.69.214.18 -> 171.69.214.17 (mm1-45a.cisco.com) [1/0/pim]
```

See the "DVMRP Interoperability Example" section at the end of this chapter for an example of how to configure a PIM router to interoperate with a DVMRP router.

Configuring a DVMRP Tunnel

The Cisco IOS software supports DVMRP tunnels to the MBONE. You can configure a DVMRP tunnel on a router if the other end is running DVMRP. The software then sends and receives multicast packets over the tunnel. This allows a PIM domain to connect to the DVMRP router in the case where all routers on the path do not support multicast routing. You cannot configure a DVMRP tunnel between two routers.

When a Cisco router runs DVMRP over a tunnel, it advertises sources in DVMRP Report messages much as it does on real networks. In addition, the software caches DVMRP Report messages it receives and uses them in its Reverse Path Forwarding (RPF) calculation. This allows the software to forward multicast packets received over the tunnel.

When you configure a DVMRP tunnel, you should assign an address to a tunnel in the following two cases:

- To enable IP packets to be sent over the tunnel.
- To indicate whether the Cisco IOS software should perform DVMRP summarization.

You can assign an IP address either by using the **ip address** interface configuration command, or by using the **ip unnumbered** interface configuration command to configure the tunnel to be unnumbered. Either of these two methods allows IP multicast packets to flow over the tunnel. The software will not advertise subnets over the tunnel if the tunnel has a different network number from the subnet. In this case, the software advertises only the network number over the tunnel.

To configure a DVMRP tunnel, perform the following tasks in interface configuration mode:

Task		Command
Step 1	Specify a tunnel interface in global configuration mode. This puts the router into interface configuration mode.	**interface tunnel** *number*
Step 2	Set the tunnel interface's source address. This is the IP address of the interface on the router.	**tunnel source** *ip-address*
Step 3	Set the tunnel interface's destination address. This is the IP address of the mrouted multitask router.	**tunnel destination** *ip-address*
Step 4	Configure a DVMRP tunnel.	**tunnel mode dvmrp**
Step 5	Assign an IP address to the interface. or Configure the interface as unnumbered.	**ip address** *address mask* **ip unnumbered** *type number*
Step 6	Configure PIM on the interface.	**ip pim [dense-mode l sparse-mode]**
Step 7	Configure an acceptance filter for incoming DVMRP reports.	**ip dvmrp accept-filter** *access-list-number* [*distance*]

See the "DVMRP Tunnel Example" section at the end of this chapter for an example of how to configure a DVMRP tunnel.

Advertising Network 0.0.0.0 to DVMRP Neighbors

The mrouted protocol is a public-domain implementation of DVMRP. If your router is a neighbor to an mrouted Version 3.6 machine, you can configure the Cisco IOS software to advertise network 0.0.0.0 to the DVMRP neighbor. Do not advertise the DVMRP default into the MBONE. You must specify whether only route 0.0.0.0 is advertised or if other routes can also be specified.

To advertise network 0.0.0.0 to DVMRP neighbors on an interface, perform the following task in interface configuration mode:

Task	Command
Advertise network 0.0.0.0 to DVMRP neighbors.	ip dvmrp default-information {originate	only}

ENABLING THE FUNCTIONAL ADDRESS FOR IP MULTICAST OVER TOKEN RING LANS

By default, IP multicast datagrams on Token Ring LAN segments use the MAC-level broadcast address 0xFFFF.FFFF.FFFF. This places an unnecessary burden on all devices that do not participate in IP multicast. The IP multicast over Token Ring LANs feature defines a way to map IP multicast addresses to a single Token Ring MAC address.

This feature defines the Token Ring functional address (0xc000.0004.0000) that should be used over Token Ring. A functional address is a severely restricted form of multicast addressing implemented on Token Ring interfaces. Only 31 functional addresses are available. A bit in the destination MAC address designates it as a functional address.

The implementation used by Cisco Systems complies with RFC 1469, *IP Multicast over Token-Ring Local Area Networks*.

If you configure this feature, IP multicast transmissions over Token Ring interfaces are more efficient than they formerly were. This feature reduces the load on other machines that do not participate in IP multicast because they do not process these packets.

The following restrictions apply to the Token Ring functional address:

- This feature can be configured only on a Token Ring interface.
- Neighboring devices on the Token Ring on which this feature is used should also use the same functional address for IP multicast traffic.
- Because there are a limited number of Token Ring functional addresses, it is possible that there are other protocols assigned to the Token Ring functional address 0xc000.0004.0000. Therefore, not every frame sent to the functional address is necessarily an IP multicast frame.

To enable the mapping of IP multicast addresses to the Token Ring functional address 0xc000.0004.0000, perform the following task in interface configuration mode:

Task	Command
Enable mapping of IP multicast addresses to the Token Ring functional address.	**ip multicast use-functional**

For an example of configuring the functional address, see the section "Functional Address for IP Multicast over Token Ring LAN Example" at the end of this chapter.

CONFIGURING ADVANCED PIM FEATURES

Perform the optional tasks in the following list to configure PIM features:

- Understanding PIM Shared Tree and Source Tree (Shortest Path Tree)
- Delaying the Use of PIM Shortest Path Tree
- Understanding Reverse-Path Forwarding
- Assigning an RP to Multicast Groups
- Increasing Control over RPs
- Modifying the PIM Router-Query Message Interval
- Enabling PIM Nonbroadcast, Multiaccess Mode

Understanding PIM Shared Tree and Source Tree (Shortest Path Tree)

By default, members of a group receive data from senders to the group across a single data distribution tree rooted at the RP. This type of distribution tree is called *shared tree*, as shown in Figure 24–2. Data from senders is delivered to the RP for distribution to group members joined to the shared tree.

If the data rate warrants, leaf routers on the shared tree may initiate a switch to the data distribution tree rooted at the source. This type of distribution tree is called a *shortest path tree* or *source tree*. By default, the Cisco IOS software switches to a source tree upon receiving the first data packet from a source.

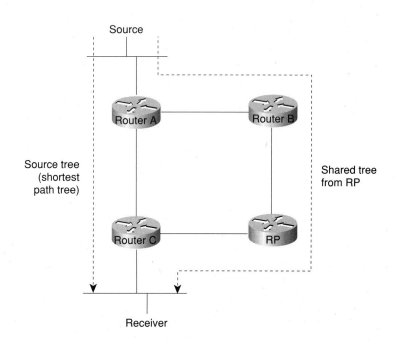

Figure 24–2
Shared tree and source tree (shortest path tree).

The following steps describe the move from shared tree to source tree in more detail:

Step 1   The receiver joins a group; leaf Router C sends a Join message toward RP.

Step 2   The RP puts link to Router C in its outgoing interface list.

Step 3   The source sends data; Router A encapsulates data in Register and sends it to RP.

Step 4   The RP forwards data down the shared tree to Router C and sends a Join message toward the source. At this point, data may arrive twice at Router C, once encapsulated and once natively.

Step 5   When data arrives natively (unencapsulated) at the RP, it sends a Register-Stop message to Router A.

Step 6   By default, reception of the first data packet prompts Router C to send a Join message toward the source.

Step 7   When Router C receives data on (S,G), it sends a Prune message for the source up the shared tree.

Step 8   The RP deletes the link to Router C from outgoing interface of (S,G). RP triggers a Prune message toward the source.

Join and Prune messages are sent for sources and RPs. They are sent hop-by-hop and are processed by each PIM router along the path to the source or RP. Register and Register-Stop messages are not sent hop-by-hop. They are sent by the designated router that is directly connected to a source and are received by the RP for the group.

Multiple sources sending to groups use the shared tree.

The network manager can configure the router to stay on the shared tree, as described in the following section, "Delaying the Use of PIM Shortest Path Tree."

Delaying the Use of PIM Shortest Path Tree

The switch from shared to source tree happens upon the arrival of the first data packet at the last hop router (Router C in Figure 24–2). This occurs because the **ip pim spt-threshold** command controls that timing, and its default setting is 0 Kbps.

The shortest path tree requires more memory than the shared tree, but it reduces delay. You might want to postpone its use. Instead of allowing the leaf router to move to the shortest path tree immediately, you can specify that the traffic must first reach a threshold.

You can configure when a PIM leaf router should join the shortest path tree for a specified group. If a source sends at a rate greater than or equal to the specified *Kbps* rate, the router triggers a PIM Join message toward the source to construct a source tree (shortest path tree). If **infinity** is specified, all sources for the specified group use the shared tree, thus never switching to the source tree.

The group list is a standard access list that controls to which groups the shortest path tree threshold applies. If a value of 0 is specified or the group list is not used, the threshold applies to all groups.

To configure a traffic rate threshold that must be reached before multicast routing is switched from the source tree to the shortest path tree, perform the following task in interface configuration mode:

Task	Command
Specify the threshold that must be reached before moving to shortest path tree.	**ip pim spt-threshold** {*kbps*	**infinity**} [**group-list** *access-list-number*]

Understanding Reverse-Path Forwarding

Reverse-Path Forwarding (RPF) is an algorithm used for forwarding multicast datagrams. It functions as described in the following list:

- If a router receives a datagram on an interface it uses to send unicast packets to the source, the packet has arrived on the RPF interface.
- If the packet arrives on the RPF interface, a router forwards the packet out of the interfaces present in the outgoing interface list of a multicast routing table entry.
- If the packet does not arrive on the RPF interface, the packet is silently discarded to prevent loops.

PIM uses both source trees and RP-rooted shared trees to forward datagrams; the RPF check is performed differently for each, as in the following:

- If a PIM router has source-tree state (that is, an [S,G] entry is present in the multicast routing table), the router performs the RPF check against the IP address of the source of the multicast packet.

- If a PIM router has shared tree state (and no explicit source-tree state), it performs the RPF check on the RP's address (which is known when members join the group).

Sparse-mode PIM uses the RPF lookup function to determine where it needs to send Joins and Prunes. (S,G) Joins (which are source-tree states) are sent toward the source. (*,G) Joins (which are shared-tree states) are sent toward the RP.

DVMRP and dense-mode PIM use only source trees and use RPF as described previously.

Assigning an RP to Multicast Groups

If you have configured PIM sparse mode, you must configure a PIM RP for a multicast group. An RP can either be configured statically in each box, or learned through a dynamic mechanism. This section explains how to statically configure an RP. If the RP for a group is learned through a dynamic mechanism (such as Auto-RP), you need not perform this task for that RP. You should use Auto-RP, which is described in the section "Configuring Auto-RP" earlier in this chapter.

PIM Designated Routers forward data from directly connected multicast sources to the RP for distribution down the shared tree.

Data is forwarded to the RP in one of two ways. It is encapsulated in Register packets and unicast directly to the RP, or, if the RP has itself joined the source tree, it is multicast forwarded per the RPF forwarding algorithm described in the preceding section, "Understanding Reverse-Path Forwarding." Last-hop routers directly connected to receivers may, at their discretion, join themselves to the source tree and prune themselves from the shared tree.

A single RP can be configured for multiple groups defined by an access list. If there is no RP configured for a group, the router treats the group as dense using the dense-mode PIM techniques.

If a conflict exists between the RP configured with this command and one learned by Auto-RP, the Auto-RP information is used, unless the **override** keyword is configured.

To assign an RP to one or more multicast groups, perform the following task in global configuration mode:

Task	Command
Assign an RP to multicast groups.	**ip pim rp-address** *ip-address* [*group-access-list-number*] [**override**]

Increasing Control over RPs

You can take a defensive measure to prevent a misconfigured leaf router from interrupting PIM service to the remainder of a network. To do so, configure the local router to accept Join messages only if they contain the RP address specified when the group is in the group range specified by the access list. To configure this feature, perform the following task in global configuration mode:

Task	Command
Control to which RPs the local router will accept Join messages.	ip pim accept-rp {*address* | auto-rp} [*access-list-number*]

Modifying the PIM Router-Query Message Interval

Route-query messages are used to elect a PIM designated router. The designated router is responsible for sending IGMP host-query messages. By default, multicast routers send PIM router-query messages every 30 seconds. To modify this interval, perform the following task in interface configuration mode:

Task	Command
Configure the frequency at which multicast routers send PIM router-query messages.	ip pim query-interval *seconds*

Enabling PIM Nonbroadcast, Multiaccess Mode

PIM Nonbroadcast, Multiaccess (NBMA) mode allows the Cisco IOS software to replicate packets for each neighbor on the NBMA network. Traditionally, the software replicates multicast and broadcast packets to all "broadcast" configured neighbors. This might be inefficient when not all neighbors want packets for certain multicast groups. NBMA mode enables you to reduce bandwidth on links leading into the NBMA network, as well as CPU cycles in switches and attached neighbors.

Configure this feature on ATM, Frame Relay, SMDS, PRI ISDN, or X.25 networks only, especially when these media do not have native multicast available. Do not use this feature on multicast-capable LANs (such as Ethernet or FDDI).

You should use sparse-mode PIM with this feature. Therefore, when each join is received from NBMA neighbors, PIM stores each neighbor IP address and interface in the outgoing interface list for the group. When a packet is destined for the group, the software replicates the packet and unicasts (data-link unicasts) it to each neighbor that has joined the group.

To enable PIM nonbroadcast, multicaccess mode on your serial link, perform the following task in interface configuration mode:

Task	Command
Enable PIM nonbroadcast, multiaccess mode.	ip pim nbma-mode

Consider the following two factors before enabling PIM NBMA mode:

- If the number of neighbors grows, the outgoing interface list gets large. This costs memory and replication time.
- If the network (Frame Relay, SMDS, or ATM) supports multicast natively, you should use it so that replication is performed at optimal points in the network.

CONFIGURING ADVANCED DVMRP INTEROPERABILITY FEATURES

Cisco routers run PIM and know enough about DVMRP to successfully forward multicast packets to receivers and receive multicast packets from senders. It is also possible to propagate DVMRP routes into and through a PIM cloud. PIM uses this information; however, Cisco routers do not implement DVMRP to forward multicast packets.

The basic DVMRP features are described in the section "Configuring Basic DVMRP Interoperability Features" earlier in this chapter. To configure more advanced DVMRP interoperability features on a Cisco router, perform the optional tasks in the following list:

- Enabling DVMRP Unicast Routing
- Limiting the Number of DVMRP Routes Advertised
- Changing the DVMRP Route Threshold
- Configuring a DVMRP Summary Address
- Disabling DVMRP Auto-Summarization
- Adding a Metric Offset to the DVMRP Route
- Rejecting a DVMRP Nonpruning Neighbor
- Configuring a Delay between DVRMP Reports

Enabling DVMRP Unicast Routing

Since policy for multicast routing and unicast routing require separate topologies, PIM must follow the multicast topology to build loopless distribution trees. Using DVMRP unicast routing, Cisco routers and mrouted-based machines exchange DVMRP unicast routes, to which PIM can then Reverse Path Forward.

Cisco routers do not perform DVMRP multicast routing among each other, but they can exchange DVMRP routes. The DVMRP routes provide a multicast topology that may differ from the unicast topology. This allows PIM to run over the multicast topology, thereby allowing sparse-mode PIM over the MBONE topology.

When DVMRP unicast routing is enabled, the router caches routes learned in DVMRP Report messages in a DVMRP routing table. PIM prefers DVMRP routes to unicast routes by default, but that preference can be configured.

DVMRP unicast routing can run on all interfaces, including GRE tunnels. On DVMRP tunnels, it runs by virtue of DVMRP multicast routing. This feature does not enable DVMRP multicast routing among Cisco routers. However, if there is a DVMRP-capable multicast router, the Cisco router will do PIM/DVMRP multicast routing interaction.

To enable DVMRP unicast routing, perform the following task in interface configuration mode:

Task	Command
Enable DVMRP unicast routing.	ip dvmrp unicast-routing

Limiting the Number of DVMRP Routes Advertised

By default, only 7000 DVMRP routes will be advertised over an interface enabled to run DVMRP (that is, a DVMRP tunnel, an interface where a DVMRP neighbor has been discovered, or an interface configured to run **ip dvmrp unicast-routing**).

To change this limit, perform the following task in global configuration mode:

Task	Command
Change the number of DVMRP routes advertised over an interface enabled to run DVMRP.	ip dvmrp route-limit *count*

Changing the DVMRP Route Threshold

By default, 10,000 DVMRP routes may be received per interface within a 1-minute interval. When that rate is exceeded, a syslog message warning that there might be a route surge occurring is issued. The warning is typically used to quickly detect when people have misconfigured their routers to inject a large number of routes into the MBONE.

To change the threshold number of routes that trigger the warning, perform the following task in global configuration mode:

Task	Command
Configure the number of routes that trigger a syslog message.	ip dvmrp routehog-notification *route-count*

Use the **show ip igmp interface** command to display a running count of routes. When the count is exceeded, "*** ALERT ***" is appended to the line.

Configuring a DVMRP Summary Address

You can customize the summarization of DVMRP routes if the default classful auto-summarization does not suit your needs. To summarize such routes, specify a summary address by performing the following task in interface configuration mode:

Task	Command
Specify a DVMRP summary address.	ip dvmrp summary-address *address mask* [metric *value*]

NOTES

At least one more specific route must be present in the unicast routing table before a configured summary address will be advertised.

Disabling DVMRP Auto-Summarization

By default, the Cisco IOS software performs some level of DVMRP summarization automatically. Disable this function if you want to advertise all routes, not just a summary. If you configure the **ip dvmrp summary-address** command and did not configure **no ip dvmrp auto-summary**, you get both custom and auto-summaries.

To disable DVMRP auto-summarization, perform the following task in interface configuration mode:

Task	Command
Disable DVMRP auto-summarization.	**no ip dvmrp auto-summary**

Adding a Metric Offset to the DVMRP Route

By default, the router increments by 1 the metric of a DVMRP route advertised in incoming DVMRP reports. You can change the metric if you want to favor, or not favor, a certain route. The DVMRP metric is a hop-count. Therefore, a very slow serial line of one hop is preferred over a route that is two hops over FDDI or another fast medium.

For example, perhaps a route is learned by Router A and the same route is learned by Router B with a higher metric. If you want to use the path through Router B because it is a faster path, you can apply a metric offset to the route learned by Router A to make it larger than the metric learned by Router B. This allows you to choose the path through Router B.

To change the default metric, perform the following task in interface configuration mode:

Task	Command
Change the metric added to DVMRP routes advertised in incoming reports.	**ip dvmrp metric-offset [in	out]** *increment*

Similar to the **metric** keyword in mrouted configuration files, the following points are true:

- When you specify **in** or no keyword, the *increment* is added to incoming DVMRP reports and is reported in mrinfo replies. The default value for **in** is 1.

- When you specify **out**, the *increment* is added to outgoing DVMRP reports for routes from the DVMRP routing table. The default value for **out** is 0.

Rejecting a DVMRP Nonpruning Neighbor

By default, Cisco routers accept all DVMRP neighbors as peers, regardless of their DVMRP capability or lack thereof. However, some non-Cisco machines run old versions of DVMRP that cannot prune, so they will continuously receive forwarded packets unnecessarily, wasting bandwidth. Figure 24–3 shows this scenario.

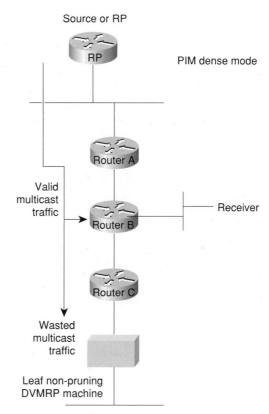

Figure 24–3
Leaf nonpruning DVMRP neighbor.

You can prevent a router from peering (communicating) with a DVMRP neighbor if that neighbor does not support DVMRP pruning or grafting. To do so, configure Router C (which is a neighbor to the leaf, nonpruning DVMRP machine) with the **ip dvmrp reject-non-pruners** command on the interface to the nonpruning machine. Figure 24–4 illustrates this scenario. In this case, when the router receives a DVMRP Probe or Report message without the Prune-Capable flag set, the router logs a syslog message and discards the message.

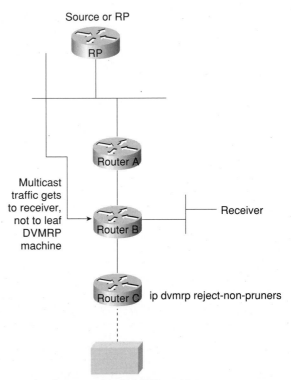

Figure 24–4
Router rejects nonpruning DVMRP neighbor.

Note that the **ip dvmrp reject-non-pruners** command prevents peering with neighbors only. If there are any nonpruning routers multiple hops away (downstream toward potential receivers) that are not rejected, then a nonpruning DVMRP network might still exist.

To prevent peering with nonpruning DVMRP neighbors, perform the following task in interface configuration mode:

Task	Command
Prevent peering with non-pruning DVMRP neighbors.	**ip dvmrp reject-non-pruners**

Configuring a Delay between DVRMP Reports

You can configure an interpacket delay of a DVMRP report. The delay is the number of milliseconds that elapse between transmissions of sets of packets that constitute a report. The number of packets in the set is determined by the *burst* value, which defaults to 2 packets. The *milliseconds* value defaults to 100 milliseconds.

To change the default values of the delay, perform the following task in interface configuration mode:

Task	Command
Configure an inter-packet delay between DVMRP reports.	**ip dvmrp output-report-delay** *milliseconds* [*burst*]

CONFIGURING AN IP MULTICAST STATIC ROUTE

IP multicast static routes (mroutes) allow you to have multicast paths diverge from the unicast paths. When using PIM, the router expects to receive packets on the same interface where it sends unicast packets back to the source. This is beneficial if your multicast and unicast topologies are congruent. However, you might want unicast packets to take one path and multicast packets to take another.

The most common reason for using separate unicast and multicast paths is tunneling. When a path between a source and a destination does not support multicast routing, a solution is to configure two routers with a GRE tunnel between them. In Figure 24–5, the UR routers support unicast packets only; the MR routers support multicast packets.

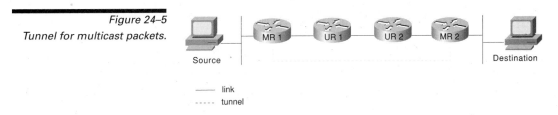

Figure 24–5
Tunnel for multicast packets.

Source

Destination

—— link
----- tunnel

In Figure 24–5, the source delivers multicast packets to the destination by using MR1 and MR2. MR2 accepts the multicast packet only if it thinks it can reach the source over the tunnel. If this is true, when the destination sends unicast packets to the source, MR2 sends them over the tunnel. This could be slower than natively sending the unicast packet through UR2, UR1, and MR1.

Prior to multicast static routes, the configuration in Figure 24–6 was used to overcome the problem of both unicasts and multicasts using the tunnel. In this figure, MR1 and MR2 are used as multicast routers only. When the destination sends unicast packets to the source, it uses the (UR3,UR2,UR1) path. When the destination sends multicast packets, the UR routers do not understand or forward them. However, the MR routers forward the packets.

To make the configuration in Figure 24–6 work, MR1 and MR2 must run another routing protocol (typically a different instantiation of the same protocol running in the UR routers), so that paths from sources are learned dynamically.

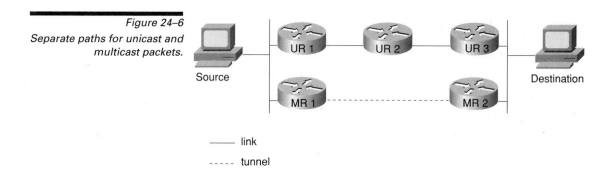

Figure 24–6

Separate paths for unicast and multicast packets.

—— link

----- tunnel

A multicast static route allows you to use the configuration in Figure 24–6 by configuring a static multicast source. The Cisco IOS software uses the configuration information instead of the unicast routing table. This allows multicast packets to use the tunnel without having unicast packets use the tunnel. Static mroutes are local to the router they are configured on and not advertised or redistributed in any way to any other router.

To configure a multicast static route, perform the following task in global configuration mode:

Task	Command
Configure an IP multicast static route.	**ip mroute** *source mask* [*protocol as-number*] {*rpf-address* | *type number*} [*distance*]

CONTROLLING THE TRANSMISSION RATE TO A MULTICAST GROUP

By default, there is no limit as to how fast a sender can transmit packets to a multicast group. To control the rate that the sender from the source list can send to a multicast group in the group list, perform the following task in interface configuration mode:

Task	Command
Control transmission rate to a multicast group.	**ip multicast rate-limit** {**in** | **out**} [**video** | **whiteboard**] [**group-list** *access-list*] [**source-list** *access-list*] *kbps*

CONFIGURING RTP HEADER COMPRESSION

Real-time Transport Protocol (RTP) is a protocol used for carrying packetized audio and video traffic over an IP network. RTP, described in RFC 1889, is not intended for data traffic, which uses TCP or UDP. RTP provides end-to-end network transport functions intended for applications with real-time requirements (such as audio, video, or simulation data over multicast or unicast network services).

The minimal 12 bytes of the RTP header, combined with 20 bytes of IP header and 8 bytes of UDP header, create a 40-byte IP/UDP/RTP header, as shown in Figure 24–7. The RTP packet has a payload of approximately 20 to 150 bytes for audio applications that use compressed payloads. It is very inefficient to transmit the IP/UDP/RTP header without compressing it.

Figure 24–7
RTP header compression.

Before RTP header compression:

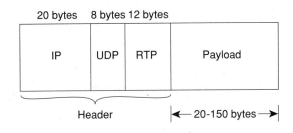

Header ⊢— 20-150 bytes —⊣

After RTP header compression:

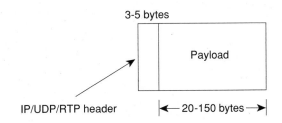

IP/UDP/RTP header ⊢— 20-150 bytes —⊣

The RTP header compression feature compresses the IP/UDP/RTP header in an RTP data packet from 40 bytes to approximately 2 to 5 bytes, as shown in Figure 24–7. It is a hop-by-hop compression scheme similar to RFC 1144 for TCP header compression. Using RTP header compression can benefit both telephony voice and multicast backbone (MBONE) applications running over slow links.

RTP header compression is supported on serial lines using Frame Relay, HDLC, or PPP encapsulation. It is also supported over ISDN interfaces.

Enabling compression on both ends of a low-bandwidth serial link can greatly reduce the network overhead if there is a lot of RTP traffic on that slow link. This compression is beneficial especially when the RTP payload size is small (for example, compressed audio payloads of 20-50 bytes). Although the MBONE-style RTP traffic has higher payload sizes, compact encodings such as Compressed Encoding for Linear Prediction (CELP) can also help considerably.

Before you can enable RTP header compression, you must have configured a serial line that uses either Frame Relay, HDLC, or PPP encapsulation, or an ISDN interface. To configure RTP header compression, perform the tasks in the following list; either one of the first two tasks is required:

- Enabling RTP Header Compression on a Serial Interface
- Enabling RTP Header Compression with Frame Relay Encapsulation
- Changing the Number of Header Compression Connections

You can compress the IP/UDP/RTP headers of RTP traffic to reduce the size of your packets, making audio or video communication more efficient. You must enable compression on both ends of a serial connection.

Enabling RTP Header Compression on a Serial Interface

To enable RTP header compression for serial encapsulations HDLC or PPP, perform the following task in interface configuration mode:

Task	Command
Enable RTP header compression.	ip rtp header-compression [passive]

If you include the **passive** keyword, the software compresses outgoing RTP packets only if incoming RTP packets on the same interface are compressed. If you use the command without the **passive** keyword, the software compresses all RTP traffic.

Enabling RTP Header Compression with Frame Relay Encapsulation

To enable RTP header compression with Frame Relay encapsulation, perform one of the following tasks in interface configuration mode:

Task	Command
Enable RTP header compression on the physical interface and all the interface maps will inherit it. Subsequently, all maps will perform RTP/IP header compression.	frame-relay ip rtp header-compression [passive]
Enable RTP header compression only on the particular map specified.	frame-relay map ip *ip-address dlci* [broadcast] rtp header-compression [active I passive]
Enable both RTP and TCP header compression on this link.	frame-relay map ip *ip-address dlci* [broadcast] compress

Changing the Number of Header Compression Connections

By default, the software supports a total of 16 RTP header compression connections on an interface. To change that number, perform the following task in interface configuration mode:

Task	Command
Specify the total number of RTP header compression connections supported on an interface.	ip rtp compression connections *number*

CONFIGURING IP MULTICAST OVER ATM POINT-TO-MULTIPOINT VIRTUAL CIRCUITS

IP multicast over ATM point-to-multipoint virtual circuits is a feature that dynamically creates ATM point-to-multipoint SVCs to handle IP multicast traffic more efficiently.

The feature can enhance router performance and link utilization because packets are not replicated and sent multiple times over the ATM interface.

Traditionally, over nonbroadcast, multiaccess networks, Cisco routers would perform a pseudo-broadcast to get broadcast or multicast packets to all neighbors on a multiaccess network. For example, assume in Figure 24–8 that Routers A, B, C, D, and E were running Open Shortest Path First protocol. Router A must deliver to Routers D and E. When A sends an OSPF Hello, the data-link layer replicates the Hello and sends one to each neighbor, known as *pseudobroadcast*, which results in four copies being sent over the link from Router A to the multi-access WAN.

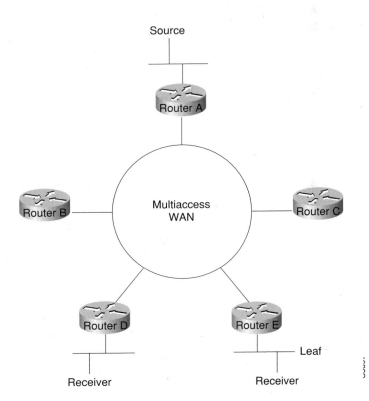

Figure 24–8
Environment for IP multicast over ATM point-to-multipoint virtual circuits.

With the advent of IP multicast, where high-rate multicast traffic can occur, that approach does not scale. Furthermore, in the preceding example, Routers B and C would get data traffic they do not need. To handle this problem, PIM can be configured in NBMA mode using the **ip pim nbma-mode** command. PIM in NBMA mode works only for sparse-mode groups. This would allow only routers D and E to get the traffic without distributing it to B and C. However, two copies are still delivered over the link from A to the multiaccess WAN.

If the underlying network supported multicast capability, the routers could handle this situation more efficiently. If the multiaccess WAN were an ATM network, IP multicast could use multipoint virtual circuits.

This works by having routers A, B, C, D, and E run sparse-mode PIM. Suppose the receiver directly connected to D joins a group and A is the PIM RP. The following sequence occurs:

1. Router D will send a PIM Join message to A.

2. When A receives the PIM Join, it sets up a multipoint virtual circuit for the multicast group.

3. Later, when the receiver directly connected to E joins the same group, E will send a PIM Join to A.

4. Router A will see that there is a multipoint VC already associated with the group, and will add E to the existing multipoint VC.

5. When the source sends a data packet, A can send a single packet over its link that gets to both D and E. The replication occurs in the ATM switches at the topological diverging point from A to D and E.

If a host sends an IGMP report over an ATM interface to a router, the router adds the host to the multipoint VC for the group.

This feature can also be used over ATM subinterfaces.

You must have ATM configured for multipoint signaling. You also must have IP multicast routing and PIM sparse mode configured. This feature does not work with dense-mode PIM.

Perform the tasks in the following sections to configure IP multicast over ATM point-to-multipoint virtual circuits. In the following list, the first task is required; the remaining tasks are optional:

- Enabling IP Multicast over ATM Point-to-Multipoint VCs
- Limiting the Number of Virtual Circuits

Enabling IP Multicast over ATM Point-to-Multipoint VCs

To enable PIM to open ATM point-to-multipoint virtual circuits for each multicast group that a receiver joins, perform the following tasks in interface configuration mode on the ATM interface:

Task		Command
Step 1	Enable IP multicast over ATM point-to-multipoint virtual circuits.	**ip pim multipoint-signalling**
Step 2	Enable point-to-multipoint signaling to the the ATM switch.	**atm multipoint-signaling**

The **atm multipoint-signaling** command is required so that static-map multipoint VCs can be opened. The router uses existing static map entries that include the **broadcast** keyword to establish multipoint calls. You must have the map list to act like a static ARP table.

Use the **show ip pim vc** command to display ATM VC status information for multipoint VCs opened by PIM.

Limiting the Number of Virtual Circuits

By default, PIM can open a maximum of 200 virtual circuits. When the router reaches this number, it deletes inactive virtual circuits so that it can open VCs for new groups that might have activity. To change the maximum number of VCs that PIM can open, perform the following task in interface configuration mode:

Task	Command
Change the maximum number of VCs that PIM can open.	ip pim vc-count *number*

Understanding Idling Policy

An idling policy uses the **ip pim vc-count** *number* to limit the number of VCs created by PIM. When the router stays at or below this *number* value, no idling policy is in effect. When the next VC to be opened will exceed the *number* value, an idling policy is exercised. An idled virtual circuit does not mean that the multicast traffic is not forwarded; the traffic is switched to vc 0. The vc 0 is the broadcast virtual circuit that is open to all neighbors listed in the map list. The name "vc0" is unique to PIM and the mrouting table.

Understanding How the Idling Policy Works

The idling policy works in the following ways:

- The only VCs eligible for idling are those with a current 1-second activity rate less than or equal to the value configured by the **ip pim minimum-vc-rate** command on the ATM interface. Activity level is measured in packets per second (pps).

- The VC with the least amount of activity below the configured **ip pim minimum-vc-rate** *pps* rate is idled.

- If the **ip pim minimum-vc-rate** command is not configured, all VCs are eligible for idling.

- If there are other VCs at the same activity level, the VC with the highest fanout (number of leaf routers on the multipoint VC) is idled.

- The activity level is rounded to three orders of magnitude (less than 10 pps, 10 to 100 pps, and 100 to 1000 pps). Therefore, a VC that has 40 pps activity and another that has 60 pps activity are considered to have the same rate, and the fanout count determines which one is idled. If the first VC has a fanout of 5 and the second has a fanout of 3, the first one is idled.

- Idling a VC means releasing the multipoint VC that is dedicated for the multicast group. The group's traffic continues to be sent; it is moved to the static-map VC. Packets will flow over a shared multipoint VC that delivers packets to all PIM neighbors.

- If all VCs have a 1-minute rate greater than *pps*, the new group (that exceeded the **ip pim vc-count** *number*) will use the shared multipoint VC.

Keeping VCs from Idling

You can configure the minimum rate required to keep VCs from being idled; by default, all VCs are eligible for idling. To configure a minimum rate, perform the following task in interface configuration mode:

Task	Command
Set the minimum activity rate required to keep VCs from being idled.	**ip pim minimum-vc-rate** *pps*

CONFIGURING AN IP MULTICAST BOUNDARY

You can set up an administratively scoped boundary on an interface for multicast group addresses. A standard access list defines the range of addresses that are affected. When a boundary is set up, no multicast data packets are allowed to flow across the boundary from either direction. The boundary allows the same multicast group address to be reused in different administrative domains.

The IANA has designated the multicast address range 239.0.0.0 to 239.255.255.255 as the administratively scoped addresses. Then this range of addresses can be reused in domains administered by different organizations. They would be considered local, not globally unique.

To set up an administratively scoped boundary, perform the following tasks beginning in global configuration mode:

Task		Command
Step 1	Create a standard access list, repeating the command as many times as necessary.	**access-list** *access-list-number* {**deny** | **permit**} *source* [*source-wildcard*]
Step 2	Configure an interface.	**interface** *type number*
Step 3	Configure the boundary, specifying the access list you created in Step 1.	**ip multicast boundary** *access-list-number*

See the section "Administratively Scoped Boundary Example" at the end of this chapter for an example of configuring a boundary.

CONFIGURING AN INTERMEDIATE IP MULTICAST HELPER

When a multicast-capable internetwork is between two subnets with broadcast-only capable hosts, you can convert broadcast traffic to multicast at the first hop router, and convert it back to broadcast at the last hop router to deliver the packets to the broadcast clients. Thus, you can take advantage of the multicast capability of the intermediate multicast internetwork. This feature prevents unnecessary replication at the intermediate routers and can take advantage of multicast fast switching in the multicast internetwork.

See Figure 24–10 and the example of this feature in the section "IP Multicast Helper Example" at the end of this chapter.

An extended IP access list controls which broadcast packets are translated, based on the UDP port number.

To configure an intermediate IP multicast helper, perform the following tasks on the first hop router beginning in global configuration mode:

Task	Command
Step 1 Specify an interface.	interface *type number*
Step 2 Configure a first hop router to convert broadcast traffic to multicast traffic.	**ip multicast helper-map broadcast** *multicast-address extended-access-list-number*
Step 3 Configure an access list.	**access-list** *access-list-number* {**deny** | **permit**} **udp** *source source-wildcard destination destination-wildcard port*
Step 4 Configure IP to forward the protocol you are using.	**ip forward-protocol udp** [*port*]

Then perform the following tasks on the last hop router beginning in global configuration mode:

Task	Command
Step 1 Specify an interface.	interface *type number*
Step 2 Configure a last hop router to convert multicast traffic to broadcast traffic.	**ip multicast helper-map** *group-address broadcast-address extended-access-list-number*

Task	Command
Step 3 Configure an access list.	**access-list** *access-list-number* {**deny** | **permit**} **udp** *source source-wildcard destination destination-wildcard port*
Step 4 Configure IP to forward the protocol you are using.	**ip forward-protocol udp** [*port*]

NOTES

On the last hop router, the **ip multicast helper-map** command automatically introduces **ip igmp join-group** *group-address* on that interface. This command must stay there for this feature to work. If you remove the **ip igmp join-group** command, the feature will fail.

STORING IP MULTICAST HEADERS

You can store IP multicast packet headers in a cache and then display them to determine any of the following information:

- Who is sending IP multicast packets to which groups
- Inter-packet delay
- Duplicate IP multicast packets (if any)
- Multicast forwarding loops in your network (if any)
- Scope of the group
- UDP port numbers
- Packet length

NOTES

This feature allocates a circular buffer of approximately 32 kilobytes.

To allocate a circular buffer to store IP multicast packet headers that the router receives, perform the following task in global configuration mode:

Task	Command
Allocate a buffer to store IP multicast packet headers.	**ip multicast cache-headers**

Use the **show ip mpacket** command to display the buffer.

ENABLING CGMP

Cisco Group Management Protocol is a protocol used on routers connected to Cisco Catalyst switches to perform tasks similar to those performed by IGMP. CGMP is necessary because the Catalyst switch cannot tell the difference between IP multicast data packets and IGMP Report messages, which are both MAC-level addressed to the same group address.

Enabling CGMP triggers a CGMP Join message. CGMP should be enabled only on 802 or ATM media, or LANE over ATM. CGMP should be enabled only on routers connected to Catalyst switches.

To enable CGMP for IP multicast on a LAN, perform the following task in interface configuration mode:

Task	Command
Enable CGMP.	**ip cgmp** [**proxy**]

When the **proxy** keyword is specified, the CGMP proxy function is enabled. That is, any router that is not CGMP-capable will be advertised by the proxy router. The proxy router advertises the existence of other non CGMP-capable routers by sending a CGMP Join message with the non CGMP-capable router's MAC address and a group address of 0000.0000.0000.

CONFIGURING STUB IP MULTICAST ROUTING

When using PIM in a large network, there are often stub regions over which the administrator has limited control. To reduce the configuration and administration burden, you can configure a subset of PIM functionality that provides the stub region with connectivity, but does not allow it to participate in or potentially complicate any routing decisions.

Stub IP multicast routing allows simple multicast connectivity and configuration at stub networks. It eliminates periodic flood-and-prune behavior across slow-speed links (ISDN and below) using dense mode. It does this by using forwarded IGMP reports as a type of Join message and using selective PIM message filtering.

Stub IP multicast routing allows stub sites to be configured quickly and easily for basic multicast connectivity, without the flooding of multicast packets and subsequent group pruning that occurs in dense-mode, and without excessive administrative burden at the central site.

Before configuring stub IP multicast routing, you must have IP multicast routing configured on both the stub router and the central router. You must also have PIM dense mode configured on both the incoming and outgoing interfaces of the stub router.

Two steps are required to enable stub IP multicast routing. One task is performed on the stub router, and the other is performed on a central router one hop away from the stub router. By definition, a stub region is marked by a leaf router. That is, the stub router (leaf router) is the last stop before any hosts receiving multicast packets or the first stop for anyone sending multicast packets.

The first step is to configure the stub router to forward all IGMP Host Reports and Leave messages received on the interface to an IP address. The reports are resent out of the next-hop interface toward the IP address, with that interface's source address. This action enables a sort of "dense-mode" Join, allowing stub sites not participating in PIM to indicate membership in multicast groups.

To configure the stub router to forward IGMP Host Reports and Leave messages, perform the following tasks in interface configuration mode. Specify the IP address of an interface on the central router. When the central router receives IGMP Host Report and Leave messages, it appropriately adds or removes the interface from its outgoing list for that group.

Task	Command
On the stub router, forward all IGMP Host Reports and Leave messages to the specified IP address on a central router.	ip igmp helper-address *ip-address*

The second step is to configure an access list on the central router to filter all PIM control messages from the stub router. Thus, the central router does not by default add the stub router to its outgoing interface list for any multicast groups. This task has the side benefit of preventing a misconfigured PIM neighbor from participating in PIM.

To filter PIM control messages, perform the following task in interface configuration mode:

Task	Command
On the central router, filter all PIM control messages based on the specified access list.	ip pim neighbor-filter *access-list-number*

For an example of stub IP multicast routing, see the section "Stub IP Multicast Example" at the end of this chapter.

LOADING SPLIT IP MULTICAST TRAFFIC ACROSS EQUAL-COST PATHS

You can now configure load splitting of IP multicast traffic across equal-cost paths. Prior to this feature, when there were equal-cost paths between routers, IP multicast packets traversed only one path. If a tunnel was configured, the same next hop was always used, and no load splitting occurred.

IP multicast load splitting is accomplished indirectly by consolidating the available bandwidth of all the physical links into a single tunnel interface. The underlying physical connections then use existing unicast load-splitting mechanisms for the tunnel (multicast) traffic.

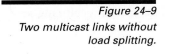

NOTES

This feature is load splitting the traffic, not load balancing the traffic.

By configuring load splitting among equal-cost paths, you can use your links between routers more efficiently when sending IP multicast traffic.

Due to reverse-path forwarding issues, splitting IP multicast traffic across physical interfaces is nearly impossible. Consider the sample topology in Figure 24–9, where Router A and Router B are connected with two equal-cost multicast links. Once a router chooses its RPF interface (Serial 0 or Serial 1), all subsequent multicast traffic is accepted only from that interface (assuming there are no routing changes). Hence, all multicast traffic uses only one link.

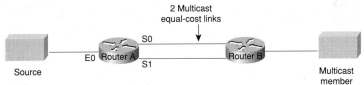

Figure 24–9
Two multicast links without load splitting.

The solution is to consolidate all the bandwidth from the equal-cost links for multicast traffic by configuring a multicast (GRE) tunnel between Router A and Router B. The routers should be made to RPF to the tunnel interface and not to any of the physical equal-cost interfaces between them. The multicast packets are then unicast across the tunnel and the underlying unicast mechanisms perform load splitting of these now unicast packets across the equal-cost links.

Use the configuration tasks in the following list to achieve this solution; the first three tasks are required:

- Configuring the Access Router
- Configuring the Router at the Opposite End of the Tunnel
- Configuring Both Routers to RPF
- Verifying the Load Splitting

Configuring the Access Router

To configure the access router end of the tunnel (the end of the tunnel near the source), perform the following tasks, beginning in global configuration mode. The tunnel mode is GRE IP by default.

Task	Command
Step 1 Configure a tunnel interface.	**interface tunnel** *number*

Task	Command
Step 2 Enable IP processing without assigning an IP address to the interface.	**ip unnumbered** *type number*
Step 3 Enable PIM on the tunnel interface.	**ip pim** {**dense-mode** I **sparse-mode** I **sparse-dense-mode**}
Step 4 Configure the tunnel source.	**tunnel source** {*ip-address* I *type number*}
Step 5 Configure the tunnel destination.	**tunnel destination** {*hostname* I *ip-address*}

Configuring the Router at the Opposite End of the Tunnel

Next, perform the following tasks on the router at the opposite end of the tunnel, beginning in global configuration mode:

Task	Command
Step 1 Configure a tunnel interface.	**interface tunnel** *number*
Step 2 Enable IP processing without assigning an IP address to the interface.	**ip unnumbered** *type number*
Step 3 Enable PIM on the tunnel interface.	**ip pim** {**dense-mode** I **sparse-mode** I **sparse-dense-mode**}
Step 4 Configure the tunnel source. This matches the tunnel destination at the opposite end of the tunnel.	**tunnel source** {*ip-address* I *type number*}
Step 5 Configure the tunnel destination. This matches the tunnel source at the opposite end of the tunnel.	**tunnel destination** {*hostname* I *ip-address*}

Configuring Both Routers to RPF

Since the use of the tunnel makes the multicast topology incongruent with the unicast topology, and only multicast traffic traverses the tunnel, you must configure the routers to RPF correctly over the tunnel. The following sections describe the two ways to do this, depending on your topology. The two ways to do this are the following:

- Configuring Load Splitting to a Stub Network
- Configuring Load Splitting to the Middle of a Network

Configuring Load Splitting to a Stub Network

If you are load splitting to a stub network, you can use a static multicast route. First perform the following task on the stub router in global configuration mode:

Task	Command
Configure a static multicast route over which to RPF from the stub router to the other end of the tunnel.	**ip mroute 0.0.0.0 0.0.0.0 tunnel** *number*

Then perform the following tasks on the router at the opposite end of the tunnel from the stub router, in global configuration mode:

Task		Command
Step 1	Configure a static route over which to RPF from the access router to the other end of the tunnel. Configure the *source* to be the network address of the network connected to the stub router.	**ip mroute** *source mask* **tunnel** *number*
Step 2	Repeat Step 1 for each network connected to the stub router.	**ip mroute** *source mask* **tunnel** *number*

Configuring Load Splitting to the Middle of a Network

You can use static mroutes in this case also, but you must make sure that Router A would RPF to the tunnel for source networks behind Router B, and Router B would RPF to the tunnel for source networks behind Router A.

Another option is to run a separate unicast routing protocol with a better administrative distance to provide the RPF. You must make sure that your multicast routers do not advertise the tunnel to your real network. For details, refer to the "Configuring an IP Multicast Static Route" section in this chapter.

If you are using a DVMRP routing table for RPF information within your network, you could configure the **ip dvmrp unicast-routing** command on your tunnel interfaces to make the routers RPF correctly over the tunnel.

Verifying Load Splitting

Load splitting works for both fast switching and process switching, but splitting the traffic among the physical interfaces is performed differently for each case. Fast switching occurs if both the incoming and outgoing interfaces are configured with the **ip mroute-cache** command. IP multicast fast switching is enabled by default. Keep the following points in mind:

- With process switching, load splitting occurs on a per-packet basis by round-robin on the equal- cost links. To verify that load splitting is working, look at the interface statistics using the **show interfaces accounting** command, and verify that the packet count is about equal for the underlying interfaces that provide the equal-cost paths.

- With fast switching, load splitting occurs on a per-flow basis. A flow is a set of traffic with the same source and destination. Once the cache is populated for the (S,G) pair, that flow is pinned to the physical interface assigned on the cache (the outgoing interface used by the first packet of the flow). If the cached interface goes down, the cache entry for the (S,G) pair is torn down and the flow is automatically switched to a different physical interface.

In the case of fast switching, you can verify that load splitting is occurring by viewing the multicast fast-switched cache with the **show ip mcache** command. The flows should be split among the underlying interfaces, as shown in the following example:

```
Router# show ip mcache

IP Multicast Fast-Switching Cache
(100.1.1.6/32, 224.1.1.1), Ethernet0, Last used: 00:00:00
  Tunnel0       MAC Header: 0F000800 (Serial1)
(100.1.1.6/32, 224.1.1.2), Ethernet0, Last used: 00:00:00
  Tunnel0       MAC Header: 0F000800 (Serial1)
(100.1.1.5/32, 224.1.1.3), Ethernet0, Last used: 00:00:00
  Tunnel0       MAC Header: 0F000800 (Serial0)
(100.1.1.5/32, 224.1.1.4), Ethernet0, Last used: 00:00:00
  Tunnel0       MAC Header: 0F000800 (Serial0)
```

For an example of load splitting IP multicast traffic across equal-cost paths, see the section "Load Splitting IP Multicast Traffic across Equal-Cost Paths Example" at the end of this chapter.

MONITORING AND MAINTAINING IP MULTICAST ROUTING

You can remove all contents of a particular cache, table, or database. You also can display specific statistics. The following sections describe each of these tasks.

Clearing Caches, Tables, and Databases

You can remove all contents of a particular cache, table, or database. Clearing a cache, table, or database can become necessary when the contents of the particular structure have become, or are suspected to be, invalid.

The following table lists the tasks associated with clearing IP multicast caches, tables, and databases. Perform these tasks in EXEC mode:

Task		Command
Step 1	Clear all group entries that the Catalyst switches have cached.	clear ip cgmp
Step 2	Delete routes from the DVMRP routing table.	clear ip dvmrp route { * I *route*}
Step 3	Delete entries from the IGMP cache.	clear ip igmp group [*group-name* I *group-address* I *interface*]
Step 4	Delete entries from the IP multicast routing table.	clear ip mroute {* I *group* [*source*]}
Step 5	Clear the Auto-RP cache.	clear ip pim auto-rp *rp-address*
Step 6	Clear RTP header compression structures and statistics.	clear ip rtp header-compression [*type number*]
Step 7	Delete the Session Directory Protocol Version 2 cache or an sdr cache entry.	clear ip sdr [*group-address* I "*session-name*"]

Displaying System and Network Statistics

You can display specific statistics such as the contents of IP routing tables, caches, and databases. This information can be used to determine resource utilization and solve network problems. You can also display information about node reachability and discover the routing path that your device's packets are taking through the network.

To display various routing statistics, perform the following tasks in EXEC mode:

Task		Command
Step 1	Query a multicast router about which neighboring multicast routers are peering with it.	mrinfo [*hostname-or-address*] [*source-address-or-interface*]
Step 2	Display IP multicast packet rate and loss information.	mstat *source* [*destination*] [*group*]
Step 3	Trace the path from a source to a destination branch for a multicast distribution tree for a given group.	mtrace *source* [*destination*] [*group*]

Task	Command
Step 4 Send an ICMP Echo Request to a multicast group address.	**ping** [*group-address-or-name*]
Step 5 Display Frame Relay RTP header compression statistics.	**show frame-relay ip rtp header-compression** [**interface** *type number*]
Step 6 Display the entries in the DVMRP routing table.	**show ip dvmrp route** [*ip-address*]
Step 7 Display the multicast groups that are directly connected to the router and that were learned via IGMP.	**show ip igmp groups** [*group-name* | *group-address* | *type number*]
Step 8 Display multicast-related information about an interface.	**show ip igmp interface** [*type number*]
Step 9 Display the contents of the IP fast-switching cache.	**show ip mcache** [*group* [*source*]]
Step 10 Display the contents of the circular cache-header buffer.	**show ip mpacket** [*source-address-or-name*] [*group-address-or-name*] [**detail**]
Step 11 Display the contents of the IP multicast routing table.	**show ip mroute** [*group-name* | *group-address*] [*source*] [**summary**] [**count**] [**active** *kbps*]
Step 12 Display information about interfaces configured for PIM.	**show ip pim interface** [*type number*] [**count**]
Step 13 List the PIM neighbors discovered by the router.	**show ip pim neighbor** [*type number*]
Step 14 Display the RP routers associated with a sparse-mode multicast group.	**show ip pim rp** [*group-name* | *group-address*]
Step 15 Display ATM VC status information for multipoint VCs opened by PIM.	**show ip pim vc** [*group-or-name*] [*type number*]
Step 16 Display how the router is doing Reverse-Path Forwarding (that is, from the unicast routing table, DVMRP routing table, or static mroutes).	**show ip rpf** *source-address-or-name*

Task	Command
Step 17 Display RTP header compression statistics.	**show ip rtp header-compression** [*type number*] [**detail**]
Step 18 Display the Session Directory Protocol Version 2 cache.	**show ip sdr** [*group*	"*session-name*"	**detail**]

IP MULTICAST CONFIGURATION EXAMPLES

This section provides the following IP multicast routing configuration examples:

- PIM Dense Mode Example
- PIM Sparse Mode Example
- DVMRP Interoperability Example
- DVMRP Tunnel Example
- RTP Header Compression Examples
- IP Multicast over ATM Point-to-Multipoint VC Example
- Functional Address for IP Multicast over Token Ring LAN Example
- Administratively Scoped Boundary Example
- IP Multicast Helper Example
- Stub IP Multicast Example
- Load Splitting IP Multicast Traffic across Equal-Cost Paths Example

PIM Dense Mode Example

The following example configures dense-mode PIM on an Ethernet interface of the router:

```
ip multicast-routing
interface ethernet 0
 ip pim dense-mode
```

PIM Sparse Mode Example

The following example configures the Cisco IOS software to operate in sparse-mode PIM. The RP router is the router whose address is 10.8.0.20.

```
ip multicast-routing
 ip pim rp-address 10.8.0.20 1
interface ethernet 1
 ip pim sparse-mode
```

DVMRP Interoperability Example

The following example configures DVMRP interoperability for configurations when the PIM router and the DVMRP router are on the same network segment. In this example, access list 1 advertises the networks (98.92.35.0, 198.92.36.0, 198.92.37.0, 131.108.0.0, and 150.136.0.0) to the DVMRP router, and access list 2 is used to prevent all other networks from being advertised (**ip dvmrp metric 0**).

```
interface ethernet 0
 ip address 131.119.244.244 255.255.255.0
 ip pim dense-mode
 ip dvmrp metric 1 list 1
 ip dvmrp metric 0 list 2

access-list 1 permit 198.92.35.0 0.0.0.255
access-list 1 permit 198.92.36.0 0.0.0.255
access-list 1 permit 198.92.37.0 0.0.0.255
access-list 1 permit 131.108.0.0 0.0.255.255
access-list 1 permit 150.136.0.0 0.0.255.255
access-list 1 deny   0.0.0.0 255.255.255.255
access-list 2 permit 0.0.0.0 255.255.255.255
```

DVMRP Tunnel Example

The following example configures a DVMRP tunnel:

```
!
ip multicast-routing
!
interface tunnel 0
 ip unnumbered ethernet 0
 ip pim dense-mode
 tunnel source ethernet 0
 tunnel destination 192.70.92.133
 tunnel mode dvmrp
!
interface ethernet 0
 description Universitat DMZ-ethernet
 ip address 192.76.243.2 255.255.255.0
 ip pim dense-mode
```

RTP Header Compression Examples

The following example enables RTP header compression for a serial, ISDN, or asynchronous interface. For ISDN, you also need a broadcast dialer map.

```
interface serial 0 :or interface bri 0
 ip rtp header-compression
 encapsulation ppp
 ip rtp compression-connections 25
```

The following example is for Frame Relay encapsulation. It enables RTP header compression on the specified map.

```
interface serial 0
 ip address 1.0.0.2 255.0.0.0
 encapsulation frame-relay
```

```
no keepalive
clockrate 64000
frame-relay map ip 1.0.0.1 17 broadcast rtp header-compression
```

IP Multicast over ATM Point-to-Multipoint VC Example

The following example enables IP multicast over ATM point-to-multipoint virtual circuits:

```
interface ATM2/0
 ip address 171.69.214.43 255.255.255.248
 ip pim sparse-mode
 ip pim multipoint-signalling
 ip ospf network broadcast
 atm nsap-address 47.00918100000000410B0A1981.333333333333.00
 atm pvc 1 0 5 qsaal
 atm pvc 2 0 16 ilmi
 atm multipoint-signalling
 map-group mpvc
router ospf 9
 network 171.69.214.0 0.0.0.255 area 0
!
ip classless
 ip pim rp-address 171.69.10.13 98
!
map-list mpvc
 ip 171.69.214.41 atm-nsap 47.00918100000000410B0A1981.111111111111.00 broadcast
 ip 171.69.214.42 atm-nsap 47.00918100000000410B0A1981.222222222222.00 broadcast
 ip 171.69.214.43 atm-nsap 47.00918100000000410B0A1981.333333333333.00 broadcast
```

Functional Address for IP Multicast over Token Ring LAN Example

In the following example, any IP multicast packets going out Token Ring interface 0 are mapped to MAC address 0xc000.0004.0000:

```
interface token 0
 ip address 1.1.1.1 255.255.255.0
 ip pim dense-mode
 ip multicast use-functional
```

Administratively Scoped Boundary Example

The following example sets up a boundary for all administratively scoped addresses:

```
access-list 1 deny 239.0.0.0 0.255.255.255
access-list 1 permit 224.0.0.0 15.255.255.255
interface ethernet 0
 ip multicast boundary 1
```

IP Multicast Helper Example

Figure 24–10 illustrates how a helper address on two routers converts from broadcast to multicast and back to broadcast.

Figure 24–10
IP multicast helper scenario.

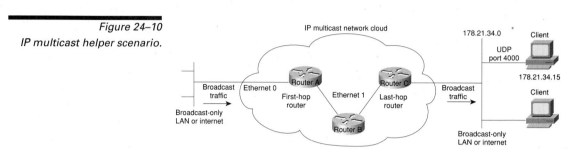

The configuration on the first hop router converts a broadcast stream arriving at incoming interface Ethernet 0 destined for UDP port 4000 to a multicast stream. The access list denies other traffic from being forwarded into the multicast cloud. The traffic is sent to group address 224.5.5.5. Because fast switching does not perform such a conversion, the **ip forward-protocol** command causes the proper process level to perform the conversion.

The second configuration on the last hop router converts the multicast stream at incoming interface Ethernet 1 back to broadcast. Again, all multicast traffic emerging from the multicast cloud should not be converted to broadcast, only the traffic destined for UDP port 4000.

First Hop Router

```
interface ethernet 0
 ip multicast helper-map broadcast 224.5.5.5 120
 ip pim dense-mode
!
access-list 120 permit any any udp 4000
access-list 120 deny any any udp
 ip forward-protocol udp 4000
```

Last Hop Router

```
interface ethernet 1
 ip multicast helper-map 224.5.5.5 178.21.34.255 135
 ip pim dense-mode
!
access-list 135 permit any any udp 4000
access-list 135 deny any any udp
 ip forward-protocol udp 4000
```

Stub IP Multicast Example

The following example configures stub IP multicast routing for Router A. Figure 24–11 illustrates this example. On stub Router A, the interfaces must be configured for PIM dense mode. The helper address is configured on the host interfaces. Central site Router B can be configured for either sparse-mode or dense-mode PIM. The access list on Router B denies any PIM messages from Router A.

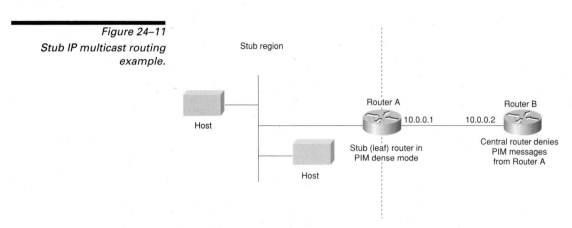

Figure 24–11
Stub IP multicast routing example.

Router A

```
ip multicast-routing
 ip pim dense-mode
 ip igmp helper-address 10.0.0.2
```

Router B

```
ip multicast-routing
 ip pim dense-mode : or ip pim sparse-mode
 ip pim neighbor-filter 1
access-list 1 deny 10.0.0.1
```

Load Splitting IP Multicast Traffic across Equal-Cost Paths Example

This example configures a GRE tunnel between Router A and Router B. Figure 24–12 illustrates the tunneled topology. The configurations follow the figure.

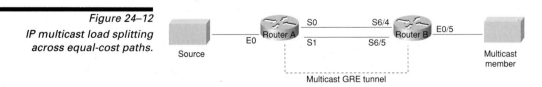

Figure 24–12
IP multicast load splitting across equal-cost paths.

Router A

```
interface tunnel 0
 ip unnumbered Ethernet0
 ip pim dense-mode : or sparse-mode or sparse-dense-mode
 tunnel source 100.1.1.1
 tunnel destination 100.1.5.3
!
interface ethernet 0
 ip address 100.1.1.1 255.255.255.0
 ip pim dense-mode : or sparse-mode or sparse-dense-mode
!
interface Serial0
 ip address 100.1.2.1 255.255.255.0
 bandwidth 125
 clock rate 125000
!
interface Serial1
 ip address 100.1.3.1 255.255.255.0
 bandwidth 125
```

Router B

```
interface tunnel 0
 ip unnumbered ethernet 0/5
 ip pim dense-mode : or sparse-mode or sparse-dense-mode
 tunnel source 100.1.5.3
 tunnel destination 100.1.1.1
!
interface ethernet 0/5
 ip address 100.1.5.3 255.255.255.0
 ip pim dense-mode : or sparse-mode or sparse-dense-mode
!
interface serial 6/4
 ip address 100.1.2.3 255.255.255.0
 bandwidth 125
!
interface Serial6/5
 ip address 100.1.3.3 255.255.255.0
 bandwidth 125
 clock rate 125000
```

CHAPTER 25

IP Multicast Routing Commands

This chapter describes the commands used to configure and monitor IP multicast routing. For IP multicast routing configuration information and examples, see Chapter 24, "Configuring IP Multicast Routing."

CLEAR IP CGMP

To clear all group entries from the Catalyst switches' caches, use the **clear ip cgmp** EXEC command.

> **clear ip cgmp** [*type number*]

Syntax	Description
type number	(Optional.) Interface type and number.

Command Mode

EXEC

Usage Guidelines

This command first appeared in Cisco IOS Release 11.1.

This command sends a CGMP Leave message with a group address of 0000.0000.0000 and a unicast address of 0000.0000.0000. This message instructs the switches to clear all group entries they have cached.

If an interface type and number are specified, the Leave message is sent only on that interface. Otherwise, it is sent on all CGMP-enabled interfaces.

Example

The following example clears the CGMP cache:

```
clear ip cgmp
```

Related Commands

Search online to find documentation for related commands.

ip cgmp

CLEAR IP DVMRP ROUTE

To delete routes from the DVMRP routing table, use the **clear ip dvmrp route** EXEC command.

> **clear ip dvmrp route** {* | *route*}

Syntax	Description
*	Clears all routes from the DVMRP table.
route	Clears the longest matched route. Can be an IP address, a network number, or an IP DNS name.

Command Mode

EXEC

Usage Guidelines

This command first appeared in Cisco IOS Release 11.0.

Example

The following example deletes route 10.1.1.1 from the DVMRP routing table:

```
clear ip dvmrp route 10.1.1.1
```

CLEAR IP IGMP GROUP

To delete entries from the IGMP cache, use the **clear ip igmp group** EXEC command.

> **clear ip igmp group** [*group-name* | *group-address* | *type number*]

Syntax	Description
group-name	(Optional.) Name of the multicast group, as defined in the DNS hosts table or with the **ip host** command.
group-address	(Optional.) Address of the multicast group. This is a multicast IP address in four-part, dotted notation.
type number	(Optional.) Interface type and number.

Default

When the command is used with no arguments, all entries are deleted from the IGMP cache.

Command Mode

EXEC

Usage Guidelines

This command first appeared in Cisco IOS Release 10.0.

The IGMP cache contains a list of the multicast groups of which hosts on the directly connected LAN are members. If the router has joined a group, it is also listed in the cache.

To delete all entries from the IGMP cache, specify the **clear ip igmp group** command with no arguments.

Example

The following example clears entries for the multicast group 224.0.255.1 from the IGMP cache:

```
clear ip igmp group 224.0.255.1
```

Related Commands

Search online to find documentation for related commands.

ip host
show ip igmp groups
show ip igmp interface

CLEAR IP MROUTE

To delete entries from the IP multicast routing table, use the **clear ip mroute** EXEC command.

clear ip mroute {* | *group* [*source*]}

Syntax	Description
*	Deletes all entries from the IP multicast routing table.
group	Can be either one of the following:
	• Name of the multicast group, as defined in the DNS hosts table or with the **ip host** command.
	• IP address of the multicast group. This is a multicast IP address in four-part, dotted notation.
source	(Optional.) If you specify a group name or address, you can also specify a name or address of a multicast source that is transmitting to the group. A source does not need to be a member of the group.

Part II

Command Reference

Command Mode
EXEC

Usage Guidelines
This command first appeared in Cisco IOS Release 10.0.

Examples .
The following example deletes all entries from the IP multicast routing table:

```
clear ip mroute *
```

The following example deletes from the IP multicast routing table all sources on the 10.3.0.0 subnet that are transmitting to the multicast group 224.2.205.42. Note that this example deletes all sources on network 10.3, not individual sources.

```
clear ip mroute 224.2.205.42 10.3.0.0
```

Related Commands
Search online to find documentation for related commands.

ip host
show ip mroute

CLEAR IP PIM AUTO-RP

To delete entries from the Auto-RP cache, use the **clear pim auto-rp** EXEC command.

> **clear ip pim auto-rp** *rp-address*

Syntax	Description
rp-address	Clears only the entries related to the RP at this address. If this argument is omitted, the entire Auto-RP cache is cleared.

Command Mode
EXEC

Usage Guidelines
This command first appeared in Cisco IOS Release 11.3.

Example
The following example deletes all entries from the Auto-RP cache:

```
clear ip pim auto-rp
```

CLEAR IP RTP HEADER-COMPRESSION

To clear RTP header compression structures and statistics, use the **clear ip rtp header-compression** EXEC command.

> **clear ip rtp header-compression** [*type number*]

Syntax	Description
type number	(Optional.) Interface type and number.

Command Mode

EXEC

Part
II

Command Reference

Usage Guidelines

This command first appeared in Cisco IOS Release 11.3.

If this command is used without an interface type and number, it clears all RTP header compression structures and statistics.

Example

The following example clears RTP header compression structures and statistics for serial interface 0:

```
clear ip rtp header-compression serial 0
```

Related Commands

Search online to find documentation for related commands.

ip rtp header-compression

CLEAR IP SDR

To delete a Session Directory Protocol (sdr) cache entry or the entire sdr cache, use the **clear ip sdr** EXEC command.

> **clear ip sdr** [*group-address* | *"session-name"*]

Syntax	Description
group-address	(Optional.) Deletes all sessions associated with the IP group address.
"session-name"	(Optional.) Deletes only the sdr cache entry with the specified name.

Command Mode

EXEC

Usage Guidelines

This command first appeared in Cisco IOS Release 11.1.

If no arguments or keywords are used with this command, the system deletes the entire sdr cache.

Example

The following example clears the sdr cache:

```
clear ip sdr
```

Related Commands

Search online to find documentation for related commands.

ip sdr cache-timeout
ip sdr listen
show ip sdr

FRAME-RELAY IP RTP HEADER-COMPRESSION

To enable RTP header compression for all Frame Relay maps on a physical interface, use the **frame-relay ip rtp header-compression** interface configuration command. To disable the feature, use the **no** form of this command.

> **frame-relay ip rtp header-compression** [active | passive]
> **no frame-relay ip rtp header-compression** [active | passive]

Syntax	Description
active	(Optional.) Compresses all outgoing RTP packets. This is the default.
passive	(Optional.) Compresses the outgoing RTP/UDP/IP header only if an incoming packet had a compressed header.

Default

Disabled.
If the command is configured, **active** is the default keyword.

Command Mode

Interface configuration

Usage Guidelines

This command first appeared in Cisco IOS Release 11.3.

When this command is used on the physical interface, all the interface maps inherit the command; that is, all maps will perform IP/UDP/RTP header compression.

Example

The following example enables RTP header compression for all Frame Relay maps on a physical interface:

```
frame-relay ip rtp header-compression
```

Related Command

Search online to find documentation for related commands.

show frame-relay ip rtp header-compression

FRAME-RELAY MAP IP COMPRESS

To enable both RTP and TCP header compression on a link, use the **frame-relay map ip compress** interface configuration command. To disable both RTP and TCP header compression, use the **no** form of this command.

frame-relay map ip *ip-address dlci* [**broadcast**] **compress**
no frame-relay map ip *ip-address dlci* [**broadcast**] **compress**

Syntax	Description
ip-address	IP address of the destination or next hop.
dlci	DLCI number.
broadcast	(Optional.) Forwards broadcasts to the specified IP address.

Default

Disabled

Command Mode

Interface configuration

Usage Guidelines

This command first appeared in Cisco IOS Release 11.3.

Example

The following example enables both RTP and TCP header compression on serial interface 1:

```
interface serial 1
 encapsulation frame-relay
 ip address 131.108.175.110 255.255.255.0
 frame-relay map ip 131.108.175.220 180 compress
```

Related Commands

Search online to find documentation for related commands.

show frame-relay ip rtp header-compression

FRAME-RELAY MAP IP RTP HEADER-COMPRESSION

To enable RTP header compression per DLCI, use the **frame-relay map ip rtp header-compression** interface configuration command. To disable the feature, use the **no** form of this command.

> **frame-relay map ip** *ip-address dlci* **rtp header-compression** [**active** | **passive**]
> **no frame-relay map ip** *ip-address dlci* **rtp header-compression** [**active** | **passive**]

Syntax	Description
ip-address	IP address of the destination or next hop.
dlci	DLCI number.
active	(Optional.) All outgoing RTP packets are compressed. This is the default.
passive	(Optional.) Compresses the outgoing RTP/UDP/IP header only if an incoming packet had a compressed header.

Default

Disabled.
If the command is configured, **active** is the default keyword.

Command Mode

Interface configuration

Usage Guidelines

This command first appeared in Cisco IOS Release 11.3.

When this command is configured, the specified maps inherit RTP header compression. You can have multiple Frame Relay maps, with and without RTP header compression.

Example

The following example enables RTP header compression on serial interface 1:

```
interface serial 1
 encapsulation frame-relay
 ip address 131.108.175.110 255.255.255.0
 frame-relay map ip 131.108.175.220 180 rtp header-compression
```

Related Commands

Search online to find documentation for related commands.

show frame-relay ip rtp header-compression

IP CGMP

To enable CGMP on an interface of a router connected to a Catalyst 5000 switch, use the **ip cgmp** interface configuration command. To disable CGMP routing, use the **no** form of this command.

> **ip cgmp [proxy]**
> **no ip cgmp**

Syntax	Description
proxy	(Optional.) Enables CGMP and the CGMP proxy function.

Default

Disabled

Command Mode

Interface configuration

Usage Guidelines

This command first appeared in Cisco IOS Release 11.1.

When enabled on an interface, this command triggers a CGMP Join message. This command should only be used on 802 and ATM media. When a **no ip cgmp** command is issued, a triggered CGMP Leave message is sent for the router's MAC address on the interface for group 0000.0000.0000 (all groups).

When the **proxy** keyword is specified, the CGMP proxy function is enabled. That is, any router that is not CGMP-capable will be advertised by the proxy router. The proxy router advertises the existence of other non-CGMP-capable routers by sending a CGMP Join message with the non-CGMP-capable router's MAC address and a group address of 0000.0000.0000.

Examples

In the following example, CGMP is enabled:

```
ip cgmp
```

In the following example, CGMP and CGMP proxy are enabled:

```
ip cgmp proxy
```

IP DVMRP ACCEPT-FILTER

To configure an acceptance filter for incoming DVMRP reports, use the **ip dvmrp accept-filter** interface configuration command. To disable this feature, use the **no** form of this command.

ip dvmrp accept-filter *access-list-number* [*distance*] **neighbor-list** *access-list-number*
no ip dvmrp accept-filter *access-list-number* [*distance*] **neighbor-list** *access-list-number*

Syntax	Description
access-list-number	Number of a standard IP access list. This can be a number from 0 to 99. A value of 0 means that all sources are accepted with the configured distance.
distance	(Optional.) Administrative distance to the destination.
neighbor-list *access-list number*	Number of a neighbor list. DVMRP reports are accepted only by those neighbors on the list.

Default

All destination reports are accepted with a distance of 0. Default settings accept reports from all neighbors.

Command Mode

Interface configuration

Usage Guidelines

This command first appeared in Cisco IOS Release 10.0. The **neighbor-list** keyword and *access-list-number* argument first appeared in Cisco IOS 11.2.

Any sources that match the access list are stored in the DVMRP routing table with *distance*.

The *distance* is used to compare with the same source in the unicast routing table. The route with the lower distance (either the route in the unicast routing table or that in the DVMRP routing table) takes precedence when computing the Reverse Path Forwarding (RPF) interface for a source of a multicast packet.

By default, the administrative distance for DVMRP routes is 0. This means that they always take precedence over unicast routing table routes. If you have two paths to a source, one through unicast routing (using PIM as the multicast routing protocol) and another path using DVMRP (unicast and multicast routing), and if you want to use the PIM path, use the **ip dvmrp accept-filter** command to increase the administrative distance for DVMRP routes. For example, if the unicast routing protocol is Enhanced IGRP, which has a default administrative distance of 90, you could define and apply the following access list so the RPF interface used to accept multicast packets will be through the Enhanced IGRP/PIM path:

```
ip dvmrp accept-filter 1 100
access-list 1 permit 0.0.0.0 255.255.255.255
```

Example

The following example applies access list 57 to the interface and sets a distance of 4:

```
access-list 57 permit 131.108.0.0 0.0.255.255
access-list 57 permit 198.92.37.0 0.0.0.255
access-list 57 deny 0.0.0.0 255.255.255.255
 ip dvmrp accept-filter 57 4
```

Related Commands

Search online to find documentation for related commands.

distance
ip dvmrp metric
show ip dvmrp route
tunnel mode

IP DVMRP AUTO-SUMMARY

To enable DVMRP auto-summarization if it was disabled, use the **ip dvmrp auto-summary** interface configuration command. To disable the feature, use the **no** form of this command.

ip dvmrp auto-summary
no ip dvmrp auto-summary

Syntax   Description

This command has no arguments or keywords.

Default

Enabled

Command Mode

Interface configuration

Usage Guidelines

This command first appeared in Cisco IOS Release 11.2.

DVMRP auto-summarization occurs when a unicast subnet route is collapsed into a classful network number route. This occurs when the subnet is a different network number than the IP address of the interface (or tunnel) over which the advertisement is sent. If the interface is unnumbered, the network number of the numbered interface the unnumbered interface points to is compared.

You might want to disable this feature if the information you want to send using the **ip dvmrp summary-address** command is the same as the information that would be sent using DVMRP auto-summarization.

Example

The following example disables DVMRP auto-summarization:

```
no ip dvmrp auto-summary
```

Related Commands

Search online to find documentation for related commands.

ip dvmrp summary-address

IP DVMRP DEFAULT-INFORMATION

To advertise network 0.0.0.0 to DVMRP neighbors on an interface, use the **ip dvmrp default-information** interface configuration command. To prevent the advertisement, use the **no** form of this command.

ip dvmrp default-information {originate | only}
no ip dvmrp default-information {originate | only}

Syntax	Description
originate	Other routes more specific than 0.0.0.0 can also be advertised.
only	No DVMRP routes other than 0.0.0.0 are advertised.

Default

Disabled

Command Mode

Interface configuration

Usage Guidelines

This command first appeared in Cisco IOS Release 10.3.

This command should only be used when the router is a neighbor to mrouted version 3.6 machines. The mrouted protocol is a public domain implementation of DVMRP.

You can use the **ip dvmrp metric** command with the **ip dvmrp default-information** command to tailor the metric used when advertising the default route 0.0.0.0. By default, metric 1 is used.

Example

The following example configures the Cisco IOS software to advertise network 0.0.0.0, in addition to other networks, to DVMRP neighbors:

```
ip dvmrp default-information originate
```

Related Commands

Search online to find documentation for related commands.

ip dvmrp metric

IP DVMRP METRIC

To configure the metric associated with a set of destinations for DVMRP reports, use the **ip dvmrp metric** interface configuration command. To disable this function, use the **no** form of this command.

> **ip dvmrp metric** *metric* [**list** *access-list-number*] [[*protocol process-id*] | **dvmrp**]
> **ip dvmrp metric** *metric* **route-map** *map-name*

> **no ip dvmrp metric** *metric* [**list** *access-list-number*] [[*protocol process-id*] | **dvmrp**]
> **no ip dvmrp metric** *metric* **route-map** *map-name*

Syntax	Description
metric	Metric associated with a set of destinations for DVMRP reports. It can be a value from 0 to 32. A value of 0 means that the route is not advertised. A value of 32 is equivalent to infinity (unreachable).
list *access-list-number*	(Optional.) Number of an access list. If you specify this argument, only the multicast destinations that match the access list are reported with the configured metric. Any destinations not advertised because of split horizon do not use the configured metric.
protocol	(Optional.) Name of unicast routing protocol, such as **bgp**, **eigrp**, **igrp**, **isis**, **ospf**, **rip**, or **static** or **dvmrp**. If you specify these arguments, only routes learned by the specified routing protocol are advertised in DVMRP report messages.
process-id	(Optional.) Process ID number of the unicast routing protocol.
dvmrp	(Optional.) Allows routes from the DVMRP routing table to be advertised with the configured *metric* or filtered.
route-map *map-name*	Unicast routes are subject to route-map conditions before being injected into DVMRP. Route-maps cannot be used for DVMRP routes.

Default

No metric is preconfigured. Only directly connected subnets and networks are advertised to neighboring DVMRP routers.

Command Mode

Interface configuration

Usage Guidelines

This command first appeared in Cisco IOS Release 10.2. The **route-map** keyword first appeared in Cisco IOS Release 11.1.

When PIM is configured on an interface and DVMRP neighbors are discovered, the Cisco IOS software sends DVMRP report messages for directly connected networks. The **ip dvmrp metric** command enables DVMRP report messages for multicast destinations that match the access list. Usually, the metric for these routes is 1. Under certain circumstances, you might want to tailor the metric used for various unicast routes. This command lets you configure the metric associated with a set of destinations for Report messages sent out from this interface.

You can use the *access-list-number* argument in conjunction with the *protocol process-id* arguments to selectively list the destinations learned from a given routing protocol.

To display DVMRP activity, use the **debug ip dvmrp** command.

Example

The following example connects a PIM cloud to a DVMRP cloud. Access list 1 permits the sending of DVMRP reports to the DVMRP routers advertising all sources in the 198.92.35.0 network with a metric of 1. Access list 2 permits all other destinations, but the metric of 0 means that no DVMRP reports are sent for these destinations.

```
access-list 1 permit 198.92.35.0 0.0.0.255
access-list 1 deny 0.0.0.0 255.255.255.255
access-list 2 permit 0.0.0.0 255.255.255.255
interface tunnel 0
 ip dvmrp metric 1 list 1
 ip dvmrp metric 0 list 2
```

Related Commands

Search online to find documentation for related commands.

debug ip dvmrp
ip dvmrp accept-filter

IP DVMRP METRIC-OFFSET

To change the metrics of advertised DVMRP routes and thus favor or not favor a certain route, use the **ip dvmrp metric-offset** interface configuration command. To restore the default values, use the **no** form of this command.

> **ip dvmrp metric-offset [in | out]** *increment*
> **no ip dvmrp metric-offset**

Part
II

Command Reference

Syntax	Description
in	(Optional.) The *increment* value is added to incoming DVMRP reports and is reported in mrinfo replies. The default for **in** is 1.
out	(Optional.) The *increment* value is added to outgoing DVMRP reports for routes from the DVMRP routing table. The default for **out** is 0.
increment	Value added to the metric of a DVMRP route advertised in a Report message.

Defaults

If neither **in** nor **out** is specified, **in** is the default.
The default for **in** is 1.
The default for **out** is 0.

Command Mode

Interface configuration

Usage Guidelines

This command first appeared in Cisco IOS Release 11.0.

Use this command to influence which routes are used, as you prefer. The DVMRP metric is in hop count.

Example

The following example adds 10 to the incoming DVMRP reports:

```
ip dvmrp metric-offset 10
```

IP DVMRP OUTPUT-REPORT-DELAY

To configure an interpacket delay of a DVMRP report, use the **ip dvmrp output-report-delay** interface configuration command. To restore the default values, use the **no** form of this command.

> **ip dvmrp output-report-delay** *milliseconds* [*burst*]
> **no ip dvmrp output-report-delay** *milliseconds* [*burst*]

Syntax	Description
milliseconds	Number of milliseconds that elapse between transmissions of a set of DVMRP report packets. The number of packets in the set is determined by the *burst* argument. The default number of milliseconds is 100 milliseconds.
burst	(Optional.) The number of packets in the set being transmitted. The default is 2 packets.

Defaults

milliseconds is 100 milliseconds
burst is 2 packets

Command Mode

Interface configuration

Usage Guidelines

This command first appeared in Cisco IOS Release 11.3.

The delay is the number of milliseconds that elapse between transmissions of sets of packets that constitute a report. The number of packets in the set is determined by the *burst* value.

You might want to change the default values, depending on the CPU and buffering of the mrouted machine.

Example

The following example sets the interpacket delay to 200 milliseconds and the burst size to 3 packets. Therefore, at the periodic DVMRP report interval, if 6 packets are built, 3 packets will be sent, then a delay of 200 milliseconds occurs, then the next 3 packets are sent.

```
ip dvmrp output-report-delay 200 3
```

IP DVMRP REJECT-NON-PRUNERS

To configure the router so that it will not peer with a DVMRP neighbor if that neighbor does not support DVMRP pruning or grafting, use the **ip dvmrp reject-non-pruners** interface configuration command. To disable the feature, use the **no** form of this command.

> **ip dvmrp reject-non-pruners**
> **no ip dvmrp reject-non-pruners**

Syntax   Description

This command has no arguments or keywords.

Default

Disabled

Command Mode

Interface configuration

Usage Guidelines

This command first appeared in Cisco IOS Release 11.0.

By default, the router accepts all DVMRP neighbors as peers, regardless of their DVMRP capability or lack thereof.

Use this command to prevent a router from peering with a DVMRP neighbor if that neighbor does not support DVMRP pruning or grafting. If the router receives a DVMRP Probe or Report message without the Prune-Capable flag set, the router logs a syslog message and discards the message.

Note that this command prevents peering with neighbors only. If there are any non-pruning routers multiple hops away (downstream toward potential receivers) that are not rejected, then a non-pruning DVMRP network might still exist.

Example

The following example configures the router not to peer with DVMRP neighbors that do not support pruning or grafting:

```
ip dvmrp reject-non-pruners
```

IP DVMRP ROUTEHOG-NOTIFICATION

To change the number of DVMRP routes allowed before a syslog warning message is issued, use the **ip dvmrp routehog-notification** global configuration command. To restore the default value, use the **no** form of this command.

> **ip dvmrp routehog-notification** *route-count*
> **no ip dvmrp routehog-notification**

Syntax

Description

Syntax	Description
route-count	Number of routes allowed before a syslog message is triggered. The default is 10,000 routes.

Default

10,000 routes

Command Mode

Global configuration

Usage Guidelines

This command first appeared in Cisco IOS Release 10.2.

This command configures how many DVMRP routes are accepted on each interface within an approximate one-minute interval before a syslog message is issued, warning that there might be a route surge occurring. The warning is typically used to detect quickly when people have misconfigured their routers to inject a large number of routes into the MBONE.

The **show ip igmp interface** command displays a running count of routes. When the count is exceeded, an "*** ALERT ***" is appended to the line.

Example

The following example lowers the threshold to 8000 routes:

```
ip dvmrp routehog-notification 8000
```

Related Commands

Search online to find documentation for related commands.

show ip igmp interface

IP DVMRP ROUTE-LIMIT

To change the limit on the number of DVMRP routes that can be advertised over an interface enabled to run DVMRP, use the **ip dvmrp route-limit** global configuration command. To configure no limit, use the **no** form of this command.

ip dvmrp route-limit *count*
no ip dvmrp route-limit

Syntax	Description
count	Number of DVMRP routes that can be advertised. The default is 7000 routes.

Default

7000 routes

Command Mode

Global configuration

Usage Guidelines

This command first appeared in Cisco IOS Release 11.0.

Interfaces enabled to run DVMRP include a DVMRP tunnel, an interface where a DVMRP neighbor has been discovered, or an interface configured to run **ip dvmrp unicast-routing**.

The **ip dvmrp route-limit** command is automatically generated to the configuration file when at least one interface is enabled for multicast routing. This command is necessary to prevent misconfigured **ip dvmrp metric** commands from causing massive route injection into the multicast backbone (MBONE).

Example

The following example changes the limit to 5000 DVMRP routes allowed to be advertised:

```
ip dvmrp route-limit 5000
```

Related Commands

Search online to find documentation for related commands.

ip dvmrp unicast-routing

IP DVMRP SUMMARY-ADDRESS

To configure a DVMRP summary address to be advertised out of the interface, use the **ip dvmrp summary-address** interface configuration command. To remove the summary address, use the **no** form of this command.

> **ip dvmrp summary-address** *address mask* [**metric** *value*]
> **no ip dvmrp summary-address** *address mask* [**metric** *value*]

Syntax	Description
address	Summary IP address that is advertised instead of the more specific route.
mask	Mask on the summary IP address.
metric *value*	(Optional.) Metric that is advertised with the summary address. The default is 1.

Default

metric *value* is 1

Command Mode

Interface configuration

Usage Guidelines

This command first appeared in Cisco IOS Release 11.2.

If there is at least a single, more specific route in the unicast routing table that matches the specified *address* and *mask*, the summary is advertised. Routes in the DVMRP routing table are not candidates for summarization.

When the **metric** keyword is specified, the summary is advertised with that metric *value*.

Multiple summary address can be configured on an interface. When multiple overlapping summary addresses are configured on an interface, the one with the longest mask takes preference.

Example

The following example configures the DVMRP summary address 171.69.0.0 to be advertised out of the interface:

```
ip dvmrp summary-address 171.69.0.0 255.255.0.0 metric 1
```

Related Commands

Search online to find documentation for related commands.

ip dvmrp auto-summary

IP DVMRP UNICAST-ROUTING

To enable DVMRP unicast routing on an interface, use the **ip dvmrp unicast-routing** interface configuration command. To disable the feature, use the **no** form of this command.

> **ip dvmrp unicast-routing**
> **no ip dvmrp unicast-routing**

Syntax   Description

This command has no arguments or keywords.

Default

Disabled

Command Mode

Interface configuration

Usage Guidelines

This command first appeared in Cisco IOS Release 10.3.

Enabling DVMRP unicast routing means that routes in DVMRP Report messages are cached by the router in a DVMRP routing table. When PIM is running, these routes may get preference over routes in the unicast routing table. This allows PIM to run on the MBONE topology when it is different from the unicast topology.

DVMRP unicast routing can run on all interfaces, including GRE tunnels. On DVMRP tunnels, it runs by virtue of DVMRP multicast routing. This command does not enable DVMRP multicast routing among Cisco routers. However, if there is a DVMRP-capable multicast router, the Cisco router will do PIM/DVMRP multicast routing interaction.

Example

The following example enables DVMRP unicast routing:

```
ip dvmrp unicast-routing
```

Related Commands

Search online to find documentation for related commands.

ip dvmrp route-limit

IP IGMP ACCESS-GROUP

To control the multicast groups that hosts on the subnet serviced by an interface can join, use the **ip igmp access-group** interface configuration command. To disable groups on an interface, use the **no** form of this command.

> **ip igmp access-group** *access-list-number version*
> **no ip igmp access-group** *access-list-number version*

Syntax	Description
access-list-number	Number of a standard IP access list. This can be a number from 1 to 99.
version	Changes IGMP version. Default is version 2.

Default

All groups are allowed on an interface.

Command Mode

Interface configuration

Usage Guidelines

This command first appeared in Cisco IOS Release 10.0.

Example

In the following example, hosts serviced by Ethernet interface 0 can join the group 225.2.2.2 only:

```
access-list 1 225.2.2.2 0.0.0.0
interface ethernet 0
 ip igmp access-group 1
```

Related Commands

Search online to find documentation for related commands.

ip igmp join-group

IP IGMP HELPER-ADDRESS

To cause the system to forward all IGMP Host Reports and Leave messages received on the interface to the specified IP address, use the **ip igmp helper-address** interface configuration command. To disable such forwarding, use the **no** form of this command.

> **ip igmp helper-address** *ip-address*
> **no ip igmp helper-address**

Syntax	Description
ip-address	IP address to which IGMP Host Reports and Leave messages are forwarded. Specify the IP address of an interface on the central router.

Default

Disabled

Command Mode

Interface configuration

Usage Guidelines

This command first appeared in Cisco IOS Release 11.2 F.

This command and the **ip pim neighbor-filter** command together enable stub multicast routing. The IGMP Host Reports and Leave messages are forwarded to the IP address specified. The reports are resent out of the next-hop interface toward the IP address, with that interface's source address. This command enables a sort of "dense-mode" Join, allowing stub sites not participating in PIM to indicate membership in IP multicast groups.

Example

The following example enables stub multicast routing on Router A, which has an outgoing interface with IP address 10.0.0.1. Router B is a central router with an incoming interface with address 10.0.0.2. Access list 1 filters PIM messages from the source (stub Router A).

Router A

```
ip multicast-routing
 ip pim dense-mode
 ip igmp helper-address 10.0.0.2
```

Router B

```
ip multicast-routing
 ip pim dense-mode : or ip pim sparse-mode
 ip pim neighbor-filter 1
access-list 1 deny 10.0.0.1
```

Related Commands

Search online to find documentation for related commands.

ip pim neighbor-filter

IP IGMP JOIN-GROUP

To have the router join a multicast group, use the **ip igmp join-group** interface configuration command. To cancel membership in a multicast group, use the **no** form of this command.

    ip igmp join-group *group-address*
    no ip igmp join-group *group-address*

Syntax	*Description*
group-address	Address of the multicast group. This is a multicast IP address in four-part, dotted notation.

Default

No multicast group memberships are predefined.

Command Mode

Interface configuration

Usage Guidelines

This command first appeared in Cisco IOS Release 10.0.

IP packets that are addressed to the group address are passed to the IP client process in the Cisco IOS software.

If all the multicast-capable routers and access servers that you administer are members of a multicast group, pinging that group causes all routers to respond. This can be a useful administrative and debugging tool.

Another reason to have a router join a multicast group is when other hosts on the network have a bug in IGRP that prevents them from correctly answering IGMP queries. Having the router join the multicast group causes upstream routers to maintain multicast routing table information for that group and keep the paths for that group active.

Example

In the following example, the router joins multicast group 225.2.2.2:

```
ip igmp join-group 225.2.2.2
```

Related Commands

Search online to find documentation for related commands.

ip igmp access-group
ping (privileged)
ping (user)

IP IGMP QUERY-INTERVAL

To configure the frequency at which the Cisco IOS software sends IGMP host-query messages, use the **ip igmp query-interval** interface configuration command. To return to the default frequency, use the **no** form of this command.

> **ip igmp query-interval** *seconds*
> **no ip igmp query-interval**

Syntax	Description
seconds	Frequency, in seconds, at which to transmit IGMP host-query messages. The can be a number from 0 to 65535. The default is 60 seconds.

Default

60 seconds

Command Mode

Interface configuration

Usage Guidelines

This command first appeared in Cisco IOS Release 10.2.

Multicast routers send host membership query messages (host-query messages) to discover which multicast groups have members on the router's attached networks. Hosts respond with IGMP report messages indicating that they wish to receive multicast packets for specific groups (that is, indicating that the host wants to become a member of the group). Host-query messages are addresses to the all-hosts multicast group, which has the address 224.0.0.1, and have an IP TTL value of 1.

The designated router for a LAN is the only router that sends IGMP host-query messages.

- For IGMP Version 1, the designated router is elected according to the multicast routing protocol that runs on the LAN.
- For IGMP Version 2, the designated querier is the lowest IP-addressed multicast router on the subnet.

If the router hears no queries for the timeout period (controlled by the **ip igmp query-timeout** command), it becomes the querier.

NOTES ——————————————————————————————————————

Changing this value may severely impact multicast forwarding.

Example

The following example changes the frequency at which the designated router sends IGMP host-query messages to 2 minutes:

```
interface tunnel 0
  ip igmp query-interval 120
```

Related Commands

Search online to find documentation for related commands.

ip pim query-interval
show ip igmp groups

IP IGMP QUERY-MAX-RESPONSE-TIME

To configure the maximum response time advertised in IGMP queries, use the **ip igmp query-max-response-time** interface configuration command. To restore the default value, use the **no** form of this command.

ip igmp query-max-response-time *seconds*
no ip igmp query-max-response-time

Syntax	Description
seconds	Maximum response time, in seconds, advertised in IGMP queries. The default value is 10 seconds.

Default

10 seconds

Command Mode

Interface configuration

Usage Guidelines

This command first appeared in Cisco IOS Release 11.1.

This command is valid only when IGMP Version 2 is running.

This command controls how long the responder has to respond to an IGMP Query message before the router deletes the group. Configuring a value less than 10 seconds enables the router to prune groups faster.

NOTES

If the hosts do not respond fast enough, they might be pruned when you don't want them to be. Therefore, the hosts must know to respond faster than 10 seconds (or the value you configure).

Example

The following example configures a maximum response time of 8 seconds:

```
ip igmp query-max-response-time 8
```

Related Commands

Search online to find documentation for related commands.

ip pim query-interval
show ip igmp groups

IP IGMP QUERY-TIMEOUT

To configure the timeout time before the router takes over as the querier for the interface, after the previous querier has stopped querying, use the **ip igmp query-timeout** interface configuration command. To restore the default value, use the **no** form of this command.

> **ip igmp query-timeout** *seconds*
> **no ip igmp query-timeout**

Syntax	Description
seconds	Number of seconds that the router waits after the previous querier has stopped querying and before it takes over as the querier.

Default

2 times the query interval

Command Mode

Interface configuration

Usage Guidelines

This command first appeared in Cisco IOS Release 11.1. It requires IGMP Version 2.

By default, the router waits twice the query interval specified by the **ip igmp query-interval** command, after which, if it has heard no queries, it becomes the querier. By default, the **ip igmp query-interval** defaults to 30 seconds, which means the **ip igmp query-timeout** defaults to 60 seconds.

Example

The following example configures the router to wait 30 seconds from the time it received the last query before it takes over as the querier for the interface:

```
ip igmp query-timeout 30
```

Related Commands

Search online to find documentation for related commands.

ip igmp query-interval

IP IGMP STATIC-GROUP

To configure the router to be a statically connected member of the specified group on the interface, use the **ip igmp static-group** interface configuration command. To remove the router as a member of the group, use the **no** form of this command.

> **ip igmp static-group** *group-address*
> **no ip igmp static-group** *group-address*

Syntax	Description
group-address	IP multicast group address of a group that the router is a member of.

Default

Disabled

Command Mode

Interface configuration

Usage Guidelines

This command first appeared in Cisco IOS Release 11.2.

When this command is configured, packets to the group are fast-switched out of this interface, provided that packets were received on the correct RPF interface. This is unlike configuring the **ip igmp join-group** command, which also causes packets to be passed up to the process level.

If the **ip igmp join-group** command is configured for the same group address as the **ip igmp static-group** command, the **ip igmp join-group** command takes precedence, and the group behaves like a locally joined group.

Example

The following example configures 239.100.100.101 on Ethernet interface 0:

```
interface ethernet 0
 ip igmp static-group 239.100.100.101
```

Related Commands

Search online to find documentation for related commands.

ip igmp join-group

IP IGMP VERSION

To configure which version of IGMP the router uses, use the **ip igmp version** interface configuration command. To restore the default value, use the **no** form of this command.

    ip igmp version {2 | 1}
    no ip version

Syntax	Description
2	IGMP Version 2.
1	IGMP Version 1.

Default

Version 2

Command Mode

Interface configuration

Usage Guidelines

This command first appeared in Cisco IOS Release 11.1.

All systems on the subnet must support the same version. The router does not automatically detect Version 1 systems and switch to Version 1, as did prior releases of the Cisco IOS software.

Configure Version 1 if your hosts do not support Version 2.

Some commands require IGMP Version 2, such as the **ip igmp query-max-response-time** and **ip igmp query-timeout** commands.

Example

The following example configures the router to use IGMP Version 1:

```
ip igmp version 1
```

Related Commands

Search online to find documentation for related commands.

ip igmp query-max-response-time
ip igmp query-timeout

show ip igmp groups
show ip igmp interface

IP MROUTE

To configure a multicast static route (mroute), use the **ip mroute** global configuration command. To remove the route, use the **no** form of this command.

ip mroute *source mask* [*protocol as-number*] {*rpf-address* | *type number*} [*distance*]
no ip mroute *source mask* [*protocol as-number*] {*rpf-address* | *type number*} [*distance*]

Syntax	Description
source	IP address of the multicast source.
mask	Mask on the IP address of the multicast source.
protocol	(Optional.) Unicast routing protocol that you are using.
as-number	(Optional.) Autonomous system number of the routing protocol you are using, if applicable.
rpf-address	Incoming interface for the mroute. If the Reverse Path Forwarding address *rpf-address* is a PIM neighbor, PIM Joins, Grafts, and Prunes are sent to it. The *rpf-address* can be a host IP address of a directly connected system or a network/subnet number. When it is a route, a recursive lookup is done from the unicast routing table to find a directly connected system. If *rpf-address* is not specified, the interface *type number* is used as the incoming interface.
type number	Interface type and number for the mroute.
distance	(Optional.) Determines whether a unicast route, a DVMRP route, or a static mroute should be used for the RPF lookup. The lower distances have better preference. If the static mroute has the same distance as the other two RPF sources, the static mroute will take precedence. The default is 0.

Default
distance: 0

Command Mode
Global configuration

Usage Guidelines
This command first appeared in Cisco IOS Release 11.0.

Part
II

Command Reference

This command allows you to statically configure where multicast sources are located (even though the unicast routing table says something different).

When a source range is specified, the *rpf-address* applies only to those sources.

Examples

The following example configures all sources via a single interface (in this case, a tunnel):

```
ip mroute 0.0.0.0 255.255.255.255 tunnel0
```

The following example configures all specific sources within a network number to be reachable through 171.68.10.13:

```
ip mroute 171.69.0.0 255.255.0.0 171.68.10.13
```

The following example causes this multicast static route to take effect if the unicast routes for any given destination go away:

```
ip mroute 0.0.0.0 255.255.255.255 serial0 200
```

IP MROUTE-CACHE

To configure IP multicast fast switching, use the **ip mroute-cache** interface configuration command. To disable IP multicast fast switching, use the **no** form of this command.

> **ip mroute-cache**
> **no ip mroute-cache**

Syntax   Description

This command has no arguments or keywords.

Default

Enabled

Command Mode

Interface configuration

Usage Guidelines

This command first appeared in Cisco IOS Release 11.0.

If fast switching is disabled on an incoming interface for a multicast routing table entry, the packet will be sent at process level for all interfaces in the outgoing interface list.

If fast switching is disabled on an outgoing interface for a multicast routing table entry, the packet is process level switched for that interface, but may be fast-switched for other interfaces in the outgoing interface list.

When fast switching is enabled (like unicast routing), debug messages are not logged. If you want to log debug messages, disable fast switching.

Example

The following example disables IP multicast fast switching on the interface:

```
no ip mroute-cache
```

IP MULTICAST BOUNDARY

To configure an administratively scoped boundary, use the **ip multicast boundary** interface configuration command. To remove the boundary, use the **no** form of this command.

    ip multicast boundary *access-list-number*
    no ip multicast boundary

Syntax	*Description*
access-list-number	Standard IP access list number identifying an access list that controls the range of group addresses affected by the boundary.

Default

There is no boundary.

Command Mode

Interface configuration

Usage Guidelines

This command first appeared in Cisco IOS Release 11.1.

You might set up a boundary to keep multicast packets from being forwarded.

Example

The following example sets up a boundary for all administratively scoped addresses:

```
access-list 1 deny 239.0.0.0 0.255.255.255
access-list 1 permit 224.0.0.0 15.255.255.255
interface ethernet 0
 ip multicast boundary 1
```

Related Commands

Search online to find documentation for related commands.

access-list (standard)

IP MULTICAST CACHE-HEADERS

To allocate a circular buffer to store IP multicast packet headers that the router receives, use the **ip multicast cache-headers** global configuration command. To disable the feature, use the **no** form of this command.

> **ip multicast cache-headers**
> **no ip multicast cache-headers**

Syntax   Description

This command has no arguments or keywords.

Default

Disabled

Command Mode

Global configuration

Usage Guidelines

This command first appeared in Cisco IOS Release 11.1.

You can store IP multicast packet headers in a cache and then display them to determine the following:

- Who is sending IP multicast packets to what groups
- Inter-packet delay
- Duplicate IP multicast packets (if any)
- Multicast forwarding loops in your network (if any)
- Scope of the group
- UDP port numbers
- Packet length

NOTES

This feature allocates a circular buffer of approximately 32 kilobytes. Do not configure this feature if you are low on memory.

Use the **show ip mpacket** command to display the buffer.

Example

The following example allocates a buffer to store IP multicast packet headers:

```
ip multicast cache-headers
```

Related Commands

Search online to find documentation for related commands.

show ip mpacket

IP MULTICAST HELPER-MAP

To allow IP multicast routing in a multicast-capable internetwork between two broadcast-only internetworks, use the **ip multicast helper-map** interface configuration command. To prevent this feature, use the **no** form of this command.

> **ip multicast helper-map** {*group-address* | **broadcast**} {*broadcast-address* | *multicast-address*} *extended-access-list-number*
> **no multicast helper-map** {*group-address* | **broadcast**} {*broadcast-address* | *multicast-address*} *extended-access-list-number*

Part II

Command Reference

Syntax	Description
group-address	Multicast group address of traffic to be converted to broadcast traffic. Use this with the *broadcast-address*.
broadcast	Specifies the traffic is being converted from broadcast to multicast. Use this with the *multicast-address*.
broadcast-address	Address to which broadcast traffic is sent. Use this with the *group-address*.
multicast-address	Specifies the IP multicast address to which the converted traffic is directed. Use this with the **broadcast** keyword.
extended-access-list-number	IP extended access list that controls which broadcast packets are translated, based on the UDP port number.

Default

No conversion between broadcast and multicast occurs.

Command Mode

Interface configuration

Usage Guidelines

This command first appeared in Cisco IOS Release 11.1.

When a multicast-capable internetwork is between two broadcast-only internetworks, you can convert broadcast traffic to multicast at the first hop router, and convert it back to broadcast at the last hop router before delivering the packets to the broadcast clients. Thus, you can take advantage of the multicast capability of the intermediate multicast internetwork. This feature prevents unnecessary replication at the intermediate routers and allows multicast fast switching in the multicast internetwork.

NOTES

On the last hop router, the **ip multicast helper-map** command introduces the **ip igmp join-group** command on that interface. That command must remain for this feature to work. If you remove the **ip igmp join-group** command, the feature fails. You can move the **ip igmp join-group** command to another interface on the same router.

Example

The following example illustrates how a helper address on two routers converts from broadcast to multicast and back to broadcast.

The configuration on the first hop router converts a broadcast stream arriving at incoming interface Ethernet interface 0 destined to UDP port 4000 to a multicast stream. The access list denies other traffic from being forwarded into the multicast cloud. The traffic is sent to group address 224.5.5.5. Because fast switching does not perform such a conversion, the **ip forward-protocol** command causes the proper process level to perform the conversion.

The configuration on the last hop router converts the multicast stream at incoming interface Ethernet interface 1 back to broadcast. Again, all multicast traffic emerging from the multicast cloud is not supposed to be converted to broadcast, only the traffic destined for UDP port 4000.

First Hop Router

```
interface ethernet 0
 ip multicast helper-map broadcast 224.5.5.5 120
 ip pim dense-mode
!
access-list 120 permit any any udp 4000
access-list 120 deny any any udp
 ip forward-protocol udp 4000
```

Last Hop Router

```
interface ethernet 1
 ip multicast helper-map 224.5.5.5 178.21.34.255 135
 ip pim dense-mode
!
access-list 135 permit any any udp 4000
access-list 135 deny any any udp
 ip forward-protocol udp 4000
```

Related Commands

Search online to find documentation for related commands.

ip forward-protocol

IP MULTICAST RATE-LIMIT

To control the rate a sender from the source-list can send to a multicast group in the group-list, use the **ip multicast rate-limit** interface configuration command. To remove the control, use the **no** form of this command.

> **ip multicast rate-limit** {**in** | **out**} [**video** | **whiteboard**] [**group-list** *access-list*]
> [**source-list** *access-list*] *kbps*
> **no ip multicast rate-limit** {**in** | **out**} [**video** | **whiteboard**] [**group-list** *access-list*]
> [**source-list** *access-list*] *kbps*

Syntax	Description
in	Only packets at the rate of *kbps* or slower are accepted on the interface.
out	Only a maximum of *kbps* will be transmitted on the interface.
video	(Optional.) Rate limiting is performed based on the UDP port number used by video traffic. Video traffic is identified by consulting the sdr cache.
whiteboard	(Optional.) Rate limiting is performed based on the UDP port number used by whiteboard traffic. Whiteboard traffic is identified by consulting the sdr cache.
group-list *access-list*	(Optional.) Specifies the access list number that controls which multicast groups are subject to the rate limit.
source-list *access-list*	(Optional.) Specifies the access list number that controls which senders are subject to the rate limit.
kbps	Kilobits-per-second transmission rate. Any packets sent at greater than this value are silently discarded. If this command is configured, the default value is 0, meaning that no traffic is permitted. Therefore, set this to a positive value if you use this command.

Default

If this command is not configured, there is no rate limit.
If this command is configured, *kbps* defaults to 0, meaning that no traffic is permitted.

Command Mode

Interface configuration

Usage Guidelines

This command first appeared in Cisco IOS Release 11.0.

If a router receives a packet and in the last second the user has sent over the limit, the packet is dropped; otherwise, it is forwarded.

For **video** or **whiteboard** to work, the **ip sdr listen** command must be enabled so the port number can be obtained from the sdr cache. If **ip sdr listen** is not enabled, or the group address is not in the sdr cache, no rate-limiting is done for the group.

Example

In the following example, packets to any group from sources in network 171.69.0.0 will have their packets rate-limited to 64 Kbps:

```
interface serial 0
 ip multicast rate-limit out group-list 1 source-list 2 64
access-list 1 permit 0.0.0.0 255.255.255.255
access-list 2 permit 171.69.0.0 0.0.255.255
```

Related Commands

Search online to find documentation for related commands.

ip sdr listen

IP MULTICAST-ROUTING

To enable IP multicast routing, use the **ip multicast-routing** global configuration command. To disable IP multicast routing, use the **no** form of this command.

> **ip multicast-routing**
> **no ip multicast-routing**

Syntax   Description

This command has no arguments or keywords.

Default

Disabled

Command Mode

Global configuration

Usage Guidelines

This command first appeared in Cisco IOS Release 10.0.

When IP multicast routing is disabled, the Cisco IOS software does not forward any multicast packets.

Example

The following example enables IP multicast routing:

```
ip multicast-routing
```

Related Commands

Search online to find documentation for related commands.

ip pim

IP MULTICAST TTL-THRESHOLD

To configure the time-to-live (TTL) threshold of packets being forwarded out an interface, use the **ip multicast ttl-threshold** interface configuration command. To return to the default TTL threshold, use the **no** form of this command.

> **ip multicast ttl-threshold** *ttl-value*
> **no ip multicast ttl-threshold** [*ttl-value*]

Syntax	Description
ttl-value	Time-to-live value, in hops. It can be a value from 0 to 255. The default value is 0, which means that all multicast packets are forwarded out the interface.

Default

0, which means that all multicast packets are forwarded out the interface.

Command Mode

Interface configuration

Usage Guidelines

This command first appeared in Cisco IOS Release 11.0.

Only multicast packets with a TTL value greater than the threshold are forwarded out the interface.

You should configure the TTL threshold only on border routers. Conversely, routers on which you configure a TTL threshold value automatically become border routers.

This command replaces the **ip multicast-threshold** command, which is obsolete.

Example

In the following example, you set the TTL threshold on a border router to 200, which is a very high value. This means that multicast packets must have a TTL greater than 200 in order to be forwarded out this interface. Multicast applications generally set this value well below 200. Therefore, setting a value of 200 means that no packets will be forwarded out the interface.

```
interface tunnel 0
 ip multicast ttl-threshold 200
```

Part
II

Command Reference

IP MULTICAST USE-FUNCTIONAL

To enable the mapping of IP multicast addresses to the Token Ring functional address 0xc000.0004.0000, use the **ip multicast use-functional** interface configuration command. To disable the feature, use the **no** form of this command.

> **ip multicast use-functional**
> **no ip multicast use-functional**

Syntax   Description

This command has no arguments or keywords.

Default

IP multicast addresses are mapped to the MAC-layer address 0xFFFF.FFFF.FFFF.

Command Mode

Interface configuration

Usage Guidelines

This command first appeared in Cisco IOS Release 11.1.

This command is accepted only on a Token Ring interface.

Neighboring devices on the Token Ring on which this feature is used should also use the same functional address for IP multicast traffic.

Because there are a limited number of Token Ring functional addresses, it is possible there are other protocols assigned to the Token Ring functional address 0xc000.0004.0000. Therefore, not every frame sent to the functional address is necessarily an IP multicast frame.

Example

The following example configures any IP multicast packets going out Token Ring interface 0 to be mapped to MAC address 0xc000.0004.0000:

```
interface token 0
  ip address 1.1.1.1 255.255.255.0
  ip pim dense-mode
  ip multicast use-functional
```

IP PIM

To enable PIM on an interface, use the **ip pim** interface configuration command. To disable PIM on the interface, use the **no** form of this command.

ip pim {dense-mode | sparse-mode ¦ sparse-dense-mode}
no ip pim

Syntax	Description
dense-mode	Enables dense mode of operation.
sparse-mode	Enables sparse mode of operation.
sparse-dense-mode	The interface is treated in the mode in which the group operates.

Default

IP multicast routing is disabled on all interfaces.

Command Mode

Interface configuration

Usage Guidelines

This command first appeared in Cisco IOS Release 10.0. The **sparse-dense-mode** keyword first appeared in Cisco IOS Release 11.1.

Enabling PIM on an interface also enables IGMP operation on that interface. An interface can be configured to be in dense mode, sparse mode, or sparse-dense mode. The mode describes how the Cisco IOS software populates its multicast routing table and how the software forwards multicast packets it receives from its directly connected LANs. In populating the multicast routing table, dense-mode interfaces are always added to the table. Sparse-mode interfaces are added to the table only when periodic join messages are received from downstream routers, or there is a directly connected member on the interface.

Dense Mode

Initially, a dense-mode interface forwards multicast packets until the router determines that there are group members or downstream routers, or until a prune message is received from a downstream router. Then, the dense-mode interface periodically forwards multicast packets out the interface until the same conditions occur. Dense mode assumes that there are multicast group members present. Dense-mode routers never send a join message. They do send prune messages as soon as they determine they have no members or downstream PIM routers. A dense-mode interface is subject to multicast flooding by default.

Sparse Mode

A sparse-mode interface is used for multicast forwarding only if a join message is received from a downstream router or if there are group members directly connected to the interface. Sparse mode assumes that there are no other multicast group members present. When sparse-mode routers want to join the shared path, they periodically send join messages toward the rendezvous point (RP). When sparse-mode routers want to join the source path, they periodically send join messages toward the source; they also send periodic prune messages to RP to prune the shared path.

Sparse-Dense Mode

An alternative to choosing just dense mode or just sparse mode is to run PIM in a single region in sparse mode for some groups and dense mode for other groups.

In sparse-dense mode, if the group is in dense mode, the interface will be treated as dense mode. If the group is in sparse mode, the interface will be treated in sparse mode. The group is "sparse" if the router knows about an RP for that group.

When an interface is treated in dense mode, it is populated in a multicast routing table's outgoing integrated list when either

- There are members or DVMRP neighbors on the interface.
- Any of the PIM neighbors on the interface have not pruned for the group.

When an interface is treated in sparse mode, it is populated in a multicast routing table's outgoing interface when either of the following is true:

- There are members or DVMRP neighbors on the interface.
- A PIM neighbor on the interface has received an explicit Join.

Examples

The following commands enable sparse-mode PIM on tunnel interface 0 and set the address of the RP router to 226.0.0.8:

```
ip pim rp-address 226.0.0.8
interface tunnel 0
 ip pim sparse-mode
```

The following commands enable dense-mode PIM on Ethernet interface 1:

```
interface ethernet 1
 ip pim dense-mode
```

The following example enables sparse-dense mode:

```
interface ethernet 1
 ip pim sparse-dense-mode
```

Related Commands

Search online to find documentation for related commands.

ip multicast-routing
ip pim rp-address
show ip pim interface

IP PIM ACCEPT-RP

To configure a router to accept Joins or Prunes destined for a specified RP and for a specific list of groups, use the **ip pim accept-rp** global configuration command. To remove that check, use the **no** form of this command.

ip pim accept-rp {*address* | **auto-rp**} [*group-access-list-number*]
no ip pim accept-rp {*ip-address* | **auto-rp**} [*group-access-list-number*]

Syntax	Description
address	RP address of the RP allowed to send Join messages to groups in the range specified by the group access list.
auto-rp	Join and Register messages are accepted only for RPs that are in the Auto-RP cache.
group-access-list-number	(Optional.) Access list that defines which groups are subject to the check.

Default

Disabled, so all Join messages and Prune messages are processed.

Command Mode

Global configuration

Usage Guidelines

This command first appeared in Cisco IOS Release 10.2.

This command causes the router to accept only (*,G) Join messages destined for the specified RP *address*. Additionally, the group address must be in the range specified by the access list.

When *address* is one of the system's addresses, the system will be the RP only for the specified group range specified by the access list. When the group address is not in the group range, the RP will not accept Join or Register messages and will respond immediately to Register messages with Register-Stop messages.

Example

The following example states that the router will accept Join or Prune messages destined for the RP at address 100.1.1.1 for the multicast group 224.2.2.2:

```
ip pim accept-rp 100.1.1.1 3
access-list 3 permit 224.2.2.2
```

Related Commands

Search online to find documentation for related commands.

access-list (standard)

Part II

Command Reference

IP PIM MESSAGE-INTERVAL

To configure the frequency at which a sparse-mode PIM router sends periodic sparse-mode Join/Prune PIM messages, use the **ip pim message-interval** global configuration command. To return to the default interval, use the **no** form of this command.

> **ip pim message-interval** *seconds*
> **no ip pim message-interval** [*seconds*]

Syntax	Description
seconds	Interval, in seconds, at which periodic sparse-mode Join and Prune PIM messages are sent. It can be a number from 1 to 65535. The default is 60 seconds.

Default

60 seconds

Command Mode

Global configuration

Usage Guidelines

This command first appeared in Cisco IOS Release 11.2.

The join-and-prune message interval should be the same for all routers in the network.

A router is pruned from a group if a Join message is not heard from it in three times the message interval specified by the *seconds* argument. By default, this is 3 minutes.

NOTES ──

Changing this value may severely impact multicast forwarding.

Example

The following example changes the PIM message interval to 90 seconds:

```
ip pim message-interval 90
```

Related Commands

Search online to find documentation for related commands.

ip igmp query-interval
ip pim query-interval

IP PIM MINIMUM-VC-RATE

To configure the minimum traffic rate to keep virtual circuits from being idled, use the **ip pim minimum-vc-rate** interface configuration command. To restore the default value, use the **no** form of this command.

> **ip pim minimum-vc-rate** *pps*
> **no pim minimum-vc-rate**

Syntax	Description
pps	Rate, in packets per second, below which a VC is eligible for idling. The default value is 0, which means all VCs are eligible for idling. The range is from 0 to 4294967295.

Part
II

Command Reference

Default

0 pps, which indicates all VCs are eligible for idling.

Command Mode

Interface configuration

Usage Guidelines

This command first appeared in Cisco IOS Release 11.3.

This command applies to an ATM interface only and also requires IP PIM sparse mode.

An idling policy uses the **ip pim vc-count** *number* to limit the number of VCs created by PIM. When the router stays at or below this *number*, no idling policy is in effect. When the next VC to be opened will exceed the *number*, an idling policy is exercised. Any virtual circuits with a traffic rate lower than the **ip pim minimum-vc-rate** are subject to the idling policy, which is described in the section "Limit the Number of Virtual Circuits" in Chapter 24, "Configuring IP Multicast Routing."

Example

The following example configures a minimum rate of 2500 pps over a VC, below which the VC is eligible for idling:

```
ip pim minimum-vc-rate 2500
```

Related Commands

Search online to find documentation for related commands.

ip pim vc-count

IP PIM MULTIPOINT-SIGNALLING

To enable PIM to open ATM multipoint switched virtual circuits for each multicast group that a receiver joins, use the **ip pim multipoint-signalling** interface configuration command. To disable the feature, use the **no** form of this command.

>**ip pim multipoint-signalling**
>**no ip pim multipoint-signalling**

Syntax   Description

This command has no arguments or keywords.

Default

Disabled. All multicast traffic goes to the static map multipoint VC as long as the **atm multipoint-signalling** command is configured.

Command Mode

Interface configuration

Usage Guidelines

This command first appeared in Cisco IOS Release 11.3.

This command is accepted only on an ATM interface. It allows optimal multicast trees to be built down to ATM switch granularity. This command can enhance router performance and link utilization because packets are not replicated and sent multiple times over the ATM interface.

Example

The following example enables PIM to open ATM multipoint switched virtual circuits for each multicast group that is joined:

```
ip pim multipoint-signalling
```

Related Commands

Search online to find documentation for related commands.

atm multipoint-signaling
ip pim minimum-vc-rate
ip pim vc-count
show ip pim vc

IP PIM NBMA-MODE

To configure a multiaccess WAN interface to be in nonbroadcast, multiaccess mode, use the **ip pim nbma-mode** interface configuration command. To disable this feature, use the **no** form of this command.

> **ip pim nbma-mode**
> **no ip pim nbma-mode**

Syntax   Description

This command has no arguments or keywords.

Default

Disabled

Command Mode

Interface configuration

Usage Guidelines

This command first appeared in Cisco IOS Release 11.0.

Use this command on Frame Relay, SMDS, or ATM only, especially when these media do not have native multicast available. Do not use this command on multicast-capable LANs such as Ethernet or FDDI.

When this command is configured, each PIM Join message is kept track of in the outgoing interface list of a multicast routing table entry. Therefore, only PIM WAN neighbors that have joined for the group will get packets sent as data link unicasts. This command should only be used when **ip pim sparse-mode** is configured on the interface. This command is not recommended for LANs that have natural multicast capabilities.

Example

The following example configures an interface to be in nonbroadcast, multiaccess mode:

```
ip pim nbma-mode
```

Related Commands

Search online to find documentation for related commands.

ip pim sparse-mode

IP PIM NEIGHBOR-FILTER

To prevent a router from participating in PIM (for example, to configure stub multicast routing), use the **ip pim neighbor-filter** interface configuration command. To remove the restriction, use the **no** form of this command.

> **ip pim neighbor-filter** *access-list-number*
> **no ip pim neighbor-filter** *access-list-number*

Syntax	Description
access-list-number	Standard IP access list that denies PIM packets from a source.

Default

Disabled

Command Mode

Interface configuration

Usage Guidelines

This command first appeared in Cisco IOS Release 11.3.

Example

The following example enables stub multicast routing on Router A, which has an outgoing interface with IP address 10.0.0.1. Router B is a central router with an incoming interface with address 10.0.0.2. Access list 1 filters PIM messages from the source (stub Router A).

Router A

```
ip multicast-routing
ip pim dense-mode
ip igmp helper-address 10.0.0.2
```

Router B

```
ip multicast-routing
 ip pim dense-mode : or ip pim sparse-mode
 ip pim neighbor-filter 1
access-list 1 deny 10.0.0.1
```

Related Commands

Search online to find documentation for related commands.

access-list (standard)
ip igmp helper-address

IP PIM QUERY-INTERVAL

To configure the frequency of PIM router-query messages, use the **ip pim query-interval** interface configuration command. To return to the default interval, use the **no** form of this command.

> **ip pim query-interval** *seconds*
> **no ip pim query-interval** [*seconds*]

Syntax	Description
seconds	Interval, in seconds, at which periodic PIM router-query messages are sent. It can be a number from 1 to 65535. The default is 30 seconds.

Default

30 seconds

Command Mode

Interface configuration

Usage Guidelines

This command first appeared in Cisco IOS Release 10.0.

Routers configured for IP multicast send PIM router-query messages to determine which router will be the designated router for each LAN segment (subnet). The designated router is responsible for sending IGMP host-query messages to all hosts on the directly connected LAN. When operating in sparse mode, the designated router is responsible for sending source registration messages to the RP. The designated router is the router with the largest IP address.

Example

The following example changes the PIM router-query message interval to 45 seconds:

```
interface tunnel 0
  ip pim query-interval 45
```

Related Commands

Search online to find documentation for related commands.

ip igmp query-interval

IP PIM RP-ADDRESS

To configure the address of a PIM rendezvous point (RP) for a particular group, use the **ip pim rp-address** global configuration command. To remove an RP address, use the **no** form of this command.

Part
II

Command Reference

ip pim rp-address *ip-address* [*group-access-list-number*] [**override**]
no ip pim rp-address *ip-address* [*group-access-list-number*]

Syntax	Description
ip-address	IP address of a router to be a PIM RP. This is a unicast IP address in four-part, dotted notation.
group-access-list-number	(Optional.) Number of an access list that defines for which multicast groups the RP should be used. This is a standard IP access list. The number can be from 1 to 100.
override	(Optional.) Indicates that if there is a conflict between the RP configured with this command and one learned by Auto-RP, the RP configured with this command prevails.

Default

No PIM RPs are preconfigured.

Command Mode

Global configuration

Usage Guidelines

This command first appeared in Cisco IOS Release 10.2.

You must configure the IP address of RPs in leaf designated routers (DRs) only. *Leaf routers* are those routers that are directly connected either to a multicast group member or to a sender of multicast messages. Leaf DRs are the only ones that need to know about RPs. Even potential DRs (that might be elected if the primary DR fails) need to be configured to know about RPs.

First-hop routers send register packets to the RP address on behalf of source multicast hosts. Routers also use this address on behalf of multicast hosts that want to become members of a group. These routers send Join and Prune messages towards the RP. The RP must be a PIM router; however, it does not require any special configuration to recognize that it is the RP. Also, RPs are not members of the multicast group; rather, they serve as a "meeting place" for multicast sources and group members.

You can configure the Cisco IOS software to use a single RP for more than one group. The conditions specified by the access list determine which groups the RP can be used for. If no access list is configured, the RP is used for all groups.

A PIM router can use multiple RPs, but only one per group.

If there is no RP configured for a group, the router will treat the group as dense using the dense-mode PIM techniques.

If the RP for a group is learned through a dynamic mechanism, such as Auto-RP, then this command might not be required. If there is a conflict between the RP configured with this command and one learned by Auto-RP, the Auto-RP information is used, unless the **override** keyword is specified.

Examples

The following example sets the PIM RP address to 198.92.37.33 for all multicast groups:

```
ip pim rp-address 198.92.37.33
```

The following example sets the PIM RP address to 147.106.6.22 for the multicast group 225.2.2.2 only:

```
access list 1 225.2.2.2 0.0.0.0
  ip pim rp-address 147.106.6.22 1
```

Related Commands

Search online to find documentation for related commands.

access-list (standard)

IP PIM RP-ANNOUNCE-FILTER

To filter incoming Auto-RP announcement messages coming from the RP, use the **ip pim rp-announce-filter** global configuration command. To remove the filter, use the **no** form of this command.

> **ip pim rp-announce-filter rp-list** *access-list-number* **group-list** *access-list-number*
> **no ip rp-announce-filter rp-list** *access-list-number* **group-list** *access-list-number*

Syntax	Description
rp-list *access-list-number*	Standard access list of RP addresses that are allowable for the group ranges supplied in the **group-list** *access-list-number*.
group-list *access-list-number*	Standard access list that describes the multicast groups the RPs serve.

Default

All RP announcements are accepted.

Command Mode

Global configuration

Usage Guidelines

This command first appeared in Cisco IOS Release 11.1.

Part
II

Command Reference

Configure this command on the PIM RP-mapping agent. If you are going to use more than one RP-mapping agent, make the filters among them consistent so that there are no conflicts in mapping state when the announcing agent goes down.

Example

The following example configures the router to accept RP announcements from RPs in access list 1 for group ranges described in access-list 2:

```
ip pim rp-announce-filter rp-list 1 group-list 2
access-list 1 permit 10.0.0.1
access-list 1 permit 10.0.0.2
access-list 2 permit 224.0.0.0 15.255.255.255
```

Related Commands

Search online to find documentation for related commands.

access-list (standard)

IP PIM SEND-RP-ANNOUNCE

To use Auto-RP to configure which groups the router is willing to act as RP for, use the **ip pim send-rp-announce** global configuration command. To deconfigure this router to be the RP, use the **no** form of this command.

> **ip pim send-rp-announce** *type number* **scope** *ttl* **group-list** *access-list-number*
> **no ip pim send-rp-announce**

Syntax	Description
type number	Interface type and number that identify the RP address.
scope *ttl*	Time-to-live value that limits the announcements.
group-list *access-list-number*	Access list that describes the group ranges for which this router is the RP.

Default

Auto-RP is disabled.

Command Mode

Global configuration

Usage Guidelines

This command first appeared in Cisco IOS Release 11.1.

Use this command in the router you want to be an RP. This command causes the router to send an Auto-RP announcement message to the well-known group CISCO-RP-ANNOUNCE (224.0.1.39). This message announces the router as a candidate RP for the groups in the range described by the access list.

Example

The following example sends RP announcements out all PIM-enabled interfaces for a maximum of 31 hops. The IP address the router wants to be identified by as RP is the IP address associated with Ethernet interface 0. Access-list 5 describes for which groups this router serves as RP.

```
ip pim send-rp-announce ethernet0 scope 31 group-list 5
access-list 5 permit 224.0.0.0 15.255.255.255
```

Related Commands

Search online to find documentation for related commands.

access-list (standard)

IP PIM SEND-RP-DISCOVERY

To configure the router to be an RP-mapping agent, use the **ip pim send-rp-discovery** global configuration command. To restore the default value, use the **no** form of this command.

ip pim send-rp-discovery scope *ttl*
no ip pim send-rp-discovery

Syntax	Description
scope *ttl*	Time-to-live value in the IP header that keeps the discovery messages within this number of hops.

Default

The router is not an RP mapping agent.

Command Mode

Global configuration

Usage Guidelines

This command first appeared in Cisco IOS Release 11.1.

Configure this command on the router designated as an RP-mapping agent. Specify a TTL large enough to cover your PIM domain.

When Auto-RP is used, the following steps occur:

1. The RP-mapping agent listens on well-known group address CISCO-RP-ANNOUNCE (224.0.1.39), which candidate RPs send to.

2. The RP-mapping agent sends RP-to-group mappings in an Auto-RP RP discovery message to the well-known group CISCO-RP-DISCOVERY (224.0.1.40). The TTL value limits how many hops the message can take.

3. PIM designated routers listen to this group and use the RPs they learn about from the discovery message.

Example

The following example limits Auto-RP RP Discovery messages to 20 hops:

```
ip pim send-rp-discovery scope 20
```

IP PIM SPT-THRESHOLD

To configure when a PIM leaf router should join the shortest path source-tree for the specified group, use the **ip pim spt-threshold** global configuration command. To restore the default value, use the **no** form of this command.

> **ip pim spt-threshold** {*kbps* | **infinity**} [**group-list** *access-list-number*]
> **no ip pim spt-threshold**

Syntax	Description
kbps	Traffic rate in kilobits per second.
infinity	Causes all sources for the specified group to use the shared-tree.
group-list *access-list-number*	(Optional.) Indicates what groups the threshold applies to. Must be a standard IP access list number. If the value is 0 or is omitted, the threshold applies to all groups.

Default

When this command is not used, the PIM leaf router joins the shortest path tree immediately after the first packet arrives from a new source.

Command Mode

Global configuration

Usage Guidelines

This command first appeared in Cisco IOS Release 11.1.

If a source sends at a rate greater than or equal to the *kbps* value, a PIM Join message is triggered toward the source to construct a source-tree.

If the **infinity** keyword is specified, all sources for the specified group will use the shared-tree. Specifying a group-list access list indicates what groups the threshold applies to.

If the traffic rate from the source drops below the threshold *kbps* value, the leaf router will, after some amount of time, switch back to the shared tree and send a Prune message toward the source.

Example

The following example sets a threshold of 4 Kbps, above which traffic to a group from a source will cause the router to switch to the shortest path tree to that source:

```
ip pim spt-threshold 4
```

IP PIM VC-COUNT

To change the maximum number of virtual circuits that PIM can open, use the **ip pim vc-count** interface configuration command. To restore the default value, use the **no** form of this command.

ip pim vc-count *number*
no ip pim vc-count

Syntax	Description
number	Maximum number of virtual circuits that PIM can open. The default is 200 virtual circuits. The range is from 1 to 65535.

Default

200 virtual circuits per ATM interface or subinterface

Command Mode

Interface configuration

Usage Guidelines

This command first appeared in Cisco IOS Release 11.3.

Example

The following example allows PIM to open a maximum of 250 virtual circuits:

```
ip pim vc-count 250
```

Related Commands

Search online to find documentation for related commands.

ip pim minimum-vc-rate
ip pim multipoint-signalling

ip pim sparse-mode
show ip pim vc

IP RTP COMPRESSION-CONNECTIONS

To specify the total number of RTP header compression connections that can exist on an interface, use the **ip rtp compression-connections** interface configuration command. To restore the default value, use the **no** form of this command.

> **ip rtp compression-connections** *number*
> **no ip rtp compression-connections**

Syntax	Description
number	Number of connections the cache supports, in the range from 3 to 256. The default is 16 connections.

Default

16 connections

Command Mode

Interface configuration

Usage Guidelines

This command first appeared in Cisco IOS Release 11.3.

Example

The following example changes the number of RTP header compression connections supported to 24:

```
interface serial 0
  encapsulation ppp
  ip rtp header-compression
  ip rtp compression-connections 24
```

Related Commands

Search online to find documentation for related commands.

ip rtp header-compression

IP RTP HEADER-COMPRESSION

To enable RTP header compression, use the **ip rtp header-compression** interface configuration command. To disable RTP header compression, use the **no** form of this command.

ip rtp header-compression [passive]
no ip rtp header-compression [passive]

Syntax	Description
passive	(Optional.) Compresses outgoing RTP packets only if incoming RTP packets on the same interface are compressed.

Default

Disabled

Command Mode

Interface configuration

Usage Guidelines

This command first appeared in Cisco IOS Release 11.3.

If you use this command without the **passive** keyword, the software compresses all RTP traffic.

You can compress IP/UDP/RTP headers to reduce the size of your packets. This is especially useful for RTP, since RTP payload can be as small as 20 bytes, and the uncompressed header is 40 bytes.

RTP header compression is supported on serial lines using Frame Relay, HDLC, or PPP encapsulation. You must enable compression on both ends of a serial connection.

This feature can compress unicast or multicast RTP packets, and hence MBONE traffic can also be compressed over slow links. The compression scheme is beneficial only when you have small payload sizes, as in audio traffic.

Example

The following example enables RTP header compression on serial interface 0 and limits the number of RTP header compression connections to 10:

```
interface serial 0
  encapsulation ppp
  ip rtp header-compression
  ip rtp compression-connections 10
```

Related Commands

Search online to find documentation for related commands.

clear ip rtp header-compression
ip rtp compression-connections
show ip rtp header-compression

Part
II

Command Reference

IP SDR CACHE-TIMEOUT

To limit how long an sdr cache entry stays active in the cache, use the **ip sdr cache-timeout** global configuration command. To restore the default value, use the **no** form of this command.

> **ip sdr cache-timeout** *minutes*
> **no ip sdr cache-timeout**

Syntax	*Description*
minutes	Time, in minutes, that an sdr cache entry is active in the cache.

Default

Disabled, which means entries are never deleted from the cache.

Command Mode

Global configuration

Usage Guidelines

This command first appeared in Cisco IOS Release 11.2.

You might want to limit how long sdr cache entries remain active because, otherwise, the source might stop advertising sdr's. You don't want to keep old advertisements needlessly.

Example

The following example causes sdr cache entries to remain in the cache for only 30 minutes:

```
ip sdr cache-timeout 30
```

Related Commands

Search online to find documentation for related commands.

clear ip sdr
show ip sdr

IP SDR LISTEN

To enable the Cisco IOS software to listen to session directory advertisements, use the **ip sdr listen** interface configuration command. To disable the feature, use the **no** form of this command.

> **ip sdr listen**
> **no ip sdr listen**

Syntax	*Description*

This command has no arguments or keywords.

Default
Disabled

Command Mode
Interface configuration

Usage Guidelines
This command first appeared in Cisco IOS Release 11.1. This command replaces the **ip sd listen** command, which is obsolete.

Session Directory Protocol (sdr) is a multicast application for setting up desktop conferencing sessions. It allocates group addresses and allows the user to specify the scope of the group and whether audio, video, or whiteboard applications will be invoked when users open the session.

Use this command to store session advertisements sent to the group. The **ip sdr listen** command merely enables the software to listen to session directory advertisements. The router joins the default session directory group (group 224.2.127.254) on the interface. Use this command to get contact information.

Example
The following example enables a router to listen to session directory advertisements:

```
ip sdr listen
```

Related Commands
Search online to find documentation for related commands.

clear ip sdr
show ip sdr

MRINFO

To query what neighboring multicast routers are peering with the local router, use the **mrinfo** EXEC command.

    mrinfo [*hostname-or-address*] [*source-address-or-interface*]

Syntax	Description
hostname-or-address	(Optional.) Queries the DNS name or IP address of the multicast router. If omitted, the router queries itself.
source-address-or-interface	(Optional.) Source address used on mrinfo requests. If omitted, the source address is based on the outbound interface for the destination.

Command Mode

EXEC

Usage Guidelines

This command first appeared in Cisco IOS Release 11.0.

The mrinfo command is the MBONE's original tool to determine what neighboring multicast routers are peering with a multicast router. Cisco routers have supported responding to mrinfo requests since Cisco IOS Release 10.2.

Now you can query a multicast router using this command. The output format is identical to DVMRP's mrouted version. (The mrouted software is the UNIX software that implements DVMRP.)

Sample Display

The following is sample output of the **mrinfo** command:

```
Router # mrinfo

192.31.7.37 (barrnet-gw.cisco.com) [version cisco 11.1] [flags: PMSA]:
  192.31.7.37 -> 192.31.7.34 (sj-wall-2.cisco.com) [1/0/pim]
  192.31.7.37 -> 192.31.7.47 (dirtylab-gw-2.cisco.com) [1/0/pim]
  192.31.7.37 -> 192.31.7.44 (dirtylab-gw-1.cisco.com) [1/0/pim]
  131.119.26.10 -> 131.119.26.9 (su-pr2.bbnplanet.net) [1/32/pim]
```

MSTAT

To display IP multicast packet rate and loss information, use the **mstat** user EXEC command.

mstat *source* [*destination*] [*group*]

Syntax	Description
source	DNS name or the IP address of the multicast-capable source.
destination	(Optional.) DNS name or address of the destination. If omitted, the command uses the system at which the command is typed.
group	(Optional.) DNS name or multicast address of the group to be displayed. Default address is 224.2.0.1 (the group used for MBONE Audio).

Command Mode

EXEC

Usage Guidelines

This command first appeared in Cisco IOS Release 11.0.

If no arguments are entered, the router will interactively prompt you for them.

This command is a form of UNIX mtrace that reports packet rate and loss information.

Sample Display

The following is sample output from the **mstat** command:

```
Router# mstat lwei-home-ss2 171.69.58.88 224.0.255.255

Type escape sequence to abort.
Mtrace from 171.69.143.27 to 171.69.58.88 via group 224.0.255.255
>From source (lwei-home-ss2.cisco.com) to destination (lwei-ss20.cisco.com)
Waiting to accumulate statistics......
Results after 10 seconds:

    Source          Response Dest    Packet Statistics For     Only For Traffic
 171.69.143.27       171.69.62.144     All Multicast Traffic     From 171.69.143.27
      :          __/   rtt  48   ms   Lost/Sent = Pct  Rate    To 224.0.255.255
      v        /       hop  48   ms   --------------------     --------------------
 171.69.143.25      lwei-cisco-isdn.cisco.com
      :        ^      ttl   1
      v        :      hop  31   ms    0/12 = 0%        1 pps    0/1 = --%  0 pps
 171.69.121.84
 171.69.121.45      eng-frmt12-pri.cisco.com
      :        ^      ttl   2
      v        :      hop -17   ms    -735/12 = --%     1 pps    0/1 = --%  0 pps
 171.69.121.4
 171.69.5.27       eng-cc-4.cisco.com
      :        ^      ttl   3
      v        :      hop -21   ms    -678/23 = --%     2 pps    0/1 = --%  0 pps
 171.69.5.21
 171.69.62.130     eng-ios-2.cisco.com
      :        ^      ttl   4
      v        :      hop  5    ms    605/639 = 95%    63 pps    1/1 = --%  0 pps
 171.69.62.144
 171.69.58.65      eng-ios-f-5.cisco.com
      :        \__    ttl   5
      v        \      hop  0    ms     4          0 pps        0     0 pps
 171.69.58.88      171.69.62.144
    Receiver       Query Source
```

Table 25–1 describes the fields shown in the display.

Table 25–1 *Mstat Field Descriptions*

Field	Description
Source	Traffic source of packet.
Response Dest	Place where the router sends the results of **mstat** command.
ttl	Number of hops required from the traffic source to the current hop.

Table 25–1 *Mstat Field Descriptions, Continued*

Field	Description
hop	Number of milliseconds of delay.
Only For Traffic From ... 0/2	0 packets dropped out of 2 packets received. If, for example, -2/2 was indicated, then there are 2 extra packets; this could indicate a loop condition.

Related Commands

Search online to find documentation for related commands.

mtrace

MTRACE

To trace the path from a source to a destination branch for a multicast distribution tree, use the **mtrace** user EXEC command.

> **mtrace** *source* [*destination*] [*group*]

Syntax	Description
source	DNS name or the IP address of the multicast-capable source. This is a unicast address of the beginning of the path to be traced.
destination	(Optional.) DNS name or address of the unicast destination. If omitted, the mtrace starts from the system at which the command is typed.
group	(Optional.) DNS name or multicast address of the group to be traced. Default address is 224.2.0.1 (the group used for MBONE Audio). When address 0.0.0.0 is used, the software invokes a weak **mtrace**. A weak **mtrace** is one that follows the RPF path to the source, regardless of whether any router along the path has multicast routing table state.

Command Mode

EXEC

Usage Guidelines

This command first appeared in Cisco IOS Release 11.0.

The trace request generated by the **mtrace** command is multicast to the multicast group to find the last hop router to the specified destination. The trace then follows the multicast path from destination to source by passing the mtrace request packet via unicast to each hop. Responses are unicast to the querying router by the first hop router to the source. This command allows you to isolate multicast routing failures.

If no arguments are entered, the router will interactively prompt you for them.

This command is identical in function to the UNIX version of mtrace.

Sample Display

The following is sample output from the **mtrace** command:

```
Router# mtrace 171.69.215.41 171.69.215.67 239.254.254.254

Type escape sequence to abort.
Mtrace from 171.69.215.41 to 171.69.215.67 via group 239.254.254.254
From source (?) to destination (?)
Querying full reverse path...
 0   171.69.215.67
-1   171.69.215.67 PIM   thresh^ 0   0 ms
-2   171.69.215.74 PIM   thresh^ 0   2 ms
-3   171.69.215.57 PIM   thresh^ 0   894 ms
-4   171.69.215.41 PIM   thresh^ 0   893 ms
-5   171.69.215.12 PIM   thresh^ 0   894 ms
-6   171.69.215.98 PIM   thresh^ 0   893 ms
```

Table 25–2 describes the fields shown in the display.

Table 25–2 *Mtrace Field Descriptions*

Field	Description
Mtrace from 171.69.215.41 to 171.69.215.67 via group 239.254.254.254	Name and address of source, destination, and group for which routes are being traced.
-3 171.69.215.57	Hops away from destination (-3) and address of intermediate router.
PIM thresh^ 0	Multicast protocol in use on this hop, and ttl threshold.
893 ms	Time taken for trace to be forwarded between hops.

Related Commands

Search online to find documentation for related commands.

mstat

PING

To send an ICMP Echo Request to a multicast group, use the **ping** EXEC command.

> **ping** [*group-name-or-address*]

Syntax	Description
group-name-or-address	(Optional.) Sends an ICMP Echo Request to the specified multicast group.

Command Mode
EXEC

Usage Guidelines
This command first appeared in Cisco IOS Release 10.2.

If you use this command with no argument, the system prompts you. We highly recommend you specify a TTL when you are prompted.

SHOW FRAME-RELAY IP RTP HEADER-COMPRESSION

To show Frame Relay's RTP header compression statistics, use the **show frame-relay ip rtp header-compression** EXEC command.

show frame-relay ip rtp header-compression [interface *type number*]

Syntax	Description
interface *type number*	(Optional.) Interface type and number.

Command Mode
EXEC

Usage Guidelines
This command first appeared in Cisco IOS Release 11.3.

Sample Display
The following is sample output from the **show frame-relay ip rtp header-compression** command:

```
Router# show frame-relay ip rtp header-compression

DLCI 17  Link/Destination info: ip 165.3.3.2
  Interface Serial0:
    Rcvd:    0 total, 0 compressed, 0 errors
             0 dropped, 0 buffer copies, 0 buffer failures
    Sent:    6000 total, 5998 compressed,
             227922 bytes saved, 251918 bytes sent
             1.90 efficiency improvement factor
    Connect: 16 rx slots, 16 tx slots, 2 long searches, 2 misses
             99% hit ratio, five minute miss rate 0 misses/sec, 0 max
```

Table 25–3 describes the significant fields in the display.

Table 25–3 *Show Frame Relay IP RTP Header-Compression Field Descriptions*

Field	Description
Interface Serial0	Type and number of interface.
Rcvd: total	Number of packets received on the interface.
compressed	Number of packets with compressed header.
errors	Number of errors.
dropped	Number of dropped packets.
buffer copies	Number of buffers that had to be copied.
buffer failures	Number of failures in allocating buffers.
Sent: total	Total number of packets sent.
compressed	Number of packets sent with compressed header.
bytes saved	Total savings in bytes due to compression.
bytes sent	Total bytes sent after compression.
efficiency improvement factor	Compression efficiency.
Connect: rx slots	Total number of receive slots.
tx slots	Total number of transmit slots.
long searches	Searches that needed more than one lookup.
misses	Number of new states that were created.
hit ratio	Number of times existing states were revised.
five minute miss rate	Average miss rate.
max	Maximum miss rate.

Related Commands

Search online to find documentation for related commands.

frame-relay ip rtp header-compression
frame-relay map ip compress
frame-relay map ip rtp header-compression
show ip rtp header-compression

SHOW IP DVMRP ROUTE

To display the contents of the DVMRP routing table, use the **show ip dvmrp route** EXEC command.

show ip dvmrp route [*name* | *ip-address*]

Syntax	Description
name	*ip-address*	(Optional.) Name or IP address of an entry in the DVMRP routing table.

Command Mode

EXEC

Usage Guidelines

This command first appeared in Cisco IOS Release 10.3.

Sample Display

The following is sample output of the **show ip dvmrp route** command:

```
Router# show ip dvmrp route

DVMRP Routing Table - 1 entry
171.68.0.0/16 [100/11] uptime 07:55:50, expires 00:02:52
    via 137.39.3.93, Tunnel3
```

Table 25–4 describes the fields shown in the display

Table 25–4   *Show IP DVMRP Route Field Descriptions*

Field	Description
1 entry	Number of entries in the DMVRP routing table.
171.68.0.0/16	Source network.
[100/11]	Administrative distance/metric.
uptime	How long in hours, minutes, and seconds that the route has been in the DVMRP routing table.
expires	How long in hours, minutes, and seconds until the entry is removed from the DVMRP routing table.
via 137.39.3.93	Next-hop router to the source network.
Tunnel3	Interface to the source network.

Related Commands

Search online to find documentation for related commands.

ip dvmrp accept-filter

SHOW IP IGMP GROUPS

To display the multicast groups that are directly connected to the router and that were learned via IGMP, use the **show ip igmp groups** EXEC command.

   show ip igmp groups [*group-name* | *group-address* | *type number*]

Syntax	Description
group-name	(Optional.) Name of the multicast group, as defined in the DNS hosts table.
group-address	(Optional.) Address of the multicast group. This is a multicast IP address in four-part, dotted notation.
type	(Optional.) Interface type.
number	(Optional.) Interface number.

Command Mode

EXEC

Usage Guidelines

This command first appeared in Cisco IOS Release 10.0.

If you omit all optional arguments, the **show ip igmp groups** command displays by group address and interface type and number all directly connected multicast groups.

Sample Display

The following is sample output from the **show ip igmp groups** command:

```
Router# show ip igmp groups

IGMP Connected Group Membership
Group Address    Interface     Uptime    Expires   Last Reporter
224.0.255.1      Ethernet0     18:51:41  0:02:15   198.92.37.192
224.2.226.60     Ethernet0     1:51:31   0:02:17   198.92.37.192
224.2.127.255    Ethernet0     18:51:45  0:02:17   198.92.37.192
226.2.2.2        Ethernet1     18:51:47  never     0.0.0.0
224.2.0.1        Ethernet0     18:51:43  0:02:14   198.92.37.192
225.2.2.2        Ethernet0     18:51:43  0:02:21   198.92.37.33
225.2.2.2        Ethernet1     18:51:47  never     0.0.0.0
225.2.2.4        Ethernet0     18:18:02  0:02:20   198.92.37.192
225.2.2.4        Ethernet1     18:23:32  0:02:55   198.92.36.128
```

Table 25–5 describes the fields shown in the display.

Table 25–5 *Show IP IGMP Groups Field Descriptions*

Field	Description
Group address	Address of the multicast group.
Interface	Interface through which the group is reachable.
Uptime	How long in hours, minutes, and seconds this multicast group has been known.
Expires	How long in hours, minutes, and seconds until the entry is removed from the IGMP groups table.
Last Reporter	Last host to report being a member of the multicast group.

Related Commands

Search online to find documentation for related commands.

ip igmp query-interval

SHOW IP IGMP INTERFACE

To display multicast-related information about an interface, use the **show ip igmp interface** EXEC command.

      show ip igmp interface [*type number*]

Syntax	Description
type	(Optional.) Interface type.
number	(Optional.) Interface number.

Command Mode

EXEC

Usage Guidelines

This command first appeared in Cisco IOS Release 10.0.

If you omit the optional arguments, the **show ip igmp interface** command displays information about all interfaces.

This command also displays information about dynamically learned DVMRP routers on the interface.

Sample Display

The following is sample output from the **show ip igmp interface** command:

```
Router# show ip igmp interface

Ethernet0 is up, line protocol is up
  Internet address is 198.92.37.6, subnet mask is 255.255.255.0
  IGMP is enabled on interface
  IGMP query interval is 60 seconds
  Inbound IGMP access group is not set
  Multicast routing is enabled on interface
  Multicast TTL threshold is 0
  Multicast designated router (DR) is 198.92.37.33
  No multicast groups joined
Ethernet1 is up, line protocol is up
  Internet address is 198.92.36.129, subnet mask is 255.255.255.0
  IGMP is enabled on interface
  IGMP query interval is 60 seconds
  Inbound IGMP access group is not set
  Multicast routing is enabled on interface
  Multicast TTL threshold is 0
  Multicast designated router (DR) is 198.92.36.131
  Multicast groups joined: 225.2.2.2 226.2.2.2
Tunnel0 is up, line protocol is up
  Internet address is 10.1.37.2, subnet mask is 255.255.0.0
  IGMP is enabled on interface
  IGMP query interval is 60 seconds
  Inbound IGMP access group is not set
  Multicast routing is enabled on interface
  Multicast TTL threshold is 0
  No multicast groups joined
```

Table 25–6 describes the fields shown in the display.

Table 25–6 *Show IP IGMP Interface Field Descriptions*

Field	Description
Ethernet0 is up, line protocol is up	Interface type, number, and status.
Internet address is... subnet mask is...	Internet address of the interface and subnet mask being applied to the interface, as specified with the **ip address** command.
IGMP is enabled on interface	Indicates whether IGMP has been enabled on the interface with the **ip pim** command.
IGMP query interval is 60 seconds	Interval at which the Cisco IOS software sends PIM router-query messages, as specified with the **ip igmp query-interval** command.

Table 25-6 *Show IP IGMP Interface Field Descriptions, Continued*

Field	Description
Inbound IGMP access group is not set	Indicates whether an IGMP access group has been configured with the **ip igmp access-group** command.
Multicast routing is enabled on interface	Indicates whether multicast routing has been enabled on the interface with the **ip pim** command.
Multicast TTL threshold is 0	Packet time-to-threshold, as specified with the **ip multicast ttl-threshold** command.
Multicast designated router (DR) is...	IP address of the designated router for this LAN segment (subnet).
Multicast groups joined: No multicast groups joined	Indicates whether this interface is a member of any multicast groups and, if so, lists the IP addresses of the groups.

Related Commands

Search online to find documentation for related commands.

ip address
ip igmp access-group
ip igmp query-interval
ip multicast ttl-threshold
ip pim

SHOW IP MCACHE

To display the contents of the IP fast-switching cache, use the **show ip mcache** EXEC command.

    show ip mcache [*group* [*source*]]

Syntax	Description
group	(Optional.) Displays the fast-switching cache for the single group. The *group* argument can be either a Class D IP address or a DNS name.
source	(Optional.) If *source* is also specified, displays a single multicast cache entry. The *source* argument can be either a unicast IP address or a DNS name.

Command Mode

EXEC

Usage Guidelines

This command first appeared in Cisco IOS Release 11.0.

Sample Display

The following is sample output from the **show ip mcache** command. This entry shows a specific source (wrn-source 204.62.246.73) sending to the World Radio Network group (224.2.143.24).

```
Router> show ip mcache wrn wrn-source

IP Multicast Fast-Switching Cache
(204.62.246.73/32, 224.2.143.24), Fddi0, Last used: 00:00:00
    Ethernet0      MAC Header: 01005E028F1800000C1883D30800
    Ethernet1      MAC Header: 01005E028F1800000C1883D60800
    Ethernet2      MAC Header: 01005E028F1800000C1883D40800
    Ethernet3      MAC Header: 01005E028F1800000C1883D70800
```

Table 25–7 describes the significant fields in the display.

Table 25–7   *Show IP Mcache Field Descriptions*

Field	Description
204.62.246.73	Source address.
224.2.143.24	Destination address.
Fddi0	Incoming or expected interface on which the packet should be received.
Last used:	Latest time the entry was accessed for a packet that was successfully fast-switched. The word "Semi-fast" indicates that the first part of the outgoing interface list is fast switched and the rest of the list is process-level switched.
Ethernet0 MAC Header:	Outgoing interface list and respective MAC header that is used when rewriting the packet for output. If the interface is a tunnel, the MAC header will show the real next hop MAC header and then, in parentheses, the real interface name.

SHOW IP MPACKET

To display the contents of the circular cache-header buffer, use the **show ip mpacket** EXEC command.

show ip mpacket [*source-address-or-name*] [*group-address-or-name*] [**detail**]

Syntax	Description
source-address-or-name	(Optional.) Displays cache headers matching the specified source address or name.

Syntax	Description
group-address-or-name	(Optional.) Displays cache headers matching the specified group address or group name.
detail	(Optional.) In addition to the summary information, displays the rest of the IP header fields on an additional line, plus the first 8 bytes after the IP header (usually the UDP port numbers).

Command Mode

EXEC

Usage Guidelines

This command first appeared in Cisco IOS Release 11.1.

This command is only applicable when the **ip multicast cache-headers** command is in effect.

Each time this command is entered, a new buffer is allocated. The summary display (when the **detail** keyword is omitted) shows the IP packet identifier, TTL, source and destination IP addresses, and a local timestamp when the packet was received.

The two arguments and one keyword can be used in the same command in any combination.

Sample Display

The following is sample output of the **show ip mpacket** command with a *group-name*:

```
Router # show ip mpacket smallgroup
IP Multicast Header Cache - entry count:6, next index: 7
Key: id/ttl timestamp (name) source group

D782/117 206416.908 (ABC-xy.company.com) 198.15.228.10 224.5.6.7
7302/113 206417.908 (school.edu) 147.12.2.17 224.5.6.7
6CB2/114 206417.412 (MSSRS.company.com) 154.2.19.40 224.5.6.7
D782/117 206417.868 (ABC-xy.company.com) 198.15.228.10 224.5.6.7
E2E9/123 206418.488 (Newman.com) 211.1.8.10 224.5.6.7
1CA7/127 206418.544 (teller.company.com) 192.4.6.10 224.5.6.7
```

Table 25–8 describes the fields in the display.

Table 25–8   *Show IP Mpacket Field Descriptions*

Field	Description
entry count	Number of packets cached (one packet for each line in the display). The cache has lines numbered from 0 to 1024.
next index	The index for the next element in the cache.
id	Identification number of the IP packet.

Table 25–8 *Show IP Mpacket Field Descriptions, Continued*

Field	Description
ttl	Current TTL of the packet.
timestamp	Timestamp sequence number of the packet.
(name)	DNS name of the source sending to the group. Name appears in parentheses.
source	IP address of the source sending to the group.
group	Multicast group address that the packet is sent to. In this example, the group address of "smallgroup."

Related Commands

Search online to find documentation for related commands.

ip multicast cache-headers

SHOW IP MROUTE

To display the contents of the IP multicast routing table, use the **show ip mroute** EXEC command.

> **show ip mroute** [*group-name* | *group-address*] [*source*] [**summary**] [**count**] [**active** *kbps*]

Syntax	Description
group-name	*group-address*	(Optional.) IP address, name, or interface of the multicast group as defined in the DNS hosts table.
source	(Optional.) IP address or name of a multicast source.
summary	(Optional.) Displays a one-line, abbreviated summary of each entry in the IP multicast routing table.
count	(Optional.) Displays statistics about the group and source, including number of packets, packets per second, average packet size, and bits per second.
active *kbps*	(Optional.) Displays the rate that active sources are sending to multicast groups. Active sources are those sending at a rate of *kbps* or higher. The *kbps* argument defaults to 4 Kbps.

Default

The **show ip mroute** command displays all groups and sources.
The **show ip mroute active** command displays all sources sending at a rate greater than or equal to 4 Kbps.

Command Mode

EXEC

Usage Guidelines

This command first appeared in Cisco IOS Release 10.0.

If you omit all optional arguments and keywords, the **show ip mroute** command displays all entries in the IP multicast routing table.

The Cisco IOS software populates the multicast routing table by creating source, group (S,G) entries from star, group (*,G) entries. The star refers to all source addresses, the "S" refers to a single source address, and the "G" is the destination multicast group address. In creating (S,G) entries, the software uses the best path to that destination group found in the unicast routing table (that is, via Reverse Path Forwarding [RPF]).

Sample Displays

The following is sample output from the **show ip mroute** command for a router operating in dense mode. This command displays the contents of the IP multicast routing table for the multicast group named *cbone-audio.*

```
Router# show ip mroute cbone-audio

IP Multicast Routing Table
Flags: D - Dense, S - Sparse, C - Connected, L - Local, P - Pruned
       R - RP-bit set, F - Register flag, T - SPT-bit set
Timers: Uptime/Expires
Interface state: Interface, Next-Hop, State/Mode

(*, 224.0.255.1), uptime 0:57:31, expires 0:02:59, RP is 0.0.0.0, flags: DC
  Incoming interface: Null, RPF neighbor 0.0.0.0, Dvmrp
  Outgoing interface list:
    Ethernet0, Forward/Dense, 0:57:31/0:02:52
    Tunnel0, Forward/Dense, 0:56:55/0:01:28

(198.92.37.100/32, 224.0.255.1), uptime 20:20:00, expires 0:02:55, flags: C
  Incoming interface: Tunnel0, RPF neighbor 10.20.37.33, Dvmrp
  Outgoing interface list:
    Ethernet0, Forward/Dense, 20:20:00/0:02:52
```

The following is sample output from the **show ip mroute** command for a router operating in sparse mode:

```
Router# show ip mroute

IP Multicast Routing Table
Flags: D - Dense, S - Sparse, C - Connected, L - Local, P - Pruned
       R - RP-bit set, F - Register flag, T - SPT-bit set
Timers: Uptime/Expires
Interface state: Interface, Next-Hop, State/Mode
```

```
(*, 224.0.255.3), uptime 5:29:15, RP is 198.92.37.2, flags: SC
  Incoming interface: Tunnel0, RPF neighbor 10.3.35.1, Dvmrp
  Outgoing interface list:
    Ethernet0, Forward/Sparse, 5:29:15/0:02:57

(198.92.46.0/24, 224.0.255.3), uptime 5:29:15, expires 0:02:59, flags: C
  Incoming interface: Tunnel0, RPF neighbor 10.3.35.1
  Outgoing interface list:
    Ethernet0, Forward/Sparse, 5:29:15/0:02:57
```

The following is sample output from the **show ip mroute** command that shows the VCD value, because an ATM interface with PIM multipoint signaling is enabled:

```
Router# show ip mroute 224.1.1.1

IP Multicast Routing Table
Flags: D - Dense, S - Sparse, C - Connected, L - Local, P - Pruned
       R - RP-bit set, F - Register flag, T - SPT-bit set, J - Join SPT
Timers: Uptime/Expires
Interface state: Interface, Next-Hop or VCD, State/Mode

(*, 224.1.1.1), 00:03:57/00:02:54, RP 130.4.101.1, flags: SJ
  Incoming interface: Null, RPF nbr 0.0.0.0
  Outgoing interface list:
    ATM0/0, VCD 14, Forward/Sparse, 00:03:57/00:02:53
```

The following is sample output from the **show ip mroute** command with the **summary** keyword:

```
Router# show ip mroute summary

IP Multicast Routing Table
Flags: D - Dense, S - Sparse, C - Connected, L - Local, P - Pruned
       R - RP-bit set, F - Register flag, T - SPT-bit set, J - Join SPT
Timers: Uptime/Expires
Interface state: Interface, Next-Hop, State/Mode

(*, 224.255.255.255), 2d16h/00:02:30, RP 171.69.10.13, flags: SJPC

(*, 224.2.127.253), 00:58:18/00:02:00, RP 171.69.10.13, flags: SJC

(*, 224.1.127.255), 00:58:21/00:02:03, RP 171.69.10.13, flags: SJC

(*, 224.2.127.254), 2d16h/00:00:00, RP 171.69.10.13, flags: SJCL
  (128.9.160.67/32, 224.2.127.254), 00:02:46/00:00:12, flags: CLJT
  (129.48.244.217/32, 224.2.127.254), 00:02:15/00:00:40, flags: CLJT
  (130.207.8.33/32, 224.2.127.254), 00:00:25/00:02:32, flags: CLJT
  (131.243.2.62/32, 224.2.127.254), 00:00:51/00:02:03, flags: CLJT
  (140.173.8.3/32, 224.2.127.254), 00:00:26/00:02:33, flags: CLJT
  (171.69.60.189/32, 224.2.127.254), 00:03:47/00:00:46, flags: CLJT
```

The following is sample output from the **show ip mroute** command with the **active** keyword:

```
Router# show ip mroute active

Active IP Multicast Sources - sending >= 4 kbps

Group: 224.2.127.254, (sdr.cisco.com)
    Source: 146.137.28.69 (mbone.ipd.anl.gov)
      Rate: 1 pps/4 kbps(1sec), 4 kbps(last 1 secs), 4 kbps(life avg)

Group: 224.2.201.241, ACM 97
    Source: 130.129.52.160 (webcast3-e1.acm97.interop.net)
      Rate: 9 pps/93 kbps(1sec), 145 kbps(last 20 secs), 85 kbps(life avg)

Group: 224.2.207.215, ACM 97
    Source: 130.129.52.160 (webcast3-e1.acm97.interop.net)
      Rate: 3 pps/31 kbps(1sec), 63 kbps(last 19 secs), 65 kbps(life avg)
```

The following is sample output from the **show ip mroute** command with the **count** keyword:

```
Router# show ip mroute count

IP Multicast Statistics - Group count: 8, Average sources per group: 9.87
Counts: Pkt Count/Pkts per second/Avg Pkt Size/Kilobits per second

Group: 224.255.255.255, Source count: 0, Group pkt count: 0
  RP-tree: 0/0/0/0

Group: 224.2.127.253, Source count: 0, Group pkt count: 0
  RP-tree: 0/0/0/0

Group: 224.1.127.255, Source count: 0, Group pkt count: 0
  RP-tree: 0/0/0/0

Group: 224.2.127.254, Source count: 9, Group pkt count: 14
  RP-tree: 0/0/0/0
  Source: 128.2.6.9/32, 2/0/796/0
  Source: 128.32.131.87/32, 1/0/616/0
  Source: 128.125.51.58/32, 1/0/412/0
  Source: 130.207.8.33/32, 1/0/936/0
  Source: 131.243.2.62/32, 1/0/750/0
  Source: 140.173.8.3/32, 1/0/660/0
  Source: 146.137.28.69/32, 1/0/584/0
  Source: 171.69.60.189/32, 4/0/447/0
  Source: 204.162.119.8/32, 2/0/834/0

Group: 224.0.1.40, Source count: 1, Group pkt count: 3606
  RP-tree: 0/0/0/0
  Source: 171.69.214.50/32, 3606/0/48/0, RPF Failed: 1203

Group: 224.2.201.241, Source count: 36, Group pkt count: 54152
  RP-tree: 7/0/108/0
  Source: 13.242.36.83/32, 99/0/123/0
```

```
Source: 36.29.1.3/32, 71/0/110/0
Source: 128.9.160.96/32, 505/1/106/0
Source: 128.32.163.170/32, 661/1/88/0
Source: 128.115.31.26/32, 192/0/118/0
Source: 128.146.111.45/32, 500/0/87/0
Source: 128.183.33.134/32, 248/0/119/0
Source: 128.195.7.62/32, 527/0/118/0
Source: 128.223.32.25/32, 554/0/105/0
Source: 128.223.32.151/32, 551/1/125/0
Source: 128.223.156.117/32, 535/1/114/0
Source: 128.223.225.21/32, 582/0/114/0
Source: 129.89.142.50/32, 78/0/127/0
Source: 129.99.50.14/32, 526/0/118/0
Source: 130.129.0.13/32, 522/0/95/0
Source: 130.129.52.160/32, 40839/16/920/161
Source: 130.129.52.161/32, 476/0/97/0
Source: 130.221.224.10/32, 456/0/113/0
Source: 132.146.32.108/32, 9/1/112/0
```

Table 25–9 explains the fields shown in the displays.

Table 25–9 *Show IP Mroute Field Descriptions*

Field	Description
Flags:	Provides information about the entry.
D - Dense	Entry is operating in dense mode.
S - Sparse	Entry is operating in sparse mode.
C - Connected	A member of the multicast group is present on the directly connected interface.
L - Local	The router itself is a member of the multicast group.
P - Pruned	Route has been pruned. The Cisco IOS software keeps this information in case a downstream member wants to join the source.
R - Rp-bit set	Indicates that the (S,G) entry is pointing towards the RP. This is typically prune state along the shared tree for a particular source.
F - Register flag	Indicates that the software is Registering for a multicast source.
T - SPT-bit set	Indicates that packets have been received on the shortest path source tree.
Timers:	Uptime/Expires.
Interface state:	Interface, Next-Hop or VCD, State/Mode.

Table 25–9 *Show IP Mroute Field Descriptions, Continued*

Field	Description
(*, 224.0.255.1) (198.92.37.100/32, 224.0.255.1)	Entry in the IP multicast routing table. The entry consists of the IP address of the source router followed by IP address of the multicast group. An asterisk (*) in place of the source router indicates all sources. Entries in the first format are referred to as (*,G) or "star comma G" entries. Entries in the second format are referred to as (S,G) or "S comma G" entries. (*,G) entries are used to build (S,G) entries.
uptime	How long in hours, minutes, and seconds the entry has been in the IP multicast routing table.
expires	How long in hours, minutes, and seconds until the entry will be removed from the IP multicast routing table on the outgoing interface.
RP	Address of the rendezvous point (RP) router. For routers and access servers operating in sparse mode, this address is always 0.0.0.0.
flags:	Information about the entry.
Incoming interface:	Expected interface for a multicast packet from the source. If the packet is not received on this interface, it is discarded.
RPF neighbor	IP address of the upstream router to the source. "Tunneling" indicates that this router is sending data to the RP encapsulated in Register packets. The hexadecimal number in parentheses indicates to which RP it is registering. Each bit indicates a different RP if multiple RPs per group are used.
Dvmrp or Mroute	Indicates if the RPF information is obtained from the DVMRP routing table or the static mroutes configuration.
Outgoing interface list:	Interfaces through which packets will be forwarded. When the **ip pim nbma-mode** command is enabled on the interface, the IP address of the PIM neighbor is also displayed.
Ethernet0	Name and number of the outgoing interface.
Next hop or VCD	Next hop specifies downstream neighbor's IP address. Virtual circuit descriptor number. VCD0 means the group is using the static-map virtual circuit.

Table 25-9 *Show IP Mroute Field Descriptions, Continued*

Field	Description
Forward/Dense	Indicates that packets will be forwarded on the interface if there are no restrictions due to access lists or TTL threshold. Following the slash (/), mode in which the interface is operating (dense or sparse).
Forward/Sparse	Sparse-mode interface is in forward mode.
time/time (uptime/expiration time)	Per interface, how long in hours, minutes, and seconds the entry has been in the IP multicast routing table. Following the slash (/), how long in hours, minutes, and seconds until the entry will be removed from the IP multicast routing table.

Related Commands

Search online to find documentation for related commands.

ip multicast-routing
ip pim

SHOW IP PIM INTERFACE

To display information about interfaces configured for PIM, use the **show ip pim interface** EXEC command.

> **show ip pim interface** [*type number*] [**count**]

Syntax	Description
type	(Optional.) Interface type.
number	(Optional.) Interface number.
count	(Optional.) Number of packets received and sent out the interface.

Command Mode

EXEC

Usage Guidelines

This command first appeared in Cisco IOS Release 10.0.

This command works only on interfaces that are configured for PIM.

Sample Displays

The following is sample output from the **show ip pim interface** command:

```
Router# show ip pim interface

Address          Interface       Mode    Neighbor  Query      DR
                                         Count     Interval
198.92.37.6      Ethernet0       Dense   2         30         198.92.37.33
198.92.36.129    Ethernet1       Dense   2         30         198.92.36.131
10.1.37.2        Tunnel0         Dense   1         30         0.0.0.0
```

The following is sample output from the **show ip pim interface** command with a **count**:

```
Router# show ip pim interface count

Address          Interface       FS   Mpackets In/Out
171.69.121.35    Ethernet0       *    548305239/13744856
171.69.121.35    Serial0.33      *    8256/67052912
198.92.12.73     Serial0.1719    *    219444/862191
```

Table 25–10 describes the fields shown in the display.

Table 25–10 *Show IP PIM Interface Field Descriptions*

Field	Description
Address	IP address of the next-hop router.
Interface	Interface type and number that is configured to run PIM.
Mode	Multicast mode in which the Cisco IOS software is operating. This can be dense mode or sparse mode. DVMRP indicates a DVMRP tunnel is configured.
Neighbor Count	Number of PIM neighbors that have been discovered through this interface. If the Neighbor Count is 1 for a DVMRP tunnel, the neighbor is active (receiving probes and reports).
Query Interval	Frequency, in seconds, of PIM router-query messages, as set by the **ip pim query-interval** interface configuration command. The default is 30 seconds.
DR	IP address of the designated router on the LAN. Note that serial lines do not have designated routers, so the IP address is shown as 0.0.0.0.
FS	An asterisk (*) in this column indicates fast switching is enabled.
Mpackets In/Out	Number of packets into and out of the interface since the box has been up.

Related Commands

Search online to find documentation for related commands.

ip pim
show ip pim neighbor

SHOW IP PIM NEIGHBOR

To list the PIM neighbors discovered by the Cisco IOS software, use the **show ip pim neighbor** EXEC command.

show ip pim neighbor [*type number*]

Syntax	Description
type	(Optional.) Interface type.
number	(Optional.) Interface number.

Command Mode

EXEC

Usage Guidelines

This command first appeared in Cisco IOS Release 10.0.

Use this command to determine which routers on the LAN are configured for PIM.

Sample Display

The following is sample output from the **show ip pim neighbor** command:

```
Router# show ip pim neighbor

PIM Neighbor Table
Neighbor Address  Interface      Uptime    Expires   Mode
198.92.37.2       Ethernet0      17:38:16  0:01:25   Dense
198.92.37.33      Ethernet0      17:33:20  0:01:05   Dense (DR)
198.92.36.131     Ethernet1      17:33:20  0:01:08   Dense (DR)
198.92.36.130     Ethernet1      18:56:06  0:01:04   Dense
10.1.22.9         Tunnel0        19:14:59  0:01:09   Dense
```

Table 25–11 describes the fields shown in the display.

Table 25–11 *Show IP PIM Neighbor Field Descriptions*

Field	Description
Neighbor Address	IP address of the PIM neighbor.
Interface	Interface type and number on which the neighbor is reachable.
Uptime	How long in hours, minutes, and seconds the entry has been in the PIM neighbor table.
Expires	How long in hours, minutes, and seconds until the entry will be removed from the IP multicast routing table.

Table 25–11 *Show IP PIM Neighbor Field Descriptions, Continued*

Field	Description
Mode	Mode in which the interface is operating.
(DR)	Indicates that this neighbor is a designated router on the LAN.

Related Commands

Search online to find documentation for related commands.

show ip pim interface

SHOW IP PIM RP

To display active rendezvous points (RPs) that are cached with associated multicast routing entries, use the **show ip pim rp** EXEC command.

     show ip pim rp [*group-name* | *group-address*] [**mapping**]

Syntax	Description
group-name	(Optional.) Name of the group about which to display RPs.
group-address	(Optional.) Address of the group about which to display RPs.
mapping	(Optional.) Displays all group-to-RP mappings that the router is aware of (either configured or learned from Auto-RP).

Command Mode

EXEC

Usage Guidelines

This command first appeared in Cisco IOS Release 10.2.

Sample Displays

The following is sample output of the **show ip pim rp** command:

```
Router # show ip pim rp

Group: 224.2.240.30, RP: 171.69.10.13, v1, uptime 1d03h, expires 00:04:17
Group: 224.1.127.255, RP: 171.69.10.13, v1, uptime 16:39:28, expires 00:04:05
Group: 224.2.127.254, RP: 171.69.10.13, v1, uptime 4d01h, expires 00:03:42
Group: 224.2.128.253, RP: 171.69.10.13, v1, uptime 12:06:25, expires 00:04:17
Group: 224.2.182.251, RP: 171.69.10.13, v1, uptime 3d10h, expires 00:03:16
```

The following is sample output of the **show ip pim rp** command when **mapping** is specified:

```
Router # show ip pim rp mapping

PIM Group-to-RP Mappings
This system is an RP
This system is an RP-mapping agent

Group(s) 224.0.1.39/32, uptime: 1w4d, expires: never
    RP 171.69.10.13 (sj-eng-mbone.cisco.com)
    Info source: local
Group(s) 224.0.1.40/32, uptime: 1w4d, expires: never
    RP 171.69.10.13 (sj-eng-mbone.cisco.com)
    Info source: local
Group(s) 239.255.0.0/16, uptime: 1d03h, expires: 00:02:28
    RP 171.69.143.25 (lwei-cisco-isdn.cisco.com), PIMv2 v1
    Info source: 171.69.143.25 (lwei-cisco-isdn.cisco.com)
Group(s): 224.0.0.0/4, Static
    RP: 171.69.10.13 (sj-eng-mbone.cisco.com)
```

Table 25–12 describes the fields in the displays.

Table 25–12 *Show IP PIM RP Field Descriptions*

Field	Description
Group	Address of the multicast group about which to display RP information.
RP	Address of the RP for that group.
v1	Indicates the RP is running PIM Version 1.
uptime	Length of time the RP has been up in days and hours. If less than 1 day, time is expressed in hours:minutes:seconds.
expires	Time in hours:minutes:seconds in which the entry will expire.
Info source	RP mapping agent that advertised the mapping.

SHOW IP PIM VC

To display ATM virtual circuit status information for multipoint VCs opened by PIM, use the **show ip pim vc** EXEC command.

show ip pim vc [*group-or-name*] [*type number*]

Syntax	Description
group-or-name	(Optional.) IP multicast group or name. Displays only the single group.
type number	(Optional.) Interface type and number. Displays only the single ATM interface.

Default

Displays VC status information for all ATM interfaces.

Command Mode

EXEC

Usage Guidelines

This command first appeared in Cisco IOS Release 11.3.

Sample Display

The following is sample output for the **show ip pim vc** command:

```
Router# show ip pim vc

IP Multicast ATM VC Status
ATM0/0 VC count is 5, max is 200
Group          VCD   Interface    Leaf Count   Rate
224.2.2.2      26    ATM0/0       1            0 pps
224.1.1.1      28    ATM0/0       1            0 pps
224.4.4.4      32    ATM0/0       2            0 pps
224.5.5.5      35    ATM0/0       1            0 pps
```

Table 25–13 describes the significant fields in the display.

Table 25–13   *Show IP PIM VC Field Descriptions*

Field	Description
ATM0/0	ATM slot and port number on the interface.
VC count	Number of virtual circuits opened by PIM.
max	Maximum number of VCs that PIM is allowed to open, as configured by the **ip pim vc-count** command.
Group	IP address of the multicast group to which the router is multicasting.
VCD	Virtual circuit descriptor.
Interface	Outgoing interface.
Leaf Count	Number of routers that have joined the group and are a member of that multipoint virtual circuit.
Rate	Rate in packets per second as configured by the **ip pim minimum-vc-rate** command.

Related Commands

Search online to find documentation for related commands.

ip pim multipoint-signalling

SHOW IP RPF

To display how IP multicast routing does Reverse-Path Forwarding (RPF), use the **show ip rpf** EXEC command.

> **show ip rpf** *source-address-or-name*

Part
II

Command Reference

Syntax	Description
source-address-or-name	Source name or address of the host for which the RPF information is displayed.

Command Mode

EXEC

Usage Guidelines

This command first appeared in Cisco IOS Release 11.0.

The router can Reverse-Path Forward from multiple routing tables (that is, the unicast routing table, DVMRP routing table, or static mroutes). This command tells you where the information is retrieved from.

Sample Display

The following is sample output of the **show ip rpf** command:

```
Router # show ip rpf 171.69.10.13

RPF information for sj-eng-mbone.cisco.com (171.69.10.13)
  RPF interface: BRI0
  RPF neighbor: eng-isdn-pri3.cisco.com (171.69.121.10)
  RPF route/mask: 171.69.0.0/255.255.0.0
  RPF type: unicast
```

Table 25–14 describes the significant fields in the display.

Table 25–14 *Show IP RPF Field Descriptions*

Field	Description
RPF information for *name* (*address*)	Host name and address that this information concerns.
RPF interface	For the given source, interface from which router expects to get packets.

Table 25–14   *Show IP RPF Field Descriptions, Continued*

Field	Description
RPF neighbor	For given source, neighbor from which router expects to get packets.
RPF route/mask	Route number and mask that matched against this source.
RPF type	Routing table from which this route was obtained, either unicast, DVMRP, or static mroute.

SHOW IP RTP HEADER-COMPRESSION

To show RTP header compression statistics, use the **show ip rtp header-compression** EXEC command.

   show ip rtp header-compression [*type number*] [**detail**]

Syntax	*Description*
type number	(Optional.) Interface type and number.
detail	(Optional.) Displays details of each connection.

Command Mode

EXEC

Usage Guidelines

This command first appeared in Cisco IOS Release 11.3.

Sample Display

The following is sample output from the **show ip rtp header-compression** command:

```
Router# show ip rtp header-compression

RTP/UDP/IP header compression statistics:
 Interface Serial1:
  Rcvd: 0 total, 0 compressed, 0 errors
     0 dropped, 0 buffer copies, 0 buffer failures
  Sent: 430 total 429 compressed,
     15122 bytes saved, 139318 bytes sent
     1.10 efficiency improvement factor
  Connect: 16 rx slots, 16 tx slots, 1 long searches, 1 misses
     99% hit ratio, five minute miss rate 0 misses/sec, 0 max.
```

Table 25–15 describes the significant fields in the display.

Table 25–15 *Show IP RTP Header-Compression Field Descriptions*

Field	Description
Interface Serial1	Type and number of interface.
Rcvd: total	Number of packets received on the interface.
compressed	Number of packets with compressed header.
errors	Number of errors.
dropped	Number of dropped packets.
buffer copies	Number of buffers that had to be copied.
buffer failures	Number of failures in allocating buffers.
Sent: total	Total number of packets sent.
compressed	Number of packets sent with compressed header.
bytes saved	Total savings in bytes due to compression.
bytes sent	Total bytes sent after compression.
efficiency improvement factor	Compression efficiency.
Connect: rx slots	Total number of receive slots.
tx slots	Total number of transmit slots.
long searches	Searches that needed more than one lookup.
misses	Number of new states that were created.
hit ratio	Number of times existing states were revised.
five minute miss rate	Average miss rate.
max	Maximum miss rate.

Part II

Command Reference

Related Commands

Search online to find documentation for related commands.

ip rtp header-compression

SHOW IP SDR

To display the session directory cache, use the **show ip sdr** EXEC command.

> **show ip sdr** [*group* | "*session-name*" | **detail**]

Syntax	Description
group	(Optional.) Displays the sessions defining the multicast group in detail format.
"session-name"	(Optional.) Displays the single session in detail format. The session name is enclosed in quotation marks (" ").
detail	(Optional.) Displays all sessions in detail format.

Command Mode
EXEC

Usage Guidelines
This command first appeared in Cisco IOS Release 11.1.

If the router is configured to be a member of 224.2.127.254 (the default sd group), it will cache sdr announcements.

If no arguments or keywords are used with this command, the system displays a sorted list of session names.

Sample Display
The following is sample output of the **show ip sdr** command:

```
Router # show ip sdr

SDR Cache - 198 entries
!Cannes Film Festival
Alan Kay: Georgia Tech Distinguished Lecture
ANL TelePresence Microscopy Collaboratory
ASC MSRC Ribbon Cutting Ceremony
audio test
Basler Fasnacht 1997 !
BayLISA meeting
Bellcore testing
Bellcore testing2
Bielsko-Biala
calren2 - private
Cannes Testing
Cbay session
CERN ATLAS
CERN LEPC meeting
CERN LHCC
CILEA pre-test for Archaeonet
cisco Beta
cisco PIM users
CMU
CMU-UKA
CRAY T3E (Course)
```

Table 25–16 describes the fields in the display.

Table 25–16 *Show IP SDR Field Descriptions*

Field	Description
SDR Cache - *x* entries	Number of entries (sessions) in the cache.
!Cannes Film Festsival	Name of session.

Related Commands

Search online to find documentation for related commands.

clear ip sdr
ip sdr cache-timeout
ip sdr listen

Index

CISCO CERTIFIED INTERNETWORK EXPERT

Cisco's CCIE certification programs set the professional benchmark for internetworking expertise. CCIEs are recognized throughout the internetworking industry as being the most highly qualified of technical professionals. And, because the CCIE programs certify individuals—not companies—employers are guaranteed any CCIE with whom they work has met the same stringent qualifications as every other CCIE in the industry.

To ensure network performance and reliability in today's dynamic information systems arena, companies need internetworking professionals who have knowledge of both established and newer technologies. Acknowledging this need for specific expertise, Cisco has introduced three CCIE certification programs:

WAN Switching

ISP/Dial

Routing & Switching

CCIE certification requires a solid background in internetworking. The first step in obtaining CCIE certification is to pass a two-hour Qualification exam administered by Sylvan-Prometric. The final step in CCIE certification is a two-day, hands-on lab exam that pits the candidate against difficult build, break, and restore scenarios.

Just as training and instructional programs exist to help individuals prepare for the written exam, Cisco is pleased to announce its first CCIE Preparation Lab. The CCIE Preparation Lab is located at Wichita State University in Wichita Kansas, and is available to help prepare you for the final step toward CCIE status.

Cisco designed the CCIE Preparation Lab to assist CCIE candidates with the lab portion of the actual CCIE lab exam. The Preparation Lab at WSU emulates the conditions under which CCIE candidates are tested for their two-day CCIE Lab Examination. As almost any CCIE will corroborate, the lab exam is the most difficult element to pass for CCIE certification.

Registering for the lab is easy. Simply complete and fax the form located on the reverse side of this letter to WSU. For more information, please visit the WSU Web page at www.engr.twsu.edu/cisco/ or Cisco's Web page at www.cisco.com.

CISCO CCIE PREPARATION LAB

REGISTRATION FORM

Please attach a business card or print the following information:

Name/Title: _____

Company: _____

Company Address: _____

City/State/Zip: _____

Country Code (_____) Area Code (_____) Daytime Phone Number _____

Country Code (_____) Area Code (_____) Evening Phone Number _____

Country Code (_____) Area Code (_____) Fax Number _____

E-mail Address: _____

Circle the number of days you want to reserve lab: 1   2   3   4   5

Week and/or date(s) preferred (3 choices):

_____

_____

_____

Have you taken and passed the written CCIE exam?   Yes   No

List any CISCO courses you have attended:

Registration fee: _____ $500 per day × _____ day(s) = Total _____

Check Enclosed (Payable to WSU Conference Office)

Charge to: _____ MasterCard or Visa exp. Date _____

CC# _____

Name on Card _____

Cardholder Signature _____

Refunds/Cancellations: The full registration fee will be refunded if your cancellation is received at least 15 days prior to the first scheduled lab day.

Wichita State University
University Conferences
1845 Fairmount
Wichita, KS 67260
Attn: Kimberly Moore
Tel: 800-550-1306
Fax: 316-686-6520